OUR ENEMIES IN BLUE

OUR ENEMIES IN BLUE
POLICE AND POWER
IN AMERICA

BY KRISTIAN WILLIAMS

SOFT SKULL PRESS • BROOKLYN NY •2004

Our Enemies in Blue

© Kristian Williams, 2004

Cover photograph by Bette Lee
Author photograph by Kristi Jo Lewis

Published by Soft Skull Press
71 Bond Street, Brooklyn, NY 11217

Distributed by Publishers Group West
www.pgw.com • 1.800.788.3123

Printed in Canada

Library of Congress Cataloging-in-Publication Data

Williams, Kristian.
  Our enemies in blue / by Kristian Williams.—1st ed.
      p. cm.
  ISBN 1-887128-85-9 (pbk. : alk. paper)
  1. Police—United States. 2. Police brutality—United States. 3.
Police misconduct—United States. I. Title.
HV8138.W615 2003
363.2'32—dc21

                              2003005745

5/05

CONTENTS

FOREWORD:
POLICE AND POWER IN AMERICA

What are police for?

Everybody thinks they know. But to assume that the police exist to enforce the law or fight crime is akin to beginning an analysis of military policy with the premise that armies exist to repel invasions. The ends an institution pursues are not always the same as those it claims to pursue.

I begin, then, with a call for skepticism, especially about official slogans and publicly traded justifications. Let us focus less on what the police say they are doing and instead assess the institution based on what it actually does. We should ask, always, who benefits and who suffers? Whose interests are advanced, and who pays the costs? Who is protected and served? Who is bullied and brutalized? The answers will tell us something of the forces directing the police, both in specific circumstances and in the larger historical sense. They will also reveal the interests the institution serves and the ends it promotes.

This book discusses much of what is worst about the police. It describes their actions largely in terms of intolerance, corruption, political repression, and violence. The first chapter, "Police Brutality in Theory and Practice," offers an overview of police violence, its prevalence, causes, and consequences. It is followed by a history of the modern police institution, beginning with "The Origins of American Policing" in chapter 2. That section traces the lineage of our modern police back to the slave patrols and other earlier forms, while chapter 3, "The Genesis of a Policed Society," weighs the significance of the new institution and considers the changing role of the state. Chapters 4 and 5—"Cops and Klan, Hand in Hand" and "The Natural Enemy of the Working Class"—continue this examination with a look at the use of police to stifle the social ambitions of racial minorities (especially African Americans) and workers. The sixth chapter, "Police Autonomy and Blue Power," discusses efforts to reform policing, especially during the twentieth century, and analyzes the relationship between reform movements and the emergence of the police as a political force. Then, "Secret Police, Red Squads, and the Strategy of Permanent Repression" and "Riot Police or Police Riots?" (chapters 7 and 8) detail intelligence operations and crowd control strategies. Chapter 9, "Your Friendly Neighborhood Police State" brings the discussion up to the present, focusing on current trends such as militarization and community policing. And the afterword, "Making Police

Obsolete," considers community-based alternatives to policing, especially those connected to resistance movements here and abroad.

Throughout, the focus is on police in their modern form, particularly in urban departments in the United States. Some discussion of earlier models will be featured as background, and conditions in other countries are sometimes described by way of comparison. Likewise, the mention of other law enforcement authorities—federal agencies, county sheriffs, private guards, and the like—will be unavoidable to the degree that they influence, resemble, or take on the duties of the municipal police.[1]

As the narrative progresses, several related trends become discernible. The first is the expansion of police autonomy and the subsequent growth of their political influence. The second is the continual effort to make policing more proactive, with the aim of preventing offenses. Related to each of these is the increased penetration of police authority into the community and into the lives of individuals. These trends are related to larger social conditions—slavery and segregation, the rise and fall of political machines, the creation of municipal bureaucracies, the development of capitalism, and so on. It is argued, in short, that the police exist to control troublesome populations, especially those that are likely to rebel. This task has little to do with crime, as most people think of it, and much to do with politics—especially the preservation of existing inequalities. To the degree that a social order works to the advantage of some and the disadvantage of others, its preservation will largely consist of protecting the interests of the first group from the demands of the second. And that, as we shall see, is what the police do.

Robert Reiner claims that "[to] a large extent, a society gets the policemen it deserves."[2] It is hard to know whether Mr. Reiner is extremely optimistic about the police or extremely cynical about society. But undeniably, the history of our society is reflected in the history of its police. Much of that history clashes with our nation's patriotic self-image. The history of America's police is not the story of democracy so much as it is the story of the prevention of democracy. Yet there is another story, an ever-present subtext—the story of resistance. It, too, drives this narrative, and if there is a reason for hope anywhere in this book, we may find it here—amidst the slave revolts, strikes, sit-ins, protest marches, and riots.

POLICE BRUTALITY IN THEORY AND PRACTICE

In April 2001, when police officer Stephen Roach killed Timothy Thomas, Cincinnati served as the stage for a classic American drama. Thomas, an unarmed teenager wanted for several misdemeanor warrants, was the fifteenth Black man the Cincinnati police had killed in six years.[1] A few days later, protesters led by the victim's mother occupied City Hall for three hours. When they were forced out, the crowd marched to the police station, growing as it went. At the police station, the demonstration escalated. Members of the crowd hit the cops with rocks and bottles, shattered the station's glass entryway, and removed the American flag outside. When the police responded with tear gas and rubber bullets, the disorder spread.[2] For three nights, hundreds of people, mostly young Black men, participated in looting and vandalism.[3] The rioting mostly consisted of window-breaking and sporadic attacks on Whites, though dumpster fires became so common that the fire department stopped responding to them.[4] The fight was by no means one-sided. The police made 760 arrests and injured an unknown number of people.[5]

In what was perhaps the most disgraceful episode of the entire affair, police fired seven less-than-lethal "beanbags" at a crowd gathered for Thomas's funeral service. Four people were hit, including two children. One victim, Christine Jones, was hospitalized with a fractured rib, bruised lung, and injured spleen. She described the incident: "It was like a drive-by shooting. All of a sudden, out of the blue, several police cars screeched to a halt at [the] intersection, jumped out of cars and just immediately started shooting people with the shotguns. No warning. No nothing."[6]

It's no secret that the police come into conflict with members of the public. The police are tasked with controlling a population that does not always respect lawful authority and may resist efforts to enforce the law. Hence, police are armed, trained, and authorized to use force in the course of executing their duty. At times, they use the ultimate in force, killing those they are charged with controlling.

Under such an arrangement, it is not surprising that officers sometimes move beyond the bounds of their authority. Nor is it surprising that the affected communities respond with anger—sometimes rage. The battles that ensue do not only concern particular injustices, but also represent deep disputes about the rights of the public and the limits of state power. On the one side, the police and the government try desperately to maintain control, to preserve their authority. And on the other, common people struggle to assert their humanity. Such riots represent, among other things, the attempt of the community to define for itself what will count as police brutality and where the limit of authority falls. It is in these conflicts, not in the courts, that our rights are established.

THE RODNEY KING BEATING: "BASIC STUFF REALLY"

On March 3, 1991, a Black motorist named Rodney King led the California Highway Patrol and the Los Angeles Police Department on a ten-minute chase. When he stopped and exited the car, the police ordered him to lie down; he got on all fours instead, and Sergeant Stacey Koon shot him twice with an electric taser. The other passengers in King's car were cuffed and laid prone on the street. An officer kept his gun aimed at them, and when they heard screams he ordered them not to look. One did try to look, and was clubbed on the head.[7]

Others were watching, however, and a few days later the entire world saw what had happened to Rodney King. A video recorded by a bystander shows three White cops taking turns beating King, with several other officers looking on, and Sergeant Stacey Koon shouting orders. The video shows police clubbing King fifty-six times, and kicking him in the body and head.[8] When the video was played on the local news, KCET enhanced the sound. Police can be heard ordering King to put his hands behind his back and calling him "nigger."[9]

The chase began at 12:40 A.M. and ended at 12:50 A.M. At 12:56, Sgt. Koon reported via his car's computer, "You just had a big time use of force . . . tased and beat the suspect of CHP pursuit, Big Time." At 12:57, the station responded, "Oh well . . . I'm sure the lizard didn't deserve it . . . HAHA." At 1:07, the Watch Commander summarized the incident (again via Mobile Data Terminal): "CHP chasing . . . failing to yield . . . passed [car] A 23 . . . they became primary . . . then tased, then beat . . . basic stuff really."[10] Koon himself endorsed this assessment of the incident. In his 1992 book on the subject, he described the altercation with Rodney King as unexceptional: "Just another night on the LAPD. That's what it had been."[11]

King was jailed for four days, but released without charges. He was treated at County-USC Hospital, where he received twenty stitches and treatment for a broken cheekbone and broken ankle. Nurses there reported hearing officers brag and joke about the beating. King later listed additional injuries, including broken bones and teeth, injured kidneys, multiple skull fractures, and permanent brain damage.[12]

Twenty-three officers had responded to the chase, including two in a helicopter. Of these, ten Los Angeles Police Department officers were present on the ground during the beating, including four Field Training Officers who supervise rookies. Four cops—Stacey Koon, Laurence Powell, Timothy Wind, and Theodore Briseno—

were indicted for their role in the beating. Wind was a new employee, still in his probationary period, and was fired. The two California Highway Patrol officers were disciplined for not reporting the use of force, and their supervisor was suspended for ten days. But none of the other officers present were disciplined in any way, though they had done nothing to prevent the beating or to report it afterward.[13]

The four indicted cops were acquitted. Social scientists have argued that the verdict was "predictable," given the location of the trial. As Melvin Oliver, James Johnson, and Walter Farrel write: "Simi Valley, the site of the trial, and Ventura County more generally, is a predominantly White community known for its strong stance on law and order, as evidenced by the fact that a significant number of LAPD officers live there. Thus, the four White police officers were truly judged by a jury of their peers. Viewed in this context, the verdict should not have been unanticipated."[14]

Koon, Powell, Wind, and Briseno were acquitted. They were then almost immediately charged with federal civil rights violations, but that was clearly too little, too late. L.A. was in flames.

A SOCIAL CONFLAGRATION

The people of Los Angeles offered a ready response to the acquittal. Between April 30 and May 5, 1992, 600 fires were set.[15] Four thousand businesses were destroyed,[16] and property damage neared $1 billion.[17] Fifty-two people died, and 2,383 people were injured seriously enough to seek medical attention.[18] Smaller disturbances also erupted around the country—in San Francisco, Atlanta, Las Vegas, New York, Seattle, Tampa, and Washington, D.C.[19]

Despite the media's portrayal of the riot as an expression of Black rage, arrest statistics show it to have been a multicultural affair: 3,492 Latinos, 2,832 Blacks, and 640 Whites were arrested, as were 2,492 other people of unidentified races.[20] While the media focused on violence (especially attacks on Whites and Korean merchants), the data tell a different story. Only 10 percent of arrests were for violent crime. The most common charge was curfew violation (42 percent), closely followed by property crimes (35 percent).[21] Likewise, the actual death toll

> definitely attributable to the rioters was under twenty. The police killed at least half that many, and probably many more. . . . Moreover, although some whites and Korean Americans were killed, the vast majority of fatalities were African Americans and Hispanic Americans who died as bystanders or as rioters opposing civil authorities.[22]

Depending on whom you ask, you will hear that the riots constituted "a Black protest," a "bread riot," the "breakdown of civilized society," or "interethnic conflict."[23] None of these accounts is sufficient on its own, but one thing is certain: The riots speak to conditions beyond any single incident.

In the five years preceding the Rodney King beating, 2,500 claims relating to the use of force were filed against the LAPD.[24] To describe just one: In April 1988, Luis Milton Murrales, a twenty-four year old Latino man, lost the vision in one eye because of a police beating. That incident also began with a traffic violation, followed by a brief chase. Murrales crashed his car into a police cruiser and tried to flee on foot. The police caught him, clubbed him, and kicked him when he fell. They resumed the beating at the Ramparts station; the attack involved a total of twenty-eight officers. One commander described his subordinates as behaving like a "lynch mob." Though the city paid $177,500 in a settlement with Murrales, none of the officers was disciplined.[25]

Such incidents, as well as the depressed economic conditions of the inner city, supplied the fuel for a major conflagration. The King beating, the video, and the verdict offered just the spark to set it off.[26]

A LESSON TO LEARN, AND LEARN AGAIN

Rodney King's beating was unusual only because it was videotaped. The community that revolted following the acquittal seemed to grasp this fact, even if the learned commentators and pious pundits condemning them did not. By the same token, the revolt itself also fit an established pattern.

In 1968, the National Advisory Commission on Civil Disorders (commonly called the Kerner Commission) examined 24 riots and reached some remarkable conclusions:

> Our examination of the background of the surveyed disorders revealed a typical pattern of deeply-held grievances which were widely shared by many members of the Negro community. The specific content of the expressed grievances varied somewhat from city to city. But in general, grievances among Negroes in all cities related to prejudice, discrimination, severely disadvantaged living conditions and a general sense of frustration about their inability to change those conditions.
> Specific events or incidents exemplified and reinforced the shared sense of grievance. . . . With each such incident, frustration and tension grew until at some point a final incident, often similar to the incidents preceding it, occurred and was followed almost immediately by violence.
> As we see it, the prior incidents and the reservoir of underlying grievances contributed to a cumulative process of mounting tension that spilled over into violence when the final incident occurred. In this sense the entire chain—the grievances, the series of prior tension-heightening incidents, and the final incident—was the "precipitant" of disorder.[27]

The Kerner report goes on to note, "Almost invariably the incident that ignites disorder arises from police action. Harlem, Watts, Newark, and Detroit—all the major outbursts of recent years—were precipitated by routine arrests of Negroes for minor offenses by white officers."[28]

A few years earlier, in his essay "Fifth Avenue, Uptown: A Letter from Harlem," James Baldwin had offered a very similar analysis:

> [T]he only way to police a ghetto is to be oppressive. None of the
> Police Commissioner's men, even with the best will in the world, have
> any way of understanding the lives led by the people they swagger
> about in twos and threes controlling. Their very presence is an insult,
> and it would be, even if they spent their entire day feeding gumdrops
> to children. They represent the force of the white world, and that
> world's real intentions are, simply, for that world's criminal profit and
> ease, to keep the black man corralled up here, in his place. . . . One
> day, to everyone's astonishment, someone drops a match in the pow-
> der keg and everything blows up. Before the dust has settled or the
> blood congeals, editorials, speeches, and civil-rights commissions are
> loud in the land, demanding to know what happened. What happened
> is that Negroes want to be treated like men.[29]

Baldwin wrote his essay in 1960. Between its publication and that of the Kerner report, the U.S. witnessed civil disturbances of increasing frequency and intensity. Notable among these was the Watts riot of 1965. The Watts riot has been said to divide the sixties into its two parts—the classic period of the civil rights movement before, and the more militant Black Power movement after.[30]

Like the riots of 1992, the Watts disturbance began with a traffic stop. Marquette Frye was pulled over by the California Highway Patrol near Watts, a Black neighborhood in Los Angeles. A crowd gathered, and the police called for backup. As the number of police and bystanders grew, the tension increased accordingly. The police assaulted a couple of bystanders and arrested Frye's family. As the cops left, the crowd stoned their cars. They then began attacking other vehicles in the area, turning them over, and setting them on fire. The next evening, the disorder arose anew, with looting and arson in the nearby commercial areas. The riot lasted six days and caused an estimated $35 million in damage. Almost 1,000 buildings were damaged or destroyed. One thousand people were treated for injuries, and 34 were killed.[31]

Fourteen years after Watts, and thirteen years before the Rodney King verdict, a similar drama played out on the other side of the country, in Miami. On December 17, 1979, the police chased, caught, beat, and killed a Black insurance salesman named Arthur McDuffie. McDuffie, who was riding his cousin's motorcycle, allegedly popped a wheelie and made an obscene gesture at Police Sergeant Ira Diggs, before leading police on an eight-minute high-speed chase. Twelve other cars joined in the pursuit, and when they caught McDuffie, between six and eight officers beat him with heavy flashlights as he lay handcuffed, face down on the pavement. Four days later, he died.[32]

Three officers were charged with second-degree murder, and three others agreed to testify in exchange for immunity. Judge Lenore Nesbitt called the case "a time bomb" and moved it to nearby Tampa, where an all-White jury had recently acquitted another officer accused of beating a Black motorist.[33] The defense then used its peremptory challenges to remove all Black candidates from the jury. The outcome was predictable: the cops were acquitted;[34] crowds then looted stores, burned buildings, and attacked White passers-by. Crowds also laid siege to the police station, breaking its windows and setting fire to the lobby.[35] When calm returned, 17 people were dead, 1,100 had been arrested, and $80 million in property had been damaged.[36] Four hundred seventeen people were treated in area hospitals, the majority of them White.[37]

Here was a key difference: In Miami, the typical looting and burning of White property were matched with attacks against White *people*. In the disorders of the 1960s, attacks against persons had been relatively rare. In three of the sixties' largest riots—those of Watts, Newark, and Detroit—the crowd intentionally killed only two or three White people. Bruce Porter and Marvin Dunn comment:

> What was shocking about Miami was the intensity of the rage direct-
> ed against white people: men, women and children dragged from
> their cars and beaten to death, stoned to death, stabbed with screw-
> drivers, run over with automobiles; hundreds more attacked in the
> street and seriously injured. . . . In Miami, attacking and killing
> white people was the main object of the riot.[38]

Among those injured in the riots was an elderly White man named Martin Weinstock. Weinstock was hit in the head with a piece of concrete and suffered a fractured skull. He was hospitalized for six days. Still, he told an interviewer:

> They should only know that I agree with their anger . . . If the peo-
> ple who threw the concrete were brought before me in handcuffs, I
> would insist that the handcuffs be removed, and I'd try to talk to
> them. I would say that I understand and that I'm on their side. I
> have no anger at all. But they'll never solve their problems by send-
> ing people like me to the hospital.[39]

Weinstock is right: violence directed against random representatives of some dominant group is hardly strategic, much less morally justifiable. But if such attacks are (as Porter and Dunn insist) "shocking," it can only be because Black anger has so rarely taken this form.

White violence against Blacks has never been limited to the destruction of their property. Even in Miami, Blacks got the worst of the violence. Of the seventeen dead, nine were Black people killed by the police, the National Guard, or White vigilantes.[40] Are these deaths somehow less shocking than those of whites?

Yet how loudly White people denounce prejudice when it is directed against them, and how quietly they accept it as it continually bears down on people of color. They indignantly point out the contradiction when those who object to prejudice employ it, and all the while adroitly ignore their own complicity in the institutions of White supremacy.

James Baldwin, again in his "Letter from Harlem," imagines the predicament of a White policeman patrolling the ghetto. "He too believes in good intentions and is astounded and offended when they are not taken for the deed. He has never, himself, done anything for which to be hated. . . . " But, Baldwin asks, "which of us has?"[41]

THE BASICS

We are encouraged to think of acts of police violence more or less in isolation, to consider them as unique, unrelated occurrences. We ask ourselves always, "What went wrong?" and for answers we look to the seconds, minutes, or hours before the incident. Perhaps this leads us to fault the individual officer, perhaps it leads us to excuse him. Such thinking, derived as it is from legal reasoning, does not take us far beyond the case in question. And thus, such inquiries are rarely very illuminating.

Of the instances of police violence I discussed above—the shooting of Timothy Thomas, the beatings of Rodney King and Milton Murrales, the arrest of Marquette Frye, the killing of Arthur McDuffie—any of these may be explained in terms of the actions and attitudes of the particular officers at the scene, the events preceding the violence (including the actions of the victims), and the circumstances in which the officers found themselves. Indeed, juries and police administrators have frequently found it possible to excuse police violence with such explanations.

The unrest that followed these incidents, however, cannot be explained in such narrow terms. To understand the rioting, one must consider a whole range of related issues, including the conditions of life in the Black community, the role of the police in relation to that community, and the history and pattern of similar abuses.

If we are to understand the phenomenon of police brutality, we must get beyond particular cases. We can better understand the actions of individual police officers if we understand the institution of which they are a part. That institution, in turn, can best be examined if we have an understanding of its origins, its social function, and its relation to larger systems like capitalism and White supremacy. Each of these topics will be addressed in later chapters, while here, as a first course, I will focus on what is known about police violence per se.

Let's begin with the basics: violence is an inherent part of policing. The police represent the most direct means by which the state imposes its will on the citizenry.[42] When persuasion, indoctrination, moral pressure, and incentive measures all fail—there are the police. In the field of social control, police are specialists in violence. They are armed, trained, and authorized to use force. With varying degrees of subtlety, this colors their every action. Like the possibility of arrest, the threat of violence is implicit in every police encounter. Violence, as well as the law, is what they represent.

DEFINING BRUTALITY

The study of police brutality faces any number of methodological barriers, not the least of which is the problem of defining it. There is no standard definition, nor is there one way of measuring force and excessive force. As a consequence, different studies produce very different results, and these results are difficult to compare. Kenneth Adams, writing for the National Institute of Justice, notes:

> Because there is no standard methodology for measuring use of force, estimates can vary considerably on strictly computational grounds. Different definitions of force and different definitions of police-public interactions will yield different rates. . . . In particular, broad definitions of use of force, such as those that include grabbing or handcuffing a suspect, will produce higher rates than more conservative definitions. . . . Broad definitions of police-public "interactions," such as calls for assistance, which capture variegated requests for assistance, lead to low rates of use of force. Conversely, narrow definitions of police-public interactions, such as arrests, which concentrate squarely on suspects, lead to higher rates of use of force.[43]

Adams himself outlines multiple definitions for use-of-force violations, focusing on different aspects of the misconduct.

> For example, "deadly force" refers to situations in which force is likely to have lethal consequences for the victim. [The victim need not necessarily die.] . . . [T]he term "excessive force" is used to describe situations in which more force is used than allowable when judged in terms of administrative or professional guidelines or legal standards. . . . "Illegal" use of force refers to situations in which use of force by police violated a law or statute. . . . "Improper," "abusive," "illegitimate," and "unnecessary" use of force are terms that describe situations in which an officer's authority to use force has been mishandled in some general way, the suggestion being that administrative procedure, societal

expectations, ordinary concepts of lawfulness, and the principle of last resort have been violated, respectively.[44]

Adding to the difficulty of comparing one set of figures with another, each of these concepts refers to standards that vary according to the agency, jurisdiction, and community involved. Even within a single agency, agreement on the interpretation of the relevant standards may not be perfect. Bobby Lee Cheatham, a Black cop in Miami, noted the different standards among the police: "To [white officers], police brutality is going up and just hitting on someone with no reason. . . . To me, it's when a policeman gets in a situation where he's too aggressive or uses force when it isn't needed. Most of the time the policeman creates the situation himself."[45]

Even where the facts of a case are agreed upon (which is rare), there may yet be intense disagreement about the relevant standards of conduct and their application to the particular circumstances. For example, in October 1997, sheriff's deputies in Humboldt County, California, swabbed pepper-spray fluid directly into the eyes of non-violent anti-logging demonstrators locked together in an act of civil disobedience. Amnesty International called the tactic "deliberately cruel and tantamount to torture." A federal judge refused to issue an injunction against the practice, however, claiming that it only caused "transient pain."[46]

This case highlights the disparate judgments possible, even given the same facts. A great many people feel about police brutality as Justice Potter Stewart felt about pornography: They can't define it, but they know it when they see it. Unfortunately, they might *not* know it when they see it. Many police tactics—the use of pressure points, the fastening of handcuffs too tightly, and the direct application of pepper spray, for example—really don't *look* anything like they feel. More to the point, in most cases, nobody *sees* the brutality at all, except for the cops and their victims. The rest of us have to rely on secondary information, usually taking one side or the other at their word.

Things get even stickier when general patterns of violence are scrutinized, even where no particular encounter rises to the level of official misconduct. *"Use of excessive force* means that police applied too much force in a given incident, while *excessive use of force* means that police apply force legally in too many incidents."[47] While the former is more likely to grab headlines, it is the latter that makes the largest contribution to the community's reservoir of grievances against the police. But, since the force in question is within the bounds of policy, the excessive use of force is more difficult to address from the perspective of discipline and administration.

All of this controversy and confusion points to a very simple fact: Police brutality is a normative construction. It involves an evaluation, a judgment, and not simply a collection of facts. David Bayley and Harold Mendelsohn explain:

> It should also be noted that police brutality is not just a descriptive category. Rather it is a judgment made about the propriety of police

behavior. . . . Since the use of the phrase implies a judgment, people may disagree profoundly about whether a particular incident, even though it involves the obvious use of force, is a case of brutality. Any discussion of police brutality is therefore encumbered by confusion about whether it applies to more than physical assaults and also by disagreement over what circumstances absolve the police from blame.[48]

In short, the technical distinctions between, say, excessive force and illegal force, while bringing some measure of precision to the discussion, lead us no nearer to a resolution of these disputes. That's because, at root, the disagreement is not about whether a rule was broken, or a law violated. The question—the real question—is one of legitimacy. The larger conflict is a conflict of values.

Let's consider this problem anew: The trouble, or part of it, comes in discerning the legitimate and illegitimate uses of violence. Abuses of authority may look very much like their less corrupt counterparts. Or, stated from a different perspective, the application of legitimate force often feels quite a lot like abuse. But there is no paradox here, not really. The state, claiming a monopoly on the legitimate use of force, needs to distinguish its own violence from other, allegedly less legitimate, uses of force. In non-totalitarian societies, authority exists within carefully prescribed, if vague (one might suggest, intentionally vague), boundaries. Action within these limits is "legitimate," similar action outside of such limits is "abuse." It's as simple as that. If the difference seems subtle, that's because it *is* subtle. In the case of police violence, the difference between legitimate and excessive force is one of degree rather than one of kind. Even the term "excessive force" implies this. Hence, where you or I see brutality, the cop sees only a day's work. The authorities—the other authorities—more often than not side with the policeman, even where he has violated some law or policy. This is, in a sense, only fair, since the police officer—unless he engages in mutiny—*always* sides with them. The main difference, then, between policing and police abuse is a rule or law that usually goes unenforced. The difference is the words.

WHY WE KNOW SO LITTLE ABOUT POLICE BRUTALITY

The preceding observations provide a framework for understanding police brutality, but tell us almost nothing about its prevalence, its forms, its perpetrators, or its victims. Solid facts and hard numbers are very hard to come by.

This dearth of information may say something about how seriously the authorities take the problem. Until very recently, nobody even bothered to keep track of how often the police use force—at least not as part of any systematic, national effort. In 1994, Congress decided to require the Justice Department to collect and publish annual statistics on the police use of force. But this effort has been fraught with difficulty. Unlike the Justice Department's other major data-collection projects—the Uniform Crime Reports provide a useful contrast—the examination of police use of force has never received adequate funding, and the reports appear at irregular intervals. Furthermore, the data on which the studies are based are surely incomplete. Many of the reports rely on local police agencies to supply their numbers, and reporting is voluntary.[49] Worse, the information, once collected and analyzed, is often put to propagandistic uses; its presentation is sometimes heavily skewed to support a law enforcement perspective. But despite their many flaws, the Justice Department reports remain one of the most comprehensive sources of information about the police use of force.

These reports represent various approaches to the issue. They measure the use of force as it occurs in different circumstances, such as arrests and traffic stops. They examine both the level of force used and the frequency with which it is employed. And some studies collect data from victims as well as police.

Unfortunately, under-reporting handicaps every means of compiling the data. One report states frankly: *"The incidence of wrongful use of force by police is unknown. . . .* Current indicators of excessive force are all critically flawed."[50] The most commonly cited indicators are civilian complaints and lawsuits. But few victims of police abuse feel comfortable complaining to the same department under which they suffered the abuse, and lawyers usually only want cases that will win— in other words, cases where the evidence is clear and the harm substantial.[51] Many people fail to make a complaint of any kind, either because they would like to put the unpleasant experience behind them, because they fear retaliation, because they suspect that nothing can be done, or because they feel they will not be believed.[52] Hence, measures that depend on victim reporting are likely to represent only a small fraction of the overall incidence of brutality.

According to a 1999 Justice Department survey, "The vast majority (91.9 percent) of the persons involved in use of force incidents said the police acted improperly. . . . Although the majority of persons with force [used against them] felt the police acted improperly, less than 20 percent of these people . . . said they took formal action such as filing a complaint or lawsuit."[53] Naturally, the victim is not always the best judge as to whether force was excessive, but in some cases, he may be the only source willing to admit that force was used at all. This provides another reason to separate questions concerning the legitimacy of violence from those concerning its prevalence.

The difficulties in measuring excessive and illegal force with complaint and lawsuit records have led academics and practitioners to redirect their attention to all use-of-force incidents. The focus then becomes one of minimizing all instances of police use of force, without undue concern as to whether force was excessive. From this perspective, other records, such as use-of-force reports, arrest records, injury reports, and medical records, become relevant to measuring the incidence of the problem.[54]

Of course, these indicators also have their shortcomings. Arrest records, medical records, and the like will surely reveal uses of violence that have not resulted in law-suits or formal complaints. But they will still underestimate the overall incidence of force, since not every case will be accurately recorded. For example, attempts to assess the prevalence of force based on arrest reports leave out those cases where force was used but no arrest was made.[55] Like the victims (though for very different reasons), the perpetrators of police violence are also likely to under-report its occurrence. And they are likely to understate the level of force used and the seriousness of resultant injuries when they do report it.[56] Individual medical records, meanwhile, are not generally available for examination, except when presented as evidence in a complaint hearing or civil trial. And even if emergency rooms were to maintain statistics on police-related injuries, many victims of violence, especially the uninsured, do not seek treatment except for the most serious of injuries.

Other indicators, such as media reports and direct observation, are similarly flawed. The media, of course, can only report on events if they know about them. Furthermore, they are unlikely to report on routine uses of force because—like the fabled "Dog Bites Man" story—it is so commonplace.[57] Direct observation is limited by the obvious fact that no one can observe everything, everywhere, all the time. And observation can lead a subject (either the officer or the suspect) to change his behavior while he is being observed. In humanitarian terms, such deterrence is all for the good, but it doesn't do much for the systematic study of police activity or the measurement of police violence.

The sad fact is that nobody knows very much about the police use of force, much less about the use of excessive force. Its prevalence, frequency, and distribution remain, for the most part, unmeasured; and there is only limited information available concerning its perpetrators, victims, forms, and causes. Nevertheless, *some* information is available through the sources mentioned above. And, imperfect though they are, the statistics they produce may point to some reliable baseline, an estimated minimum to which we can refer with a fair amount of certainty. With that aim in mind, and with not a little trepidation, we should turn our attention to the data that are available, and consider what they indicate.

A LOOK AT THE NUMBERS

According to a 1996 Justice Department survey, 20 percent of the American public had direct contact with the police during the previous year. Most of these contacts took the form of traffic stops, and most were unremarkable. Only 1 in 500 residents was subject to the use of force or the threat of force. Three years later, the Justice Department repeated the study, this time with a sample almost fifteen times as large. The results were nearly identical: 21 percent of the population had contact with the police in 1999, and 1 in 500 fell victim to violence or threats of violence.[58]

Now, that may not sound like a lot of people, until you realize that "1 in 500" is a polite way of saying "nearly half a million"—an estimated 471,000 people in 1996 and 422,000 in 1999.[59] Four-hundred thousand people, if we got them all together, would make for a fair-sized city, larger than Atlanta, Georgia, and almost as large as Fresno, California.[60] And when you orient yourself to the fact that this city could be reproduced *every year*, you start to get some picture of how common police violence really is.

Another way of looking at the figures is that, out of every 100 people the police come into contact with, they will threaten or use force against one of them (0.96 percent). This rate is nearly twice as high for Blacks and Hispanics, who experience force (or the threat thereof) in 2 percent of their interactions with the police.[61]

Among these 422,000 people, the most common form of violence they suffered involved being pushed or grabbed.[62] Approximately 20 percent were threatened, but not subject to actual physical violence. At the other end of the curve, another 20 percent reported injuries.[63] More than three-quarters of the victims (76 percent) characterized the force as excessive,[64] and the "vast majority (92 percent) of persons experiencing [the] threat or use of force said the police acted improperly."[65]

According to a Justice Department study of six police agencies,[66] police use force in 17.1 percent of all adult custody arrests (or 18.9 percent, if we include threats of force). Suspects, in contrast, use force against the police in less than 3 percent of arrest cases. More specifically, suspects employ weaponless tactics in 1.9 percent of arrests, and use weapons in 0.7 percent. Police, meanwhile, use weaponless tactics in 15.8 percent of arrests, and use weapons in about 2.1 percent.[67] The police, in short, use force far more often than it is used against them.

With police using force in about one of every six arrests, it strikes me as an inescapable fact that police violence is quite routine, but most studies resist this conclusion, insisting that the use of force is exceptional.[68] The police themselves seem untroubled by the level of violence within their departments. According to a National Institute of Justice study on "Police Attitudes Toward Abuse of Authority," 24.5 percent of police surveyed "agreed" or "strongly agreed" that "It is sometimes acceptable to use more force than is legally allowable to control someone who physically assaults an officer"; 31.1 percent contended that "Police are not permitted to use as much force as is often necessary in making arrests"; and 42.2 percent felt that "Always following the rules is not compatible with getting the job done."[69]

Interestingly, 62.4 percent of police feel that officers in their department "seldom. . . . use more force than is necessary to make an arrest." Sixteen percent maintained that police never do, and 21.7 percent said that police sometimes, often, or always use excessive force.[70] Sociologist Rodney Stark, writing well before the study in question explained this tendency to understate the incidence of violence: "[If] each policeman only loses his temper once or twice a year and roughs someone up, a very large number of citizens will get roughed up during the year. Thus, their violence may seem occasional to individual policemen, when in fact for the force as a whole it is routine."[71]

Of course, the propensity for violence is not distributed evenly throughout police departments. The Independent Commission on the Los Angeles Police Department (also called the Christopher Commission) noted:

> Of nearly 6,000 officers identified as involved in a use of force . . .
> from January 1987 through March 1991, more than 4,000 had less
> than five reports each. But 63 officers had 20 or more reports each.
> The top 5 percent of officers ranked by number of reports accounted
> for more than 20 percent of all reports, and the top 10 percent
> accounted for 33 percent.[72]

These numbers may not be as comforting as they first seem. For one thing, 6,000 cops is still quite a lot, even when the occasions of their violence are spread over four years. In fact, it seems the Christopher Commission fell into precisely the trap that Rodney Stark described: By emphasizing the idea that most officers rarely use force, they demonstrate that brutality is *individually* rare, while obscuring the fact that it is *collectively* common. Four thousand officers, with fewer than five reports each, together could have as many as 16,000 such reports. Moreover, the unruly 5 percent, in numerical terms, would add up to about 300 officers.[73] One retired LAPD sergeant told the Christopher Commission that there were at least one or two cops in every division who regularly use excessive force.[74] This would imply that not only is brutality routine, it is widespread.

But, however common police brutality may be, its victims are not a perfect cross-section of the American public. In 1999, for example, 86.9 percent of the victims of police violence were male, and 55.3 percent were between the ages of sixteen and twenty-four.[75] While most victims were White (58.9 percent), Blacks and Hispanics were victimized in numbers significantly out of proportion to their representation in the general population. Hispanics make up 10.2 percent of the population nationally, but accounted for 15.5 percent of those victimized by the police. Blacks constitute 11.4 percent of the population, and 22.6 percent of those facing police violence.[76] Of those killed by police from 1976 to 1998, 42 percent were Black.[77]

These figures, which I have recited with relatively little comment, offer only a very limited representation of police violence. The studies producing these numbers, with their statistics and their charts, seem altogether too sanitized. They should, to do the subject justice, come smeared with blood, with numbers surrounded by chalk outlines. The real cost of police violence, the human cost, is too easily forgotten, figured away, buried under a mountain of decimal points. We must not allow that to happen. We must bear in mind, always, that each of these statistics represents a tragedy. Behind each there lies real pain, humiliation, indignity, often injustice, and sometimes death. Our understanding of police brutality relies on our ability to hear the scream behind the statistic. Once we do, the rage of L.A., of Miami, of Cincinnati becomes comprehensible. Their fires may burn inside us.

EXPLAINING AWAY THE ABUSE

In *Uprooting Racism*, Paul Kivel makes a useful comparison between the rhetoric abusive men employ to justify beating up their girlfriends, wives, or children and the publicly traded justifications for widespread racism. He writes:

> During the first few years that I worked with men who are violent I was continually perplexed by their inability to see the effects of their actions and their ability to deny the violence they had done to their partners or children. I only slowly became aware of the complex set of tactics that men use to make violence against women invisible and to avoid taking responsibility for their actions. These tactics are listed below in the rough order that men employ them. . . .

(1) *Denial*	"I didn't hit her."
(2) *Minimization*	"It was only a slap."
(3) *Blame*	"She asked for it."
(4) *Redefinition*	"It was mutual combat."
(5) *Unintentionality*	"Things got out of hand."
(6) *It's over now*	"I'll never do it again."
(7) *It's only a few men*	"Most men wouldn't hurt a woman."
(8) *Counterattack*	"She controls everything."
(9) *Competing victimization*	"Everybody is against men."[78]

Kivel goes on to detail the ways these nine tactics are used to excuse (or deny) institutionalized racism. Each of these tactics also has its police analogy, both as applied to individual cases and in regard to the general issue of police brutality.[79]

Here are a few examples:

(1) Denial

"The professionalism and restraint displayed by the police officers, supervisors, and commanders on the 'front line' . . . was nothing short of outstanding."[80]

"America does not have a human-rights problem."[81]

(2) Minimization

The injuries were "of a minor nature."[82]

"Police use force infrequently."[83]

(3) Blame

"This guy isn't Mr. Innocent Citizen, either. Not by a long shot."[84]

"They died because they were criminals."[85]

(4) Redefinition

It was "mutual combat."[86]

"Resisting arrest."[87]

"The use of force is necessary to protect yourself."[88]

(5) Unintentionality

"[O]fficers have no choice but to use deadly force against an assailant who is deliberately trying to kill them."[89]

(6) It's over now

"We're making changes."[90]

"We will change our training; we will do everything in our power to make sure it never happens again."[91]

(7) It's only a few men

"A small proportion of officers are disproportionately involved in use-of-force incidents."[92]

"Even if we determine that the officers were out of line . . . it is an aberration."[93]

(8) Counterattack

"The only thing they understand is physical force and pain."[94]

"People make complaints to get out of trouble."[95]

(9) Competing Victimization.

The police are "in constant danger."[96]

"[L]iberals are prejudiced against police, much as many white police are biased against Negroes."[97]

The police are "the most downtrodden, oppressed, dislocated minority in America."[98]

Another commonly invoked rationale for justifying police violence is:

(10) The Hero Defense.

"The police routinely do what the rest of us don't: They risk their lives to keep the peace. For that selfless bravery, they deserve glory, laud and honor."[99]

"[W]ithout the police . . . anarchy would be rife in this country, and the civilization now existing on this hemisphere would perish."[100]

"[T]he police create a sense of community that makes social life possible."[101]

"[T]hey alone stand guard at the upstairs door of Hell."[102]

This list is by no means exhaustive, but it should offer something of the tone that these excuses can take. Many of these approaches overlap, and often several are used in conjunction. For example, LAPD Sgt. Stacey Koon offers this explanation for the beating of Rodney King:

> From our view, and based on what he had already done, Rodney King was trying to assault an officer, maybe grab a gun. And when he was not moving, he seemed to be looking for an opportunity to hurt somebody, his eyes darting this way and that. . . .
>   So we'd had to use force to make him respond to our commands, to make him lie still so we could neutralize this guy's threat to other people and himself.
>   The force we used was well within the guidelines of the Los Angeles Police Department; I'd made sure of that. And, I was proud of the professionalism [the officers had] shown in subduing a really monster guy, a felony evader seen committing numerous traffic violations.[103]

In three paragraphs, Koon employs minimization, blame, redefinition, unintentionality, counterattacks, competing victimization, and the Hero Defense. As is usual, his little story stresses the possible danger of the situation, and elsewhere Koon emphasizes the generalizable sense of danger that officers experience: "[W]e'd all thought that maybe we were getting lured into something. It's happened before. How many times have you read about a cop getting killed after stopping somebody for a speeding violation?"[104]

The danger of the job is a constant theme in the defense of police violence. It is implicit (or sometimes explicit) in about half of the excuses listed above. By pointing to the dangers of the job, the excuse-makers don't only defend police actions in particular circumstances (which might actually have been dangerous), but as often as not take the opportunity to mount a general defense of the police. This is a clever bit of sophistry, as cynical as a Memorial Day speech during wartime. It's one thing to make a banner of the bloody uniform when discussing a case where the cops actually *were* in danger, but quite another to do so when they *might have been* in danger, or only *thought* that they were.

The fact that policing is risky, by this view, seems to justify in advance whatever measures the police feel necessary to employ. This point lies at the center of the Hero Defense. Its genius is that it is so hard to answer. Few people are indifferent to the death of a police officer, especially when they feel (though only in some vague, patriotic kind of way) that it occurred because the officer was selflessly working—as former Philadelphia City Solicitor Sheldon Albert put it—"so that you and I and our families and our children can walk on the streets".[105] The flaw of the Hero Defense, however, is both simple and, if you'll pardon the term, fatal: Policing is not so dangerous as we are led to believe.

THE DANGERS OF THE JOB

In 2001, 140 cops were murdered on the job. Most of these (71) were killed in the September 11 attacks on the World Trade Center and the Pentagon. The remaining 69 deaths represent 65 separate incidents, most commonly domestic disturbances and traffic stops. Additionally, 77 officers died in on-duty accidents.[106]

The 2001 figures are exceptional, skewed by the fact that more cops died in one day than in the entire rest of the year combined. Outside of the World Trade Center attack, only three officers were intentionally killed in the entire northeastern United States. If we bracket the anomaly of September 11, we get a more representative picture of the dangers police face: more officers died in accidents (77) than were murdered (69).[107] This is not unusual. Between 1995 and 2000, 360 cops were murdered and 403 died in accidents. To take just one year's figures, 135 cops died in 2000; this number represents 51 murders and 84 accidents.[108]

Naturally it is not to be lost sight of that these numbers represent human lives, not widgets or sacks of potatoes. But let's remember that there were 5,915 fatal work injuries in 2000.[109] Policing may be dangerous, but it is not the most dangerous job available. In terms of total fatalities, more truck drivers are killed than any other kind of worker (852 in the year 2000).[110]

A better measure of occupational risk, however, is the rate of work-related deaths per 100,000 workers. In 2000, for example, it was 27.6 for truck drivers. At 12.1 deaths per 100,000, policing is slightly less dangerous than mowing lawns, cutting hedges, and running a wood-chipper: Groundskeepers suffer 14.9 deaths per 100,000. By occupation, the highest rate of fatalities is among timber cutters, at 122.1 per 100,000.[111] By industry, mining and farming are the most dangerous. "The mining industry recorded a rate of 30.0 fatal work injuries per 100,000 workers in 2000, the highest of any industry and about 7 times the rate for all workers. Agriculture recorded the second highest rate in 2000 (20.9 fatalities per 100,000 workers)."[112] The rate for all occupations, taken together, is 4.3 per 100,000 workers.[113]

Where are the headlines, the memorials, the honor guards, and sorrowful renderings of taps for these workers? Where are the mayoral speeches, the newspaper editorials, the sober reflections that these brave men and women died, and that others risk their lives daily, so that we might continue to enjoy the benefits of modern society?

Policing, it seems, is the only industry that both exaggerates and advertises its dangers. It has done so at a high cost, and to great advantage, though, as is so often

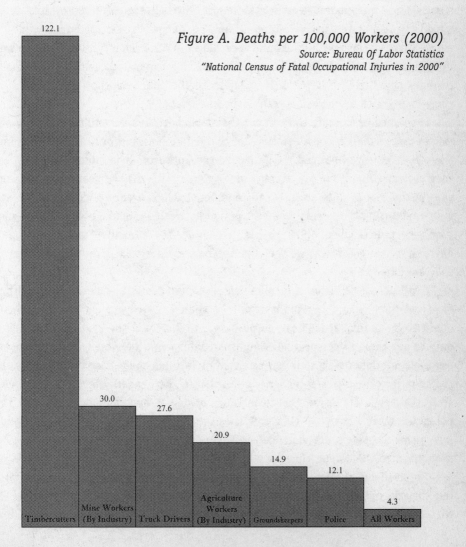

Figure A. Deaths per 100,000 Workers (2000)
Source: Bureau Of Labor Statistics
"National Census of Fatal Occupational Injuries in 2000"

the case, the costs are not borne by the same people who reap the benefits. The overblown image of police heroism, and the "obsession" with officer safety (Rodney Stark's term), do not only serve to justify police violence after the fact; by providing such justification, they legitimize violence, and thus make it more likely.[114] The exaggerated sense of danger has helped to re-order police priorities to the detriment of the public interest.

Stark argues that "the police ought to understand clearly that they are being paid to take a certain degree of risk and that their safety does not come before public safety or the common good. Unfortunately, the police typically place their safety first and in recent years we have come to accept this priority."[115] By way of counterpoint, Stark describes the performance of the U.S. Marshals deployed to protect James Meredith during his September 1962 entrance into the University of Mississippi. Two hundred Marshals faced off with a crowd of 2,000 Whites determined to prevent the school's integration. The Marshals stood for hours, while the crowd attacked them with bricks and sporadic sniper fire. Twenty-nine Marshals were injured, but they never broke ranks or fired their weapons. "Recalling this episode, consider how little we have come to expect of the police and how greatly we have come to share their obsession with their own safety."[116]

The police exaggerate the dangers they face, both in a general sense and in particular cases, where bloodied victims are charged with assault or resisting arrest, and the officer is left unharmed.[117] The fact is the police produce more casualties than they suffer. "Since 1976, an average of 79 police officers have been murdered each year in the line of duty. . . . "[118] All together, 1,820 law enforcement officers were murdered during the twenty-two-year period between 1976 and 1998.[119] In the same time, the police killed 8,578 people, averaging 373 annually—more than one a day.[120] If we do the math, we see that the police kill almost five times as often as they are killed.

I will surely be accused of ghoulishly keeping score, of measuring the differences where I should be emphasizing the shared tragedy, of subtracting when I ought to be adding. It isn't my purpose here to disregard the deaths of the police, only to put them in perspective. The disparity between the violence police face and the violence they use is striking, especially if we remember that the available statistics reflect the officers' tendency to overstate the dangers they face and understate their own use of force, both in terms of degree and frequency. The fact that police use more force than they face is incontrovertible; it is left for us to wonder how often the police use violence—in some cases, deadly force—that is out of all proportion to the danger they face.

The available studies tell us very little about the prevalence of excessive force, but they do indicate that the police use violence more often, at higher levels, and with deadlier effects, than they actually encounter it.[121] This disparity should not be surprising, considering the nature of policing—the imperative to maintain control at all times, in every situation (hardly a realistic goal), the training to use escalating levels of force to gain compliance, and authority unhindered by genuine oversight. Policing, as I said earlier, is inherently violent; this violence, generally speaking, seems to be of an offensive—rather than defensive—character. In essence, the police are professional bullies. And like all bullies, the thing they most fear is an even fight. As Kenneth Bradley, a Miami-Dade Metro officer sees it: "I don't get paid to get hurt, and I don't get paid to fight fair. "[122] No wonder, then, that the violence used *by* the police far outstrips anything used *against* them.

INSTITUTIONALIZED BRUTALITY

Given such pervasive violence, it is astonishing that discussions of police brutality so frequently focus on the behavior of individual officers. Commonly called the "Rotten Apple" theory, the explanation of police misconduct favored by police commanders and their ideological allies holds that police abuse is exceptional, that the officers who misuse their power are a tiny minority, and that it is unfair to judge other cops (or the department as a whole) by the misbehavior of the few.[123] This is a handy tool for diverting attention away from the institution, its structure, practices, and social role, pushing the blame, instead, onto some few of its agents.[124] It is, in other words, a means of protecting the organization from scrutiny, and of avoiding change.

Despite the official insistence to the contrary, it is clear that police organizations, as well as individual officers, hold a large share of the responsibility for the prevalence of police brutality.[125] Police agencies are organizationally complex, and brutality may be promoted or accommodated within any (or all) of its various dimensions. Both formal and informal aspects of an organization can help create a climate in which unnecessary violence is tolerated, or even encouraged. Among the formal aspects contributing to violence are the organization's official policies, its identified priorities, the training it offers its personnel,[126] its allocation of resources, and its system of promotions, awards, and other incentives.[127] When these aspects of an organization encourage violence—whether or not they do so intentionally, or even consciously—we can speak of brutality being promoted "from above." This understanding has been well applied to the regimes of certain openly thuggish leaders—Bull Connor, Richard Daley, Frank Rizzo,[128] Daryl Gates, Rudolph Giuliani (to name just a few)—but it needn't be so overt to have the same effect.

On the other hand, when police culture and occupational norms support the use of unnecessary violence, we can describe brutality as being supported "from below." Such informal conditions are a bit harder to pin down, but they certainly have their consequences. We may count among their elements insularity,[129] indifference to the problem of brutality,[130] generalized suspicion,[131] and the intense demand for personal respect.[132] One of the first sociologists to study the problem of police violence, William Westley, described these as "basic occupational values," more important than any other determinant of police behavior:

> [The policeman] regards the public as his enemy, feels his occupation to be in conflict with the community and regards himself as a pariah. The experience and the feeling give rise to a collective emphasis on secrecy, an attempt to coerce respect from the public, and a belief that almost any means are legitimate in completing an important arrest. These are for the policeman basic occupational values. They arise from his experience, take precedence over his legal responsibilities, are central to an understanding of his conduct, and form the occupational contexts with which violence gains its meaning.[133]

Police violence is very frequently over-determined—promoted from above and supported from below. But where it is not actually encouraged, sometimes even where individuals (officers or administrators) disapprove of it, excessive and illegal force are nevertheless nearly always condoned. Among police administrators there is the persistent and well-documented refusal to discipline violent officers; and among the cops themselves, there is the "code of silence."

In its 1998 report, Human Rights Watch noted the inaction of police commanders:

> Most high-ranking police officials, whether at the level of commissioner, chief, superintendent, or direct superiors, seem uninterested in vigorously pursuing high standards for treatment of persons in custody. When reasonably high standards are set, superior officers are often unwilling to require that their subordinates consistently meet them.[134]

Even where officers are found guilty of misconduct, discipline rarely follows. For example, in 1998 New York's Civilian Complaint Review Board issued 300 findings against officers; fewer than half of these resulted in disciplinary action.[135]

LAPD Assistant Chief Jesse Brewer told the Christopher Commission:

> We know who the bad guys are. Reputations become well known, especially to the sergeants and then of course to lieutenants and captains in the areas. But, I don't see anyone bringing these people up and saying, "Look, you are not conforming, you are not measuring up. You need to take a look at yourself and your conduct and the way you're treating people" and so forth. I don't see that occurring. . . . The sergeants don't, they're not held accountable so why should they be that much concerned[?] . . . I have a feeling that they don't think that much is going to happen to them anyway if they tried to take action and perhaps not even be supported by the lieutenant or the

captain all the way up the line when they do take action against some individual.[136]

Rank-and-file cops, likewise, are extremely reluctant to report the abuses they witness. Some of this reluctance, surely, is a reflection of their superiors' indifference. (After all, if nothing's going to come of it, why report it?) But their peers also enforce this silence. A National Institute of Justice study on police integrity discovered

> a large gap between attitudes and behavior. That is, even though officers do not believe in protecting wrongdoers, they often do not turn them in.
> More than 80 percent of police surveyed reported that they do not accept the "code of silence" (i.e., keeping quiet in the face of misconduct by others) as an essential part of the mutual trust necessary to good policing. . . . However, about one-quarter (24.9 percent) of the sample agreed or strongly agreed that whistle blowing is not worth it, more than two thirds (67.4 percent) reported that police officers who report incidents of misconduct are likely to be given a "cold shoulder" by fellow officers, and a majority (52.4 percent) agreed or strongly agreed that it is not unusual for police officers to "turn a blind eye" to other officers' improper conduct. . . . A surprising 6 in 10 (61 percent) indicated that police officers do not always report even serious criminal violations that involve the abuse of authority by fellow officers.[137]

We should remember that these numbers reflect the reluctance of police to report misconduct *when they recognize it as such*. Given police attitudes about the use of force, when nearly a quarter of officers (24.5 percent) think it acceptable to use illegal force against a suspect who assaults an officer,[138] we can reasonably conclude that the police report their colleague's excessive force only in the rarest of circumstances.

I have, to this point, concentrated on the means by which violence ,and excessive force in particular, is institutionalized by police agencies. That is, I have discussed the ways police organizations produce and sanction violence, even outside the bounds of their own rules and the law. This examination has provided a brief sketch of the way the institution shapes violence, but has not thus far considered the implications of this violence for the institution. It seems paradoxical that an institution responsible for enforcing the law would frequently rely on illegal practices. The police resolve this tension between nominally lawful ends and illegal means by substituting their own occupational and organizational norms for the legal duties assigned to them. Westley suggests:

> This process then results in a transfer in property from the state to the colleague group. The means of violence which were originally a property of the state, in loan to its law-enforcement agent, the

police, are in a psychological sense confiscated by the police, to be conceived of as a personal property to be used at their discretion.[139]

From the officers' perspective, the center of authority is shifted and the relationship between the state and its agents is reversed. The police become a law unto themselves.

This account reflects the attitudes of the officers, and explains many of the institutional features already discussed. It also identifies an important principle of police ideology, one that (as we shall see in later chapters) has guided the development of the institution, especially in the last half-century. But Westley's theory also raises some important questions. Chief among these: Why would the state allow such a coup?

THE POLICE, THE STATE, AND SOCIAL CONFLICT

We might also ask: To what degree is violence the "property" of the state to begin with? At what point does the police co-optation of violence challenge the state's monopoly on it? When do the police, in themselves, become a genuine rival of the state? Are they a rival to be used—as in a system of indirect rule—or a rival to be suppressed? Is there a genuine danger of the police becoming the dominant force in society, displacing the civilian authorities? Is this a problem for the ruling class? Might such a development, under certain conditions, be to their favor? These are real questions, and we will get to them.

For now, let us concentrate on the question of why the state (meaning, here, the civil authorities) would let the police claim the means of violence as their own. Police brutality does not just happen; it is *allowed* to happen. It is tolerated by the police themselves, those on the street and those in command. It is tolerated by prosecutors, who seldom bring charges against violent cops, and by juries, who rarely convict. It is tolerated by the civil authorities, the mayors, and the city councils, who do not use their influence to challenge police abuses. But why?

The answer is simple: Police brutality is tolerated because it is what people with power want.

This surely sounds conspiratorial, as though orders issued from a smoke-filled room are circulated at roll call to the various beat cops and result in a certain number of arrests and a certain number of gratuitous beatings on a given evening. But this isn't what I mean, or not quite. Instead, the apparent conflict between the law and police practices may not be so important as we tend to assume. The two may, at times, be at odds, but this is of little concern so long as the interests they serve are essentially the same. The police may violate the law, as long as they do so in the pursuit of ends that people with power generally endorse, and from which such people profit. This idea may become clearer if we consider police brutality and other illegal tactics in relation to lawful policing: When the police enforce the law, they do so unevenly, in ways that give disproportionate attention to the activities of poor people, people of color, and others near the bottom of the social pyramid.[140] And when the police violate the law, these same people are their most frequent victims. This is a coincidence too large to overlook. If we put aside, for the moment, all questions of legality, it must become quite clear that the object of police attention, and the target of police violence, is overwhelmingly that portion of the population that lacks real power. And this is precisely the point: Police activities, legal or illegal, violent or nonviolent, tend to keep the people who currently stand at the bottom of the social hierarchy in their "place," where they "belong"—at the bottom. This is why James Baldwin said that policing was "oppressive" and "an insult."

Put differently, we might say that the police act to defend the interests and standing of those with power, those at the top. So long as they serve in this role, they are likely to be given a free hand in pursuing these ends and a great deal of leeway in pursuing other ends that they identify for themselves. The laws may say otherwise, but laws can be ignored.

In theory, police authority is restricted by state and federal law, as well as by the policies of individual departments. In reality, the police often exceed the bounds of their lawful authority, and rarely pay any price for doing so. The rules are only as good as their enforcement, and they are seldom enforced. The real limits to police power are established not by statutes and regulations—since no rule is self-enforcing—but by their leadership and, indirectly, by the balance of power in society.

So long as the police defend the status quo, so long as their actions promote the stability of the existing system, their misbehavior is likely to be overlooked. It is when their excesses threaten this stability that they begin to face meaningful restraints. Laws and policies can be ignored and still provide a cover of plausible deniability for those in authority. But when misconduct reaches such a level as to prove embarrassing, or so as to provoke unrest, the authorities may have to tighten the reins—for a while.[141] Token prosecutions, minimal reforms, and other half-measures may give the appearance of change, and may even serve as some check against the worst abuses of authority, but they carefully fail to affect the underlying causes of brutality. It would be wrong to conclude that the police never change. But it is important to notice the limits of these changes, to understand the influences that direct them, and to recognize the interests that they serve. Police brutality is pervasive, systemic, and inherent to the institution. It is also, as we shall see, anything but new.

THE ORIGINS OF AMERICAN POLICING

In February 1826, Aziel Conklin, the Captain of the Watch in New York's third district, was suspended—but later reinstated—after a conviction for assault and battery.[1] This incident was not especially unusual at the time. Even now, it would only stand out because cops are so rarely convicted, regardless of the evidence against them. Yet if the licensed use of violence is not new, the system employing it today looks very different than that of the 1820s. And if the abuse of authority is itself a constant feature of government, the nature of that authority has undergone substantial changes.

CHARACTERISTICS OF MODERN POLICE

Policing itself is not a distinctly modern activity.[2] It has existed in some form, under numerous political systems, in disparate locations, for centuries. Most of the institutions historically responsible for law enforcement would not be recognizable to us as police. Colonial America, for example, had nothing like our modern police departments.

> The earliest specialized police were watchmen. . . . However, although their function was certainly specialized, it is not always clear that it was policing. Very often they acted only as sentinels, responsible for summoning others to apprehend criminals, repel attack, or put out fires.[3]

It was not until the middle of the nineteenth century that most American cities had police organizations with roughly the same form and function as our contemporary departments.

Though most historians agree it was in the mid-1800s that police forces throughout the United States converged into a single type, it has been surprisingly difficult to enumerate the major features of a modern police operation. David Bayley defines the modern police in terms of their public auspices, specialized function, and professionalism,[4] though he does also mention their non-military character[5] and their authority to use force.[6] Richard Lundman offers four criteria: full-time service, continuity in office, continuity in procedure, and control by a central governmental authority.[7] Selden Bacon, meanwhile, suggests six characteristics:

(a) citywide jurisdiction,
(b) twenty-four hour responsibility,
(c) a single organization responsible for the greater part of formal enforcement,
(d) paid personnel on a salary basis,
(e) a personnel occupied solely with police duties,
(f) general rather than specific functions.[8]

Raymond Fosdick argues that the defining mark of modern police departments is their organization under a single commander.[9] And Eric Monkkonen takes as his sole requirement the presence of uniforms.[10]

Two of these criteria are easily done away with. The use of uniforms is neither a necessary nor a unique feature of modern policing. Some police officers, especially detectives, do not wear uniforms, and are no less modern for that fact. Furthermore, even within the history of law enforcement, uniforms predate the modern institution. The London Watch, for example, was uniformed in 1791.[11] Likewise, though most police agencies are headed by a single police chief, this is not always the case, and has not always been the case, even in departments that are distinctly modern. Police boards of various kinds have moved in and out of fashion throughout the modern period, especially at the cusp of the nineteenth and twentieth centuries.

The civilian character of the police is more problematic, and, precisely because it *is* problematic I will put it aside as a suggested criterion for modern police. The relationship between policing and the military has always been complex and controversial, and if current trends are any indication, it will remain so for some time. Given the ambiguous and shifting character of the police, it seems unwise to generalize about its essentially civilian—or military—nature, and I do not wish to define away the problem at the expense of a more nuanced analysis.[12]

Those characteristics remaining may be divided into two groups. The first are the defining characteristics of police:

(1) the authority to use force,
(2) a public character and accountability (at least in principle) to some central governmental authority, and
(3) general law enforcement duties (as opposed to limited, specified duties such as parking enforcement or animal control).

These traits, I think, are essential to any organization that claims to be engaged in policing.

The second set comprises those criteria distinguishing *modern* policing from earlier forms. These include:

(1) the investment of responsibility for law enforcement in a single organization,

(2) citywide jurisdiction and centralization,

(3) an intended continuity in office and procedure,[13]

(4) a specialized policing function (meaning that the organization is only or mainly responsible for policing, not for keeping the streets clean, putting out fires, or other extraneous duties),

(5) twenty-four-hour service, and

(6) personnel paid on a salary basis rather than by fee.

"Policing" Characteristics	"Modern" Characteristics
Authority to Use Force	Single Organization
Public; Accountable to Central Governmental Authority	City-Wide Jurisdiction; Centralized Control
General Law Enforcement Duties	Continuity in Office and Procedure
	Specialized Function
	24-Hour Service
	Salaried Personnel
	Preventive Orientation

Figure B.   Characteristics of Modern Policing

There is one final characteristic that deserves consideration. The development of policing has been guided in large part by an emerging orientation toward preventive rather than responsive activity. Though this idea was firmly established by the time modern departments took the stage, it was not until quite some time later that specific techniques of prevention entered into use, and the degree to which the police do, or can, or should act to prevent crime remains even now a matter of intense debate.

Rather than use these factors to draw a sharp line demarcating a clearly identifiable set of modern police (a line most police departments will have crossed and re-crossed), I propose we use these criteria to place various organizations on a continuum as being *more* or *less* modern depending on the degree to which they display these characteristics.[14] I have listed the traits above in order of what I take to be their relative significance. This approach may seem a bit impressionistic, but I think the picture it offers is helpful in understanding the evolution of police systems. For the most part, the creators of the new police did not see themselves as marching inexorably toward an ideal of modern policing. Instead, they adapted preexisting institutions to the demands of new circumstances, evolving their systems slowly through a process of invention and imitation, improvisation and experimentation, promise and compromise, trial and error. The rate of progress was unsteady, its path wavering, its advances frequently reversed, and its direction determined by a variety of factors including political pressure, scandals, wars, riots, economics, immigration, budget constraints, the law, and sometimes crime.

There is a further advantage to this approach: It acknowledges the fact of continuing development and leaves open the possibility of further modernization. Hence, rather than a revolution of modernity, occurring between 1829 and about 1860, we are faced with a much more protracted process. We find police departments approaching their modern form quite a while earlier; and yet, we can recognize that these same departments may not be fully modernized, even now.[15] In short, this view avoids the tendency to treat our contemporary institution as the final product of earlier progress, as an end-point marking completion, and instead situates it as one stage in an ongoing process.

ENGLISH PREDECESSORS

Many people find it astonishing that the police have predecessors. They seem to imagine that the cop has always been there, in something like his present capacity, subject only to the periodic change of uniform or the occasional technological advance. Quite to the contrary, the police have a rich and complex history, if an ugly one. Our contemporary institution owes much of its character to those that came before it, including those offices imported or imposed during the colonial period. These in turn have their own stories, closely linked to the creation of modern states. It is worth considering this lineage and the forces that propelled change, from one form of control to another.

During the time between the fall of Rome and the rise of modern states, policing—like political authority—became quite decentralized. "Gradually, new superordinate kingdoms were formed, delegating the power to create police but holding on to the power to make law."[16] Within such arrangements, policing initially took an informal mode, such as that of the frankpledge system in England.[17] Under this system, families grouped themselves together in sets of ten (called "tythings") and collections of ten tythings (called "hundreds"). The heads of these families pledged to one another to obey the law. Together they were responsible for enforcing that pledge, apprehending any of their own who violated it, and combining for mutual protection. If they failed in these duties, they were fined by the sovereign.[18]

Under the frankpledge system, the responsibility for enforcing the law and maintaining order fell to everyone in the community.

> Our extremely modern concept of a specialized police force did not then exist. Neither was there any public means for repressing or preventing crime, as distinguished from its detection and the apprehension of offenders. The members of each tything were simply bound to a mutual undertaking to apprehend, and present for trial, any of their number who might commit an offense.[19]

This arrangement relied on the social conditions present in small communities, especially the sense of interpersonal connection and interdependence. But we should be careful of romanticizing this idyllic scenario. The frankpledge system was imposed by the Norman conquerors as a means of maintaining colonial rule. Essentially, they forced the conquered communities to enforce the Norman law.[20]

Still, the system was rather limited in its authoritarian uses, as it depended on a common acceptance of the law. Hence, English sovereigns later found it necessary to supplement the frankpledge with the appointment of a *shire reeve*, or sheriff, to act in local affairs as a general representative of the crown. The sheriff was responsible for enforcing the monarch's will in military, fiscal, and judicial matters, and for maintaining the domestic peace.[21] Sheriffs were appointed by and directly accountable to the sovereign. They were responsible for organizing the tythings and the hundreds, inspecting their weapons and, when necessary, calling together a group of men to serve as a *posse comitatus*, pursuing and apprehending fugitives. The sheriffs were paid a portion of the taxes they collected, which led to abuses and made them rather unpopular figures.[22] Eventually, following a series of scandals and complaints, the sheriff's powers were eroded and some of his responsibilities were assigned to new offices, including the coroner, the justice of the peace, and the constable.[23] According to the 1285 Statute of Winchester, the constable was responsible for acting as the sheriff's agent. Two constables were appointed for every hundred, thus providing more immediate supervision of the tythings and hundreds.[24]

> [The constable's] early history is closely intertwined with military affairs and with martial law; for after the Conquest the Norman marshals, predecessors of the modern constable, held positions of great dignity and were drawn for the most part from the baronage. As leaders of the king's army they seem to have exercised a certain jurisdiction over military offenders, particularly when the army was

engaged on foreign soil, and therefore beyond the reach of the usual institutions of justice. The disturbed conditions attending the Wars of the Roses brought the constables further powers of summary justice, as in cases of treason and similar state crimes. They therefore came to be a convenient means by which the English kings from time to time overrode the ordinary safeguards of English law. These special powers, originating in the "law marshal," were expanded until they came to represent what we know as "martial law."[25]

Beyond his original military function, and the additional job of serving the sheriff, the constable was also responsible for a host of other duties, including the collection of taxes, the inspection of highways, and serving as the local magistrate. Ironically, as the *posse comitatus* came increasingly to act as a militia, the constable was without assistance in policing. "The ancient custom of making 'hue and cry' after criminals, with the entire countryside up in arms and joining the hunt, lapsed into disuse. The civil police officer began to emerge."[26] By the end of the thirteenth century, the constable was no longer connected to the tything; he acted instead as an agent of the manor and the crown.[27] By the beginning of the sixteenth century, the constable's function was quite limited; constables only made arrests in cases where the justice of the peace issued a warrant.[28]

Around the middle of the thirteenth century, towns of notable size were directed by royal edict to institute a night watch.[29] This was usually an unpaid, compulsory service borne by every adult male. Carrying only a staff and lantern, the watch would walk the streets from late evening until dawn, keeping an eye out for fire, crime, or other threats, sounding an alarm in the event of emergency. "Charlies"—so called because they were created during the reign of Charles II[30]—were unarmed, untrained, under-supervised, often unwilling, and frequently drunk.

In 1727, Joseph Cotton, the Deputy Steward of Westminster, visited St. Margaret's Watchhouse and complained that there was "neither Constable, Beadle, Watchman, or other person (save one who was so Drunk that he was not capable of giving any Answer) Present in, or near the said Watchhouse." A few years later, in 1735, John Goland of Bond Street complained to the Burgesses that he had been robbed three times in five years, noting that he "generally finds the Watchmen drunk, and wandering about with lewd Women. "[31]

The watch thus represented neither a significant bulwark against crime nor a major source of power for the state. Yet the watch continued in various forms for six hundred years.

During the eighteenth century, the London Watch underwent a long series of reforms.[32] While neglect of duty and drunkenness remained major complaints, most of the characteristics of modern police were introduced to the watch in this period, first in one locale and then in the others. "The goal was a system of street policing that was honest, accountable, and impartial in its administration and operation. . . . "[33]

Toward this end, the West End parishes of St. James, Piccadilly, and Saint George, Hanover Square began paying watchmen in 1735; most other parishes adopted the practice within the next fifty years.[34] During this same time, more men were hired, hours of operation were expanded, command hierarchies and plans of supervision were drafted, minimum qualifications established, record-keeping introduced, and pensions offered.[35]

> By 1775, Westminster and several neighboring parishes had a night watch system that was both professional and hierarchical in structure, charged with preventing crime and apprehending night walkers and vagabonds. While police authority did remain divided between several local bodies and officials, decentralization was not necessarily synonymous with defectiveness. These parochial authorities put increasing numbers of constables, beadles [church officials], watchmen, and [militia] patrols on the street, paid and equipped them. They spent increased amounts of time disciplining them when they were delinquent and increasing amounts of money on wages.[36]

Thus, during the eighteenth century the London Watch came very nearly to resemble the modern police department that replaced it.

The watch was also supplemented by various private efforts, including a "river police" created by local merchants and taken over by the government in 1800.[37] "By 1829 London had become a patchwork of public and private police forces . . . supported by vestries, church wardens, boards of trustees, commissioners, parishes, magistrates, and courts-leet."[38] Among this mix, we find one group worthy of special notice—the thieftakers, forerunners of the modern detective. Despite their name, thieftakers were less interested in catching thieves than in retrieving stolen property and collecting rewards. And the easiest way to do that was to act as a fence for the thieves, returning the goods and splitting the fee. Until his execution in 1725, Jonathan Wild was England's most prominent thieftaker, controlling an international operation that included warehouses in two countries and a ship for transport.[39]

Such was the state of policing when Robert Peel, the Home Secretary, proposed a plan for a citywide police force. This body, the Metropolitan Police Department—now nicknamed "Bobbies" after their creator, but commonly called "crushers" by the public of the time[40]—adopted many of the innovations previously introduced in the local watch, adding to these a new element of centralization.[41] It thus fulfilled most of the criteria defining modern policing.

Peel based this effort on his experiences in Ireland, where he had introduced the Royal Irish Constabulary in 1818.[42] Hence both the traditional watch and the police system that came to replace it were informed by the experience of colonial rule. They were each created by foreign conquerors to control rebellious populations. Peel had seen the difficulties of military occupation and understood the need to establish some sort of legitimacy. He crafted his police accordingly—first in Ireland, and then, with revisions, in England.[43] In London the police uniforms and equipment were selected with an eye toward avoiding a military appearance, though critics of the police idea still drew such comparisons.[44]

In 1829, citing a rise in crime (especially property crime), Parliament accepted Peel's proposal with only a few adjustments.[45] The most important of these compromises excluded the old City of London from the jurisdiction of the Metropolitan Police. The old City of London (about one square mile, geographically) retained its own police force, which in 1839 was reorganized on the Metropolitan model.[46] Meanwhile, the watch and river police were preserved and proved for some time more effective than the new Metropolitans.[47] Still, though they lacked citywide jurisdiction and sole policing authority, the London Metropolitan Police are generally credited as the first modern police department.

Some historians treat the modern American police as a straightforward application of Peel's model. As we shall see, however, policing in the United States followed a separate course, motivated by different concerns and producing unique institutional arrangements. In fact, I shall argue that American policing systems, especially those designed for slave control, neared the modern type well before Peel's reforms.

COLONIAL FORERUNNERS

The American colonies mostly imported the British system of sheriffs, constables, and watches, though with some important differences. Sheriffs at first were appointed by governors, and made responsible for apprehending suspects, guarding prisoners, executing civil processes, overseeing elections, collecting taxes, and performing various fiscal functions.[48] Corruption in all of these duties was quite common, with sheriffs accepting bribes from suspects and prisoners, neglecting their civil duties, tampering with elections, and embezzling public funds.[49] The sheriff was empowered to make arrests when issued a warrant, or without one in certain circumstances, and was given additional duties during emergencies, but during the colonial period the office was only tangentially concerned with criminal law.[50]

The constable's duties were similarly varied. He was charged with summoning citizens to town meetings, collecting taxes, settling claims against the town, preparing elections, impressing workers for road repair, serving warrants, summoning juries, delivering fugitives to other jurisdictions, and overseeing the night watch. In addition, he was, in theory, expected to enforce all laws and maintain the Crown's peace.[51] In practice, however, constables were paid by a system of fees, and tended to concentrate on the better-paying tasks.[52]

In the seventeenth and eighteenth centuries, both the sheriff and the constable were elected positions.[53] Still, they were not popular jobs; many people refused to serve when elected,[54] and the authority of each office was commonly challenged, sometimes by violence. In 1756, for example, Sheriff John Christie was killed when trying to make an arrest. James Wilkes was convicted, but was soon pardoned by Governor Sir Charles Hardy, who reasoned that Wilkes

> had imbibed and strongly believed a common Error generally prevail-
> ing among the Lower Class of Mankind in this part of the world that
> after warning the Officer to desist and bidding him to stand off at
> his Peril, it was lawful to oppose him by any means to prevent the
> arrest.[55]

The fact that such a view would be respected, despite its legal inaccuracy, says a great deal about the weakness of the sheriff's position.[56]

Neither of these offices was designed for what we now consider police work, and neither ever fully adapted itself to that function.[57] Constables survived into the twentieth century, though only as a kind of rural relic.[58] Sheriffs, meanwhile, retained many of their original duties—especially those concerning jails—and in some places still patrol the unincorporated areas of counties, though even in this respect state police forces sometimes supersede them.

Rather than invest much authority in these offices, the colonial government relied primarily on informal means of policing. As public nuisances arose concerning the behavior of slaves, the delivery of goods, sanitation, street use, gambling, and the like, the local government responded by instituting regulations. These would general-ly be ignored. To remedy this deficiency, the civil authorities called on the family and church to use their influence to bring about compliance. Where that failed, they would establish a system of fines (for violators) and rewards (for informers). They might then direct the constable to enforce the laws, or else appoint special informers concerned only with that particular law. Eventually towns began consolidating these positions and appointing general officers called marshals.[59]

Citizens were further expected to participate in law enforcement through the night watch.

> The character of the nightwatch varied from time to time. Sometimes
> it was composed entirely of civilians forced to take their regular turn
> as watchmen or pay for a substitute to replace them. At other times,
> especially during the intercolonial wars, the militia took over the
> watch. At still other times, a paid constable's watch was used, or cit-
> izens themselves were paid to guard the city.[60]

As in England, the watch was charged with keeping order, reporting fires, sounding an alarm when crimes were discovered, detaining suspicious persons, and sometimes suppressing riots and lighting street lamps.[61]

The Boston Watch was in many respects typical. All men over eighteen years old were required to serve in person or provide a substitute. Ministers and certain public officials were exempted from duty. The state legislature ordered the watchmen to "see that all disturbances and disorders in the night shall be prevented and suppressed" and gave them the

> authority to examine all persons, whom they have reason to suspect of any unlawful design, and to demand of them their business abroad at such time, and whether they are going; to enter any house of ill-fame for the purpose of suppressing any riot or disturbance.[62]

They were further instructed to

> walk in rounds in and about the streets, wharves, lanes, and principal inhabited parts, within each town, to prevent any danger by fire, and to see that good order is kept, taking particular observation and inspection of all houses and families of evil fame.[63]

New York provided similar instruction in 1698. The watchmen were told to go

> round the City Each Hour in the Night with a Bell and there to proclaime the season of the weather and the Hour of the night and if they Meet in their Rounds Any people disturbing the peace or lurking about Any persons house or committing any theft they take the most prudent way they Can to Secure the said persons.[64]

Like the modern police, the colonial watch was public in character and accountable to a central authority, usually either a town council or state legislature. Unlike the modern police, however, the watch had only limited authority to use force, with no training and usually no equipment for doing so. As far as "modern" characteristics go, the watch shared responsibility for enforcement with the constables, sheriffs, and sometimes other inspectors. Thus it was not the major body responsible for law enforcement. Its personnel rotated with deliberate frequency, and in many places it only patrolled part of the year. Hence, it lacked continuity in office and procedure. While the watch was concerned with crime, it was often more concerned with other dangers, especially fire and military attack; thus it lacked the specialized policing function. Except in times of emergency, the watch only patrolled at night ,offering no twenty-four-hour service. And for the most part, its personnel were not paid at all. In sum, by our criteria, the colonial watch may be counted as a policing effort, but in no way did it constitute a modern police agency.

The standard story in the history of policing, if we may speak of such a thing, presents the modern American police force as a direct adaptation of the night watch, following the English pattern.[65] But this story leaves out significant stages in the development of American policing. Or, put differently, it omits an entire branch of the American police family tree.

> In fact, the first major reform of the traditional system did not occur in any of the big northeastern cities in the mid-1800s but in the cities of the Deep South in a much earlier period. As early as the 1780s Charleston introduced a paramilitary municipal police force primarily to control the city's large population of slaves. In later years, Savannah, New Orleans, and Mobile did the same.[66]

These police forces, generally called City Guards, were distinct from both the militia and the watch. They were armed, uniformed, and salaried; they patrolled at night but kept a reserve force for daytime emergencies. In most respects, they resembled modern American police departments to the same degree as did the London Metropolitan Police of 1829.

Of course, these City Guards did not arise out of nothing. To understand their origin, we should consider the peculiar institutions of Southern society, its social and economic systems and the police measures that arose to preserve them.

SLAVE PATROLS

Relying on a slave economy, the American South faced unique problems of social control, especially in areas where White people were in the minority. Regardless of their own economic class or ethnic background, Whites were haunted by the prospect of a slave revolt. They became utterly obsessed with controlling the lives of Black people, free and slave, and developed a deep and terrible fear of any unsupervised activity in which Blacks might engage.[67] As a result, the South developed distinctive policing practices. Called "slave patrols," "alarm men," or "searchers," by the authorities who appointed them, they were known as "paddyrollers," "padaroles," "padaroes," and "patterolers" by the populations they policed.[68]

Michael Hindus cites three related reasons why the criminal justice system in the South developed along different lines than it did in the North: 1) tradition, 2) social and economic development, and 3) slavery.[69] Of these three, slavery exerted the most powerful influence. It held a central place in Southern society, in the social and political as well as the economic life of the region. For many Southerners, a future without slavery was literally inconceivable.[70] Thus the whole of Southern society was, at times, directed to the defense of the "peculiar institution." Where the demands of slavery conflicted with the region's traditions and social development—and to a lesser extent when it interfered with economic development—the maintenance of the slave system was nearly always preferred.[71]

Faced with the difficulties of keeping a major portion of the population enslaved to a small elite, Southern society borrowed from the practices of the Caribbean, especially Barbados. There, slaveowners used professional slave catchers and militias to capture runaways, while overseers were responsible for maintaining order on the plantations. The weaknesses of this system led to the creation of slave codes, laws directed specifically to the governing of slaves. Beginning in 1661, the slave code shifted the responsibilities of enforcement from the overseers to the entire White population. Shortly thereafter, in the 1680s, the militia began making regular patrols to catch runaways, prevent slave gatherings, search slave quarters, keep order at markets, funerals, and festivals, and generally intimidate the Black population.[72]

> The final move in policing Barbadian slaves in the seventeenth century came with the importation of two thousand professional English soldiers, who were installed on plantations as intimidating "militia tenants." Arriving between 1696 and 1702, they did not perform manual labor but instead functioned exclusively as slave control forces. Their presence served the White colonists' purposes well: throughout the eighteenth century only one slave rebellion attempt was reported in Barbados.[73]

During the same period, South Carolina passed laws restricting the slaves' ability to travel and trade, and created the Charleston Town Watch. Beginning in 1671, this watch consisted of the regular constables and a rotation of six citizens. It looked for any sign of trouble—fires, Indian attacks, or slave gatherings. The laws also established a militia system, with every man between sixteen and sixty years old required to serve.[74]

In 1686, South Carolina passed a law enabling any White person to apprehend and punish runaway slaves.[75] A few years later, the 1690 Act for the Better Ordering of Slaves *required* "all persons under penalty of forty shillings to arrest and chastise any slave out of his home plantation without a proper pass."[76] Those who captured runaways would receive a reward.[77]

In 1704, fears of a Spanish invasion, combined with the ever-present threat of a slave revolt, led South Carolina to form its first official slave patrols. The colony faced two types of danger and divided its military capacity accordingly. Henceforth, the militia would guard against outside attack, and the patrol would be left behind to protect against insurrection.[78]

Patrollers would gather from time to time and, as instructed by the law,

> ride from plantation to plantation, and into any plantation, within the limits or precincts, as the General shall think fit, and take up all

slaves which they shall meet without their master's plantation which
have not a permit or ticket from their masters, and the same
punish.[79]

In 1721, the law was revised to shift its focus from runaways to revolts. The new law
ordered the patrols to "prevent all caballings amongst negros, by dispersing of them
when drumming or playing, and to search all negro houses for arms or other offensive weapons."[80] The patrollers seized other goods as well, alleging them to be stolen,
and were permitted to keep for their own whatever they took.[81]

The patrol was essentially an institutionalized extension of the more informal
system described by the 1686 law. The law's intention was, foremost, to divide the
means of protecting the city so that both internal and external threats could be met
simultaneously. It did not represent an effort to specialize slave control, or to
reduce the obligations of each White citizen, or to interfere with the personal
authority of the slave owner. But whatever the intention behind it, the law did, or
threatened to do, all three.

> Reform required increasing the amount of time each man devoted to
> protecting the safety and property of others, which was repugnant to
> Southern white ideas of individual freedom and, indirectly, their
> sense of personal honor. No white man should have to cower before
> slaves, it was thought, and patrols were an unequivocal manifesta-
> tion of white fear. Southern honor required the individual to protect
> his name and family without the assistance of courts or the commu-
> nity; patrols, by their very nature, were communal, intrusive in the
> master-slave relationship, and implied that the individual alone
> could not adequately control his bondsmen.[82]

Slave patrols were both a product of White racism, vital to the survival of slavery, and a manifest contradiction of the ideology and culture it was meant to protect. "To admit that danger existed was to concede the possibility of fear; to admit
that slaves posed a threat could undermine confidence in an entire way of life."[83] Of
course, to ignore the threat of insurrection could prove equally as dangerous. The
patrols were created to defend slavery, but their effectiveness was limited by the
same ideology that justified the slave system.

For Southern Whites, slavery was valued, in part, as a means of maintaining the
entire social order and a deeply cherished way of life. It would not be an exaggeration to say that they imagined that the slave system upheld civilization itself, in
part by controlling the group that most threatened it—the slaves. This racist ideology was self-reinforcing, and provided for its own defense.

> As long as Charlestonians believed that blacks were the sole threat to
> order, white supremacy served in lieu of a police force. In such a
> racially stratified society, with few legal rights accorded to the black

man, every white person, by virtue of his skin, had sufficient authority over blacks.[84]

So, rather than develop more formal means of control, Southern ideology encouraged a reliance on informal systems rooted in racism. This was not only true of the police function, but of all authority. While the rest of the country developed systems of authority that were formal, legalistic, and centered on the state, the South maintained a unique commitment to a system that was informal, personalistic (characterized by deference and paternalism), diffused, and in which the state was kept deliberately weak. When compared to Northern cities of the nineteenth century, plantation life seems positively feudal. "In other words, the plantation was a sort of governmental unit as to the police control of the slave, and to its head, the slaveowner, was given in large measure the sovereign management of its affairs under certain restrictions."[85] The arrangement was, in the fullest, traditional sense of the word, patriarchal; not only slaves, but also White women and children were subject to the personal authority of male heads of households.[86] Any intercession in these relationships was apt to be viewed negatively. Slaveowners felt that any outside intervention—especially that of the state—represented not only a usurpation of their authority but also a personal slight, implying that the master was not up to the task of controlling his slaves.[87]

This sentiment, an important aspect of Southern "honor," created a major impediment to the effective control of the Black population. It discouraged White elites from enhancing the means of social control.

> [O]nly the state (through the agency of the courts, councils, and militia) could force whites to act in concerted fashion to protect their own self-interest. And some state legislatures, like South Carolina's, simply refused to reform patrol practices in order to coerce more public service from their constituents.[88]

Progress, here, came not as the result of continual efforts at critique and improvement, but in a rush during times of crisis, typically following real or rumored revolts. Aside from minor alterations in 1737 and 1740, the patrol system established in 1704 survived, virtually unchanged, until 1819. The 1737 and 1740 acts limited the personnel of the patrols, first to landowners of 50 acres or more, and then to slaveowners and overseers.[89] But in 1819, the state legislature—spurred by two separate slave revolts shortly before—again made all "free white males" aged 18 to 45 liable for patrol duty, without compensation. Substitutes could be sent, for a fee, and discipline came in the form of fines.[90] After this revision, the structure and activities of the patrols remained relatively unchanged until the Civil War.[91]

While "[the patrol system in] South Carolina seems to have been the oldest, most elaborate, and best documented," other colonies followed suit.[92] Georgia, Tennessee,

Kentucky, and Mississippi all had similar arrangements, with variations. In Georgia, slave patrols were also responsible for disciplining disorderly Whites, especially vagrants.[93] In Tennessee, the law required slaveowners to provide patrols on the plantations themselves, in addition to those that rode between plantations. In Kentucky, after a series of revolts, some cities established round-the-clock patrols. And in Mississippi, the first patrols were federal troops; these were gradually replaced by the militia, and then by groups appointed by county boards.[94]

Until 1660, Virginia relied more on indentured European servants than on African slaves, though both groups sought to escape their bonds. Initially, the colonists used the hue and cry to mobilize the community and recapture runaways. In 1669, the colonial legislature began offering a reward (paid in tobacco) to anyone who returned a runaway. And in 1680, as the slave population grew, slaves were required to carry passes, as debtors and Native Americans already had been. Slaves were singled out for special enforcement measures beginning in 1691, when the legislature required sheriffs to raise posses for their recapture. In 1727, this responsibility was transferred to the militia, creating the colony's first slave patrol. At first the militia only patrolled as needed, but after a failed rebellion in 1730, it began regular patrols two or three times each week. In 1754, county courts began paying patrollers and requiring reports from their captains. After that point, Virginia's patrols remained essentially the same until the Civil War.[95]

North Carolina's system developed along similar lines, driven by the same concerns. The colony required passes for slaves, debtors, and Native Americans beginning in 1669. In 1753, patrols were instituted. Called "searchers," the patrols were initially responsible for searching the slaves' homes, but couldn't stop them between plantations. This function reflected the motives behind their creation: the lawmakers were more afraid of revolts than escapes. In 1779, paid patrols were established, with expanded powers for searching the homes of Whites and stopping slaves whenever they were off the plantation.[96] With this they came to closely resemble the patrols already in place elsewhere, and after 1802 they were placed under the auspices of the county court, rather than the militia.[97]

Whether supervised by the militia or the courts, whether chiefly concerned with escapes or revolts, whether paid or conscripted, whether slaveowners or poor Whites, the rural patrols all engaged in roughly the same activities and served the same function. "Throughout all of the [Southern] states during the antebellum period, roving armed police patrols scoured the countryside day and night, intimidating, terrorizing, and brutalizing slaves into submission and meekness."[98] They patrolled together in "beat companies", on horseback and usually at night.[99] Along the roads they would stop any Black person they encountered, demand his pass, beat him if he was without one, and return him to the plantation or hold him in the jail. For this, they carried guns, whips, and binding ropes.[100]

They would search slaves' homes, and sometimes the homes of disreputable Whites, looking for illegal visitors, weapons, and stolen goods. Guns and horses were confiscated as a matter of course, as were linen and china;[101] slaves weren't allowed to have anything too valuable. Books and paper were often confiscated as well; education itself was deemed subversive.[102]

The patrols would break up any unsupervised gathering of slaves, especially meetings of religious groups the patrollers themselves disliked. Baptist and Methodist services were specifically targeted.[103] One former slave, Ida Henry, recalled an assault against her mother:

> De patrollers wouldn't allow de slaves to hold night services, and one night dey caught me mother out praying. Dey stripped her naked and tied her hands together and wid a rope tied to de handcuffs and threw one end of de rope over a limb and tied de other end to de pummel of a saddle on a horse. As me mother weighed 'bout 200, dey pulled her up so dat her toes could barely touch de ground and whipped her.[104]

Patrollers couldn't legally interfere with a slave carrying a pass.[105] But patrollers would often harass Blacks whom they felt to be traveling too far, or too often.[106] Moses Grandy, a former slave, verified that the law did little to restrain the patrollers:

> If a negro has given offense to the patrol, even by so innocent a matter as dressing tidily to go to a place of worship, he will be seized by one of them, and another will tear up his pass; while one is flogging him, the others will look another way; so when he or his master makes complaint of his having been beaten without cause, and he points out the person who did it, the others will swear they saw no one beat him.[107]

Other abuses were also common. Black women faced sexual abuse at the hands of patrollers, both when they were found on the road and during searches of their homes.[108] Patrollers sometimes kidnapped free Blacks and sold them as slaves.[109] They also frequently threatened Blacks with mutilation, sometimes with a basis in law: between 1712 and 1740, South Carolina law required escalating tortures for captured runaways, from slitting the nose to severing one foot.[110]

Masters sometimes complained about the abuses directed against the slaves, but courts were generally reluctant to award damages or discipline the patrollers, for fear of undermining the patrol system.[111] The main restraint on the actions of patrollers was the economic value of the slave's life; slaves were rarely killed, since the local government would then have to compensate the owner.[112] In general, however, the patrols were invested with vast authority and wide discretion, as a North Carolina court explained in 1845:

[Patrols] partake of a judicial or quasi-judicial and executive character. Judicial, so far as deciding upon each case of a slave taken up by
them; whether the law has been violated by him or not, and adjudg-
ing the punishment to the inflicted. Is he off his master's plantation
without a proper permit or pass? Of this the patrol must judge and
decide. If punishment is to be inflicted, they must adjudge, decide,
as to the question: five stripes may in some cases be sufficient,
while others may demand the full penalty of the law.[113]

To summarize, the state control of slave behavior advanced through three stages.
First, legislation was passed restricting the activities of slaves. Second, this legislation
was supplemented with requirements that every White man enforce its demands. Third,
over time this system of enforcement gradually came to be regulated, either by the
militia or by the courts. The transition between these second and third steps was a slow
one. Each colony tried to cope with the unreliable nature of private enforcement, first
by applying rewards and penalties, and later by appointing particular individuals to
take on the duty. Volunteerism was eventually replaced with community-sanctioned
authority in the form of the slave patrols. Among the factors determining the rate of
this transition and the eventual shape of the patrols were the date of settlement, the
size of the slave population, the size of the White population, threats of revolt, geography, and population density.[114] As this suggests, slave patrols developed differently in
the more populous cities than in the countryside.

CITY GUARDS

Slave control was no less a priority for urban Whites than for their country kin.
The growing numbers of Blacks in cities were of obvious concern to the White population, and their concentration in distinct neighborhoods presented an unnerving
reminder of the possibility of revolt.

In many respects, the cities followed the lead of the plantations. There, too,
Blacks—slaves especially, but free Blacks as well—were singled out by the law, and
specialized enforcement mechanisms arose to insure compliance. These agencies
"went by a variety of names, including town guard, city patrol, or night police,
although their duties were the same: to prevent slave gatherings and cut down on
urban crime."[115]

In the initial stage, enforcement would be entrusted to private individuals and
the existing watch, but after some period the town might petition the legislature
for the funds to form a permanent patrol, with the same group on duty each night.[116]
The urban patrols, then, did not evolve from the watch system; rather, adapted from
the rural slave patrols, they came to supplant the watchmen. Charleston formed a
City Guard in 1783. It wore uniforms, carried muskets and swords, and maintained a

substantial mounted division. Unlike the watchmen, who walked their beats individually, the City Guard patrolled as a company.[117]

Louis Tasistro, who traveled through Charleston in the 1840s, described the patrol: "the city suddenly assumes the appearance of a great military garrison, and all the principal streets become forthwith alive with patrolling parties of twenties and thirties, headed by fife and drum, conveying the idea of a general siege."[118] A few years later, in the early 1850s, J. Benwell, an English visitor to Charleston, described the reaction of Blacks to the mounting of the guard: "It was a stirring scene, when the drums beat at the Guard house in the public square . . . to witness the negroes scouring the streets in all directions, to get to their places of abode, many of them in great trepidation, uttering ejaculations of terror as they ran."[119]

Throughout the first part of the nineteenth century, similar urban patrols were created in Savannah, Mobile, and Richmond. The Savannah guard carried muskets and wore uniforms as early as 1796. It was later equipped with horses and pistols.[120] Richmond's Public Guard was formed in 1800, after the discovery of a planned rebellion. It was assigned to protect public buildings from insurrections, and was made responsible for punishing any slaves it found out after curfew.[121]

The urban patrols, and the laws they enforced, were modeled on the system designed for the plantations. But cities with developing industries had different needs than did the surrounding rural areas. For one thing, the large numbers of Blacks present in the city often lived in one part of town, away from their masters, making it impossible to maintain the sort of intimate knowledge of the slave's comings and goings essential to the plantation system. Furthermore, rigid restrictions on daily travel were not even desirable, proving inconvenient for the budding industries.[122] As burgeoning industries sought out cheap sources of labor, the practice of "hiring out" slaves became increasingly common. Under this arrangement, slaves paid the master a stipulated fee, and were then free to take other jobs at wages.[123] The regulations on travel, then, had to be more flexible for slaves to do their work.[124]

As the masters "capitalize[d] their slaves,"[125] the bondsmen became, literally, wage slaves. Industrialization in Southern cities thus not only created new demands for social control, but threatened to alter the entire institution of slavery.

> The slavery system was based essentially on the agricultural regime
> and no other. Its system of control was fixed on the basis of the
> slave's forever remaining a "field hand" or at best remaining attached
> to the plantation. But the city had other work for the slave to do
> which rendered the original plan of regulation cumbersome and
> unsuitable.[126]

Given the White population's preoccupation with controlling Blacks, the practice of hiring out slaves was quite controversial. As late as 1858 it was denounced in a grand jury "Report of Colored Population." Spelling out the concerns of the White community, the report states:

> The evil lies in the breaking down of the relation between master and slave—the removal of the slave from the master's discipline and control and the assumption of freedom and independence on the part of the slave, the idleness, disorder and crime which are consequential, and the necessity thereby created for additional police regulations to keep them in subjection and order, and the trouble and expense they involve.[127]

In other words, economic changes related to industrialization and urban life relaxed the master's personal control over the slave but did not reduce the racist obsession with slave control. Additional responsibilities thus fell to the state.

Between 1712 and 1822 South Carolina banned the practice of hiring out slaves, but these laws went almost entirely unenforced, and other means of control emerged.[128] Beginning in 1804, Charleston established a nightly curfew for the Black population—free and slave alike.[129] A few years later a statewide nine o'clock curfew was established. Free Blacks were required to carry a pass from their employers, and patrols beat those who didn't have their "free papers."[130] A stricter law was passed in Pendleton in 1835, instructing the patrol to "apprehend and correct all slaves and free persons of color" on the streets after nine at night, "whether such slave or free person of color have a pass or not."[131]

In Charleston the law requiring passes gradually gave way to a system of badges for slaves being hired out. This procedure allowed the state the opportunity to regulate the practice of hiring out slaves, and entitled it to a share of the master's fee (that is, really, of the slave's wages).[132] Slowly, Charleston began to pre-figure the segregated South of the twentieth century: In 1848, the city limited the right of Blacks to use the public parks; in 1850, Blacks were banned from bars altogether.[133]

Meanwhile, throughout South Carolina, town after town asked the state legislature to transfer control of the slave patrols from the county courts or state militia to the local government. Camden won that power in 1818. Columbia followed in 1823.[134] Georgetown requested it in 1810, but was not granted it until 1829.[135] Ten years later, the legislature granted all incorporated South Carolina towns the power to regulate patrol duty.[136]

The patrols' work was not always popular. Peter Cutting, the head of the Georgetown Guards, soon found his house burned to the ground.[137] Around the same time "A Citizen" wrote in to the Charleston paper: "I think it is dangerous for a person to send out his slave *even with a pass*."[138] But the most common complaint was that the guards did not do their job. Grand juries frequently cited them for "shameful neglect of patrol duty," a term covering absenteeism, drinking on duty, and patrolling in a slipshod fashion.[139]

Whatever the faults of these patrols, the White citizens of the American South relied on them to alleviate their anxieties about slave rebellions. These anxieties changed with the growth of the urban population, and the patrols changed with them, eventually approaching the model of a modern police force.

Still, though they provided a transition between the militia and the police, and despite their resemblance to other functionaries responsible for slave control, the patrols represented a distinct mode of policing. While originally bound up with the militia system, the patrols served in a specialized capacity distinguishing them from the rest of the militia. Furthermore, the authority over the patrols came more and more to shift from the militia to the courts, and then to the city government, implying that patrolling was regarded as a civil rather than military activity.[140]

The patrols also, in certain respects, resembled the watch. The watch, even in Northern cities, was issued specific instructions concerning the policing of the Black population. Boston, for example, instituted a curfew for Blacks and Native Americans, beginning in 1703;[141] in 1736 the watch was specifically ordered to "take up all Negro and Molatto servants, that shall be unseasonably Absent from their Masters [sic] Families, without giving sufficient reason therefore."[142] But while the watch was told to keep an eye on Blacks along with numerous other potential sources for trouble, the slave patrols (and later, the City Guards) were more specialized, focusing almost exclusively on Blacks. In fact, it is this racist specialization that—more than anything else—distinguished the slave patrols from other police types and accelerated their rate of development.

> The reliance upon race as a defining feature of this new colonial creation reveals the singular difference that set slave patrols apart from their European antecedents. Although slave patrols also supervised the activities of free African Americans and suspicious whites who associated with slaves, the main focus of their attention fell upon slaves. Bondsmen could easily be distinguished by their race and thus became easy and immediate targets of racial brutality. As a result, the new American innovation in law enforcement during the eighteenth and early nineteenth centuries was the creation of racially focused law enforcement groups in the American south.[143]

With this specialization came expanded powers—to search the homes of Blacks, to mete out summary punishment, and to confiscate a broad range of valuables without need to demonstrate further suspicion. Moreover, their relationship to the militia meant that patrols generally carried firearms, whereas the watch did not.[144]

While the slave patrols did anticipate the creation of modern police, it must still be remembered that they were not *themselves* modern police. Of the two sets of criteria listed earlier, the slave patrols satisfy those of a police endeavor: they were public, authorized—indeed, instructed—to use force, and had general enforcement powers ,if only over certain segments of the population. They do not, however, seem very modern, by the second set of criteria. They were certainly not the main law enforcement body, and they usually only operated at night. Arrangements for pay and continuity of service varied by location, but they were generally no more advanced than was typical of the watch. The patrols did have citywide—and sometimes broader—jurisdiction, and they were accountable to either the militias or the courts, or later, to special committees.[145] And perhaps more than any police force before them, the patrols had a preventive orientation. Rather than respond to slave revolts, as the militia had done, or take off after runaways like the professional slave catchers the patrol aimed to prevent rebellions and sometimes operated to keep the slaves from even leaving the plantation.

The slave patrol, which began as an offshoot of the militia, and came to resemble modern police, thus provides a transitional model in the development of policing. As the militia adapted to the needs of a rural, agrarian, slave society, it evolved into a new form that surpassed the original. The slave patrols, when confronted with the conditions of a proto-industrialized city—where slavery itself was facing obsolescence—underwent a similar metamorphosis.

CHARLESTON: "KEEPING DOWN THE NIGGERS"

In 1671, the South Carolina's Grand Council created a watch for Charles Town, consisting of the regular constables and a rotation of six citizens. They guarded the city against fire, Indians, slave gatherings, and other signs of trouble, and detained lawbreakers until the next day.[146] The law creating the watch was renewed in 1698, with an addendum citing the increase in the Black population:

> And whereas, negroes frequently absent themselves from their masters or owners [sic] houses, caballing, pilfering, stealing, and playing the rogue, at unseasonable hours of the night Be it therefore enacted, That any Constable or his deputy, meeting with any negro or negros, belonging to Charles Town, as such unseasonable times as aforesaid, and cannot give good and satisfactory account of his business, the said constable or his deputy, is required to keep the said negro or negros in safe custody till next morning.[147]

For this work, the constable was to receive a fee from the owner of the detained slave. In 1701, the exact language of this law was repeated, though the fee was increased and the constable was further instructed to administer a severe beating.[148]

In 1703, as a wartime measure, the governor established a paid watch, and added special duties related to sailors and bars. This experiment was short-lived, however, and seventeen months after its creation it was replaced with a volunteer patrol organized by the militia.[149] This organization was essentially the slave patrol. In 1721, it again merged with the militia. Its function was broadened, giving patrollers authority over a large part of the working class besides the slaves. The new law instructed patrollers

> to use their utmost endeavor to prevent all caballings amongst negroes, by dispersing of them when drumming or playing, and to search all negro houses for arms or other offensive weapons; and farther, are hereby empowered to examine all white servants they shall meet with, out of their master's business, and the same (if they suspect to be runaway, or upon any ill design) to carry such servant immediately to be whipped, or punished as he shall think fit, and then send him home to his master; and also, if they meet with any idle, loose or vagrant fellow that cannot give good account of his business, shall also carry such vagrant fellow to a magistrate.[150]

By 1734, this body was again removed from the militia, and was explicitly referred to as a slave police. By this time the patrollers were all armed and mounted, and were ordered to search the homes of all Blacks, pursue and capture escaped slaves, and kill any slave who used a weapon against them. Until the end of the colonial period, the Parish of Saint Philip (which includes Charleston) had two separate patrols—the two largest in the state.[151]

By 1785, these patrols were incorporated into the Charleston Guard and Watch. This body was responsible for arresting vagrants and other suspicious persons, preventing felonies and disturbances, and warning of fires.[152] But one guard described his job succinctly as "keeping down the niggers."[153] Indeed, slave control was the aspect of their work most emphasized by the public officials, and given highest priority by the guard itself. "With very minor differences, their orders here were a summation of those given the rural patrols in the preceding hundred years, with the major and natural exception that they did not inspect plantations."[154]

The organization of the Charleston Guard and Watch represented a significant advance in the development of policing.[155] The force contained a developed hierarchy and chain of command, consisting of a captain, a lieutenant, three corporals, fifty-eight privates, and a drummer. Each was given a gun, bayonet, rattle (for use as a signal), and a uniform coat. Some acted as a standing guard; the rest were divided into two patrols—one for St. Philip's Parish, and the other for St. Michael's. The captain issued daily reports, and all the men were paid.[156] The same group patrolled every night, and discipline and morale received a level of attention unique at the time.[157]

By our earlier criteria, there can be no question that the Charleston Guard and Watch were involved in policing. They were authorized to use force, had general enforcement responsibilities, and were publicly controlled. They were also exceptionally modern. The guard was the principal law enforcement agency in Charleston, enjoyed a jurisdiction covering the entire city (and some of the surrounding countryside), served a specialized police function, and had a preventive orientation. It also established organizational continuity and paid its personnel by salary. In fact, lacking only twenty-four-hour service, the Charleston Guard and Watch may count as the first modern police department, predating the London Metropolitan Police by more than thirty years.

Charleston, being subject to the pressures of maintaining a slave system in an urban area with an industrializing economy, underwent an intense period of innovation, just around the time of the American Revolution. Its efforts to control the Black population put it in the lead in the development of modern policing. But once policing mechanisms were in place, the authorities felt little need to tamper with them. When change again appeared on the agenda—following the discovery of a plan for insurrection in 1822—the authorities instituted reforms that had been developed previously in other cities.[158] During the intervening years, Charleston's advances were surpassed by those of another Southern city, facing similar but distinct social pressures.

NEW ORLEANS: "BARBARISM," "DESPOTISM," AND "A SYSTEM OF VIOLENCE"

Occupying a strategic position for both economic and military uses, the city of New Orleans has changed hands numerous times. But, until the Civil War, each subsequent regime agreed on one basic principle: the utter suppression of the Black race. In succession, the French, Spanish, and American governments enacted very nearly the same set of laws for this purpose, controlling the social, economic, and political life of the Black community and regulating the work, travel, education, and living arrangements of Black people in the city. Louis XIV instituted a "Code Noir" in 1685, which Sieur de Bienville, the founder of the French colony of Louisiana, copied; the Spanish retained it as their own while they controlled the city; and the Americans re-enacted it as the "Black Code."[159]

In 1804, as the Black population nearly equaled that of the White,[160] New Orleans sought out special mechanisms for enforcing these laws. At the time, two separate night patrols were in effect—a militia guard, to protect against outside attack, and a watch, called the "seranos," whose primary duty was lighting the street lamps. But in 1804 the militia organized a mounted patrol specifically to enforce the Black Codes.[161] This unit only survived a few months, however. After repeated conflicts between the English-speaking militia guard and the French-speaking army, the patrol was disbanded in 1805, replaced with the Gendarmerie.

The Gendarmerie, while nominally a military unit, functioned more as a slave patrol than anything else. The law establishing it made this clear:

> They will make rounds in suspected places where slaves can congre-
> gate, particularly on Sundays. They will break up these assemblies,
> foresee and prevent uproars and gambling, and declare confiscated
> all moneys found for their own profit. . . . The officers accompanied
> by all or part of their troop, and equipped with orders from the
> mayor, shall search negro huts on plantations, but only after looking
> for and then notifying the overseer or owner of their actions, as well
> as inviting them to be present at the search. And all fire-arms,
> lances, swords, etc. that shall be found in the said cabins will be
> confiscated and deposited in the City arsenal.[162]

The Gendarmerie also arrested slaves traveling without passes and maintained a reserve of officers for daytime emergencies.[163]

While drawn from the military, this group was directed by the mayor, magistrates, and other civil officials, and was paid through a combination of salaries, fees, and rewards. Half mounted, half on foot, and all wearing blue uniforms, the same men patrolled every night.[164] In many respects, then, the New Orleans patrol closely resembled the Charleston Guard of the same period, but it survived only briefly. In February 1806 the city council abolished the Gendarmerie, citing the cost of horses and the poor quality of the men.[165] That same year, the council created a City Guard, modeled after and performing the same functions as the Gendarmerie, though less militaristic in demeanor and lacking the horses.[166] Aside from two years when there was no patrol, this body survived until 1836.[167]

In the 1830s the City Guard came under attack in the newspapers, courtrooms, and among politicians. In 1834, the *Louisiana Advertiser* accused the police of "bar-barism" and "despotism." It urged the city council to

> dispense with the sword and pistol, the musket and bayonet, in our
> civil administration of *republican* laws, and adopt or create a system
> more congenial to our feelings, to the opinions and *interests* of a free
> and prosperous people, and more in accordance with the spirit of the
> age we live in.[168]

That same year a committee of the city council decried the Guard's violent treatment of suspects, saying that "the moment they lay hands on a prisoner they at once commence a system of violence towards him."[169] It was police violence, the committee argued, that caused the forceful resistance of both prisoners and passers-by acting from "just indignation."[170]

In 1830, the death of the first person killed by a New Orleans cop prompted much of the criticism,[171] but an underlying xenophobia was also at work, and the native-born population openly expressed distaste for the immigrant-dominated Guard. Another important demographic shift may also help explain this backlash against the Guard: during the 1830s and 1840s the White population increased by 180 percent, while the Black population increased at a much slower rate (41 percent).[172] Hence, with whites in the overwhelming majority, fears of a slave revolt were less present, while ethnic tensions among White groups were increasingly pronounced. "A military-style police to protect against the danger of slave rebellion no longer compensated for the day-to-day irritation of respectable citizens who found their increasingly alien policemen too menacing and too lacking in deference."[173] In short, both the initial militarization and the eventual de-militarization of New Orleans' police were the product of the ethnic fears of the city's ruling class.

In 1836, the city council did away with the military model of policing. In its place they put a system of twenty-four-hour patrolling along distinct beats. The blue uniforms were replaced with numbered leather caps like those worn by watchmen in other cities. A Committee of Vigilance was elected to supervise them. This revision brought New Orleans into line with the watch system as it existed in Northern cities, and represented a substantial break from the Charleston model.[174] Still, the new organization retained the most modern features of the City Guard, and added to them 24-hour service. Hence, in 1836, the New Orleans city government approved the adoption of a public body, accountable to a central authority, authorized to use force, and assigned general law enforcement duties. This body would be the main agency of law enforcement, with citywide jurisdiction, organizational continuity, a specialized policing function, and twenty-four-hour operations. And, as its inheritance from the slave patrol, it would be oriented toward the prevention of various disorders. In short, it would have all the major features of a modern police department.[175] As luck would have it, however, this organization never materialized.

As the city government was busy redesigning the police services, the state government was redesigning the entire municipal administration. In March 1836, the Louisiana state legislature divided New Orleans along the borders of its ethnic neighborhoods, creating three distinct municipalities, and preventing the just-settled police reforms from taking effect. Motivated by ethnic and economic rivalries, the plan maintained a common mayor and Grand Council, but divided the administration of services—including the police—into three districts. The city stayed so divided until 1852.[176]

Each department adopted a new, non-military approach, and retained some features of the old City Guard—namely, its public character, its authority to use force, its general law-enforcement duties, twenty-four-hour patrols, the goal of organizational continuity, its specialized police function, and its preventive orientation. However, none of the three could be counted as the chief law enforcement agency in the city because none had citywide jurisdiction. Furthermore, while in theory each police force was accountable to the General Council, in practice they were solely controlled by the district government and little effort was made to coordinate among them.[177]

The General Council met only once each year, leaving the practical management of the city's affairs to municipal councils.[178] This arrangement actually exacerbated the ethnic tensions that led to the city's division in the first place, and neighborhood rivalries now found official expression in the structure of government.[179] In effect, the two sets of changes—fragmentation of the city government and re-structuring of the police—laid the groundwork for the development of neighborhood-based and ethno-centric political machines, with the police taking a central role.

> During the 1840s and early 1850s control of the police force had become an increasingly important issue in municipal politics because of its value as a source of patronage and its influence in elections. After the restoration of unitary government in the city in 1852, the police played an even larger role in the manipulation of elections and resorted more frequently to intimidation and violence.[180]

Even after formal consolidation in 1852, the police functioned as separate, district-based organizations, controlled more by local political bosses than the general city government.[181]

The machines' influence was palpable. For example, when the American Party (the "Know-Nothings") gained control of the city in March 1855, they immediately removed all immigrants from the police force, reducing it from 450 to 265 members.[182] After that, the police stood aside while Know-Nothings prevented immigrants from voting; sometimes police aided the effort.[183] Opposition parties likewise fought for control of the polls. In the election of June 1858, a Vigilance Committee seized the state arsenal and police headquarters, with the stated purpose of insuring a fair election.[184] Similar actions were taken in 1888 by the Young Men's Democratic Club, who—armed with rifles—surrounded the polls to prevent Know-Nothings and police from interfering with Democratic party voters.[185]

Corruption didn't end at the polls. Less politically driven misconduct was also common. Naturally, vice laws created opportunities for corruption at all levels, and throughout the nineteenth century scandals were common. In 1854, a new chief, William James, began a vigorous campaign to enforce the laws against gambling, liquor, and other vice crimes. As his reward, the Board of Police fired him and eliminated his office.[186]

Meanwhile, though state law forbade carrying concealed weapons and made no exception for police, many cops did begin carrying guns, especially revolvers, illicitly. This practice was condoned, and sometimes advocated by supervisors, and eventually gained the mayor's approval as well. Predictably, a lack of training led to numerous accidents, often with police casualties.[187]

Brutality and violence were also common, and during the 1850s several New Orleans cops were tried for murder. Most of these cases involved personal disputes, and the victims were frequently cops themselves.[188]

> Less severe episodes of violence were legion. In a sample of cases
> covering a twenty-one-month period during 1854-1856, the Board of
> Police adjudicated forty-three cases of assault, assault and battery,
> or brutality by policemen, dismissing thirteen of the accused from
> the force and penalizing nine others with fines or loss of rank.[189]

Of course it is still worth noting that, of the 672 cases adjudicated by the Board of Police during this same period, the majority of them—59.2 percent—dealt with the dereliction of duty. Abuses of authority came at a distant second, comprising 17.4 percent of the cases.[190]

Ironically, both sorts of complaints may have resulted from the same features of the job. Lack of discipline was certainly a factor of each. But the complaints may also reflect public disagreement about what it was the police were supposed to be doing. Respectable middle-class Protestants and temperance crusaders were eager to have the police enforce laws regulating gambling, prostitution, drinking, and other vice and public order offenses. The lower-class and immigrant communities, who often enjoyed these activities, were apt to feel that the police were intruding where they weren't wanted or needed. The poor complained that they were treated unfairly or with unnecessary force; the respectable classes felt that the police weren't doing their jobs so long as such vice persisted. This dispute directly reflects the struggle for control of the municipal government, and in a different sense, the debate about the nature of democracy—neither of which was resolved in the nineteenth century.

New Orleans made the transition from Southern plantation politics to Northern machine politics, with the police occupying a central role in the process. Indeed, this transition was in many respects aided by the simultaneous shift from a distinctly Southern model of policing (based on the slave patrol) to a Northern style (resembling the watch).

> The most distinctive features of early southern police forces were
> uniforms, formidable weapons, and wages (rather than fees or com-
> pulsory unpaid service); around-the-clock patrolling and unification
> of day and night forces came later. In the 1840s and 1850s northern
> cities adopted the twenty-four-hour patrol, organizational unity, and
> wages for patrolmen; uniforms and fire-arms followed later (often
> northern policemen armed themselves with guns without official
> authorization or even against the law). New Orleans participated in
> both types of reform, adopting the southern model in the period
> 1805-1836 and shifting to the northern model in the years 1836-
> 1854.[191]

This shift was significant, but not absolute; as a result, New Orleans foreshadowed many of the qualities of the modern police—qualities that finally crystallized in New York in 1848.

NEW YORK: "ALMOST EVERY CONCEIVABLE CRIME"

In New York, as in New Orleans, the move toward modern policing was closely tied to the reconstitution of city government. In 1830 the state legislature divided the city's common council into a board of aldermen and a board of assistant alder-men, each elected annually by ward. Distinct executive departments were formed, and the mayor was assigned the responsibility to see that the laws were enforced. A year later, the council gave him some of the authority he needed to meet that demand, putting him at the head of the watch.[192]

In the spring of 1843, Mayor Richard H. Morris proposed another round of reforms designed to reorganize the city government and consolidate the police. The state legislature authorized the city to create and manage a single, centralized police department—specifically a "Day and Night Police" consisting of 800 officers. Under this plan, each ward would have its own patrol, and the officers had to live in the wards where they worked. The councilors would nominate officers from their ward, and the mayor would appoint them. This plan was finally accepted in May 1845.[193]

The new police ranked as extremely modern by the criteria listed earlier: a single organization was entrusted with the exclusive responsibility for law enforcement, served a specialized police function, patrolled twenty-four hours a day, and employed salaried personnel.[194] In fact, New York City is often credited with having the first modern department in the United States. As we've seen, its claim to this title is debatable. The Day and Night Police marked a step forward in a nationwide progression, drawing from and solidifying ideas already in circulation elsewhere. But if New York's police did not invent the model, they set the standard for the rest of the country. At the same time, they also set a new standard for political interference.

The mayor's power to appoint officers of all ranks made it clear that the new police force would be politically driven. An officer's job came as a reward for his political loyalty, and to keep the job he needed to support the officials who appointed him.[195] Even if the politicians themselves did not demand such support, it was nevertheless built into the system. Since any incoming councilman would be likely to replace the present police with those of his own choosing, the police understood that to keep their jobs they had to keep their patrons in power. Thus the police came to represent not only a means of securing political support through patronage, but also of ensuring influence through more direct means. In 1894, the Lexow Commission concluded that in a very large number of the election districts in the city of New York, almost every conceivable crime against the elective franchise was either committed or permitted by the police, invariably in the interest of the dominant Democratic organization of the city of New York, commonly called Tammany Hall.

The Committee's report goes on to document police involvement in the

Arrest and brutal treatment of Republican voters, watchers, and workers; open violations of the election laws; canvassing for Tammany Hall candidates; invasion of election booths; forcing of Tammany Hall pasters upon Republican voters; general intimidation of the voters by the police directly and by Tammany Hall election district captains in the presence and with the concurrence of the police; colonization of voters; illegal registration and repeating, aided and knowingly permitted by the police; denial of Republican voters and election district officers of their legal rights andprivileges . . . and on and on.[196]

Political corruption was not new to the city, and law enforcement had always had a role in it. But the political use of the Day and Night Police extended the established pattern and reached a new level of malfeasance. The watch had previously been used as a source of patronage, as political parties filled its ranks with their supporters.[197] But the watch offered only a hint of the political uses to which the police could be put; a more developed example was provided by the marshals. Marshals, who operated more or less like constables, were created in the early nineteenth century to enforce laws that had previously been left to the attention of civilian informants.[198] While the watch was a resource for rewarding supporters with jobs, the marshals were becoming an active force in local politics—a force that Tammany Hall would harness and direct for its own ends. Placed under the mayor's command, the marshals provided one means of controlling the city council.

There were only one hundred marshals, but this force could exert great influence upon the primary meetings at which candidates for the general election were chosen. The marshals often had enough political influence in the wards to block the nomination of a candidate for alderman or assistant alderman, and sometimes they had sufficient power to ensure the nomination of their favorites.[199]

The new Day and Night Police replaced the watch and the marshals, concentrating police power—and its political potential—in a single agency.[200] Predictably, the police expanded their political role in new directions, becoming a tool for ambitious politicians to increase their influence. The career of Fernando Wood gives some idea of the uses to which police could be put.

Wood, a Democrat, ran for mayor on a reform platform and was elected in 1854. He began his term by launching an ambitious campaign against vice crimes, but quickly turned the effort to his own advantage. Saloons, gambling houses, and brothels were shut down—unless their owners supported the mayor's political machine.[201] While declaring, "I know no party and recognize no political obligation,"[202] Wood disciplined police along strictly partisan lines and was willing to impose all sorts of political obligations on the officers under his command. Police were required to make financial contributions to the mayor's re-election campaign, and many were ordered to canvass for him as well.[203] Those on duty ignored irregularities in polling, and two officers—Petty and Hanley—inspected all the ballots in the first ward, beating anyone who voted against the mayor. When Wood was re-elected, the *Tribune* estimated the police had been worth 10,000 votes.[204]

But while the Democrats retained the mayoralty and controlled both boards of the council, the Republicans held the governor's mansion and the state assembly, sharing the senate with the Know-Nothings. In 1857 the state legislature passed the Metropolitan Police Bill, creating a new police force with jurisdiction over Kings (Brooklyn), Westchester, Richmond, and New York (Manhattan) counties, and dissolving the existing municipal police. A five-member board was established to oversee the new department, and no Democrats were appointed to it.[205] *Harper's Weekly* noted: "Of this change the practical effect will be to transfer the patronage of our city police to Albany."[206]

Wood refused to acknowledge the legitimacy of the Metropolitan Police Law and ordered the police to obey only his authority. Eight hundred officers and fifteen captains sided with Wood, and about half as many joined the Metropolitans. For two months the city had two competing police forces, resulting in occasional street fights and brawls in the station houses. The conflict reached its peak when fifty Metropolitans tried to arrest Wood; 500 municipal police came to his defense, attacking the Metropolitans with their clubs and forcing a retreat. Finally, in July, after an appeals court ruled in favor of the Metropolitans, Wood dissolved the municipal police.[207]

The Metropolitan Police Department lasted until 1870, when another series of power struggles led to its reorganization. In the 1869 election the Democrats won control of the mayor's office, the governorship, and the majority of the legislature. William M. Tweed proposed a new city charter and invested $600,000 in its passage. Under the new charter, the mayor appointed the police board, and the police controlled the board of elections, selected all inspectors and clerks, guarded the polls, and supervised the counting of the ballots.[208]

In this, too, New York set the standard for the rest of the country. Political machines arose throughout the Northeast and, to a lesser degree, in parts of the West and the South as well. In every case, the police department served as the strong arm of the machine—regardless of which party held power, or whether the department answered to the city or state government.

The police, as we know them, came into maturity at about the same time as the urban political machine. And while the machine's growth depended crucially on the police, their relationship was not that of equals. The cops were the tools of the machine. As tools they were used, as tools they were refined, and as very important tools they were fought over. Neither the political machines nor any part of them invented the police for this purpose, but they were well adapted to it, and—without submitting to teleological reasoning—we should consider the implications of this fact for policing, and for political authority.

THE GENESIS OF A POLICED SOCIETY   3

In the context of nineteenth-century municipal government, New York's Tammany Hall was exceptional only in the level of its success. Similar machines emerged in nearly every American city. Powerful neighborhood bosses arose and affiliated, gaining control through a system of patronage and protection, keeping it through increased applications of the same means, and administering civil affairs along lines which were not merely partisan, but personalistic as well. Favoritism became the central principle of local government.

> The machine was urban America's outstanding contribution to the art of municipal government. Exemplified by Tammany Hall, it emerged in New York, Philadelphia, and other eastern cities in the early and middle nineteenth century and in Chicago, Kansas City, San Francisco, and other western cities not long after. A highly decentralized outfit, the machine was an association of loosely affiliated and largely autonomous ward organizations whose power depended on their ability to get out the vote on election day. Whether allied with the Democrats, as in New York, the Republicans, as in Philadelphia, or neither party, as for a while in San Francisco, the ward bosses operated in much the same way in most American cities. They gave out contracts to local businessmen, found and if need be created jobs for recent immigrants, provided opportunities for aspiring politicians, and otherwise exchanged material inducements for political loyalty. In return for delivering the vote, the ward bosses demanded a good deal to say not only about the policies of the mayor's offices and city councils but also about the operations of the police departments and other municipal agencies.[1]

Under the machines, the resources of the government were the spoils of victory, belonging less to the public than to the reigning faction. Thus, quite removed from the ideal of deliberative democracy, elections were neither contests of principle nor gauges of the public will, but battles between rival cliques—battles fought as often in the streets as at the polls. And these battles determined the distribution of jobs, services, and graft. Elections decided who made the law, supplied public services, and controlled the city treasury. And more importantly, they decided whose friends would fill public jobs, which neighborhoods would receive attention or suffer neglect, which illicit businesses would continue operation, and whose palm would be greased in the process.

POLITICAL MACHINES: THE GANG AND THE GOVERNMENT

> The gang and the government are no different.[2]

> What is property? Proudhon asked. And his answer, somewhat para-
> doxically: Property is theft.
> What is government? we ask ourselves now. And again a paradox
> comes in reply: Government is crime.[3]

Corruption was the foundation and the defining characteristic of the political machine. Edward C. Banfield and James Q. Wilson offer a more formal definition: "A political 'machine' is a party organization that depends crucially upon inducements that are both *specific* and *material*. . . . "[4] Put more simply, "Machine government is, essentially, a system of organized bribery."[5] But perhaps even this puts too pleasant a face on it, for machines did not use only bribery to get what they wanted; they used whatever means were available to them, including threats, fraud, blackmail, and actual violence. Machines were concerned about power and resources, not principles—and certainly not democracy.[6] Principles were espoused, of course, as justification for their actions, to differentiate one party from another, and to gain and maintain the allegiance of a constituency committed to such values. But it was typical of machine politics that principles were always secondary to the demands of power.

The privileging of power over principle meant that every aspect of the government's activity was directed towards maintaining the ruling clique's control. By the same token, every resource at the city's disposal was available as a reward for the machine's supporters. The police served in both capacities. Hiring, discipline, transfers, and promotions were all governed by the convenience of the machine organization. Hence, whenever control of the city government changed hands, turnover in the police department was sure to follow. Without regard for the qualifications of the individual officer, each party dispensed with the supporters of the other and replaced them with their own. Very nearly full turnover of police personnel followed the Los Angeles election of 1889, the Kansas City election of 1895, and the Chicago and Baltimore elections of 1897.[7]

In the 1907 Louisville election, when a Republican was unexpectedly elected mayor, every captain was reduced to a patrolman, and Republicans (many lacking in police experience) were appointed in their place. When the Democrats won in the following election, the process was reversed. Again in 1917, the Republicans gained control and fired 300 from a department of 429. Everyone above the rank of sergeant was replaced.[8]

In New York, positions were so sought after that appointments relied on political sponsorship or outright bribery, or sometimes both. Hence, from the first moment, the importance of political influence and bribes was made clear to new recruits.[9] A patrolman's position typically sold for $300 and required the approval of the district leader.[10] Higher positions cost more. In 1893, Timothy Creeden paid a commissioner $15,000 to be promoted from sergeant to captain. As a captain's salary was only $3,000 each year, it is obvious that he would need to rely on graft to even pay for his job.[11]

Even when civil service tests were instituted in the 1880s, conditions remained largely the same. Politicians circumvented civil service requirements either by appointing partisan boards, administering the exams in essay style, or by requiring the civil service commission to provide three qualified candidates for every open position and allowing police officials to choose among them.[12] Experiments with state-level police boards proved equally unhelpful. The creation of state boards, a partisan maneuver by design, only transferred the control of patronage from one group to another—as indeed it was intended to do. Likewise, bipartisan boards, rather than eliminating political spoils, merely divided them between the two strongest parties, to mutual advantage.[13]

Nor did political interference end once an officer was hired. Police with powerful friends proved nearly impossible to discipline, no matter how corrupt, brutal, or negligent they might be. Even such routine matters as going on patrol and wearing uniforms were difficult to enforce.[14]

Since each officer's career was politically controlled from beginning to end, the police became ardent supporters of their patrons. Police support was central to the survival of the machines: For much of the nineteenth century New York's Board of Elections was under the supervision of the police board. The commissioners chose the polling places, drew up the voting districts, had the ballots and voter registration lists printed, and appointed the polling inspectors and clerks. The police department itself verified the registration lists, guarded the polls, and counted the votes.[15] Mayor William R. Grace described this system as "a standing menace to the safety and purity of the ballot box, and tend[ing] to render the police of the city its masters rather than its servants."[16] Tammany Police Commissioner John Sheehan once bluntly stated that control of the police was more important than how the votes were cast.[17]

This power tended to magnify the significance of the administrative branch, and bolstered the influence of the mayor especially.[18] The career of Boston's Josiah Quincy anticipated the trend. Beginning in 1823, Quincy was elected mayor six times. In 1829, he was dubbed "The Great Mayor," a title which probably reflected the extent of his power more than the quality of his performance. During his term, Quincy chaired every important committee, allowing him to build an efficient administration and, as importantly, consolidate power under his personal leadership. At the same time, Quincy maintained his influence in the wards with the assistance of the nascent police apparatus. Central to this effort was the creation of a new office—Marshal of the City—which, lacking precedent and statutory limits, could be made to fit whatever demands the mayor placed on it. The marshal served as head constable, commanded the night watch, acted as the city's chief health officer, prosecuted minor cases, and took on additional responsibilities after the creation of a day police in 1838.[19]

The power of the marshal reached its peak during the term of Marshal Francis Tukey, who took office in 1846. Within the first year of Tukey's command the number of officers on the force was doubled, a detective division added, and a special night force created.[20] But there were limits to how far this power would be allowed to develop. In 1851, the police voted as a bloc for Benjamin Seaver in the mayoral election, acting under the assumption that he would bar Irish immigrants from joining the force. Seaver won, but did not ban Irish police. Apparently the night police had crossed a line when they marched to the polls en masse. Seaver responded by firing all the night duty officers, dissolving that branch of the force, and leaving its patrols entirely in the hands of the barely existent night watch. Over the course of the next year, power was systematically moved away from the marshal and toward the mayor and the aldermen. In April 1852, the aldermen limited the marshal's tenure to one year. Two months later, they replaced the position with that of Chief of Police. While Tukey was not fired outright, neither was he named the new chief.[21] The Boston *Semi-Weekly Atlas* drew a comparison: "The Great Caesar fell for his ambition."[22] The lesson was clear: the police were a tool for the political machine; they would not be allowed to develop as a political force in their own right.

This balance could be difficult to maintain, though, since police were so central to the functioning of the machines. The police served the interests of political machines in three key ways: police jobs served as rewards for supporters; police controlled the elections; and police regulated illicit businesses, deciding which would be allowed to operate and under what conditions.[23]

> Contrary to the conventional wisdom, the police did not suppress vice; they licensed it. From New York's Tenderloin to San Francisco's Barbary Coast and from Chicago's Levee to New Orleans' French Quarter, they permitted gamblers, prostitutes, and saloon keepers to do business under certain well-understood conditions. These entrepreneurs were required to make regular payoffs, which ranged, according to the enterprise and the community from a few dollars to a few hundred dollars per month, and to stay inside the lower- and lower-middle-class neighborhoods. . . . [24]

In this way vice laws, and liquor laws especially, proved a useful tool for political machines to enhance their power. Protection money provided a source of funding, and selective enforcement allowed political bosses to discipline their supporters and put their competitors out of business.[25]

In New York, precinct captains used detectives to collect protection money.[26] In other places, the landlord would collect it as a part of the rent, then pass it on to the police. He would say to the proprietor of the saloon or brothel: "You can have this house for two hundred dollars, with police protection, or one hundred dollars if you take care of yourself."[27]

Police detectives, like the thieftakers before them, were more interested in retrieving stolen property and collecting rewards than in catching crooks. Of course, the easiest way to get hold of stolen goods was to work with the thieves. In exchange for immunity and a portion of the reward, thieves would supply detectives with their loot. The detectives would return the stolen items to the rightful owners—minus whatever sum they claimed as a reward. Many professional criminals would not work outside of such a framework, and these deals could be quite profitable for the cops. Between January 1, 1855, and April 30, 1857, Robert Bowyer of the New York Police Department earned $4,700 in rewards—more than twice his salary for the same period.[28]

Sometimes, no effort would be made to retrieve the stolen property, or to return it to the victim. Pickpockets and con artists were generally allowed to go about their business unmolested so long as they cut the cops in on the action. The profits then worked their way up the political food chain. The cops were required to give a portion of their take to their commanders, the local politicians, and their affiliates, thus avoiding any punishment.[29]

Shakedowns weren't restricted to illicit enterprises, either. Legitimate businesses could also be inconvenienced by strict enforcement of the law and were vulnerable to the disruption caused by routine harassment. Builders, bootblacks, produce merchants, and other peddlers had to pay off the beat cop, or else they might be taken in for blocking the sidewalks.[30]

The system of bribery and extortion that was nineteenth-century policing far surpassed anything that could be termed individual misconduct, or even organizational deviance; it resembled nothing so much as institutionalized corruption, state-sponsored crime. Graft and the abuse of power were not merely allowed, they were expected, required, and enforced—within the police department and throughout the city administration. The political machine may best be understood as an exercise in government of, by, and for corruption. This fusion of government and criminality follows a certain kind of logic. In "War Making and State Making as Organized Crime," Charles Tilly argues that:

Banditry, piracy, gangland rivalry, policing, and war making all belong on the same continuum. . . . [C]onsider the definition of a racketeer as someone who creates a threat and then charges for its reduction. Governments' provision of protection, by this standard, often qualifies as racketeering. To the extent that the threats against which a given government protects its citizens are imaginary or are the consequences of its own activities, the government has organized a protection racket.[31]

The history of American cities gives concrete expression to Tilly's theoretical claim.[32] In the classic political machines, government agencies and organized criminal enterprises were not only moral equivalents, they often comprised the same people. Nineteenth-century policing did not just resemble racketeering, it *was* racketeering, unmistakably.

The police were a central component of this system. Both the protection schemes that insured the cooperation of the underworld and the brawling gangs that controlled the polls on election day depended on, at the very least, the acquiescence of the police. In many respects the development of the political machines depended upon the simultaneous development of the modern police. At the same time, the modernization of policing made possible important advances in municipal government. In particular, the police provided the means by which the power of local government could be consolidated into a single coherent system. In this respect, the rise of political machines resembled the earlier rise of the state itself. A brief comparison of these processes may tell us something about the engineering of power and the uses of policing in establishing its claims.

MACHINE POLITICS, STATE POWER, AND MONOPOLIES OF VIOLENCE

In general terms, we can discern a common principle underlying the creation of local political machines and that of national states: "A tendency to monopolize the means of violence makes a government's claim to provide protection, in either the comforting or ominous sense of the word, more credible and more difficult to resist."[33] Tilly further identifies four activities characteristic of states:

1) making war (defeating external rivals);
2) making states (destroying internal rivals);
3) protection (defending clients from their enemies); and,
4) extraction (acquiring the resources to do the other three).[34]

Cities have not, since the colonial period, usually been forced to contend with external rivals, and thus have not been concerned with making war. But the other three activities find clear analogies in the activities of city governments, especially during the machine period. And at both the national and the municipal levels, "all [these activities] depend on the state's tendency to monopolize the concentrated means of coercion."[35]

Philadelphia's history illustrates some more specific parallels. In the first half of the nineteenth century, urban growth had spread beyond the city's jurisdiction, practically uniting it with nearby townships over which it had no authority. The urban area was divided between several municipalities, and these were divided geographically into neighborhoods, politically into wards, and socially along religious and ethnic lines, with a strong correlation between these sets of divisions. It was nearly impossible to keep order. Catholics and Protestants fought in the streets, White mobs attacked Blacks and abolitionist speakers, and the city government could do practically nothing, even within the limited area of its authority.[36] The localized, ward-based system of city politics inhibited the government's ability to enforce its will within the neighborhoods. Yet, in the course of a few years, Philadelphia was transformed from a fragmented megalopolis with only a nominal central authority to a modern city with a unified city government, a citywide political machine, and a police system to enforce the will of each.

Much of the disorder in nineteenth-century Philadelphia was perpetrated, oddly, by the city's volunteer fire departments. Neighborhood-based fire companies adopted the ethnic and religious identities of their members, and often saw themselves as the champions of their neighborhood's traditional culture and honor. Firefighting became a source of neighborhood pride, and offered an opportunity to settle scores against rival groups. Demographic shifts and overlapping jurisdictions led to frequent turf wars; firemen would often fight one another while a blaze continued unabated. When opportunities for battle did not present themselves, they were sometimes created: Fire companies would set fires in other precincts and then ambush their rivals.[37]

These brawls became neighborhood affairs, involving large sections of the community. Many of the fire companies affiliated with youth gangs, some with names like "Killers," "Rats," and "Bouncers."[38] As the police at the time were also organized into separate ward organizations, they were ill suited for suppressing such riots. Not that they were eager to, either; the cops generally felt little inclination to interfere with these battles, except in support of their neighborhood company.

This situation put conflicting pressures on the political system. On the one hand, it created demands for more centralization, for government-run fire departments and a single police force capable of suppressing disorder. On the other hand, ward leaders saw the political potential of the fire companies and were quick to avail themselves of this additional source of election-day muscle.[39] The balkanized state of the city therefore left local political bosses in a bit of a bind. Their personal fiefdoms were inextricably tied to the ward-based structure of government; it allowed them a distinct realm of influence and a base of support for pursuing their agenda in the citywide political arena. But the exercise of this authority relied on a certain minimum degree of public order, which this same ward structure, with its rivalries and fragmentation, constantly threatened.

The outcome of this dilemma is revealing. In 1850, a "marshal's" police force was created for the entire city of Philadelphia. Police in the suburbs and the four city districts continued to act independently, but were also called on to cooperate with the marshal's force.[40] The first marshal, John Keyser, recruited the new police directly from the youth gangs associated with Nativist fire departments, reasoning that he could form a "strong-armed force prepared to slug it out with fire gangs."[41] By co-opting the most militant element of the fire companies and consolidating them into a single, citywide force, the marshal's police organization afforded the new cops the opportunity to defeat their traditional rivals and greatly enhanced the power of the city government, as well as, for a time, that of the Nativist party machine.

Catholic gangs and fire companies, while overpowered, were not especially impressed with their rivals' new authority. One gang, the Bleeders, told in a song of being attacked by "a band of ruffians . . . they called themselves Police."[42] And when the Nativists lost control of the city government, Keyser's replacement—a Democrat— filled the force with Democrats also recruited from fire company gangs.[43]

In 1854, the Legislature revised the city's charter to cover the entire contiguous urban area, incorporating outlying districts into the city.[44] The new charter required a centralized police department and allowed for a city-controlled fire department as well. The mayor was given the power to appoint police officers and set the department's rules, and the city council was responsible for determining the size and organization of the force. The council created an 820-man department, divided between fourteen precincts corresponding to the ward districts. One alderman was elected to serve as magistrate in each district, and a single marshal was appointed to oversee the entire operation.[45] In effect, this arrangement put the new police directly in the service of the reigning political machine.[46]

But the consolidation of power may not have been everything the ward leaders had hoped for. In many respects, the beginnings of a central authority relied on a corresponding decline in local power. The survival of the central power structure demanded the eventual elimination of its potential rivals. So long as local political bosses could command their own sources of power, the central government as a whole was necessarily vulnerable. Again we find a parallel with the creation of the nation-state.

> In one way or another, every European government before the French Revolution relied on indirect rule via local magnates. The magnates collaborated with the government without becoming officials in any strong sense of the term, had some access to government-backed force, and exercised wide discretion within their own territories. . . .

Yet the same magnates were potential rivals, possible allies of a rebellious people.

Eventually, European governments reduced their reliance on indirect rule by means of two expensive but effective strategies: (a) extending their officialdom to the local community and (b) encouraging the creation of police forces that were subordinate to the government rather than to individual patrons, distinct from war-making forces, and therefore less useful as the tools of dissident magnates.[47]

Likewise, in Philadelphia, so long as the central government was dependent upon the cooperation of the ward bosses, the government's influence was quite limited and no one faction could be assured of permanent dominance. Faced with difficulties resembling those of the early European states, Philadelphia's local government followed a similar course.

> [In England,] Tudor demilitarization of the great lords entailed four complementary campaigns: eliminating their personal bands of armed retainers, razing their fortresses, taming their habitual resort to violence for the settlement of disputes, and discouraging the cooperation of their dependents and tenants.[48]

In Philadelphia, all four aims were accomplished with one masterstroke: the creation of a citywide police force allowed the limited consolidation of the city government. The ward-based militants were either co-opted into the police or defeated by them. While no fortresses existed to be pulled down, the ward leaders were made increasingly vulnerable; their position came to depend as much on their status within the machine, citywide, as on their influence in their own ward. Interward battles were either avoided by the new system or forcibly resolved by the new police. And the cooperation and loyalty of ward residents, once owed to their local boss, became attached to the new citywide machine.

Philadelphia did not become a nation-state, of course, or even a city-state. But the authority of the city government was produced by very similar means, and in this process the creation of modern policing played a central role. The new police were not simply one aspect of a modernizing city government; they also represented a means of consolidating power within the modernizing government. But as the city consolidated power, it embarked on the first of a series of adaptations that would strengthen the government itself at the expense of the local leaders, eventually leading to the decline of the machine system.[49]

Centralization, even in meager form, not only changed the distribution of power, but also tended to transform the institutions that shared power. The modernization of the police allowed for a major advance in the organization and efficiency of the political machine, and with it the power of the municipal government. With a single police force in place, power could be, if not quite centralized, at least somewhat solidified. This step proved a major boon to the reigning machine, and provided one means for the machine to exert influence in wards where popular support was weak. As it did, however, it began the process by which control was shifted both upward and toward the center.[50] Inadvertently, the creation of a citywide police force both drew up the blueprint and laid the groundwork for the creation of other municipal bureaucracies, and the eventual destruction of the ward-based machine system.[51] While somewhat ironic, this turn of events represents a continuation of the trends that had shaped the development of law enforcement as it approached the modern period—specifically, the growing emphasis on prevention, the tendency to expand police duties, and the move toward specialized agencies. Each of these three factors contributed to the process of modernization, but the ideal of prevention occupied a special place as a guiding principle of police development.

THE PREVENTIVE IDEAL, GENERALIZED POWERS, AND SPECIALIZATION

The idea of preventing crime has long been the avowed aim of policing, but it has undergone significant revision over time. In the London Night Watch Acts of 1737 and 1738, crime prevention was explicitly cited as the goal of the watch, though it is unclear how the body was supposed to contribute to this aim.[52] The instructions offered the Philadelphia Watch in 1791 were only slightly more explicit:

> [T]he said constable and watchmen, in their respective turns and courses of watching, shall use their best endeavors to prevent murders, burglaries, robberies and other outrages and disorders within the city, and to that end shall, and they are hereby empowered and required to arrest and apprehend all persons whom they shall find disturbing the peace, or shall have cause to suspect of any unlawful and evil design.. [53]

By 1800, the preventive rationale had been refined. The watch's role was to ensure that criminals would be punished, and the guarantee of punishment (it was hoped) would be sufficient to deter crime.[54] To this end, in 1794, the St. Marylebone Watch Committee resolved unanimously "that in case any Robbery be committed within the Parish, the Watchmen in whose Walk the same shall happen be absolutely discharged." Several other London districts adopted a similar standard, though eventually the limits of the system had to be admitted. A few months later, St. Marylebone's committee relented, acknowledging that "many Robberies are committed within this Parish without the possible knowledge of the Watchmen. . . . "[55]

Watchmen were thought to deter crime by their mere presence and they could detain people they suspected of criminal acts, but the watch was not a detective force and had no means for discovering the culprits after a crime was committed.[56] The odds, then, were against apprehension. While the idea behind the watch was preventive, the watch's methods were essentially reactive, and even their reactive capabilities were quite limited.

When Robert Peel created the London Metropolitan Police in 1829, the prevention of crime was singled out as the new body's chief concern:

> It should be understood, at the outset, that the principal object to be attained is *'the Prevention of Crime.'*
> To this great end every effort of the Police is to be directed. The security of person and property, the preservation of the public tranquillity, and all the other objects of a Police Establishment, will thus be better effected than by the detection and punishment of the offender, after he has succeeded in committing the crime.[57]

Nevertheless, the Metropolitans remained unsure of *how* to prevent crime. In the decades that followed, they essentially replicated the patrols of the watch, with even less success.[58]

In the U.S., "the term 'preventive police' was used frequently and loosely. Preventive seemed to mean that by their presence the police would inhibit the commission of crime and that they would deal with potentially serious crimes before they reached the crisis stage."[59] This crude notion of prevention developed into a more serious and ambitious program as time passed, and came to inform the expansion of police powers. In Boston, for example, in 1850 the police were authorized to order any group of three or more people to "move on" or suffer arrest.[60]

Of course, most of what the police did was still responsive, and most actual crimefighting still took place after the crimes had been committed. But the preventive ideal was clearly gaining an articulation, and slowly techniques were developed to bring the practice closer to the principle. The preventive ideal both prompted the expansion of police power and helped shape the specialized focus on crime.

It is worth noting the tension between these two trends: If police powers expand over too large a range of duties, policing loses its character. The police come to resemble generalized inspectors, and enforcement of the criminal law becomes a secondary matter. But, if enforcement is overly specialized, the police are in effect replaced by a series of guards, traffic wardens, thieftakers, bounty hunters, and whatnot.

Constables, sheriffs, and marshals, as servants of the court or sovereign, were assigned general responsibilities. The slave patrols developed from the other end of the spectrum, beginning with a few select duties and accumulating responsibilities and power over time. This second path was the more straightforward route toward modernization because, rather then serving primarily as officers to the crown or the court, the slave patrols existed solely as a means of preserving the status quo through the enforcement of the slave codes. As soon as they separated from the militia, they existed as law-enforcement bodies, and new duties were added accordingly.

The tension between specialization and generalization did not vanish with the creation of the modern police. The police retained many duties that were quite remote from their alleged purpose of preventing crime and enforcing the criminal law. Robert Fogelson explains:

> In the absence of other specialized public bureaucracies, the authorities found the temptation almost irresistible to transform the police departments into catchall health, welfare, and law enforcement agencies. Hence the police cleaned streets and inspected boilers in New York, distributed supplies to the poor in Baltimore, accommodated the homeless in Philadelphia, investigated vegetable markets in St. Louis, operated emergency ambulances in Boston, and attempted to curb crime in all these cities.[61]

In fact, even today, the police continue to hold duties quite removed from the enforcement of the law and the prevention of crime. In many cities cops still direct traffic, license parades, escort funerals, remove panhandlers, quiet loud parties, find lost children, advise urban planners, make presentations to civic groups and school children, operate Boys and Girls Clubs, and perform other tasks quite outside their stated purview.

As Fogelson implies, this tendency developed in part because the police offered a means for the local government to enforce its will, regulate the behavior of the citizens, and generally keep an eye on things with unprecedented efficiency and regularity. It thus became a constant temptation to use this power in new and expanding ways, often to the detriment of the specialized law-enforcement function.

Further specialization then relied on the development of additional bureaucracies to take on these extraneous duties.

> The police were valued especially for the flexibility which made them adaptable to new demands. But when better machinery was developed the government did not hesitate to transfer their responsibilities. The creation of the sewer, health, street, and building departments all diminished the role of the police in local administration.[62]

Policing is thus tied to a more general trend in government administration, the rise of bureaucracies. The development of modern police both depended on and promoted the creation of other municipal bureaucracies. In the first place, the creation of other bureaucracies allowed the police to specialize. Second, the consolidation of police forces facilitated a more general move toward bureaucratization by providing a model for these same bureaucracies to adopt. For both of these reasons, the modernization of the police was a key component in the modernization of city government.[63] But the impact of the new police was not restricted to its effect on municipal administration. Policing was also closely connected to the economic conditions attending widespread industrialization, and the consequent expansion of the cities themselves.

URBANIZATION AND INDUSTRIALIZATION

When the modern police first appeared, Eastern cities were experiencing a wave of expansion, fueled by industrialization. It is no accident that industrial society produced new means of social control, since it also created new risks for disorder. Put simply, in an increasingly complex society, there was more that could go wrong. While the sheer numbers and diversity of the population contributed to this complexity, specialization—especially in the production and distribution of goods—and increased social stratification were probably more important. These factors acted together to depress or reduce the standard of living for the greatest portion of the cities' residents, creating conflict between economic classes and increasing friction between ethnic and religious groups.[64] Selden Bacon suggests:

> These three factors of social change, the rise in specialization, the
> stratification of classes, and the lowering of standards and conse-
> quent limitation of activities brought about by increasing numbers,
> all created problems in the maintenance of a harmonious and secure
> society; the techniques of enforcement present in the 16th, 17th,
> and 18th centuries were unable to meet these problems. The family,
> the local church, the neighborhood, and the existing governmental
> agencies could not cope with the situation. In fact, there is a good
> deal of evidence to show that the changes were weakening all these
> institutions, especially as they helped bring about the mobility and
> individualism so characteristic of American society.[65]

Cyril D. Robinson and Richard Scaglion argue along similar lines, placing the advent of modern policing in the context of the emerging capitalist system. They present four interdependent propositions:

(1) the origin of a specialized police function depends upon the division of society into dominant and subordinate classes with antagonistic interests;
(2) specialized police agencies are generally characteristic only of societies politically organized as states;

(3) in a period of transition, the crucial factor in delineating the modern specialized police function is an ongoing attempt at conversion of the social control (policing) mechanism from an integral part of the community structure to an agent of an emerging dominant class; and

(4) the police institution is created by the emerging dominant class as an instrument for the preservation of its control over restricted access to basic resources, over the political apparatus governing this access, and over the labor force necessary to provide the surplus upon which the dominant class lives.[66]

There is much to recommend this as a general scheme, though it seems to exaggerate the role of elite foresight and planning at the expense of after-the-fact opportunism. It does more to characterize the result than the process, assuming that the outcome corresponds with some original intention. Robinson and Scaglion's account offers a useful outline of the preconditions necessary for the creation of the modern police, but the long and complex process of transition from pre-modern to modern policing suggests a more complicated picture than their theory would indicate, especially in regard to the relationship between economic elites and the state. While it is certainly true that the ruling class came to use the police as an instrument for the expansion and preservation of their power, it seems like a stretch to say that they *created* the institution *for* that end.

As we have seen, the first significant advances toward modern policing appeared in the South, where elite attitudes about the state were characteristically ambivalent. The maintenance of slave laws originally relied upon informal, universal enforcement requirements reminiscent of the frankpledge; every White member of the community had the responsibility to uphold the law. The Southern system of slave control underwent a full transition from this informal policing system, through various stages of specialization, to its apex in the creation of the quite modern Charleston police force.[67] Clearly this transformation relied on social stratification, the existence of a political state, and the use of the policing function to maintain the racial and economic status quo—that is, to protect the interests of the slaveowners. However, while police powers were intentionally divorced from the community and invested in a specialized group, this change was not—as Robinson and Scaglion's model might imply—instigated at the behest of the slaveowners, but to some degree accomplished over their objections and despite their resistance. It was instead *political* elites who created slave patrols as a guard against the political threat of revolt more than against the economic dangers of escape. While the state functioned in the interests of the ruling class, it was not yet an agent of the ruling class, but a competing nexus of power, and a challenge to the aristocratic pretensions of the slave owners.

In cities, industrialization and its accompanying entourage of social changes led to the breakdown of the informal means of social control that had proved mostly sufficient to that point.[68] Cities thus produced advances in social control that the plantation system hadn't needed and likely would have eschewed. In Southern cities like Charleston, the City Guards picked up where the patrols had fallen short, in the control of slaves and free Blacks on hire. In Northern cities, industrialization produced similar needs to control the workforce. Rather than rely on personal authority and social deference as on the plantation, or on the influence of the family and church, as in smaller New England towns, industrial cities of the North created governmental systems that were universalistic and routinized.[69]

Faced with similar challenges relating to urbanization, industrialization, and the rise of capitalism, elites in different cities responded in markedly similar ways, sometimes consciously borrowing from each other and sometimes unwittingly reproducing models and techniques that were in use elsewhere, keeping what succeeded and discarding that which failed to suit their purposes. And as this process advanced, they transformed the mechanisms of law enforcement and created a new, distinctive institution—the modern police.

The New York Municipal Police came to define the type. But it would be wrong to think of the New York police as simply a modern watch, or as a Northern slave patrol, or as a set of American Bobbies[70], though it was somewhat analogous to all three. In New York, as elsewhere, the police appeared when broad social trends intersected with local crises and the particular needs of the city. Of course, the authorities only responded to the crises on a rather shallow level, never acknowledging the underlying causes that produced them. Instead, local elites preferred to blame the crises of urbanization on the moral shortcomings of the poor, and the idea of the "dangerous classes" was born.

> In the years preceding the rise of police departments in London and in the United States, middle-class and elite members of society attributed crime, riot, and public drunkenness to the members of the "dangerous classes." The image was that of a convulsively and possibly biologically criminal, riotous, and intemperate group of persons located at the base of society. Their actions were seen as destroying the very fabric of society.[71]

The particular population identified with the dangerous classes varied by locale. In England, the dangerous classes consisted of the urban poor, vagrants and prostitutes in particular. In the northern United States, it was the immigrant lower class; in Boston, the term was especially applied to Irish Catholics.[72] The term was not used much in the South, but the dangerous classes found an analogy in the Black population, and especially the slaves. In addition to their association with crime and disorder, the dangerous classes also represented an alien presence, a group with different values whose behavior was therefore suspicious as if by definition.[73] The Boston Council reported:

In former times the Night Watch with a small constabulary force, were quite sufficient to keep the peace in a city proverbial for its love of order and attachment to the laws and remarkable for the homogenous character of its population. But the rapid development of the system of railroads and of the means of communication, with all parts of Europe, together with other causes have brought among us great numbers who have not had the benefit of a New England training and who have heretofore been held in restraint rather by fear of the lawgiver than respect for the law.[74]

Moreover, criminal behavior was understood as a threat to the social order, not merely to its real or potential victims. Theft obviously challenged the sanctity of private property, but more to the point, drunkenness and vagrancy seemed to threaten the standards of diligence and self-control central to Protestant morality and crucial to an economic system dependent on regularity, predictability, and a disciplined workforce.[75]

Crime and criminality were thus constructed to reflect the ideological needs of elites. Criminality was less a matter of what people did than of what they represented.[76] The idea of the dangerous classes was intimately tied to the prevailing economic order in each place, and had profound implications for the systems of social control they adopted.

Slavery was not primarily a penal institution, though that was one of its results. In addition to its role in the southern labor and social system, the plantation kept under confinement and control the one class that was most threatening to the social order. Similarly, the prison was not primarily a labor system, but it mandated labor for rehabilitation, profit, and internal order. The prison adopted many features of the factory system and justified forced labor of convicts because of the moral uplift it provided.[77]

Both systems supplied large-scale, unpaid labor for the propertied classes, deprived the workers of their most basic civil liberties and political rights, and relied on corporal punishment and shaming for discipline.[78] Furthermore, in both cases the economic systems created the class of people they were then at such pains to control: the slaves in the plantation system, and the immigrant working class in industrialized cities.

While elite anxieties about the dangerous classes supplied the impetus for new forms of social control, other concerns also helped to shape the emerging institutions. The modern police system, unlike less formal means of control, actually required very little of ordinary citizens in the way of enforcement, and exposed the respectable classes to almost no personal danger. And, though supplying an organized force under control of the government, it avoided the unseemly image of a military occupation, since police—in the North, at least—patrolled alone or in pairs, and were sparingly armed. Furthermore, an impersonal system was to be preferred over either a military model or a more informal arrangement because, ironically, it was less obviously a tool of the ruling classes.[79]

To the degree that industrialization and urbanization created changes related to the diversity of the urban population, economic specialization, and social stratification, they certainly produced new challenges of social control. But the question remains, what did those difficulties have to do with crime? Put differently, it might be asked: Were the dangerous classes criminal? Or were they criminalized?

THE DEMAND FOR ORDER

It is generally assumed that the police were created to deal with rising levels of crime caused by urbanization and the increasing numbers of immigrants. John Schneider describes the typical accounts:

> The first studies were legal and administrative in their focus, confined mostly to narrative descriptions of the step-by-step demise of the old constabulary and the steady, but often controversial evolution of the professionals. Scholars seemed preoccupied with the politics of police reform. Its causes, on the other hand, were considered only in cursory fashion, more often assumed than proved. Cities, it would seem, moved inevitably toward modern policing as a consequence of soaring levels of crime and disorder in an era of phenomenal growth and profound social change.[80]

I will refer to this as the "crime and disorder" theory.

Despite its initial plausibility, the idea that the police were invented in response to an epidemic of crime is, to be blunt, exactly wrong. Furthermore, it is not much of an explanation. It assumes that "when crime reaches a certain level, the 'natural' social response is to create a uniformed police force. This, of course, is not an explanation but an assertion of a natural law for which there is little evidence."[81]

It may be that slave revolts, riots, and other instances of collective violence precipitated the creation of modern police, but we should remember that neither crime nor disorder were unique to nineteenth-century cities, and therefore cannot on their own account for a change such as the rise of a new institution. Riotous mobs controlled much of London during the summer of 1780, but the Metropolitan Police did not appear until 1829. Public drunkenness was a serious problem in Boston as early as 1775, but a modern police force was not created there until 1838.[82] So the crime-and-disorder theory fails to explain why earlier crime waves didn't produce modern police. It also fails to explain why crime in the nineteenth century led to *policing*, and not to some other arrangement.[83]

Furthermore, it is not at all clear that crime was on the rise prior to the creation of the modern police. In Boston, for example, crime went down between 1820 and 1830,[84] and continued to drop for the rest of the nineteenth century.[85] In fact, crime was such a minor concern that it was not even mentioned in the marshal's report of 1824.[86] And the city suffered only a single murder between 1822 and 1834.[87]

Whether or not *crime* was on the rise, after the introduction of modern policing the number of *arrests* increased.[88] The majority of these arrests were for misdemeanors, and most were related to victimless crimes, or crimes against the public order. They did not generally involve violence or the loss of property, but instead concerned public drunkenness, vagrancy, loitering, disorderly conduct, or being a "suspicious person."[89] In other words, the greatest portion of the actual business of law enforcement did not concern the protection of life and property, but the controlling of poor people, their habits and their manners. Sidney Harring wryly notes: "The criminologist's definition of 'public order crimes' comes perilously close to the historian's description of 'working-class leisure-time activity.'"[90] The suppression of such disorderly conduct was only made possible by the introduction of modern police. For the first time, more arrests were made on the initiative of the officer than in response to specific complaints.[91] Though the charges were generally minor, the implications were not: the change from privately initiated to police-initiated prosecutions greatly shifted the balance of power between the citizenry and the state.

A critic of this view might suggest that the rise in public order *arrests* reflected an increase in public order *offenses*, rather than a shift in official priorities. Unfortunately, there is no way to verify this claim. (The increase in arrests does not provide very good evidence, since it is precisely this increase the hypothesis seeks to explain.) However, if the tolerance for disorder was in decline, this fact, coupled with the existence of the new police, would be sufficient to explain the increase in arrests of this type.[92]

The Cleveland police offered a limited test of this hypothesis. In December 1907, they adopted a "Golden Rule" policy. Rather than arrest drunks and other public order offenders, the police walked them home or issued a warning. In the year before the policy was established, Cleveland police made 30,418 arrests, only 938 of which were for felonies. In the year after the Golden Rule was instituted, the police made 10,095 arrests, 1,000 of which were for felonies.[93] Other cities implemented similar policies, in some cases, reducing the number of arrests by 75 percent.[94]

Cleveland's example demonstrates that official tolerance can reduce arrest rates. This suggests an explanation for the sudden rise in misdemeanor arrests during the previous century: If official *tolerance* can *reduce* arrest rates, it makes sense that official *intolerance* could *increase* the number of arrests. In other words, during the nineteenth century crime was down, but the demand for order was up, at least among those people who could influence the administration of the law.

Although the *problems* of the streets—the fights, the crowds, the crime, the children—were nothing new, the "problem" itself represented altered bourgeois perceptions and a broadened political initiative. An area of social life that had been taken for granted, an accepted feature of city life, became visible, subject to scrutiny and intervention.[95]

New York City's campaign against prostitution certainly followed this pattern. During the first half of the nineteenth century, the official view on prostitution transformed from one of complacency to one of moral panic. Beginning in the 1830s, when reform societies took an interest in the issue, it was widely claimed that prostitution was approaching epidemic proportions. Probably the number of prostitutes did increase: The watch estimated that there were 600 prostitutes working in 1806, and 1,200 in 1818. In 1856, Police Chief George Matsell set the figure at 5,000. But given that the population of the city increased by more than six times between 1820 and 1860, the official estimates actually showed a *decrease* in the number of prostitutes relative to the population.[96]

Enforcement activities, however, increased markedly during the same period. In 1860, ninety people were committed to the First District Prison for keeping a "disorderly house." This figure was five times that of 1849, when seventeen people were imprisoned for the offense. Likewise, prison sentences for vagrancy rose from 3,173 for the entire period covering 1820–1830, to 3,552 in 1850 and 6,552 in 1860. As prostitutes were generally cited for vagrancy, since prostitution itself was not a statutory offense, the proportion of female "vagrants" steadily rose: Women comprised 62 percent of those imprisoned for vagrancy in 1850 and 72 percent in 1860.[97]

This analysis does not solve the problem, but merely relocates it. If it was not crime but the standards of order that were rising, what caused the higher standards of public order? For one thing, the relative absence of serious crime may have facilitated the rise in social standards and the demand for order.

A fall in the real crime rate allows officially accepted standards of conduct to rise; as standards rise, the penal machinery is extended and refined; the result is that an increase in the total number of cases brought in accompanies a decrease in their relative severity.[98]

Once established, the police themselves may have helped to raise expectations. In New York, Chief Matsell actively promoted the panic over public disorder, in part to quiet criticism of the new police.[99] More subtly, the very existence of the police may have suggested the possibility of urban peace and made it seem feasible that most laws would be enforced, not indirectly by the citizenry, but directly by the state.[100] And the new emphasis on public order corresponded with the morality of the dominant Protestant class and the demands of the new industrialized economy, ensuring elite support for policing.

This intersection of class bias and rigid moralism was particularly clear concerning, and had special implications for, the status of women. In many ways, the sudden furor over prostitution was typical. As the social mores of the Protestant ruling class came to define legal notions of "public order" and "vice," the role of women was redefined and increasingly restricted. "Fond paternalistic indulgence of women who conformed to domestic ideals was intimately connected with extreme condemnation of those who were outside the bonds of patronage and dependence on which the relations of men and women were based."[101] As a result, women were held to higher standards and subject to harsher treatment when they stepped outside the bounds of their role. Women were arrested less frequently than men, but were more likely to be jailed and served longer sentences than men convicted of the same crimes.[102] Enforcement practices surrounding the demand for order thus weighed doubly on working-class women, who faced gender-based as well as class-based restrictions on their public behavior.

At the same time, the increased demand for order came to shape not only the enforcement of the law, but the law itself. In the early nineteenth century, Boston's laws only prohibited *habitual* drunkenness, but in 1835 *public* drunkenness was also banned. Alcohol-related arrests increased from a few hundred each year to several thousand.[103] In 1878, police powers were extended even further, as they were authorized to arrest people for loitering or using profanity.[104] In Philadelphia, meanwhile, "after the new police law took effect, the doctrine of arrest on suspicion was tacitly extended to the arrest and surveillance of people in advance of a crime."[105]

This scrutiny of the dangerous classes was at least partly an outgrowth of the preventive orientation of the new police. Built into the idea that the cops could prevent crime is the notion that they can predict criminal behavior. This preventive focus shifted their attention from actual to potential crimes, and then from the crime to the criminal, and finally to the potential criminal.[106] Profiling became an inherent element of modern policing.

So, contrary to the crime-and-disorder explanation, the new police system was not created in response to spiraling crime rates, but developed as a means of social control by which an emerging dominant class could impose their values on the larger population.

This shift can only be understood against a backdrop of much broader social changes. Industrialization and urbanization produced a new class of workers and, with it, new challenges for social control. They also produced opportunities for social control at a level previously unknown. The police represented one aspect of this growing apparatus, as did the prison, and sometime later, the public school. Furthermore, the police, by forming a major source of power for emerging city governments, and for those who would control them, also contributed to the development of other bureaucracies and increased the possibilities for rational administration. The reasons for these developments have been made fairly clear, but the means by which the police idea evolved and spread deserves further explication.

IMITATION, EXPERIMENTATION, EVOLUTION

Studies of police history that focus on the experience of a particular city often inadvertently imply that the police in New York, for example, or Philadelphia, or Boston, developed independently based on the unique needs and specific circumstances of that city.[107] This perspective obscures a very important aspect of police development, namely the degree to which city administrators consciously watched the innovations of other cities, drawing from them as suited their needs.[108] This system of communication and imitation explains the sudden appearance of very similar police organizations in cities all across the country in a relatively short period of time. For though it took a very long time for the characteristics of modern policing to develop, once they crystallized into a coherent form, the idea spread very quickly.[109]

Of course, the practice of borrowing police models from elsewhere was not itself new. American cities borrowed their earliest law enforcement mechanisms from European cities, especially London and Paris.[110] Georgia modeled its slave patrols on those already established in South Carolina, which were themselves copied from similar systems in Barbados; later it became common for towns to copy the patrolling techniques of others nearby.[111] Thus it is not especially surprising that New York, Philadelphia, Baltimore, Boston, and Washington, D.C., all took inspiration from the Metropolitan Police of London.[112]

But, the English influence on American policing should not be over-stated. Imitation occurred, but it was not total. Instead, "America's borrowing from England was selective. The general form of innovation came from England, although Americans modified and transformed English patterns to fit their particular culture."[113] Hence, the two countries prescribed very different relationships between the officers and the communities they patrolled. In England, the Bobbies were recruited from the countryside and from the lower ranks of the army. They were housed in barracks, denied the vote, and made accountable to Parliament rather than to the local authorities. In the United States, the police were expected to be a part of the communities they served. They were to act not only as police, but as citizens and neighbors as well.[114] A more telling difference lay in the extent and nature of local political influence in policing. In America, "Political parties contested vigorously to control police patronage and power, which . . . precluded American departments from following exactly their supposed model, the London Metropolitan Police."[115]

American cities also looked to each other for ideas. When Boston resolved "to imitate, as far as may be, the system of London," it also mentioned the reforms of New York and Philadelphia, and noted that Baltimore, Brooklyn, and other cities were moving in the same direction.[116] And in 1843, the legislative committee investigating better means of policing riots in Philadelphia spent two months collecting ideas from other cities.[117]

While less well documented, innovations originating in particular districts, or in the countryside, came to be incorporated into the practices of city police. This certainly occurred in Charleston, where the police had a direct lineage from the slave patrols. A similar process took place in London, where the use of full-time officers, the system of beat patrols, the focus on crime prevention, and even a bureaucratic structure were all developed in the parishes under the watch system, and then consolidated in 1829.[118]

If the practice of imitation shows how cities came to create police departments that closely resembled one another's, the process of experimentation helps to explain why they settled on the particular model they did. Because each city adjusted its organization in a number of ways, either in response to local pressures or based on innovations of its own, variations emerged that could then be tested by experience. Those judged to be successful were retained, and those that failed were abandoned. A kind of natural selection took place. Only the ideas deemed successful in one city survived to be reproduced elsewhere. In principle, this process could result in a diversity of policing mechanisms, and at times has done so—witness the contrast between the seventeenth-century plantation system and that of New York City during the same period. But as cities faced similar pressures related to population growth, industrialization, increased stratification, and the like, they came to adopt shared measures of success. As a result, older models, which had survived in some places for a very long time, were suddenly outmoded and replaced.

As Bacon outlines it, when social changes caused the traditional means of control to fail, variations of enforcement were adopted. Generally these were aimed at particular populations—slaves, the poor, immigrants—or trouble spots—ghettos, plantations, saloons, etc. Specialists in enforcement arose, and then unified into general enforcement bodies.[119] The move from informal systems of racial dominance to slave patrol, to police, may be understood as following this pattern. In New York, policing developed along similar lines: The watch was expanded, the constable's duties extended, the marshal's office created, and eventually a modern police force replaced them all.

The new agencies drew heavily from their predecessors in matters related to organizational structure, methods, and purpose. By incorporating the best of the recent innovations, the new types out-competed the disparate organizations they first imitated and then replaced. But it would be wrong to think of such changes as

only ever representing real progress. In fact the nature of experimentati
cally guarantees otherwise. Innumerable innovations were introduced, on
abandoned a short time later. Reforms were implemented, and quickly revers

It would be tedious to trace out every dead branch on this family tree, b
only consider the successes would run the risk of distorting the picture of devel
ment, presenting a circuitous route as a straight-away for the sake of preserving th
neatness of our map. To make the point briefly, I will borrow Bacon's taxonomy of
the failed types:

> Some of the variations in enforcement brought about by the failure
> of the primary groups, particularly the failure of the family, to main-
> tain order and security may be noted: the use of religious officers,
> such as the tythingman and warden; the use of the military; the
> attempt to secure order by having legislators and justices act as
> police; the trial of policing by posse, by citizen watch, by citizen
> informer; the practice of employing special men paid by fee; the
> experiments with private police and substitutes . . . for the most
> part, these all failed.[121]

Experimentation moved cities from one type of law enforcement to the next, but
we should not exaggerate the empiricist nature of the process. Far from following a
carefully controlled program and employing the scientific method, progress occurred
on an improvisational basis in response to short-term political considerations. Many
adaptations were accepted, or abandoned, not on their practical merits but for
strictly partisan reasons.

> Americans have rarely if ever agreed on the proper scope and
> function of the police and . . . such conflicts have molded
> police performance in a variety of ways. Most police adminis-
> trators have responded to whichever group was making the
> most noise at the moment rather than following a consistent
> and thought-out line of policy.[122]

These political conflicts helped to shape the institution, just as the practice of
imitation and the process of constant revision did. But behind it all is the simple
fact that institutions, like organism species, must adapt to their environment or die.
Policing, as an institution, did a great deal better than just survive. As it adapted
to the social conditions of the early to mid nineteenth century, it became not only
the product, but also the producer of social change.

As policing changed, it grew in importance, and in turn changed the society that had created it. The development of modern police facilitated further industrialization, it consolidated the influence of political machines, it led to the creation of new bureaucracies and advances in municipal government, and it made possible the imposition of Protestant moral values on the urban population. Also, and more basically, it allowed the state to impose on the lives of individuals in an unprecedented manner.

Sovereignty—and even states—are older than the police. "European kingdoms in the Middle Ages became 'law states' before they became 'police states,'"[123] meaning that they made laws and adjudicated claims before they established an independent mechanism for enforcing them. Organized police forces only emerged when traditional, informal, or community-maintained means of social control broke down. This breakdown was in each case prompted by a larger social change, often a change that some part of the community resisted with violence, such as the creation of a state, colonization, or the enslavement of a subject people.[124] It is at the point where authority is met with resistance that the organized application of force becomes necessary.[125] Each development detailed here has conformed to this general patern: the creation of the offices of the sheriff and the constable, the establishment of the watch, the deployment of slave patrols, the transition to City Guards, and finally the rise of the modern police.

The aims and means of social control always approximately reflect the anxieties of elites. In times of crisis or pronounced social change, as the concerns of elites shift, the mechanisms of social control are adapted accordingly. In the South, the institution of the slave patrol developed in stages following real or rumored insurrections. Later, complex factors conspired to produce the modern police force. Industrialization changed the system of social stratification and added a new threat, or set of threats, subsumed under the title of the "dangerous classes." Moreover, while serious crime was on the decline, the demand for order was on the rise owing to the needs of the new economic regime and the Protestant morality that supported it. In response to these conditions, American cities created a distinctive brand of police. They borrowed heavily from the English model already in place, but also took ideas from the existing night watch, the office of the constable, the militia, and the slave patrols.

At the same time, the drift toward modern policing fit nicely with the larger movement toward modern municipal government, best understood in terms of the emerging political machines, and later tied to the rise of bureaucracies.

The extensive interrelation between these various factors—industrialization, increasing demands for order, fear of the dangerous classes, pre-existing models of policing, and the development of citywide political machines—makes it obvious that no single item can be identified as the sole cause for the move toward policing. History is not propelled by a single engine, though historical accounts often are. Scholars have generally relied on one or one set of these factors in crafting their explanations, with most emphasizing those surrounding the sudden and rapid expansion of the urban population, especially immigrant communities.

Urbanization certainly had a role, but not the role it is usually assumed to have had. Rather than producing widespread criminality, cities actually produced widespread civility; as the population rose, the rate of serious crimes dropped.[126] The crisis of the time was not one of law, but of order—specifically the order required by the new industrial economy and the Protestant moralism that supplied, in large part, its ideological expression.

The police provided a mechanism by which the power of the state, and eventually that of the emerging ruling class, could be brought to bear on the lives and habits of individual members of society.

> The new organization of police made it possible for the first time in generations to attempt a wide enforcement of the criminal code, especially the vice laws. But while the earlier lack of execution was largely the result of weakness, it had served a useful function also, as part of the system of compromise which made the law tolerable.[127]

In other words, the much-decried inefficiency and inadequacy of the night watch in fact corresponded with the practical limitations on the power of the state.[128] With these limits removed or overcome, the state at once cast itself in a more active role. Public safety was no longer in the hands of amateur nightwatchmen, but had been transferred to a full-time professional body, directed by and accountable to the city authorities. The enforcement of the law no longer relied on the complaints of aggrieved citizens, but on the initiative of officers whose mission was to prevent offenses. Hence, crimes without victims needn't be ignored, and potential offenders need never be given the opportunity to act. In both instances the new police were doing what would have been nearly inconceivable just a few years before.

It was in this way that the United States became what Allan Silver calls "a policed society."

> A policed society is unique in that central power exercises potentially violent supervision over the population by bureaucratic means widely diffused throughout civil society in small and discretionary operations that are capable of rapid concentration.[129]

The police organization allowed the state to establish a constant presence in a wide geographic area and exercise routinized control by the use of patrols and other surveillance. Through the same organization, the state retained the ability to concentrate its power in the event of a riot or other emergency, without having to resort to the use of troops or the maintenance of a military presence. Silver argues that the significance of this advance "lay not only in its narrow application to crime and violence. In a broader sense, it represented the penetration and continual presence of central political authority throughout daily life."[130] The populace as a whole, even if not every individual person, was to be put under constant surveillance.

The police represent the point of contact between the coercive apparatus of the state and the lives of its citizens. Put this way, the characteristics of modern policing may come to sound more ominous—the specialized function, the concentration of power in a centralized organization, the constant application of that power over the entire city, the separation of the police from the community, and a preventive aim. While in some ways a more rational application of traditional means, the organizations that developed in this direction were fundamentally different from the ones they replaced. With the birth of modern policing, the state acquired a new means of controlling the citizenry, one based on its experiences, not only with crime and domestic disorder, but with colonialism and slavery as well. If policing was not in its inception a totalitarian pursuit, the modern development of the institution has at least been a major step in that direction.

COPS AND KLAN, HAND IN HAND

In the later nineteenth century, as political machines, industrialization, and the new police reshaped urban society, politics in the South faced additional complexities in the aftermath of the Civil War. There, many of the trappings of machine politics were present—corruption, abuses of power, favoritism, and street brawls—but with a difference. The status of the newly freed Black population became *the* political question of the day. The Republican Party, dominant following the war, developed a constituency among Black voters eager to assert themselves, and relied on the occupying Union army to suppress opposition. The Democratic Party aligned itself with disenfranchised Confederate veterans, deposed planters, former slaveowners, and the other reactionary remnants of Southern society, including many poor Whites ideologically attached to the old order.[1] The coercive force of the Democratic party was embodied in secret terrorist societies and vigilante groups including the Black Cavalry, the Men of Justice, the Young Mens' Democratic Clubs, the Knights of the White Camellia, and the Ku Klux Klan.[2] As the Klan gained a prominence in 1868, it concentrated on discouraging Black voters, intimidating Republican candidates, and defeating proposed Radical constitutions.[3] But the Klan's defense of White supremacy quickly expanded beyond such narrow political goals.

RECONSTRUCTION AND REDEMPTION: WHO WON THE WAR?

During the Reconstruction period, vigilante actions and policing were often indistinguishable. The Klan, which saw itself as a force for order, especially against Black criminality[4], took up night-riding, at times in regular patrols. Its members stopped Blacks on the roads, searched their homes, seized weapons and valuables, interrogated them about their voting plans, and often brutalized them.

> Bands of a dozen or more disguised men rode about regularly after dark, calling or dragging Negroes from their homes and threatening, robbing, beating, and occasionally killing them. Some white Republicans received the same treatment. Most of this activity followed a common pattern. Klansmen nearly always searched for and confiscated any guns they found; in a few locations they made a blanket requirement that Negroes deposit their guns at a certain place by an assigned date or face a whipping. Generally they quizzed

their victims about their voting intentions at the forthcoming election. If a freedman answered that he planned to vote for Grant he was likely to be whipped; if he said he planned to vote for Seymour or else stay home he was more likely to get off with a warning and the loss of his gun. In some cases, blacks were robbed of money, watches, and other possessions.[5]

In many places, the Klan totally regulated the social lives of the Black population, breaking up worship services, opposing the creation of Black schools, often with success, and establishing and enforcing a system of passes for Black workers.[6]

In less routine actions, White mobs sometimes attacked individual Blacks, Black political assemblies, and White Republicans. These attacks often involved the police as participants, or even leaders.

For example, in April 1866, after a crowd of Black veterans prevented the police from arresting two of their comrades, the police led White mobs through the streets of Memphis attacking Blacks. Mounted squads headed by police rode through Black neighborhoods, beating anyone they found on the streets and setting fire to schools, churches, and homes. The attack lasted four days, until martial law was declared. Forty-six Blacks and two Whites died; ninety-one houses, twelve schools, and four churches were burned.[7]

That July in New Orleans, the police led a military-style attack against a convention of Union loyalists composed mostly of Blacks. On July 30, as the delegates gathered at the Mechanics Institute, crowds of White men collected on the streets, many cops and firefighters among them. As a procession of a hundred or so Black delegates approached the Mechanics Institute, a fight broke out. It is disputed what, precisely, led to the fight, but it is generally agreed that a White policeman fired the first shot. The Blacks returned fire and hurried into the building. Between 1,000 and 1,500 whites surged in after them, breaking down doors, firing into the assembly hall, and clubbing the delegates.[8]

A *New Orleans Times* reporter described the scene following the massacre:

> Out of the Senate Chamber, once more in the cross passage, pass through the hall, here is the last step of the main stairway. Blood is on it. The white wall is smeared with blood in the track of what had been a live man's shoulder leaning up against it. Blood on the next step. Blood marks higher up on the walls, blood and marks of sanguinary struggle from the top to the bottom. . . . A door opens outward on the stairway leading down into the vaults. The first thing noticed is a bloody handmark, blood-spots line the white walls on the side, and blood spots the steps. . . . It is with a sensation of sickening horror that you leave all the scenes and respectfully picking your way through cast off hats and shoes that are all over every floor of the building, find yourself in the open street, the sidewalk of which ran with blood.[9]

With the convention in ruins, the police led bands of Whites around the city, beating any Blacks they encountered and shooting at those who fled. The majority of the victims had no connection to the convention. At least thirt-eight people were killed, and many times that number wounded. Overwhelmingly, the victims were Black.[10]

That afternoon, bodies were piled into baggage cars. Many of the wounded were loaded in with the dead, and witnesses later swore to seeing police systematically shooting those who stirred.[11] No one was prosecuted for the massacre, though a Congressional committee concluded that it had been planned by a group of police, mostly Confederate veterans.[12] They were assisted by a Know-Nothing group called, appropriately, "the Thugs" and a vigilante regiment named "Hay's Brigade," acting under the leadership of police Sergeant Lucien Adams and Sheriff Harry T. Hays, respectively.[13]

These two examples, especially the Mechanics Institute massacre, illustrate the character of such attacks. As Melinda Hennessey explains,

> The actions of whites in many of the Reconstruction riots, however, had less in common with mob rule than with the organized character of paramilitary units. . . . Antebellum militias and slave patrols gave southern whites experience in local military organization, and this trend continued in the locally based Confederate military units.[14]

Whites adhered not only to the values of the slave system, but its methods as well.

The central role of the police in these two disturbances was unfortunately typical of the period. In her comprehensive study of Reconstruction-era unrest, Hennessey finds, "In only three riots, including Mobile in 1867, Vicksburg in 1875, and Charleston in 1867, did the police or sheriff try to quell the disturbance, and in a third of the riots, the police or sheriff's *posse* led the violence."[15] Examples of police-led violence include the election riots in Savannah in 1868, Baton Rouge in 1870, and Barbour County, Alabama, in 1874.[16] Perhaps the starkest case occurred in Camilla, Georgia, where in 1868 Sheriff Munford J. Poore deputized the town's entire White male population to prevent a Black political procession;[17] a military investigation found that the sheriff made no effort to control the posse and "was a party to the wanton and unnecessary destruction of life which subsequently ensued."[18]

Where legal authorities were not themselves complicit with the terrorists, they found themselves among the terrorized; they were powerless to stop Klan activity, prosecute offenders, protect their own constituencies, or in some cases, defend themselves. For officers sincere in their duties, the situation was desperate. In Warren County, Georgia, Sheriff John C. Norris faced constant harassment for his efforts to enforce the law; eventually he was crippled in a Klan ambush. The weakness of his position might be indicated by the fact that, though he could identify his attackers, he did not press charges.[19] The impotence of local authorities was particularly felt in areas where they were dependent on the federal government for their power. As the federal government became increasingly reluctant to insert itself—especially militarily—into local affairs, city and county officials were left vulnerable. Sheriff Joseph P. Doyle of Madison County, Alabama, worried, "I have nobody to protect me."[20]

When Klan-type violence occurred, arrests were unusual, prosecutions rare, and convictions almost unknown. The attitudes—and sometimes, involvement—of police officers and sheriffs certainly impeded the enforcement of the law, but this was only one of many obstacles standing in the way of convictions. Prosecutors were unwilling to press such cases, and magistrates were often glad to dismiss them. Klansmen frequently dominated juries, including grand juries and coroner's juries. Witnesses and victims, like Sheriff Norris, were intimidated and refused to testify, while Klan members were eager to swear false alibis on one another's behalf.[21]

The law, when it did oppose Klan activity, did so in times and places where the Klan was politically weak.

> Wherever Union men were numerous and sufficiently well organized to sustain the local authorities. . . . [Arkansas Governor Powell] Clayton encouraged sheriffs to mobilize them as posses, and they were used to good effect. Thus the sheriff of Carroll County managed to quell the small-scale terror there, even if he failed to catch the criminals. In Fulton County, where the governor had to send in reinforcements from other counties and make use of Monk's Missouri volunteers, the policy contributed to a mutual escalation but was ultimately successful.[22]

Even then, the usual form of conflict was not open warfare or even vigorous enforcement of the law, but a kind of rivalry or dual power. The police and the Klan became counterbalancing forces rather than outright antagonists. Under such conditions, police may have limited the Klan's worst atrocities, but they did little to protect Blacks from routine abuse and intimidation.[23] Likewise, the Klan, while not usually driving the sheriff out of town or making good on their threats against him, limited the scope of his authority and greatly restricted his agenda, especially where the sheriff was a Republican. In Homer, Louisiana, the sheriff gave up policing whole areas of the parish where the Klan was strongest.[24] One Texan sheriff found it impossible to raise a posse against Klan activity; White citizens told him derisively to "call on your nigger friends."[25]

But usually, law enforcement agents were unwilling to move against the Klan, even when they were backed by federal military force.[26] And they were almost never willing to avail themselves of the one source of power that may have been most readily mobilized against Klan activity: the Black population. Even when faced with widespread lawlessness, White officials proved unwilling to arm and rally their Black constituency.[27] It may be that they worried such a move would create a panic among Whites and provoke further violence, or it may be that they feared creating a Black resistance that they could not then control.[28] Whatever the reasons, the result was disastrous for American Blacks.

As renegade states were reincorporated into the Union and the federal commitment to Reconstruction waned, Blacks were returned to something very much like their previous status.[29] When Democrats attained control of state legislatures and local governments, they passed a series of "Black Codes" designed to regulate the former slaves and restore a system of White supremacy, based not on the private institution of slavery, but on publicly established segregation.[30] Blacks were, whether by law, custom, or by Klan intimidation, commonly forbidden to own land, run businesses, work on railroads, change employers, travel, or vote.[31] This was termed, in the parlance of Southern whites, "Redemption." For Blacks, it was more like damnation.

SLAVE PATROLS REVISITED

During the Reconstruction period, the line between legal and extra-legal authority became extremely hazy. The Klan took on criminal violence in the defense of an archaic view of law and order, and the local authorities, especially the police, were either incapable or unwilling to challenge them. In many cases, the police were actually complicit with Klan violence, and it seemed that the two organizations pursued the same ends, sometimes using the same means. These common features were not arrived at by chance. Both the police and the Klan were adaptations of an earlier and deeply entrenched Southern institution, the slave patrols.[32]

> In the new regime of Reconstruction, Southern whites were forced to adopt laws and policing methods that appeared racially unbiased, but they relied upon practices derived from slave patrols and their old laws that had traditionally targeted blacks for violence. To resolve this apparent contradiction, the more random and ruthless aspects of slave patrolling passed into the hands of vigilante groups like the Klan. . . . Meanwhile, policemen in Southern towns continued to carry out those aspects of urban slave patrolling that seemed race-neutral but that in reality were applied selectively. Police saw that nightly curfews and vagrancy laws kept blacks off city streets, just as patrollers had done in the colonial and antebellum eras.[33]

The slave patrols helped form the character of both the police and the Klan. Like the slave patrols, the Klan was organized locally, operated mostly at night, drew its members from every class of White society, enforced a pass system and curfew, broke up Black social gatherings and meetings, searched homes, seized weapons, and enforced its demands through violence and intimidation.[34] A former slave, J.T. Tims, remarked, "There wasn't no difference between the patrols and the Ku Klux that I know of. If th'd ketch you, they all would whip you."[35]

As a part of this same tradition, minorities, especially Blacks, became the objects of police control,[36] the targets of brutality, and the victims of neglect.[37] Perhaps the clearest inheritance from this tradition is the racial characterization of criminality—the criminalizing of people of color, and Black people especially. Presently understood in terms of "profiling," the practice is much older than the current controversy. Under slavery, "Bondsmen could easily be distinguished by their race and thus became easy and immediate targets of racial brutality."[38] The only thing new about racial profiling is the term, which makes prejudicial harassment seem procedural, technical, even scientific.

PROFILES AND PREJUDICE

One critic of racial profiling, David Harris, defines the concept in terms of more general police techniques. He writes:

> *Racial* profiling grew out of a law enforcement tactic called *criminal* profiling. *Criminal* profiling has come into increasing use over the last twenty years, not just as a way to solve particular crimes police know about but also as a way to predict who may be involved in as-yet-undiscovered crimes, especially drug offenses. *Criminal* profiling is designed to help police spot criminals by developing sets of personal and behavioral characteristics associated with particular offenses. By comparing individuals they observe with profiles, officers should have a better basis for deciding which people to treat as suspects. Officers may see no direct evidence of crime, but they can rely on noncriminal but observable characteristics associated with crime to decide whether someone seems suspicious and therefore deserving of greater police scrutiny.
>   When these characteristics include race or ethnicity as a factor in predicting crimes, *criminal* profiling can become *racial* profiling. *Racial* profiling is a crime-fighting strategy—a government policy that treats African Americans, Latinos, and members of other minority groups as criminal suspects on the assumption that doing so will increase the odds of catching criminals.[39]

Harris is right that racial profiling is a sub-set of criminal profiling, but he has the genealogy reversed. As we saw in previous chapters, long before the police used high-discretion tactics and vice laws to regulate the lives of the immigrant working class, their predecessors in law enforcement were using race as *the* factor directing their activities. Harris overlooks a crucial feature of this history: Both the slave patrols and the laws they enforced existed for the express purpose of controlling the Black population. There was no pretense of racial neutrality, and so there was less concern with the abstract aim of controlling "crime" than with the very concrete task of controlling Black people. Blacks were, in a sense, criminalized, but more importantly, they were permanently deemed objects for control. As cities industrialized, White workers formed another troublesome group. Efforts to control these new "dangerous classes" were more legalistic and impartial—in form—if not in application) than those directed against the slaves. Laws against vagrancy, gambling, prostitution, loitering, cursing, and drinking—the nineteenth-century equivalent of our current war on drugs—brought the habits of the poor into the jurisdiction of the police, and the police directed their suspicions accordingly. Thus, contrary to Harris' account, racial profiling gave birth to the broader category of "criminal profiling", not the other way around.

What may distinguish our contemporary notion of "profiling" from simple prejudice is the idea that suspicious characteristics can somehow be scientifically identified and formulated into a general type in order to rationally direct police suspicions. It is the war on drugs that has most recently popularized profiling, initially because of the work of Florida Highway Patrol officer, and later Volusia County sheriff, Bob Vogel. Vogel formulated a list of "cumulative similarities" that he used in deciding whether to search a vehicle. These included factors like demeanor, discrepancies in the vehicle's paperwork, overcautious driving, the model of the car, and the time of the trip. In the mid-1980s, after Vogel made several particularly impressive arrests, the DEA adopted similar techniques in its training of local law enforcement.[40]

The scientific basis of Vogel's system is questionable—his "cumulative similarities" were based on a sample of thirty cases[41]—and its application even more worrisome. While Vogel claims that race was never a factor in his approach,[42] his deputies' behavior tells a different story. Blacks and Hispanics represented 5 percent of the drivers on the roads his department patrolled. But according to a review of 148 hours of videotape from cameras mounted in squad cars, minorities made up 70 percent of the people stopped and 80 percent of those searched. Of the 1,100 drivers appearing on the tapes, only nine were issued tickets.[43]

Likewise, under "Operation Pipeline" the DEA told the police *not* to consider race as a factor, while continuously emphasizing the race of suspected drug dealers.[44] The results were predictable. According to a 1999 report by the California legislature's Task Force on Government Oversight, two-thirds of those stopped as part of Operation Pipeline were Latinos. The report noted the systematic nature of this bias:

> It should be emphasized that this program has been conducted with the support of CHP [California Highway Patrol] management.

Individual officers involved in these operations and training programs have been carrying out what they perceived to be the policy of the CHP, the Department of Justice, and the Deukmejian and Wilson Administrations. Thus we are not faced with "rogue" officers or individual, isolated instances of wrongdoing. The officers involved in these operations have been told repeatedly by their supervisors that they were doing their jobs exactly right.[45]

THE FLAWED LOGIC OF RACIAL PROFILING

The theoretical groundwork for racial profiling was in place long before the DEA popularized its current form. Writing in the middle of the twentieth century, LAPD Chief of Police William H. Parker defended the police saturation of minority neighborhoods. His views anticipate those supporting the use of other race-based police tactics. They are worth quoting at length:

> Deployment is often heaviest in so-called minority sections of the city. The reason is statistical—it is a fact that certain racial groups, at the present time, commit a disproportionate share of the total crime. Let me make one point clear in that regard—a competent police administrator is fully aware of the multiple conditions which create this problem. There is no inherent physical or mental weakness in any racial stock which tends its [sic] toward crime. But—and this is a "but" which must be borne constantly in mind—*police field deployment is not social agency activity.* In deploying to suppress crime, we are not interested in *why* a certain group tends toward crime, we are interested in maintaining order. The fact that the group would not be a crime problem under different socio-economic conditions and might not be a crime problem tomorrow, does not alter today's tactical necessities. Police deployment is concerned with *effect*, not cause. . . .
>
> At the present time, race, color, and creed are useful statistical and tactical devices. So are age groupings, sex, and employment. If persons of one occupation, for some reason, commit more theft than average, then increased police attention is given to persons of that occupation. Discrimination is not a factor there. If persons of Mexican, Negro, or Anglo-Saxon ancestry, for some reason, contribute heavily to other forms of crime, police deployment must take that into account. From an ethnological point of view, Negro, Mexican, and Anglo-Saxon are unscientific breakdowns; they are a fiction. From a police point of view, they are a useful fiction and should be used as long as they remain useful.
>
> The demand that the police cease to consider race, color, and creed is an unrealistic demand. *Identification is a police tool, not a police attitude.* If traffic violations run heavily in favor of lavender colored automobiles, you may be certain, whatever the sociological reasons for that condition, we would give lavender automobiles more than average attention. And if these vehicles were predominantly found in one area of the city, we would give that area more than average attention.[46]

These remarks clearly outline the logic of racial profiling, and reflect the flaws of such logic. Parker tries to deny police bias by relocating it from the individual to the institutional level. He then defends institutional bias by denying individual prejudice. He also attempts to justify institutionalized racism by casting it in "statistical" terms. Hence, we're reassured that race-based police tactics are not based on "a police attitude" or on a belief in the inherent criminality of people of color, while at the same time we are urged to accept practices designed to target specific populations.

Parker explains unequal police attention with reference to variations in crime rates among different groups. No evidence is offered concerning these variations, but they are said to be the product of unidentified "multiple conditions," which we are assured are not the business of the police. The possibility that policing may preserve or contribute to these "socio-economic conditions" is not discussed, though the function of policing is identified as "maintaining order."

Put differently, Parker tries to justify the police department's discrimination with reference to *other discrimination*. If this line of reasoning is accepted, then so long as an overall system of White supremacy exists, no particular aspect of it can be faulted. Landlords could justify discrimination in housing, or bankers in lending, just by noting that "the reason is statistical," that "for some reason" unemployment is higher among "certain racial groups." Employers could justify discrimination in hiring by explaining that, statistically speaking, certain groups tend to be less qualified. And so on. The moral and political faults of such reasoning are obvious, but there is a logical fallacy as well. An individual's ability to pay the rent, to perform a job, or to obey the law, cannot be judged on the basis of the statistical performance of a group to which she belongs.

Darrell Huff explains the problem this way:

> A correlation of course shows a tendency which is not often the ideal
> relationship described as one to one. Tall boys weigh more than short
> boys on the average, so this is a positive correlation. But you can
> easily find a six-footer who weighs less than some five-footers, so
> the correlation is less than 1. . . . Even if education generally
> increases income, it may easily turn out to be the financial ruin of
> Joe over there. Keep in mind that a correlation may be real and
> based on real cause and effect—and still be almost worthless in
> determining action in any single case.[47]

In the end, Parker's argument is circular; the premises assume the conclusion. It calls for intensive scrutiny of people of color based on a "disproportionate share of the total crime" committed by them. And how do we know they commit more crimes? Because of their contact with the criminal justice system, obviously![48] David Harris explains the problem simply:

In the case of consensual crimes such as drug activity and weapons offenses, arrest and incarceration rates are particularly poor measures of criminal activity. They are much better measures of *law enforcement activity*. . . . Arrest statistics tell us that police arrest disproportionate numbers of African American males for drug crimes. This reflects decisions made by someone in the police department—the chief, lieutenants, street-level supervisors, or even individual officers themselves—to concentrate enforcement activity on these individuals.[49]

While admitting that the very categories of race are "unscientific" and "a fiction," Parker argues that race is a "useful fiction" and so should be maintained. But we should ask, useful for what? Presumably for identifying criminals, or rather for identifying *suspects*. That is, race is a "useful fiction" for delineating groups of people to be *treated as suspects* by the police.

The analogy to the color of the car implies that the use of race as an indicator is fortuitous, that it is something of an accident. Of course, it is nothing of the sort.[50] It is more paradigmatic than fortuitous, a matter of design rather than happenstance. Race, unlike car color, is used as a profiling tool because society as a whole uses race as a marker of privilege or privation. And according to Parker's theory, race-based tactics are useful in crime control for just that reason.

Today's law enforcement administrators still seek to justify police practices by appealing to racist conceptions of crime and criminality. In 1999, the New Jersey Attorney General's office issued a report showing that during the two previous years (1997 and 1998), 40 percent of motorists stopped on the New Jersey Turnpike and 80 percent of those searched were minorities.[51] According to Carl Williams, the superintendent of the New Jersey State Police, that's because "The drug problem is mostly cocaine and marijuana. It is most likely a minority group that's involved with that."[52]

Studies in other states reveal a common pattern. Following a 1995 lawsuit, the Maryland State Police were required to keep data on every traffic stop that led to a search. Temple University's John Lamberth analyzed the data from 1995 and 1996. He found that while Blacks represent 17 percent of Maryland's driving population and can be observed to drive no differently than Whites, 72 percent of those stopped and searched were Black. Fully one-half of the Maryland State Police traffic officers stopped Blacks in at least 80 percent of their stops. One officer stopped Blacks in 95 percent of his stops, and two *only* stopped Blacks.[53]

Likewise, a 1999 Ohio state legislator's review of 1996 and 1997 court records revealed that Black drivers in Akron were 2.04 times as likely as all other drivers to receive tickets. In Toledo, they were 2.02 times as likely; and in Columbus and Dayton, 1.8 times.[54] Researchers with North Carolina State University found that in 1998, Blacks were 68 percent more likely than Whites to be searched by the North

Carolina Highway Patrol.[55] And a 2002 Justice Department report concluded that, nationwide, "police were more likely to conduct a search of the vehicle and/or driver in traffic stops involving black male drivers (15.9%) or Hispanic male drivers (14.2%), compared to white male drivers (7.9%)."[56]

More recently, the *Boston Globe* analyzed 764,065 traffic tickets from the period April 2001 to November 2002 and found that Blacks and Hispanics are ticketed at a rate twice that of their portion of the Massachusetts population. And once ticketed, Blacks are 50 percent more likely than Whites to have their cars searched.[57] Likewise, the LAPD's statistics from July to November 2002 show that Black motorists were stopped at rates far outstripping their portion of the local population: 18 percent of the drivers pulled over were Black, while Blacks make up only 10.9 percent of the city's populace. Of those pulled over, Blacks and Latinos were significantly more likely to be removed from the car than were Whites: 22 percent of Blacks and 22 percent of Latinos were removed from the vehicle, as opposed to 7 percent of Whites. And once out of their cars, Blacks and Latinos were more likely to be searched: 85 percent of Blacks and 84 percent of Latinos were searched, as compared to 71 percent of Whites.[58]

The studies show another thing as well: Race is useless as an indicator of criminality. In Maryland, where 70 percent of those searched were Black, the rate at which searches produced evidence of a crime was about the same for Blacks as for Whites—28.4 percent and 28.8 percent, respectively.[59] While Blacks and Latinos accounted for 78 percent of those searched at the south end of the New Jersey Turnpike during the year 2000, evidence was more reliably found by searching Whites: 25 percent of Whites searched had contraband, as compared to 13 percent of Blacks and 5 percent of Latinos.[60] According the 1998 North Carolina study, 26 percent of those Blacks searched, and 33 percent of the whites searched, were found to possess contraband.[61] In Massachusetts, 16 percent of Whites searched were found to possess drugs, as compared to 12 percent of Blacks and 10 percent of Hispanics.[62]

The evidence absolutely contradicts the idea that racial profiling is useful in getting drugs, or guns, or criminals, off the streets. If we insist on viewing the police as crime-fighters, profiling can only be seen as a mistake, a persistent disaster. But if we suspend or surrender this noble view of police work, and look instead at the actual consequences of what the cops do, profiling makes a certain kind of sense; it follows a sinister logic. Racial profiling is not about crime at all; it's about controlling people of color.

CONSEQUENCES OF PROFILING

On February 4, 1999, Amadou Diallo, a twenty-two-year-old West African immigrant, was killed by New York City police officers while standing in front of his own home. The four cops—Sean Carrol, Edward McMellon, Kenneth Boss, and Richard Murphy—fired a total of forty-one shots. Nineteen hit him. Diallo was unarmed, and had committed no crime.[63] He was simply in the wrong place at the wrong time, and Black.

Stephen Worth, a lawyer for the Patrolman's Benevolent Association explained the shooting: "He is acting strange, he fits the rapist's description in a generic way. . . . The reason they are shooting him is they think he has a gun."[64] Worth refused to elaborate on Diallo's "strange" behavior, the "description" he matched, or why the police would think he was armed. But witnesses later helped to fit the shooting into a broader pattern; they told the *Village Voice* that earlier in the evening the same officers—members of the elite Street Crimes Unit—were stopping and searching numerous Black men, seemingly at random. Such behavior fits the unit's established *modus operandi*. In 1997 and 1998 the Street Crimes Unit stopped and searched 45,000 men, mostly Blacks and Latinos; it made 9,000 arrests.[65] Eric Adams, a police lieutenant and the head of 100 Blacks in Law Enforcement Who Care, remarked: "This is the unit that's been given carte blanche to do as it will to the people of the City of New York, especially the African-American community."[66]

Amadou Diallo was not a criminal. He was not, in any real sense, a suspect. He matched a "generic" description. He fit the profile. He was a young Black man, and that was enough. He became, quite literally, a target. The police gunned him down as he stood in his doorway. They fired forty-one shots.

Diallo's shooting represents only one cost of racial profiling, the losses calculated in terms of bodies, bulletholes, scars, and stitches. But there are other victims, other costs, counted in years, marked off in cell blocks, ringed with razor wire. Race-based policing contributes to the overrepresentation of minorities, especially Blacks, in the criminal justice system. According to a 1997 Justice Department report, "Lifetime Likelihood of Going to State or Federal Prison," 16.2 percent of Blacks and 9.4 percent of Hispanics will be imprisoned during their lifetime, as compared to 5.1 percent of the total population and 2.5 percent of Whites. The figures focusing exclusively on men are even more startling: An individual Black man has a greater than one-in-four chance of being imprisoned during his lifetime (28.5 percent), as compared to one-in-six for Hispanic men (16 percent), and one-in-twenty-three for White men (4.4 percent).[67]

When the statistics reflect recidivism rates, the disparity grows: "Among non-Hispanic men, blacks are 6.5 times more likely than whites to serve some time in prison during their life, but 8.7 times more likely to be in prison on any one day."[68]

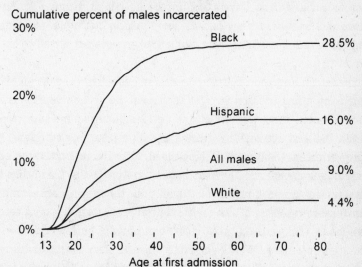

Percentage of U.S. males likely to ever go to prison, based on constant 1991 rates of first incarceration, by age, race, and Hispanic origin

Cumulative percent of males incarcerated

Black — 28.5%

Hispanic — 16.0%

All males — 9.0%

White — 4.4%

Age at first admission

Source: Bonzcar and Beck, "Lifetime Likelihood."

These numbers may give some indication as to why racial profiling persists despite its demonstrable failure as a tool for stopping crime: Police and prisons have replaced patrols and plantations as the means by which White society maintains its control over Black people. Michael Hindus clearly articulates the continuity between the new forms of control and the old: "Antebellum South Carolina had accepted three equations: slaves with crime, blacks with slaves, and imprisonment with slavery. After emancipation, the state found new modes of race control."[69]

CRIME AND CONTROL

The racial politics of police suspicion are well illustrated by the North Carolina State Bureau of Investigation's "Operation Ready-Rock." In November 1990, forty-five state cops, including canine units and the paramilitary Special Response Team, laid siege to the 100 block of Graham Street in a black neighborhood of Chapel Hill. Searching for crack cocaine, the cops sealed off the streets, patrolled with dogs, and ransacked a neighborhood pool hall. In terms of crime-control, the mission was a flop. Although nearly 100 people were detained and searched, only 13 were arrested, and none of those convicted. Nevertheless, and despite a successful class action lawsuit, the cops defended their performance and no officers were disciplined for their role.[70]

When applying for a warrant to search every person and vehicle on the block, the police had assured the judge, "There are no 'innocent' people at this place. . . . Only drug sellers and drug buyers are on the described premises."[71] But once the clamp-down was underway, they became more discriminating: Blacks were detained and searched, sometimes at gunpoint, while Whites were permitted to leave the cordoned area.[72]

The Chapel Hill episode followed a pattern familiar from the LAPD's racially coded anti-gang efforts, which were at their peak just a couple of years before. In February and March, 1988, the LAPD targeted so-called drug areas for sweeps involving between 200 and 300 officers. During the nine raids carried out in these eight weeks, they arrested 1,500 people, impounded 500 cars, and interrogated hundreds of suspected gang members.[73] The next month, in April 1988, L.A. Police Chief Daryl Gates announced the beginning of "Operation Hammer," concentrating similar actions in ten square miles of the South Central area. Over the next several weeks, the police made 1,453 arrests, mostly for violations of curfew, disorderly conduct, and other minor offenses. Of those arrested, only 32 were charged with felonies and 1,350 (90 percent) were released without any charges at all. Hundreds of other Black youths were not arrested, but were stopped, identified, and had their names entered into a computerized gang register. About half of those with gang files were later shown not to be gang members. Sociologist Randall Sheldon concluded, "The overall purpose was merely social control (of African-American youth) rather than a serious attempt at reducing crime."[74]

Around the time Operation Hammer reached its zenith, in August 1988, the LAPD raided a number of apartments at 39th Street and Dalton Avenue. In the process, they assaulted residents and used sledgehammers and axes to destroy walls, furniture, and appliances.[75] Southwest Division Captain Thomas Elfont ordered officers to "level" the targeted building and "make [it] uninhabitable." Sergeant Charles Spicer underscored these orders at the scene, telling the officers, "This is a Class-A search—that means carpets up, drywall down."[76] Police investigators later documented 127 separate acts of police "vandalism," and the city paid over $3.4 million in subsequent lawsuits. Three cops, including a captain, were charged with vandalism and acquitted; another pled no contest. Of the 88 cops involved, 24 were promoted to supervisory positions within three years.[77]

The Christopher Commission faulted this approach for creating a schism between the police and the community:

> Because of the concentration and visibility of gangs and street drug
> activities and higher rates of violent and property crime in Los
> Angeles' minority communities, the Department's aggressive style—

its self-described "war on crime"—in some cases seems to become an attack on these communities at large. The communities, and all within them, become painted with the brush of latent criminality.[78]

The Christopher Commission assumed that it is the war on crime that motivates the police to target minority communities. But this relationship might well be reversed: Racism propels the war on crime, with race-neutral rhetoric as a justifying pretext.

Imagine for a moment that certain crimes were demonstrated to be committed by White people far out of proportion with their percentage of the population. No one in the White community would stand for the generalized suspicion and heightened levels of police contact that should follow from this fact according to the logic of profiling. In fact, we needn't invent hypothetical scenarios to test this claim:

> Although whites are a disproportionate percentage of all drunk drivers, for example, and although drunk driving contributes to the deaths of more than 10,000 people each year, none of the defendants of anti-black or brown profiling suggests that drunk driving roadblocks be set up in white suburbs where the "hit rates" for catching violators would be highest.[79]

This simple observation is masked by the fact that White people are both the dominant group and, in the country as a whole, the numerical majority. One might suggest that there are just too many White people for a useful profile to be based on such a broad category. But note that this objection assumes a level of individualization among White people that the practice of profiling denies in regard to people of color.[80] The rationale behind profiling relies on the racist judgment that White skin is the "norm" and that a profile must, to be effective, or justifiable, be based on some "deviance."[81] I argued in the preceding chapter that profiling is a central aspect of modern policing. Bayley and Mendelsohn reason along similar lines, noting that police work largely consists of looking for things that seem out of place.

> The fact that policemen are alert for incongruity probably does militate against minority persons. . . . Living in a middle-class society dominated by whites, Negroes especially, and the poor as well, are likely to appear "out of place" more often than others. They not only are more "visible" to policemen by virtue of their expected association with crime, but they have more opportunity to be "visible."[82]

This approach to policing not only identifies certain groups as the objects of official control, but also limits the mobility of people of color, and thus limits their access to many resources and opportunities otherwise widely available. That is, racial profiling reinforces existing patterns of segregation. Harris notes:

Racial profiling has behavioral as well as emotional costs. It may cause many people of color to plan their driving and travel routes in certain ways, to take (or not take) particular jobs, even to wear clothing and behave in ways that minimize their potential to attract police attention. They may simply stay out of places and neighborhoods where they will 'stand out'—where police may feel they don't "belong." . . .[84]

Where the demands of the economy conflict with those of segregation, the enforcement of White supremacy may take a different, but familiar form. In the Indianapolis suburb of Carmel, for example, a communications company relies largely on Black workers from outside the immediate area. After an embarrassing lawsuit, the police department issued the workers special tags for their vehicles. These would signal to the police that they should be allowed to pass through the area. Harris compares this with the pass system in apartheid-era South Africa.[85] But closer analogies are available: Passes, as we've seen, were a major feature of the slave system, were then applied to free Blacks, and survived Emancipation as a means of limiting the mobility of Black people.

Race-based policing, and especially the fear of Black criminality, has a more subtle function as well: maintaining the ideological basis of White solidarity and indirectly controlling the political allegiances of White people. While people of color are the targets of racial profiling, there are actually two audiences for such police activity. Profiling serves to humiliate and threaten those who are targeted; even when it does not lead to criminal sanctioning, it serves as a not-very-subtle reminder of their "place." And it helps to align White people with the power structure by convincing them that the state protects them from people of color.[86]

I have argued that racial profiling has more to do with maintaining White supremacy than with fighting crime. On the one hand, profiling is over-inclusive; a great many innocent people are treated with suspicion for no reason besides their race. On the other hand, White people are, somehow, exempt from the statistical reasoning used to justify profiling. With this in mind, it is worth considering the status of crimes associated with dominant groups. Rather than producing profiles and leading to concentrated enforcement, these crimes are downplayed, legitimized, treated leniently, or even decriminalized.[87] Thus, the possession of crack cocaine is punished much more harshly than that of powder cocaine.

People convicted of possessing five grams of crack get a minimum prison term of five years. It takes 500 grams of powder to draw the same sentence. Those serving time for crack tend to be disproportionately black. . . . Powder is more in use among whites.[88]

And let's not forget the enormous range of corporate crimes that are essentially handled as violations of administrative rules or as civil matters rather than as criminal conspiracies.[89]

If the social control function operates as this argument suggests, it follows the same pattern as nineteenth-century public order arrests, and may be presumed to fulfill a similar function. Allen Steinberg concludes that in the nineteenth century

> the primary lesson of the minor police cases was that the public disorder of the lower classes was subject to the repressive activity of the state. . . . The exceptional treatment of "respectable" miscreants proved the rule. Their indiscretions could be overlooked because the larger problem of public disorder was a problem of the lower classes.[90]

WHITE LAWS, WHITE POWER

Laws have been passed, and interpreted, and enforced in ways designed to maximize the control White people exercise over people of color. But they have also been broken, and ignored, and underenforced with the same aim in mind. When the demands of White supremacy and the requirements of the law have conflicted, the maintenance of White supremacy has almost always appeared higher on the police agenda. Police illegality and complicity in White terror continue in an unbroken sequence from Reconstruction to today.

In the early twentieth century, police re-established their ties to the newly reconstituted Klan. During the 1920s, Klansmen were enlisted to aid the authorities in their fight against the evils of alcohol and Communism. In 1930, John G. Murphy, a member of the Alabama Knights of the Ku Klux Klan, testified before the House Special Committee to Investigate Communist Activities (also called the Fish Committee) that the Klan helped the Birmingham police and the FBI keep track of Communists by following Communist Party organizers, identifying people at their meetings, and so on.[91] In other places, whole Klaverns were deputized for Prohibition raids, and many cops signed up in the "Invisible Empire."[92] The extent of joint membership was often startling. In 1922, when Los Angeles District Attorney Thomas Lee Woolwine raided area Klan headquarters and seized their records, he discovered that Los Angeles Chief of Police Louis D. Oaks, Sheriff William I. Trager, and U.S. Attorney Joseph Burke were all connected to the Klan. The police chief and police judge in nearby Bakersfield were both members, as were seven Fresno officers, twenty-five cops in San Francisco, and about a tenth of the public officials and police in the rest of California's cities.[93]

Further north, in Portland, Oregon, the connection between the police and the Klan was public knowledge. In 1923, the *Portland Telegram* reported that the police bureau was "full to the brink with Klansmen."[94] At times, this relationship was officially sanctioned, as when the police bureau deputized one hundred Klansmen specially selected by Grand Dragon Fred Gifford, designating them "Portland Police Vigilantes." Of course, Klan membership was not limited to policemen. The Portland-based Klan No. 1 boasted 15,000 members, and on March 3, 1923, it hosted a banquet featuring Governor Walter Pierce and Mayor George L. Baker.[95]

When the Klan was at the peak of its power in Colorado, it counted among its members many prominent businessmen, state representatives and senators, the Colorado secretary of state, four judges, two federal narcotics agents, and scores of police. In Denver, the mayor, city attorney, manager of public safety, two deputy sheriffs, the chief of police, and a police inspector were all Klan members.[96] Former mayor George D. Begole claimed that the Klan controlled the civil service commission, fire department, and police.[97]

During the 1930s, about 100 Michigan cops, including the chief of police in Pontiac, joined either the Klan or its successor organization, the Black Legion. The Black Legion, in addition to attacking racial minorities, embarked on a deliberate campaign targeting the left; they beat and sometimes murdered suspected radicals, bombed their offices, and burned their homes.[98] An investigation in New York found 407 cops belonging to the pro-fascist Christian Front.[99]

In his memoirs, Atlanta Police Chief Herbert Jenkins described the Klan's influence in Southern police departments:

> In the thirties in Atlanta and throughout the South it was helpful to join the Ku Klux Klan to be an accepted member of the force. This was your ID card, the badge of honor with the in group, and it was unfortunately often an allegiance stronger than the policeman's oath to society.
> Not every member of the Atlanta force belonged to the Klan but those who did not had very little authority or influence. The Klan was powerful in that it worked behind the scenes with certain members of the Police Committee and the City Council. A well-liked and respected member of the department who was not a Klan member could still get promoted through the ranks if supported by the Klan. But as he owed his rank to the Klan he could never defy them for fear of his job—and his life. The Klan was like a kind of Mafia in dirty sheets.[100]

Also during the early part of the twentieth century, the police again played a significant role in the nation's numerous race riots. Starting the century out badly, on August 15, 1900, a fight between Blacks and New York City police escalated into a riot, with Irish mobs in the streets attacking Black passers-by. Police refused to protect Black citizens, and in many cases joined in on the attacks. Despite considerable evidence, the police commissioners refused to discipline their officers, noting that Black witnesses "displayed a strong and bitter feeling while under examination."[101]

The police took a more active role in the Detroit riot of 1943. The disorder began on June 20, with a short-lived skirmish between Black and White patrons at the Belle Isle amusement park. More of a brawl than a riot, really, more of a fight than a brawl, the initial conflict was over nearly as soon as it began. The police interposed, arresting several Blacks and sending the rest away. But a rumor spread that a Black man had raped a White woman during the encounter, and soon White mobs were attacking Black patrons at the Roxy theater. The disorder soon spread throughout the (White) Woodward neighborhood, and crowds beat, stabbed, and shot Blacks, and stoned their cars. Around the same time, a rumor spread through the Black neighborhoods of Hastings and Adams that White sailors had thrown a Black woman and her baby into a lake at Bell Isle. Blacks began attacking whites in the area and breaking the windows in White-owned businesses.[102]

The police attacked Black crowds with clubs and, where looting was most prevalent, shot at anyone inside the stores. Black bystanders were ordered to "run and not look back;" many were shot as they did. Police also used hit-and-run tactics against small groups of Blacks quite removed from the riot area: They would pull up in a squad car near a group of Blacks; several officers would then jump out, beat them, get back in the car, and drive away.[103] That night, a cop was shot in a vacant lot near Vernor Highway; he returned fire and the assailant was killed. Nevertheless, the police retaliated against the entire neighborhood. They laid siege to an apartment building at 290 East Vernor, shining searchlights on the building and firing into it with revolvers, rifles, and machine guns. They eventually forced the residents out with tear gas and beat them as they fled. Then the apartments were ransacked, doors kicked in, locks broken, furniture overturned. Money, jewelry, and liquor were stolen.[104]

In an article titled "The Gestapo in Detroit," NAACP attorney and later Supreme Court Justice Thurgood Marshall reported, "They used 'persuasion' rather than firm action with white rioters, while against Negroes they used the ultimate in force: night sticks, revolvers, riot guns, sub-machine guns, and deer guns."[105] He concluded:

> This record of the Detroit police demonstrates once more what all Negroes know only too well: that nearly all police departments limit their conception of checking racial disorders to surrounding, arresting, maltreating, and shooting Negroes. Little attempt is made to check the activities of whites.[106]

Of the thirty-four people killed, twenty-five were Black and nine were White; the police killed seventeen Blacks and no Whites.[107] Judge George Edwards of the United

States Court of Appeals for the Sixth Circuit, described the riot as "open warfare between the Detroit Negroes and the Detroit Police Department."[108]

BIRMINGHAM: BULL CONNOR AND THE LAW

Shortly after World War II, resistance to White supremacy began to accumulate a critical mass. Nearly a century after the Civil War, Blacks had had enough, more than enough, of empty promises and the thin imitation of freedom that had been their lot since the end of slavery. Tired of being excluded and exploited, sick of segregation and second-class citizenship, they determined to, as James Forman put it, either "sit at the table," or "knock the fuckin' legs off" of it.[109] First in the South, but soon throughout the country, Blacks were demanding their due of White society. And Whites, as ever, were serious about not giving it to them.

The police occupied their traditional place, standing firmly in the way of African-Americans' efforts to win their rights. The situation demanded nothing new of the police, though in times of crisis their function may have been a bit clearer than usual, as the rhetoric of legal impartiality slipped further and further away from them. Birmingham's Police Chief, Bull Connor, put it plainly: "We don't give a damn about the law. Down here we make our own law."[110] It was a startling admission from a man sworn to uphold the law, but undoubtedly true.[111]

Connor and his police department epitomized a type of law enforcement characteristic of the time, though sadly persisting to the present day. Most famously, in 1963, Birmingham became the shame of the nation when television footage showed demonstrators with the Southern Christian Leadership Conference being beaten by Connor's officers, attacked with police dogs, and sprayed with fire hoses. Reverend Fred Shuttleworth had to be taken away in an ambulance. Connor expressed his disappointment: "It should have been a hearse."[112]

Connor's disdain for Shuttleworth had a long history. In 1958, when the reverend's home had been bombed, Connor publicly accused Shuttleworth of doing it himself.[113] The accusation, made without evidence, came in the midst of a bombing campaign commonly known to be the work of the Klan. Black homes and Jewish synagogues were attacked so often that one part of the city was nicknamed "Dynamite Hill." The fire department, which was also under Connor's control, generally let the buildings burn down entirely, and the police made no serious efforts to investigate the attacks.[114] Connor preferred to blame civil rights workers for stirring up trouble.

Connor expressed special animosity for "out-of-town meddlers" like the Freedom Riders—Blacks and Whites traveling together to desegregate interstate bus lines.[115] In 1961, the Congress of Racial Equality (CORE) Freedom Rides came through Birmingham. Connor had the Riders arrested, drove them to the Tennessee line, and left them stranded on the highway.[116] When they returned, on Mother's Day 1961, they were beaten by a group of Klansmen while Connor watched from a nearby office building.[117]

As we shall see, the Mother's Day incident illustrates not only the extent to which the police shared the aims of organized racist groups—I am tempted to say *other* organized racist groups—but also actively cooperated with them. This connection was not incidental. Nor was it an isolated occurrence. To understand something of its depth, we should turn briefly to examine the career of Gary Rowe.

THE STRANGE CAREER OF GARY ROWE

Gary Rowe was an FBI infiltrator in the Ku Klux Klan, working in that capacity from 1959 to 1965.[118] Though not personally sympathetic to the Klan, he had, by his own admission, "beaten people severely, had boarded buses and kicked people, had [gone] into restaurants and beaten them with blackjacks, chains, pistols."[119] All this he did while on the FBI payroll. Rowe reported, sometimes in advance, about attacks on Blacks at a county fair, at sit-ins, and on Freedom Rides, including advanced warning about the Mother's Day attack of 1961. When he asked why nothing was done to stop the assault, his FBI handler told him, "Who the hell are we going to report to? . . . The police department helped set [it] up."[120]

And indeed they had. In April 1961, Detective Sergeant Tom Cook, the commander of the Birmingham Police Department red squad, provided the Klan with a list of civil rights groups, the locations of their meetings, and the names of their members. He went on to offer them full access to the red squad's files. As it happened, the man Cook passed the information to was Gary Rowe. Ironically, Cook told Rowe that the Eastview Klavern had been infiltrated by the feds, and promised to help them learn the identity of the snitch.[121] Rowe was actually a triple agent, assigned by the Klan to attend civil rights meetings and report back. He also gave these reports to the FBI.[122]

Together, Cook and Rowe organized a series of meetings between Birmingham Klan leader Hubert Pape, Imperial Wizard Robert Shelton, Bull Connor, and themselves. At these meetings, they planned a response to the Freedom Rides. The Klan would meet the bus at the terminal, and the police would wait at least 15 minutes before arriving.[123] Connor recommended beating and stripping any Blacks who entered the restroom. "[Make] them look like a bulldog got hold of them," he said. Cook added: "I don't give a damn if you beat them, bomb them, murder or kill them. I don't give a shit. I don't want them in Alabama when you're through with them."[124]

The plan went through as agreed. By the time the police showed up, the Freedom Riders had been beaten with iron bars, and most of the Klansmen had gone. Those remaining were sent away rather than being arrested.[125]

Rowe had informed the FBI of the plan, and the FBI dutifully put it in their files, while allowing the Klan to move ahead. Rowe's handler claimed that there was nothing they could do, because of the involvement of the local police. But the FBI also played a further role in the Mother's Day attack: Government documents released during a 1978 lawsuit revealed that the FBI had provided the Birmingham police with the details of the Freedom Rider's plan, knowing that the information would reach the Ku Klux Klan.[126] Thus the Birmingham police provided a conduit for information to pass between the FBI and the KKK, while maintaining the federal government's shield of plausible deniability. And Rowe, by monitoring Klan activity and reporting to the feds, served to confirm that the information they provided reached its intended audience.

The FBI finally used Rowe against the Klan in 1965, after the murder of Viola Liuzzo. Rowe and three others shot Liuzzo as she drove demonstrators back to Selma after a march to Montgomery.[127] Leroy Moton, who was traveling with Liuzzo, described the shooting:

> I looked at my watch. It was like eight o'clock, and I reached over
> for the radio and that's when I felt this glass and everything hit me
> in the face, and the car goin' off the road. Mrs. Liuzzo, last thing
> she said was, "I was just thinkin' of this song, 'Before I'll be a slave,
> I'll be buried in my grave.'" By the time she got "grave" out, that's
> when she was shot. That's when the glass started hittin' me in the
> face. We ran into an embankment, a ditch, came out of it, and ran
> into a fence. And I reached over and called her, shook her. She did-
> n't say anything. That's when I turned the motor off and the lights.
> This other car came back, stopped, and I looked over my left shoul-
> der and I seen it, and I saw the door open and I passed out for
> about a half hour. I understand they thought I was dead, too.
> Because the blood was on my face from the glass hittin' me. They
> figured I was dead. Only the good Lord saved me.[128]

The FBI had seventy agents in the area at the time of the attack, but made no move to prevent the violence.[129] Worse, the police may have had a role in marking Liuzzo as a target: At a press conference after the murder, a Klan spokesman cited details of her life drawn from the files of the Detroit Police Department's Special Investigations Bureau.[130]

The Klansmen were eventually arrested for murder, and acquitted. The Justice Department then prosecuted them for civil rights violations. Based on Rowe's testimony, they were convicted and sentenced to the maximum of ten years.[131]

A Senate Committee later summed up his career:

Rowe provided the FBI with a great deal of information on planned and actual violence by the Klan throughout his years as an informant. . . . Only rarely, however, did Rowe's information lead to the prevention of violence or arrests of Klan members. There were several reasons for this, including the difficulty of relying on local police to enforce the law against the Klan in the early 1960s, the failure of the Federal Government to initially mobilize its own resources, and the role of the FBI as an investigative rather than police organization.[132]

The "investigative" rather than "police" mission of the FBI was a political fiction popular at the time, providing a technical excuse for federal inaction. Actually, Section 3052, Title 18 of the U.S. Administrative Code empowered the FBI to make arrests without warrants "for any offense against the United States committed in their presence." Historian Howard Zinn notes: "The FBI makes arrests in kidnappings, bank robberies, drug cases, espionage cases. But not in civil rights cases? Then not only were black people second-class citizens, but civil rights law was second-class law."[133]

The availability of Federal Marshals for law enforcement purposes also remained conveniently forgotten.[134] Whatever Rowe's own intentions, the inaction of his superiors was certainly culpable, and their explanations disingenuous.

MISSISSIPPI: "FOR UNDERNEATH HER BORDERS THE DEVIL DRAWS NO LINE"[135]

Even where White violence was at its most extreme, even where Blacks were most oppressed, the federal government was loath to act. Its position, for most of a century, had been that Blacks were on their own, or, put differently, that local officials were free to treat them in whatever way they saw fit. When the federal government was moved to act, it was usually because some particular atrocity created a national uproar. One such event was the 1964 disappearance of three civil rights workers in the Mississippi back country.

On June 21, 1964, Michael Schwerner, James Chaney, and Andrew Goodman traveled to Philadelphia, Mississippi, to investigate a fire at a Black church. They never returned. This was just one of many instances of violence and intimidation visited upon the participants of the Mississippi Summer Project organized by the Council of Federated Organizations (COFO), a coalition including the Student Nonviolence Coordinating Committee (SNCC), CORE, the National Council of Churches, and the NAACP. The violence used against civil rights workers was audacious and severe. But more staggering was the violence against the Black community at large. Chaney, Goodman, and Schwerner weren't the only three men to disappear in Mississippi that summer. They're just the three who made headlines; they're just the three we remember. When Whites disappeared, people noticed. And Schwerner and Goodman were White. When Black people disappeared, who cared? Who took notice? Black folks could vanish,Black folks could hang, without stirring even a mutter from the nation's newspapers, without so much as a report from the FBI.[136]

Dave Dennis, a field secretary for CORE, draws out the point:

> During the time they were looking for the bodies of Chaney,
> Schwerner, and Goodman, they found other bodies throughout the
> state. They found torsos in the Mississippi River, they found people
> who were burned, they even found a few bodies of people on the
> side of the roads. As soon as it was determined that these bodies
> were not the three missing workers, or one of the three, these deaths
> were forgotten. That's what we were talking about in terms of what
> the Freedom Summer was all about, in terms of why it was necessary
> to bring that attention there. Because people forget, and if it had
> just been blacks there, they would have forgotten again. It would
> just have been three black people missing.[137]

Following the disappearances, COFO collected 257 affidavits for use in a lawsuit against Neshoba County Sheriff Lawrence Rainey, among others. Fifty-seven of these were selected as typical and printed as the *Mississippi Black Paper*.[138] The lawsuit, *Council of Federated Organizations et al. v. L.A. Rainey et al.* was filed on July 19, 1964. It alleged:

> Murders, bombings, burnings, beatings, terrorization and intimidation
> continue throughout the state at a steadily increasing tempo without
> any attempts by state or local authorities to prevent them. In many
> instances, the police themselves were—and are—directly involved or
> [have] tacitly or openly encouraged—and encourage—the form of
> brutalization being employed.

As documentation, COFO provided:

> Approximately 90 affidavits as to illegal acts of Mississippi law
> enforcement officers against civil rights workers and the Negro citi-
> zens of Mississippi, including physical violence, intimidation, harass-
> ments, unprovoked arrests, and prolonged unjustified incarceration
> which are daily continuing . . . approximately 35 affidavits as to the
> failure of Mississippi law enforcement officers to take any or ade-
> quate steps to safeguard civil rights workers and Negro citizens
> against physical violence and property destruction although fully
> warned in advance of the possibility of their occurrence, all of which
> is daily continuing . . . approximately 35 affidavits as to the failure
> of the law enforcement officers of Mississippi to prosecute known
> perpetrators of violence, destruction and terrorism against the per-
> sons and property of civil rights workers and Negro citizens, all of
> which is daily continuing.[139]

The *Black Paper* makes for disturbing reading. At times, it is distinctly reminiscent of the statements former slaves made about the patrols. One young woman testifies:

> On February 6, 1962, when I was 19, I was walking with a young man down a Clarksdale street when Clarksdale police officers _____ and _____ stopped us and accused me of having been involved in a theft. I was taken to jail by the officers and they forced me to unclothe and lie on my back. One of the officers beat me between my legs with a belt. A few minutes later, the other officer began to beat me across my naked breasts.[140]

The range of abuses described is astonishing, sometimes within even a single deposition. Douglas MacArthur Cotton, for example, tells of being followed by the McComb police as he canvassed for a mock election: "Police followed me wherever I went, stood beside me on the front porch of people, photographing them and taking their names while I was talking to them."[141] More terrifying, he also attests to the abuse of prisoners: "On approximately July 20, Willie Carnell was hung by his hands to the cell bars for 30 hours. Guards accused him of 'singing.'"[142] These documents help to situate Goodman, Schwerner, and Chaney's disappearance—their murder—within a broader pattern of ongoing violence.

In her deposition, Rita Schwerner, the wife of one of the missing men, tells of the numerous threats they received, and the constant harassment by police officers. She remembers one occasion, when her husband went to bail out picketers who had been arrested. The desk sergeant told him: "If you get any more of these damn kids arrested, Schwerner, I'm going to get you, and that's a promise."[143]

Such threats were not made, or taken, lightly. Someone did "get" Michael Schwerner. And Andrew Goodman. And James Chaney. After a long investigation, the FBI found an informant who was willing to talk. He led them to an earthen dam where the three men were buried and told investigators what happened on the night the three men disappeared: Deputy Cecil Price arrested Schwerner, Goodman, and Chaney. He released them in the middle of the night, and then pulled them over again. This time, Price put them in his car and drove them to a deserted area, where Klansmen shot and killed them.[144]

> The participation of a law officer was evidently considered vital to the conspiracy. Not only would the civil rights workers be more likely to stop for a marked police car, southern lynch mobs had traditionally had their victims handed over to them by the police, a convenience that lent the proceeding a shade of social legitimacy.[145]

Nineteen men were charged with conspiracy to deprive the activists of their civil rights. Among them were Sheriff Rainey, Deputy Price, and a Philadelphia, Mississippi police officer.[146] In October 1967, a jury of Mississippi Whites convicted Price and six Klansmen.[147] Price was sentenced to six years, and served four.[148]

Rainey, who was not part of the original conspiracy but aided in the cover-up, was acquitted. But he was removed from his position as sheriff, and never regained the office.[149] Though Rainey retained his freedom and racist violence continued, the trial ended a terrible reign in Neshoba County. During his time in law enforcement, Rainey, who voiced open support for the Klan[150], had been involved in a great many beatings, arbitrary arrests, and incidents of harassment directed against Blacks and civil rights workers. He had also been a party to at least two suspicious shootings in addition to those of Chaney, Schwerner, and Goodman. In one case, he had—gun drawn—approached a Black couple sitting in a parked car, and ordered them out. When the man complied, Rainey shot and killed him. That was in October 1959; Rainey had been a Philadelphia, Mississippi, police officer. Shortly thereafter he became a Neshoba County sheriff's deputy, and was party to a second shooting. He and Sheriff Hop Barnett were transporting a handcuffed Black man to the state mental hospital when, they say, he reached for one of their guns. Barnett shot him, fatally.[151]

A torch had been passed, Barnett to Rainey, Rainey to Price. With Price in prison and Rainey disgraced, history granted us a moment of hope. But hope is not the same thing as justice. Three good men lay in their graves, needlessly, and others—unnamed, uncounted—continued to rot in riverbeds, ditches, and swamps. There would be more. Other, larger torches had been passed a century before, from slave patrol to police, from slave patrol to Klan. These fires still burned, an unholy, fiery cross.

SELMA, ALABAMA: BLOODY SUNDAY

Violence continued elsewhere in the South, with police in the vanguard and the Klan in the wings. Birmingham was only the most notorious example of police repression. Throughout the South, cops followed Bull Connor's example.

Albert Truner described a march in Marion, Alabama, near Selma:

> As we went out of the church to begin the actual march—we got
> about half a block from the door—the sheriff and several troopers
> halted us. We were told that we was an unlawful assembly and that
> we had to disband the demonstration and go back to the church. We
> had planned already to have a prayer at that point. We had Reverend
> [James] Dobynes who got down to pray. And they took Reverend
> Dobynes, who was on his knees immediately behind me, and they
> just started beating him right there on the ground. That was proba-

bly the viciousest thing I have ever seen. They beat him, and they took him by his heels and drug him to jail. At that point, they had state troopers all over the city, and plainclothes people, a lot of citizens really was involved. They beat black people wherever they found them.[152]

One man, Jimmy Lee Jackson, was severely beaten by state troopers and then shot at close range. He died as a result on February 26, 1965.[153]

Jackson's death served to mobilize increasing numbers of people and inspired civil rights groups to escalate their actions. A march was planned in response to Jackson's murder—from Selma to Montgomery, on Sunday, March 7. Governor George Wallace prohibited the march, saying that it would be impossible to protect the demonstrators. Ignoring or defying him, 600 people gathered in Brown's Chapel in Selma. As the crowd moved out of the church building and through the town, they were attacked by state police under the command of John Cloud, and by the deputies of Sheriff Jim Clark. The police used clubs, tear gas, cattle prods, horses, and dogs. Seventeen people were hospitalized as a result, including an eight-year-old. Forty others were treated at Good Samaritan Hospital and released.[154] March 7, 1965, became known as "Bloody Sunday."

The violence in Selma forced President Johnson's hand on the civil rights issue. On March 15, in a televised address to Congress, he announced that he would introduce voter registration legislation, underscoring his intentions with the movement's slogan, "We shall overcome."[155] Howard Zinn explains the change in policy: "Selma became a national scandal, and an international embarrassment for the Johnson administration."[156] But the nation's sheriffs were not embarrassed by the violence; even less were they moved by Johnson's speech. Barely a year after he led the attack at Selma, they elected Sheriff Jim Clark to head their national association.[157]

PANTHERS AND POLICE

The country's sheriffs weren't the only ones unimpressed by LBJ's gesture. While the White establishment was wringing its hands over integration, voter registration, and the free speech rights of Black people, the civil rights movement was transforming itself, redefining its goals to keep pace with its successes, rethinking its tactics in light of its defeats. A new militancy emerged. The sweet tune of "We shall overcome" gradually faded into the background, replaced by the more forceful cries of "Black Power!"—and, in Watts, "Burn, baby, burn!"[158]

Emblematic of the new militancy, the Black Panther Party for Self Defense appeared in Oakland in 1966. Formed by Huey Newton and Bobby Seale, the Panthers offered a comprehensive ten-point program for addressing the injustices facing the

Black community.[159] In keeping with the principles of their program, the Panthers provided free breakfasts for school children, ran free medical clinics, gave away shoes and clothing, and most famously, organized armed patrols against police brutality.[160]

The Panthers' politics were surely enough to raise the ire of White elites, and the sight of Blacks with guns created something of a panic among government officials. The Panthers posed a challenge to White society and, in the form of the patrols, to the police in particular. Of course some response was expected, but the viciousness of the government attack was remarkable, even by the standards of the time. Harassment, arrests, and violence were constant threats.[161]

In 1969 alone, police raided Panther offices in San Francisco, Los Angeles (twice), Chicago (three times), Denver, Sacramento, and San Diego. In nearly every case, several Panthers were arrested. In at least two of the raids, office equipment and food (for distribution in the community) were destroyed. One Panther was killed in L.A., two in Chicago. By the end of the year, thirty Panthers were charged with capital offenses, forty faced life imprisonment, fifty-five faced sentences of up to thirty years, and another 155 were either in jail or in hiding.[162]

Not all the attacks on Panthers involved raids, arrests, or gun battles. Drivers with Black Panther bumper stickers complained of routine harassment by the police. In 1969, a professor at California State College in Los Angeles decided to test their claims. He assembled a group of fifteen student volunteers—five Black, five White, five Mexican; three men and two women in each group—all with perfect driving records. They affixed to their vehicles orange and black bumper stickers featuring a picture of a panther and the words "Black Panthers." Within two hours one of the students had received a ticket for an "incorrect lane change." On the fourth day of the experiment, one student was forced to quit because he had received three tickets and was in danger of losing his license. Three others reached the three-ticket limit within a week. After seventeen days, the $500 fund to pay for tickets hit zero, and the experiment officially ended. All the participants removed the stickers from their cars. A total of thirty-three citations had been issued, with no variation according to race, sex, style of dress, or type of vehicle. Some of the cars were searched, and a White woman was questioned at length about her reasons for supporting "criminal activity."[163]

Police tactics were not limited to raids, arrests, and petty harassment. Disinformation, the use of informants to create rifts within the Party, and the promotion of violent rivalries between the Black Panthers and similar organizations also hampered the Panthers' efforts. This was, of course, precisely the point. The Panthers personified everything that White society most feared: Black people, armed and smart, militant, radical, and organized. In attacks on the Panthers, the racist undertones of police actions often came to the surface. In 1968, members of a New York police organization, the Law Enforcement Group, packed a courtroom where Panthers were being tried and beat Panther supporters with blackjacks in the hallway outside.[164] They shouted slogans such as "Win with Wallace!" and "White Power!"[165]

SINCE THE SIXTIES

While it's uncommon these days to hear police chiefs publicly sounding like Bull Connor, and while police departments have added increasing numbers of minorities to their ranks, the use of the police to control people of color and guard White supremacy continues in a refined form. Race-based tactics remain in prominent use, racist ideology still exercises a strong pull on individual officers, and racist organizing within law enforcement has entered a new phase.

Michael Novick of People Against Racist Terror lists more than fifty incidents of police involvement in racist organizing between 1976 and 1994. His chronology represents occurrences across the country and describes the involvement of police, prison guards, and federal agents in building racist organizations, attacking minorities, and ignoring or engaging in Klan-style terrorism.[166]

To give just a brief sample, from Novick's list and elsewhere: In 1978, the Klan publicly revealed its penetration of police agencies in northern Mississippi.[167] In 1980, the San Diego Police Department assigned a reserve officer to infiltrate the Klan. Through him, the department provided funding, equipment, and other assistance to a petition drive to place noted White supremacist Tom Metzger on the ballot for Congress.[168] In Chicago's 1983 mayoral race, members of "Police for Epton" sided with a White Republican against Black candidate Harold Washington. Police decorated their uniforms with plain White buttons, or buttons with a circle and slash around a picture of a watermelon. The media also uncovered a plot to target Black neighborhoods for mass arrests on the eve of the election; the idea was subsequently abandoned.[169]

A couple of years later, in 1985, Alex Young was fired from the Jefferson County, Kentucky police force after passing data from police files to the KKK. Young had earlier founded the department's chapter of Confederate Officers Patriot Squad (COPS).[170] In 1988, former Youngstown, Pennsylvania, police chief David Gardner was indicted for providing armed guards to protect a counterfeiting operation run by the White supremacist group Posse Comitatus.[171] Two White LAPD homicide detectives were reprimanded in 1989 for displaying the flag of apartheid South Africa on their squad car.[172] Around the same time, two Black cops complained that Nazi and Klan literature was being circulated in the stationhouses. Soon thereafter, one of the whistle-blowers, Donald Jackson, was attacked by White Long Beach officers. They threw him through a plate-glass window.[173]

In June 1991, Indianapolis Police officer Wayne Sharpe shot and killed Edmund Powell, a Black man suspected of shoplifting. Sharpe claimed Powell attacked him with a nail-studded board, but witnesses said that Powell was lying on the ground when Sharpe shot him. It was soon learned that Sharpe had killed a Black burglary suspect ten years before and had briefly been involved with the National Socialist White People's Party. A jury awarded Powell's family $456,000, but Sharpe was never disciplined.[174]

In September of that same year, a class action suit against the Los Angeles County Sheriff's Office cited 130 abuses occurring within 104 days, mostly against Blacks and Latinos. The lawsuit covered 69 warrantless searches, 31 uses of excessive force, and 16 incidents described by attorney James Foster as "outright torture, meaning interrogations with stun guns, beating victims into unconsciousness, holding a gun in a victim's mouth and pulling the trigger on an empty chamber." Foster attributed much of the violence to a racist gang of deputies called the Vikings.[175] A simultaneous scandal affected the LAPD when a Klan group was found to be operating in the Foothill Division—home of the officers who beat Rodney King.[176]

The next year, as the Rodney King case went to trial, the Klan organized rallies in Simi Valley with the slogan "Support the Police." Neither the Simi Valley police chief nor the Ventura County sheriff ever repudiated this support, though they were called on to do so by members of the local community.[177] Also in the wake of the Rodney King beating, police officers, especially Black officers, who agreed to testify before the Christopher Commission found themselves ostracized and sometimes threatened by their colleagues. One Black cop, Garland Hardeman, discovered a chalk outline in front of his locker, marked to indicate two bullet wounds in the head.[178] After testifying before the Commission, another officer found a hangman's noose tied to his telephone.[179]

Most recently, in March 2003, FBI Special Agent Joseph Thompson acknowledged ties between police, the Klan, and the National Alliance—probably the largest Nazi organization in the country. When Chester James Doles, the Georgia organizer for the National Alliance and a longtime Klan member, was arrested on gun charges, Agent Thompson testified at his bail hearing: "Mr. Doles has a support network including law enforcement." Thompson explained that the involvement of police "vastly increase[s] the capacity of the network" because cops "can look the other way."[180]

GREENSBORO: DEATH AND THE KLAN

Throughout the twentieth century, as overt racism grew ever less respectable, the long-established partnership between police and racist extremists was intentionally obscured. When it was no longer possible to deputize entire Klaverns, or to brag of Klan support in political campaigns, the two types of organizations returned to something like their Reconstruction-era roles: The police defending White supremacy through overt and legalistic means, the Klan (and similar groups) pursuing the same ends through agitation and terrorism. The cop-Klan consensus persisted, but more quietly; joint action continued, but secretly. It was and is no less deadly. The events of November 3, 1979, proved that.

In Greensboro, North Carolina, on November 3, 1979, Klansmen and members of the American Nazi Party, acting together as the United Racist Front, gunned down demonstrators assembled for a "Death to the Klan" rally organized by the Communist Workers Party. Five labor leaders and community organizers—Jim Waller, Sandi Smith, Bill Sampson, Cesar Cauce, and Mike Nathan—were killed, and ten other people were wounded.[181]

At the time of the attack, the Greensboro Police Department tactical squad was, literally, out to lunch, and routine patrols were mysteriously absent.[182] Afterward, while slow to move against the Nazis, the police were quick to arrest eight anti-Klan demonstrators, charging them with planning a riot.[183]

One of the Klansmen, Eddie Dawson, was a paid informant for the Greensboro Police Department (and, previously, for the FBI).[184] Dawson later stated that he was "in charge" of the attack. He recruited the Klansmen and arranged the meeting with the Nazis.[185] But he had a great deal of assistance in planning the massacre. The police supplied him with a copy of the parade permit, which noted the starting place and route of the march.[186] And a BATF agent, Bernard Butkovich, also infiltrated the United Racist Front and provided them with guns.[187]

Let me say that again clearly: An agent of the Greensboro Police Department assembled this band of assassins, drew up the plan, and saw the mission through to completion. Meanwhile, an agent of the Bureau of Alcohol, Tobacco, and Firearms provided them weapons. And both agencies stood aside while a bloodbath ensued.[188]

The killers were tried twice. First for murder, then for civil rights violations. Both times they were acquitted by all-White juries, despite video evidence provided by local television stations.[189] Finally, in 1985, a lawsuit awarded three plaintiffs $390,000. The jury found three Nazis, two Klansmen, a police informant, and two cops liable for the wrongful death of Michael Nathan, but, strangely, insisted that there had been no conspiracy.[190]

WHITE SHEETS, BLUE UNIFORMS

The police did not create the racism in American society. If anything, it's the other way around. But the police have, since their inception, enforced and defended the racist status quo—by controlling slaves, maintaining segregation, resisting civil rights efforts, and generally terrorizing the Black community and other people of color.

This function has remained constant even when the laws have changed. Even when it has conflicted with their official duties, the police have acted as a repressive force against the interests of people of color.

It will surely be objected that I have singled out the police unfairly. It will be pointed out, by critics at both ends of the political spectrum, that all of Southern society—perhaps, all of American society—has been implicated in racist violence. It is hardly surprising that policemen were also involved.

Were my point simply that *individual* police officers were complicit, this complaint would be well grounded. But it overlooks two major features of my argument: first, that the involvement of the police is different than the involvement of, say, dentists or auto mechanics; second, and more importantly that the cop-Klan connection is *institutional*, not merely individual.

The participation of police officers in White supremacist organizations and racist violence is different than the involvement of other people because the police are often professionally as well as personally involved. They use their professional position to advance the aims of the group, they use their standing in the community to legitimize vigilante violence, and they are often considered attractive recruits for just these reasons. The same may be true of certain other occupational groups as well—journalists, clergy, politicians—but cops engage in these crimes when they have sworn to stop them. To understand this contradiction we must view it, not only in terms of personal prejudice and individual action, but as a sustained institutional relationship.

Historically, the police and the Klan have operated as parallel and, in general, mutually reinforcing types of organizations. Cops, like other officials, have sometimes drawn on the political support of the Klan to buttress their own authority. Conversely, the police can offer some degree of validation to Klan activity by lending it their support, or less directly, by refusing to treat racist violence as crime. At times the police have supplied the institutional nucleus around which vigilante activity could orbit.

The police, as an institution, have shared many of the aims, methods, and values of Klan-type groups. During the Reconstruction period, for example, police authority and vigilante activity neatly paralleled one another. In part, the similarities may be understood in terms of a family resemblance: Both the police and their young cousins, the night-riders, were still chronologically very near to their common ancestor, the slave patrols. But more importantly, in the South during this period, the very basis and constitution of authority, and the nature of legality itself, as well as the particular laws, were hotly contested. Local elites remained loyal to the vanquished Confederacy, mourned their lost cause, and held dear the values that had so long supported the racial and economic system of slavery, while the new status quo, amorphous and exhilarating, often relied for its preservation on the presence of federal troops. Under such conditions, it could be expected that the categories of legality and illegality, legitimate authority and illegitimate force, and order and disorder, would become confused.

What is remarkable is the degree to which the resemblance between the police and the Klan has persisted. It may tell us a great deal about the real function and fundamental character of the police that, after more than a century of institutional development, legalism, bureaucratization, professionalization, and more than one hundred years since the death of the Confederacy, they would continue to behave like racist terrorists. The police have persisted in denying Blacks the rights guaranteed to them by the Constitution, have actively sought to frustrate their efforts to exercise such rights or become in a real sense full citizens, and have resorted to the most vicious, brutal, and often patently unlawful means to do so. These facts can leave no doubt as to the institution's priorities when the demands of White supremacy clash with those of the law. The police cannot be considered simply the custodians of the legal order, but must be seen as the guardians of the social order as well.[191] That they defend it wearing blue uniforms rather than white sheets is a matter of only minor importance.

THE NATURAL ENEMY OF THE WORKING CLASS

> I have no particular love for the idealized "worker" as he appears in the bourgeois Communist's mind, but when I see an actual flesh-and-blood worker in conflict with his natural enemy, the policeman, I do not have to ask myself which side I am on.[1]
>
> —George Orwell

The Greensboro massacre of 1979 represented a racist attack against people of color, but it also marked an attack on the rights of working people. The "Death to the Klan" rally was organized as part of an effort to end the harassment of poultry workers as they fought to form a union, and most of those killed were union organizers.[2] Such pairings of racist oppression and class exploitation have been the historical norm; slavery, for example, was a system of production as well as a system of race control.

Though there are divergences between race and class, the means for control in each area have always been very closely linked. This connection is perhaps never clearer than when racist means are used to suppress the resistance workers mount against capitalism, as in Greensboro, or, to take an earlier example, as in 1885, when Mayor Joseph Guillote of New Orleans responded to a levee workers' strike by ordering the police to arrest any Black man who "did not want to work."[3]

Control of the lower classes has been a function of policing at every point since the institution's birth, and has served as one of the major determinants of its development. In the South, the police first approached their modern form after a long process of experimentation and development in the official means of controlling the slave population. This mandate was over-determined, required both by the demands of White supremacy and by the economic needs of the plantation system. The mechanisms developed to control slaves eventually expanded in each direction, as slave patrols were charged with regulating the behavior of free Blacks *and* that of poor Whites, especially indentured servants. As modern capitalism took shape, the new industrial working class posed new challenges to the social order, and the police institution evolved to meet them. Like the slaves, these "dangerous classes" were marked as permanent objects for police control, and their lives became increasingly regulated by specially designed laws, selective enforcement, and heightened scrutiny.

THE MAJESTIC EQUALITY OF THE LAWS

> The law, in its majestic equality, forbids rich and poor alike to sleep under bridges, beg in the streets or steal bread.[4]
>
> —Anatole France

In 1876, the Report of the General Superintendent of Police in Chicago warned: "There is in every large city, a dangerous class of idle, vicious persons, eager to band themselves together, for purposes subversive to the public peace and good government."[5] The police, in Chicago and elsewhere, took as their main task the control of this dangerous class, especially when the poor "banded themselves together," but also, and more routinely, in the course of daily life. The police concentrated their enforcement activities in poor neighborhoods, armed with the tools of physical violence and a variety of laws prohibiting public order offenses, vice crimes, and a great deal of other activities associated with the working class.[6]

It was a short step from selective enforcement to the criminalization of poverty itself and of poor people as a group. While the wealthy were treated leniently by the courts, the poor were sometimes convicted where no crime was even alleged. In Philadelphia, in 1839, Sarah Hays and Thomas Firth were jailed for the non-offense of kissing in public. The mayor admitted that there was no law prohibiting such behavior, but based on the reputation of the neighborhood where they were arrested, he ordered them jailed just the same.[7] In short, the laws themselves targeted the poor, the courts issued harsher judgments against poor defendants, and the police treated poor people with intense suspicion. The instructions to the Philadelphia police explained: "As a general thing, any idle, able-bodied poor man has no right to complain if the eye of the police follows him wherever he roams or rests. His very idleness is an offense against all social laws."[8]

This tradition of class control continues today, in many forms, including urban "quality-of-life" and "zero-tolerance" policies, the war on drugs, and "gang suppression" efforts that seem aimed at disrupting the normal course of neighborhood life.[9] One of the clearest examples of class bias in law enforcement, in the nineteenth century and today, is the persecution of the homeless. Beginning in the 1870s, cities around the country began vigorously enforcing laws against "vagrancy," and mounted special efforts to limit the mobility of migrant workers (in the parlance of the day, "tramps"). For nothing other than the crime of being poor, vagrants and tramps were forced out of town, subject to violence, and oftentimes imprisoned for as long as six months.[10] While contemporary laws are careful to proscribe certain *behavior* rather than poverty per se, statutes prohibiting trespassing under bridges, sleeping on sidewalks, and panhandling clearly have the same effect as the vagrancy laws of the earlier period.

The practices surrounding the enforcement of these laws are often simply cruel, involving intimidation, violence, seizing and never returning identification, and the destruction of personal possessions. In the fall of 1993, I was witness to an incident in which numerous police officers, all wearing latex gloves, moved methodically through Lafayette Park in Washington, D.C., seizing the belongings of the people who lived in the park—sleeping bags, backpacks, pieces of tarpaulin. With the White House in the background, the police carried the items to a nearby garbage truck, where they were unceremoniously crushed. Similar incidents have been reported in Miami, where a court ruled the practice illegal,[11] and in Detroit, where social service providers blamed the crackdown on pressure from area businesses.[12]

In these cases the police put their energies toward attacking, rather than protecting, some of society's most vulnerable members. This use of resources only makes sense when viewed in the context of vast disparities in wealth. The continual harassment of the destitute reinforces their low social standing, stigmatizes poverty, keeps the poor under the supervision and control of the criminal justice system, and in all these ways serves to preserve existing inequalities. Given this perspective, routine attacks against the poor seem ruthlessly rational, and the suppression of organized labor becomes altogether too predictable.

STRIKEBREAKERS, PINKERTONS, AND POLICE

The role of the police as union-busters and strikebreakers was an outgrowth of their position in the class structure and their function regulating the behavior of workers for the convenience of the new capitalist economy. After about 1880, whenever strikes were anticipated, the police made special preparations to control, and thereby defeat, the workers' efforts. Police were sometimes housed on company property for the duration of the conflict. In addition to attacking picketlines and rallies, they increased patrols in working-class neighborhoods, stepped up enforcement of public order laws, and took pains to close the meeting halls and bars where strikers gathered.[13] Arbitrary arrests were common, and strikers were sometimes held on minor charges or without charges until the strike was over. The police also intercepted union organizers and radicals traveling to areas affected by strikes; the unionists and "reds" were usually interrogated, sometimes with third-degree methods, and released at the town line with a stern warning to stay away.[14]

Writing in 1920, Raymond Fosdick described something of the range of police tactics, and the uses to which they were put:

> The police are often used on behalf of employers as against employees in circumstances which do not justify their interference at all.
> This has been especially true in the handling of strikes. Lawful pick-

eting has been broken up, the peaceful meetings of strikers have been brutally dispersed, their publicity has been suppressed, and infractions of ordinances which would have gone unnoticed had the violators been engaged in another cause, have been ruthlessly punished. Sometimes, too, arrests have been made on charges whose baselessness the police confidentially admit. "We lock them up for disorderly conduct," a chief of police told me when I asked him about his policy in regard to strikes and strikers. "Obstructing the streets" is another elastic charge often used on such occasions. Sometimes the arbitrary conduct of the police passes belief. Newspapers favoring the strikers' cause have been confiscated and printing establishments closed on the supposition that they would "incite to riot." Meetings of workingmen have been prohibited or broken up on the theory that the men were *planning* a strike, and specific individuals have been denied the right to speak for the reason that they were "labor organizers." "I have this strike broken and I mean to keep it broken," a director of public safety told me, as if breaking strikes were one of the regular functions of the police.[15]

Such coercive activity is now generally considered the exclusive domain of governments, but the use of violence to break strikes was at first the right and responsibility of private employers. In the period immediately following the Civil War, company guards were sometimes relied on to perform this function, while in other cases the company reimbursed the city government for expenses incurred during strikes.[16] Either way, capitalists facing unruly workers were caught between the desire to directly control strikebreaking activity, and the expense and difficulty of maintaining security forces at the necessary level. It was under these conditions that the Pinkerton Detective Agency grew to national prominence, achieving special notoriety for its use of an agent provocateur against the radical miners organization, the Molly Maguires.[17] By the mid-1880s, the Pinkertons had become part of the standard response to labor trouble, and their dual roles as spies and leg-breakers were often sanctified by deputization into local police departments.[18]

In the coal fields of Pennsylvania, recurring unrest led the coal companies to dispense with the Pinkerton middle-men and maintain an industry police of their own, the "Coal and Iron Police." For a fee of $1 per officer, the state conferred police powers upon these company-controlled guards.[19] In 1915, the Commission on Industrial Relations noted with disapproval that

one of the greatest functions of the State, that of policing, [was] virtually turned over to the employers or arrogantly assumed by them . . . , [and] criminals employed by detective agencies [were] clothed, by the process of deputization, with arbitrary power and relived of criminal liability for their acts.[20]

During the early twentieth-century Progressive Era, such civic-minded concerns, matched with the employers' unwillingness to bear the full cost of strike-breaking, shifted responsibility for these duties to the public police.

The creation of the state police illustrates this process clearly. After the 1902 Great Anthracite Strike, President Theodore Roosevelt appointed a body to investigate the conflict and make recommendations concerning the unresolved disputes. The Anthracite Coal Strike Commission, as it was called, took this task a step further, recommending thoroughgoing changes in the policing of strikes. After quite a few damning words about the strikers,[21] the commission concluded: "Peace and order . . . should be maintained at any cost, but should be maintained by regularly appointed and responsible officers . . . at the expense of the public."[22] In May 1905, Pennsylvania Governor Samuel Pennypacker signed into law an act creating a state police force.[23]

The Pennsylvania State Constabulary proved an effective force against strikes, since it recruited from across the state, thus minimizing the influence of any particular officer's ties to the local community.[24] The Pennsylvania State Federation of Labor called for the organization's elimination and published a volume of evidence against the state police. Titled *The American Cossack*, the book collects witness statements, newspaper accounts, legislative debate, and other material. A typical story comes from S. P. Bridge of New Alexandria, Pennsylvania, dated February 21, 1911:

> Gentlemen:
> State Police came to New Alexandria July 31, 1910, Sunday. The State Constabulary are of no use in this country to farmers or workingmen. They make all efforts to oppress labor.
> Six of them were stationed at this town for a period of two months for the benefit of the coal company. Their duty was in and around the works.
> At the time they were here there was trouble between them and the miners. There was a camp located within two hundred feet of my house. There were three State Constabulary and two deputy sheriffs went into camp. They rode their horses over men, women, and children. They used their riot clubs freely on the miners without cause or provocation.
> One of the men had to be sent to the hospital, one received a broken arm, one woman was clubbed until she was laid up for two weeks. . . . They used their clubs on everyone that protested against their conduct and I was an eye-witness to the affair.
> There were no lives lost and no one hurt before their arrival.
> The majority of citizens are not in favor of the Constabulary.
> I cannot see that anyone but the coal company is benefited by the Constabulary.
> Yours truly,
> S.P. Bridge.[25]

Another statement is unusual only for its source. Hugh Kelley, the Chief of Police in South Bethlehem, wrote:

> When the constabulary arrived here, February 26, 1910, neither the burgess nor myself, as chief of police, were informed of their arrival. They were in charge of the sheriff. . . . They beat people standing peaceably on the street; men were arrested and taken to the plant of the Steel Company and there confined.
> They started out on our streets, beat down our people without any reason, whatever, and they shot down an innocent man, Joseph Zambo, who was not on the street, but was in the Majestic Hotel. One of the troopers rode up on the pavement at the hotel door and fired two shots into the room, shooting one man in the mouth and another (Zambo) through the head. . . . There was no disturbance of any kind at this hotel, the Majestic was the headquarters of the leaders who were conducting the strike. . . . Troopers went into the houses of people without warrant and searched the inmates, drove people from their own doorsteps. They beat an old man, at least, sixty years of age. Struck him with a riot stick and left him in a very bad condition. This is only one of a dozen similar cases.[26]

The law creating the Pennsylvania State Constabulary intended the new body "as far as possible, to take the place of the police now appointed at the request of various companies."[27] It is hard to think of a more literal description of their role. Whereas strikers had previously had their heads cracked by guards in private employ, or police leased to the company, which comes to the same thing, they increasingly had the honor of having their heads cracked by impartial public servants, authorized by the government and funded by the tax. By investing this responsibility in the state itself, the ruling class made provision for the more regular and predictable service of its needs, with the costs shared—in a sense, socialized—and, for that matter, at least some portion of the costs borne by the workers themselves.[28]

Though Pennsylvania did not boast the first state police force, it did pioneer the current type. Earlier state forces were either military organizations, vice squads, or short-lived civil rights agencies.[29] But following the success of the Pennsylvania State Constabulary, the idea of a state police force took hold across the country. By 1919, of the six existing state police departments, all but one were modeled after Pennsylvania's. Ten years later, there were twenty-five such departments. And by 1940, every state had one.[30]

However, with or without a state police force, the independence of the police in relation to the larger companies was somewhat illusory. And in the 1920s, following the federally directed Red Scare, distinctions between union-busting and law enforcement practically dissolved. In Philadelphia, the police issued a proclamation on March 21, 1921, that they would not interfere with union meetings "so long as the meeting is orderly and not of radical character, but all meetings of radical character will be prohibited or broken up."[31] The policy offered the police license to attack any union meeting, since it was assumed all labor organizing was Communist in nature.

At times, anti-union campaigns drew on a practice familiar from the efforts to control African-Americans; police formed alliances with, actively cooperated with, and provided official cover for the activities of right-wing vigilante groups. In Los Angeles, for example, the police joined in a partnership with the American Legion, deputizing members of its "law and order committee." The American Legion then commenced a series of raids against meetings of the Industrial Workers of the World (the IWW, or the "Wobblies"). In the first such raid, four Wobblies were hospitalized and five were arrested for "inciting a riot." A few months later, in April 1921, the IWW's offices and meeting halls were again raided, its supporters arrested, and men, women, and children beaten with ax handles. Those identified as leaders were driven to the desert, beaten unconscious, and abandoned. Though many of the victims could identify their attackers, no charges were ever filed. The pattern continued for years. In June 1924, a vigilante mob, organized in part by the police, attacked the IWW hall with clubs and guns. They destroyed the furniture in the building, beat many of the men and women present, tarred and feathered the leaders, and deliberately scalded several children with hot coffee.[32] While the police ignored these offenses, and sometimes actively protected the perpetrators, they simultaneously engaged in aggressive enforcement practices against the unionists. Between 1919 and 1925 the LAPD arrested 504 union organizers; 124 were convicted of "criminal syndicalism," a charge designed to stifle union activity and specifically targeting the IWW.[33]

So while actual union-busting activity remained a joint venture between public and private forces, during the Progressive Era the authority to use or license violence slowly moved out of private hands, solidifying the state's theoretical monopoly on it. Despite the continual re-configuration of the public/private split in terms of funding and control, the police mission during strikes remained basically the same: to defend the company's interests, to preserve the status quo.

Where conflicts arise between workers and bosses, between the rights of one class and the interests of the other, the machinery of the law is typically used as a weapon against the poor. And where the law is contrary to the demands of powerful corporations, the police act not from principle or legal obligation, but according to the needs of the ruling class. This tendency shouldn't surprise us, if we remember the lengths to which the cops have gone in the defense of White supremacy, even as laws and policies have changed.[34] With class, as with race, it is the status quo that the police act to preserve and the interests of the powerful that they seek to defend, not the rule of law or public safety. The law, in fact, has been a rather weak guide for those who are meant to enforce it.

For example, the Interchurch World Movement's Commission of Inquiry reported that:

> During the [1919 Steel Strike] violations of personal rights and personal liberty were wholesale; men were arrested without warrants, imprisoned without charges, their homes invaded without legal process, magistrates' verdicts were rendered frankly on the basis of whether the striker would go back to work or not.[35]

Thus, in a time of crisis, the pretense of law enforcement was given up in favor of naked repression and class warfare. The police, the jails, and the courts acted to serve, not the law, but the interests of business.

This tendency was occasionally tempered by the attitudes of other elites, or by those of the officers themselves. James Richardson notes that countervailing forces within the community, or especially within the city government, did sometimes neutralize the police:

> In grappling with the dilemmas posed by community polarization, the police tended to follow the lines of power and influence. . . . If the authorities favored the workers or were at least neutral, the police remained neutral. If on the other hand, political leaders and newspapers viewed the strikers as un-American radicals or a threat to the town's prosperity by making industry reluctant to locate there, then the police acted as agents of employers in their strikebreaking activities.[36]

Richardson's point is well taken, but it must be remembered that such neutrality must, in a class-based society, remain suspect. Bruce Smith, an early scholar of policing, makes the point clearly:

> The substitution of non-union labor for union labor is perfectly legal, and the police are bound to give protection against any and all interference with the right to work. The effective performance of this duty . . . frequently "breaks the strike," and the police, whether local or state, are charged with conducting a strike-breaking operation. At such times, evenhanded justice almost necessarily operates to the ultimate advantage of vested property rights.[37]

Even where police do not deliberately side with the employers, class bias is nevertheless built into their role. An exhaustive recounting of labor battles, police attacks on picket lines, and unlawful arrests cannot be supplied here, but two case studies may offer some sense of the usual police role.

THE LAWRENCE TEXTILE STRIKE:
BREAD AND ROSES, BAYONETS AND CLOTH

In 1912, Massachusetts law reduced the workweek for women and children from fifty-six hours to fifty-four. The American Woolen Company complied with the letter of the law, if not the spirit; it reduced the work week, but also made corresponding cuts in pay. In Lawrence, Massachusetts, where 60,000 people depended on the earnings of the 25,000 textile workers, and where the average wage was $8.76 per week, 25 cents more or less made an enormous difference in the workers' ability to feed their families.[38] Thus, on January 11, when the workers received their paychecks and discovered the reduction, they walked out—first at the Everett cotton mill, and the following day at the Washington mill. The Washington workers marched to the Wood mill, shut off the power, and called out the workers there. By that evening, 10,000 were on strike.[39] By the end of the month, the strike had spread to other industries, and 50,000 people in a town of 86,000 were striking.[40] One picket sign expressed the workers' position clearly, capturing both the desperation of the moment and the hope for a better future: "We want bread and roses too."[41]

The repression of the strike was immediate and intense. Arbitrary arrests and summary judgments became the order of the day, and many strikers were sentenced to one-year prison terms without ever having the opportunity to put forth a defense.[42] Leaders were marked for more serious charges, and extreme measures were taken to discredit the union. When dynamite was discovered in a cobbler's shop, police and press alike were quick to blame the strikers, though there was no evidence to support such a conclusion. The tactic backfired. First, a school board member, John C. Breen, was arrested, tried, convicted, and fined $500 for planting the dynamite.[43] Then, Ernest W. Pitman, president of Pitman Construction Company, implicated himself and several other business leaders in a confession to the District Attorney. Pitman revealed that the incident had been planned by one of the textile companies, leading to conspiracy charges against Fred E. Atteaux, the president of the Atteaux Supply Company, and William M. Wood, the president of the American Woolen Company.[44]

Regardless of the scandal, union leaders were generally blamed for any violence, not only the violence of the strikers, but that used against them as well. On January 29, when striking workers attempted to block the mill gates, the police and the militia attacked, and a riot ensued. An Italian striker, Anna Lo Pizzo, was shot and killed. Witnesses identified the culprit as officer Oscar Bemoit, but two IWW leaders were arrested instead. Neither of the two men—Joseph Ettor and Arturo Giovannitti—had been present when the shooting occurred, but the complaint alleged that "before said murder was committed, as aforesaid, Joseph J. Ettor and Antonio (sic) Giovannitti did incite, procure, and counsel or command the said person whose name is not known, as aforesaid, to commit the said murder. . . . "[45] The police later named Joseph Caruso as an accomplice and "Salvatore Scuito" as the gunman, though no one of that name was ever located.[46]

Martial law was declared on January 30, the day after the shooting. Colonel E. LeRoy Sweetser was given charge of twelve companies of infantry, two cavalry units, fifty cops from the Metropolitan Park Force, and twenty-two companies of militia. Citizens were forbidden to meet or talk in the streets, and Lo Pizzo's funeral was broken up by a cavalry charge. Mass arrests became common, and strikers were rousted from their homes and taken to jail. A Syrian striker, John Ramy, was stabbed with a bayonet and subsequently died. But the strike grew. The textile companies kept the looms running, but only as a kind of propaganda; they had no workers to operate them, and thus no product.[47] Joseph Ettor commented from jail: "Bayonets cannot weave cloth."[48]

On February 5, the Italian Socialist Federation proposed evacuating the strikers' children. Supplies could thus be saved and the children decently cared for by sympathetic families. In the three days following, they received 400 offers to take in the children. The Socialist Women's Committee and a committee of the IWW took applications and inspected the homes. On February 10, 119 children were sent to New York under the supervision of four women, two of them nurses. A week later, 103 more were sent to New York, and 35 others to Barre, Vermont. This exodus was embarrassing for both the government and the mill owners, and on February 17, Colonel Sweetser announced that no more children would be allowed to leave.[49] But if the socialist foster-care system was embarrassing, the attempt to disrupt it was absolutely scandalous. On February 24, when 40 children tried to leave for Philadelphia, they found the train station full of police. A member of the Women's Committee of Philadelphia later testified before a House committee about what happened next:

> When the time approached to depart, the children arranged in a long line, two by two, in orderly procession, with their parents near to hand, were about to make their way to the train when the police closed in on us with their clubs, beating right and left, with no thought of children, who were in the most desperate danger of being trampled to death. The mothers and children were thus hurled in a mass and bodily dragged to a military truck, and even then clubbed, irrespective of the cries of the panic stricken women and children.[50]

No further effort was made to interfere with the children, and on March 12, the American Woolen Company agreed to a new pay rate.[51] The workers voted to end the strike, but the struggle was not over. New slogans appeared: "Open the jail doors or we will close the mill gates."[52] As the September 30 trial date for Ettor, Giovannitti, and Caruso approached, textile workers in Lawrence, Haverhill, Lowell, Lynn, and elsewhere threatened to strike if they were convicted. As a demonstration of their seriousness, 15,000 staged a one-day strike a few days before the trial was set to start. The police attacked the strikers, arresting 14, and almost 2,000 were fired and blacklisted. But the strikers had already seen worse, and knew something of their own strength. Amid threats of further strikes, the mill owners were forced to back down, and after fifty-eight days of trial all three defendants were acquitted.[53]

THE 1934 SAN FRANCISCO GENERAL STRIKE AND A "REIGN OF TERROR"

In 1934, the West Coast witnessed an extended, and at times bloody, conflict between dockworkers represented by the International Longshore Association (ILA) and the business interests represented by the Waterfront Employers Union and the Industrial Association. Principally, the conflict concerned the control of the long-shore hiring hall and related issues of scheduling, seniority, and of course wages. The bosses preferred to arbitrate the dispute, and the union leadership was willing to compromise, but the workers had other ideas. A strike began on May 9 among longshore workers in San Francisco, and quickly spread to maritime and related industries, reaching up and down the coast.[54] It stalled the economy of the entire country, but the center of conflict remained in San Francisco, where it escalated through a series of bloody battles to become a general strike.[55]

Violence was a major feature of the San Francisco strike, a tool used by both sides. Strikers commonly beat up scabs, and sent "sanitary" or "clean-up" crews to patrol the waterfront with bats.[56] The bosses, however, mostly relied on the violence of the state, especially the police. This was a convenient relationship, as it legit-imized anti-strike violence and shifted the target of public outrage away from the employers and onto the police. David Selvin emphasizes the point:

> [T]he police even more than the strikebreakers became the strikers' chief antagonist. The role of the strikebreaker was soon stabilized and contained, while police came to serve, day by day, as the employers' virtual private assault force. When the clashes came, as they did, the police—not the strikebreakers—were pitted against the strikers.[57]

The violence started early, and escalated throughout the strike. On the first day, the police dispersed 500 picketers with relative ease. By the end of the month, how-ever, the pickets were fighting back, hurling bricks at the police. The cops then used clubs, gas, and eventually shotguns to break up groups of strikers.[58]

The most serious violence accompanied efforts to operate the docks, especially attempts to move goods to or from the ports.[59] On July 3, 1934, the police created a corridor down King Street to Pier 38, guarded by a police line on one side and a row of box cars on the other. As trucks approached, the police sought to break up the crowd of strike supporters. They attacked with clubs, teargas, and gunfire, injuring many in the crowd as well as numerous bystanders. A stray bullet wounded a teller in the nearby American Trust Company. Strikers retaliated by throwing rocks, bricks, and tea rgas containers back at the police. At least two strikers were shot, one killed, and eleven hospitalized, and nine cops were injured.[60] The ILA issued a statement on the encounter: "Striking pickets were clubbed down and rode over by the police who a short time ago were supposed to be the friends of these same workers. The strike cannot and will not be settled by force."[61]

But force seemed to be the authorities' preferred means of convincing the workers to return to their jobs. On July 5, the entire San Francisco Police Department was put on strike duty.[62] The fighting was concentrated in the area surrounding Pier 38 and Rincon Hill. But the police also moved in on a crowd at Steuart and Mission, near the ILA hall. Suddenly a car carrying two police inspectors appeared in the intersection. The inspectors stepped out of the car, fired their pistols into the crowd, and then fled as the crowd hurled rocks and bricks at them.[63] Two men died in the attack—Howard S. Sperry, a longshoreman, and Nick Counderakis (aka, Nick Bordoise), a Communist. A third man, Charles Olsen, was also shot, but survived.[64] When the injured were taken to the ILA's clinic, the police fired into the building and filled it with tear gas. As the unionists barricaded themselves in the hall, the telephone rang: "Are you willing to arbitrate now?"[65]

That evening 1,700 National Guard troops were deployed, armored cars patrolled the streets, and the Embarcadero, the street nearest the waterfront, was enclosed in barbed wire and guarded with machine guns. But the military fortifications fell short of their objective: the work remained undone. Two hundred fifty ships sat idle along the coast. Even when a military guard made it possible for scabs to unload and move cargo, it just sat in the warehouses, where Teamster truckers refused to touch it.[66] As in Lawrence, the state was reminded of the practical limits of its reliance on force.

By the end of the day, in addition to Sperry and Bordoise, one other worker had been killed, and at least 115 hospitalized.[67] Thus July 5 came to be termed "Bloody Thursday." Strike leader Harry Bridges called it a "reign of terror." He said: "It was an attack by armed men against unarmed peaceful pickets. It was a massacre of workers by the shipowners through the police."[68] The next day, the corner of Steuart and Mission was covered with flowers. Chalked on the street were the words: "Two men killed here, murdered by police."[69]

One week later, 4,000 truck drivers walked out, marking the move toward a general strike. They were quickly joined by butchers, machinists, welders, laundry workers, culinary workers, cleaners and dyers, and boilermakers. Thirteen unions, representing 32,000 workers, joined the strike.[70] The Teamsters picketed the city's southern limits, guarding the only vehicular route to the city. There they turned back, and sometimes turned over, non-union trucks. A strike committee issued permits for hospital supplies, food, and other necessary services, but the city could not function as usual.[71] Signs began appearing in shop windows: "Closed, Out of Supplies," "No Gas, Due to the Strike," "Closed for the duration," and "Closed till the boys win."[72]

The next day the authorities declared an emergency. The police began stockpiling weapons, swore in 500 special officers, and created an "anti-radical and crime prevention bureau."[73] Eighteen hundred cops and 4,500 National Guard troops were now on strike duty, reinforced with machine guns, tanks, and artillery.[74] Meanwhile, across the bay, 15,000 building trades workers laid down their tools and walked off their jobs. They were joined by 27,000 workers affiliated with the Central Labor Council.[75]

On July 17, the second day of the general strike, the police launched a coordinated attack. That morning a group of uniformed officers and plainclothes detectives raided the Maritime Workers Industrial Union office, breaking down the door, destroying office equipment and furniture, smashing windows, seizing records, and arresting everyone present, often delivering a beating in the process. This was the first of a daylong series of similar raids, not only in San Francisco, but throughout the state. Police, National Guard troops, and vigilantes attacked radical hangouts, strike kitchens, newspapers offices, and even a school. About 300 people were arrested.[76]

Shortly thereafter, on July 20, the strike committee voted to end the General Strike, though the longshore and maritime workers continued striking on their own.[77] The announcement was met with another wave of police raids and vigilante attacks.[78] Eleven days later, the last strikers returned to work. The strike had lasted eighty-two days and involved 30,000 dock workers. Seven were killed, hundreds were hospitalized, and thousands were treated at the ILA clinic. There were 938 arrests in San Francisco alone.[79]

In arbitration, the workers won a raise and a 30-hour week, but were only granted partial control of the hiring hall, falling short of their most important demand.[80] The strike delivered real gains, but not the decisive victory the workers wanted. In this case, they proved unwilling to accept even a minor defeat, and the class war shifted from a campaign of massive, often deadly, battles to one of quick, bloodless, guerrilla actions. Both the longshore and the ship workers immediately instigated a series of on-the-job actions against unfair and dangerous conditions.[81] And, perhaps as importantly, they changed the face of their unions and the labor movement overall. Looking back on the strike a few years later, Thomas G. Plant told a conference of longshore employers:

> Most of us heaved a big sigh of relief, and felt that the old peace and order would soon be restored. But the old order had changed. The old union had said to us, "We believe our interests are common

with yours; we will cooperate with you in every way. . . . " The new union was to say to us, "We believe in the class struggle, that there is nothing in common between our interests and yours, therefore, we will hamper you at every turn, and we will do everything we can to destroy your interests, believing that by doing so we can advance our own."[82]

CLASS WAR IN THE 1990s AND TODAY

The role of the police in suppressing organized labor during the period before World War II is well-documented and relatively uncontroversial. What is often over-looked, however, is their continuation in this role since that time. The police have undergone a great many changes in the half-century since World War II, but their position in the class structure and their role in the class war have remained very much the same.

For example, sixty-five years after the San Francisco General Strike, on the opposite side of the country, dockworkers were again facing a threat to their union—a recalcitrant company backed by the armed might of the state. In October 1999, Nordana Line, a Danish shipping company, announced that it would end its contract with the ILA and started using non-union workers to unload its ships. Union members began picketing the port in Charleston, South Carolina, sometimes damaging equipment, blocking access to machinery, and intimidating non-union workers.[83] On January 20, 2000, the police intervened with a massive display of force. Six hundred officers from the State Law Enforcement Division, the State Highway Patrol, the Charleston County Sheriffs Office, and the police departments of Charleston, North Charleston, and Mount Pleasant assembled in riot gear at the port's gates, a helicopter buzzing overhead.[84] Just after midnight, about two hundred workers marched from the union hall to the docks, chanting "ILA, ILA, ILA." As the workers tried to break through the police lines, the cops pushed them back with their shields. The fight escalated from there, with workers throwing rocks and bottles, and the police using clubs, teargas, and rubber bullets to drive the crowd back toward the union hall. At least ten workers, and probably many more, were injured, most of them African-Americans.[85]

Nine workers were arrested, charged with misdemeanor trespassing. Those charges were dismissed when the accused agreed to perform community service, but South Carolina Attorney General and gubernatorial candidate Charlie Condon filed felony riot charges against five of the workers—Kenneth Jefferson, Elijah Ford, Jr., Peter Edgerton, Ricky Simmons, and Peter Washington, Jr. Condon explained the importance of prosecution: "In South Carolina, a citizen's right not to join a union is absolute and will be fully protected." At the same time he announced "a comprehensive plan for dealing with union violence and attacks on police which involves jail, jail, and more jail."[86]

The state of South Carolina placed the Charleston Five under house arrest for more than a year while they awaited trial; if found guilty, the men faced five years in prison. But after a massive, international solidarity campaign, ranging from "Free the Charleston Five" posters in windows around town, to rallies at the statehouse, to threats to close ports around the world on the first day of the trial, Condon removed himself from the case.[87] The new prosecutor downgraded the charges to misdemeanors in exchange for "no contest" pleas; each of the five was sentenced to thirty days, or a fine (ranging from $100 to $309). Nordana, in the meantime, returned to its agreement with the ILA.[88]

This sort of intersection between race politics and class conflict is not unique to the South. On June 15, 1990, the Los Angeles police trapped and beat striking janitors as they marched through the Century City business district. The janitors, who were mostly Latino, were organized as part of the Service Employee's International Union's "Justice for Janitors" campaign; they were demanding that International Service Systems (ISS) recognize their union. As the march entered Century City, the 300 demonstrators found themselves surrounded by nearly 100 police. The cops blocked the exits and proceeded to arrest and beat them. Ninety people were injured, nineteen of them seriously. Workers reported broken bones, a concussion, and a miscarriage as a result. Ironically, the violence brought more attention to the workers' cause than the march itself ever would have, and nine days later ISS recognized the union.[89]

Perhaps the clearest recent case of police-managed strikebreaking is that of the Detroit Newspaper Strike (and later, lockout). In July 1995, when 2,600 employees of the *Detroit News* and the *Detroit Free Press* went on strike, the newspapers (together, the Detroit News Agency) responded by hiring 2,000 private security guards, supplied by Vance International, and by giving money to police in the suburb of Sterling Heights, where the papers' production plants are located. Police initially confiscated clubs and other weapons from Vance guards, but after the Detroit News Agency's first donation—a sum of $115,921—the cops' attitudes changed.[90] Police ignored harassment and violence on the part of the guards, even when several Vance agents beat a striker so severely they split his skull.[91] But strike sympathizers were arrested for even minor infractions, such as blowing the horns of their cars to show support for the strike.[92]

The cops also perpetrated their own violence against the workers. Most notoriously, on August 19, 1995, a picketer named Frank Brabenec was beaten by the Sterling Heights police. A widely published photograph showed a uniformed officer dragging Brabenec along the ground while a plainclothes cop, later identified as Lt. Jack Severance, kicked him.[93] A couple weeks later, on Saturday, September 2, the police attacked picketlines with pepper spray. The unions happened to be holding a rally nearby, and 4,000 supporters rushed to the site of the conflict. The cops called for reinforcements from twenty-two police agencies, and a sixteen-hour stand-off ensued, during which time trucks could not enter or leave the plant. Two days later, on Labor Day, a smaller crowd fought with the security guards.[94] Those first few weeks set the tone for the next five-and-a-half years, until December 2001, when the unions finally gave in. Only a third of the striking workers were rehired—at lower wages, of course.[95]

It is hard to know how much of the blame for this defeat really falls to the police, especially given the poor planning of the unions, media hostility, and court orders limiting the number of strikers on picketlines.[96] But it is easy to see what the cooperation of the police was worth to the Detroit News Agency. During the course of the strike, the company donated nearly a million dollars to the Sterling Heights police. Police violence escalated accordingly, and crowds took to chanting "Bought and paid for!" when the cops arrived.[97] Mayor Dennis Archer explained that riot police helped to preserve "a good business climate."[98]

CLASS CONFLICT: CONTINUITY AND CHANGE

These recent events indicate how little has changed over the course of a century. Naturally, strikes and other labor actions still focus on many of the same issues, since there is a permanent conflict of interest between workers and their employers when it comes to matters of pay, hours, and control. And in the clashes between workers and capital, the police continue to line up on the side of capital. But the differences between these later disputes and those of the early twentieth century are also clear enough. Violence persists, but at lower levels. Battles between police and workers, while sometimes bloody, are rarely deadly.[99]

These reduced levels of violence are the result of a shift in the form of class conflict: unionization, collective bargaining, and even strikes have been formalized, institutionalized, and subject to legal regulation. Increasingly, this development has taken the struggles of workers out of the factories and the streets and placed them instead in courthouses and government offices.[100] Companies, then, have come to rely less on police or Pinkerton thuggery to keep the workers in line. At the same time, the militancy of the labor movement overall has suffered a sustained decline, and the power within unions has shifted away from the rank and file and toward the official leadership, the paid staff, and their legal advisors.[101]

This process was already taking hold at the time of the San Francisco General Strike of 1934. In fact, the strike may be seen as the workers' direct resistance to the institutionalization of class conflict on two fronts: first, in their refusal to submit substantive issues to arbitration; and second, in following the leadership of rank-and-file members like Harry Bridges, rather than obeying the orders of union officials.[102] The depth of this resistance—the degree to which workers refused to play by the prescribed rules, and rejected the given definitions of victory and defeat—is evident in the continuation of the struggle even after they had returned to work. The strike ended, but the workers did not surrender. They, in effect, moved the conflict to an arena where the influence of the union officials, the courts, and the police could be minimized, and where the strength of the workers was greatest: on the shop floor.

The institutionalization of class conflict has changed unions and strikes, certainly; it has also changed the means of controlling the working class, and the role of the police in particular. Police tactics, strategies, and organization have all changed as the forms of conflict have changed. All the while, the basic aims of policing—control of the powerless, defense of the powerful—have remained essentially the same. The relationship between these changes and continuities will be examined in the chapters that follow.

POLICE AUTONOMY AND BLUE POWER

The ongoing history of police anti-labor action seems at odds with the growth of militant police unions in the latter part of the twentieth century.[1] Nevertheless, the police *have* organized unions, and in many cases their unions occupy a central place in the constellations of local political power. In addition to advocating improved wages and working conditions, prosecuting grievances, and forestalling (or sometimes preventing) discipline against individual officers, the unions also have a strong hand in the creation of public policy, inside and outside their respective departments. Few changes in public safety or security policies can be made without the tacit approval of the police unions, and the officers' associations are routinely consulted on changes in the criminal code, or in city policies that might indirectly affect police work. When controversies arise concerning the police, their actions, or their role in society, it often falls to the unions to detail the "law and order" perspective. The organization's agenda may then dominate the debate, or even define its terms.

This influence has been hard-won and always controversial. The police union's development, between the end of the nineteenth century and today, has been tightly braided with changes concerning standards of public morality, the shape of municipal government, race relations, and of course, class conflict. Embedded within every strand of this cord, exposed with every tangle and snare, lies a question about the nature of democracy, and about the role of police power in a democratic society.

FROM STRIKEBREAKERS TO STRIKERS (AND BACK AGAIN)

Beginning in the late nineteenth century, police in many cities belonged to social organizations, called either "Patrolmen's Benevolent Associations" (PBAs) or "Fraternal Orders of Police" (FOPs). The two types of organizations functioned along similar lines, providing their members insurance and promoting their overall health and well-being. The main differences were that, whereas the PBAs were only open to patrolmen and were strictly independent, the FOPs were open to any officer and were affiliated nationally.[2] Both groups petitioned for better working conditions, an effort that the authorities tolerated so long as there was no move toward unionization.[3] The rank and file crossed that line during World War I, when a steep rise in the cost of living pushed several organizations to apply for charters from the American Federation of Labor. In a break with its previous position, the AFL granted the charters, and the police unionized in several cities, including Cincinnati, Washington, Los Angeles, St. Paul, Fort Worth, and most famously, Boston.[4]

Unhappy with long hours, low pay, favoritism, and the sorry condition of their stationhouses, on August 15, 1919, members of the existing police association, the Boston Social Club, voted to affiliate with the AFL.[5] They thus created the Boston Police Union Number 16 of the American Federation of Labor.[6] Less than a month later, on September 8, Police Commissioner Edwin Upton Curtis responded by suspending nineteen union supporters. The Boston Police Strike began the next day.[7]

Approximately three-quarters of the Boston Police Department joined the strike, creating a politically uncomfortable situation made worse by rampant crime and widespread disorder.[8] Almost immediately, small crowds gathered around craps games on the Boston Common. By the evening of September 9, the disorder had escalated to the point of looting. Crowds overturned parked cars, and numerous gang rapes were reported.[9] Some rowdies took the opportunity to settle scores with striking police. Crowds gathered at stationhouses and pelted the strikers with mud, rocks, bottles, and rotten fruit as they left the building.[10] A South Boston Vigilance Committee was formed and tried to keep order, but its volunteers were savagely beaten.[11]

The rioting ended when 3,000 State Guard troops, scab police, and a provost navy guard unit broke up the crowds.[12] The State Guard killed three people in the process, including one bystander and one person who was fleeing. A fourth was killed as the soldiers broke up the craps games on the Common, and two more died when the militia attacked a group of boys trying to steal a manhole cover. By September 11, eight were dead and more than seventy injured—twenty-one seriously, several of them children. More than $300,000 in property had been damaged or stolen.[13] On September 12, the striking patrolmen voted unanimously to end the strike if only their suspended colleagues would be reinstated. Instead, Curtis fired all the striking police.[14] The State Guard patrolled until December 12.[15]

Following the strike's defeat, many states passed laws forbidding police unions, and the AFL revoked the charters of all its police locals.[16] Isolated from the rest of the labor movement and lacking political support, the new unions were crushed in city after city. Local governments then raised wages so as to remove any incentive for re-forming the unions. Immediately after the strike, the starting salary for Boston police was increased to $1,400 per year. (Only a few months before it had been as low as $730).[17] Between 1919 and 1929, police wages increased by 30 percent in Detroit, 50 percent in Chicago, 70 percent in Los Angeles, and 100 percent in Oakland. By 1929, patrolmen earned between $1,500 (in Cincinnati) and $2,500 (in New York), which put them on par with most skilled laborers.[18]

This strategy worked to neutralize rank-and-file organizing throughout the 1930s, restricting their activity to the lobbying tactics of the early PBAs.[19] But in the 1940s, unionization was again on the agenda, and by 1944 the AFL had police unions in 168 cities.[20] In the name of preserving their neutrality, police departments generally responded to this new wave of organizing in the same way they had before—barring the organizations and firing union supporters.[21]

In the 1950s, after the NYPD defeated a Transport Worker's Union drive by offering the officers concessions,[22] Commissioner George Monaghan established Rule 225: "No member of the police force of the city of New York shall become a member of any labor union." He reasoned that the rule was necessary

> to protect the policemen from influences or commitments which
> might impair their ability to perform their duties impartially and
> without fear or favor, or might tend to weaken or undermine the dis-
> cipline and authority to which they must necessarily be subjected.[23]

Appeals to the "neutrality" of the police are questionable, given their historical use against strikes and unions. Monaghan's second reason probably comes closer to the truth: Unionization was seen as a threat to the control of police commanders.

Whatever the justification, restrictions against unionization proved ineffectual, and some commanders were forced to try other approaches in order to preserve their control. In 1941, the AFL supported an FOP organizing drive in the Detroit Police Department. The department harassed officers who supported the drive, fired its leaders, and procured court orders barring unionization, but half of the patrolmen joined the organization anyway. The next year, however, the FOP lost ground when the Detroit Police Officers Association (DPOA) was formed with the backing of police commanders.[24] Carl Parsell, who served as the DPOA president in the late sixties, explained: "It started out basically a company union under their guidance, under their control. They gave you the rights at their pleasure."[25]

Things took a different turn in New York, though a similar strategy was in evidence. The PBA sued to protect itself from Rule 225, and won. The court found that the department could bar "organizations of policemen affiliated with nonpolice labor associations or officered by non-policemen," but could not interfere with the PBA's activities.[26]

The distinction became relevant in June 1958, when the Teamsters publicly announced an effort to unionize the police. The announcement put pressure on the PBA leadership to produce results,[27] and it also gave police managers an incentive to cooperate with the PBA rather than face the stronger muscle of the Teamsters. A *Journal-American* editorial suggested:

The surest way of slapping down Hoffa would be for Mayor Wagner, Commissioner Kennedy, and the representatives of the Patrolmen's Benevolent Association to begin exploring methods by which such grievance machinery would be set up with proper safeguards all around.[28]

This is, more or less, what occurred. After the Teamsters' drive was defeated, PBA President John Cassese set about winning gains for his organization's members. By 1961, lobbying, lawsuits, and job actions—including ticket speed-ups and slow-downs—had won the PBA a dues check-off, protections against management retaliation, and a formal grievance system.[29] Two years later, Mayor Robert Wagner, whose father had authored the National Labor Relations Act, extended collective bargaining rights to police officers, and the PBA won better wages and retirement benefits as a result.[30] In exchange, the PBA agreed to a no-strike clause and a bar from affiliating with other unions.[31]

The leaders of the police associations, PBA and FOP alike, were only too glad to protect their positions from the competition of the Teamsters or American Federation of State, County, and Municipal Employees (AFSCME), but no-strike provisions proved more difficult to enforce. The authorities learned this the hard way in 1967 when the Detroit police staged a sick-out (nicknamed the "Blue Flu"). A year later, the Newark police did the same, and the Chicago cops threatened their own Blue Flu epidemic.[32] In 1969, the Atlanta FOP organized "Operation No Case," in which the police issued fewer tickets and overlooked minor offenses.[33] The next year, Atlanta officers repeated the tactic without union approval, initiating a ten-week slowdown.[34] The trend continued throughout the seventies, with strikes in Baltimore, Cleveland, Memphis, and New Orleans.[35] When faced with a walkout or slowdown, the authorities usually decided that the pragmatic need to get the cops back to work trumped the city government's long-term interest in diminishing the rank and file's power.[36]

The Detroit sick-out provides an interesting illustration of the forces at work in these conflicts. The action began on May 16, 1967, with a ticket slow-down. The police continued to pull over speeding motorists, thus technically enforcing the law. But they issued warnings rather than citations.[37] Overnight the number of traffic tickets dropped to one-half its previous level. Between May 16 and June 14, the number of tickets was down 66.9 percent compared to the previous thirty days, and 71.5 percent relative to the same period a year before. It's estimated that the effort cost the city about $15,000 each day.[38] On June 6, the DPOA escalated the conflict when its members voted to stop volunteering for overtime. The following week, police commanders responded to the disruption by suspending 61 officers. Then, on June 15, 323 cops called in sick.[39]

DPOA President Carl Parsell denied that the action constituted a strike, but said: "Policemen for the first time are joining the labor movement. They are beginning to think and act like a trade union."[40] The city filed a lawsuit against the DPOA, instituted emergency 12-hour shifts, and alerted the National Guard. The strike not only continued, but grew. On June 17, 800 of the city's 2,700 officers were absent. Of these, 170 had been suspended, 459 were "sick," and 15 cited family emergencies. As the conflict escalated, each side grew increasingly eager to find a resolution, and on June 20, a tentative agreement was reached. The next day, the police returned to work.[41]

The proposed agreement granted the DPOA changes in policy and discipline, and established a grievance procedure, but it was not at all clear that the fight was over, or which side would prevail. All "non-economic" issues were settled, but there was still the matter of wages, and the deal had to be approved by the city council.[42] The tension persisted. Commanders had only a tenuous grasp on the loyalties of their subordinates. But then a funny thing happened: The Detroit riot of 1967. With the Black community in open revolt, the cops, the city government, and local elites very quickly rediscovered their previous affinity. In bringing the labor dispute to a close, the specially appointed Detroit Police Dispute Panel noted: "Far more than the interests of the police officers themselves is involved. As has become obvious in recent months . . . the police force is the first line of defense against civil disorder."[43] The cops got their raises.[44]

In contrast to the defeated strike of 1919, the labor skirmishes of the 1960s and 1970s solidified the positions of the police associations and had the somewhat paradoxical effect of buttressing the top-to-bottom unity of the departments. The unions asserted increasing levels of influence over departmental policy, and the police management used the unions to win rank-and-file cooperation.[45] Such management-union partnerships reinforced the institution's cohesion, allowed disparate parts of the organization to develop a community of interests, and provided a means for settling disputes and resolving grievances. But they retained traditional taboos against autonomous rank-and-file action and meaningful expressions of solidarity with other labor organizations.[46]

Whereas the Boston strike had been ignominiously defeated, the Detroit strike was resolved in a way that strengthened both the department and the union. Clearly, a lot had changed during the intervening half-century. The relevant differences were not limited to shifts in policing and labor organizing, but also concerned the overall character and function of municipal government.

THE DEATH OF THE MACHINES

During the early twentieth century Progressive Era, police departments were subject to a battery of reforms, changing the institution's structure, aims, and personnel.

These reforms were not motivated by concerns about racism or brutality so much as they constituted one part of a general effort to re-invent urban government.

It is not hard to see why reform was needed. Under political machines, there was little to distinguish an official's personal attachments, interests, loyalties, and obligations from the duties, responsibilities, powers, and benefits of his office. Authority rested as much in the informal and decentralized ward networks as in the government itself or the offices of the various municipal departments. Positions were filled strictly along partisan lines or as personal favors; there was no pretense of professionalism or impartiality. Discipline was lax, corruption was sanctified, and bribery was a major source of income at every level of the hierarchy. In this context, it was the job of the police to protect illicit businesses, extort money from honest citizens, rig elections, and otherwise enforce the will of neighborhood bosses. So long as they were successful in these central tasks, it made little difference to the machine bosses whether the cops engaged in petty crime, neglected their legal duties, were rude in their encounters with the public, or used violence unnecessarily.[47]

As a result, police legitimacy was sorely lacking. This problem was aggravated by a long series of scandals implicating departments around the country in organized crime and other types of corruption. For example, at the turn of the century, Los Angeles Mayor Arthur Harper, Police Chief Charles Sebastian, and a local pimp formed a syndicate in order to monopolize prostitution in the city; the police were used to suppress competition and protect the syndicate's operations. In 1912, Herman Rosenthal, a professional gambler, accused the New York City Police of protecting gambling houses; he was murdered on his way to meet with the district attorney. The next year, San Francisco papers revealed that a group of detectives had recruited a gang of con-men, offering protection in return for 15 percent of the total take (an estimated gross of $300,000 annually). And during Prohibition, dozens of Cincinnati cops sold confiscated liquor and offered protection to bootleggers in return for a share of the profits.[48] Such scandals largely discredited the police departments and the machines to which they were attached.[49] But the Progressive agenda offered a map toward legitimacy.

Seeking to replace the machine system, Progressive reformers looked to business and the military for organizational models. Schools, for instance, were reorganized on a corporate model, whereas the police were structured according to a military design.[50] This military analogy provided a positive ideal of what the police could be—a disciplined, hierarchically organized force, with the chief holding nearly absolute power. More specifically, the reformers offered three recommendations for change: departments should be centralized; the quality of personnel should be improved; and police operations should be narrowly focused on crime control, with an emphasis on prevention.[51]

Toward these ends, police departments were divided, as far as possible, into specialized units with a streamlined chain of command and an articulated hierarchy. Chiefs were given more control and discipline was moved from external boards, which were deemed "political," to internal "professional" mechanisms. Civil service procedures were instituted, age and education requirements were established, and character checks and psychological exams were introduced.[52]

But the success of the Progressive movement was uneven overall. Despite the trend toward centralization and rationalized management, little changed in the areas of policy or procedure, and neighborhood precinct stations retained much of their autonomy.[53] Police chiefs did not, on the whole, receive the lifetime tenure Progressives proposed.[54] And the police still had a broad range of duties, even after specialization. In fact, contrary to the rhetoric of the time, the police function did not so much narrow, as it shifted to meet new demands for social order.[55]

Yet modest successes had a profound impact on the character of government. Around the country, political machines were beginning to decay. The localized, personalistic, and unabashedly corrupt machine system was giving way to a new kind of public administration. In theory, the new system was very nearly the opposite of the old; it operated legalistically, acting according to general principles and enforcing rules impersonally. City government was becoming bureaucratized.[56]

BUREAUCRATIZATION AND BOURGEOIS CONTROL

Police reforms contributed in several ways to the rise of bureaucracy. The narrowing of the police function promoted bureaucratic development, not only within police departments, but throughout the city government. As elections, health regulations, licensing, and welfare duties were removed from the list of police responsibilities, other municipal departments—other bureaucracies—were created to take over these tasks. A similar process occurred within departments, as civilians began performing clerical, technical, and related work.[57]

The efforts to improve personnel also promoted increased bureaucratization. Cops were assigned civil service status or military rank, barred from accepting rewards, paid higher salaries, received better training, and hired and promoted on the basis of exams.[58] By rationalizing the selection of personnel and the delivery of services, the new procedures reduced the opportunities for personal favors and patronage, thus cutting machine bosses off from their means of securing support.[59]

Centralization, likewise, reduced the importance of the local precincts and undercut an important base for the ward organizations.[60] It also made it possible for such specialized functions as vice control, record-keeping, internal investigations, and detective work to be removed from the precincts and assigned to squads controlled by headquarters. By 1930, such squads abounded—riot squads, prohibition squads, narcotics squads, gambling squads, homicide squads, robbery units, auto theft teams, missing persons bureaus, bomb squads, bicycle squads, motorcycle squads, juvenile divisions, red squads, units to handle particular ethnic groups, records divisions, and internal affairs.[61] This reorganization limited the opportunities for corruption and, again, put power in the hands of the police chief rather than ward bosses or precinct commanders.[62]

But despite the specialization, civil service procedures, and administrative centralization, police departments became only incomplete, imperfect bureaucracies. Though governed in principle by general rules, police organizations lacked elements of managerial control implicit in the bureaucratic ideal.

> The concept of control adopted by modern management requires that every activity in production have its several parallel activities in the management center: each must be devised, recalculated, tested, laid out, assigned and ordered, checked and inspected, and recorded throughout its duration and upon completion. The result is that the process of production is replicated in paper form before, as, and after it takes place in physical form.[63]

This demand was incompatible with the dispersed and highly discretionary activities that characterized police activity and made policing a source of power for the state. Officers on the street never approached the ideal of the impartial bureaucrat, nor was there much effort to transform them into such. Rules were crafted, records kept, promotions and assignments somewhat rationalized, but the cop on the beat was expected and required to exercise just the sort of individual discretion and situational judgment denied to his counterpart on the lower rungs of proper bureaucracies. This allowed corruption, prejudice, favoritism, and political influences some amount of latitude on the street—where the police did their work—while limiting these factors in the offices of management, where policy was set.[64]

The military aspects of reform were just as limited. Some departments adopted military ranks, instituted drilling, and began requiring target practice, but discipline was not established along military lines, in part because of the resistance of patrolmen's associations.[65] In short, cops became neither soldiers nor bureaucrats; they did, however, cease acting as the pawns of the political machines.

Reformers quickly learned that this administrative independence cut both ways:

> While civil service procedures reduced some of the politician's power over the policemen's working life, they also reduced policemen's receptivity to reform leadership. Increasingly, the police could follow their own lead, independent both of the party organizations and the innovative administrations.[66]

Hence, while the new system of administration diminished the influence of machine bosses, it did so by bolstering the position of municipal bureaucracies as independent seats of power. While sometimes frustrating reform efforts, this arrangement was not wholly disadvantageous for the city administrators, mayors, and politicians, as it let them disavow the police department's excesses without needing to do anything to stop them. If authority was invested exclusively in the police chiefs, then the chiefs would also incur whatever blame was directed at the department, though they faced few consequences of public disfavor.[67] But even the position of the chief of police was not necessarily so strong as it appeared, and discipline was generally limited by the need to maintain the loyalty of those in his command.

> It is exceedingly rare that a ranking police officer can take positive charge of police action, and even in the cases where this is possible, his power to determine the course of action is limited to giving the most general kinds of directions. But like all superiors, police superiors do depend on the good will of the subordinates. . . . Thus, they are forced to resort to the only means available to insure a modicum of loyalty, namely, covering mistakes. The more blatantly an officer's transgression violates an explicit departmental regulation the less likely it is that his superior will be able to conceal it. Therefore, to be helpful, as they must try to be, superiors must confine themselves to white-washing bad practices involving relatively unregulated conduct, that is, those dealings with citizens that lead up to arrests. In other words, to gain compliance with explicit regulations, where failings could be acutely embarrassing, command must yield in unregulated or little regulated areas of practice.[68]

The protection that the individual officer once received from his political patron was thus transferred to his superior officers. In a formal sense, the police faced more discipline, while in practice they continued to engage the public—or certain parts of it—according to their own judgment. Hence, bureaucratization increased the autonomy of the department as a whole and, ironically, preserved the discretion enjoyed by officers at the lowest ranks.

Yet this gap in accountability was not particularly worrisome to reformers of the time. The Progressive movement, while often credited with improving the quality of public services and reducing corruption, was not especially concerned with protecting the rights of the poor. Reform efforts were not led by immigrant workers, who constituted the usual victims of the police abuse, but by the business and professional classes.[69] The Progressive agenda reflected the ideology and interests of this constituency.[70] By promoting bureaucratic reform, these "respectable" classes sought to ensure their own control over the workings of the local governments. J. W. Hill, an influential reformer in Des Moines, wrote: "The professional politician must be ousted and in his place capable business men chosen to conduct the affairs of the city." Likewise, I. M. Earle, the general counsel of the Bankers Life Association and a reform advocate, explained, "When the plan [for a commission government] was adopted, it was the intention to get businessmen to run it."[71]

Put simply, the reformers hoped to break the machines and, at the same time, push working-class immigrants out of politics. Because immigrants generally lived together in distinct neighborhoods, they had been well placed to influence the ward-based machines. So Progressive reforms replaced districted elections with city-wide contests and strengthened the mayor's office to the detriment of the ward councilors.[72] The Progressive reforms thus practically limited popular access to government.[73] Meanwhile, other efforts were underway to restrict suffrage, assimilate immigrant children, and regulate the numbers of new immigrants.[74]

Progressive efforts encouraged legalistic administration and promoted transparency, but these gains were only really extended to the White, Protestant, native-born, English-speaking middle and upper classes. The transition, then, was from a populist gangsterism to an elitist republicanism. The Progressive movement replaced machine politics with class rule.

Edward C. Banfield and James Q. Wilson explain this transformation:

> The machine provided the politician with a base of influence deriving from its control of lower-income voters. As this base shrinks, he becomes more dependent on other sources of influence—especially newspapers, civic associates, labor unions, business groups, and churches. "Nonpolitical" (read nonparty) lines of access to the city administration are substituted for "political" ones. Campaign funds come not from salary kickbacks and the sale of favors, but from rich men and from companies doing business with the city. Department heads and other administrators who are able to command the support of professional associations and civic groups become indispensable to the mayor and are therefore harder for him to control. Whereas the spoils of office formerly went to "the boys" in the delivery [voting] wards in the form of jobs and favors, they now go in the form of urban renewal projects, street cleaning, and better police protection to newspaper [public opinion] wards.[75]

The poor did not control, or especially benefit from, the political machines. But the machines required their participation and offered them something in return. The emerging bureaucracies of the Progressive Era, in contrast, were designed to limit their participation. The poor did not control these either, and the new system offered them terribly little.

Machine rule was replaced with the more subtle power of the capitalist class. Whereas before local government was administered according to strictly material incentives, it was now guided by administrative norms and the formal rules of bureaucracy, backed with the moral standards and political ideology of the

Protestant bourgeoisie. This victory was ironic, in a sense, because Progressive rhetoric centered on "taking the police out of politics," and conversely, "taking the politics out of policing." Though the reforms did grant police commanders a fresh independence from the demands of politicians, the idea of taking the politics out of policing was doomed at the outset, as ridiculous a notion as taking the politics out of government. As Robert Fogelson put it:

> Far from being mere administrative bodies that enforced the law,
> kept the peace, and served the public, the police departments were
> policy-making agencies that helped to decide which laws were
> enforced, whose peace was kept, and which public was served. Much
> like the courts, schools, and other vital institutions, the police
> thereby exercised a great deal of influence over the process of mobil-
> ity, the distribution of power, and the struggle for status in urban
> America. To put it bluntly, no institution which had so great an
> impact on the lives and livelihoods of so many citizens could have
> been separated from the political process. Nor, so long as the nation
> was committed to democracy and pluralism, should it have been.
> None of the reform proposals—neither the schemes to centralize the
> police forces, upgrade their personnel, and narrow their function nor
> the appeals to transform them along the lines of a military organiza-
> tion—could have changed this situation.[76]

In effect, the city government was wrested from the grip of the political machines, and the police were removed from the control of the city government, but the bourgeoisie exercised a high level of influence over both the city government and the police. The Progressive Era saw simultaneously an increase in state autonomy and the full rise of capitalist class hegemony.

To understand this concurrence, we must recognize that "hegemony" is not synonymous with dictatorial rule.[77] It is more subtle, more flexible, and therefore also more insidious and more resilient. It is characterized less by the direct issuing of orders than by the setting of agendas, the framing of debate, the articulation of standards, the valuation of alternatives, and the delineation of available options.[78] It is through hegemony that the ruling class creates a bounded sphere of institutional autonomy. Without need of conspiracies or actual censorship, its ideological ascendancy determines in advance which issues will be raised, which debates will be aired, and ultimately, whose interests will be considered and whose rights respected.

PROFESSIONALIZATION: A CONSPIRACY AGAINST THE LAITY

> All professions are conspiracies against the laity.[79]
> —Bernard Shaw

Despite the limitations of their actual reforms, the Progressives' ideology prevailed, and a perspective that was both nativist and bureaucratic became the accepted view of newspapers, churches, commercial organizations, civic associations, universities, and other opinion-makers.[80] It also, predictably, found an audience among police administrators.

A second wave of police reform originated from within law enforcement.[81] More specifically, it was brought to policing by newcomers to the field. During the 1930s, depressed economic conditions made police work attractive to the large numbers of men seeking steady employment. Police departments became more selective,[82] and the sudden influx of middle-class officers, many of whom shared the values of the Progressive reformers, changed the character of the institution. This "new breed" of officer found their backgrounds and ideals in conflict with the lowly status of their jobs and the ideology of the departments, but thanks to the civil service procedures, they soon moved through the ranks and into command positions.[83]

The new police reformers retained Progressive assumptions about the purpose of the police, the need for its leaders to be autonomous, and the nature of political legitimacy, but were motivated by their own immediate frustration with the low level of respect accorded the occupation.[84] Despite the previous wave of reforms, the police remained ineffective and often corrupt. Departments were badly managed, with little forward planning, poor supervision, and no rational division of labor. Though formal standards and bureaucratic civil service procedures did exist, the personnel were poorly trained and generally undisciplined.[85]

Faced with these conditions, the "new breed" sought to professionalize policing, and thereby raise their social standing. Beginning in the late 1920s and early 1930s, they developed a model of professionalism that achieved prominence in police circles by mid-century. This model emphasized strict admission standards, extensive training, a high level of technical knowledge, and a devotion to service and a commitment to the public interest.[86] By becoming a profession, the reasoning went, police could improve the quality of their work, raise their own status, and further insulate themselves from outside interference.[87]

The professional movement overlapped chronologically with the latter part of the Progressive Era, and the new reforms continued some of the efforts begun by the Progressives, finding more success in many areas. For example, they continued the project of reorganizing departments along functional lines and managed to close more precincts, extending the reliance on special squads and streamlining the hierarchy.

While these changes did further diminish the influence of neighborhood bosses (whose power was already in decline), they often just shifted corruption from the wards to the squads.[88] In a textbook case of failed reform, Chicago Mayor Richard Daley responded to a 1960 burglary ring scandal by replacing Police Commissioner Timothy J. O'Connor with reform luminary O .W. Wilson. Wilson set about professionalizing the department, removing corrupt or incompetent commanders, instituting a system of promotions based on seniority and competitive exams, and closing seventeen of the thirty-eight district stations, but corruption continued unabated.[89] A 1964 Justice Department report revealed that a score of Chicago cops, including an internal affairs investigator, were running a protection racket.[90]

Reformers took steps to regulate the quality of the personnel, using physical examinations, education requirements, character checks, and the civil service process to weed out undesirable applicants.[91] Whether these measures succeeded in "improving" the quality of recruits is another matter. Critics at the time denounced the professional ideology as elitist,[92] and in many cities, the new requirements were used to prevent racial minorities from joining the force.[93]

The reform commanders seemed to want to fill departments with recruits whose backgrounds and values resembled their own, but the practical consequences of these changes were not what their advocates had intended. When the economy recovered from the Depression, the "professionalized" departments had trouble attracting and keeping recruits. The pay had not kept pace with that of other occupations, prestige was still lacking, and new officers could only enter the department at the lowest level.[94] Since the best cops did not always advance through the ranks, and the worst were seldom removed, stagnation set in. The quality of leadership suffered, and the police became increasingly isolated.[95]

Compared to the Progressives, the advocates of professionalization had more success in instituting their prescribed reforms, but they did no better in achieving their ultimate aims. The status of the police did not equal that of doctors and lawyers, and the departments were only mildly cleaner than before. But the main effect of professionalization was to increase police autonomy. And professionalization, like bureaucratization, not only institutionalized that autonomy, but helped to legitimize it.[96] The discourse surrounding professionalization encouraged institutional problems to be thought of in technical terms, and thus referred to the "experts"—the police. Issues of accountability and oversight were thus framed as professional matters with which the uninitiated should not be trusted to interfere. In other words, professionalization sought to take the issues of police power and accountability outside of the realm of the political.

The move toward professionalization embodied both a continuation of and a reaction against the bureaucratization of policing. The advocates of professionalization, usually police administrators, envisioned their project as an extension of the bureaucratic reforms, with an increased emphasis on the quality of recruits and higher public esteem for the occupation. Carl Klockars argues from this basis that the term "professional" was primarily of rhetorical value:

> The fact is that the "professional" police officer, as conceived by the professional police model, was understood to be a very special kind of professional, a kind of professional that taxes the very meaning of the idea. The distinctive characteristic of the work of professionals is the range of discretion accorded them in the performance of their work. By contrast, the police view of professionalism was exactly the opposite. It emphasized centralized control and policy, tight command structure, extensive departmental regulation, strict discipline, and careful oversight. While the professional model wanted intelligent and educated police officers and the technological appearance of modern professionals, it did not want police officers who were granted broad, professional discretion. It wanted obedient bureaucrats.[97]

The rank-and-file officer, on the other hand, had a very different notion of what professionalization implied: "The professionally-minded patrolman wants to act according to his evaluation of the situation and not according to some bureaucratic directive."[98] Professionalization very clearly promoted police autonomy, but it was deeply ambivalent about what this meant for the management of departments. Did professionalization only require the autonomy of the institution relative to the civilian authorities? Or did it also demand the autonomy of the patrolman relative to departmental control? In practice the second followed from the first, as commanders sought to protect themselves from criticism. Rather than exposing abuses and disciplining the officers, internal affairs investigators and unit commanders took their task as the defense of the department as a whole, and especially of the officers under their command.[99]

> Most high-ranking officials were prone to praise the efforts of their units and, in the face of clear evidence to the contrary, to shift the responsibility to other parts of the force or other branches of government. If this tactic failed, they were ready to deny responsibility on the grounds that . . . they had few effective sanctions over their subordinates.[100]

Professionalization, again like the earlier reform effort, continued to put supervisors in the position of covering for their subordinates.

At the same time as the "professional" police were asserting a new independence, they also adopted strategies that increased their presence in the lives of the urban poor and people of color. The professional model encouraged police leaders to take seriously the elusive goal of preventing crime. Making the most of the new squad structure, the police sought to reduce the opportunity for crime, experimenting with vehicular patrols, saturation tactics, and high-discretion techniques like "stop-and-search" or "field interrogation."[101] For example, in the late 1950s, the San Francisco police used each of these approaches in tandem. Chief Thomas Cahill created an "S Squad" ("S" standing for "saturation") to be deployed in high-crime areas, with instructions to stop, question, and search suspicious characters. During its first year, the S Squad stopped 20,000 people, filed 11,000 reports, and made 1,000 arrests. Most of those they stopped were Blacks and young people.[102]

The preventive aims of the professionals led the police to intervene in situations that had previously gone unnoticed, were ignored, or were not even criminal. This encroachment promoted a generalized distrust on both sides, as police grew ever more suspicious of the public and the public (especially the Black community) grew increasingly resentful of the police.[103] As we have seen, this tension bore bitter fruit in the years that followed.

UNIONIZATION AND BLUE POWER

Today's police unions are the bastard children of the mid-century professionals. Though earlier union efforts had met with little success, the fissures and contradictions of the professional agenda helped create conditions that made unionization possible. While the rhetoric of professionalization lent legitimacy to demands for higher pay and greater autonomy, the prescriptions of the reformers alienated the regular officers and produced additional strife with the public. This situation created new tensions within police departments and brought the idea of unionization back to the surface.

Though coming as a direct result of the attempts to professionalize policing, union organizing efforts were of a quite different character. The movement for police unions reflected a working-class labor perspective rather than a middle-class professional agenda, and found its support with the mass of patrol officers rather than with commanders. The International Association of Chiefs of Police recognized this difference as crucial, and described unionization as sounding "the death knell of *professionalization*."[104]

The influence of unionization has extended far beyond such basic matters as wages, working conditions, and grievances. Unionization, like the previous two waves of reform, had the general effect of increasing the institutional autonomy of the department[105] and the autonomy of individual officers.[106] But unionization took the latter as one of its principle aims, and for that matter, sought to provide the lowest-level officers collective power over the institution as a whole.[107]

As the police unions grew, they set about negotiating policy matters, including those governing patrols, deployment, and discipline.[108] The agenda quickly broadened to include "questions of social policy, including which type of conduct should be criminal, societal attitudes toward protest, the procedural rights of defendants, and the sufficiency of resources allocated to the enforcement of the criminal law."[109] These efforts represented "a phenomenon new to American society: the emergence of the police as a self-conscious, organized, and militant political constituency, bidding for far-reaching political power in their own right."[110]

The police also returned to open electioneering—like in the machine days, but with a difference. Rather than owing allegiance to their patrons and taking orders from the ward bosses, the police had developed into a constituency for the politicians to wow and woo. Police support could make or break a candidate, and once in office the politician owed his allegiance to the cops, rather than the other way around.[111]

Some politicians made the most of the new balance of power. Philadelphia police commissioner, and later mayor, Frank Rizzo deftly exploited the political potential of the department, building himself a career while at the same time amplifying the power of the police and increasing their independence. Under Rizzo's guidance, the police department became the unrivaled center and base of his power.[112]

It wasn't long before police unions started producing their own candidates, and served in some places as a ladder into office. In 1969, Wayne Larking, who had served as head of the Police Officer's Guild, was elected to the Seattle City Council.[113] That same year, Charles Stenvig, a former police detective and the business manager of the Minneapolis Police Officer's Federation, was elected mayor, having run solely on a law-and-order platform.[114] Stenvig convinced patrolmen to campaign for him. When an interviewer asked an officer, "Did you introduce yourself as a patrolman?" the officer responded: "Sure. That was the whole point. The idea was to convince people that a cop would know how to bring peace back to the community."[115]

At times, such political efforts, especially electioneering, crossed lines of decorum. In 1964, many departments had to issue special orders to prevent officers from wearing Goldwater or Wallace buttons on their uniforms, or from putting campaign stickers on squad cars. Some cops even handed out campaign literature while on duty.[116]

In each arena, whether their efforts involved electioneering, lobbying, or strikes, the police pursued a conservative agenda—specifically one that increased the power, autonomy, and central role of law enforcement. L.A.'s Fireman's and Policemen's Protective League ("Fi-Po") represented the direction of the new activism; it lobbied for counter-subversive laws, promoted right-wing rallies, sponsored conservative speakers, and sold businesses a blacklist naming union organizers and radicals.[117]

"NO JUSTICE! NO POLICE!"

In July 1966, New York supplied the first real test of this newfound power. Mayor John Lindsay made good on one of his campaign promises, restructuring the city's police complaint board to include a civilian majority. The Police Benevolent Association immediately and vigorously attacked the plan, eventually forcing the issue to the ballot. The PBA then sponsored an extensive ad campaign and individual officers put anti-review board signs on their cars, distributed literature, and harassed those who campaigned in favor of the board, often while on duty.[118]

The anti-review board propaganda openly appealed to public anxieties about civil unrest and crime—two issues, in the context of the time, with obvious racial overtones. One poster showed a young girl at the entrance to a subway; its text read: "The Civilian Review Board must be stopped. Her life, your life, may depend on it."[119] Another poster showed a riot-torn street, cluttered with rubble and lined with damaged storefronts. The caption stated: "This is the aftermath of a riot in a city that *had* a civilian review board."[120] An August 18, 1966, *Reporter* editorial titled "License to Riot" worked from the same theme: "Did you see the pictures of those Cleveland riots, of Negro thieves running wild, in and out of wrecked establishments, arms loaded? And did you see the cops standing by, idly watching the debauchery? That was the result of a Police Review Board."[121]

As the November election approached, police tactics became more brazen. The PBA and their supporters packed a meeting about the review board, chaired by Councilman Theodore S. Weiss. Former FBI agent William Turner described the scene:

> Thousands of off-duty policemen in uniform, with service revolvers strapped on and wearing PBA buttons (the buttons were later removed at the request of the police commissioner) tightly ringed City Hall and packed its corridors. Many carried signs with such slogans as "What About Civil Rights For Cops," [and] "Don't Let The Reds Frame The Police." Adding to the spectacle were dozens of American nazis and John Birch Society members toting American flags and shouting encouragement to the police.[122]

The New York review board was defeated by a two-to-one margin—1,313,161 to 765,468.[123] Elsewhere during the same period, similar battles were fought more quietly, with police associations convincing city councils or mayors to refuse proposals for review boards—sometimes even dismantling existing boards. Such was the story in Los Angeles, Denver, Cincinnati, Seattle, Detroit, Newark, San Diego, Hartford, Baltimore, San Francisco, and Philadelphia.[124]

But it is worth noting that the police were not univocal in their opposition to civilian review. In many cases, associations of Black officers openly favored the review proposals.[125] In New York, when one such group, the Guardians, released a statement expressing their support of the mayor's proposal, a PBA spokesman protested, "they put their color before their duties and their oath as policemen."[126] It seems that the PBA saw its own political agenda as determining the scope and content of official police duty.

This view was given a fuller expression in August 1968, when PBA President John Cassese issued his own orders concerning police behavior during demonstrations. Cassese instructed PBA members, "If a superior tells a man to ignore a violation of the law, the policeman will take action notwithstanding that order."[127] When the PBA finally published its full guidelines they turned out to be more bark than bite, as they mostly just paraphrased existing laws and policies, but the episode demonstrated something of the PBA's aims.[128] In particular, it suggested an emerging system of dual-power within police agencies, with commanders and union-leaders sometimes sharing and sometimes competing for control. This situation was a natural outgrowth of earlier struggles for departmental autonomy, like the fight against the Civilian Review Board.

In the course of these conflicts, the political ambitions of the police became more aggressive: They not only sought to insulate themselves from all outside control, but also wanted to exercise control over other areas of the government and public policy. Henry Wise, a lawyer for the Patrolmen's Benevolent Association, was very optimistic about the organization's potential: "We could elect governors, or at least knock 'em off. I've told them [the police] if you get out and organize, you could become of one [of] the strongest political units in the commonwealth."[129]

By the end of the 1960s, the trajectory of these developments was clear, and elites started to worry. The *New York Times* opined, "[A] city cannot be ruled by its police force, any more than a free nation can be ruled by its military establishment."[130] The police, both in their departments and in their unions, were coming to represent a force that could rival that of the civil authorities. In 1968, Boston Mayor Kevin White confessed, "Are the police governable? Yes. Do I control the police, right now? No."[131] In 1972, L.A. city administrative officer C. Erwin Piper said Fi-Po had "more political clout than any other group in city government."[132]

Unfortunately, the period of police militancy has outlasted many of the social conditions that produced its rise, and police activism continues to have major political consequences. In 1992, when New York Mayor David Dinkins proposed a civilian review committee, the PBA mounted a protest-cum-riot, which Acting Commissioner Raymond Kelly described as "unruly, mean-spirited and perhaps criminal."[133] According to Kelly's report, 10,000 off-duty cops took over the steps of City Hall, blocked traffic on the Brooklyn Bridge, damaged property, and assaulted passersby. The response of the on-duty officers was "lethargic at best."[134] Several officers, including one captain and two sergeants, failed to hold police lines, and a uniformed officer, Michael P. Abitabile, waved protesters through the police barricades while shouting racial slurs.[135] Police Chief David W. Scott later said, "I'm disappointed in the fact that police officers would violate the law."[136]

The demonstration carried obvious racial overtones. Signs read, "Dinkins, we know your true color—yellow bellied," and "Dear Mayor, have you hugged a drug dealer today?" T-shirts urged, "Dinkins must go!" And demonstrators chanted, "The mayor's on crack" and "No justice! No police!"[137] Kelly's report suggests that the demonstration was self-defeating, as "the inability of the on-duty personnel assigned to police the demonstration has raised serious questions about the department's willingness and ability to police itself."[138] I would actually say that it *answered* those questions, but the disagreement is academic; the demonstration had greater practical consequences, helping to launch the candidacy of Rudolph Giuliani. Giuliani, who spoke at the rally, was elected mayor following Dinkins and immediately set about expanding police power.[139] In retrospect, the September 16 rally has all the flavor of a municipal-level coup.

Police activism, especially in the guise of union activity, remains somewhat perplexing. The historical development is clear enough, but politically it is troublesome, especially for the left. The whole issue presents a nest of paradoxes: The police have unionized, and struck—but continue in their role as strikebreakers.[140] They have pitted themselves against their bosses and the government, but represent a threat to democracy rather than an expression of it. They have resisted authority for the sake of authoritarian aims, have broken laws in the name of law and order, and have demanded rights that they consistently deny to others.

This situation is sometimes thought to create a bind for those who both support the rights of workers *and* demand that police be accountable to the community. But the dilemma here is illusory. The demands of solidarity—true solidarity—are with the oppressed, and against the police. Working people cannot afford to extend solidarity to the police, and we cannot let the reactionary goals of police unions restrain us in our attacks on injustice. Confusion in this matter represents a set of related misconceptions; these can be resolved by clearly examining the class status of the police and the nature of their organizations.

WAGE SLAVES AND OVERSEERS

The class position of the police is complex, and even contradictory.

Individual officers may consider themselves "working class" for any of a variety of reasons. First, there is the fact that, even after the period of professionalization, most officers are still drawn from working-class backgrounds. There is also the persistent sense that, regardless of income, the job has little social status attached to it. And finally, there is the nature of the work itself. "After all, police work is often physical, sometimes dirty, involves shift-work, and brings officers into contact with undesirable elements of society."[141]

The police have certainly faced their share of uncomfortable and unfair working conditions. In the nineteenth century, police received low pay, unless one counts graft, worked long shifts, were given no vacations, enjoyed little job security, and had no guarantee of income if they were injured or of support for their families if they were killed.[142] Such standards are appalling, for certain, but most workers were no better off.[143] In the twentieth century, the pressures of bureaucratization and professionalization were often resented by the officers at the lowest levels. Bureaucratization increased discipline, eliminated political patronage and protection, and supplied rule-bound prescriptions for police action. Professionalization represented, from the perspective of the old-school cops, an unnecessary intrusion of elitist organizational goals at the expense of a traditional hard-nosed approach. Both reform movements created structural tensions within the police departments that later motivated the drive toward unionization.

But the proletarian aspects of policing are only half the equation. Though individually they receive just a meager portion of capitalism's benefits, the police represent both the interests and the power of the ruling class. Like managers, police control those who do the work, and they actively maintain the conditions that allow for profitable exploitation.[144]

The police thus occupy a dual position as workers and overseers, but this is not a fatal contradiction: A worker can be made to discern "his own" interests, apart from the interests of the working class as a whole. This is the origin of the so-called "middle class," which is really a section of the working class bought off by the capitalists to manage their affairs.[145] Class status, in this regard, is determined neither by income nor by ownership, but by power relations:

> Since the authority and expertise of the middle ranks in the capitalist corporation represent an unavoidable delegation of responsibility, the position of such functionaries may best be judged by their relation to the power and wealth that commands them from above, and to the mass of labor beneath them which they in turn help to control, command, and organize.[146]

The peculiar distinction of this middle stratum is that its members share in *both* the power and rewards of the upper classes, *and* in the alienation of the workers they control.[147] This basic fact requires elites to treat police differently than other workers, seeking through ideology and material incentives to separate them from the mass of workers, and the labor movement especially, tying the interests of the police to those of capitalism and the state.[148] This trick is accomplished through peculiar means, using what is ostensibly a labor organization: the police union.

POLICE UNIONS AREN'T UNIONS

The status of police unions, and their relationship to the labor movement as a whole, has always been troublesome. When the NYPD challenged the legality of the Patrolman's Benevolent Association in 1951, the court ruled that the PBA could organize police and could negotiate contracts precisely because it was *not* a union. According to the court, the police could join "associations" like the PBA and FOP, but not any organization that had either non-police leadership or affiliation with nonpolice unions.[149] This ruling represented something of a compromise position, seeking both to preserve the "neutrality" of police action against strikes and to respect the officers' right to free association.

As legal reasoning goes, that's not very impressive. New York City Police Commissioner Stephen P. Kennedy, who strongly resisted the PBA's demands for recognition in the late 1950s, argued that the distinction between an independent association and a union was meaningless: "When an organization acts like a union, talks like a union, makes demands like a union and conducts itself like a union, it cannot be heard to say that it is not a union."[150] But the legal status of police associations is at most a secondary matter. The practical effect of the ruling was to privilege the PBAs and FOPs over the Teamsters and AFSCME. Police managers were then quick to recognize (in some cases, to *create*) associations, especially when facing a Teamsters organizing drive. The associations gave police management a means of establishing agreed-upon conditions while still discouraging autonomous rank-and-file action and solidarity with other workers.[151]

Police associations thus developed in relative isolation from the rest of the labor movement, while building close ties with the command hierarchy within the departments. This fact points to two related reasons why police unions are not legitimate labor unions. First, as is discussed above, the police are clearly part of the managerial machinery of capitalism. Their status as "workers" is therefore problematic.[152] Second, the agendas of police unions mostly reflect the interests of the institution (the police department) rather than those of the working class.[153]

When the PBA organized in New York, collective bargaining rights were traded for no-strike agreements and a bar from affiliating with other unions. During the same period, police unions around the country were defecting from AFSCME to form police-only locals.[154] Almost twenty years later, in 1970, the NY PBA took this dissociation further than the law required, moving to break parity with other city employees, including firefighters, corrections deputies, and sanitation workers.[155] This is telling, and not just because it shows the lack of solidarity between police associations and the rest of the working class. It indicates that police associations organize more along institutional rather than class lines. That is, they organize police *as police*, not as workers.

The police exhibit an institutional unity that is fundamentally different than the class consciousness underlying union activity. The chief difference is that, despite fissures along race lines, disputes between superiors and subordinates, and intra-departmental rivalries, a sense of shared identity extends to every branch of police organizations and is felt at every level, from the highest commander to the rookie on the beat. This solidarity helps the commanders maintain the loyalty of their troops and, as mentioned before, it also leads cops of all ranks to cover up for each other. Not only do street cops hide one another's mistakes from those above them, but superiors shield subordinates from outside scrutiny.[156]

Such managerial complicity reinforces the sense of identity and group cohesion, thus reducing the possibilities for conflict within the department. And as the rank and file have become a more vocal, and more powerful, political constituency, some commanders have extended this strategy in order to share in the benefits of militancy.[157] A savvy commander can secure the loyalty of his troops by participating in their revolt, providing himself with the platform for leadership and at the same time retaining a militant force prepared to back him up in clashes with civil authorities.

Police unions exercise influence over departments in ways other unions can only envy. However, apart from localized, usually individuated, grievances, the officers and their managers share interests, perspectives, and a sense of identity. In the end, their institutional identification is superior to their class consciousness. To a very large extent, police departments achieve internal peace by subsuming the interests of both workers and managers to those of the institution. Even economic issues, like wages and hours, become common ground for cops and their bosses: both want increases in department budgets. The officers, of course, enjoy a higher standard of living as a result, and police administrators can look forward to more funding, larger departments, better morale, and an easier time attracting recruits. For this reason some scholars describe police contract negotiations as exercises in "collusive bargaining."

Margaret Levi explains:

> As the literature on private labor unions so often illustrates, collective bargaining often serves as a device of social control. It channels conflict and sets its terms. But collusive bargaining goes one step further: it enables management and labor negotiations to cooperate actively with each other. (In order to convince their constituencies of their motives the bargaining teams fight publicly, but privately they compromise.) By engaging in collusive bargaining, city leaders gain credibility with the public for being tough, gain some assurance of relatively uninterrupted service delivery, and regain some power to make programmatic innovations. Of course, in return, they must grant some of the union's demands.[158]

Union leaders, meanwhile, put on a similar act for the benefit of their constituency. As a result, they are able to deliver gains to the union members and retain their positions of influence, all without the risks of genuine conflict.

As an example of this collusive approach, Levi cites the relationship between the Fraternal Order of Police and Atlanta Police Chief John Inman: "The chief found the FOP was sympathetic enough to his policies to become a much-needed ally, and the FOP discovered it could gain promotions and respect. . . . However, this alliance also contributed to the racism of the police labor organization."[159] In this way, antagonisms between labor and management become secondary to their shared, institutional aims. As both press to increase the power, resources, and autonomy of the institution, they form a community of interests, an alliance against the meddling of city officials or the competing demands of other government agencies.

Such an alliance bears the markings of corporatism. Colin Crouch and Ronald Dore define "a corporatist arrangement" as:

> An institutional pattern which involves an explicit or implicit bargain (or recurring bargaining) between some organ of government and private interest groups (including those promoting "ideal interests"—"causes"), one element in the bargain being that the groups receive certain institutionalized or *ad hoc* benefits in return for guarantees by the groups' representatives that their members will behave in certain ways considered to be in the public interest.[160]

They go on to cite both historical and recent examples:

> The doctors and lawyers of medieval England—as well as the civil engineers and all the other professional groups which got their charters in the nineteenth century—were granted monopoly privileges (the right to decide who should and who should not be allowed to sell certain kinds of services) in exchange for promises to make sure that the professional standards of those who did sell those services—their skills and their morals—were what the public had a right to expect. More modern forms—this time the granting by the state of an *ad hoc* concession rather than an institutionalized privilege—include, for instance, the bargains sometimes struck in the 1960s and 1970s in Britain between the British Rail management, the railway unions, and the government: more state funds for railway modernization provided that the unions would agree to get their members to accept productivity improvements and changes in the work practice.[161]

They could also have pointed to, more notoriously, the economic system of Fascist Italy.[162]

Leaving aside the question of police fascism, corporatist arrangements in policing have taken both the "medieval" and the "modern" forms that Crouch and Dore describe. As the historical comparisons indicate, each phase of police reform has tended toward corporatist arrangements—bureaucratization and professionalization under the "medieval" model, and unionization in a more "modern" guise. Currently, the "medieval" aspects find an analogy in the relations between police departments and governments, wherein bargaining is implicit, and the "modern" are in evidence with the three-party relations between the union, the departments, and the government. However, with the police the corporatist deal is not between the state and some outside group (as in Crouch and Dore's idealized scenario), but between various sections of the state. Specifically, it is an agreement between the elected civil authorities (the government), the police commanders (the department), and the representatives of the rank-and-file officers (the union).[163]

This alignment between workers and management is not unique to police labor relations, but a common feature of many public or semi-public institutions. In the wave of public employee unionization of the 1960s, many public service workers—not just cops—began to demand changes in the way their work was organized, and sometimes sought to influence the social conditions that affected their work. But whereas teachers and social workers rallied against discrimination, inequality, and the meager remedies of the Great Society, the police turned sharply to the right. For example, a major demand of the 1967 Chicago social workers' strike was the provision of additional services for clients. Teachers' unions frequently demand smaller classes and better material. The police, in contrast, advocate longer prison sentences, fewer safeguards against brutality, and new weaponry.[164]

In each case, the workers seek to make common cause with their clients, but the clientele of the various agencies are quite different. Smaller classes benefit both teachers and students; additional social services are good for the people who receive them and for the people who provide them. But, such provisions likely inconvenience taxpayers, other portions of the government (who compete for the funds), and the business and government elites who feel they can surely find "better" uses for the money and have little sympathy for the plight of public school students and the poor. In the case of the police, these relationships are exactly reversed: The police defend the interests of elites, and it is the poor who are burdened.[165] Thus, the social function of policing provides a permanent basis for the conservative orientation of police unions.

In turn, police associations provide a stronghold for the most reactionary aspects of the profession, elements that the command hierarchy is often at pains to disavow.[166] When the police command cannot, for legal or political reasons, resist demands for civilian oversight, for more diversity in the department, or for redress in particular cases, the union can defend the departmental status quo. Historically, most police associations barred Black members,[167] and police in Detroit and St. Louis threatened strikes to keep Blacks off the force. The police departments accommodated the White officers in various ways, sometimes by refusing to hire Blacks, in other cases by keeping Black officers out of uniform, restricting them to Black neighborhoods, or prohibiting them from arresting Whites.[168] As recently as 1995, a group of Black LAPD officers sued the Police Protective League for its role in preserving discrimination on the force, describing the union as a "bastion of white supremacy."[169]

Police unions are also on hand to defend particular officers whose misbehavior becomes embarrassing to the department and who therefore cannot be protected by their supervisors. For instance, when officer Doug Erickson was fired for shooting twenty-two times at a fleeing suspect, the Portland Police Association spent over $100,000 taking the case to arbitration; Erickson was reinstated as a result.[170]

The police union represents an extreme of autonomy, protecting officers of the lowest rank from authority both inside and outside the department. This has the effect of distributing some kinds of power toward the bottom of the formal hierarchy:

> Certainly if the police chief or police commissioner ignores legislative mandates or other directives from policy-makers, he must suffer the consequences, whereas even the rookie patrolman soon learns the art of camouflaging both inefficiency and policy infractions. In this sense, not only does the individual officer, acting in an isolated instance, make a subjective judgment as to how he should intervene in a particular situation, but when these discretionary judgments are made by officers on a wholesale basis, as they frequently are, it takes on the character of administrative and policy decisions being made by officers at the lowest level of the hierarchy.[171]

The careful tension between departmental policy and officer autonomy has its benefits for both the commanders and the line officers. Though police regulations do notoriously little to actually regulate officer conduct, they do provide a layer of plausible deniability between commanders and the routine activities of their troops. That is, the rules help to insulate commanders from responsibility for misconduct while at the same time police unions defend the rank and file from meaningful discipline. This arrangement allows for the formal appearance of a rigorous command and control while maintaining maximum discretion at the lowest levels of the organization. The command staff can minimize the criticism it faces through the manipulation of formal policies and bureaucratic shuffling, but concessions granted at this level need not affect much of what happens on the street.

Of course, discipline *does* exist and can be quite stringent when it comes to certain procedural or organizational matters—scheduling, the chain of command, uniforms, budgets, and so on. But both discipline and discretion exist within carefully delineated bounds according to the needs and aims of the institution. Discipline fails and discretion is preserved in those areas where it is most convenient for the department that it be so—that is, when the police come into contact with the public. The public cares very little about whether cops are issued light blue or dark blue shirts, whether they stand at attention during roll call, whether they work eight- or ten-hour shifts, are dispatched in pairs or alone, etc.,but these are just the sort of matters over which management exercises the most control. Those elements with which the public is especially concerned—when and how force is used, how the police deal with a noisy but peaceful drunk, the basis on which people are treated with suspicion—these are left to the individual officer's discretion.

Here is a convenient rule of thumb: Police will be disciplined when their behavior threatens the smooth operation of the institution. But there is a corollary to this: To the degree that officers collectively control the department, discipline will be weaker, as elites will have to bargain for access to the institution's power. This is one effect of police unionization.

Police labor action reminds local governments that they have created for themselves a rival to their own power. Unlike private-sector strikes, which threaten the bosses' ability to make a profit, public worker strikes threaten the local government's ability to provide services or, in the case of the police, to rule. They work by disrupting the city government's access to the institutions by which it achieves its ends. While a sit-down strike may raise the specter of workers controlling industry— since there is a natural continuum between workers' shutting down a plant, occupying it, and running it themselves—analogous actions by the police would fall on a different continuum and foreshadow less blissful social arrangements. If the police continued to patrol, make arrests, and otherwise conduct surveillance and distribute violence but without direction from the local government, this would amount to a transfer of power from the one institution to the other. It would portend the possibility of direct rule by the police.

In 1919 it was thought, clumsily, that this was a threat to be repressed. And such repression has occurred since then, when police excesses create the conditions for unrest or otherwise threaten the status quo. But police ambitions cannot be permanently repressed if the cops are to continue in their capacity, reliably suppressing the unruly portions of the population. And so, through a long series of reforms and negotiations, a strategy of co-optation developed, and with it emerged the instrument for balancing police loyalty with the demands of a semi-autonomous organization.

These instruments are generally called *unions*, though that misnomer—like so many others in "police science"—relies on a false analogy to other, dissimilar organizations. Police unions provide the means by which the officers can collectively negotiate with the civil authorities, determine together the rate and conditions under which loyalty may be ensured—loyalty to the police commanders, civil authorities, and the ruling class, respectively. It is not the loyalty of the individual officers that is at stake: They are not freelancers or mercenaries negotiating a fee for service. Rather, it is the loyalty of the institution that the officers collectively, through their union, may not control but *can* disable. Interestingly, this not only increases the power and autonomy of the union, but of the entire department, relative to the rest of the city government. The officers may, under rare conditions, even use their associations to compete with the civil authorities for control. Such power struggles are generally of short duration, but their effects can be long-lasting. They demonstrate the limit of police loyalty and the threat of mutiny—really, the usurpation of the institution—and in so doing they help to set the price for that loyalty. When that price is agreed on, the police again become fully available for the uses to which the ruling class, the state authorities, and their own commanders would put them.

As police organize, lobby, and strike, it seems that their negotiations have as much to do with the elites' access to, and the smooth functioning of, the police institution itself as with wages and working conditions. In this, police bargaining resembles less the struggles of exploited workers than the agreements formed between sovereigns and their intermediaries in the creation or expansion of states.[172] In fact, in at least one sense, police associations are best conceived of as semi-autonomous, but constitutive, parts of the state.

THE POLICE UNION AS A SEMI-AUTONOMOUS COMPONENT OF THE STATE

The independent organization of police officers has done a great deal to protect both individual cops and whole departments from meaningful oversight. Unionization has thus served to preserve patterns of abuse and discrimination, while at the same time advancing the agenda of law enforcement on the social and political fronts. This development represents, as per William Westley's analysis of police brutality, the collective usurpation of governmental authority and the means of violence.

> This process then results in a transfer in property from the state to the colleague group. The means of violence which were originally a property of the state, in loan to its law-enforcement agent, the police, are in a psychological sense confiscated by the police, to be conceived of as a personal property to be used at their discretion.[173]

But whereas Westley analyzed police brutality in terms of the informal, "psychological" confiscation of authority, union negotiations formalize the officers' claim to partial control of the institution and, by implication, its capacity for violence.[174]

Our earlier discussion of police brutality led us to pose a series of questions we are now primed to address. These were: To what degree is violence the "property" of the state? At what point does the police co-optation of violence challenge the state's monopoly on it? When do the police, in themselves, become a genuine rival of the state? Are they a rival to be used—as in a system of indirect rule—or a rival to be suppressed? Is there a genuine danger of the police becoming the dominant force in society, displacing the civilian authorities? Is this a problem for the ruling class? Might such a development, under certain conditions, be to their favor?

These questions suggest another, prior, question: *What is the state?* Let us begin with that.

It may seem odd to talk about an independent private organization, such as a police association, as a constitutive part of the state. The tendency is to think of the state as a monolithic institution claiming an exclusive right to the use of force. But this conception of state power is overly simple, both in terms of the state's actual operation and in terms of its historical development.

The state is not a unitary organization, but rather a complex network, with components termed "the welfare state," "the police state," etc., and with extensions identified as "the military-industrial complex," "the prison-industrial complex," and so on. Martin J. Smith defines the state as "a set of institutions which provide the parameters for political conflict between various interests over the use of resources and the direction of public policy."[175] As the state becomes increasingly differentiated and its power ever more diffuse, its precise edges become difficult to define and the public/private distinction grows hazy.[176] What has sometimes been hailed as a post-modern end to state sovereignty is in reality the modern state reaching maturity, drawing in additional elements, incorporating new sources of influence and legitimacy, and adjusting the balance of power accordingly.

Organizations and power networks win influence over the state according to their ability to aid or impede its operation (or to contribute to the aims of other institutional actors). Sometimes this influence will be established through sharp conflict and the decisive victory of one faction over another. More usually, however, it will be settled through a process of negotiation and bargaining. The latter is generally preferable, not only because it carries fewer costs than all-out battle, but also because by sharing power the various interests can oftentimes increase the power that is there to be shared.

> Within these networks, power is not simply wielded instrumentally by the autonomous state over social actors, or conversely by dominant social groups over a neutral or powerless state. Rather, power is to some extent *created* within these networks. . . . [I]t arises out of a relationship of dependence between state and social actors. Each actor provides something that the other cannot obtain on its own, and the power (or autonomy) of each is hence increased by the relationship.[177]

In the case of police officers, police administrators, police departments, and police unions, this dynamic is at work simultaneously on several levels. Individual officers share in the authority of the department, while the department maintains its power through the concerted efforts of its individual members. By joining together in independent associations, the member officers can effectively shape the policies and operations of the department, and can sometimes influence the policies and priorities of the government more broadly. When police unions and administrators make common cause, they can pressure the civil authorities to increase the power, resources, and independence of the department, because, to a certain extent, the civil authorities are always dependent on the cooperation of the police to defend their power and enforce their will.[178] Meanwhile, as the departments become more prominent as institutions, the share of power controlled by administrators and the unions increases proportionately, and the department finds itself well placed to form alliances with other government agencies, and sometimes private enterprises, enhancing the bargaining power of each.[179] And, in the process, departmental administrators and union leaders alike can increase their personal influence.[180]

This analysis is in keeping with the historical development of the state. Charles Tilly explains:

> Because no ruler or ruling coalition had absolute power and because classes outside the ruling coalition always held day-to-day control over a significant share of the resources rulers drew on for war, no state escaped the creation of some organizational burdens rulers would have preferred to avoid. A second, parallel process also generated unintended burdens for the state: as rulers created organizations either to make war or to draw the requisites of war from the subject population—not only armies and navies but also tax offices, customs services, treasuries, regional administrations, and armed forces to forward their work among the civilian population—they discovered that the organizations themselves developed interests, rights, perquisites, needs, and demands requiring attention on their own.[181]

Within this theoretical framework, it is possible to briefly reinterpret the history of policing. The use of legitimate violence, which was originally the "property" of individual slaveholders, heads of households, and various secular and ecclesiastic authorities, was slowly formalized and consolidated. On the local level, this process produced slave patrols and then police. Initially, the police were highly dependent on local patrons and served as the instruments of political machines. As the capitalist class and its middle-class supporters took control of the government, the police were transformed to a tool of class rule. The destruction of the machines, however, required the creation of formal bureaucracies, which quickly came to develop interests of their own and started to formulate their own demands. The police were the prototypical bureaucracy, and the following wave of professionalization only further decreased their dependence on the municipal administration while reinforcing the organization's loyalty to the ruling class. The police rebellion came when the lowest ranking officers reacted against the demands of professionalization while taking advantage of the autonomy it granted. They organized independently and began presenting demands at every level—of administrators, of city and state officials, of legislatures, and of society. Because a strike would disrupt the city government's power and therefore also weaken the state's protection of the ruling class's interests, the rank and file held enough control over the state's coercive apparatus to credibly threaten its access to force, even if they could not fully mobilize this force for their own purposes. By this telling, the coup of police unionization did not represent a sharp break from the institution's previous development, but instead signaled a new step in the pre-existing pattern. The emergence of the police as social and political actors marked the maturity of the institution.

The police have always been thugs, but they have traditionally been thugs in the service of elites. The crises of the 1960s produced an outbreak of police hooliganism directed against the citizenry (especially Blacks, students, and radicals) and a revolt against their own commanders and the civil authorities. The police, in short, became self-conscious political actors seeking to defend their own interests, advance their own agenda, act under their own authority, and increase their already substantial power. Such a development is very dangerous for a wavering democracy like that of the United States.

An uneasy truce has developed between the cops and the civil authorities. Police departments have been granted a great deal of autonomy concerning their policies, procedures, and discipline. This allows for peace between the civil authorities and the police while maintaining a degree of plausible deniability concerning misconduct, as long as abuse is directed against suitable targets: racial minorities and the poor.

So, to answer our earlier questions: *To what degree is violence the "property" of the state?* In the United States, the state has increasingly exercised monopolistic control over legitimate violence, especially since the early nineteenth century. However, given the networked nature of power relations constituting the state, the means of violence have always been invested in some particular institution or set of institutions that carried, to a greater or lesser degree, the potential for independent action.

At what point does the police co-optation of violence challenge the state's monopoly? When do the police, in themselves, become a genuine rival of the state? Are they a rival to be used (as in a system of indirect rule) or a rival to be suppressed? Given their unique bargaining position (only the military can compete with the cops' potential for organized violence), the possibility of police dominance of the government cannot be discounted. So far, they have not achieved permanent ascendancy in any city, and nationally their influence has been rather limited. On the other hand, since their inception the police have been increasingly central to any power network that succeeds in controlling local government, and there is no indication that this trend is being reversed.

Of course, so long as the faction that maintains control of the apparatus of violence remains loyal to, and incorporated within, the network that is the state, the development of semi-autonomous police institutions may actually bolster the power of the state, especially in times of crisis when that power is challenged. Under these conditions, though it may require shifting power and resources to the criminal justice system at the expense of other state enterprises, the police may—in part *because* of their high level of independent organization—be effectively used by the dominant group. But if the police mutiny for either material or ideological reasons, or if they begin to make demands that the government cannot accommodate, police control of institutional resources may threaten the power of civil authorities. Under such conditions, the civil authorities will feel compelled to break the police unions for the sake of preserving their own position.

Is there a genuine danger of the police becoming the dominant force in society, displacing the civilian authorities? A simple armed revolt would invite intervention at the state or federal level, and would surely fail. But, it is conceivable that the police could seize control of a local government if they proceeded with a combination of electoral and bully-boy tactics, on the Rizzo and Giuliani model. For the police to seize control nationally, they would either need to be networked on that level to a greater extent than they are at present, or else gain the assistance of some other institution (e.g., the military).

Is this a problem for the ruling class? Might it, under certain conditions, be to their favor? Logically speaking, it is possible that police-rule would favor the ruling class. For example, capitalists may feel that the cops are more willing or able to defend their interests than are the civilian authorities. This may especially be the case if the authorities are so divided as to threaten regime collapse, while the police retain the unity necessary to take control and keep order. The significance of the 1967 riots for the Detroit police strike is precisely this: The state is more tolerant of some rivals than others, more willing to accept some challenges to its power than others, and more ready to bargain with its long-term allies than to face defeat at the hands of immediate antagonists. As rebellions go, a police rebellion is particularly likely to gain the support of elites. For though police autonomy diminishes the power of the courts, civil government, and the rule of law vis-á-vis the police. It tends on the whole to preserve the inequalities extant in the status quo, including the inequalities inherent in these other institutions.

Of course, a full-force police state may make economic demands that prove inconvenient for business and would almost certainly hinder the fully autonomous operation of industry. But under certain conditions, especially those of social crisis, the ruling class may prefer the stability of police or military rule, with all its accompanying constraints, to the possibility of facing extinction in the course of revolution. (It was just such considerations that led the middle and upper classes to support Franco in Spain, and later, Pinochet in Chile.)[182] More likely, however, is a "soft" coup, by which the police gradually gain a dominant position within the local government, though never becoming the only voice. The police could then form the center and base for a new kind of machine, building the necessary alliances with other social actors, but keeping the power in the stationhouse rather than in the wards. Formally representative structures could remain in place while the police use their power to squash dissent, engineer campaigns, and shape policies—making the most of their practical monopoly on organized violence. This would seem the natural ideal of "Blue Power," and while it may prove compatible to the needs of capitalism, it is an obvious threat to democracy.

The police have been transformed from a wholly dependent tool of the political machines to an independent source of power. I noted in an earlier chapter that the development of modern police forces marked an unprecedented incursion on the part of the state into the lives of citizens, and signified in retrospect a clear step toward totalitarianism.[183] As the police institution has evolved, it has become a major source of power not only *for* the state, but *within* the state. This achievement represents another step in the same direction: As the institutions of violence become more autonomous, they isolate themselves from democratic control. This is bad enough, surely, but as these same institutions gain influence over policy and social priorities, they inhibit the representative aspects of other parts of government. Blue Power reduces the possibility of democracy.

While the police were undergoing their metamorphosis, from instrument of the machines to bureaucratic apparatus of class rule, to independent political force, they were simultaneously challenging democracy in other ways and expanding their social influence in some surprising directions. The task of the police in preserving race and class hierarchies made them experts in suppressing dissent, and police departments quickly developed specializations in this regard. More recently, as we shall see, these same designs have led them to seek ever-more involvement and greater shares of influence in aspects of social life quite removed from law enforcement.

SECRET POLICE, RED SQUADS, AND THE STRATEGY OF PERMANENT REPRESSION

7

Police intervention during industrial strife has had a complex legacy, producing detailed riot control strategies and specialized units to handle political intelligence. Judging by appearances, one might not think that these two sets of activities have very much to do with each other. Riot cops wear full protective gear and operate in ways that are by definition very public. The stereotypical trenchcoat aside, police spies usually wear no uniform at all, and their activities are often covert. The targets are generally unaware of police intelligence activity; the public at large barely recognizes its existence. But historically, red squads were formed with crowd control in mind, and took on their secret police functions later.[1] Separate divisions currently handle these duties, but their operations remain connected at the root. The riot cop and the secret policeman provide the two faces of political repression.[2]

HAYMARKET: "ANARCHY IS ON TRIAL."

The role of police in crushing dissent, and the place of intelligence work within that pursuit, began to take shape in 1886 in response to the movement for an eight-hour workday. In May of that year, the nation saw a wave of strikes demanding "Eight hours for work. Eight hours for sleep. Eight hours for what you will."[3] Much of the action was centered in Chicago, where on May 1, 40,000 workers walked off the job, and were joined a few days later by 25,000 more.[4]

On May 3, police shot and killed four workers picketing the McCormick Harvester Works. Enraged, August Spies, an anarchist, printed a forceful handbill calling for an open-air meeting on May 4 in Haymarket Square. The flier was headed "Workingmen, To Arms," and encouraged workers to come prepared to defend themselves.[5]

The rally began as a typical affair. Three thousand people came to listen to speeches, but as the evening wore on and storm clouds gathered, their numbers dwindled to just a few hundred. At last, when the final speaker was on stage, 180 police appeared and ordered the crowd to disperse. In response, someone from the crowd—it has never been determined who—threw a bomb into the line of police. Seventy-six cops were injured, seven later died. The police immediately opened fire, killing about a dozen of the crowd and injuring 200 more, as well as hitting some of their own.[6]

The Haymarket bomb cost the eight-hour movement dearly, dividing the radicals from their natural base of support—unionists—and setting off the first serious red scare in American history.[7] On May 5 and 6, police under the leadership of Captain Michael J. Schaack made more than fifty raids against newspaper offices, union halls, and other radical meeting spots.[8] State Attorney Julius Grinnell urged the cops, "Make the raids first and look up the law afterwards."[9] Schaack apparently decided not to bother with the law at all. His published notes detailed seventy interrogations conducted during this period; they revealed that prisoners had been denied lawyers, food, water, and medical treatment.[10] Meanwhile, around the country, state legislatures hurriedly passed laws limiting the rights of labor unions, and courts began convicting strikers en masse.[11] This climate of political repression lasted well into the 1890s.

Of those arrested, eight anarchists were charged with murder: August Spies, Albert Parsons, Adolph Fischer, Samuel Fielden, Michael Schwab, Louis Lingg, Oscar Neebe, and George Engel. While it was never learned who threw the bomb, it was certainly none of these men. Most of them weren't even at the Haymarket. Those who were there were on the speaker's platform, in plain sight. Nevertheless, after a highly irregular and explicitly political trial,[12] all eight were convicted and seven were sentenced to hang. Neebe was sentenced to fifteen years.

The tool for convicting innocent men of a capital offense was the claim that they had urged others to violence, and were therefore responsible for the violence that occurred. The prosecutor had originally sought to prove that the defendants had executed the bombing themselves. Failing that, he resorted to a theory that they had conspired together to kill policemen, crafting a plot carried out by another, unknown person. But there was no evidence for any such plot. So instead, the case came to rely on the allegation that the person who threw the bomb had been driven to do so by the defendants' anarchistic writings and fiery speeches. Over the objections of the defense, the prosecutor read aloud the fiercest anarchist writings he could lay his hands on.[13] Some of these were written by the defendants, others were not. Nobody paid much attention to such details, as the purpose of this "evidence" was purely prejudicial.

State's Attorney Julius Grinnell put it this way, as he addressed the jury:

> Law is on trial. Anarchy is on trial. These men have been selected, picked out by the grand jury and indicted because they were leaders. They are no more guilty that the thousands who follow them. Gentlemen of the jury; convict these men, make examples of them and you save our institutions, our society.[14]

That it was anarchy on trial, Albert Parsons agreed. He wrote to a friend:

> There is no evidence . . . that I or any of us killed, or had anything
> to do with the killing of policemen at the Haymarket. None at all.
> But it was proven clearly that we were, all of us, anarchists, social-
> ists, communists, Knights of Labor, unionists. It was proven that
> three of us were editors of labor papers; that five of us were labor
> organizers and speakers at workingmen's mass meetings. They, this
> class court, jury, law and verdict, have decided that we must be put
> to death because, as they say, we are "leaders" of men who denounce
> and battle against the oppression, slavery, robbery and influences of
> the monopolists. Of these crimes against the capitalist class they
> found us guilty beyond a reasonable doubt, and, so finding, they
> have sentenced us.[15]

Parsons, Spies, and Engel eventually did hang. Lingg committed suicide while
awaiting execution. The survivors first had their sentences commuted to life imprisonment, and six years later were pardoned by Governor John Altgeld. Altgeld made
it clear in issuing his pardon that he did so because "much of the evidence given at
the trial was a pure fabrication . . . "[16]

Unfortunately, Haymarket established the pattern that anti-radical campaigns
would follow for the century to come. The basic elements are present: In a climate
of conflict and political polarization, an incident of dubious origin provides the pretext for suppressing radical movements. Raids, arrests, and media smear campaigns
lead up to a criminal trial, at which the defendants' political views and associations
are presented as evidence.

The authorities involved in the Haymarket affair, Captain Schaack especially,
pioneered the use of radical-hunting as a means of building a career, consolidating
power, and lining one's pockets at the same time. Schaack used his position for
shameless self-promotion, casting himself as a first-class sleuth, bragging about
conspiracies he had supposedly unearthed and plots he had foiled, and even writing
a book on the matter, *Anarchy and Anarchists*. On top of this, Schaack gained control of a slush fund established by the conservative "Chicago Citizens' Association"
and used its resources to bribe witnesses, hire informers, and pay for other related
investigative expenses. In addition to this considerable sum, it was later revealed
that he had, on more than one occasion, personally accepted bribes and helped himself to a great deal of the "evidence" seized in various raids.[17]

Schaack quickly became dependent on the role he had created for himself, the
great anarchist hunter. To justify continued operations, he began creating the conspiracies he was to uncover. In 1889, Police Chief Frederick Ebersold told the *Chicago
Times*:

> Captain Schaack wanted to keep things stirring. He wanted bombs to
> be found here, there, all around, everywhere. I thought people would

lie down to sleep better if they were not afraid their homes would be blown to pieces any minute. But this man, Schaack . . . wanted none of that policy. . . . After we got the anarchist societies broken up, Schaack wanted to send out people to organize new societies right away. . . . He wanted to keep the thing boiling, keep himself prominent before the public.[18]

Haymarket was not the first police excursion into the realm of political spying, but it did signify the beginning of a new trend.

The Haymarket tragedy . . . marked the emergence of a new form of policing: anarchists were indiscriminately surveilled not only as a means of crime suppression, but for ideological reasons alone. . . . This style of ideological warfare against anarchism broke ground for subsequent similar police initiatives against socialism and communism.[19]

REPRESSION 101

There's nothing surprising about the antagonism between anarchists and authorities. Anarchists oppose the powerful and the institutions that maintain their power, especially the state. They don't like bosses, bureaucrats, politicians, landlords, or cops. And, for the most part, the feeling is mutual.

The state's reaction to such opposition is equally unsurprising. It is the nature of power to preserve itself, and this requires that efforts to change the structures of society be actively opposed by those who profit from the existing order. "Repression is a process by which those in power try to keep themselves in power by consciously attempting to destroy or render harmless organizations and ideologies that threaten their power."[20] Repression may be accomplished through propaganda, indoctrination, and other ideological means, or when these fail, through more direct means like harassment, imprisonment, and violence.

More specifically, "political repression . . . in the context of policing, may be defined as police behavior motivated or influenced in whole or in part by hostility to protest, dissent, and related activities perceived as a threat to the status quo."[21] In addition to the means listed above, repression may involve a much broader range of both overt and covert activities, including surveillance, false arrest, media smear campaigns, the use of disinformation, burglary, blackmail, infiltration, sabotage, the promotion of factionalism, entrapment, threats, brutality, assassinations, and torture.

The form repression takes and the intensity with which it is applied will depend on a variety of factors, including the aims of the target group, its popularity, its strengths and weaknesses, its methods, and the goals, popularity, and relative strength or vulnerability of the government. But whatever its shape, the purpose of repression remains essentially the same. Based on his experiences in Northern Ireland, Kenya, Cyprus, and elsewhere in the crumbling British empire, military strategist Frank Kitson described the task facing a government when rebellion surfaces:

> Translated into normal terms, the aim of the government is to regain if necessary and then retain the allegiance of the population, and for this purpose it must eliminate those involved in subversion. But in order to eliminate the subversive party and its unarmed and armed supporters, it must gain control of the population.[22]

Repression is a tricky business. And it is complicated by the fact that the initiative seems to always rest with the subversives. Rebellions may brew, discontent spread, revolutionaries prepare their forces, all before the government even realizes it is facing a threat. Intelligence work is intended to fill this gap.

The Senate Select Committee to Study Government Operations With Respect to Intelligence Activities (the Church Committee) outlines the three types of intelligence activities:

> The first is intelligence collection—such as infiltrating groups with informants, wiretapping or opening letters. The second is dissemination of material which has been collected. The third is covert action designed to disrupt and discredit the activities of groups and individuals deemed a threat to the social order. These three types of "intelligence" activity are closely related in the practical world. Information which is disseminated by the intelligence community or used in disruptive programs has usually been obtained through surveillance.[23]

Furthermore, the same techniques may be used for more than one goal simultaneously. Surveillance has its obvious uses in collecting information, but conspicuous surveillance may also be used to harass the target, breed paranoia and feelings of persecution, and so on. Likewise, informants can supply information, but they can also be used to disrupt a group's organizing efforts, engaging in routine sabotage, provoking rivalries and in-fighting, and encouraging illegal (especially violent) activities that can discredit the organization.

The specific strategies and techniques involved have been developed over time, with the twentieth century representing a period of particular advancement. The degree of actual activity has ebbed and flowed, for the most part following the level of dissident political activity particularly dissent from the left. At the national level, this work has been centered in the federal intelligence agencies—the FBI, the CIA, Army Intelligence—but has also come to involve, at times, practically every federal agency and every branch of government. At the local level, the bulk of intelligence work has been shared between the police and innumerable private agencies, beginning with the Pinkertons. Within police departments, the branches responsible for keeping the lid on subversives have gone under a wide variety of names, including the "Radical Bureau," the "Anarchist Squad," the "Bomb Squad," the "Intelligence Division," the "Industrial Squad," the "Bureau of Special Services," the "Special Investigations Bureau," and others. For the sake of regularity, I will refer to them here primarily under the generic term "red squad."

THE RED SQUADS

New York City's red squad got a head start on the rest of the country.

On January 13, 1874, in what came to be termed the "Tompkins Square Riot," 7,000 people took to the streets in a demonstration against unemployment, and the police responded by ruthlessly beating them. Following that debacle, the police department began assigning detectives to spy on socialist and union meetings.[24] Within just a few years, their operations expanded enormously. In 1895 and 1896 the NYPD tapped 350 phones, including those of churches.[25]

This pattern was repeated in cities around the United States. The police began by attacking public events, especially demonstrations. They rigorously enforced laws, forcibly dispersed crowds, and expended a great deal of energy trying to identify and nab individual agitators who, they assumed, must be responsible for any such disturbance. This latter pursuit quickly developed to the point where police targeted entire organizations, sending informants to their meetings.[26] The creation of special branches devoted to this task took hold after 1900, prompted by labor unrest, the increased popularity of socialism, and a wave of immigration.[27]

The role of the red squads further expanded during World War I, thanks in part to Attorney General A. Mitchell Palmer and his curious notion of national security. Local cops aided the Justice Department first in 1917, with a series of raids against the Industrial Workers of the World. IWW headquarters were raided in eleven cities and hundreds of union leaders were arrested, allegedly for interfering with the draft. The red squads repeated their performance two years later, beginning in 1919, as they provided support for Justice Department raids on a wide range of leftist organizations, resulting in 4,000 arrests and almost 1,000 deportations.[28] Local police agencies found support for these endeavors among the members of the American Protective League, a volunteer organization formed during the war to combat espionage and sabotage, round up draft-dodgers, and spy on immigrants. Many APL "volunteers" were actually off-duty cops; others were deputized to assist in raids.[29]

During this same period, laws regulating demonstrations, meetings, and leafleting granted the police broad powers to determine when, where, and what speech would be allowed. It thus became the explicit function of the police to suppress the free exercise of political speech.[30]

As the Great Depression produced a swell of activism and unrest, police practices shifted toward a focus on intelligence operations rather than direct intervention. Intelligence became a distinct pursuit, very nearly its own profession, increasingly removed from law enforcement. While the potential for such a division had been present as early as 1886, it became institutionalized during the 1930s as red squads paid less attention to public disorder and more to the organizations and movements behind such discord.[31]

This change in emphasis was accompanied by a marked escalation in tactics. Increasing numbers of informants were employed against an ever-wider array of organizations. The most spectacular abuses, of course, are those directed from the top. During the 1930s, Los Angeles' red squad had been used to target the mayor's critics and political opponents, even to the point of outright blackmail. At the same time, active disruption of organizations became a higher priority, often greatly overreaching the authority granted the police, and even directly violating the law. For instance, the head of the Los Angeles red squad, Captain Earl Kynette, was convicted and imprisoned in connection with a 1938 car bomb explosion that critically injured a member of a reform group, the Citizen's Independent Investigating Committee, which had been leading a campaign against police corruption, an effort certain to draw the ire of the authorities.[32]

Kynette's zealotry led not only to a prison term, but to the dissolution of his squad as well. Shortly after his conviction, the City Council eliminated its funding. Elsewhere in the country, red squads fell victim to their own success. In the conservative climate of the 1950s, they faced a repeat of Captain Schaack's problem: a shortage of subversives. The response to this situation was two-fold. In part, red squads focused again on their historical opponents, labor unions. At the same time, they were granted a new mission as auxiliary forces in the Cold War. But while the FBI still relied on local police for a great deal of information, the special units saw their numbers and resources dwindle.[33] As a result, red squads became increasingly isolated within local departments and their activities became even more removed from regular police work.

The upheavals of the sixties and the seventies made police spying a priority again, but did nothing to reverse the federalization of intelligence, the specialization of red squad operations, or their organizational culture and its distance from other police not to mention the citizenry. Instead, as police were continually called on to suppress what seemed to be ever-growing social movements, these characteristics only solidified. As the role of red squads expanded and the number of officers involved grew, the flaws, faults, and excesses of intelligence agencies, perhaps of intelligence per se, increased in magnitude and became more readily apparent.

A RENAISSANCE OF REPRESSION

During the 1960s, in city after city, red squads suddenly swelled like an unpleasant fungus. Detroit's intelligence unit had only six members at the end of the 1950s; by 1968 that number had grown to seventy. In most places, the rate of growth was accelerated spectacularly at the very end of the decade. Between 1968 and 1970, the New York City red squad went from sixty-eight uniformed officers to ninety (plus fifty-five others assigned to undercover work). During the same period, Los Angeles increased its squad from eighty-four officers to 167.[34] The Chicago Police Department had 500 intelligence officers at the end of the decade, and Illinois State Police Superintendent James T. McGuire estimated that more than 1,000 federal, state, and local operatives were working in the area undercover.[35]

As the popular movements developed—first the civil rights movement, then student movements, anti-war efforts, and a host of others—the police understanding of these campaigns, their objectives, and the conditions producing them seriously lagged. The police response, as though from habit, was to blame a conspiracy and seek out the agitators creating all this turmoil. Hence identification procedures retained their central place in the strategy of repression, and photography became a sort of obsession. As with infiltration, wiretapping, and the collection of dossiers, photography was easily exploited as a means of intimidation as well as data gathering.[36] At times, intimidation became the *primary* function of police photography; cops would take numerous pictures at close range or, alternately, show their "subject" photographs of herself when she hadn't realized she was under surveillance. Conspicuous surveillance was often accompanied by other forms of harassment as well, including slashed tires, verbal abuse, and arbitrary arrests.[37]

As the role of surveillance was extended, the number and type of subjects increased as well. By the end of the 1960s, many red squads were building straightforward enemies lists, going after people outside of any radical movement. For example, after the 1968 Democratic Convention, the Chicago police maintained files on churches and members of the clergy, newspaper columnists and radio commentators, an ACLU attorney, the League of Women Voters, the Parent-Teacher Association, the chair of Sears and Roebuck, the president of Notre Dame University, State's Attorney Bernard M. Carey, prosecuting attorney Barnabas Sears, Dan Walker (author of the Walker Report on the 1968 Democratic Convention, and later governor), U.S. Senator Charles Percy, seven sitting or former aldermen, fifteen members of the Illinois General Assembly, the chair of the First National Bank, Chicago Bears runningback Gayle Sayers, and Congressional Representative Ralph Metcalf.[38] A few years later, Philadelphia Mayor Frank Rizzo created a special thirty-three-member intelligence unit, answerable directly to him. The unit's sole purpose was to investigate two of Rizzo's political adversaries, city councilor Peter J. Caniel and city council president George X. Schwartz.[39]

As the range of targets grew, so did the range of tactics—first to improve surveillance and then, as is the pattern, harass leaders, cripple organizations, and interfere with their political efforts. Wiretaps and mail opening came very much into fashion during this period.[40] As in the thirties, informers were employed in increasing numbers, with a key difference—whereas previously infiltration was done primarily by private detectives or civilian volunteers, in the 1960s it became the norm to use police officers themselves.[41]

Interestingly, the specialization of undercover work did nothing to abate the agent's development from passive observer to saboteur, and then, from saboteur to provocateur. In fact, informers often suggested the plan, supplied the weapons, drove the car, and then made the arrest. ACLU attorney Frank Donner observes, "The most common *provocateur* is simply a professional police agent who coldly engineers a single provocative act designed to 'set up' leaders for roundup and arrest."[42]

An infiltrator's success didn't always rely on discrediting an organization or bringing legal action against them. For example, in 1967 the New York Police Department sent Richard Lyons, a civilian, into the Veterans and Reservists Against the War (V&R). During the two years he was a member, he advocated that the V&R attack soldiers with tear gas, burn GI weapons authorization cards (a federal offense), charge police lines during demonstrations, and carry replica machine guns. Each suggestion was firmly rejected in favor of legal and nonviolent tactics. Nevertheless, when he was finally exposed in 1968, the knowledge that they had been infiltrated greatly added to feelings of demoralization and contributed to the V&R's collapse.[43]

In part, the work of infiltrators represented a move away from reactive practices and toward a proactive, anticipatory approach. Hence, red squads justified many of their activities with the claim that they were necessary in order to prevent violence. On the contrary, infiltrators often *encouraged* violence, as the V&R case shows. And the red squads' methods carried with them inherent barriers to law enforcement. For example, information gathered illegally was usually inadmissible in court, and the reluctance to identify informants greatly limited their utility in actual prosecutions.[44]

Add to this the fact that so much of the "information" police gathered was hopelessly off base. One Chicago cop told a Cook County Grand Jury that he listed as a "member" of an organization anyone who attended two of its public meetings. This "information" was passed on to the FBI, and disseminated from there.[45] More recently, in 2002, files leaked to activist groups revealed that the Denver Police Department had used the label "criminal extremist" as a default category when no other description seemed to apply. Featured under this heading were political activists, members of the clergy, troubled students, and, for some reason, people who had received honors from the department itself. A commission appointed by the mayor determined that none of the 3,400 files could be legitimately maintained, and ordered them destroyed. But the files, and their inaccuracies, had already been passed on to other agencies.[46]

The harm of such exaggeration is multiplied as misinformation is spread from one agency to others. For example, in 1973 the Seattle Police Department's intelligence division opened a file on a local Chicano activist. The American Friends Service Committee described the report's transformation as it changed hands.

> It began: "Modus Operandi—participant in demonstrations, support-
> ing UFW x Safeway (sic), establishment of El Centro." His only police
> record is for failure to disperse during a demonstration. By 1976,
> however, in describing him to the Portland Police Intelligence
> Division, Seattle Police stated, "M.O. Chicano activist—advocates ter-
> rorist acts." There is no information in the SPD intelligence files to
> support such a defamatory and damaging claim.[47]

Inaccuracies and distortions are phenomena familiar to anyone who reads even standard police reports, but the potential for mis-reporting is amplified by the nature of undercover work (especially when informants are paid for the information).

> Both the pressures and inducements, along with the sense of guilt
> that requires the betrayer to find some justification for his betrayal,
> tend to produce tainted information. All too frequently it is inaccu-
> rate, highly selective, and based on sinister and unwarranted infer-
> ences. Where a literal version of a target's utterances would seem
> innocent, the informer will insist on stressing the connotations; con-
> versely, where the language is figurative or metaphysical [sic] the
> informer reports it as literally intended. Most important of all, he
> seizes on the transient fantasies of the powerless—rhetoric and
> images not intended to be acted upon—and transforms them into
> conspiracies whose purpose and commitment are wholly alien to
> their volatile and ambiguous context.[48]

These interpretive practices underscore the symbolic value of red squad files. At first a simple administrative tool for collecting and organizing evidence, these files, like so much in the field of intelligence, quickly became a means of intimidation, and eventually became an end in themselves, serving to legitimize the red squad's other activities.[49]

More often than not, the reported violence was only a much-exaggerated pretext for heavier repression. Frank Donner describes the pattern as it appeared in Philadelphia:

> Based on information typically supplied by a street tipster or casual
> informant, or "discovered" through several weeks of intensive sur-

veillance by the CD [the Civil Disobedience Unit], police would raid a private residence where they assertedly found explosives, guns, or inflammatory literature. A torrent of Rizzo-inspired publicity would then link the raided premises and the seized material to a group of militants, which, it usually suggested, was part of a larger and more powerful movement. Front-page stories under banner headlines would quote Rizzo's blood-chilling description of the plot, miraculously aborted, and the closeness of the city's escape from destruction. Bail would be set at astronomical levels, but prosecution of the culprits usually faltered. After long delays (months and even years), the back pages of the newspapers whose front pages had originally blazed with reports of the sensational arrests would limply record that the prosecution had been dropped altogether or the defendants plead guilty to lesser charges (usually possession of weapons) or other, unrelated charges.[50]

The Philadelphia branch of the Student Nonviolent Coordinating Committee (SNCC) was destroyed by just such a "dynamite plot," as was the Revolutionary Action Movement and, after several such raids, the Philadelphia chapter of the Black Panther Party.[51]

COINTELPRO: THE FBI'S GREATEST HITS

The Black Panthers bear the uneasy distinction of being the most targeted organization of the late 1960s, perhaps the most targeted organization of all American history. The Panthers were persecuted—there is no other word—by a campaign, code-named COINTELPRO for "COunter INTELligence PROgram". COINTELPRO was explicitly designed, in the words of FBI Director J. Edgar Hoover, "to expose, disrupt, misdirect, discredit, or otherwise neutralize the activities of black nationalist, hate-type organizations and groupings, their leadership, spokesmen, membership, and supporters, and to counter their propensity for violence and civil disorder."[52]

The Church Committee offers more detail:

COINTELPRO tactics included:
—Anonymously attacking the political beliefs of targets in order to induce their employers to fire them;
—Anonymously mailing letters to the spouses of intelligence targets for the purpose of destroying their marriages;
—Obtaining from IRS the tax returns of a target and then attempting to provoke an IRS investigation for the express purpose of deterring a protest leader from attending the Democratic National Convention;

—Falsely and anonymously labeling as Government informants members of groups known to be violent, thereby exposing the falsely labeled member to expulsion or physical attack;

—Pursuant to instructions to use "misinformation" to disrupt demonstrations, employing such means as broadcasting false orders on the same citizens' band radio frequency used by demonstration marshals to attempt to control demonstrations, and duplicating and falsely filling out forms soliciting housing for persons coming to a demonstration, thereby causing "long and useless journeys to locate these addresses". . . . [53]

The Church Committee report devotes a small section specifically to "Cooperation Between the Federal Bureau of Investigation and Local Police Departments in Disrupting the Black Panther Party." It details file sharing practices involving the FBI and the police in San Diego, Oakland, Los Angeles, and Chicago, as well as FBI-instigated raids in San Diego and Chicago, and an FBI-directed disinformation campaign in Oakland.[54] What the report *doesn't* say is that between December 1967 and December 1969, twenty-eight Panthers were killed as the result of police attacks.[55] It would require another book to consider all of these cases in detail, but a couple of examples may be quite telling.

In Chicago, efforts to disrupt the Black Panther Party focused on a young leader named Fred Hampton. First, the FBI tried to trigger a feud between the Panthers and a local street gang, the Blackstone Rangers. FBI operatives sent Ranger leader Jeff Fort an anonymous letter claiming that Hampton had ordered his assassination. This tactic seems to have been selected in hopes of producing violence. The FBI memo describing it reads:

> It is believed that the [letter] may intensify the degree of animosity between the two groups and occasion Forte [sic] to take retaliatory action which could disrupt the BPP or lead to reprisals against its leadership. . . . Consideration has been given to a similar letter to the BPP alleging a Ranger plot against BPP leadership; however, it is not felt that this would be productive principally because the BPP . . . is not believed to be as violence prone as the Rangers, to whom violent type activity—shooting and the like—is second nature.[56]

When the letter failed to produce the desired results, the FBI moved on to more direct means of neutralizing Hampton.

On the morning of December 4, 1969, at 4 A.M., fourteen police armed with submachine guns literally shot their way into Hampton's apartment. The police fired ninety-eight rounds, killing Fred Hampton and Mark Clark, head of the Peoria, Illinois BPP, and injuring three others. Only a single round of fire was returned—by

Clark, as he died. Hampton was shot five times—three times in the chest, and then twice in the head.

The raid had been planned a few weeks before by COINTELPRO operative Roy Mitchell and two cops assigned to a special unit under the direction of State's Attorney Edward V. Hanrahan. Mitchell had met with Hampton's body guard, William O'Neal, and received from him a detailed floorplan of the apartment, including the location of Hampton's bed. He also arranged for O'Neal to drug Hampton with a barbiturate on the night in question. A week after the raid, Robert Piper, the Chicago COINTELPRO section head, requested a $300 bonus for O'Neal.[57]

In this case we see local police, under the direction of the FBI, serving as nothing other than a death squad.

Four days after the Chicago raid, forty SWAT officers and more than 100 backups launched a similar attack in Los Angeles. Under the leadership of red squad detective Ray Callahan, and again working from a floorplan provided by an FBI informant, the police began their offensive at 5:30 in the morning. This time, however, the target, Panther leader Elmer "Geronimo" Pratt, was not in his bed. The opening burst of gunfire missed him altogether. The Panthers held the police off until the media arrived and a crowd had formed; then, they surrendered. Six were wounded and thirteen arrested, but no one was killed.[58]

The raid was a dud, but the campaign against Pratt continued, eventually resulting in his arrest for the 1968 robbery and murder of Caroline Olsen in Los Angeles. Pratt maintained that he was at a Black Panther Party meeting in Oakland when the crime was committed, a fact verified by other testimony.[59] The defense sought to support the alibi with the FBI's phone tap records, but the feds wouldn't cooperate. They first denied that the telephone at the Oakland BPP office was tapped, then admitted that it was but refused to turn over the records on "national security" grounds, and finally produced the records, except for those from the period relevant to the murder case, which they claimed were lost.[60] Pratt was convicted of first degree murder and sentenced to life in prison.

The conviction rested on the testimony of Julius Butler, a former party member who claimed that Pratt had admitted to the murder. The prosecutor failed to mention that his key witness was on the police payroll, and Butler vehemently denied it under oath, saying he'd "never been in all the world a snitch."[61] Years later, documents surfaced identifying Butler as a paid informant for the FBI, LAPD, and District Attorney's office.[62] Furthermore, an FBI report from June 1970 frankly admitted the bureau's interest in Pratt: "Constant consideration is given to the possibility of utilization of counter-intelligence measures with effort being directed toward neutralizing Pratt as an effective B.P.P. functionary."[63] After years of legal delays, in 1997 a conservative Reagan-appointed judge, Everett W. Dickey, overturned Pratt's conviction.[64] Pratt, now going under the name Geronimo ji Jaga, spent twenty-seven years as a political prisoner, nearly a third of that in solitary confinement.[65]

BEYOND COINTELPRO

COINTELPRO was only one aspect of the relationship between local red squads and the federal government. Beginning in 1968, the Law Enforcement Assistance Administration supplied grants to intelligence units for training and equipment.[66] At about this same time, the Justice Department's Interdivisional Information Unit (IDIU) provided the means for intelligence agencies at all levels, and from around the country, to share information. According the Church report, this established a system through which

> the Attorney General received the benefits of information gathered
> by numerous agencies, without setting limits to intelligence report-
> ing or providing clear policy guidance. Each component of the struc-
> ture—FBI, Army, IDIU, local police, and many others—set its own
> generalized standards and priorities, resulting in excessive collection
> of information about law abiding citizens.[67]

Nor was this the extent of federal involvement: Throughout the late 1960s New York City's red squad gave daily briefings to Army intelligence.[68] In Chicago, the U.S. Army Region I, 113th Military Intelligence Group not only trained and traded information with the local police, but participated in interrogations.[69]

Never willing to be left out of the action, the CIA offered a six-week training course for local law enforcement personnel, teaching cops the basics of surreptitious entry, photographic surveillance, electronic eavesdropping, and the manufacture and use of explosives. Members of at least forty-four state, county, and municipal police departments received this training, and in return the locals helped the agency gather information, protect informants, and harass its critics.[70]

Since the practices of local cops inevitably came to resemble those of the organizations that trained, funded, supplied, and directed them, it is worth considering the conduct of these federal agencies. The Church Committee summed it up:

> Too many people have been spied upon by too many Government
> agencies and to [sic] much information has been collected. The
> Government has often undertaken the secret surveillance of citizens
> on the basis of their political beliefs, even when these beliefs posed
> no threat of violence or illegal acts on behalf of a hostile foreign
> power. The Government, operating primarily through secret inform-
> ants, but also using other intrusive techniques such as wiretaps,
> microphone "bugs", surreptitious mail opening, and break-ins, has

swept in vast amounts of information about the personal lives, views, and associations of American citizens. Investigations of groups deemed potentially dangerous—and even of groups suspected of associating with potentially dangerous organizations—have continued for decades, despite the fact that those groups did not engage in unlawful activity. Groups and individuals have been harassed and disrupted because of their political views and their lifestyles. Investigations have been based upon vague standards whose breadth made excessive collection inevitable. Unsavory and vicious tactics have been employed—including anonymous attempts to break up marriages, disrupt meetings, ostracize persons from their professions, and provoke target groups into rivalries that might result in deaths. Intelligence agencies have served the political and personal objectives of presidents and other high officials. While the agencies often committed excesses in response to pressure from high officials in the Executive branch and Congress, they also occasionally initiated improper activities and then concealed them from officials whom they had a duty to inform.[71]

With this in view, the political operations touched on here, and the abuses that accompanied them, cannot be dismissed as the excesses of individual, over-zealous officers, or even as the dysfunctions of particular departments. Instead, they should be understood as systematic in nature, institutional in scope, affecting the entire country, and, despite their purported aims, undermining democracy. This is certainly true of the most flagrant abuses, but it may also be true of "legitimate" intelligence operations. However restrained, intelligence activities function to suppress dissent and undercut basic political liberties. Yale University Law Professor Thomas Emerson explains:

The very process of investigating political activities, involving the questioning of friends, neighbors, employers and other government agents, is intimidating. The compiling of dossiers, which may be the basis of internment in the event of emergency or of other reprisals, is threatening. The very existence of agents, informers, and possible agents provocateurs is chilling. Opportunities for partisan abuse of intelligence powers become available and tempting. Freedom of expression cannot exist under these conditions.[72]

Secret police are always the enemies of democracy.

LOOKING AT THE LEFT

At every level of government, campaigns against dissent have tended to focus disproportionately on the activities of the left. In 1975 a former detective leaked to the press a list of organizations with files maintained by the Baltimore Police

Department's Inspectional Service Division. Three of the 125 groups listed were classified as right-wing. Other categories included "subversive, extremist, civil rights, left-wing, pacifist, miscellaneous, and civic." The NAACP, the ACLU, the American Friends Service Committee, and the Southern Christian Leadership Conference all had files, as did a tenants' group and a tutoring program.[73]

A similar list was leaked to the Citizen's Commission on Police Repression concerning LAPD surveillance activity during the year 1975. Of two hundred organizations listed, twenty could be considered violent. Twenty others were crossed off, suggesting that they had been removed from the surveillance roster; These were mostly conservative groups, beginning with the John Birch Society. Of the 160 remaining, the vast majority were liberal, leftist, or Third World solidarity groups.

> A numbered grading system, from one to six, classified the degree of dangerousness attributed to each organization. For example, Women's Strike for Peace and the World Peace Council were graded number one ("Communist or affiliated or sympathetic with the Communist Party"); the Southern Christian Leadership Conference and the National Council of Churches were rated number two ("Public advocacy of social or political change through violence or law-violation"); in categories three and four (violence-prone groups), we find the Klan and others . . . ; category five ("Participation in or advocacy of any activity intended to create disorder") included the National Organization for Women and the United Farm Workers of America; category six was assigned to, among others, the Black Social Workers' Union and the Pakistan-American Friendship League.[74]

Police in Portland, Oregon, likewise maintained secret files on elected officials, people attending political lectures, soup kitchens, a free dental clinic, day care centers, food co-ops, a bicycle repair collective, and other community groups. A report on rape crisis centers reads: "We can expect that these safe houses and this hotline communication network will probably be used for movement of wanted fugitives in the case of future terrorist acts. . . ."[75] The file "South Africa—Anti" contained the birth dates, phone numbers, class schedules, and grades of six high school students who wrote letters against apartheid. The "IRA" file listed the names of hundreds of people who signed a petition against the mistreatment of political prisoners. The "Cults" file included the 1983 annual report of the First Unitarian Church.[76] The file labeled "Terrorism, Misc.—Oregon" featured information on Physicians for Social Responsibility, the Portland State University Hispanic Student Union, and Ecumenical Ministries of Oregon.[77]

Police suspicion of reformers and radicals was not simply a reflection of the level of activity on the left, nor was the left more prone to violence than the right. Instead, this pattern indicates a deeply ingrained ideological bias on the part of police, especially intelligence sections.[78] This bias has consistently found two complementary expressions: hostility to the left, and alliance with the right.[79] For this reason, red squad files have commonly been shared with right-wing groups. The Los Angeles police traded files with the Western Goals Foundation, an organization started by John Birch Society leader and former Congressman Larry McDonald, and Research West, a private organization funded by FBI agents. Similar arrangements existed throughout the 1960s in most large American cities, including New York, Philadelphia, Chicago, Detroit, Cleveland, Buffalo, and Birmingham.[80]

At times these relationships went further, as police made use of right-wing paramilitary and vigilante groups to carry out campaigns of violence or dirty tricks. The Legion of Justice, for example, conducted a series of burglaries, beatings, and arson attacks on behalf of the Chicago red squad.[81] Less spectacular but nearly as disturbing, in 1980 New Hampshire State Police worked with a private pro-nuclear group headed by Lyndon LaRouche in order to infiltrate the anti-nuclear Clamshell Alliance.[82] Corporate America also got in on the act. A 1974 lawsuit, *Benkert v. Michigan*, revealed that the Detroit Intelligence Unit had been sharing files with the Chrysler Corporation, in some cases recommending Chrysler fire employees with radical political views. Chrysler, for its part, provided the police with information on its workers and helped place informants among militants on the job.[83]

The left as a whole has certainly received more than its fair share of unwanted police attention, but the police give particular scrutiny to those who criticize them. In March 1978, the Coalition Against Police Abuse (CAPA) received a partial list of LAPD officers. CAPA's secretary, Georgia Odom, appeared on the list. CAPA and the Citizen's Commission on Police Repression quietly circulated the list, and two more infiltrators were discovered.[84]

In Philadelphia, the police undertook a prolonged struggle against a community paper called the *Free Press* after it ran a series of articles detailing police abuses. Reporters were harassed, searched, arrested, beaten, and slandered in the police-friendly corporate media. Their apartments and cars were burglarized. Their employers and schools were pressured to fire them and withdraw scholarships. The *Free Press* only survived by seeking and receiving federal court protection.[85]

Obviously the police have an institutional interest in defending themselves against criticism. But, it is worth noting the extent to which they treat dissent of any sort, absolutely any pressure toward social change, with animosity. This hostility to dissent should be understood not simply in terms of individual conservatism, but as an institutional feature of the entire criminal justice system—and perhaps even of the state as a whole. Alan Wolfe explains:

> It is not so much that the state acts mechanistically, always moving to support one group and repress the other, as it is that a regularized bias exists in the operations of the democratic state that tends to support the interests of the powerful against those who challenge them. . . .

Despite some variations, when the state acts in a liberal democratic society such as that of the United States, it acts in a biased
fashion. . . . It is partial to the dominant interests, hostile to those
whose power is minimal. By nearly all of its actions, it reproduces a
society in which some have power at the expense of others, and it
moves to support the "others" only when their protests are so
strong that the "some" stand to lose all they have gained.
   It follows that repression will similarly not be a neutral phenomenon but will have a class bias. We can predict, with good accuracy,
that when the state intervenes to repress an organization or an
ideology, it will be a dissenting group, representing relatively powerless people, that will be repressed and the interests upheld will
be those of the powerful.[86]

Two natural outgrowths of this bias are the criminalization of ideologies (rather than behavior), and the judgment of guilt based on association. These, in turn, are each bound up with police efforts to prevent unrest, rather than simply responding to it. For example, Detective Sergeant John Ungvary, the head of the Cleveland red squad, told a Senate committee, "[I]f we had a law whereby we can charge all of them [Black nationalists] as participants or conspirators . . . it would be far better than waiting for an overt act."[87] As the police attempt to prevent unrest, assumptions about dissenting organizations' aims come to stand in for evidence of any indi-vidual guilt.[88] This attitude, and the activity it inspires, creates a chilling effect that harms not only those groups actually under attack, but any group that fears simi-lar treatment.

THE DEATH OF THE RED SQUADS?

Paradoxically, the silencing of dissent may itself undercut the public's faith in the government's benevolence. The 1970s were characterized by massive public dis-trust of governing bodies—especially the federal intelligence agencies, but also their local counterparts. Along with the Watergate scandals, other startling revela-tions shook public confidence in the government. A researcher for the Pentagon, Daniel Ellsberg, leaked the Defense Department's secret history of the Vietnam War, revealing that the public had been deceived about the aims and methods of the war and, specifically, about American atrocities.[89] Anonymous persons similarly released a series of documents stolen from the FBI office in Media, Pennsylvania, detailing the operations grouped under the heading COINTELPRO.[90] It is quite ironic that the best tool for proving official misconduct by federal agencies turned out to be their own cherished files.

In an effort to salvage credibility, Congressional committees and special prose-cutors tried to "come clean." Even the intelligence agencies themselves tried to rehabilitate their public image; COINTELPRO and similar programs were quickly discontinued. And on the local level, opponents of police spying took the opportunity to move against the red squads.

So what kills a red squad? In Washington, D.C., it was a combination of lawsuits and pressure from the city council. In Birmingham, it was the success of civil rights efforts, and the shift of power that accompanied it. Official investigations and a change in local statutes did in the Baltimore unit. A series of court rulings, a change in political climate, the election of a liberal mayor, attacks in the media, and a sudden loss of allies conspired against the red squad in Detroit. A series of scandals finally cost the Los Angeles unit the last of its credibility, leading to its break-up. In Philadelphia, it was the combination of a Federal Civil Rights Commission investigation, lawsuits, judicial rulings, and a loss of public support stemming from widespread corruption. In Seattle, a city ordinance outlawed the red squad's activities. In Memphis and Chicago, lawsuits produced consent decrees limiting political investigations. A change in political climate brought New York city a liberal mayor and police commissioner; combined with lawsuits, court rulings, and an overall loss of credibility, the change of administration spelled doom for the red squad. Of the various weapons used against the red squads, the most common was litigation.[91] But the political climate may well have been more important to the success of such legal action than either the law or the facts of the case.

Author Ken Lawrence describes the limits of legal victories:

> [Legal reforms are] more reflective of the political climate than they are a way of creating a favorable climate. So, it's a mistake to regard a legal forum as itself a particularly useful way to create an improved political situation. . . . If you win an injunction, that's more a sign that you have prevailed in changing the political climate. But it doesn't for a minute mean that it's going to place any serious restraint on the actions of the police.[92]

Success is rarely total, or permanent. Political repression didn't end with the defeat of the red squads, any more than it ended with the termination of COINTELPRO, the death of J. Edgar Hoover, the resignation of Nixon, or the retirement of Captain Schaack decades before. Repression continues as a permanent feature of capitalist society and as a central function of the state. The changes necessary to remove it, then, are far deeper than anything that we can expect from the courts.

Judges issued a series of favorable rulings; however, as Donner put it, "the plaintiffs won all the battles but lost the war."[93] Maintaining the conditions established by the courts was a separate fight, and a difficult one, since even judges themselves proved very reluctant to enforce the rules the courts established.[94] And police actively resisted reform, sometimes through lawyerly quibbling, sometimes by dragging their feet, sometimes through dirty tricks.

In 1976, Judge James Montante ordered the Detroit Police Department and the Michigan State Police to turn their files over to the people listed in them. Four years later, the state police finally complied with this order. The Detroit police never did. Instead, Mayor Coleman Young simply dissolved the red squad and transferred its files to other units in the department.[95] Elsewhere, the police responded to lawsuits by destroying files, thus preempting the legal discovery process, the court's attempt to inspect them, and any possible orders to make them public. This occurred in Memphis, Seattle, Chicago, and in a case involving the Mississippi Highway Patrol.[96]

In Los Angeles, the police hid the files and claimed they had been destroyed.[97] Red squad detective Jay Paul rescued over 100 cartons of documents, storing them in several locations, including his own home. More than a dozen cops helped Paul with the move. Several others, including lieutenants and captains, knew this was happening, allowed it, and even approved the use of department resources and staff time to assist in the effort.[98]

In 1983, Portland Police Bureau intelligence officer and John Birch Society member Winfield Falk undertook a similar task, stealing files that were headed for the shredder, taking them home, and adding to them on his own for several years.[99] Ranging from a 1924 Communist Party membership card to a 1986 anti-apartheid flier, the files contained information on 576 organizations and more than 3,000 individuals.[100]

Falk's files provide an unnerving glimpse at the tactics employed by police agents. They detail the use of informants, and a 1972 document offers explicit instructions on infiltrating and disrupting dissident groups.[101] COINTELPRO-style dirty tricks are similarly discussed: When a Black activist's mother overheard someone offer to sell her son dynamite, she accused the police of trying to entrap the young man. Officer Mike Salmon took a report and forwarded it to the head of intelligence, Lieutenant Melvin "Corky" Hulett, along with a note: "I'm sending this direct to you, bypassing records, and I'll let you decide what to do with the report. For all we know what Mrs. Anderson says is true (it sounds sneaky, but a good idea)."[102]

Many of the files contain no allegations of criminal wrongdoing, but focus instead on personal information, including financial records, job applications, speculation about the subject's sexual orientation, and family photos.[103] Collecting such information on people not suspected of crimes has been against Police Bureau policy since 1975, and after 1981 it violated state law as well. But many of Falk's reports were addressed to senior officers, indicating that police commanders knew what he was up to.[104] While careful to deny knowledge of the files' existence, former Portland Police Chief Penny Harrington recounted an episode in 1985, when Falk called her to report on the activities of liberal city councilors, alleging they were out to "take over the city government."[105] Harrington wasn't surprised to hear that Falk had kept the files for his own use: "That was happening all over the country at that time. . . . Files were end-ing up in people's garages and basements."[106]

File rescues have occurred as recently as November 1990, when San Francisco Police Chief Willis Casey shut down his department's red squad. Instead of destroy-ing the squad's files, officer Tom Gerard moved them to his home. From there he dis-tributed the documents to the Anti-Defamation League of B'nai B'rith who passed them on to the Israeli government, and also to the apartheid government of South Africa. In total, Gerard maintained files on thousands of Arab Americans, thirty-six Arab groups, thirty-three anti-apartheid groups, 412 "pinko" organizations, 349 right-wing groups, and thirty-five skinhead gangs, as well as the ACLU, the National Lawyer's Guild, *Mother Jones* magazine, the United Auto Workers, the board of direc-tors of KQED (a public television station), the Black Studies Department at San Francisco University, Democratic politicians, and journalists. When Gerard's opera-tion was discovered, it touched off a major scandal. But Richard Hirschhaut, execu-tive director of the Anti-Defamation League Central Pacific Region, shrugged off the controversy: "[T]he relationship we had with him . . . was the same as with thou-sands of police officers around the country."[107] Indeed, when the SFPD and FBI raid-ed B'nai B'rith offices in San Francisco and Los Angeles, they discovered that the organization was keeping computerized files on nearly 10,000 people. Approximately 75 percent of the data in the files had been obtained illegally from police, federal agents, or the Department of Motor Vehicles.[108]

As municipal red squads closed up shop, the burden of political repression was moved off of city police departments and onto county or state agencies. At the end of the 1970s, as city police were getting out of the spy business, at least officially, state units were formed in California, Connecticut, Maryland, Michigan, New Jersey, New York, Ohio, New Hampshire, and Georgia.[109]

A simultaneous charade was being played out at the federal level.

> By discontinuing use of the term "COINTELPRO," the Bureau gave the *appearance* of acceding to public and congressional pressure. In reali-ty, it protected its capacity to continue precisely the same activity under other names. Decentralization of covert operations vastly reduced the volume of required reporting. It dispersed the remaining documentation to individual case files in diverse field offices, and it purged these files of any caption suggesting domestic covert action.[110]

From the FBI's perspective, the problem with COINTELPRO was that it created a paper trail leading to its exposure. The solution, then, lay not in discontinuing the oper-ation, but in decentralizing it, thus making it far less vulnerable.

One innovation, the Joint Terrorism Task Force (JTTF), allowed both local and federal agencies to sidestep restrictions on their activities by working together. JTTFs are comprised of agents from numerous local, state, and federal agencies, and head-ed by the FBI. Since local cops are ostensibly acting as federal agents, their activities are not subject to the supervision of local authorities and the information they col-lect remains secret.[111] The FBI meanwhile can rely on these other agencies to do the heavy lifting, thus avoiding the unseemly impression of excessive federal involve-ment. Accountability disappears in a bureaucratic shell game.

Really, this is an old story: When New York's "Anarchist Squad" was disbanded in 1914, its responsibilities were shifted to the bomb squad. Overt harassment was replaced with clandestine operations, and within a few months the bomb squad had an undercover unit.[112] A similar tale can be told about the Detroit red squad, which was abolished in 1939 after a far-reaching scandal, only to be revived a few months later with World War II as a justification. Its activities were then taken up in coop-eration with the FBI.[113]

At least some of those responsible for the reforms of the late seventies and early eighties knew about this history, and understood how fragile their gains really were. Richard Gutman, an attorney with the Alliance to End Repression, said in 1982:

> History teaches that the intensity of political surveillance is not con-stant. It ebbs and flows. When the political establishment feels its power or policies threatened, political surveillance will resume. That resumption may be marked by a court-ordered revision of our injunc-tion based upon "changed circumstances." . . . [114]

And indeed, eighteen years later, the Chicago consent decree fell. In keeping with Gutman's prediction, the court decided that:

> The era in which the Red Squad flourished is history, along with the Red Squad itself. The instabilities of that era have largely disap-peared. Fear of communist subversion, so strong a motivator of con-stitutional infringements in those days, has disappeared along with the Soviet Union and the Cold War. Legal controls over the police, legal sanctions for infringement of constitutional rights, have multi-plied. The culture that created and nourished the Red Squad has evaporated. The consent decree has done its job.[115]

The consent decree's final test began in 1996, when the Democratic National Convention was set in Chicago and Active Resistance, an anarchist "counter-con-vention," was scheduled to coincide with it. Despite court-mediated limits on such activities, police, both in uniform and in civilian clothing, lurked around the anar-chists' meeting halls, and patrol cars frequently cruised by, slowing down when pass-ing a conference participant on her way in or out. Police even conducted surveil-lance from a helicopter, hovering over the conference area while participants ate a picnic lunch. Witnesses reported being followed, threatened, photographed, and questioned by police, and the cops repeatedly attempted to gain entry to the meeting space. A demonstration connected with Active Resistance was attacked by police using horses and nightsticks, and those arrested were interrogated about their political views, their participation in protest activity, and related matters.[116] Finally, on August 29, 1996, the conference space was raided by several officers wearing uniforms but no badges. They ordered everyone to the ground, pushing down or pepper-spraying those who refused. They searched conference participants' belongings, and seized papers they deemed "subversive to the government of the United States."[117]

When the Alliance to End Repression, joined by the Active Resistance organizers and others, sued to enforce the consent decree, Judge Joan Gottschall rejected out of hand the testimony of numerous witnesses and found that the police had not violated the court order.[118] Following her ruling, a U.S. Appeals Court accepted the city's motion to lift most of the restrictions the consent decree had established, citing changes in the political climate, in police culture, and in the mission of intelligence agencies. But whatever the court might think, the attack on Active Resistance in 1996 foreshadowed similar police tactics, overt and secret, used against the larger wave of protest activity beginning in 1999.[119] It also showed that the guys in the trenchcoats were still up to their old tricks.

THE UNREPORTED REPRESSION

The eighties and nineties are commonly thought to be times of social peace and political conservatism. Yet these two decades were punctuated with surges of activism concerning nuclear disarmament, U.S. policies in Central American, gay and lesbian rights, the AIDS crisis, abortion rights, the Gulf War, police brutality, immigrants' rights, the environment, prison expansion, and economic globalization.[120] And, as before, these movements were met with repression and police interference.

For example, in 1986 Christopher McKinney was arrested during a demonstration against President Reagan's proposed missile defense system. He filed a lawsuit, and in doing so unearthed an intelligence operation involving the local police, the U.S. Marshals, the Air Force, and Lockheed. With federal direction, two Sunnyville, California, cops, Tom Piatanesi and Dave White, had infiltrated student peace groups. Piatanesi later identified activists to be arrested at the demonstration.[121]

In Portland, Oregon, in 1993, a scuffle broke out between youth at a punk rock show and the riot police who had surrounded the venue and refused to let them leave. Thirty-one people were arrested, among them Douglas Squirrel. Squirrel had left the show early but was arrested anyway because, as police spokesperson Derrick Foxworth explained, police files identified him as the "leader of the anarchists."[122]

Files released during the trial revealed an extensive pattern of political surveillance, much of it in violation of Oregon law. In particular, informants had been used against groups with no criminal history, including those lobbying for a civilian board to hear complaints against the police. Squirrel was acquitted, and a subsequent lawsuit produced a ruling limiting police surveillance activities to those attached to an ongoing criminal investigations. Despite the judge's ruling, the surveillance continued. After a 1998 protest against the bombing of Iraq, another activist, Dan Handelman, was surprised to see his name in a police report, with a brief synopsis of his political work:

> The Peace and Justice Works Iraq Affinity Group has held numerous protests in the Portland area concerning U.S. involvement with Iraq. This group is headed by a subject named Dan Handleman [sic] who has been very active in calling for, arranging, and sponsoring these demonstrations.[123]

Handelman was not arrested at the event, and this political information, likely drawn from other files, had no bearing on any criminal case.

Together these examples show that the police are loath to respect any restrictions placed on their operations, whether by the legislature or by the courts, and that the obsession with agitators remains alive and well. In fact, though not yet apparent on the larger scale, there are indications of COINTELPRO-style abuses and even outright atrocities during the Reagan-Bush-Clinton years.

Consider, for instance the case of Judi Bari, bombed by persons unknown, then unsuccessfully framed by the Oakland police and the FBI. Bari was seriously injured on March 24, 1990, when a pipe bomb exploded under the seat of her car. Darryl Cherney was also in the vehicle, and was also injured, though not as badly. The two were members of the radical environmental group Earth First! and were in the midst of organizing a civil disobedience campaign against logging in Northern California. In the weeks before the attack, they had received numerous death threats, which the police declined to investigate. When the bomb exploded, the cops, under the always helpful guidance of the FBI, were quick to blame the victims: Bari and Cherney were arrested for transporting explosives and branded in the media as terrorists. Unfortunately for the cops, the physical evidence did not match the official theory that Bari and Cherney were knowingly transporting explosives. The damage to the car, and to Bari herself, indicated that the bomb was under the driver's seat, not in the back seat where the police said it had been. The DA declined to prosecute, the police refused to look for other suspects, and Bari and Cherney sued.[124]

The lawsuit brought forth evidence suggestive of possibilities far more sinister than simple incompetence, including details of an FBI-run bomb school held on lumber company property weeks before the explosion. In the course of the training,

Special Agent Frank Doyle simulated a bombing identical to that which injured Bari and Cherney a month later.[125] The jury became convinced that Bari and Cherney's civil rights had been violated, and in June 2002, awarded them $4.4 million. The jury explicitly recognized the political motivations behind the police misconduct: Violations of the plaintiffs' First Amendment rights represented 80 percent of the damages.[126] One unnamed juror told the *Press Democrat*, "There were too many lies and manipulation of the evidence. And way too much guilt by association. Law enforcement isn't supposed to do that."[127] Another juror concurred, saying, "Now every time I hear anything about the FBI where they made an arrest I question it. That's what this experience taught me."[128] But for Bari, justice delayed really was justice denied; she died of cancer while the case was still in litigation.

During the last quarter of the twentieth century, however, no set of events are as dramatically damning of police intelligence operations as the Philadelphia Police Department's campaign against MOVE. MOVE is a radical afrocentric, anti-technology organization inspired by the teachings of John Africa. After neighbors lodged noise and sanitation complaints against the group, police used eight-foot-high fences to blockade a four-block area around the home of the organization's members. From May 1977 until March 1978, the Powelton neighborhood came to resemble an armed camp. Under the command of red squad Lieutenant George Fencl, the area was only accessible through a police checkpoint. Residents were required to show ID to enter, and were escorted to their homes by police; friends and family were only permitted inside if they had been previously listed by residents, and if they received police approval. Residents could only leave their homes with permission from the police.[129] The whole operation cost $2 million, required 1,000 officers, and ended with a shoot-out. One cop was killed, and eighteen other people injured—twelve police and firefighters, six members and supporters of MOVE. This was immediately followed by the beating of MOVE leader Delbert Africa as he tried to surrender.[130]

A few years later, the neighborhood suffered another poorly conceived police action. Allegedly trying to serve four arrest warrants, cops fired into the MOVE house, and then used a helicopter to bomb the building. Eleven people were killed, including five children.[131] Sixty-one homes were destroyed in the fire that followed, leaving 250 people homeless. A commission established to study the incident found that police gunfire had prevented the residents of the house from evacuating, and noted that the "firing of over 10,000 rounds of ammunition in under ninety minutes at a row house containing children was clearly excessive and unreasonable."[132] The courts have tended to agree with this assessment, and the City of Philadelphia has paid more than $33 million in damages related to the incident. Still, no government official has ever faced criminal charges for the massacre. In sharp contrast, Ramona Africa, the one adult survivor, spent the next seven years in prison.[133]

Like so many others, this atrocity was the joint work of local and federal authorities. MOVE members cataloged the weaponry used against them: tear gas, water canons, shotguns, Uzis, M-16s, Browning Automatic Rifles, M-60 machine guns, a 20mm anti-tank gun, and a 50-caliber machine gun, plus, of course, a bomb. The Bureau of Alcohol, Tobacco, and Firearms granted the police special permission for this arsenal, and the FBI provided 37.5 pounds of C-4 plastic explosives several months before the final attack.[134] Philadelphia's first Black mayor, W. Wilson Goode, justified the military approach: "What we have out there is war." MOVE's neighbors had a different word for it. As they gathered on the streets, their homes burning, they chanted at the police, "Murder! Murder!"[135]

"A NEW DAY IN SECRET GOVERNMENT"

In terms of official repression, the twenty-first century may come to surpass the twentieth. Repressive operations have only escalated, and accelerated, since the September 11, 2001, attacks on the Pentagon and the World Trade Center. Both the domestic security forces and the military have used the climate of fear following the attacks to justify radical expansion of their activities. Around the country, police pressed for increased powers and sought relief from the limits imposed in the 1970s.[136] And the FBI took the opportunity to expand its JTTF program, adding twenty-one new task forces, so that there is one attached to each of its fifty-six field offices.[137]

Just weeks after the attacks, Congress did its part to advance the domestic espionage agenda, passing the Uniting and Strengthening America by Providing Appropriate Tools Required to Intercept and Obstruct Terrorism (USA Patriot) Act.

The *Washington Post* described the law:

> Molded by wartime politics and passed . . . in furious haste, the new anti-terrorism bill lays the foundation for a domestic intelligence-gathering system of unprecedented scale and technological prowess, according to both supporters and critics of the legislation. . . . The bill effectively tears down a legal fire wall erected 25 years ago during the Watergate era. . . . [138]

Or, as the ACLU's Dave Fidanque put it, "this is the dawn of a new day in secret government."[139]

The Patriot Act represents the Palmer Raids and Watergate-style black-bag jobs, rolled into one and stamped with Congressional approval.[140] Passed and signed on October 26, 2001, this law expanded the definition of "terrorism," reduced the legal rights of immigrants, and granted the police greater powers to conduct surveillance, while limiting judicial oversight.[141]

The Patriot Act created a new crime, that of "domestic terrorism." According to the ACLU:

> The new offense threatens to transform protesters into terrorists if they engage in conduct that "involves acts dangerous to human life." . . . Then, under this law, the dominos begin to fall. Those who provide lodging or other assistance to these "domestic terrorists" could have their homes wiretapped and could be prosecuted.[142]

The effect is to formalize guilt by association, allowing the secretary of state to designate any group that has ever engaged in violence as a "terrorist organization." Those who have lent assistance to such groups, whether or not their assistance was connected to terrorism, are subject to scrutiny, including searches and wiretaps. Worse still, the secretary can *secretly* designate a group as terrorist, and the decision to detain an individual lies with the attorney general, not the courts.[143]

The ACLU elaborates:

> Non-citizens could also be detained or deported for providing assistance to groups that are not designated as terrorist organizations at all, as long as activity of the group satisfies an extraordinarily broad definition of terrorism that covers virtually all violent activity. . . . Such groups as the World Trade Organization protesters, the Vieques protesters and even People for the Ethical Treatment of Animals (PETA), would, on the basis of minor acts of violence or vandalism, meet this overbroad definition.[144]

The law also damages privacy rights by encouraging secret searches, increasing eavesdropping, and removing many protections for confidential information. Section 213 allows police to search a person's property without notifying them that a warrant has been issued. Likewise, Section 216 allows for increased surveillance of electronic communication, removes most restrictions on the use of wiretaps, and substantially limits the role of judicial review, essentially giving law enforcement a free hand to monitor telecommunications. As the ACLU points out, "Most of the changes apply not just to surveillance of terrorists, but instead to all surveillance in the United States."[145] By authorizing such practices while preventing any effective oversight, the law opens the door for more and greater abuses of power. By legitimizing many tactics previously used illicitly, it makes it easier for police to play more dirty tricks behind the scenes.

The Patriot Act also restructured the American security forces and shifted their priorities. The law increased information-sharing between the FBI, CIA, NSA, INS, and Secret Service, and granted them access to previously off-limits grand jury information.[146] Section 203 allows the CIA to share information with whomever they chose, including foreign governments.[147] While the CIA is still barred from performing domestic police or intelligence functions, it *is* allowed to cooperate with the agencies that do this work.[148] The FBI, meanwhile, "must shift its primary focus from investigating and prosecuting past crimes to identifying threats of future terrorist attacks. . . ."[149]

As if the Patriot Act weren't enough, a year later Congress bolstered the power of the security forces, this time ordering the largest bureaucratic reorganization since the creation of the Defense Department. The Homeland Security Act, passed in November 2002, incorporated 170,000 employees from 22 agencies into an integrated domestic anti-terrorism apparatus, the Department of Homeland Security.[150] The Homeland Security Department will centrally manage tasks related to sharing information, monitoring electronic communications, regulating the borders, responding to emergencies, and coordinating local anti-terrorism efforts.[151] It includes 74,300 armed federal agents and takes on many of the tasks formerly performed by the INS, Customs, the Coast Guard, and the Border Patrol.[152] Additionally, under Title II of the Homeland Security Act, the Directorate of Information Analysis and Infrastructure Protection is charged with creating a database on individuals' credit card purchases, telephone calls, banking transactions, and travel. This information is to be used to create profiles with which to identify future suspects.[153]

The Bush administration has extended its reach even further. Through a series of executive orders, administrative rules, and memoranda, President George W. Bush and Attorney General John Ashcroft have openly ignored even the meager restrictions established by the Patriot and Homeland Security laws, not to mention the limits spelled out in the Bill of Rights. A September 20, 2001, executive order allows the INS to hold a person, without charges, for an unspecified "reasonable period of time."[154] According to an October 31, 2001, interim regulation, detainees *who have been ordered released by a court* may still be held until the order can be appealed. Another interim regulation issued on the same date allows federal authorities to monitor privileged attorney-client communications.[155] And new Department of Justice rules allow local and state police to be deputized for immigration control.[156]

Perhaps most chilling, a November 2001 executive order authorized the use of military tribunals to try "enemy combatants," including U.S. citizens.[157] As the Center for Constitutional Rights points out, this order

> gives the President the power to decide who will be tried under the new system, to create the rules by which trial will proceed, to appoint those who will serve as judge, prosecutor, and defense attorney, to set penalties once guilt is determined (including death) and to decide all appeals.[158]

These unilateral extensions of executive power have prompted predictable court battles, the final outcomes of which have yet to be determined.[159]

While legal maneuvering and bureaucratic in-fighting leave a great many details in flux, the overall direction of events is clear enough: toward government secrecy, away from individual privacy; expanding state power, diminishing individual rights.[160] John Ashcroft sounds eerily like a certain former FBI director as he explains the administration's intentions: "We are doing everything we can to identify those who would hurt us, to disrupt them, to delay them, to defeat them."[161]

As with the Palmer Raids and the internment of Japanese Americans during World War II, the rights of immigrants have been hardest hit, though the level of actual impact has been difficult to measure. While the government has been quite enthusiastic about locking up the tired, the poor, the huddled masses, it has been less eager to say exactly how many people have been detained. The last officially released total placed the number at 1,147, a figure human rights advocates suspect is deceptively low.[162]

Many detainees are held incommunicado. They are commonly denied legal representation and their families are not told where—or in some cases, *whether*—they are in custody.[163] While Ashcroft calls the detainees "suspected terrorists," none have been charged with a crime related to terrorist activity.[164] In fact, the Justice Department estimates that only ten or twelve of those being held are connected to Al Qaeda, and documents released under the Freedom of Information Act show that, of the first 725 arrested, 300 were of no interest to any investigation of terrorism.[165] Yet in a clear inversion of the presumption of innocence, the detainees are held under the pretext of minor immigration violations until the authorities become convinced of their innocence; they are then either released or deported.[166] Georgetown University Law professor David Cole points out the obvious:

> The real reason for their incarceration is not that they worked without authorization or took too few academic credits, for example. Rather, the government used these excuses to detain them because it thinks they just might have valuable information, because it suspects them but lacks evidence to make a charge, or simply because the FBI is not yet convinced that they are innocent.[167]

In a typical case, Hady Hassan Omar, an Egyptian national, fell under suspicion because he made plane reservations from a Kinko's computer. On the basis of this questionable conduct, he was arrested, held for two months, and then released without charges.[168] Or, to take another case: Shahin Hajizadeh, a legal resident awaiting his permanent status, appeared at the INS office in Los Angeles to comply with regulations requiring the registration and fingerprinting of all Middle Eastern men over sixteen years of age. He was detained, kicked in the ribs by a guard, and placed in an overcrowded cell without adequate food, water, or bathroom facilities. He was then transferred to a cold cell in the desert town of Lancaster, allowed to sleep for about an hour, moved back to L.A., and released.[169]

Hajizadeh was just one of hundreds of Middle Eastern men detained while attempting to comply with the new rules. As usual, the government refused to cite exact figures, but put the number arrested somewhere "in the low two hundreds."[170] Civil rights activists, attorneys representing the detainees, and anonymous immigration officials put the number between 500 and 700.[171] Most of those detained were in the country legally. The registration requirements thus present immigrants with a classic catch-22: Either comply with the law and risk detention, or violate the law and risk arrest.

Abdallah Higazy's experience was less typical, but just as revealing. On September 11, 2001, Higazy had been staying at the Millennium Hilton Hotel, with a view of the World Trade Center. Like everyone else in the building, he abandoned his room when hijacked airliners collided with the twin towers. Later, as Hilton employees cataloged the property left behind, a security guard reported finding an aviation radio in Higazy's room. Higazy initially denied that the radio was his, but was arrested and spent a month in solitary confinement. Then, during an FBI interrogation, he confessed to aiding the attacks. But something unexpected happened: An American pilot contacted the hotel to claim his aviation radio, and the case against Higazy disintegrated. The security guard, a former Newark cop named Ronald Ferry, admitted that he had lied to investigators about where he found the radio. He was sentenced leniently, receiving six months of weekend detention.[172]

It would be a mistake, however, to put all the blame on Ferry. The FBI's role in this near-disaster also deserves some scrutiny. Our first question should be: How exactly did they convince an innocent man to confess? And our second: Why did the investigators take Ferry at his word? Even a cursory check would have drawn his credibility into question, since he had been fired from the Newark Police Department for drug-related misconduct. But, as the U.S. Attorney in the case explained:

> Given what the Government knew . . , the information [Ferry provided] seemed more than merely plausible. . . . [The government] knew that, on September 11, Mr. Higazy was staying at the hotel next to the WTC, on the 51st floor, in a room with a view of the WTC. . . . It knew that one of his duties in the Egyptian Air Corps was to repair aviation radios. . . . [I]t knew that a number of the September 11 hijackers were Egyptian nationals; and it knew that Mr. Higazy is an Egyptian national.[173]

In other words, as federal authorities saw it, they had no reason to doubt the word of a dirty cop and every reason to suspect a foreign student.

Despite its happy ending, at least when compared to the alternative: imagine if the pilot had never come back for his radio, this case remains deeply troubling and does not bode well for the nationwide terrorist dragnet. In the context of official panic and diminished rights, Higazy was accused by an unreliable informant, arrested, held in solitary confinement, and repeatedly interrogated; he was ultimately induced to confess to a crime of which he was innocent.

That's the danger of witchhunts: An eager inquisitor will always find someone to burn.

RETHINKING UNREST

We've come a long way since Haymarket.

Originally, police repression focused on the behavior of crowds; surveillance allowed the cops to respond quickly to any disturbance. But as the police began to view their role more in terms of preventing trouble, the use of surveillance increased, and intelligence operations became specialized.[174] Police attention fell, not only on demonstrations and individual leaders, but on meetings, organizations, and entire movements.

By the 1970s, it was clear that something was lacking in the theory behind domestic intelligence work, and that the actual practice had reached far beyond whatever strategy there may once have been. The cops clung to a conspiracy model for understanding subversion, but their targets included individuals quite removed from any radical tendency whatever. The police became obsessed with ideology, but continually misread the intentions of peaceful groups and even pressed them toward violent action. Police aggressively sought to preempt subversion and prevent unrest, yet remained essentially reactive in their stance toward existing social movements.

When theory advanced to address this confusion, it was the work of neither an American nor, strictly speaking, a policeman. Instead, the person who realigned the theory and practice of repression was the aforementioned British military commander Frank Kitson.

Kitson based his doctrine on an analysis of rebellions, outlining three stages of a subversive campaign: preparation, nonviolence, and insurgency. The security forces need to be ready at every stage, beginning with the preparatory stage when everything seem calm. Despite its aims, the old model remained essentially reactive; it only responded at the second stage, when political activity became visible. Kitson's hope was to prevent the "enemy" from ever reaching the second stage.[175] He wrote:

Looking in retrospect at any counter-subversion or counter-insurgency campaign, it is easy to see that the first step should have been to prevent the enemy from gaining an ascendancy over the civil population, and in particular to disrupt his efforts at establishing his political organization. In practice this is difficult to achieve because for a long time the government may be unaware that a significant threat exists, and in any case in a so-called free country it is regarded as the opposite of freedom to restrict the spread of a political idea.[176]

Kitson saw that previous efforts at preventing unrest had begun too late, after a threat had already developed. The task at hand was to prevent subversive ideas from finding a popular audience. Clearly, intelligence must play a central role in this pursuit.

Kitson's analysis reflected an important break from assumptions fundamental to the police ideology. The earlier obsession with conspiracies and agitators reflected a conservative view of society: the political order was fundamentally stable, unrest was anomalous and irrational, dissent was not prompted by social conditions but by Communist plots. As Frank Donner notes:

To equate dissent with subversion, as intelligence officials do, is to deny that the demand for change is based on real social, economic, or political conditions. A familiar example of this is the almost paranoid obsession with the "agitator." Intelligence proceeds on the assumption that most people are reasonably contented but are incited or misled by an "agitator," a figure who typically comes from "outside" to stir up trouble. The task is to track down this sinister individual and bring him to account: all will then be well again.[177]

Working from these premises, the police were incapable of understanding social movements when they arose, and could do practically nothing to prevent them. Eventually, the shortcomings of this approach necessitated the shift to COINTELPRO tactics and the covert disruption of radical movements. But COINTELPRO, too, was essentially reactive: it sought to dis-organize existing movements and isolate them from their constituencies, but could not prevent them from arising in the first place. Kitson corrected for these problems by abandoning the conservative stance. His analysis suggests that society exists in a state of permanent conflict; this would require a strategy of permanent repression, on the model of counter-insurgency efforts.[178] Rather than focusing solely on activists, political repression must be understood in terms of controlling whole populations.

The shift from anti-Communism to anti-terrorism is minor compared to the move from conspiracy theories to counter-insurgency. The latter has broadened the scope of intelligence operations and, at the same time, informed the direction of other police work. In crowd control actions and community policing programs, as well as in the work of the red squads, the emphasis is increasingly placed on preemptive and proactive efforts. In each case, police seek to enlist the support of reliable portions of the population when conditions are stable, and to neutralize disruptive elements before they present a threat.

The broader implications of this strategy, and the practical efforts to implement it, will be considered in the chapters that follow.

RIOT POLICE OR POLICE RIOTS?

Despite the efforts of the intelligence agencies, opposition movements continue to arise, occasionally developing to the point of unrest. Naturally, when uprisings occur, the authorities must put them down. Governments necessarily have a stake in controlling political protest, especially when it becomes forceful enough to disrupt the usual course of things—that is, when it becomes an effective threat to the status quo. No one with an interest in retaining power can allow things to go so far as to actually jeopardize their ability to rule. But this presents a problem for the rulers of an alleged democracy, with its promises of civil rights, free speech, popular assembly, and the pretense that the people are actually in the driver's seat. Open repression may exacerbate a crisis and undercut the state's claim to legitimacy, while acquiescence may make the government seem weak and will surely carry with it unfavorable policy implications. There can be no question of whether to control political protest, but there is a clear question as to how this may best be accomplished.[1]

SEATTLE, 1999: DANCE PARTY, STREET FIGHT, NO-PROTEST ZONE

The 1999 Seattle demonstrations against the World Trade Organization (WTO) precipitated a sharp controversy in the theory of crowd control, calling into question police strategies of the previous twenty-five years.

On the morning of November 30, 1999, tens of thousands of people filled downtown Seattle in protest against the World Trade Organization. Protesters surrounded the venue for the WTO's ministerial conference, blocking the delegates' access to the meeting and shutting down a large portion of the city. The protests were overwhelmingly peaceful; many took the form of dance parties in the street. On the demonstrators' side, the much-decried "violence" and "rioting" amounted to only a few broken windows and some tear gas thrown back in the direction of the police.

For most of that day, the police were helpless to restore order. They stood in small groups, blocking random streets, accomplishing nothing. Occasionally tear gas was used, and the police would advance a block, but that was all. For one day, the streets belonged to jubilant crowds. Shops were not open, cars could not pass, the

WTO meeting was stalled at the outset. By nightfall, a curfew was in place and the National Guard was on patrol. It was announced that no more demonstrations would be allowed in the area of the conference. Police chased a crowd from downtown to the nearby Capitol Hill neighborhood, attacking everyone in the street along the way. The residents of Capitol Hill fought back, and a pitched battle ensued. The fighting continued late into the night.

On December 1, the streets belonged to the cops. Early that morning, the police arrested more than 600 people just outside the "No-Protest Zone." Police were shown on national television indiscriminately firing tear gas, rubber bullets, and other "less-lethal" munitions. Beatings were common; not only protesters, but bystanders and reporters were attacked. Still the demonstrations continued. On December 2, several hundred people surrounded the jail, demanding their comrades be released. A compromise was reached when the authorities allowed lawyers in to see the prisoners, the first legal access since the arrests began.

In the end, the protesters won. The WTO meeting started late and ended in failure; no new trade agreements were reached. Most of those arrested were released, with charges dropped. And Norm Stamper, Seattle Chief of Police, resigned in disgrace. People—workers, students, environmentalists, human rights activists—stood together against the WTO, the city government, the police, the National Guard, and the corporate powers they all represent. And the people won. Before the smoke had even cleared, authorities around the country were asking what had gone wrong and, more importantly, how they could prevent it from happening again.[2]

ASSESSING THE POLICE RESPONSE: "WHAT NOT TO DO"

Everyone agrees that the police action at the WTO was an unmitigated disaster. A city council committee charged with reviewing the events noted, "This city became the laboratory for how American cities will address mass protests. In many ways, it became a vivid demonstration of what *not* to do."[3]

From a civil rights perspective, the 1999 WTO ministerial was marked by a virtual prohibition on free speech, a plague of arbitrary arrests, and widespread police brutality. The ACLU described the situation this way:

> Realizing it had lost control of the scene, the City then over-reacted. It violated free speech rights in a large part of downtown. Under the direction of the Seattle Police Department, police from Seattle and nearby jurisdictions used chemical weapons on peaceful crowds and people walking by. Losing discipline, police officers committed individual acts of brutality. Protesters were improperly arrested and mistreated in custody.[4]

The city council's description of the events bears the standard characteristics of a police riot:

> Our inquiry found troubling examples of seemingly gratuitous assaults on citizens, including use of less-lethal weapons like teargas, pepper gas, rubber bullets, and "beanbag guns," by officers who seemed motivated more by anger or fear than professional law enforcement.[5]

And police commanders admit that they lost control, not only of the streets, but of their troops as well.

> An essential element for the successful execution of any plan is the ability to control operations once officers are deployed. Unfortunately, in several respects the command and control arrangements for WTO broke down early in the operation.[6]

Nevertheless, from the law-and-order side, the protests represented a vast sea of lawlessness, complete with attacks against police and property. The Seattle Police Department After-Action Report describes the protests from the police perspective:

> Numerous acts of property damage, looting, and assaults on police were committed. Officers were pelted with sticks, bottles, traffic cones, empty chemical irritant canisters, and other debris. Some protesters used their own chemical irritants against police, and a large fire was set in the intersection at 4th and Pike.[7]

What's remarkable is not so much the dispute between the police and civil rights advocates, not to mention the protesters, but the level of conflict between the city council and the police. Some of this was surely opportunistic posturing, a typical political game, with politicians scrambling to cover their asses, point accusing fingers, and associate themselves with the winners. But the dispute also represents a sharp split between the perspective of the city council, as presented in its Accountability Committee Report, and that of the police, argued mostly by proxy, in a report prepared by an independent consulting firm, R. M. McCarthy and Associates. Not only are their analyses in conflict—in places, even the *facts* they cite are at odds—but their suggested remedies are in direct opposition.

Funded by the mayor's office, the McCarthy and Associates report was written primarily by three retired law enforcement officers from New York and Los Angeles. They describe every step of the SPD's WTO operation and urge a more forceful response when dealing with future civil disobedience. They recommend establishing the siege-like atmosphere of December 1 well before any demonstrations begin, arguing that

had a restrictive safety zone been established, protest areas designated outside of the zone, and additional personnel from other agencies been planned for and deployed in a pre-emptive manner on
November 26, the results would likely have been different.[8]

The report also suggests that the police response didn't go far enough in the
suppression of civil rights. "The review team believes the decision to allow any previously scheduled marches or demonstrations to proceed after violence had erupted
was unwise."[9] Furthermore, it recommends amending police policy by removing
instructions that crowds be moved or dispersed "peacefully," and adding explicit
orders to make as many arrests as possible.[10] Luckily, elected officials are likely to
balk at such draconian measures. Describing the McCarthy report as a "crude and
unsatisfying" document, the City Council's Review Committee reached almost entirely opposing conclusions.[11]

Rather than pressing for a more forceful response, the city council's committee
suggested that in many cases the police would have done better to have done nothing at all. "Members of the public, including demonstrators, were victims of ill-con-
ceived and sometimes pointless police actions to 'clear the streets'."[12] Aside from its
brutality, such an approach is often self-defeating. For example, "The unintended
consequence of police actions on Capitol Hill was to bring sleepy residents out of
their homes and mobilize them as 'resistors.'"[13]

Despite the objections to the McCarthy report, its recommended tactics are by
now familiar in the setting of any large anti-globalization event. We've seen this
pattern repeated time and again in Washington, D.C., Philadelphia, and Los Angeles,
as well as in Prague, Quebec City, Gothenburg, and Genoa,[14] and, with variations, in
more recent anti-war protests.[15]

EARLY STRATEGIES

There is more at stake in this debate than the blame for the WTO debacle. Each
of these reports represents one side in an ongoing dispute over the principles of
crowd control. Spanning slightly more than a hundred years, this controversy has
been shaped by a series of similar crises, instances in which the police orthodoxy
proved disastrous.

Prior to the Great Railroad Strike of 1877, civil disturbances were essentially
handled like any other military engagement, with the possible exception that
crowds would be ordered to disperse before the police or militia charged with clubs
or opened fire. During the Draft Riots of 1863, for example, New York Police
Commissioner Thomas Acton ordered those under his command to "Take no prisoners." George Walling, the commander of the twelfth precinct, was even more specif-

ic in his instructions: "Kill every man who has a club."[16] I will term this the strategy of "Maximum Force."

Such an approach may have had a certain efficacy against localized revolts, unplanned riots, or drunken mobs, but it met with greater difficulty in 1877 when more than 100,000 railroad workers, enraged by cuts to their already meager wages, went on strike and prevented the companies from moving their freight.[17] The turmoil was too vast for local police to control, and the militia proved unreliable.

"In Pittsburgh, the city where strike-related violence climaxed, militia displayed opposite extremes of indiscipline: fraternization and panic."[18] The commander of the Pittsburgh militia later testified:

> Meeting on the field of battle you go there to kill . . . but here you had men with fathers and mothers and brothers and relatives mingled in the crowd of rioters. The sympathy was with the strikers. We all felt that these men were not receiving enough wages.[19]

The Philadelphia militia, which was also sent to Pittsburgh, displayed no such sympathy. The *New York Times* reported that they "fired indiscriminately into the crowd, among whom were many women and children."[20] Rather than fleeing, the crowd was enraged; the militia was forced to retreat. Likewise, in Reading, when troops killed eleven strikers, the general population only grew more furious. Strike supporters looted freight, tore up tracks, and armed themselves with rifles from the militia's own armory. When reinforcements arrived, they sided with the crowds and threatened their colleagues, "If you fire at the mob, we'll fire at you."[21]

These same problems arose in every city facing strikes. In Newark, Ohio, and Hornellsville, New York, militia men openly fraternized with strikers, much to the dismay of their commanders. In Martinsburg, West Virginia, the commander of the Beverly Light Guards telegraphed the governor, worried by his troops' sympathy with the strikers. In Harrisburg, Morristown, and Altoona, Pennsylvania, the militias surrendered. Half of the soldiers in the Maryland Sixth Regiment broke into an undisciplined retreat during a Baltimore street fight. And in Lebanon, Pennsylvania, a company of militia mutinied.[22]

In the end, a combination of attrition, fatigue, and military force won out over the striking workers.[23] But still, the authorities were very disappointed. They immediately set about building the militias into well-disciplined machines, capable of quelling riots or, more to the point, breaking strikes.[24] During this period, the state militias were reconstituted into the modern National Guard.[25] Military training was imposed and matters of discipline rigidly enforced, including inspections by regular Army officers. In addition, more emphasis was placed on recruitment, and armories were built throughout the North.[26]

These changes in the organization, training, discipline, and culture of the Guard were accompanied by new articulations of crowd control strategies. A number of manuals suddenly appeared spelling out the strategy for stifling unrest. These books were generally unconcerned with the social causes of disorder, content to blame them on agitators of various sorts. Most continued to advocate the principle of Maximum Force: They predicted increased militancy among workers, and offered increased state violence as the remedy.[27] E. L. Molineux, the commander of the New York National Guard, wrote: "In its incipient stage a riot can be readily quelled . . . if met bodily and resisted at once with energy and determination. Danger lurks in delay."[28]

A milder version of the doctrine did emerge, and gained popularity among local commanders. According to this "Show of Force" (my term) theory:

> Strikes and riots were outbursts that could be controlled—perhaps even prevented—by shows of authority which even rowdy workers were presumed to respect, or by shows of force which workers would fear. From these premises it followed that the function of the militia on riot duty was as much demonstrative, even theatrical, as it was coercive. The goal was to disperse rioters, not—as General Vodges would have it—to corner them and wipe them out.[29]

And if this could be accomplished without firing a shot, so much the better. One manual stated, "[A] strong *display* of a well-disciplined and skillfully handled force will in most instances be sufficient in itself to suppress a riot."[30]

This presumption was later shown to be false: A large police presence is not so much preventive as it is provocative. Such errors were at least partly a product of the theory's underlying premise that rioters are psychologically deranged rather than politically or economically motivated. In any case, the practical consequence of the Show of Force theory was a new demand for dress uniforms, public drilling, and parades.[31] It was not shown to reduce the likelihood of class conflict or to prevent strikes.

In the 1880s, a wave of immigration made the authorities less reluctant to use force against striking workers.[32] And after the Haymarket incident of 1886, the Show of Force approach was almost entirely abandoned in favor of more direct responses: "[T]acticians [came] to favor the use of force over shows of force."[33] Tellingly, racist comparisons between workers and Native Americans became more common. In 1892 the *Army and Navy Register* opined, "The red savage is pretty well subdued . . . but there are white savages growing more numerous and dangerous as our great cities become greater."[34] This analogy was not merely rhetorical; many of the same units were used against strikers as against indigenous peoples.

The Maximum Force approach did have its disadvantages. "Fire tactics appropriate for conventional warfare . . . jeopardized innocent lives, invited public condemnation, and . . . simply did not work in the urban terrain where most riots took place."[35] As the National Guard's reputation for brutality grew, so did sympathy for those who opposed them, especially striking workers. At the same time, Maximum Force was out of step with the authorities' overall strategy in handling strikes, as the government and businesses came to rely more and more on the pacifying effects of concessions.[36] Nevertheless, and despite atrocities like the Ludlow Massacre,[37] Maximum Force remained the dominant approach well into the twentieth century.

RATIONALIZING FORCE

It was not until World War I and its accompanying Red Scare that the Maximum Force doctrine was revised. State violence was then rationalized, broken into discrete, ordered stages. This change represented one component in an early effort to take some of the conflict out of class conflict. "In short, repealing bellicose post-Haymarket formulas for riot control was part of a multifaceted drive to wreck the Left, strip the working class of radical leaders, and put progressive managers in their place."[38]

Of the new crowd-control strategists, the most influential was Henry A. Bellows, an officer in the Minnesota Home Guard and the author of *A Manual for Local Defense* (1919) and *A Treatise on Riot Duty for the National Guard* (1920). In these works, he drew a distinction between crowds and mobs, and argued that the key was to keep a crowd from becoming a mob. Ideally this could be accomplished by preventing crowds from forming in the first place—or, failing that, by breaking up any crowd that did form and doing so before it had the chance to transform into a mob. The crowd should be dispersed with as little actual violence as possible, but without hesitating to use whatever force was necessary.[39] Bellows wrote, "Practically every riot can be prevented without bloodshed . . . if sufficient force can be brought to bear on it in time."[40]

Army Major Richard Stockton and New Jersey National Guard Captain Saskett Dickson expressed a similar view in their *Troops on Riot Duty: A Manual for the Use of the Armed Forces of the United States*. They wrote:

> Troops on riot duty should keep in mind the fact that they are called upon to put down disorder, absolutely and promptly, *with as little force as possible*, but it should be remembered, also, that in the majority of cases the way to accomplish these ends is to use at once every particle of force necessary to stop all disorder.[41]

The new theorists sought a doctrine by which force would be prescribed in proportion to the difficulty of dispersing the crowd. They thus advocated using tactics suited to the particular situation.

In terms of tactics, giving priority to prevention demanded what later military thinkers would call doctrines of "sequence of force" or "flexible response." Simply put, the idea was to adapt levels of forces [*sic*] to levels of perceived menace, escalating to fire-power only as a last resort. . . . All of the writers of 1918-1920 endorsed the initial use of verbal warnings, bayonets, rifle butts, or hoses, as alternatives to firepower.[42]

By 1940, the Show of Force doctrine had been reinserted as the first step of this progression.[43]

In this way, the doctrine of Maximum Force was transformed into that of Escalated Force, which remained the standard approach to crowd control until the 1970s.

As its name indicates, the escalated force style of protest policing was characterized by the use of force as a standard way of dealing with demonstrations. Police confronted demonstrators with a dramatic show of force and followed with a progressively escalated use of force if demonstrators failed to abide by police instructions to limit or stop their activities.[44]

Such force took different forms. Sometimes, arrests immediately followed even minor violations of the law, or were used to target and remove "agitators," whether or not a law had been broken. Other times, police used force instead of making arrests, either to break up the crowd or to punish those who disobeyed them.[45]

Figure D. Escalated Force

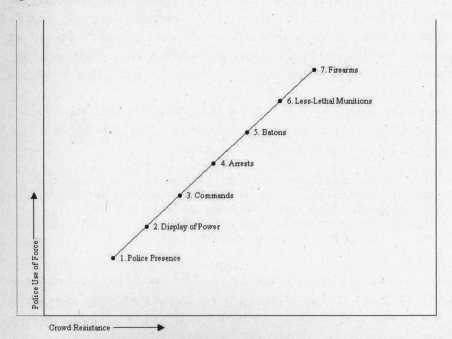

THE APPLICATIONS AND IMPLICATIONS OF ESCALATED FORCE

According to the theory, force is only used in proportion to the threat posed by the crowd. The reality is often quite different. The police response to protests is determined by something more than the behavior of protesters. In fact, the actions of the crowd may not even be the most important factor. Others may include police preparedness and discipline, the presence of counter-demonstrators, the number of participants, media coverage, and the political calculus surrounding the event—that is, what people with power, and the police leaders in particular, stand to gain or lose by attacking the event or letting it alone. These factors can be classed into six groups:

(1) the organizational features of the police;
(2) the configuration of political power;
(3) public opinion;
(4) the occupational culture of the police;
(5) the interaction between police and protesters; and,
(6) police knowledge.[46]

Even when the police do respond in proportion to the threat, their victims often include peaceable demonstrators and innocent bystanders, along with the hooligans. Widespread violence is by its nature imprecise. And questions of "guilt" or "innocence," like those pertaining to constitutional rights, are of secondary concern, if indeed they are considered relevant at all. Dispersal operations are not designed to uphold the law or to protect public safety; often the police action itself will represent the most serious violation of the law and constitute the greatest threat to the safety of the community. Instead of the law or public safety, the police are concerned with establishing control, maintaining power.[47]

> Well-known demonstrations in which police used the escalated force approach include those in the Birmingham civil rights campaign (May 1963), the 1968 Chicago Democratic National Convention, and the confrontation between student protesters and National Guard soldiers at Kent State University (May 1970). During each of these demonstrations, police or soldiers used force in an attempt to disperse demonstrators, even demonstrators who were peacefully attempting to exercise their First Amendment rights—as the vast majority of them were.[48]

These events, while large in scope and attracting a great deal of media attention, were not uncharacteristic of Escalated Force operations. In many ways, they were sadly typical. While Kent State, where the victims were White, has come to symbolize the murder of student protesters, it was not the first or last time that students were shot in the name of keeping order. In May 1967, three years before Kent State, a Black student was killed at Jackson State College in Mississippi. In February 1968, three students were killed at South Carolina State College. One was killed in Berkeley in May 1969, and another at North Carolina Agricultural and Mechanical College that same month. One was killed in Santa Barbara in February 1970. In March 1970, twelve were shot, but no one killed, at State University of New York, Buffalo. Most famously, in May 1970, four were murdered at Kent State. That same month, twenty were shot just down the road at Ohio State (all survived), and four-teen were shot (again) at Jackson State, two of whom died. In July 1970, one was killed at the University of Kansas, Lawrence, and another at the University of Wisconsin, Milwaukee. Two years later, in November 1972, two more students were killed at the University of New Orleans.[49]

Predictably, urban Blacks received even worse treatment. In the Detroit upris-ing of 1967, forty-three people were killed, thirty-six of whom were Black. Twenty-nine of these deaths were definitely attributable to police, National Guard troops, or the Army. The remaining thirteen died from any of a variety of causes: Some were shot by store owners, some died in fires, two were electrocuted by fallen power lines. No deaths were directly attributable to the violence of the crowds. Despite the rhet-oric surrounding them, Black uprisings in the sixties "were marked by a relative absence of violence committed by rioters against people. Careful examination of the casualty lists shows that police and military inflicted the vast majority of fatalities and injuries on blacks in the riot area."[50]

A GLIMPSE AT 1968

These facts speak to the level of police violence, but they say very little about its prevalence in crowd control situations. For that, we should consider a sample of police actions during a specific time frame, for example, during the year 1968, a banner year remembered for producing rebellions around the world. While 1968 was in this respect exceptional, it may also—for the same reasons—be seen to typify the official response to unrest. It certainly provided numerous, widely varied exam-ples for comparison.

In January 1968, San Francisco police broke ranks and charged into the crowd at an anti-war demonstration, beating protesters. San Francisco also saw numerous rampages by the police department's Tactical Squad throughout the year, especially in the Haight-Ashbury neighborhood. During one such attack, a Black plainclothes officer was beaten by his White colleagues. During another, off-duty Tactical Squad officers moved through the Mission district, clearing sidewalks and assaulting pedes-trians. Two officers went to trial for that stunt.[51]

Three Blacks were killed and almost fifty others injured when police and National Guard troops opened fire at a February demonstration against a White-only bowling alley in Orangeburg, South Carolina. Most of the wounded were shot in the back.[52]

In March, New York City police attacked a Yippie demonstration at Grand Central Station. Offering no opportunity for the crowd to disperse, they indiscriminately beat members of the crowd that had gathered. The same tactic was repeated at another Yippie march in April, this time in Washington Square.[53] Later that same month, Students for a Democratic Society held a demonstration at Rockefeller Center. Jeff Jones, an SDS organizer, described the event as "very militant, it turned into a street fight. I think there were eight felony and fourteen misdemeanour [sic] arrests. There were beatings on both sides."[54] A week later, on April 29, 1968, New York City police used clubs to clear some of the same students from occupied buildings at Columbia University. Police emptied the occupied buildings and then moved through the campus, beating any students they could find, whether or not they had been involved in the occupation.[55] One hundred thirty-two students and four faculty were injured.[56] Also in New York that fall, 150 off-duty cops filled a Brooklyn courthouse and beat several Black Panthers who were there to observe a trial.[57]

A week before he was assassinated, Martin Luther King, Jr., led 15,000 people on a march through Memphis, expressing solidarity with the city's striking garbage collectors. The police and National Guard used clubs and tear gas to break up the march, killing one person in the process.[58] In April, following King's murder, 202 riots occurred in 175 cities across the country, with 3,500 people injured and 43 killed, mostly at the hands of police.[59]

Also in April, a peace march of 8,000 moved slowly through downtown Chicago. Having been refused a parade permit, marchers stayed on sidewalks and obeyed the traffic signals. Nevertheless, in an incident foreshadowing the Democratic National Convention later that year, a line of police pushed the crowd into the streets; quickly, another line of cops pushed them back to the sidewalks. The situation quickly degenerated. Ignoring the orders of their superiors, police broke ranks, chasing and beating members of the crowd. A panel convened to study the incident and laid the blame with Mayor Richard Daley and other city officials who set the tone for the action by denying the required permits.[60]

In June, cops attacked a crowd of Berkeley students listening to speeches about the Paris uprising, setting off several days of fighting.[61] In July, police responded forcefully to racial unrest in Paterson, New Jersey. A grand jury later condemned the police for engaging in "terrorism" and "goon squad" tactics. The jury reported that teams of cops intentionally vandalized Black-owned businesses and severely beat individual Blacks and Puerto Ricans, as an example to others.[62] In August, Los Angeles exploded after police attacked a crowd at the Watts Festival. Three people were killed and thirty-five injured.[63]

That winter, when students at San Francisco State College went on strike to demand a Black Studies program, college president S. I. Hayakawa declared a state of emergency, ordered classes to resume, and called in police to make sure that they did.[64] (Hayakawa is perhaps best remembered for his assertion, "There are no innocent bystanders.")[65] Skirmishes followed throughout December, during which individual officers broke from their units and charged into crowds of students. News photos showed police holding protesters while other cops maced them.[66] The strike was finally defeated in January when police started making mass arrests, resulting in several felony convictions.[67]

This chronology is undoubtedly incomplete, but it makes the point: police violence against crowds, sometimes perfectly innocuous gatherings, was utterly common.[68] It was as frequent as it was extreme. Nevertheless, one event stands out as the paradigmatic police riot—the 1968 Democratic National Convention in Chicago.

ANATOMY OF A POLICE RIOT

Televised footage of the 1968 Democratic National Convention shocked the nation.[69] Mobs of police were filmed beating protesters, bystanders, and reporters viciously and indiscriminately. Over a hundred people were hospitalized as the result of police violence.[70] Senator Abraham Ribicoff spoke on the floor of the convention against the "Gestapo tactics in the streets of Chicago."[71] George McGovern described the scene as a "blood bath," also making comparison to "Nazi Germany."[72]

Norman Mailer commented:

> What staggered the delegates who witnessed the attack—more accurate to call it the massacre, since it was sudden, unprovoked, and total—on Michigan Avenue, was that it opened the specter of what it might mean for the police to take over society. They might comport themselves in such a case not as a force of law and order, not even as a force of repression upon civil disorder, but as a true criminal force; chaotic, improvisational, undisciplined, and finally—sufficiently aroused—uncontrollable.[73]

Mailer's characterization of police behavior closely matches that produced by more systematic studies. Daniel Walker, in his authoritative report on the DNC, notes, "Fundamental police training was ignored; and officers, when on the scene, were often unable to control their men."[74] Walker's report offers this example:

> A high-ranking Chicago police commander admits that on [at least one] occasion the police "got out of control." This same commander appears in one of the most vivid scenes of the entire week, trying desperately to keep individual policemen from beating demonstrators as he screams, "For Christ's sake, stop it!"[75]

Such a breakdown in command, when paired with the widespread and excessive use of force, is perhaps the defining mark of the classic police riot.[76] In his book, *Police Riots: Collective Violence and Law Enforcement*, sociologist Rodney Stark offers a six-step outline as to how these riots unfold:

(1) "Convergence"—There must be substantial numbers on both sides.

(2) "Confrontation"—Either police actions attract hostile crowds, or police deem some gathering illegal and move in to break it up.

(3) "Dispersal"—Police attempt to break up the crowd.

(4) "The Utilization of Force"—Police use force against the crowd.

(5) "The Limited Riot"—Excessive or punitive force ends once the crowd is dispersed. The limited police riot is often signified by the disintegration of police formations into small autonomous groups, charging into crowds, chasing fleeing individuals, and beating people up.

(6) "The Extended Police Riot"—Attacks continue even after the crowd has dispersed. Extended riots are most common in densely populated areas, like college campuses or urban ghettos. Then, police attacks often attract new crowds, thus renewing confrontations.[77]

There are a number of factors that, in the right circumstances, give police actions this trajectory. Among them are specific crowd control tactics, operational deficiencies, the machismo inherent to cop culture,[78] and a paranoid ideology that leads police to overestimate the threat crowds pose.[79]

On the tactical level, Stark notes:

> The incapacities and misconceptions of the police contribute to the occurrence of police riots in a number of ways. First, simply massing the police together, given their lack of discipline and tactical competence, provides an opportunity for them to attack crowds. Second, massive displays of police power provoke demonstrators and tend to produce confrontations and deeper conflicts. Third, police tactics mislead policemen about what is expected of them and increases [sic] their anxiety and hostility. The obsession with officer safety leads to overpreparedness, overreaction, and a disregard for the general safety.[80]

Add to this an habitual reliance on violence, and the production of a riot seems quite predictable.[81]

These difficulties are exacerbated by organizational weaknesses common to police departments, namely the lack of internal discipline. The tactics of riot control are generally derived from the military, but the police proved to be a very different type of organization than the Army. "To put it bluntly: the American police cannot perform at the minimum levels of teamwork, impersonality, and discipline which these military tactics take for granted."[82] For example, in the Detroit riot of 1967, the police and National Guard were responsible for establishing order on one side of town; U.S. Army paratroopers were assigned to the other side. Within a few hours, the Army had restored order in their area, having fired 201 rounds of ammunition and having killed one person. The police and Guard, in contrast, fired thousands of rounds and killed twenty-eight people, while the disorder continued.

> These dramatic and critical differences seem to have stemmed from discipline. The paratroopers had it, the police and guardsmen did not. The Army ordered the lights back on and troopers to show themselves as conspicuously as possible; the police and the guardsmen continued shooting out all lights and crouched fearfully in the darkness. The troopers were ordered to hold their fire, and did so. The police and guardsmen shot wildly and often at one another. The troopers were ordered to unload their weapons, and did so. The guardsmen were so ordered, but did not comply.[83]

The Guard, whose training approximates that of the Army, may have lost discipline in part because of how they were deployed. The police effectively dis-organized the National Guard by converting it into a police force. One National Guard commander complained:

> They sliced us like baloney. The police wanted bodies. They grabed [sic] Guardsmen as soon as they reached the armories, before their units were made up, and sent them out—two on a firetruck, this one in a police car, that one to guard some installation. . . . The Guard simply became lost boys in the big town carrying guns.[84]

In the case of the 1968 Democratic convention, other factors also came into play, in particular the attitudes of civil authorities. Walker mentions, "Chicago police [had been led] to expect that violence against demonstrators, as against rioters, would be condoned by city officials."[85] In fact, this expectation was validated; Mayor Daley continued to defend his officers long after his excuses could be considered in any way credible.[86] One further fact complicates the picture: Much of the convention-week violence was planned. Some reporters received warnings from cops with whom they were friendly; they were told the police intended to target members of the media.[87] With these facts in mind, the police riot seems to take on a different air. The cops did not simply panic; they knew what they meant to do. While internal discipline broke down, the police action as a whole filled its intended role. Indeed, the cops had been encouraged, and then protected, by the mayor. Certain commanders may have been appalled by what they saw or may simply have been afflicted by the managerial need to assert their authority in a crisis, but this did nothing to affect the behavior of the institution as a whole.

Finally, it should be noted that the Escalated Force strategy itself contributes to the likelihood of a police riot. The police riot, by Stark's analysis, moves along exactly the same lines as the Escalated Force model. (In fact, Stark refers to his six-stage articulation as an "Escalation Model.")[88] The crowd control operation ends and the riot begins at the point where discipline breaks down. The implementation of the Escalated Force strategy tends to race toward this point. In practice, police commanders "tend to maximize rather than minimize the use of force in order to maximize officer safety and to maximize dispersal" even though "command control and tactical integrity tend to collapse in contact with crowds and as greater force is applied."[89] In other words, as the amount of force is increased, the likelihood that discipline will be lost and that excessive force will be used also increases. This lapse, as we've seen, was generally either tolerated or actively encouraged by local authorities; in any case, it was a predictable consequence of placing large numbers of police in tense circumstances, with neither the training nor the organization, not to mention to inclination, to respond with restraint.

While the Escalated Force model did not always produce police riots, it also did practically nothing to reduce the odds that they would occur. In one sense, the police riot can be understood as the last step in the Escalated Force sequence.

During the sixties, three additional problems with Escalated Force became clear. First, the deployment of large numbers of cops often created a confrontation that could have otherwise been avoided. Second, the rigid enforcement of the law and the quick recourse to force provoked crowds and sometimes led to violence. And third, as a strategy for restoring order, Escalated Force failed. Stark observes, "There was a strong negative correlation between the amount of force applied and the cessation of rioting in Detroit."[90]

REVISING THE THEORY

Following the disasters of the late sixties, some people started to question the wisdom of a police strategy designed to "escalate" violence. Several commissions were set up to study the disturbances of the sixties, their causes, and the police response to them. Most prominent among these were the Kerner, Eisenhower, and Scranton Commissions. All three bodies concluded that police actions against crowds often intensified, and in some cases provoked, civil disorder. They also recognized that the dangers of the Escalated Force model were not only tactical, but political.

The Scranton Commission wrote, "[T]o respond to peaceful protest with repression and brutal tactics is dangerously unwise. It makes extremists of moderates, deepens the divisions in the nation and increases the chances that future protests will be violent."[91]

Consequently, these boards recommended a number of changes in police handling of demonstrations. The Kerner Commission, for instance, advocated a strategy emphasizing manpower over firepower, prevention over reaction, and increased management and regimentation of the police. A new strategy, "Negotiated Management," was born.

Negotiated Management was designed to correct for the excesses of the Escalated Force model. Under the Negotiated Management approach,

> Police do not try to prevent demonstrations, but attempt to limit the amount of disruption they cause. . . . Police attempt to steer demonstrations to times and places where disruption will be minimized. . . . Even civil disobedience, by definition illegal, is not usually problematic for police; they often cooperate with protesters when their civil disobedience is intentionally symbolic.[92]

Under Negotiated Management, arrests are used only as a last resort, and force is kept to a strict minimum. Rather than trying to disperse the crowd, the police plan so as to contain it. Rather than responding to disorder with force, the police calculate their tactics so as to defuse potentially explosive situations. The innovation of this approach lies in the understanding that de-escalation is sometimes possible.

> [T]he three most significant tactical tendencies characterizing protest policing in the 1990s appear to be (a) underenforcement of the law; (b) the search to negotiate; (c) large scale collection of information. [Beginning in the 1980s, police strategy was] dominated by the attempt to avoid coercive interaction as much as possible. Lawbreaking, which is implicit in several forms of protest, tends to be tolerated by the police. Law enforcement is usually considered as less important than peacekeeping. This implies a considerable departure from protest policing in the 1960s and 1970s, when attempts to stop unauthorized demonstrations and a law-and-order attitude in the face

of the "limited rule-breaking" tactic used by the new movements maneuvered the police repeatedly into "no-win" situations.[93]

Under the new model, police focus on preventing a disturbance, rather than responding to one, seeking to control demonstrations through a system of permits and a series of negotiations with protest organizers.[94] Elements such as the time of the event and the route of the march are agreed upon, and organizers are encouraged (or sometimes required) to provide their own marshals to exercise discipline over the group as a whole.

A model application of Negotiated Management is described by John Brothers in his article "Communication Is the Key to Small Demonstration Control." Brothers documents a series of anti-apartheid actions on the University of Kansas campus and details the Kansas University Police Department's response. Between April 29 and May 9, 1985, the campus was the site of three "moderate-sized" demonstrations and several small ones, including some accompanied by civil disobedience. Sixty-five arrests were made, but there were no injuries, no property damage, and no violence on either side. This small miracle was accomplished by establishing friendly relations with the demonstrators and being patient enough to let crowds dwindle on their own. Police kept their presence to a minimum, and carefully crafted a non-aggressive demeanor in part by not donning riot gear. They also provided refreshments on hot days, and waited to receive complaints before issuing citations. By these means, police won the cooperation of organizers, who met with them regularly to outline their plans.[95]

Clearly this approach is better suited to a political system that espouses ideals of freedom and popular sovereignty, but the ultimate aim of Negotiated Management remains the same as that of Escalated Force—or even Maximum Force, before that— to control dissent, to render protest ineffective.

Looking now at the Scranton, Eisenhower, and Kerner reports, what strikes the reader is the apparent schizophrenia of them all. They decry social injustice with criticisms of racial discrimination, prison conditions, and the plight of the urban poor. They push for greater inclusivity at all levels of society. But they also denounce the activities by which attention was successfully brought to these problems, and change effected. The Eisenhower report explicitly denounces civil disobedience; and, the Scranton report insists that those responsible for campus unrest be disciplined.[96] These reports push for rigorous adherence to Constitutional guarantees of free speech and the like, while at the same time offering precise instruction on the means of limiting, containing, and controlling protests.

It is tempting to read such documents as well-intentioned but politically naive defenses of the rule of law. But, rather more appropriately, one might also understand them as handbooks for social managers and others responsible for controlling dissent.[97] Taken as such, the reports' advocacy of civil liberties and the principle of minimal force reflect the sophistication of the liberal approach to repression.

Negotiated Management was an innovation in the means of crowd control, but the basic aim remains unchanged. Both Negotiated Management and Escalated Force represent a defense of the status quo. Brothers' article, for example, emphasizes again and again the "neutrality" of the police, but notes that their plans were designed to "minimize the impact of the event upon the media."[98] Presumably, had the demonstrations aimed at goals besides media attention, the police would have sought to minimize their impact in those areas as well.

The Eisenhower Commission offers the Peace Moratorium March of November 15, 1969, as an example of the success of Negotiated Management:

> The bulk of the actual work of maintaining the peacefulness of the proceedings was performed by the demonstrators themselves. An estimated five thousand "marshals," recruited from among the demonstrators, flanked the crowds throughout. Their effectiveness was shown when they succeeded in stopping an attempt by the fringe radicals to leave the line of the march in an effort to reach the White House. . . . [99]

The nature of such an arrangement is not lost on those who study law enforcement. The academic literature describes marshals who "'police' other demonstrators,"[100] and who have a "*collaborative* relationship" with the authorities.[101] This is essentially a strategy of co-optation. The police enlist the protest organizations to control the demonstrators, putting the organization at least partly in the service of the state and intensifying the function of control.

PLAYING BY THE RULES

The Negotiated Management model has its weaknesses as well. Its success requires a certain kind of cop and a certain kind of protest. If either is unavailable, Negotiated Management becomes impossible.

The Philadelphia police department made a very early attempt at this softer approach, and failed for lack of the right cop. In 1964, Police Commissioner Howard Leary created a "Civil Disobedience" unit charged with both keeping order and protecting the civil rights of demonstrators. This unit was to be headed by an officer proven to be calm, patient, and friendly. His job was to build a relationship with protest leaders and work with them to keep the peace. The unit never functioned as it was intended to. Instead, it quickly degenerated into a domineering red squad.[102] This quick return to the antagonistic approach was the result of several deeply rooted features of the police as a group, including the rejection of compromise and conciliatory tactics, an obsession with agitators and conspiracies, and the system of political sponsorship that guided promotion into the unit.[103]

Police/protester cooperation requires a fundamental adjustment in the attitude of the authorities. The Negotiated Management approach demands the institution-alization of protest. Demonstrations must be granted some degree of legitimacy so they can be carefully managed rather than simply shoved about. This approach has, until recently, de-emphasized the radical or antagonistic aspects of protest in favor of a routinized and collaborative approach.

Naturally such a relationship brings with it some fairly tight constraints as to the kinds of protest activity available. Rallies, marches, polite picketing, symbolic civil disobedience actions, and even legal direct action such as strikes or boycotts are like-ly to be acceptable, within certain limits. Violence, obviously, would not be tolerat-ed. Neither would property destruction. Nor would any of the variety of tactics that have been developed to close businesses, prevent logging, disrupt government meet-ings, or otherwise interfere with the operation of some part of society. That is to say, picketing may be fine, barricades are not. Rallies are in, riots are out. Taking to the streets, under certain circumstances, may be acceptable; taking over the factories is not. The danger for activists is that they might permanently limit themselves to tac-tics that are predictable, non-disruptive, and ultimately ineffective.[104] On the other side, Negotiated Management opens a pitfall for police wherein they may come to rely on this cooperative arrangement. If the police assume that activists will conduct themselves within the bounds set by this approach, they leave themselves open for some nasty surprises.

Essentially, this is what happened to the Seattle police in 1999. According to the SPD's After Action Report, police planners adopted a Negotiated Management strategy early on and failed to consider contingencies that would make other options necessary. Despite well-publicized plans to disrupt the WTO conference, the police decided to "Trust that Seattle's strong historical precedents of peaceful protest and our on-going negotiations with protests groups would govern the actions of demonstrators."[105] On November 30, their mistake must have been only too obvious. When the institutional framework of protest was challenged, the coopera-tive relationship proved fragile and the basis of the Negotiated Management model was undermined. Not only did radicals refuse to play the game by its usual rules, even respectable protest groups were unable to keep their members in line. For example, when police changed the route of the officially sanctioned union march, hoping to keep union members away from the center of the disturbance, they were surprised when several thousand of the marchers ignored the marshals, left the route, and joined the fray.[106]

The SPD offered this analysis of their mistake: "While we needed to think about a new paradigm of disruptive protest, we relied on our knowledge of past demonstrations, concluding that the 'worst case' would not occur here."[107] Such blindness is a typical fault of police agencies. Equally typical is the panic that follows a defeat, a panic felt not only in Seattle, but around the country, resulting in the sudden shift in police tactics at demonstrations nationwide.

> Changes and learning processes of the police are initiated by an analysis of problematic public order interventions, that is, the police learn from their failures. . . . The importance of the body of past experience, however, seems such that it prevents the police from anticipating change. Tactical and strategic errors in confrontations with new movements and protest forms may trigger off a relapse into an antagonistic protest policing style.[108]

In the wake of Seattle, the use of force has received a new emphasis. Riot gear, tear gas, mass arrests, and widespread violence have again become common features of demonstrations. While police violence has always been a possibility, it has lately come to resemble an open threat. Some of this is surely deliberate. The threat of violence is an effective tool for suppressing the attendance at a gathering, especially among portions of the population who are more routinely subject to police attack. It also serves to criminalize dissent. When members of the public see the police in riot gear, it is easy to assume that the crowd they are monitoring is dangerous, or even criminal.[109] But some of the police reliance on force is the product of desperation. They simply don't know what to do, and while they figure it out, the old-fashioned, straightforward head-knocking approach seems like a safe bet.

A TERRORIST STRATEGY

The police and other authorities are frantically trying to find new footing in their handling of protests. Naturally, their mistakes in Seattle figure prominently in the developing analysis.

While everyone acknowledges that the police needed to be better prepared if they wanted to maintain control in Seattle, it is hotly disputed what, precisely, they should have been prepared for. The McCarthy report implies that the police should have been trained, armed, and organized as though to repel an invasion.[110] The city council's committee notes that the cops weren't even ready to implement the plan that they had and condemns the subsequent civil rights abuses and police violence. Essentially, the city council's committee thinks the problem was not with the Negotiated Management strategy, but with its implementation. They urged, not more force, but increased accommodation.

> It is clear to the committee that demonstrators who sought arrest— in order to underline their statements of principle—should have been

accommodated by police. Tear gas is a cruel implement to use against persons trying to make deeply-felt statements against what they view as injustice.[111]

But the city council's perspective on this situation may rely on a misconception about what the protesters hoped to accomplish. Rather than seek symbolic arrests to "underline their statements of principle," protesters intended to directly interfere with the WTO's work by blockading the conference and disrupting its proceedings. The police didn't understand this until the disruption was underway; the city council seems never to have figured it out.

The McCarthy and Associates report implies that where Negotiated Management failed on November 30, Escalated Force succeeded on December 1. If this is true, then the lesson the police should take from Seattle is that the Negotiated Management model is one strategy of control, but that to rely on it exclusively is to court disorder. The use of force must always be prepared for, if only as a backup.

The LAPD has adopted just such a two-track approach, alternating between Negotiated Management and Escalated Force strategies according to the circumstances. Two incidents from the 2000 Democratic National Convention suffice to make the case.

On August 14, after a concert in one of the designated protest areas,[112] police cut power to the stage, declared the event an unlawful assembly, and gave approximately 10,000 people 20 minutes to leave through a single exit. A short time later, the cops attacked, charging with horses and firing rubber bullets. The *Los Angeles Times* reported, "In addition to rubber bullets, police also used pepper spray and projectile beanbags, striking many of the protesters and some bystanders as they fired indiscriminately for more than an hour."[113] Jesse Jackson termed the police action "unnecessary brutality"; Commander David Kalish called it "a measured, strategic response."[114] They may both be right. The ACLU described the event precisely, referring to it as "an orchestrated police riot."[115]

A few days later, the cops showed a different face when thirty-seven people sat down in front of the notorious Ramparts division police station and refused to leave.

> The civil disobedience action . . . attempted to focus on the brutality, corruption, and violence of the LAPD. . . . However, some of the organizers had collaborated closely with the Ramparts police prior to the action to work out the details of the arrests, and had followed some suggestions of the police in order to avoid what they feared would be the cops going berserk if taken by surprise. After presenting the police chief with a list of demands, one of the arrestees shook hands amicably with him as the cameras flashed. Ironically, the result was a PR/media opportunity to showcase the civility and non-violent behavior of the cops.[116]

This incident shows the effective co-optation of protest when it proceeds through collaborative channels. It also shows the disciplining effect of police violence: the threat of violence motivates protesters to negotiate ahead of time, and allows the cops to set the rules. As per the McCarthy team recommendations, a hybrid approach may incorporate Escalated Force as the primary strategy of control, with Negotiated Management serving as a tool for police to establish boundaries. This approach works as a modification of the Good Cop/Bad Cop routine: If the Bad Cop is bad enough, he may only need to act in minor or symbolic ways to keep the crowd in line. Negotiation with the Good Cop starts to look more attractive, as does playing by the rules. This, in essence, is the strategy of political terrorism. The threat of violence is made clear at every turn, and a politically useful climate of fear is carefully developed in order to control the population.[117] Terrorism and co-optation are thus subsumed under a single system.

This is something we should learn to expect: the strategic use of both the Good Cop and the Bad Cop to control and, ultimately, to neutralize dissent.

ORGANIZATIONAL CHANGES

If the 2000 Democratic convention is any indication, it would seem that the biggest change since 1968 is the broadened range of tactics available to police. Police commanders have gained the ability to restrain officers when a Good Cop approach is in order. This is made possible by organizational changes connected, both historically and conceptually, to the process of militarization.

Historically, the federal government prompted the development of Negotiated Management: The approach was shaped by the various commission reports, Supreme Court rulings, the development of the National Park Service permit system, and the availability of crowd control training at the U.S. Army Military Police School.[118] (In this respect, local police have followed a course similar to that of the National Guard, which was militarized after the 1877 strike wave.) This new training was specifically designed according to the recommendations of the Kerner and Eisenhower reports.[119]

The Negotiated Management model arose at the same time and from the same sources as the militarization of the police. To make sense of this, it is important to understand that *militarization* does not only refer to police tactics and weaponry, but also to their mode of organization.[120] The Kerner report argued for it explicitly:

> The control of civil disturbances . . . requires large numbers of disciplined personnel, comparable to soldiers in a military unit, organized and trained to work as a team under a highly unified command and control system. Thus when a civil disturbance occurs, a police department must suddenly shift into a new type of organization with

different operational procedures. The individual officer must stop acting independently and begin to perform as a member of a closely supervised, disciplined team.[121]

In short, it is military discipline that makes Negotiated Management a possibility, restraining the individual officers while maintaining the potential for a coordinated attack. This requires careful planning for the operation itself, and a high level of discipline among the officers, so that each one acts according to the established plan.[122] Hence, militarization may *increase* the organization's overall capacity for violence, but may *decrease* individual acts of brutality, owing to a higher level of discipline.[123]

Previously, individual acts of brutality were tolerated or encouraged as a means of controlling the population through terror. But this approach can be limiting, as it renders negotiation and co-optation unlikely. Militarization formalizes the strategy of violence at the institutional level. It thus maintains discipline and employs force more selectively, with direction from above.

Ironically, while the conventional wisdom associates militarization with the Escalated Force approach (and contrasts it with community policing), in point of fact militarization is essential to Negotiated Management.[124] Moreover, as we shall see, militarization is a key component of community policing.

YOUR FRIENDLY NEIGHBORHOOD POLICE STATE

The difficulties of crowd control have shown the need for police to balance their reliance on force against the possibility of containment, negotiation, and the co-optation of leadership. Over-reliance on either approach is likely to lead to disaster: Naked repression can create or escalate resistance and discredit authorities, while resting on the framework of institutionalized dissent can leave the state's forces unprepared for tactical innovations or renewed militancy among protesters. The challenge for police is to chart a middle course between the WTO protests in Seattle and the massacre at Kent State.

Though drawn from their experiences with protests and riots, these lessons have come to shape the development of police strategy overall. They have thus given rise to the seemingly incongruous but in fact complementary trends of militarization and community policing.

BRINGING THE WAR HOME

"Militarization" is a buzz-word, popular chiefly among critics of the police. The term is in some sense pejorative, as military incursions into the domestic sphere are taboo in liberal democracies. But militarization is rarely defined, and the use of the word is often superficial. This is true in two senses: First, the term is sometimes chosen more for its sinister connotations than for any literal meaning; second, it is used to describe the most obvious aspects of policing—the equipment, uniforms, and weaponry. By implication, armored cars, riot gear, and assault rifles evidence militarization; the friendly cop on the beat does not.

This dichotomy is false, and dangerous. It misconstrues the nature of militarization and underestimates its impact. Militarization affects not only police paraphernalia, but the police mission, the roles of violence and intelligence, police ideology, rhetoric, training, and organization. A leading scholar of militarization, Peter Kraska, offers this definition:

> *Militarization* . . . can be defined in its broadest terms as the social process in which society organizes itself for the production of violence or the threat thereof.[1]

He goes on to list the following "tangible indices of this sort of high-modern militarization:"

1. A blurring of external and internal security functions leading to a targeting of civilian populations, internal "security" threats, and a focus on aggregate populations as potential internal "insurgents"

2. An avoidance of overt or lethal violence, with a greater emphasis placed on information gathering and processing, surveillance work, and less-than-lethal technologies

3. An ideology and theoretical framework of militarism that stresses that effective problem solving requires state force, technology, armament, intelligence gathering, aggressive suppression efforts, and other assorted activities commensurate with modern military thinking and operations

4. Criminal justice practices guided by the ideological framework of militarism, such as the use of special-operations paramilitary teams in policing and corrections, policing activities that emphasize military tactics such as drug, gun, and gang suppression, and punishment models based on the military boot camp

5. The purchasing, loaning, donation, and use of actual material products that can be characterized as militaristic, including a range of military armaments, transportation devices, surveillance equipment, and military-style garb

6. A rapidly developing collaboration, at the highest level of the governmental and corporate worlds, between the defense industry and the crime control industry

7. The use of military language within political and popular culture, to characterize the social problems of drugs, crime, and social disorder[2]

By these standards, the contemporary American police department is highly militarized in ways that its nineteenth-century counterpart was not.[3]

Developments in crowd control and intelligence have each placed the police on this course, as have police ideology and the institution's rapidly advancing mode of organization. Of course, the rhetoric of policing and of police reform has long made use of a military analogy, though in practice this amounted to little more than instituting ranks and requiring firearms training.[4] But following the crises of the 1960s, this analogy was suddenly taken far more seriously. The rhetoric, of course, never really went out of style,[5] but it gained a more literal reading than had been possible before. Radicals were calling on America to "Bring the war home," and policymakers very quietly decided to do just that.

FROM OCCASIONAL SHOOT-OUTS TO ROUTINE PATROL

The authorities responded to the disorder of the 1960s by increasing the cops' funding, upgrading their equipment, and reorganizing departments along more military lines.[6] To this end, the National Institute of Justice (NIJ) was founded in 1968, and it immediately set about transferring Defense Department technology to the police. Over the next ten years, the NIJ outfitted police with military wonders like night vision goggles, soft body armor, forensic and computer equipment, surveillance devices, and retired Army helicopters.[7]

Police planning also quickly turned in a more martial direction. In 1969, the NYPD began planning construction of its Command and Control Center. For models, it visited military installations like the Pentagon and the Strategic Air Command Headquarters. Mayor John Lindsay described the new center aptly as a "war room."[8] Meanwhile, in Los Angeles, Daryl Gates was reinventing the Metro Division of the LAPD:

> Breaking from LAPD tradition, we formed sixteen military-type squads with a sergeant in charge of each ten-man squad, and then we meshed them into two platoons, each headed by a lieutenant. They were given missions for which they were responsible. They developed the approach and the tactics without direction from above. Their only admonishment was to maintain departmental policy and rules.[9]

Gates' adaptation of military organization to law enforcement was remarkable, and it did not end with the squad and platoon structures. Military tactics were soon adopted as well, most famously with the creation of the SWAT team.

The Los Angeles Police Department's Special Weapons And Tactics team became the first of many similar units generically termed "Police Paramilitary Units" or PPUs.[10] SWAT was developed in secret during the late sixties, and trained with marines at Camp Pendleton.[11] Though ostensibly designed to handle snipers, the team's first mission was a 1969 raid on the headquarters of the Black Panther Party. A shoot-out ensued, follow by a long stand-off. Growing impatient, the SWAT team requested and received a Marine Corps grenade launcher, but the Panthers surrendered before it could be put to use.[12] Shortly thereafter, SWAT raided a house where members of the Symbionese Liberation Army (SLA) were hiding out. Again, a shoot-out ensued, followed by a long standoff. This time SWAT asked for fragmentation grenades and Gates refused. But no matter; when police fired teargas into the house it caught fire and burned to the ground. Six SLA members died in the blaze.[13] Gates later expressed his concern: "At the moment my main concern was whether Patty Hearst had been inside. I didn't give a shit about the others."[14] Apparently his regard for the neighbors was no higher. No effort had been made to evacuate the neighborhood before the raid or during the stand-off. Nearby homes were damaged in the fire, and several houses were riddled with bullets.[15]

The LAPD SWAT team was deployed 200 times in its first two years.[16] Since then, paramilitary police units have become a nationwide phenomenon, and their rate of use has sharply increased. In 1980, PPUs were deployed 2,884 times across the country. Fifteen years later, in 1995, that number had risen to 29,962.[17]

In part, PPUs are deployed more often simply because there are more of them to deploy. Many small departments have formed their own paramilitary units, whereas before they relied on those of larger cities or the state police in the rare event of an emergency. After all, how often do the campus police at the University of Central Florida face sniper fire, a barricaded suspect, or a hostage situation? Yet they have their own SWAT team.[18]

Many factors promoted the spread of paramilitary units, including the existence of a ready-to-use model, the availability of equipment[19] and training,[20] and the professional prestige attached to the highly specialized teams. The nationwide craze for SWAT teams marks an advance in the militarization of the police, but as importantly, the factors sustaining this trend also indicate militarization.

Perhaps more troubling than the replication of the SWAT model is the expansion of the SWAT mission. Since 1994, Fresno California has used its PPU, the Violent Crime Suppression Unit (VCSU), to patrol its southwest ghettos. Wearing black fatigues, combat boots, and body armor, the officers routinely patrol with MP-54 submachine guns, helicopters, and dogs. First deployed after a wave of gang violence, including attacks on police officers, the VCSU quickly went from raiding houses to stopping cars, interrogating "suspicious persons," and clearing people off of street corners. These street corner sweeps represent an impressive display of force, beginning with a pyrotechnic flash-bang grenade. Police then move in with their guns drawn, sometimes supported by a canine unit. Everyone in the area is forced to the ground, and civilian dogs are shot on sight. The "suspects" in the area are photographed, interrogated, checked for warrants, and entered into a computerized database.[21] One Fresno cop explains the intended scope of these files: "If you're twenty-one, male, living in one of these neighborhoods, been in Fresno for ten years and you're *not* in our computer—then there's definitely a problem."[22]

The VCSU produces impressive figures marking its activity. Since it started patrolling Fresno's streets, misdemeanor arrests have increased 48.3 percent. Meanwhile, the unit averages one shooting every three months.[23]

Fresno is not alone in its use of paramilitary police for routine patrol. By 1999, there were 94 departments across the country similarly deploying their SWAT teams.[24] One commander described his department's approach:

> We're into saturation patrols in hot spots. We do a lot of work With
> [sic] the SWAT unit because we have bigger guns. We send out two,

two-to-four-men cars, we look for minor violations and do jump-outs, either on people on the street or automobiles. After we jump-out the second car provides periphery cover with an ostentatious display of weaponry. We're sending a clear message: if the shootings don't stop, we'll shoot someone. . . .[25]

The application of paramilitary techniques in routine, non-emergency law enforcement situations has been termed the "normalization" of paramilitary units.[26] This process works in two complementary directions. First, the scope of activity considered appropriate for specialized units becomes ever wider. In military jargon, this is referred to as "mission creep," a suitably unpleasant sounding term.[27] Second, the increased use of the specialized team promotes the view that their military organization, skills, and equipment are well suited to general police work; the regular police then come to resemble the paramilitary units.[28] Both tendencies advance the militarization of the police, and both have been encouraged by the current efforts at drug prohibition.

THE DRUG WAR AND OTHER DANGEROUS HABITS

The tendency for mission creep, the temptation to use specialized forces for a widening range of activities, is surely understandable. The reasoning, from a managerial perspective, is pretty clear. Where such units exist, commanders are loath to "waste" their capabilities. To justify their continued existence, in particular their continued funding, they must be used. Inactivity is bureaucratic suicide. So the mission of these units expands. As it expands, their operations become normalized.

> Because riots and hostage-takings are relatively rare, SSU [Denver's Special Service Unit] has had a lot of time on its hands, notwithstanding its demanding training requirements. So in its spare time, which has amounted to 90 percent, it has been doing saturation patrolling.[29]

Saturation patrolling offers one solution for the need to keep the paramilitary teams busy between emergencies. Likewise, mundane police duties can be framed as "emergencies," or alternately, the cops may actually *create* emergencies. This, in essence, is what the police do when they use paramilitary units to perform "warrant work."

"Warrant work" is actually something of a misnomer, since many departments claim that they don't need a warrant when they fear that evidence would be destroyed during the time it takes to contact a judge.[30] The searches at issue are usually drug-related. One commander describes the procedure: "[O]ur unit storms the residence with a full display of weaponry so we can get the drugs before they're flushed."[31] Paramilitary units usually specialize in "no-knock" or "dynamic" entries, meaning they avoid announcing their presence until they've knocked down the door and are charging into the house. The LAPD, in its characteristic style, gave its SWAT team an armored car with a battering ram attached; rather than breaking down the door, the cops drive the vehicle straight through the wall.[32]

No-knock entries are dangerous for everyone involved—cops, suspects, bystanders. The raids usually occur before dawn; the residents are usually asleep, and are disoriented by the sudden intrusion. There is no warning, and sleepy residents may not always understand that the men breaking down their door are police. At the same time, police procedures allow terribly little room for error. Stan Goff, a retired Special Forces sergeant and SWAT trainer, says that he teaches cops to "Look at hands. If there's a weapon in their hands during a dynamic entry, it does not matter what that weapon is doing. If there's a weapon in their hands, that person dies. It's automatic."[33]

Predictably, these raids sometimes end in disaster. When the Visalia, California, SWAT team raided Alfonso Hernandez's apartment in 1998, the teenager opened fire, injuring one officer. The police fired back without restraint, hitting Hernandez 39 times and killing him on the spot. Some of their bullets traveled through walls into neighboring apartments. In addition to Hernandez, another man in the apartment, Emiliano Trevino, was killed. Trevino was seeking refuge in a corner when he was shot five times.[34]

No-knock raids are inherently dangerous but, in most cases, altogether avoidable. That is because there is usually no emergency before the raid begins.[35] Even if we take current drug laws for granted, it is clear that this approach places citizens and police alike at unnecessary risk. The fact that such risks are considered normal, and thought to represent an acceptable price for maintaining current policy, says a great deal about the prevalence of militarized thinking. As Peter Kraska remarks:

> Only an intensive ideology of militarism could drive much of the police institution into believing that forced invasions of people's private residences using police units designed around the Navy Seals model for the purpose of conducting a crude investigation into minor drug law infractions are a reasonable and beneficial crime control tactic.[36]

For their part, police sometimes complain that the "war" metaphor—against crime, or against drugs—is not taken literally enough. Never one for understatement, former LAPD Chief Daryl Gates once told the Senate Judiciary Committee: "The casual drug user should be taken out and shot." When *Los Angeles Times* reporter Ron Ostrow asked him if he meant that, the Chief was glad to explain:

Yeah, Ron, I did. . . . if we have people who smoke a little pot or snort a little coke, who simply want to go out and party and use drugs, I think they ought to be taken out and shot, because if this is a war on drugs, they are giving aid and comfort to the enemy.[37]

Self-righteousness and self-interest often lean on each other suspiciously. Behind their moral platitudes and somber denunciations, the police have always been major beneficiaries of vice—drugs, gambling, prostitution. In the nineteenth century, selective enforcement of vice laws stood to profit the individual cops, their commanders, and their political masters. The police stood at the center of a multi-faceted protection racket. The threat of raids kept the owners of illegal saloons, gambling houses, brothels, and opium dens obedient and willing to pay the going rate; or, the promise of protection might be withheld for either political or commercial reasons, to eliminate a source of income for a rival political faction, or to give the competitive edge to a loyal client. And the thing that made all this corruption possible was the puritanical obsession with other people's recreation.[38]

At the end of the twentieth century, things looked a little different. At the lowest levels of the law enforcement ladder, the police still sometimes sold protection to street-level drug dealers, pimps, and prostitutes; or, conversely, they offered them the opposite of protection, robbing them of guns, drugs, and money, assaulting them, and making no arrest.[39] As bad as this was, it was only a small-time, illegal version of official policy. On a much wider scale, and with much lower risk, entire departments were involved in exactly the same sort of extortion, under the guise of asset forfeiture.

First introduced by a 1970 anti-racketeering law (the irony here is sickening), the practice of seizing drug money and other property has been expanded repeatedly, most notably by the 1984 Comprehensive Crime Control Act. The 1984 law allowed local and state authorities to seize the assets of suspected drug dealers, try the cases in federal court, and keep up to 90 percent of the loot for departmental use. Forfeiture cases are not considered criminal proceedings—in fact, no one need be charged with a crime at all—and so the hearings carry a lower standard of proof. Cases involving assets under $100,000 are handled in administrative hearings, not even reaching civil court. More questionable still, prosecutors sometimes reduce charges when defendants agree to surrender their assets without a fight.[40]

Racial profiling innovator and Volusia County (Florida) Sheriff Bob Vogel, used these laws quite adeptly. Between 1989 and 1992, he confiscated $8 million in property based on searches conducted during motor vehicle stops. Of those who "forfeited" their property, 85 percent were Black and 75 percent were never charged with a crime.[41]

The forfeiture law provided the local cops with a major incentive for prioritizing drug busts. As the money came in, many departments reinvested it in the drug war, upgrading their arsenals with military hardware.[42] But in addition to the financial gains, drug raids promised political and bureaucratic benefits as well. Asset forfeiture opened another major source of funding for local departments, making the police less reliant on their local governments' budget processes, and therefore also less subject to the control of mayors and city councils.

It is hard to overstate the impact drug policy has had on policing. The national obsession with controlling drug use has provided a rationale for racial profiling, legitimized prison expansion and draconian sentencing laws, eroded constitutional protections against warrantless searches, promoted federal intervention and military involvement in local law enforcement, and helped enormously to militarize the police.[43] It has also provided a convenient justification for widening the scope of police activity.

COMMUNITY POLICING: THE RETURN OF OFFICER FRIENDLY[44]

If the aggressive, armored paramilitary unit represents one face of contemporary policing, the other is that of the smiling, chatty, cop on the beat. One is the image of militarization; the other is that of community policing.

"Community policing," like "militarization," is a jargon term. It is loosely defined and sometimes used to mean only "something desirable." "Community policing" is thrown around quite a lot by both critics of the police and by the cops' policy-level allies, but the term is mostly used by those who advocate its programs. What, precisely, they advocate is the matter of quite some controversy.[45]

Community policing largely grew out of innovations developed during the 1970s. The seventies and eighties were periods of extreme experimentation in law enforcement, as departments across the country struggled to recover from the defeats of the 1960s. As the years progressed, the new ideas were either refined or abandoned, and those remaining gradually coalesced under the rubric of community policing. This legacy, plus the community policing premise that law enforcement strategies should be adapted to local conditions and local needs, has resulted in a baffling variety of programs operating under the same label, and has made generalizing about them very difficult.

Community policing largely evolved from the earlier notion of "team policing," under which a group of officers shared responsibility for a particular area.[46] From this base, community policing slowly came to incorporate novelties like decentralized command, storefront mini-stations, directed (rather than random) patrol, neighborhood watch groups, permanent assignments, neighborhood liaisons, door-to-door surveys, public forums, crime prevention trainings, citizen advisory boards, meetings with religious and civic leaders, foot patrols, bike patrols, police-sponsored community activities and social functions, a focus on minor offenses, educational and recreational programs for young people, citizen volunteer opportunities, and community organizing projects.[47]

Common features seemed to connect many of the more successful programs, and these slowly formed the basis for the community policing perspective. Sociologist Gary Cordner groups the elements of community policing into philosophical, strategic, tactical, and organizational dimensions. Philosophically, community policing is characterized by the solicitation of citizen input, the broadening of the police function, and the attempt to find solutions based on the values of the local community. Organizationally, community policing requires that departments be restructured such as to decentralize command, flatten hierarchies, reduce specialization, civilianize staff positions, and encourage teamwork. Strategically, community policing efforts reorient operations away from random patrols and responding to 911 calls, towards more directed, proactive, and preventive activities. This reorientation requires a geographic focus, and encourages cops to pay attention to the sources of disorder as well as to the crimes themselves. Tactics that sustain community policing efforts are those that encourage positive citizen interactions, partnerships, and problem solving.[48]

A 1994 report written by the Community Policing Consortium, representing the International Association of Chiefs of Police, the National Sheriff's Association, the Police Executive Research Forum, and the Police Foundation, and published by the Department of Justice, identifies the two "core components" of community policing as "community partnership and problem solving."[49] Sociologists Jerome Skolnick and David Bayley concluded, based on a study of six police departments renowned as innovators and trend-setters, that the governing premise of community policing was "that the police and the public are co-producers of crime prevention."[50]

By the early 1990s "Community Policing" was the official religion of police nationwide, even if nobody knew exactly what it meant.[51] Even Daryl Gates, the embattled and abrasive former Chief of Police in Los Angeles, explicitly advocated community policing in his 1992 memoir,[52] which only underscores questions about the term's use. If the notorious LAPD has, as Gates insists, been practicing community policing since the 1970s, then what *doesn't* count as community policing? If the term covers everything, then does it mean anything?

Perhaps I'm being unfair. After all, the LAPD did invent some of the paradigmatic community policing programs, including DARE (Drug Abuse Resistance Education) and the neighborhood watch.[53] But the clash between the LAPD's uncivil image and that of the personable neighborhood beat cop gets to the heart of the confusion about what is and is not community policing. There is a difference between adopting stand-alone *programs* and taking on community policing as an overall organizational *strategy*. The Los Angeles police may have recognized early on the need for community partnerships, but it, like most departments, has pursued these partnerships unevenly, haphazardly, and without changing the basic orientation of the police force.

On the other hand, community policing is not at all incompatible with the hard-nosed, militarized tactics for which Gates' department became famous, or infamous. Of the two major strands of community policing programs, "peace corps policing" and "order maintenance policing," the latter seems to actually *promote* just the sort of excess that Gates favored. Peace corps policing "emphasized community empowerment, cultivating constructive relationships with disenfranchised minority groups, and establishing partnerships between the public and the police."[54] The "order-maintenance" model "seeks to 'clean up' a community proactively, thereby reducing the potential for crime and diminishing citizens' fears."[55] Linking the two is an emphasis on problem solving and a sense that police business extends beyond the most basic matters of law enforcement.[56] Hence, both approaches are proactive, prevention-oriented, concerned with the fear of crime as well as with crime itself, and they generally fit within the framework of community policing as it is laid out above. Where differences exist, they tend to be matters of emphasis rather than principle. In fact, peace corps and order maintenance approaches are sometimes employed in tandem, and, together or separately, they dovetail with militarization to form a coherent, strategic whole. To resolve this seeming paradox, we should consider what the police hope to accomplish with community policing, and what advantages they take from their community partnerships.

COMMUNITY POLICING AND POLICY COMMUNITIES

The first thing to notice about community policing is the degree to which it seeks to undo the reforms of the Progressive and professional eras. These earlier reformers sought to centralize command, introduce bureaucratic management practices, close neighborhood precincts, do away with foot patrols, narrowly focus on crime control, increase specialization within the departments, and generally sever the connections between the police and the public.[57] These efforts were never fully successful, but that is hardly the point. The point is that they move in exactly the opposite direction from many of the recommendations made by community policing advocates.

To make sense of this reversal, we need to recognize that community policing seeks to address a different set of problems than those faced by the Progressives or the professionals. There is no longer any need for capitalists to wrest city governments away from Tammany-style political machines, and police unionization has done more to improve the typical patrol officer's standard of living than the move toward professionalization ever did. More subtly, the police have largely established their institutional autonomy, and have developed extensive means to defend it. In fact, since the late sixties, they have moved beyond their quest for independence and have begun to pursue political power.

Here, perhaps, we can discern a pattern. Historically, the means of social control have adapted in response to crises, to challenges faced by the existing authorities. Slave patrols evolved gradually in response to slave revolts. The rise of capitalism produced new class tensions and higher demands for order; one result was the modern police.[58] Is it a coincidence, then, that the three most pronounced trends in contemporary policing—unionization, militarization, and community policing—gained their momentum during a period of profound social tension and overt political conflict?

This puts it dramatically, but it's no secret that community policing arose as a response to the crises of the 1960s. Society was in a state of upheaval and elites were wracked with panic, at One Police Plaza and Parker Center no less than in the White House and the Pentagon.[59] The immediate clash was resolved through a combination of concessions and repression, but before the fight was even over, the authorities were in training for a rematch.

The shortcomings of social control in the Civil Rights and anti-war periods are not difficult to discern. Misplaced intelligence efforts meant that the security forces were often caught unawares by rebellions, and heavy-handed crowd control tactics exacerbated disorder where it arose.[60] Meanwhile, government lawlessness, both domestically and in the field of foreign policy, eroded the citizens' faith in the system. The continuation of such conditions threatened to render the country ungovernable.[61] The authorities had to reassess their approach to social control.

> The fact that police actions triggered many of the riots and then
> could not control them revealed to everyone the price of having a
> police department backed only by the power of the law, but not by
> the consent, much less active support, of those being policed.[62]

The resulting police experiments, which eventually blended into the community policing approach, were born of the desire to correct for the shortcomings of the earlier bureaucratic-professional model. They sought to build a bond between the police and the public in hopes that this would increase police legitimacy, give them better access to information, intensify their penetration of community life, and expand the police mission.[63] All of this, in theory, should make the populace easier to police and heighten the level of police control.

The first task of any community policing strategist is to make police authority legitimate in the eyes of the community. Herman Goldstein, a community policing advocate, identifies "the ultimate potential in community policing" as

> the development of a reservoir of respect and support that could greatly increase the capacity of police officers to deal with problems with less need to resort to the criminal process or to the coercive force that officers derive from their uniform, their weapon, their badge, or the knowledge that they can summon reinforcements.[64]

The means by which this legitimacy is established are sometimes subtle. Even the mechanisms through which the community is supposed to voice its concerns often become forums for the police to promote their own agenda. The most common of these is the citizen survey. Under the guise of collecting information about neighborhood problems and community attitudes, the surveys carefully frame questions to reinforce the fear of crime and present the police as problem solvers. They also suggest a conservative view concerning the causes of crime (drugs, a tolerance for disorder), the people who commit crimes (young people, gang members, strangers), and the solutions to the crime problem (law enforcement).[65] The surveys function twice in this regard—first, in the collection of the data, and then, in the presentation of the results.[66] Community meetings work the same way, turning an atmosphere of inclusiveness and participation to propagandistic ends:

> Although the meetings are supposedly held to deal with the community's concerns, these concerns are defined by police within the framework of how best to reduce crime. The "communication" is frequently a one-way lobby for the police and *their* concerns.[67]

Other features of community policing, like foot patrols and storefront offices, serve to increase friendly contact between police and the residents in the neighborhoods they patrol. All of these practices, it is hoped, can reduce the friction between the cops and the community, encourage communication, build trust, and humanize the individual officers in the eyes of the neighborhood residents.

When legitimacy is established, the police can rely more on the cooperation of the citizenry, rather than resorting to coercive force. Citizen participation

> can run the gamut from watching neighbors' homes, to reporting drug dealers, to patrolling the streets. It can involve participation in problem identification and problem solving efforts, in crime prevention programs, in neighborhood revitalization, and in youth-oriented educational and recreational programs. Citizens may act individually or in groups, they may collaborate with the police and they may

even join the police department by donating their time as police department volunteers, reserves, or auxiliaries.[68]

Moreover, the police are not just encouraged to mobilize individuals, but to draw existing civic groups into their efforts and, where necessary, to set up new organizations to provide the support they need. Hence, the new-found trust would give the police access to, and influence over, community resources that may have otherwise had their law enforcement potential overlooked—or that may have served as centers for resistance. It also provides the police department with additional leverage with which to further its agenda with the rest of the government.

Goldstein, for one, specifically encourages police to act as organizers and advocates in the community. He writes:

> After analyzing the problem, officers involved in these projects conduct an uninhibited search for alternative responses. They may settle on one of the responses identified above as commonly used in community policing, or they may go a step further, perhaps pressuring municipal agencies to carry out existing responsibilities or to invest new resources in an area. They may push for changes in the policies of other government agencies or advocate legislation that would enable police to deal more effectively with a problem that clearly warrants arrest and prosecution.[69]

Hence, community policing advances the autonomy of the institution and encourages police interference with the functions of the rest of the government. It provides an incentive to political action, and threatens to blur the separation of powers and invert the principles of civilian control.

The aim is to turn an ever-widening range of institutions into tools for law enforcement. This goal is made explicit in the tactics of "third-party policing." Third-party policing occurs when the authorities convince or require an uninvolved individual or organization to take actions designed to minimize disorder or prevent crime.[70] Popularized by the "problem-oriented" perspective, third-party policing often involves the use or threat of civil or administrative sanctions to force bar owners, landlords, social service agencies, and others in contact with criminal suspects or disorderly persons to apply pressure such as to control their behavior. A bar owner, under threat of losing his liquor license, may agree to hire bouncers or eschew certain types of entertainment (e.g., nude dancers or hip-hop music). Landlords may be urged to install better lighting, report suspicious activity, and evict tenants whom the police deem to be problems.[71] Social service agencies may be asked to exercise additional control over their clients. The police may also move further up the social ladder. If a social service agency proves uncooperative, its landlord or funding sources may also be asked to bring their influence to bear.

Third-party policing, like many of the tactics that fall within the scope of community policing, operates by co-opting community resources and existing sources of power.[72] The Community Policing Consortium report puts it politely:

> Community policing does not imply that police are no longer in authority or that the primary duty of preserving law and order is subordinated. However, tapping into the expertise and resources that exist within communities will relieve police of some of their burdens. Local government officials, social agencies, schools, church groups, business people—all those who work and live in the community and have a stake in its development—will share responsibility for finding workable solutions to problems that detract from the safety and security of the community.[73]

In other words, community policing is a strategy for making the community's total "expertise and resources" available to the police. The ultimate goals of policing—"the primary duty of preserving law and order"—are unchanged, and police authority is not diminished. But community policing does allow some parts of the community to share in police power, acting as adjuncts to the police institution.

Police power is extended further into the community, but the balance of power between the police and the community remains heavily weighted, always, in favor of the police. Former LAPD Chief William Parker complained, "I'm a policeman, not a social worker."[74] Under community-police cooperation schemes, social workers, as well as teachers, public health officials, bus drivers, bartenders, landlords, could register the corresponding complaint: *"I'm not a cop."* Community policing, especially in the form of third-party policing, is less a matter of policing-as-social-work than social-work-as-policing, without the need for any Foucauldian camouflage.

The overall result of these efforts is to increase the police role in the community, meaning that the coercive apparatus of the state will be more involved with daily life. The state, and the police in particular, will have more opportunities for surveillance, and can exercise control in a variety of ways besides arrests, citations, or physical force. This shift can be made to sound like demilitarization, liberalization, or democratization,[75] but it is instead just a smarter approach to repression. The goal of community policing is to reduce resistance before force is required.

What we've traced out here is the path from legitimacy to hegemony. The ultimate goal of community policing is to increase the power of police, and this represents the most stable limit on the community's role as "co-producers" of crime control. The police and the community may form a "partnership," but the police always remain the senior partner.[76]

The demands of community policing may sound contradictory: the police are to rely on community's support, but remain in control; community input should shape police priorities, but without granting the community power. The corporatist model again becomes useful in understanding the police-community partnership.[77] Santa Ana (California) police Lieutenant Hugh Mooney tells of his role in the neighborhood:

> This is my area. . . . I am their spokesman. . . . I support them 100 percent. If I have to argue with them, I do it here, and we work things out. Then, when I do go before my peers and superiors I tell them exactly what my people feel. . . . I represent them.[78]

Of course, this is only half the equation. The other half is that Lt. Mooney also represents the Santa Ana Police Department to the residents of the neighborhood where he serves; he presents the organization's perspective, promotes its agenda, and couches its demands in acceptable terms.

Where the police succeed in establishing such relationships, and in using them to increase their power, they create what Martin J. Smith calls a "policy community."

> Policy communities increase state autonomy by establishing the means through which state actors can intervene in society without using force. By integrating state and society actors, they increase the capabilities of the state to make and implement policy. They create state powers that would not otherwise exist and, more importantly, they increase the autonomy of actors in a policy area by excluding other actors from the policy process. . . . It is state actors who determine the rules of the games, the parameters of policy and the actors who will have access to the policy community.[79]

Hence, what may be presented in terms of democratic engagement and greater inclusion tends overall to favor the state's interests and reinforce state power. Negotiation and co-optation provide the means for the state to extend its influence. Thus potential sources of resistance can be neutralized—or even turned to the state's advantage—by their incorporation into a policy community, in this case one centered around and dominated by the police department.[80] In some sense, the client groups become incorporated into the state itself. It makes little difference whether the client organization is a police union,[81] a social service agency, a church, a school, another governmental body, or a neighborhood watch group. By organizing on a sufficient scale the police can greatly enhance their own power, not only *over* these agencies, but *through* them, while acquiring relatively few additional burdens for themselves. So long as the police maintain control over the network as a whole, no one component of it is likely to make demands that cannot be easily accommodated or safely ignored.

This is the secret to a friendly police state: As the police more fully penetrate civil society, and as they gain the cooperation of the citizenry and its various organizations, they become less reliant on their own access to violence.

Or do they? Do they instead, perhaps, become ever less tolerant of resistance and disorder, ever more forceful in their own demands?

THE HARD EDGE OF COMMUNITY POLICING

In the wake of the Rodney King beating, the Christopher Commission noted with alarm that distrust of the police was commonplace, especially among Blacks and Latinos. As a remedy, the commission issued a broad slate of recommendations, many centering on the full adoption of a community policing perspective as the guiding philosophy of the LAPD. Giving credit where it was due, the Commission's report listed already-existing LAPD programs that made use of community policing strategies. The report specifically mentioned DARE, the short-lived Community Mobilization Project, in which police attended block meetings and arranged for Boy Scout troops to remove graffiti, and Operation Cul-de-Sac.

> In "Operation Cul-de-Sac," police erect barriers on streets in high crime areas so that motorists cannot drive through a neighborhood. The most ambitious use of this program occurred in a 30-block area of the Newton district of South-Central Los Angeles. The LAPD set up two cul-de-sacs in the section and erected small barriers on other streets. The zone was saturated with officers on foot, horse, and bicycle. "Open to Residents Only" and "Narcotics Enforcement Area" signs were posted. The aim was to discourage drug dealers and gang members from driving through the area. At the same time, debris was removed from alleys and graffiti scrubbed off walls.[82]

The Christopher Commission report went on to voice concerns about the intensive deployment of officers, the specific targeting of high-crime areas, the "illusory" nature of the reduction in crime, and citizen complaints that the area had been converted into an "armed camp."[83] But despite its reservations, the commission saw value in the program, and more importantly, saw its place within the overall framework of community policing.

This combination of militaristic tactics and community policing ideology is less mysterious than it might initially appear. The community policing focus on problem solving can easily tend towards a zero-tolerance approach with a strong emphasis on pubic order, rather than on crime per se.[84]

> Zero-tolerance policing refers to the strict enforcement of all criminal and civil violations within certain geographical hot spots (a code word for lower-income, minority areas) using an array of aggressive tactics such as street sweeps, proactive enforcement of not just the law but "community order," and a proliferation of drug raids on private residences.[85]

The effect is to criminalize an ever-wider range of public order offenses and minor nuisances, some of which might not even really be illegal. Hence, standard features of urban life that may previously have been considered mere irritations, inconveniences, annoyances, or eccentricities, suddenly become matters for police attention.

Worst of all, the new intolerance sometimes make crimes of the most human, humanizing, and humane parts of city life, the aspects that make it tolerable, or for some people, possible. Skateboarding, graffiti, loud parties, and other signs of "disorder" make cities more interesting than they would otherwise be. More importantly, though, the focus on public order can shut down soup kitchens and make the streets altogether uninhabitable for those who have nowhere else to live.

In 1993, San Francisco mayor and former police chief Frank Jordan introduced the Matrix program, which deliberately targeted the homeless for aggressive enforcement of quality-of-life laws. For two years, pre-dawn police raids broke up homeless camps in Golden Gate Park. Elsewhere in the city, shanty towns were leveled with bulldozers, and activists with Food Not Bombs were repeatedly arrested for the crime of serving free food.[86] Such efforts can push those already at the margins of society—the young, the poor, people of color—out of public spaces altogether, making room (it is hoped) for posh restaurants and trendy boutiques.

Community policing is intimately connected with urban renewal, neighborhood revitalization, and ultimately, gentrification. "Places abandoned by the government and the police for decades—inner cities, railroad yards, and river-front properties are being reclaimed because they are now seen as valuable locations for capital investment."[87] Consider the response of two academic advocates of community policing, Jerome Skolnick and David Bayley, to Santa Ana Police Chief Raymond Davis' efforts to make the destitute unwelcome in the downtown area. Davis formed an alliance with local business owners, who pressured judges to issue stiffer sentences for public order violations.[88] Skolnick and Bayley don't pause to worry about the separation of powers, or about private businesses interfering with the judiciary, or about the human rights implications of targeting one class of people for prosecution to benefit another class, always targeting the poor, for the benefit of the rich. Instead, our astute academicians consider removal of poor people as part and parcel of restoring order. And rather than addressing the social and economic causes of poverty, they go so far as to blame the poor for *causing* economic decline:

> Drunks loiter and sleep in front of stores, urinate in alleys, panhandle, and otherwise annoy the sort of person who might be interested in purchasing a meal, a pair of shoes, or a floor lamp in downtown Santa Ana. The more the downtown area became a haven for habitual drunks and transient street criminals, the more precipitous its decline.[89]

Despite all the happy talk about "community involvement" and "shared problem solving," in practice certain populations generally get counted among the problems to be solved rather than the community to be involved. Priorities identified by the "community" may suspiciously coincide with the interests of business owners and real estate developers.

FIXATING ON BROKEN WINDOWS

The theoretical justification for the sudden focus on minor offenses is what is known as the "Broken Windows" doctrine. Though actually quite old,[90] the Broken Windows idea owes its name and current popularity to March 1982 *Atlantic Monthly* article by James Q. Wilson and George L. Kelling.[91] They argue that if minor disorder is allowed to persist, it leads to both public fear and to serious crime, because it establishes the sense that the area is uncared for.

> We suggest that "untended" behavior also leads to the breakdown of community controls. A stable neighborhood of families who care for their homes, mind each other's children, and confidently frown on unwanted intruders can change, in a few years or even a few months to an inhospitable and frightening jungle. A piece of property is abandoned, weeds grow up, a window is smashed. Adults stop scolding rowdy children; the children, emboldened, become more rowdy. Families move out, unattached adults move in. Teenagers gather in front of the corner store. The merchant asks them to move; they refuse. Fights occur. Litter accumulates. People start drinking in front of the grocery; in time, an inebriate slumps to the sidewalk and is allowed to sleep it off. Pedestrians are approached by panhandlers. . . .
>   Such an area is vulnerable to criminal invasion. Though it is not inevitable, it is more likely that here, rather than in places where people are confident they can regulate public behavior by informal controls, drugs will change hands, prostitutes will solicit, and cars will be stripped. . . . muggings will occur.[92]

By this reasoning, it is not just crime and the fear of crime that demand police attention but the entire range of factors affecting the "quality of life."[93]

Aside from its implicit class-bias,[94] the Broken Windows theory seems to assign inordinate importance to keeping one's lawn tidy. It seems frankly implausible that litter and abandoned cars lead to rape and murder in the vague but direct way Wilson and Kelling suggest.[95] Their thesis assumes that once we enter the continuum of disorder, we will naturally drift toward the hellish extreme. Moreover, the zero-tolerance conclusion does not necessarily follow from the Broken Windows premise. If panhandlers and dilapidated buildings serve as indicators of disorder, and thus promote crime, then public safety should be better advanced by the state's welfare functions rather than its policing functions, and there is no reason to subordinate the one to the other. Rather than investing resources in law enforcement, government funds would be better used to reduce poverty, provide housing, and help lower-income families to keep up their homes, efforts that do not require any involvement on the part of the police.[96]

But even if we accept the Broken Windows theory as Wilson and Kelling present it, there are still good reasons not to make the police responsible for the maintenance of order. For one thing, many aspects of "order" are not reflected in the law. Charging the police with maintaining order without the pretense of law comes uncomfortably close to outright bullying. Second, where "order" is distinct from "law," it would seem to invest in the police the power to determine for themselves what counts as proper behavior. This is a dangerous enough precept to be avoided in its own right. Both of these worries can be somewhat alleviated if laws are changed to reflect the prevailing standards and to invest the police with order maintenance duties de jure as well as de facto.

But this also should be resisted. First, it may raise troubling questions about the separation of powers, especially where the police themselves lobby for such laws. And more importantly, we should always hesitate to rely on the police to solve problems that can be addressed in other ways or that we can stand to leave unresolved. There are political reasons for this position: In the interest of individual liberty, it is better not to expand police power or turn community problems into a source of police legitimacy. But there is also an underlying ethical principle, that violence should be always and only a last resort. When we mark something—a behavior, a person, a "hot spot" location—as an object for police control, we also authorize an unknown level of violence to be applied to ensure compliance. The police represent, in Carl Klockars' phrase, the state's "nonnegotiably coercive force."[97] That is ultimately why they are there.

A noisy drunk may be bothersome, to be sure. It is possible that, as so may business owners seem to believe, panhandlers keep patrons away. And a group of teenagers sulking on the street corner can make for an unnerving walk home. But few of us would feel justified using violence to address these difficulties. And neither should the police. But violence—or its threat—is implicit in every police interaction and manifests at times when it is undeniably inappropriate.

To authorize police action is to authorize violence; to direct the police to act against such minor offenses—or non-offenses—as loitering or public drunkenness is to authorize violence in circumstances where very few people would consider it justified.[98]

THE FUTURE (AND PAST) OF PUBLIC ORDER

One precursor of the Broken Windows doctrine was Oakland's "Beat Health" program. Under the auspices of Beat Health, police were encouraged to take an interest in the social environment where they patrolled, arranging for abandoned cars to be towed, litter picked up, graffiti scrubbed away. As in Santa Ana, the Oakland program had a close connection to the city's downtown renewal program. Local businesses funded the Oakland Police Department's "Fourth Platoon," which used foot patrols, bike patrols, horse patrols, motorcycle patrols, canine units, helicopters, and two Special Duty Task Forces to enforce public order laws in the downtown corridor. Police made use of a wide range of tactics, from gentle admonishments to open harassment, warrant checks, arrests, and violence.[99] The NAACP reported a rise in police brutality as a result.[100]

Denver provides another early example of this philosophy in action. In 1980 the Denver Police began deploying directed foot patrols, focusing on minor offenses in areas where young people gathered. The plan was quickly deemed a success, and expanded to deal with homeless campers and panhandlers, especially in commercial areas. The foot patrols were supplemented with motorcycle patrols and dubbed "ESCORT" (Eliminate Street Crime On Residential Thoroughfares).[101] Skolnick and Bayley enthusiastically report:

> ESCORT officers are specialized in the enforcement of laws dealing with behavior in public places. One might call this skilled harassment. Working the streets' busy hours, 10 A.M. to 2 A.M. divided into two shifts, ESCORT officers are told to "find a rock and kick it." That means combing the streets for minor violations by people who live persistently in the narrow space between respectability and criminality. . . . These people are hit for any infraction that can be found, from rowdyism to the use of drugs, from propositioning to illegal parking, from procuring to causing a disturbance.[102]

The zero-tolerance perspective came to inform not only the enforcement of the law, but the law itself: On July 1, 1983, the Denver city government made loitering illegal.[103]

Much of this pattern is familiar from the nineteenth century, when the newly formed police were immediately set to the job of keeping the urban poor in line. The bulk of police attention was not directed toward serious crime, but to vice and public order, which is a nice way of saying that they tried to control the morality, habits, and social life of the urban working classes.[104] A similar task is implied by Wilson and Kelling's nostalgic reminiscences about the cop on the beat:

> [T]he police in this earlier period assisted in that reassertion of authority by acting, sometimes violently, on behalf of the communi-

ty. Young toughs were roughed up, people were arrested "on suspicion" or for vagrancy, and prostitutes and petty thieves were routed. "Rights" were something enjoyed by decent folk. . . .[105]

Historian Samuel Walker argues that "the tradition of policing cited by Wilson and Kelling. . . never existed," but that's not quite true.[106] While unrecognizably distorted by Wilson and Kelling's rosy description, the nineteenth century did witness a very real increase in the demand for order, a demand met with police action. Pleasantries and circumlocutions aside, the tradition Wilson and Kelling seek to revive is not that of the station-house soup kitchen, but that of the vagrancy law and the saloon raid. This is why Walker's protestation misses the point: The reactionary idealization of the past is a rhetorical device, not an historical hypothesis. It does not seek the truth about the past in order to learn the truth about the present; it tells lies about the past to support lies about the present. Thus, it makes little difference whether the nineteenth-century cop was on better terms with the community or did a better job of maintaining order, so long as that faded Norman Rockwell image of the neighborhood cop can be used to justify repressive police tactics *now*. If the trick works, policing in the twenty-first century may resemble, very closely, that of the nineteenth.

INOCULATED CITY:[107] THE NEW NEW YORK

Always proud to crystallize an emerging model, the New York Police Department provides the paradigm case of zero-tolerance policing. After Rudolph Giuliani's police-backed rise to the mayor's office, the former prosecutor immediately set about transforming the city according to his own view of public order. Within months, the crackdown had been directed against—not only petty criminals, vagrants, and drunks—but peep shows, street vendors, and cabbies.[108]

The mastermind behind Giuliani's police state strategy was NYPD Commissioner William Bratton. Bratton, inspired by Wilson and Kelling's "Broken Windows" article, had previously dabbled with zero-tolerance and quality-of-life measures in the subway system as the head of the Transit Police. The subway cops started using plainclothes officers to catch turnstile-jumpers, put uniformed cops on the trains, and used the loudspeaker to announce periodic sweeps. These sweeps, code-named "Operation Glazier,"[109] were ostensibly to remove drunks, though the later use of police dogs indicates another purpose.[110] Christian Parenti comments, "Such sweeps, still in effect from time to time, are simple political semaphore from the state to the people: 'We have the guns, we have the dogs, you will obey.'"[111] Other symbolism reinforced the message: Bratton issued the subway cops 9mm semiautomatic handguns and uniforms chosen for their military character, "commando sweaters with epaulets, very military".[112] Meanwhile, an extensive ad campaign reassured the public: "We're Taking the Subway Back—for You."[113]

As head of the NYPD, Bratton was able to experiment on a much broader scale. Seeing an intolerable array of disorder everywhere he looked, Bratton took his subway strategy to New York City's streets: "*Quality of Life*. Boom boxes, squeegee people, street prostitutes, reckless bicyclists, illegal after-hours joints, graffiti—New York was being overrun. We called Police Strategy Number 5 'Reclaiming the Public Spheres of New York.' It was the linchpin strategy."[114]

The first casualties of the Bratton's obsession with order were, as elsewhere, the homeless. Squeegee workers in particular suddenly found their efforts to eke out a living by washing windshields at intersections treated as the first priority of New York's finest.[115] Police cleared "squeegee corners" every two hours, and started making arrests rather than issuing citations.[116] Soon, the police were hard at work breaking up the homeless encampments under the city's bridges.[117] Then they moved on to other sections of the population: truants, and then students;[118] prostitutes and their clients; then, the workers and customers in the legal branch of the sex industry; squatters; bus drivers and cabbies; and eventually, jay-walkers.[119]

Almost immediately, complaints against the police began to rise. In 1994, 37 percent more complaints were filed than in the year before; by 1996 the police were receiving 56 percent more complaints than in 1993.[120] Nevertheless, once New York was making headlines with its aggressive police tactics, Bratton's methods spread. Philadelphia cops started pursuing kids cutting class, handcuffing them like criminals. Boston police started cracking down on street merchants and beggars.[121] A Washington, D.C., Metro Police officer explained his department's zero-tolerance efforts: "[The administrators] want to see numbers, so we're arresting people and locking them up for almost nothing."[122] Indianapolis instituted "quality of life enforcement" in 1997 with funds from the federal Community Oriented Policing program.[123] The Miami police department's focus on safe shopping led a half dozen Miami cops to kick, pepper spray, and shackle Lewis Rivera, a homeless man eating at a shopping mall; an hour later Rivera was dead.[124] Even Portland, Oregon, has tried to become the new New York, with a law against sitting on the sidewalk, and neighborhood campaigns targeting churches that feed the homeless.[125] Bratton himself has recently taken his considerable skills to the Los Angles Police Department, where he began his term as police chief with promises to target graffiti, begging, and gangs.[126]

MILITARIZATION IN THE COMMUNITY POLICING CONTEXT

Given the popularity of the Broken Windows theory and the world-wide rush to imitate the New York police, we can begin to understand the use of paramilitary teams to conduct routine patrols. As a zero-tolerance tool, SWAT teams have a lot going for them. One officer explains:

> We conduct a lot of saturation patrol. . . . We focus on "quality of life" issues like illegal parking, loud music, bums, neighbor troubles. We have the freedom to stay in a hot area and clean it up—particularly gangs. Our tactical enforcement team works nicely with our department's emphasis on community policing. . . .[127]

While not exactly building community partnerships, these saturation patrols do represent an extreme form of the kind of proactive, preventative, geographically-focused operations at the center of the community policing approach. Such uses of SWAT teams provide a clear instance of the intersection between community policing and militarized tactics, equipment, ideology, and organizational structures. The connection is empirically indisputable: Many police departments esteemed for their community policing efforts use paramilitary units for patrols and other routine operations.[128] Commanders have been known to move between community policing posts and paramilitary assignments, sometimes occupying both positions simultaneously.[129] And funds designated for community policing programs are frequently used to pay for SWAT operations.[130]

The use of SWAT teams for neighborhood patrols is striking, but it is not by any means the only point of contact between militarization and community policing. Beginning in 2001, the D.C. Metropolitan police established links to hundreds of video cameras strategically positioned around the city. Adapted from military technology, the cameras continuously survey federal buildings and national monuments, public streets, subway and train stations, schools, and, thanks to the business association, stores in Georgetown. Heading the project is Stephen J. Gaffison, the former Justice Department director of community policing programs. He describes the system:

> The video technology is state-of-the-art, fully computerized switching equipment that is very similar to what you would find in a NASA or defense command center. . . . I don't think there's really a limit on the feeds it can take. . . . We're trying to build . . . the capacity to tap into not only video but databases and systems across the region.[131]

D.C.'s high-tech surveillance network, currently the most advanced in the country, is not intended to guard against normal street crime, but for use in emergencies, to help route traffic, and, tellingly, to monitor political demonstrations.[132] Here military technology and community policing leadership are combined for a project seemingly removed from crime-control. Again, as with PPU patrols, the question is not whether there is a connection between community policing and militarization, but how to interpret this connection.

Kraska and Kappeler suggest that the demands of reformers help to link community policing and militarization:

> Contemporary police reformers have asked the police to join together in problem-solving teams, to design ways to take control of the streets, to take ownership of neighborhoods, to actively and visibly create a climate of order, and to improve communities' quality of life. . . .[133]

If we accept the idea of "quality of life" implicit in zero-tolerance police practices, then militarized policing does all of these things. What is more, efforts to do all of these may actually tend to promote militarization.

Community policing is not a specific program, but a strategy; militarization is as much about organization as it is about high-tech weaponry. It is possible that community policing and militarization can exist independently, but the two have a definite affinity. Strategies create demands on the organizations responsible for implementing them.[134] Community policing is no exception. It requires, as we have seen, a decentralized command, officers working in teams, and highly discretionary police action.

Decentralization and discretion may not sound like features of a military organization, but it is a mistake to contrast them with strict hierarchy and active discipline. Military discipline is not bureaucratic control; it is not meant to eliminate discretion, but to shape or guide it. Bureaucrats apply pre-scripted rules to a given situation, with a minimum of personal latitude. Soldiers are expected to follow orders, adhere to regulations, and act in accordance to military doctrine, but the application of these various codes must be determined to a very large extent "on the ground" by widely dispersed units acting with a minimum of direct supervision.[135] Military discipline therefore builds in a degree of discretion.

> [S]ophisticated military managers increasingly prefer the initiative of the self-starter to the blind obedience of the automaton. Suspicious of excessive bureaucratic rigidity, they seek to cultivate in professional soldiers the disposition to act in conformity with the spirit of a command rather than formalistically with its letter. A felicitous way to do this is to formulate orders to junior officers (and where possible, to the troops themselves) in terms of mission objectives.[136]

Discipline is the internalized voice of authority. It is distinguished from rote obedience by the adoption of the values, aims, and methods of the institution.[137] It requires obedience, at a bare minimum, and may be established and maintained in part through punishment. But a well-disciplined soldier, like a well-trained dog,[138] will behave properly even when direct orders are unavailable and no punishment is threatened. Orders from superiors still supersede individual judgment, but fewer such orders are necessary. By the same means, an organization can decentralize its command and maintain a rigid hierarchy with overall direction coming always from above.

The NYPD command structure shows how these various organizational elements—decentralization, discretion, teamwork, discipline—can be meaningfully combined, while at the same time demonstrating how a militarized organization can pursue community policing strategies. As commissioner, Bratton streamlined the departmental bureaucracy and introduced a new management style. This worked in two directions. It returned much of the day-to-day control to the precinct level, but it also established performance evaluations and required precinct commanders to track weekly crime statistics. At the crux of the new system was a computerized method of analyzing crime statistics, called "Compstat."

Twice a week, all the commanders would meet and review the situation in one precinct.[139] This left each commander with enormous freedom to determine the day-to-day operations of his precinct. But every few weeks the entire precinct's performance would be brought under close scrutiny, and the commander would have to answer some hard questions:

> I want to know why these shootings are still happening in that housing project! What have we done to stop it? Did we put Crime Stoppers tips in every rec room and every apartment? Did we run a warrant check on every address at every project, and did we relentlessly pursue those individuals? What is our uniform deployment there? What are the hours of the day, the days of the week that we are deployed? Are we deployed in a radio car, on foot, on bicycle? Are they doing interior searches? Are they checking the rooftops? How do we know we're doing it? What level of supervision is there? When they're working together in a team with a sergeant and four cops, do they all go to a meal together? When they make an arrest, does everyone go back to the precinct or does one person go back? Are we giving desk-appearance tickets to people who shouldn't be getting them? What are we doing with parole violators? Do we have the parole photos there to show? Do we know everybody on parole? Parolees are not allowed to hang out with other parolees, they're not allowed in bars. Of the 964 people on parole in the Seventy-fifth Precinct, do we know the different administrative restrictions on each one, so when we interview them we can hold it over their heads? And if not, why not?[140]

The grilling could be intense, and it put pressure on the precinct commanders to get results. This pressure then moved down the chain of command, affecting every level and every branch of the New York Police Department. Bratton describes the effect:

> We created a system in which the police commissioner, with his executive core, first empowers and then interrogates the precinct commander, forcing him or her to come up with a plan to attack crime. But it should not stop there. At the next level down, it should be the precinct commander, empowering and interrogating the platoon commander. Then, at the third level, the platoon commander should be asking his sergeants, "What are we doing to deploy on this tour to address these conditions?" And finally, you have the sergeant at roll call—"Mitchell, tell me about the last five robberies on your post"; "Carlyle, you think that's funny, it's a joke? Tell me about the last five burglaries"; "Biber, tell me about those stolen cars on your post"—all the way down until everyone in the entire organization is empowered and motivated, active and assessed and successful.[141]

This organizational structure demonstrates the possibility of combining tight command and control with individual discretion. Compstat allows the higher-level administrators to establish the organization's values and goals; precinct-level commanders set strategy for their areas; and street-level officers have the discretion to adopt the particular tactics they think suitable. Information moves up and down the chain of command, decision making is consistently deferred to lower levels, and power is concentrated at the top. In this sense, Compstat has as much to do with militarization as does SWAT.

This analysis goes some way toward resolving the apparent tensions between community policing and militarization, but a puzzle remains. Remember that theorist-advocates commonly claim that community policing requires, or at least promotes, "civilianization."[142] If anything undermines the coherence of militarized community policing, surely this does.

But what does "civilianization" mean? "Civilianization" refers to the use of civilians to perform police department functions that don't require the authority of sworn officers. These tasks can range from clerical work and communications, to training and forensic analysis, to equipment maintenance, and in extreme cases taking reports and performing minor investigations.[143] "An assumption behind all this, of course, is that civilians do not supplant sworn officers. Civilianization in Houston, for example, was designed in part to put more uniforms on the street."[144] In other words, when a department is "civilianized," the actual number of armed, uniformed officers available for duty *increases*. Thus, civilianization is not in any sense incompatible with militarization.

To sum up: Community policing, as a strategy of social control, stresses proactive efforts to create order and focuses on problem solving, broadly construed.

This emphasis can come to justify zero-tolerance policing efforts, and specifically the use of paramilitary units for routine police work. The degree to which SWAT teams and community policing campaigns have come to share personnel and funding demonstrates the close linkage between the two. Furthermore, the type of organization, discipline, team-work, officer discretion, and even civilianization suggested by community policing all tend toward a military model. All of this indicates that community policing is not only compatible with, but may actually promote, militarization. On the broader view, when we look at police action both in terms of its strategic and organizational aspects, the picture emerging is that of a Kitsonian counter-insurgency program.

COMMUNITY POLICING + MILITARIZATION = COUNTER-INSURGENCY

The ability to concentrate power in the event of an emergency (e.g., a riot) has been shown to require a shift toward military operations.[145] But the ability to penetrate communities is enhanced if the police have the consent (or acquiescence) of those communities. This requires legitimacy, and a softer service-oriented, or "peace corps" approach. Complicating things further, military organization requires strict, almost automatic, discipline and tight command and control; community policing requires discretion, localized decision-making, and a great deal of organizational flexibility. But the two aspects achieve strategic coherence when viewed in the framework of counter-insurgency.[146]

Drawing from the work of British military strategist Frank Kitson, modern counter-insurgency stresses the need to *prevent* disorder, rather than simply repressing it where it occurs.[147] This aim requires that the authorities make nice with the local populace, creating in the community a sense that their rule is stable and legitimate. But it also requires heavy intelligence about the condition of the community, the sources of conflict, grievances, prevalent attitudes, and the efforts of troublemakers. To both these ends, counter-insurgency theorists encourage the authorities to actively penetrate the local community. Community penetration allows for ready access to intelligence, lets the state present itself as a benevolent problem-solver, and more subtly gives it the means to co-opt community institutions that might otherwise provide a base for resistance. All of this can be recognized in the community policing agenda.

The neighborhood watch structure specifically mirrors counter-insurgency efforts. Kitson writes:

> Following the procedure used by the French Army in Algiers, the policeman or soldier in charge of each strong point [strategic area]

might then appoint one local inhabitant to be responsible for each street who would be instructed to appoint an individual to be responsible for each block and so on down to one individual responsible for each family. The avowed reason for doing this would be to facilitate requests by the people themselves for help. . . .[148]

A December 2002 article in the *Portland Tribune* demonstrates the utility of such a system. A front-page photograph shows ten cops in helmets, bulletproof vests, combat boots, and blue fatigues aiming pistols and assault rifles at a suspect's house. The cops in the picture were members of the Northeast Precinct senior neighborhood officer unit, a team that focuses on quality of life issues. The raid was authorized by a warrant based on six months of intensive surveillance, surveillance conducted not by police but by neighbors who kept logs recording the traffic in and out of the house, disputes among the tenants, and any suspicious behavior. Police Chief Mark Kroeker identified the effort as a central aspect of Portland's community policing strategy: "We have a police bureau that is understaffed, underfunded and overwhelmed. But we have a community that is willing to work, willing to help."[149]

Community policing turns the citizenry into the eyes and ears of the state and by the same means creates a demand for more aggressive tactics. This is where street sweeps, roadblocks, saturation patrols, zero-tolerance campaigns, and paramilitary units come into the picture. SWAT, in particular, was created as part of a counterinsurgency plan, a fact of which Daryl Gates is quite proud:

> [We] began reading everything we could get our hands on concerning guerrilla warfare. We watched with interest what was happening in Vietnam. We looked at military training, and in particular we studied what a group of marines, based at the Naval Armory in Chavez Ravine, were doing. They shared with us their knowledge of counterinsurgency and guerrilla warfare.[150]

Of course, many community policing advocates fail to recognize the symbiotic relationship between the soft and the tough approaches. Goldstein, for example, cautions that

> a department could not long tolerate a situation in which officers in a residential area go out of their way to demonstrate that they are caring, service-oriented individuals, while other officers assigned to a roving task force make wholesale sweeps of loitering juveniles in that community.[151]

Goldstein is simply wrong. Recent studies of SWAT activity show that departments *can* tolerate the juxtaposition between outreach and smack-down. In fact, some departments deliberately choose this Good Cop/Bad Cop strategy.[152] Community policing operations can legitimate such sweeps by mobilizing conservative elements of the community, especially businesses and property owners.[153] One LAPD officer describes the role of community support:

> When the community cooperates and tells you who has been doing things, why they have been doing them, and how long they have been doing them, you jump at the chance to get the sons-of-bitches. The community don't help that much, so you got to take what you can get while you can get it! Because the community may change its mind, so you got to act quickly and decisively, or else you'll lose the opportunity. That's why when we know the community is behind us, we're going to be aggressive, break their asses and put their butts in jail.[154]

Or, beginning at the other pole, an initial crackdown can repress active opposition, opening the political space for Peace Corps-type efforts and outreach to "responsible" community leaders.[155] In military terms, the sweeps work to secure territory, and community organizing efforts constitute a battle for the hearts and minds of the populace.[156]

If this description sounds exaggerated, we should consider New York Police Department Deputy Commissioner Jack Maple's plans for "Operation Juggernaut":

> We'll take the city back borough by borough. . . .
> You go into Queens. . . . You stay there for six months with eight hundred officers. There are some bad areas: the 103, the 110, the 113, the 114 precincts. You do everything that works: buy-and-bust operations, quality-of-life enforcement, warrants, guns, the whole thing. It works, we know it works. We do our job and take out the drug organizations and clean up Queens. Now we have it under control.
> After six months, you downgrade by about twenty percent, you leave six hundred officers in Queens as a standing army and slide two hundred over to Brooklyn North, plus another seven hundred. We give Brooklyn North the same treatment for four months, leave several hundred there and slide the rest to Brooklyn South and then Staten Island. When we've cleaned up there, we leave some and move to the Bronx. We finish with Manhattan. Within a year we kill crime in New York.[157]

Likewise, the chief of police in one unidentified city described the role of paramilitary units in his community policing strategy:

> It's going to come to the point that the only people that are going to be able to deal with these problems are highly trained tactical teams with proper equipment to go into a neighborhood and clear the neighborhood and hold it; allowing community policing officers to come in and start turning the neighborhood around.[158]

This is a direct adaptation of military thinking, intended to address the shortcomings of the traditional law enforcement approach. Former Army intelligence officer Thomas Marks explains:

> Police are relatively ineffective in dealing with hard-hit areas, of course, because they violate the most elementary rules of counter-insurgency. They do not systematically seize and clear areas, leaving behind "militia." Rather, they chase the guerrilla "main forces" over hill and dale.[159]

Since the early 1990s the police have been actively trying to correct for this tendency. What we are seeing, as a result, is neighborhood safety transformed in the image of national security.

Understood in terms of counter-insurgency, community policing represents an approach to establishing and maintaining police control over the community, an approach enhanced by the insights of military experiences in restless colonies. Organizationally, militarization provides the model by which the police can work in teams, enhance officer discretion, and maintain tight command and control; community policing efforts, meanwhile, create the infrastructure for intelligence gathering and co-optation. Strategically, community policing strives toward directed, proactive action, with a geographic focus and attention to the causes of disorder; military planning gives a central role to intelligence work and takes an aggressive approach to confronting the enemy. Hence, military tactics are used to clear and hold contested areas, while community policing programs seek to create partnerships that bring the police legitimacy, information, and access to community resources. Ideologically, community policing serves to legitimize military-type efforts, while the rhetoric of a "war on crime" can be used to mobilize the community to aid the police. And of course, the threats of a militarized "Bad Cop" encourage cooperation with the "Good Cop's" community policing projects.

MEET THE NEW COP, SAME AS THE OLD COP

Modern policing has a dual nature—going back to its origins. The twin developments of community policing and militarization are an extension of the initial advantages of policing identified by Allan Silver: 1) widespread surveillance and discretionary action penetrating the community; and, 2) the capacity for rapid concentration and swift, forceful action.[160] The state has sought to develop its potential in each of these directions while maintaining a single organization responsible for enforcement.

The form of discretionary action has changed, from foot patrols to vehicle patrols, to a combination of the two. And thanks to technological advances and organizational innovations, the rapid concentration of police once reserved for emergencies is becoming a standard response to crime and disorder. The discrete and discretionary aspects are likewise available for increasing coordination. All the while, the penetration of the community increases, not only through patrol and surveillance, but also by the co-optation of community institutions.

These developments are, in one sense, quite new. But they come as the latest in a long series of institutional shifts and political realignments, the most significant of which I have traced out in the chapters preceding.

Our story so far has followed two related threads. The first is the institutional development of the police, from informal system to formal, from the militia-based slave patrols, to prototype City Guards, to modern municipal departments. The modern departments themselves began as the strong arms of corrupt political machines, then developed through the processes of bureaucratization and professionalization, only to be reshaped by the internal crisis surrounding unionization and its "collusive"—if uneasy—resolution. The second narrative concerns the relationship of this institution to the rest of society, roughly divided between "elites" (capitalists, landlords, politicians, bureaucrats) and the "masses" (the rest of us). The first story is characterized by a continually increasing measure of autonomy; the second by the institution's service to elites at the expense of the masses. I have suggested that the increased autonomy has been traded for loyalty to the elites, and is consistently used to further their interests.

The current era of policing began in response to the social conflict of the 1960s. As a result of that period's turmoil, policing underwent a change that drew together the two historical currents; the police became fully a political power unto themselves. They could not govern independently—no single body in our society can—but they suddenly came into their own as a center of power. This was the logical result of the long progression toward institutional autonomy, but it emerged as an unexpected consequence of the internal conflict between rank-and-file officers and their commanders. When the rank and file rebelled and began exerting influence of their own, this naturally shifted the balance of power within the institution. As it happened, the change was beneficial to both parties: Re-distributing power downward, the institution was able to seize for itself an additional measure of autonomy and the police achieved a sense of having political, as well as occupational, interests in common.

The emergence of the police as a political force changed the institution's relationship to social and political elites. No longer simply the servants of the ruling class, the cops became an interest group for whose loyalty the elites had to bargain. Rather than merely acting as agents of the most powerful faction, police leaders—

both administrators and union representatives—became power brokers themselves, capable of entering into or withdrawing from alliances with other powerful social actors.

In a related way, the relationship with the masses also changed. Rather than simply appealing to the "silent majority" or relying on the John Birch Society to organize "Support Your Local Police" campaigns, police began organizing their own political efforts and developing their own constituency. Part of this happened through the police union, political action committees, and grassroots support for "tough on crime" or "victims' rights" lobbying. Part of it happened through the departments themselves, under the rubric of community policing. At the same time, police departments were taking on the organizational form, tactics, weaponry, and ideology of the military, and modeling their operations after counter-insurgency programs. This complex set of developments sometimes creates paradoxes and strategic ambiguities, but each aspect of it moves along the same trajectory: Police power is increased, and democracy suffers a proportional loss.

AFTERWORD:
MAKING POLICE OBSOLETE

It is traditional, in a book such as this, to end with recommendations as to how the police can be made more efficient, more effective, less corrupt, less brutal, and so on. Those recommendations are almost always addressed to policy-makers and police administrators. Usually the recommendations are more technical than political, meaning that they offer detached advice on what, in the broadest sense, may be considered the *means* of policing—strategies of patrol, crowd control, interrogation techniques, use of force policies, organizational schemes, accountability mechanisms, morale boosters, affirmative action—while taking for granted, but rarely identifying, the *ends* of policing. They do not usually raise substantive questions about the police role in society, the need for police, or alternatives to policing.

I am going at things from quite the opposite angle. My recommendations are not addressed to those with power, but to the public. They are decidedly political and avoid the technical. I have, throughout this book, scrutinized the police role, examined its implications for democracy and social justice, and questioned the ends the cops serve. I turn now to briefly consider whether we can do without police.

CHALLENGING THE CONVENTIONAL WISDOM

In his essay "The Manufacture of Consent," Noam Chomsky advises, "If you want to learn something about the propaganda system, have a close look at the critics and their tacit assumptions. These typically constitute the doctrines of the state religion."[1]

With this in mind, it is interesting to note the things that scholars will not admit, the possibilities that they leave unexamined. In the "serious" literature, it is a nearly universal assumption that the police are a necessary feature of modern society.[2]

Rodney Stark writes, "It is vulgar nonsense to be anti-police. Our society could not exist without them."[3]

Carl Klockars echoes the point: "[N]o one whom it would be safe to have home to dinner argues that modern society could be without police."[4]

Dozens of similar quotations are available for anyone who wishes to find them. Yet in one sense these particular remarks are unusual. I present them here because they come from authors whose critical insights have been invaluable to my work on this book, and because they clearly state what others quietly take as given. Most authors do not even bother to *assert* that the police are necessary, much less argue the point. They feel no requirement to identify social needs that the police meet, because the role of the police, as they see it, is simply beyond dispute. It is outside the boundaries of debate. It is unquestionable; the alternative, unthinkable. In this context, the defensive comments of Stark and Klockars read less like arguments in favor of police and more like evasive maneuvers against the accusation that the authors might somehow oppose the cops. Their statements serve as a kind of loyalty oath, a promise to remain within the borders of acceptable opinion.

But the assumption that the police represent a social inevitability ignores the rules of logic: If we accept that police forces arose at a particular point in history, to address specific social conditions, then it follows that social change could also eliminate the institution. The first half of this syllogism is readily admitted, the second half is heresy. Almost no scholarly work takes the possibility seriously.[5]

It is a bad habit of mind, a form of power-worship, to assume that things must be as they are, that they will continue to be as they have been.[6] It soothes the conscience of the privileged, dulls the will of the oppressed. The first step toward change is the understanding that things can be different. This is my principal recommendation, then: We must recognize the possibility of a world without police.

CRIME AS A SOURCE OF STATE POWER

There is a question that haunts every critic of police—namely, the question of crime, and what to do about it. This is a real concern, and it deserves to be taken seriously. The fact is, the police *do* provide an important community service—offering protection against crime. They do not do this job well, or fairly, and it is not their chief function, but they do it, and this brings them legitimacy.[7] Even people who dislike and fear them often feel that they need the cops. Maybe we can do without omnipresent surveillance, racial profiling, and institutionalized violence, but most people have been willing to accept these features of policing, if somewhat grudgingly, because they have been packaged together with things we cannot do without—crime control, security, and public safety. It is not enough, then, to relate to police power only in terms of repression; we must also remember the promise of protection, since this legitimates the institution.

Because the state uses this protective function to justify its own violence, the replacement of the police institution is not only a goal of social change, but also a means of achieving it. The challenge is to create another system that can protect us from crime, and can do so better, more justly, with a respect for human rights, and with a minimum of bullying. What is needed, in short, is a shift in the responsibility for public safety, away from the state and toward the community.

THE THREAT OF COMMUNITY

In the earlier discussion of community policing, I argued that community policing constituted, in part, an effort to co-opt community resources and put the community in the service of police objectives.[8] I did not, at the time, dwell on the reasons underlying this, but the attempt at co-optation points to a fact that ought not be overlooked: community is a source of power.

> Community is not simply the territory within which crime is to be controlled, it is itself a *means* of government: its detailed knowledge about itself and the activities of its inhabitants are to be utilized, its ties, bonds, forces and affiliations are to be celebrated, its centres of authority and methods of dispute resolution are to be encouraged, nurtured, shaped and instrumentalized to enhance the security of each and all.[9]

Where possible, the state seeks to draw on this power and direct it to its own ends. Community policing is one such attempt. In exchange for protection, the police negotiate for access to this power network, insinuate themselves deeply within it, and try to shape its activities to suit their interests.

One major difficulty facing the state in its efforts to harness community power is the fact that this power is generally underdeveloped.

> Community is defined by two characteristics: first, a web of affect-laden relationships among a group of individuals, relationships that often crisscross and reinforce one another . . . , and second, a measure of commitment to a set of shared values, norms, and meanings, and a shared history and identity—in short, to a particular culture.[10]

Such webs of affinity are often painfully lacking from modern urban life[11]—and where they exist, they do not generally come in easily manageable bureaucratic packages awaiting official "partnerships" with police. In fact, there is inherent tension between the idea of police and the ideals of community.

> The modern police are, in a sense, a sign that community norms and controls are unable to manage relations within or between communities, or that communities themselves have become offensive to society. The bottom line of these observations is that genuine communities are prob-

ably very rare in modern cities, and, where they do exist, have little interest in cultivating relationships of any kind with police.[12]

Where genuine communities exist, they are sometimes even hostile to the police. In such cases, the authorities view community power not as an additional source of legitimacy, information, and infrastructural development, but as a rival that must be suppressed. The state has no choice but to interfere with the means of community action when the community falls into "enemy" hands—that is, when it resists state control or makes demands beyond those the state is willing to accept. This rule holds whether the enemy is described in political or criminal terms. The rationale is the same whether the authorities are interfering with grassroots political organizing, or whether they're disrupting neighborhood life in the name of "gang suppression."[13] The danger in these cases is not the *lack* of community, but the *existence* of a community that the state does not control. The police response is the domestic equivalent of destroying a village in order to save it.

In brief, the state seeks to mobilize community power in support of government goals, or else to suppress the sources of power opposed to its goals. Either way, the state recognizes the potential for community power, its promise and its threat.

This carrot-and-stick attitude may be unsettling, but the underlying analysis suggests some hopeful possibilities: If the community is a source of power, then it could exercise this power for its own ends, rather than those of the state. If, as community policing advocates argue, community involvement is the key to controlling crime, then this suggests that communities could develop public safety systems that do not rely on the state. The state's efforts to maintain legitimacy thus, ironically, point the way to its destruction.

> Both state-sponsored and citizen-initiated attempts at community crime prevention are based on the recognition, however unsystematized, that formal, bureaucratic responses to crime which are both temporally and spatially removed from the commission of crime can never approach the efficacy of more informal, more immediate forms of community social control. Equally recognized by the state officials is that citizen-initiated and citizen-controlled forms of justice threaten the legal basis of the state itself. The essence of formal state law—the foundation of state society—is that removal from individuals and communities of their rights to directly define what constitutes correct behavior within that community and to take direct action against incorrect behavior. The substitution of state justice for popular justice is generally argued as the only viable alternative to mob rule and vigilantism. Counterposing state justice to vigilante justice, however, is a false dichotomy which obscures a third alternative. The alternative is organized, community forms of popular justice operated and controlled by private citizens, not by employees of the state.[14]

The thought that such community-based measures could ultimately replace the police is intriguing. But if it is to be anything more than a theoretical abstraction or a utopian dream, it must be informed by the actual experiences of struggle.

LABOR GUARDS, DEACONS, AND PANTHERS

Luckily, history does not leave us without guidance. The obvious place to look for community defense models is in places where distrust of the police, and active resistance to police power, has been most acute. There is a close connection between resistance to police power and the need to develop alternative means of securing public safety.

In the United States, the police have faced resistance mainly from two sources: workers and people of color, especially African Americans. This is unsurprising given the class-control and racist functions that cops have fulfilled since their beginning. The job of controlling poor people and people of color has brought the cops into continual conflict with these parts of society. It has bred resistance, sometimes in the form of outright combat—riots, shoot-outs, sniper attacks. At other times, resistance has led to political efforts to curtail police power, or direct attempts to replace policing with other means of preserving order.

The role of the police in breaking strikes did not escape the attention of the workers on the picketline.[15] In the early twentieth century, labor unions worked strenuously to oppose the creation of the state police and to dissolve them where they existed. These efforts led, for a time, to restrictions on the use of state cops against strikers, but this victory has been practically forgotten today.[16] More significant, for the purposes of this discussion, are the unions' efforts to keep order when class warfare displaced the usual authorities.

The classic example is the Seattle General Strike of 1919. Coming to the aid of a shipbuilders' strike, 110 union locals declared a citywide sympathy strike and 100,000 workers participated. Almost at once the city's economy halted, and the strike committee found itself holding more power than the city government. The strike faced three major challenges: starvation, state repression, and the squeamishness of union leaders. Against the first, the strikers themselves set about insuring that the basic needs of the population were met, issuing passes for trucks carrying food and other necessities, setting up public cafeterias, and licensing the operation of hospitals, garbage collectors, and other essential services.[17] Recognizing that conditions could quickly degenerate into panic, and not wanting to rely on the police, they also organized to ensure the public safety. The "Labor War Veteran's Guard" was created to keep the peace and discourage disorder. Its instructions were written on a blackboard at its headquarters:

The purpose of this organization is to preserve law and order without the use of force. No volunteer will have any police power or be allowed to carry weapons of any sort, but to use persuasion only.[18]

In the end, the Seattle General Strike was defeated, caught between the threat of military intervention and the fading support of the AFL's international officers.[19] While the strike did not end in victory, it did demonstrate the possibility of working-class power, the power to shut down the city, and also the power to run it for the benefit of the people rather than for company profit. The strike was broken, but it did not collapse into chaos. Mayor Ole Hanson noted, while denouncing the strike as "an attempted revolution," that "there was no violence . . . there were no flashing guns, no bombs, no killings."[20] Indeed, there was not a single arrest related to the strike, though later there were raids, and other arrests decreased by half.[21] Major General John Morrison, in charge of the federal troops, marveled at the orderliness of the city.[22]

Almost fifty years later, more sustained efforts at community defense grew out of the civil rights movement. As the militancy of the movement increased and its perspective shifted toward that of Black Power, African Americans prepared to defend themselves, first against Klansmen and cops, later against crime in the ghetto. As early as 1957, Robert Williams armed the NAACP chapter in Monroe, North Carolina, and successfully repelled attacks from the Ku Klux Klan and the police.[23] Soon other self-defense groups appeared in Black communities throughout the South. The largest of these was the Deacons for Defense and Justice, which claimed more than 50 chapters in the Southern states. The Deacons made it their mission to protect civil rights workers and the Black community more generally. Armed with shotguns and rifles, they escorted civil rights workers through dangerous back country areas, and organized twenty-four-hour patrols when racists were harassing Blacks in Bogalusa, Louisiana. They also eavesdropped on police radio calls and responded to the scene of arrests to discourage the cops from overstepping their bounds.[24]

Williams and the Deacons influenced what became the most developed community defense program of the period: the Black Panther Party for Self Defense. The Panthers, most famously, "patrolled pigs."[25] Visibly carrying guns, they followed police through the Black ghetto with the explicit aim of preventing police brutality and informing citizens of their rights.[26] When police misbehaved, their names and photographs appeared in the *Black Panther* newspaper.[27]

The Panthers also sought to meet the community's needs in other ways—providing medical care, giving away shoes and clothing, feeding school children breakfast, setting up housing cooperatives, transporting the families of prisoners for visitation days, and offering classes during the summer at "Liberation Schools." These "survival programs" sought to meet needs that the state and the capitalist economy were neglecting, at the same time aligning the community with the Party and drawing both into opposition with the existing power structure.[28]

The strategy was applied in the area of public safety as well. The Panthers' opposition to the legal system is well known: They patrolled and sometimes fought the police, they taught people about their legal rights, and they provided bail money and arranged for legal defense when they could. But the Panthers also took seriously the threat of crime, and sought to address the fears of the community they served. With this in mind, they organized Seniors Against a Fearful Environment (SAFE), an escort and bussing service in which young Blacks escorted the elderly on their business around the city.[29]

At the same time, the Panthers sought reforms to democratize and decentralize the existing police. In Berkeley, they proposed a 1971 ballot initiative to divide the city into three police districts—one for the predominantly Black area, one for the campus area, and one for the affluent Berkeley Hills. Each district would elect a board to oversee policing in their area, and the officers themselves would be required to live in the neighborhoods they patrolled.[30] The campaign marked a straightforward attempt to establish community control over a major source of state power, the police. Writing in the *Nation*, Jerome Skolnick acknowledged the strength of this approach. He predicted: "In all probability, the proposal will lose. . . . But whether it wins or loses, it will have an effect. It will demand that its critics come up with something better, and it will probably promote change, if not this year, or precisely this way."[31] The measure failed at the ballot, but it succeeded in demonstrating sizable opposition to the current state of policing. Over all, one-third of Berkeley voters voted for the proposal; in the campus area, two-thirds voted in favor.[32] Even in defeat, the plan represented a challenge to the status quo.

Meanwhile, the Black Panther Party enjoyed massive support around the country. According to a 1970 Harris poll of African Americans, 43 percent of those interviewed said that the Black Panther Party represented their views; 66 percent said the Panthers' activities gave them a sense of pride; 86 percent stated that even if they disagreed with the Party's views, Black people had to stand together and defend themselves; and half said they felt that sympathy for the Party was growing.[33] The Panthers' support was grounded in the Black community, but it was not limited to the Black population. Other ethnic groups noted the Panthers' successes and began organizing along similar lines, creating groups like the Young Lords, the Brown Berets, and the Patriot Party.[34] To radicals of the time, the Panthers represented the vanguard of a revolution; to FBI leader J. Edgar Hoover, they were "the greatest threat to the internal security of the country,"[35] and accordingly they faced what is probably the most intensive political repression in American history.[36]

These cases are instructive, perhaps as much for their limitations as for the positive example they offer. In each historical instance, the initiative taken to defend the community was extraordinary, and the relationship between collective self-defense and conflict with the state was clear. But the efforts were abridged, cut short by external pressures and internal tensions. The 1919 Seattle Strike, however well it may prefigure a society where the workers are in control, was never intended as a revolution.[37] The provisions the unions offered were necessary and remarkable, but they were only seen as short-term measures. The presumption, always, was that when the strike was won, the city would return to normal. The Panthers had more ambitious aims, but their revolution was attacked from without and disrupted from within.

More developed models arise, predictably, where revolutionary movements are more advanced, more successful, and stronger. For examples, we must look beyond our own borders, and turn our attention to the struggles of colonized people in South Africa and Northern Ireland.[38]

SOUTH AFRICA: POPULAR JUSTICE AND STATE POWER

No one said that revolution would be easy. Writing his influential how-to for repression regimes, counter-insurgency expert Frank Kitson explained that

> the leaders of a subversive movement have two separate but closely related jobs to do: they must gain the support of a proportion of the population, and they must impose their will on the government either by military defeat or by unendurable harassment.[39]

What Kitson failed to note are the burdens that accompany success in these endeavors. As a revolutionary movement gains the support of the population, it acquires, intentionally or not, responsibilities that it must meet to maintain this support. Increasingly the population will turn to the revolutionary movement, and not the government, to meet their needs. And to the degree that the harassment campaign is successful, the authorities will be likely to abdicate their responsibilities, adding to the legitimacy of the revolutionaries, but also obliging them to meet additional demands. If the movement can do so, while withstanding whatever repressive measures are directed against it, it may be able to transfer power to itself and away from the state.

This is essentially what happened in South Africa. The apartheid government was never particularly concerned with meeting the needs of the population, so the anti-apartheid civic organizations took on many welfare functions, including services related to banking, childcare, insurance, healthcare, and assistance to the elderly and unemployed.[40] Meanwhile, the African National Congress (ANC) engaged in a campaign to, in the words of Nelson Mandela, "make government impossible."[41] This strategy had clear implications for crime control. The South African police were famously indifferent to crime in the Black townships, and the Black population was none too eager to cooperate with the cops.[42] This created a vacuum in the area of conflict resolution and public safety, and local communities painstakingly evolved institutions to fill it.

In the 1970s, townships established community courts modeled on traditional chieftain structures. These *makgotla* were patriarchal and conservative, dominated by older men, upholding traditional hierarchies of gender and age, and participating in the local government. Slowly, over the course of two decades, the *makgotla* were replaced by "People's Courts"—and later, "Street Committees"—connected to the growing resistance movement. As these forms spread, younger people gained a more prominent place, as did—eventually—women.[43]

These new committees were elected in public meetings and made responsible for preserving order and resolving disputes in their areas.[44] Though sometimes relying on physical punishment, often at a brutal extreme,[45] the Street Committees tended to emphasize restorative justice rather than retributive justice. Hence they focused less on punishment than on healing, on putting things right and preserving the community.[46]

Under apartheid, the police estimated there were 400 Street Committees operating throughout the country.[47] In many places, the organizations have survived into the post-apartheid era. According to a 1998 survey of Guguletu, Cape Town, 95 percent of respondents reported that there was a Street Committee on their street, 58 percent said they attended the Street Committee's meetings, and 69 percent thought that the committee did a good job. When asked "Where do you go for help if a young man in your family does not obey his parents?" 41 percent said that they would go to the Street Committee. When asked where they would go if the neighbors played their music too loud, 69 percent said they would take the complaint to the Street Committee. About two-thirds (66 percent) said they would go to the Street Committee "If a boy in the street stole a radio from your house."[48] In addition to minor criminal cases, neighborhood disputes, and family troubles, Street Committees also handle grievances against employers, merchants, and creditors.[49] Though violence is still sometimes used, most cases are settled peacefully. Many Street Committees no longer employ corporal punishment at all, relying instead on public shaming, financial restitution, community service, or at the most severe, banishment from the area.[50]

The persistence of the Street Committees indicates something of the tensions between the aims of the anti-apartheid movement and the means it employed. The ANC sought to avail itself of popular direct action *and* to establish a new state. It achieved both, and is left trying to reconcile the two. Since 1994, the new government has been willing to acknowledge the legitimacy of the Street Committees, but in exchange it has insisted that they cooperate with the police.[51] At the same time, the police often refuse to become involved with minor disputes, referring them instead to the Street Committees; cops have even been known to allow extra-legal violence to persist without interference.[52] Of course, the need for such violence is different in the new political context: In the post-apartheid era, vigilantism is more a response to the state's inefficiency than to its oppressive nature—that is, it is a reaction to the state's weakness rather than to its overbearing might.[53] But the Street Committees may themselves help keep the government weak. Localized, democratic systems of justice undermine the state's monopoly on force and challenge its authority to define lawful behavior and good order. Daniel Nina writes:

> Through the experience of popular justice, communities in South Africa are able to define what type of "legality" they want in their residential area. Moreover, a community is able to define how it wants to solve conflicts within its geographic boundaries. Communities, through their elected representatives, have developed their own notion of justice which differs from that of the state. In many circumstances, the community notion of justice epitomizes values of equality and social responsibility which are either not recognized or denied by the state.[54]

POPULAR JUSTICE IN NORTHERN IRELAND: THE OTHER PEACE PROCESS

In Northern Ireland, the search for popular justice has followed a similar path as in South Africa, and it continues to move in quite promising directions. There, too, the insurgents have sought out popular support while subjecting the authorities to unrelenting harassment; and the authorities have again responded with a mix of repression and neglect. In 1969, after Loyalist attacks on Catholic neighborhoods, Republican residents formed Citizen Defense Committees for their own protection. These committees built and supervised barricades and maintained continuous foot patrols.[55] As a consequence, the Royal Ulster Constabulary (RUC) simply gave up policing militant areas of West Belfast and Derry.

With extraordinary levels of unemployment and poverty, and without state intervention, these "no-go" areas became extremely vulnerable to crime. So Catholics elected Community Councils responsible for welfare and justice in their neighborhoods and created "People's Courts" to hear minor cases. Petty criminal matters and neighborhood disputes were usually resolved through restitution or community service, but serious offenses were referred to the Irish Republican Army (the IRA).

When the People's Courts broke down after a couple of years, the IRA had little choice but to take over their crime control efforts.[56] This role fell to the paramilitaries for several reasons. First, it was widely felt that the IRA had already established its responsibility for protecting the community, and many residents were demanding that something be done about crime. Second, crime posed a security risk, since the police were liable to use petty criminals as informers.[57] And third, crime had a destabilizing and corrosive effect on the very communities the Republican forces depended on for support.

Unwilling to cede ground to Republican forces, the RUC has since sought to reassert its authority in these areas, but its efforts have not been terribly successful. Security concerns made it difficult to police Catholic areas. The police were slow in their response to calls, and they often brought soldiers with them when they arrived. Worse, the cops tried to recruit crime victims as informants; those unwilling to serve as snitches publicly exposed and vocally denounced these clumsy efforts. All this occurred in a context of continual human rights abuses, and only increased the Catholic distrust of the authorities. In many areas residents became entirely unwilling to cooperate with the police, refusing even to report crimes.[58]

But the IRA has not had an easy time of it, either. The IRA is not a police force. It had few resources to devote to investigations or corrections, little time or patience for due process considerations and human rights concerns. Hence, the IRA response to crime usually took the form of threats, beatings, property destruction, knee-cappings, expulsions, shootings, and executions.[59] This was typically unpleasant for all concerned. The accused had practically no chance of presenting a defense and faced punishment out of proportion to the crime. Innocent people were punished, sometimes killed.[60] IRA volunteers, meanwhile, were burdened with the job of beating up petty crooks when they wanted to be making things difficult for the British.[61] And worst of all, from a revolutionary standpoint, the friction created by this situation threatened to isolate the revolutionaries from their constituency.[62]

One Republican activist explained the dilemma:

> [T]he conflict has created a cycle of dependency, where the community expects the movement [the IRA] to deal with anti-social crime, the IRA feels responsible and must act but lacks the resources to deal with it other than through violence and the result is damaging the kids who are after all part of the community.[63]

This dependency worked two ways: The IRA depended on the Catholic community for protection, discretion, and support; the community relied on the IRA to protect it from crime, the state, and the Loyalists.[64] The difficulty arose when protecting the community from crime undercut the community's support for the paramilitaries.

To resolve the dilemma, Republican activists have sought a means to "disengage responsibly,"[65] ideally by empowering the community to address anti-social behavior directly, without relying on either the IRA or the police. Republican activists approached a group of academics—criminologists and conflict resolution experts—and asked them to design a system that did not rely so much on breaking people's legs. The scholars obliged, publishing their recommendations in a Blue Book. The authors of the Blue Book, in extensive consultation with the local communities, set out to design a restorative justice system that met the following criteria: community involvement and support; nonviolence and operating within the law; proportionality of the sanctions to the offense; due process and a guarantee of human rights; consistency; engagement in the community; contact with community programs; and, adequate resources.[66]

With the endorsement of Sinn Fein, Community Restorative Justice (CRJ) programs based on the Blue Book have been implemented on a trial basis.[67] In 1999, four pilot projects were established in Republican areas of Belfast and Derry.[68] The IRA pledged its support for the process, ending punishment beatings and referring cases to the CRJ.[69] In the first year, the new programs handled 200 cases, clearing 90 percent of them. By the end of 2001, 1,200 cases had been processed through the program, including complaints about noise, family conflicts, burglaries, property damage, and chronic offenders. Between 15 percent and 20 percent of these cases would previously have been handled with violence.[70] Since 1999, the CRJ programs have been quickly reproduced throughout Northern Ireland.[71]

As recommended by the Blue Book, the Community Restorative Justice programs use mediation and family group counseling, monitor the agreements they negotiate, and employ charters outlining the rights and responsibilities of community members. Also recommended in the Blue Book, but not implemented by the pilot programs, were the use of professional investigators, community hearings, and boycotts of persistent offenders.[72] Tellingly, the RUC opposes the program, leading one IRA spokesman to quip, "the opposition of the RUC to the programme is the finest recommendation it could receive."[73]

LOOKING BEYOND THE STATE

Obviously, none of the models described in this chapter are perfect, but they do suggest the possibility of crime control without police, and perhaps even without the state.[74] Unfortunately, they don't follow this idea through to its most radical conclusion. Neither the ANC nor the IRA sought to do away with policing, or to replace the state with another system of social organization. They sought or seek not the elimination of the state, but the creation of new states. So when the ANC won the 1994 elections, it did not attempt to dismantle the state's police apparatus, but instead tried to incorporate the Street Committees into it. And, despite Sinn Fein's continued refusal to cooperate with the existing police, it has made it perfectly clear that restorative justice is *not* intended to replace state policing.[75] Likewise, the Blue Book states: "It was never an objective of this process to supplant the official criminal justice system."[76]

But, whether or not the organizations responsible recognize the full implications of these crime-control activities, the possibilities they suggest are extraordinary. What's clear is that in neither case were the people dependent upon the state to protect them—quite the opposite! Such efforts thus present the opportunity to shift power away from the state. Based on his observations in Natal, South Africa, Daniel Nina concludes "that there could be peace when the formal sovereign is not in control . . . [but] only if the structures of popular participation are running democratically and are accountable to the immediate community in which they operate."[77]

If we accept community control as a desirable end, and take seriously the possibility that it could be achieved without police, that leaves us with the hard work of finding an alternative system suitable to a diverse and disjointed society like that of the United States.[78] This is not the place to detail a full model, but it is worth mentioning some of the features a viable proposal must include.

THE SEARCH FOR LEGITIMACY

No universal model of popular justice is currently available. Despite their similarities, the differences between Street Committees and Community Restorative Justice are quite important. Rebekah Lee and Jeremy Seekings, who studied the Street Committees, are skeptical of Blue Book-type efforts to remove violence from the process. They write:

> It is tempting to try to distinguish between a non-violent and restitutive form of popular justice, rooted in and accountable to the "community," and a violent and punitive form of popular justice executed by irresponsible and "lawless" individuals. "Community courts" (organized, responsible, restrained) are often contrasted with "vigilantism," (spontaneous, reckless and brutal), and it is claimed that strengthening "community courts" will lead to less "vigilantism." There is some truth in this. But the reality is not neat and tidy. Many communities will sanction the use of violence in a wide range of conditions, sometimes to an extent that seems excessive to observers. . . . In a township like Guguletu most forms of vigilantism do not entail actual physical violence: disputes within families or between neighbors or even between people on different streets are settled through compensation or undertakings to change one's behavior. But behind these settlements lies the threat of ostracism or

of violence, and violence is widely used against rebellious juveniles. Vigilantism is *implicit* in even the most peaceful forms of community court. . . . In other words, there seems to be a tacit acceptance of violent forms of vigilantism if it is initiated by or has the consent of street committees or other legitimate local institutions.[79]

Likewise, the Blue Book authors are critical of the South African model:

[W]e are not sure that any form of "direct democracy" such as specially elected street and neighborhood committees would be workable. While this is the pattern in some South African models and has been tried in Belfast . . . we believe it would be hard to implement in today's modern, differentiated communities.[80]

They go on to specifically criticize the reliance on violence:

After considerable discussion, it was agreed that the presence of violence as a sanction in a community justice system had a considerably de-legitimizing effect. . . . This was despite the fact that several of the community justice systems examined (notably South Africa) had included the use of violent sanctions as punishment for offending.[81]

This disagreement points to a more fundamental concern, one that will largely determine the success or failure of any democratic or community-based system— namely, that of legitimacy. More important than the questions of "law" or "violence" is the competition between the state and the revolutionaries to acquire and maintain political support. Lee and Seekings note the popular support for some types of violence, and specifically explain that its acceptability depends on the legitimacy of the institutions authorizing it. The Blue Book authors, likewise, do not denounce violence per se (remember, they hope someday to cooperate with the police), but they strongly recommend against its use in the contemporary context of Northern Ireland because it is likely to de-legitimize the restorative justice efforts. This strikes me as politically wise: Given the history of the conflict, the earlier involvement of the IRA in crime-control, the widespread distrust of the RUC, and the continued tensions in the region cease-fire or no, it seems highly probable that any officially sanctioned violence will be viewed in partisan terms and undercut the CRJ's efforts. In both these cases, there is a close correlation between public interpretations of violence and political legitimacy.

The Blue Book suggests these indicators of legitimacy: due process, nonviolence, the reintegration of offenders back into the community, proportionality between offenses and sanctions, the community-spirited motivation of participants, and effectiveness.[82] Structurally, it recommends the program be connected to other community efforts, be located in identifiable neighborhoods of manageable size, coordinate operations between neighborhoods, represent the diversity of the community, and include former combatants and prisoners.[83] It also advises that volunteers be extensively trained in the principles of restorative justice, nonviolence, human rights.[84]

Harry Mika and Kieran McEvoy identify seven elements necessary for legitimacy:

(1) *Mandate* is the broadly-based license for program development which is secured through basic research (audit) in areas to ascertain needs and resources.

(2) *Moral authority* [is] the bas[i]s upon which the community acquiesces power and authority to representative members.

(3) *Partnership* is the sense of restorative initiatives emanating from the community, empowering and building capacity in the community, parlaying local resources to the ends of antisocial crime control and prevention in the community, addressing needs of community members who are victims and offenders, and working constructively with other community groups, associations, and organizations.

(4) *Competence* involves the purposive and long term development of appropriate skill sets among individuals and organizations in conflict resolution including training materials and courses. Generally, competence involves program performance at a level sufficient to satisfy key program objectives (addressing needs of victims and offenders, community safety, crime prevention, and the like), thereby both demonstrating and affirming community capacity to respond to antisocial behavior and find justice for its members.

(5) *Practice* includes establishment of standards for justice processes, protection of participants, and responsiveness to the community.

(6) *Transparency* involves mechanisms for public scrutiny, local management and control, and opportunities for public input.

(7) Finally, *accountability* refers to ongoing program monitoring and evaluation, to ascertain compliance with published standards, as well as program impact and effectiveness."[85]

It is no accident that many of the listed criteria represent practical limitations on the organization's power, and especially, on the possibility for abuses of that power.[86] There are dangers to popular justice that cannot be ignored. The Blue Book identifies the major weaknesses of the earlier Republican arrangement: inconsistency, a lack of training, few resources, a paramilitary character, the absence of accountability, the removal of the community from the process, and the reliance on the IRA.[87] There is also the danger that informal systems could be used to settle personal grudges, attack political rivals, or give expression to the community's prejudices.[88] The chief hazard, as one Irish feminist organization worried, is the "danger of groups being mirror-images of the forces they are combating in terms of tactics and attitudes, even if their objectives remain revolutionary."[89]

These dangers provide clear guidance for those who wish to fight oppression. Underlying the search for justice is a simple principle: Revolutionary institutions cannot be immune to the demands we place on existing institutions—demands for democracy, accountability, transparency, and most of all, real community control.

THE BIG PICTURE

Modest demands can be the seeds of major upheaval.

The demands for human rights, for community control, for an end to harassment and brutality—the basic requirements of justice—ultimately pit us against the ideology, structure, interests, and ambitions of the police. The modern police institution is at its base racist, elitist, undemocratic, authoritarian, and violent. These are the institution's major features, and it did not acquire them by mistake.

The order that the police preserve is the order of the state, the order of capitalism, the order of White supremacy. These are the forces that require police protection. These are the forces that created the police, that support them, sustain them, and guide them. These are the ends the police serve. They are among the most powerful influences in American society, and some of the most deeply rooted.

In this sense, our society cannot exist without police. But this needn't be the end of the story. A different society is possible.

NOTES

Foreword: Police and Power in America

1 For example, large, bureaucratic, and paramilitary sheriffs departments—like those in Los Angels County and Cook County—are almost indistinguishable from municipal police. In contrast, police in very small communities often have more general duties and personal ties to the people they encounter; these officers will be more "sheriff-like."

David N. Falcone and L. Edward Wells, "The County Sheriff as a Distinctive Policing Modality," in *Policing Perspectives,* eds. Larry K. Gaines and Gary W. Cordner (Los Angeles: Roxbury Publishing Company, 1999), 48–49 and 52.

2 Robert Reiner, *The Blue-Coated Worker: A Sociological Study of Police Unionism* (Cambridge: Cambridge University Press, 1978), 269.

Chapter 1: Police Brutality in Theory and Practice

1 "NAACP: Police 'Declared War' on Blacks," *Cincinnati Post,* April 9, 2001, http://www.cincypost.com/2001/apr/9/reay040901.html (accessed April 25, 2002).

2 "Protest Spills Into the Streets," *Cincinnati Post,* April 10, 2001, http://www.cincypost.com/2001/apr/10/prot041001.html (accessed April 25, 2002).

3 Craig Garretson, "On 4th Night, All Quiet: Curfew Brings Calm to City Streets," *Cincinnati Post,* April 13, 2001, http://www.cincypost.com/2001/apr/13/curfew041301.html (accessed April 25, 2002).

4 Andrew Conte and Barry M. Horstman, "City Declares Curfew," *Cincinnati Post,* April 12, 2001, http://www.cincypost.com/2001/apr/12/unrest041201.html (accessed April 25, 2002).

5 Jennifer Edwards, "Beanbag Guns Fired at Peaceful Marchers," *Cincinnati Post,* April 16, 2001, http://www.cincypost.com/2001/apr/16/bnbags041601.html (accessed April 25, 2002).

6 Quoted in Edwards, "Beanbag Guns."

A police investigation revealed that six members of the SWAT team were responsible for the attack, two of them instructors at the Cincinnati Police Training Academy. Jennifer Edwards, "No Explanation Given Yet in Beanbag Case," *Cincinnati Post,* April 17, 2001, http://www.cincypost.com/2001/apr/17/shoot041701.html (accessed April 25, 2002).

7 Independent Commission on the Los Angeles Police Department [The Christopher Commission], *Report of the Independent Commission on the Los Angeles Police Department* (July 9, 1991), 6–7.

8 Christopher Commission, *Report,* 3.

9 Quoted in Christopher Commission, *Report,* 8.

10 Quoted in Christopher Commission, *Report,* 14. Ellipses in original.

11 Stacey C. Koon with Robert Deitz, *Presumed Guilty: The Tragedy of the Rodney King Affair* (Washington, D.C.: Regnery Gateway, 1992), 22.

12 Christopher Commission, *Report,* 8 and 15.

13 Christopher Commission, *Report,* 11 and 13.

14 "The second development that made the outcome of the trial predictable, in retrospect, was the defense attorneys' ability to put Mr. King, instead of the four white police officers, on trial. . . . It is our contention that the jury agreed with the defense attorneys' portrayals of Mr. King as dangerous and uncontrollable, and thus rendered a verdict in favor of the four white police officers, notwithstanding the seemingly irrefutable videotaped evidence." Melvin Oliver et al., "Anatomy of a Rebellion: A Political-Economic Analysis," in *Reading Rodney King: Reading Urban Uprising,* ed. Robert Gooding-Williams (New York: Routledge, 1993), 119–120.

15 Charles E. Simmons, "The Los Angeles Rebellion: Class, Race, and Misinformation," in *Why L.A. Happened: Implications of the '92 Los Angeles Rebellion,* ed. Haki R. Madhubuti (Chicago: Third World Press, 1993), 150.

16 Oliver et al., "Anatomy of a Rebellion," 118.

17 David O. Sears, "Urban Rioting in Los Angeles: A Comparison of 1965 with 1992," in *The Los Angeles Riots: Lessons for the Urban Future,* ed. Mark Baldassare (Boulder: Westview Press, 1994), 238.

18 Oliver et al., "Anatomy of a Rebellion," 118.

19 Robin D. G. Kelley, "'Slangin' Rocks . . . Palestinian Style': Dispatches from the Occupied Zones of North America," in *Police Brutality*, ed. Jill Nelson (New York: W.W. Norton & Company, 2000), 50.

20 Oliver et al., "Anatomy of a Rebellion," 134.

21 Joan Petersilia and Allan Abrahamse, "A Profile of Those Arrested," in *The Los Angeles Riots: Lessons for the Urban Future*, ed. Mark Baldassare (Boulder: Westview Press, 1994), 141.

22 Paul A. Gilje, *Rioting in America* (Bloomington: Indiana University Press, 1996), 174–75.

23 David Sears uses these terms to characterize the various explanations of the disturbance. Sears, "Urban Rioting," 248–250.

24 Christopher Commission, *Report*, 55.

25 Christopher Commission, *Report*, 57–58.

26 Oliver et al., "Anatomy of Rebellion," 120.

27 National Advisory Commission on Civil Disorders [The Kerner Commission], *Report of the National Advisory Commission on Civil Disorders* (New York: E.P. Dutton & Co., Inc., 1968), 117–18.

28 Kerner Commission, *Report*, 206.

29 James Baldwin, "Fifth Avenue, Uptown: A Letter From Harlem," in *Nobody Knows My Name: More Notes of a Native Son* (New York: The Dial Press, 1961), 65–67.

30 Bob Blauner, "Whitewash Over Watts: The Politics of the McCone Commission," in *Still the Big News: Racial Oppression in America* (Philadelphia: Temple University Press, 2001), 115.

31 Kerner Commission, *Report*, 37–38; and Sears, "Urban Rioting," 238.

32 Bruce Porter and Marvin Dunn, *The Miami Riot of 1980: Crossing the Bounds* (Lexington, Massachusetts: Lexington Books, 1984), 33 and 36–38.

33 Porter and Dunn, *Miami Riot*, 37.

34 Porter and Dunn, *Miami Riot*, 38 and 43.

35 Porter and Dunn, *Miami Riot*, 62–63.

36 Porter and Dunn, *Miami Riot*, xiii.

37 Porter and Dunn, *Miami Riot*, 53–54.

38 Porter and Dunn, *Miami Riot*, xiii.

39 Quoted in Porter and Dunn, *Miami Riot*, 55–56.

40 These vigilantes acted not from panic, or in self-defense, but in planned drive-by attacks. Porter and Dunn, *Miami Riot*, 71.

41 Baldwin, "Letter from Harlem," 66.

42 See, for example: Egon Bittner, "The Capacity to Use Force as the Core of the Police Role," in *The Police and Society: Touchstone Readings*, ed. Victor E. Kappeler (Prospect Heights, Illinois: Waveland Press, 1999).

43 Kenneth Adams, "What We Know About Police Use of Force," in *Use of Force by Police: Overview of National and Local Data* (Washington, D.C.: United States Department of Justice, National Institute of Justice and the Bureau of Justice Statistics, October 1999), 3.

44 Adams, "Police Use of Force," 4.

45 Quoted in Danny Goodgame, "Police Operate in World of Hostility," *Miami Herald*, July 25, 1979.
For more on this point, see: Adams, "Police Use of Force," 10.

46 Both quoted in Amnesty International, *United States of America: Rights for All; Race, Rights and Police Brutality* (London: Amnesty International, September 1999), 23.
The United Nations Convention Against Torture and Other Cruel, Inhuman or Degrading Treatment or Punishment defines torture as "any act by which severe pain or suffering, whether physical or mental, is intentionally inflicted on a person for such purposes as obtaining from him or a third person information or a confession, punishing him for an act he or a third person has committed or is suspected of having committed, or intimidating or coercing him or a third person, or for any reason based on discrimination of any kind, when such pain or suffering is inflicted by or at the instigation of or with the consent or acquiescence of a public official or other person acting in an official capacity." U.N. General Assembly, "Convention Against Torture and Other Cruel, Inhuman or Degrading Treatment or Punishment" [General Assembly Resolution 39/46: December 1984] *Basic Human Rights Instruments* (Geneva: United Nations Centre for Human Rights; and Turin: International Centre of the ILO, 1998), 116.
The use of torture is not so remote from the practices of American policing as many people would like to believe. According to U.S. district court Judge Milton Shadur, it was "common knowledge that in the early to mid-1980s, Chicago Police Cmdr. Jon Burge and many officers working under him regularly engaged in the physical abuse and torture of prisoners to extract confessions." In fact, the allegations against Burge cover a twenty-year span from 1973 to 1993. A Chicago Police Department Office of Professional Standards investigation identified about fifty victims, and dozens of inmates claim that Burge extracted false confessions from them. Burge's tactics included electric shock, Russian Roulette, beatings, and suffocating inmates with typewriter covers.
Steve Mills and Janan Hanna, "Counsel to Probe Torture by Police," *Chicago Tribune*, April 25, 2002, http://www.chicagotribune.com/news/chi-0204250299apr25.story (accessed April 2002).

47 Tom McEwan, *National Data Collection on Police Use of Force* (United States Department of Justice, Bureau of Justice Statistics and National Institute of Justice, April 1996), 46. Emphasis in original.

48 David Bayley and Harold Mendelsohn, *Minorities and the Police: Confrontation in America* (New York: The Free Press, 1969), 125.

49 Amnesty International discusses these problems in greater detail. Amnesty International, *Race, Rights, and Police Brutality,* 31.

50 Adams, "Police Use of Force," 10. Emphasis in original.

51 McEwan, *National Data Collection,* 63–64.

52 Charles J. Ogletree, Jr. et al., *Beyond the Rodney King Story: An Investigation of Police Misconduct in Minority Communities* (Boston: Northeastern University Press, 1995), 52–53.

53 Patrick A. Langan et al., *Contacts Between Police and the Public: Findings from the 1999 National Survey* (United States Department of Justice, Bureau of Justice Statistics, February 2001), 34.
   This study represents one promising variation on the victim-reporting approach—the victim survey. Of course, the survey still relies on the victim's willingness to discuss the abuse (with a representative of the Justice Department, no less), but it does not rely on the victim's initiative in reporting it.

54 Adams, "Police Use of Force," 10.

55 Joel Garner and Christopher Maxwell, "Measuring the Amount of Force Used By and Against the Police in Six Jurisdictions," in *Use of Force by Police: Overview of National and Local Data* (Washington, D.C.: United States Department of Justice, National Institute of Justice and the Bureau of Justice Statistics, October 1999), 27.

56 McEwan, *National Data Collection,* 67.

57 Sociologist (and former reporter) Rodney Stark explains that the American news media are not well suited for covering chronic social problems and face additional hurdles when reporting on police abuse because they rely on police for information concerning other stories. Rodney Stark, *Police Riots: Collective Violence and Law Enforcement* (Belmont, California: Focus Books, 1972), 217–18.

58 Langan, et al. "Contacts Between Police and the Public," iii.
   This figure only represents the number of victims. It does not indicate how many distinct incidents of violence occurred, their severity, or the number of police involved. Also, because of the surveying methods used, it almost certainly under-represents the experiences of certain populations—the homeless, to cite an obvious example.

59 Langan, et al. "Contacts Between Police and the Public," iii and 2.

60 Atlanta had 416,474 residents in 2000. Fresno had 427,652. "Top 50 Cities in the U.S. by Population and Rank, 1990 and 2000," in *Time Almanac 2002,* ed. Borgna Brunner (Boston: Information, Please, 2002), 201.
   Our hypothetical metropolis would be the thirty-ninth largest city in the United States.

61 Langan, et al. "Contacts Between Police and the Public," 2.

62 Langan, et al. "Contacts Between Police and the Public," 3.
   In nearly half (49.7 percent) of arrests involving force, the most severe tactic reported was classified as a "grab." Garner and Maxwell, "Measuring the Amount of Force," 41.

63 Langan, et al. "Contacts Between Police and the Public," 2.
   The police themselves report that force is used at a much lower rate. "The IACP [International Association of Chiefs of Police] calculation of the use-of-force rate is based on dispatched calls for service. For example, based on 1995 data reported by 110 agencies [in the United States], the police use-of-force rate was 4.19 per 10,000 responded-to calls for service, or 0.0419 percent." Mark A. Henriquez, "IACP National Database Project on Police Use of Force," in *Use of Force by Police: Overview of National and Local Data* (Washington, D.C.: United States Department of Justice, National Institute of Justice and the Bureau of Justice Statistics, October 1999), 21.

64 Langan, et al. "Contacts Between Police and the Public," 24.

65 Langan, et al. "Contacts Between Police and the Public," 2.

66 Charlotte-Mecklenburg (North Carolina) Police Department; Colorado Springs (Colorado) Police Department; Dallas (Texas) Police Department; Saint Petersburg (Florida) Police Department; San Diego County (California) Sheriff's Department; and, the San Diego (California) Police Department. Garner and Maxwell, "Measuring the Amount of Force," 25.

67 Garner and Maxwell, "Measuring the Amount of Force," 30–32.
   Chemical weapons like pepper spray were the type most commonly used by police (being employed in 1.2 percent of all adult arrests). The second most common weapon was the flashlight, being used in 0.5 percent of arrests. Batons were used somewhat less frequently, in 0.2 percent of arrests. If we class batons and flashlights together as clubs, we learn that such weapons were used in 0.7 percent of arrests, and threatened twice as often (in 1.5 percent of arrests). Handguns were used in 0.1 percent of arrests, and shotguns or rifles in another 0.1 percent. Oddly, "firearms are infrequently used but are the most frequent weapon displayed." Counting handguns, shotguns, and rifles, guns were displayed in 3.1 percent of the arrests, and used in 0.2 percent. Garner and Maxwell, "Measuring the Amount of Force," 30–31.
   It is worth remembering that, even when they are not drawn or brandished, police firearms are always, to some extent, on display.

68 See, for example: Adams, "Police Use of Force," 3 and 5; Garner and Maxwell, "Measuring the Amount of Force," 25, 30, 33, and 41; and McEwan, *National Data Collection,* 41. It's hard to know what to say about

such views, except perhaps to suggest that the researchers are not giving the numbers the weight they deserve.

One exception is the NAACP's report on police brutality, based on testimony and documents from six cities around the country. They found that "Excessive Force has become a standard part of the arrest procedure." Ogletree et al., *Beyond the Rodney King Story*, 29.

69 David Weisburd et al., *Police Attitudes Toward Abuse of Authority: Findings from a National Survey* (United States Department of Justice, National Institute of Justice: May 2000), 2.

70 Weisburd et al., *Police Attitudes*, 3.

71 Stark, *Police Riots*, 74.

72 Christopher Commission, *Report*, 36.

73 Christopher Commission, *Report*, 40.

74 Christopher Commission, *Report*, 169.

75 Erica Leah Schmitt et al., *Characteristic of Drivers Stopped by Police, 1999* (United States Department of Justice, Office of Justice Programs and Bureau of Justice Statistics, March 2002), 14.

"Persons ages 16 to 29 were 34.5 percent of the estimated 44 million who had a police contact but 68.1 percent of those experiencing force during a contact. Persons age 32 or less accounted for about 75 percent of all persons who reported experiencing police use of force. The median age of those experiencing force was 23." Langan, et al., "Contacts Between Police and the Public," 29.

76 Langan et al.,"Contact Between Police and the Public," 4 and 24; and Schmitt, et al., *Drivers Stopped by Police*, 14–16.

Police racism will be discussed at greater length in chapter 4.

77 Jodi M. Brown and Patrick A. Langan, *Policing and Homicide, 1976–98: Justifiable Homicide by Police, Police Officers Murdered by Felons* (United States Department of Justice, Bureau of Justice Statistics, March 2001), iii.

"From 1976 to 1998, young black males (black males under age 25) made up about 1 percent of the population but 16 percent of felons killed by police in justifiable homicides; young white males made up about 8 percent of the population but 16 percent of felons killed by police. " Brown and Langan, *Policing and Homicide*, 8.

Police officers, for the most part, do not feel that these statistics reflect prejudice on the part of their colleagues. Only 17 percent thought that "Police officers often treat whites better than they do blacks and other minorities." (57.8 percent of the cops surveyed disagreed, and 25.2 percent strongly disagreed.) Likewise, even fewer (11.1 percent) suspected that "Police officers are more likely to use physical force against blacks and other minorities than against whites in similar situations." (55.6 percent disagreed and 33.3 percent strongly disagreed.) Weisburd et al., *Police Attitudes*, 6.

The opinions of police diverge sharply according to the race of the officer. Among Black cops, 51.3 percent think that the police treat whites better than Blacks, but only 11.9 percent of White cops agree. Concerning the use of force, the difference is even greater: 57.1 percent of Black cops and 5.1 percent of their White colleagues think police use force more readily against Blacks. Weisburd, et al., *Police Attitudes*, 9.

Perhaps more surprising, "Use of force appears to be unrelated to an officer's personal characteristics, such as age, gender, and ethnicity." Adams, "Police Use of Force," 6. (This claim is, by Adam's own admission made only "with moderate confidence," based on an analysis of the available data. Given our current state of knowledge about police violence, it can hardly be conclusive.)

78 Paul Kivel, *Uprooting Racism: How White People Can Work for Racial Justice* (Gabriola Island, British Columbia: New Society Publishers, 1996), 40. I have added the numbers here for the reader's convenience.

79 This parallel was brought to my attention by the Portland Copwatch Women's Caucus at a May 17, 2001, training.

Unfortunately, the analogy between police brutality and domestic violence is oftentimes entirely literal. In September 1997, Chief Soulsby of the D.C. Metropolitan Police told Human Rights Watch that "domestic violence is one of [the department's] worst behavior problems." Quoted in Human Rights Watch, *Shielded From Justice: Police Brutality and Accountability in the United States* (New York: Human Rights Watch, 1998), 381.

D.C. is not alone. Between 1990 and 1997, the LAPD investigated 227 domestic violence cases involving officers as perpetrators. In Boston, domestic violence is the single most common reason police are arrested. Human Rights Watch, *Shielded From Justice*, 211 and 149.

80 Seattle Police Department, *The Seattle Police Department After Action Report: World Trade Organization Ministerial Conference; Seattle, Washington; November 29–December 3, 1999* (April 4, 2000), 2.

81 Arch Puddington, "The Extent of Police Brutality is Exaggerated," in *Police Brutality: Opposing Viewpoints*, ed. Helen Cothran (San Diego: Greenhaven Press, Inc., 2001), 29.

82 The phrase is from LAPD sergeant Stacey Koon's report of Rodney King's arrest. Koon describes King's injuries: "Several facial cuts due to contact with asphalt. Of a minor nature. A split inner lip. Suspect oblivious to pain." Quoted in Christopher Commission, *Report*, 9.

83 Adams, "Police Use of Force," 3.

84 Sgt. Stacey Koon, describing Rodney King. Koon, *Presumed Guilty*, 18.

85 Cincinnati Police Sergeant Harry Roberts, after the killing of Timothy Thomas: "We didn't kill fifteen black men. We killed fifteen criminals who resisted arrest. They didn't die because they were black. They died because they were criminals." Quoted in Jennifer Edwards, "Police Union Defends Deaths," *Cincinnati Post*, April 14, 2001, http://www.cincypost.com/2001/apr/14/union041401.html (accessed April 25, 2002).

86 San Francisco Mayor Willie Brown, describing an incident in which three off-duty cops attacked two men to rob them of a bag of fajitas. Quoted in Lance Williams, "SFPD Indictments; The Mayor's Reaction: He Protects His Friends, Feuds With the D.A.," *San Francisco Chronicle*, March 3, 2003 (database: NewsBank Full-Text newspapers, accessed March 4, 2003).

87 "Well, there are cases. For example, when you stop a fellow for routine questioning. Say a wise guy, and he starts talking back to you and telling you you are no good and that sort of thing. You know you can take a man in on a disorderly conduct charge but you can practically never make it stick. So what you do in a case like that is to egg the guy on until he makes a remark where you can justifiably slap him and then if he fights back you can call it resisting arrest." Quoted in William A. Westley, *Violence and the Police: A Sociological Study of Law, Custom, and Morality* (Cambridge, Massachusetts: The MIT Press, 1970), 124.

88 "The use of force is necessary to protect yourself. You should always show that you are the boss. Make them respect the uniform and not the man. Suppose you are interrogating a guy who says to go fuck yourself. You are not supposed to take that." Quoted in Westley, *Violence and the Police,* 126.

89 Portland Police Association *Rap Sheet* editor Loren Christensen. Quoted in Dan Handelman, "Police Shootings . . . We're Tired of *Having To* Write About This," *The People's Police Report* 13 (January 1998): 2.

90 Portland Police Officer Ed Riddell, concerning an incident during which police shot and killed an epileptic Latino man inside a psychiatric hospital. Quoted in Steve Duin, "Silver Medals for the Guys with the Golden Guns," *Oregonian*, November 21, 2002.

91 LAPD Chief Daryl Gates, announcing his finding that two cops acted within policy when they shot and killed a mentally unbalanced African American woman who threw a knife at them. Quoted in Daryl F. Gates with Diane K. Shah, *Chief: My Life in the LAPD* (New York: Bantam Books, 1992), 199.

92 Adams, "Police Use of Force," 8.

93 Daryl Gates, to the media, regarding the Rodney King beating. Quoted in Gates, *Chief,* 316

94 A Black NYPD officer told Nicholas Alex: "There are a lot of Negroes, the only thing they understand is a boot in the right direction. They are not different than a lot of children. The only thing they understand is physical force and pain." Quoted in Nicholas Alex, *Black in Blue: A Study of the Negro Policeman* (New York: Appleton-Century-Crofts, 1969), 155.

95 Sergeant Dennis Mullen, Atlanta Police Department Office of Professional Standards. Quoted in Human Rights Watch, *Shielded From Justice,* 41.

A similar sentiment was expressed by Detroit Police Department Chief Investigator Thomas Elder, who said that people who file complaints "are not part of the community in a positive way." Quoted in Human Rights Watch, *Shielded From Justice,* 181.

96 Robert Coles, "A Policeman Complains," *New York Times Magazine,* June 13, 1971, 11.

97 Seymour Martin Lipset, "Why Cops Hate Liberals—And Vice Versa," in *The Police Rebellion: A Quest for Blue Power,* ed. William J. Bopp (Springfield, Illinois: Charles T. Thomas, Publisher, 1971), 38.

98 This grotesque overstatement originated with former LAPD Chief William Parker. Quoted in Robert M. Fogelson, *Big-City Police* (Cambridge, Massachusetts: Harvard University Press, 1977), 239.

99 Duin, "Silver Medals."

100 August Vollmer. The full quotation is: "Whatever else may be said of the American police, this fact should be more widely known; namely, that without the police and the police organizations, with all their many defects, anarchy would be rife in this country, and the civilization now existing on this hemisphere would perish." Quoted in Center for Research on Criminal Justice, *The Iron Fist and the Velvet Glove: An Analysis of the U.S. Police* (Berkeley, California: Center for Research on Criminal Justice, 1975), 21.

101 "In responding to the mandate for order maintenance, the police create a sense of community that makes social life possible. Where police are unwilling or unable to play this moral leadership role or define the community boundaries of right conduct, the quality of life declines and the existence of every other cherished value may be jeopardized. Where the civil libertarian fears repression and the denial of due process, others see the emancipation from fear and the creation of community as the result of police peacekeeping activities." Gary W. Sykes, "Street Justice: A Moral Defense of Order Maintenance Policing," in *The Police and Society: Touchstone Readings,* ed. Victor E. Kappeler (Prospect Heights, Illinois: Waveland Press, Inc., 1999), 142.

102 This poetic exaltation first appeared in the *FBI Law Enforcement Bulletin* in 1967. Quoted in Robert Reiner, *The Blue-Coated Worker: A Sociological Study of Police Unions* (Cambridge, Massachusetts: Cambridge University Press, 1978), 5.

103 Koon, *Presumed Guilty,* 20–21.

Koon was so proud of the job he had done that when he learned of the video his first thought was that it should be used for training purposes: "This is great! They got it on tape! Now we'll have a live, in the field film to show police recruits. It can be a real life example of how to use escalating force properly. Watch what the suspect does. If he moves, control him. If he doesn't, cuff him. The guys are going to love this one. It's true stuff." Koon, *Presumed Guilty,* 22.

NOTES FOR PAGES 20-24

104 Koon, *Presumed Guilty*, 19.

105 Quoted in "Response of City Officials to the Federal Charges," *Philadelphia Inquirer*, August 19, 1979.

106 FBI National Press Office, press release (United States Department of Justice, Federal Bureau of Investigation: May 15, 2002).

107 FBI (May 15, 2002).

108 Sourcebook of Criminal Justice Statistics, 328, table 3.164, www.albany.edu/sourcebook/1995/pdf/t3164.pdf (accessed May 17, 2003).

109 Bureau of Labor Statistics, *National Census of Fatal Occupational Injuries in 2000* (United States Department of Labor, Bureau of Labor Statistics, August 14, 2001), 1.

110 Bureau of Labor Statistics, *Occupational Injuries in 2000*, 3 and 4.

111 Bureau of Labor Statistics, *Occupational Injuries in 2000*, 4.
   The rate of deaths is a more reliable indicator of danger than the rate of work-related injuries: deaths are more reliably reported, and the severity of injuries varies enormously.

112 Bureau of Labor Statistics, *Occupational Injuries in 2000*, 3.

113 Bureau of Labor Statistics, *Occupational Injuries in 2000*, 4.

114 Stark, *Police Riots*, 135.

115 Ibid.

116 Ibid.

117 Ogletree et al., *Beyond the Rodney King Story*, 43.

118 Brown and Langan, *Policing and Homicide*, iv.

119 Brown and Langan, *Policing and Homicide*, 19.

120 Brown and Langan, *Policing and Homicide*, 1.

121 The police are also injured at a lower rate than those they oppose. IACP data indicates that "About 10 percent of 2,479 officers using force sustained injuries. Less than 1 percent of the injuries were major; none resulted in death. About 38 percent of the subjects were injured as the result of police use of force, including approximately 1.5 percent with major injures. (Data spanning the 1995–97 period indicate that of 75,082 use-of-force incidents, 3,274, or about 4 percent, resulted in officer injuries, all but 39 minor.)" Henriquez, "IACP National Database Project," 21.

122 Quoted in Goodgame, "World of Hostility."

123 An anonymous NYPD sergeant told *New York Times Magazine*: "Look, in any organization, you'll find no-good people. There are rotten apples right in my own back yard; our precinct has some crazy cops who are ready to use machine guns on the 'college kids and niggers,' that's how they are called. But for every cop like that I can find you two that you'd just have to admire." Quoted in Coles, "A Policeman Complains," 74.

124 "The effect of the rotten apple theory is to offer scapegoats to public indignation and to evade basic questions about the organization and character of police institutions." Stark, *Police Riots*, 10.

125 Lundman uses the term "organizational deviance" to describe behavior that violates rules or norms mandated by those outside the department, but that is nevertheless supported by internal organizational norms. "Police misconduct is organizational deviance when actions violate external expectations for what the department should do. Simultaneously, the actions must be in conformity with internal operating norms, and supported by socialization, peers, and the administrative personnel of the department." Richard J. Lundman, *Police and Policy: An Introduction* (New York: Holt, Rinehart, and Winston, 1980), 141.
   One book outlines the competing explanations in terms of "Rotten Apples" and "Rotten Barrels." Charles H. McCaghy, et al., *Deviant Behavior: Crime, Conflict, and Interest Groups* (Boston: Allyn and Brown, 2003), 244.

126 In her statement before the NAACP, one former Miami officer described a field training exercise in which she was reprimanded for not using force against a mentally ill man who shouted at her. Ogletree et al., *Beyond the Rodney King Story*, 19.
   Two of the four cops who beat Rodney King had participated in a training exercise earlier that evening, focusing on baton techniques. Christopher Commission, *Report*, 12.

127 In 1990, a White Indianapolis police officer received his department's medal of valor for shooting an unarmed African-American robbery suspect. Human Rights Watch, *Shielded From Justice*, 190.
   In 2002, Portland (Oregon) Police Chief Mark Kroeker stirred controversy by awarding medals to each of the 12 officers involved in fatal shootings during the two previous years. Duin, "Silver Medals."

128 Rizzo advised his officers to "break their heads before they break yours." Quoted in James T. Fyfe, "Police Use of Deadly Force: Research and Reform," in *Policing Perspectives: An Anthology*, eds. Larry K. Gaines and Gary W. Cordner (Los Angeles: Roxbury Publishing Company, 1999), 429.
   Fyfe's research quantifies the results of Rizzo's leadership: "Overall, the [Philadelphia Police Department's] police homicide rates were 2.09 [civilians killed annually, per 1,000 officers] while Rizzo was police commissioner; 2.29 while he was mayor; and 1.05 after he was out of office (as compared to the annual PPD homicide rate of 0.61 over 1950–1960 . . .)." Fyfe concludes that "knowing what Frank Rizzo was doing was far more valuable for estimating the PPD homicide rate than were data on public homicides." Fyfe, "Police Use of Deadly Force," 417.

282

129 "To a considerable extent the police regard all citizens as 'outsiders'—as unsympathetic and a threat to order—because the police are a distinctive and relatively socially isolated subculture." Stark, *Police Riots*, 124.

See also: Victor E. Kappeler et al., "Breeding Deviant Conformity: Police Ideology and Culture," in *The Police and Society: Touchstone Readings*, ed. Victor E. Kappeler (Prospect Heights, Illinois: Waveland Press, Inc., 1999), 251 and 252.

130 According to one study, police consider excessive force to be of "intermediate seriousness." Asked to evaluate the severity of eleven misconduct cases, police ranked brutality seventh, just ahead of covering up an officer-involved traffic accident (number 8), and below management favoritism (number 6), accepting kickbacks (number 4), accepting bribes (number 2), and theft (number 1). Carl B. Klockars, et al., *The Measurement of Police Integrity* (U.S. Department of Justice, National Institute of Justice, May 2000), 3.

131 Fogelson described the police as suffering from "a strong sense of alienation, a sharp feeling of persecution, and other severe anxieties which for want of a better term might be called occupational paranoia." This disorder was characterized by complaints about the incompetence of the civil authorities, a "frenzied reaction to criticism from outside," and advocacy of reactionary and draconian measures. Fogelson, *Big-City Police*, 120.

See also: Stark, *Police Riots*, 92–93.

132 In 1994, NYPD officer Bernard Cawley testified before the Mollen Commission: "We'd just beat people in general . . . to show who was in charge." Quoted in Human Rights Watch, *Shielded From Justice*, 268.

Cawley admitted to involvement in 400 beatings, using nightsticks, flashlights, and lead-lined gloves. Only one citizen ever filed a complaint against him, and no officers did. Human Rights Watch, *Shielded From Justice*, 272.

133 William A. Westley, "Violence and the Police," in *Police Patrol Readings*, ed. Samuel G. Chapman (Springfield, Illinois: Charles C. Thomas, 1964), 284.

134 Human Rights Watch, *Shielded From Justice*, 62.

135 Amnesty International, *Race, Rights, and Police Brutality*, 28.

136 Quoted in Christopher Commission, *Report*, 32.

137 Weisburd et al., *Police Attitudes*, 5.

Many supervisors share this perspective: 16.7 percent agreed or strongly agreed that whistle blowing is not worth it. Almost as many (16.4 percent) felt that it was acceptable to use illegal levels of force against a suspect who assaults an officer, and 7.6 percent (about one in every 13 supervisors) felt that the Code of Silence was an essential part of policing. Weisburd et al., *Police Attitudes*, 11.

The Christopher Commission found that police commanders often enforce the code of silence by singling out whistle blowers for discipline. Christopher Commission, *Report*, 170.

138 Weisburd et al., *Police Attitudes*, 2.

139 Westley, "Violence and the Police," 289–90.

140 William Chambliss explains the institutional basis for this tendency: "The bureaucratic requirement that police action be designed to maximize rewards and minimize strain for the organization leads to looking for crime among the powerless and ignoring the crimes of the powerful." William J. Chambliss, *Power, Politics, and Crime* (Boulder, Colorado: Westview Press, 1999), 100.

This idea will be expanded in later chapters.

141 "The [Christopher] Commission also spoke with a deputy chief who . . . stated that the discipline imposed by the [Los Angeles Police] Department is more severe for conduct that embarrasses the Department than for conduct that reflects improper treatment of members of the public. By way of example, he said that an officer caught in a liaison with a prostitute is likely to receive more severe discipline than an officer who beats an individual. A former high ranking officer with broad experience within the Department also corroborated this view, telling us that excessive force is treated leniently because it does not violate the Department's internal moral code." Christopher Commission, *Report*, 166.

This pattern seems to hold at all levels of discipline. For instance, in June 1999, there were 655 former cops in federal prison. The majority of them were serving time for corruption, not brutality. Amnesty International, *Race, Rights, and Police Brutality*, 28.

Chapter 2: The Origins of American Policing

Typically, comparative police histories discuss various cities in the order by which they came to attain modern police forces. So London would be first, if the volume considers English cities, and then New York, Boston, and so on. My approach breaks from this formula, presenting the cities instead in the order by which they reached progressively higher states of police development. Charleston appears first because its contribution to the modern type came very early. This approach preserves the sense of historical development leading to the appearance of modern policing; and it retains the sense that the modern police represent one stage in this sequence—not the inevitable end-point. In other words, I have tried to approach the matter of development prospectively rather than retrospectively, while still limiting the exploration of dead-ends and historical cul-de-sacs.

NOTES FOR PAGES 29–35

1 Selden Daskan Bacon, "The Early Development of the American Municipal Police: A Study of the Evolution of Formal Controls in a Changing Society, vol. 1" (PhD diss., Yale University, 1939; Ann Arbor: University Microfilms International [facsimile], 1986), 206-8.

2 In general terms, "Modernity is distinguished on economic, political, social and cultural grounds. For example, modern societies typically have industrial, capitalist economies, democratic political organization and a social structure founded on a division into social classes. There is less agreement on cultural features, which are said to include a tendency to the fragmentation of experience, a commodification and rationalization of all aspects of life, and a speeding up of the pace of daily life. Modernity has required new systems of individual surveillance, discipline and control. It has emphasized regularity and measurement in everyday life." *The Peguin Dictionary of Sociology*, Nicholas Abercrombie et al. (London: Penguin Books, 2000), s.v. "Modernity."

3 David H. Bayley, "The Development of Modern Policing," in *Policing Perspectives: An Anthology*, eds. Larry K. Gaines and Gary W. Cordner (Los Angeles: Roxbury Publishing Company, 1999), 67-68.

4 "Policing in the modern world is dominated by organizations that are public, specialized, and professional. What is new about policing is the combination of these attributes rather than any of the attributes themselves." Bayley, "Development of Modern Policing," 75.

5 Bayley, "Development of Modern Policing," 69.

6 "In policing, the defining task is the application of physical force within a community." Bayley, "Development of Modern Policing," 67.

7 Richard J. Lundman, *Police and Policing: An Introduction* (New York: Holt, Rinehart, and Winston, 1980), 17.

8 Bacon, "Early Development of the Modern Municipal Police, vol. 1," 6.

9 Raymond B. Fosdick, *American Police Systems* (New York: The Century Company, 1920), 67.

10 Eric H. Monkkonen, *Police in Urban America, 1860–1920* (Cambridge: Cambridge University Press, 1981), 53.

11 Clive Emsley, *The English Police: A Political and Social History* (London: Longman, 1991), 19.

12 The militarization of the police is discussed in detail in chapter 9.

13 Emergency measures such as National Guard patrols are thereby excluded.

14 This continuum has obviously been designed with city police in mind. Some county, state, and federal agencies may also count as modern police organizations. Clearly, different standards would apply.

15 There are two sets of implications to this treatment of modernization. First, current trends like militarization may be viewed in terms of an ongoing process of modernization. Second, this view allows for the possibility that emerging characteristics might overtake the traditional policing characteristics, thus fundamentally altering the nature of the institution. For example, our contemporary public, government-controlled police agencies may someday be superseded by private corporate-controlled organizations fulfilling similar functions. Whether such organizations should be counted as "police," "company guards," or "private armies" is very much open for debate, and probably cannot be decided without knowledge of the particulars of the institution.

16 Bayley, "Development of Modern Policing," 62.

17 "Informal policing refers to a system where community members are jointly responsible for the maintenance of order. Absent are persons whose sole responsibility is policing." Lundman, *Police and Policing*, 15.

18 Bruce Smith, *Rural Crime Control* (New York: Institute of Public Administration, 1933), 36.

19 Smith, *Rural Crime Control*, 36.

20 Monkkonen, *Police in Urban America*, 33.

21 Smith, *Rural Crime Control*, 38.

22 Bayley, "Development of Modern Policing," 62.

23 Smith, *Rural Crime Control*, 39-42.

24 Bayley, "Development of Modern Policing," 62-63.

25 Smith, *Rural Crime Control*, 75.

26 Smith, *Rural Crime Control*, 76.

27 "Under this system, the constable became subordinated first to the lord of the manor and eventually to the justice of the peace (who was frequently also the lord of the manor). As feudalism ended, capitalism developed as an economic system, and the nation-state formed. Thus, in gross, the origin of the English police in its modern form and function can be said to be consistent and coincident with the origin of the English state. . . . "
Cyril D. Robinson and Richard Scaglion, "The Origin and Evolution of the Police Function in Society: Notes Toward a Theory," *Law and Society Review* 21.1 (1987): 147.

28 Smith, *Rural Crime Control*, 76.

29 Emsley, *English Police*, 9.

30 Elaine A. Reynolds, *Before the Bobbies: The Night Watch and Police Reform in Metropolitan London, 1720–1830* (Stanford, California: Stanford University Press, 1998), 169.

31 Quoted in Reynolds, *Before the Bobbies*, 16 and 18.

32 Emsley, *English Police*, 19-22.

33 Reynolds, *Before the Bobbies*, 61.

34 Reynolds, *Before the Bobbies*, 4.

35 Reynolds, *Before the Bobbies*, 62-68 and 77-78.

36 Reynolds, *Before the Bobbies,* 57.
 Beadles were daytime officers responsible for enforcing liquor laws and poor laws, directing traffic, keeping order in church, and sometimes supervising the watch. Reynolds, *Before the Bobbies,* 10 and 24.

37 Lundman, *Police and Policing,* 17; and Reynolds, *Before the Bobbies,* 76.

38 Bayley, "Development of Modern Policing," 63. A courts-leet was a judicial hearing traditionally held by the lord of the manor and attended by residents of his promise.

39 Philip John Stead, *The Police in Britain* (New York: Macmillan, 1985), 16–17.

40 Quoted in Wilbur R. Miller, "Police Authority in London and New York, 1830–1870," *The Journal Of Social History* (Winter 1975): 92.

41 "Finally, when we combine our better understanding of the elements, process, personnel, and motivations that were involved in police reform in London during the whole period from 1735 to 1829, it becomes clear that Robert Peel's reform in 1829 was not revolutionary. It rationalized and extended but did not alter existing practices. . . . The change was carried out with the input and cooperation of local authorities, although not all were confident as to its benefits. The new police took on the functions of the old and did them in much the same fashion, drawing on the experience and expertise of the parish watch system. Many of the people who staffed the new police had staffed the parochial system." Reynolds, *Before the Bobbies,* 164.

42 "Peel's previous experience as an under secretary in the War and Colonies Office had prepared him somewhat in the management of alien, poverty stricken, and rebellious populations. Moreover, his staunch Protestantism and unwillingness to grant political rights to Catholics made him ideologically perfect to run the affairs of Ireland, at least from the English point of view." Monkkonen, *Police in Urban America,* 37.

43 Monkkonen, *Police in Urban America,* 38.

44 Emsley, *English Police,* 26.

45 Reynolds, *Before the Bobbies,* 4 and 164.

46 Emsley, *English Police,* 31.

47 Shortly after the Watch was disbanded, the vestry clerk of St. Thomas, Southwark reported to Lord Melbourne: "The generality of the Inhabitant Householders expresses much dissatisfaction at the policeman being so seldom seen and consider that they are not so well protected as they were under the old nightly watch. And the parish is much more frequently annoyed by disturbances in the night. " Quoted in Reynolds, *Before the Bobbies,* 158.

48 Smith, *Rural Crime Control,* 42–43.

49 Smith, *Rural Crime Control,* 45.

50 Roger Lane, *Policing the City: Boston 1822–1885* (Cambridge, Massachusetts: Harvard University Press, 1967), 7.

51 Smith, *Rural Crime Control,* 79; and Bacon, "Early Development of the Modern Municipal Police, vol. 1," 91–92.

52 Douglas Greenberg, *Crime and Law Enforcement in the Colony of New York, 1691–1776* (Ithaca, NY: Cornell University Press, 1976), 160–61.

53 David N. Falcone and L. Edward Wells, "The County Sheriff as a Distinctive Policing Modality," in *Policing Perspectives: An Anthology,* eds. Larry K. Gaines and Gary W. Cordner (Los Angeles: Roxbury Publishing Company, 1999), 42.

54 Greenberg, *Crime and Law Enforcement,* 164–65.

55 Quoted in Greenberg, *Crime and Law Enforcement,* 160.

56 Likewise, the fact that this presumption has been exactly reversed may serve as some measure of the increase in police authority. Nowadays, resisting arrest is unlawful even if the arrest itself is unjustified. And once a person has been warned that he is under arrest the police may generally use whatever force is necessary to restrain him.

57 Bruce Smith, *Police Systems in the United States* (New York: Harper and Brothers, 1940), 105.

58 The 1931 Report of the (Virginia) Commission on County Government described the constable's office as being "of ancient origin," "employ[ing] ancient methods," and "having outlived its usefulness." The Commission concluded that "the proper administration of justice will be promoted by its abolition." Quoted in Smith, *Rural Crime Control,* 87–88.

59 Bacon, "Early Development of the Modern Municipal Police, vol. 1," 8–9.

60 Greenberg, *Crime and Law Enforcement,* 167.

61 Monkkonen, *Police in Urban America,* 34.

62 Quoted in Lane, *Policing the City,* 10.

63 Quoted in Lane, *Policing the City,* 11.

64 Quoted in Greenberg, *Crime and Law Enforcement,* 156.

65 Marvin Dulaney complains: "Most scholars have dutifully traced the origins of the American police back to England and ignored the influences of the slave patrol and racism on the American police heritage." W. Marvin Dulaney, *Black Police in America* (Bloomington, Indiana: Indiana University Press, 1996), 127.

66 Dennis C. Rousey, *Policing the Southern City: New Orleans, 1905–1889* (Baton Rouge: Louisiana State University Press, 1996), 3.

67 For a thorough discussion of White fears, see: Herbert Aptheker, *American Negro Slave Revolts* (New York: International Publishers, 1987), 18–52.

White fears of insurrection may have reached the level of paranoia, but they were in no way baseless. Aptheker cites 250 documented rebellions or conspiracies involving ten or more slaves. Aptheker, *American Negro Slave Revolts*, 162.

See also: Harvey Wish, "American Slave Insurrections Before 1961," in *Black Protest: 350 Years of History, Documents, and Analyses*, ed. Joanne Grant (New York: Fawcett Columbine, 1968), 29–38; and William F. Cheek, *Black Resistance Before the Civil War* (Beverly Hills, California: Glencoe Press, 1970), especially chapter 4, "Slave Insurrections, North and South."

68 Sally E. Hadden, *Slave Patrols: Law and Violence in Virginia and the Carolinas* (Cambridge, Massachusetts: Harvard University Press, 2001), 36 and 109; H. M. Henry, "The Police Control of the Slave in South Carolina," PhD diss., Vanderbilt University, 1913 (Emory, Virginia: 1914), 31; and Philip L. Reichel, "Southern Slave Patrols as a Transitional Police Type," in *Policing Perspectives: An Anthology*, eds. Larry K. Gaines and Gary W. Cordner (Los Angeles: Roxbury Publishing Company, 1999), 85.

69 Michael Stephen Hindus, *Prison and Plantation: Crime, Justice, and Authority in Massachusetts and South Carolina, 1768–1878* (Chapel Hill: University of North Carolina Press, 1980), xxiv–xxvi.

70 "Slavery was not only an economic and industrial system, and as such felt to be a burden by the non-slaveholder; but more than that, it was a gigantic police system, which the poor man in the up-country as well as the wealthy planter in the lowlands did not know how to replace." Henry, "Police Control," 154–55.

71 The depth of this preference is astonishing, and its influence on Southern priorities proved self-defeating. "Many intransigent southerners never yielded the notion that the [Civil] war itself was of no importance if the slave system was not maintained. Even in 1865, with defeat almost imminent, and the conscription of slaves being seriously considered, still the preservation of the slave system remained a greater priority than the war effort. Some Confederate congressmen claimed that granting freedom to slaves who fought for the Confederacy would subvert their basic contention that slavery was the natural condition for blacks and make victory irrelevant. Rather than compromise in any way on the slavery issue, the South preferred to lose the war." Mary Frances Berry, *Black Resistance, White Law: A History of Constitutional Racism in America* (New York: Allen Lane, 1994), 67–68.

72 Hadden, *Slave Patrols*, 10–11 and 13.

73 Hadden, *Slave Patrols*, 14.

74 Hadden, *Slave Patrols*, 15–16.

75 Henry, "Police Control," 31.

76 Quoted in Robert F. Wintersmith, *Police and the Black Community* (Lexington, Massachusetts: Lexington Books, 1974), 18.

77 Hadden, *Slave Patrols*, 17.

78 Hadden, *Slave Patrols*, 19–20.

In 1770, South Carolina Lieutenant Governor William Bull wrote: "The defense of the province as far as our own power can avail, is provided for by our militia against foreign and Patrols against domestic enemies." Quoted in Hadden, *Slave Patrols*, 43.

79 Quoted in Reichel, "Southern Slave Patrols," 83.

80 Quoted in Reichel, "Southern Slave Patrols," 83; and Bacon, "Early Development of the Modern Municipal Police, vol. 1," 580.

81 Henry, "Police Control," 33.

82 Hadden, *Slave Patrols*, 70.

83 Hadden, *Slave Patrols*, 138.

84 Hindus, *Prison and Plantation*, 37–38.

85 Henry, "Police Control", 78–79.

86 I am indebted to Shira Zucker for drawing my attention to this aspect of Southern culture.

87 Hadden, *Slave Patrols*, 130.

88 Hadden, *Slave Patrols*, 70.

89 Henry, "Police Control," 33–34; and Hadden, *Slave Patrols*, 73.

The 1740 act explained: "Many irregularities have been committed by former patrols arising chiefly from their drinking too much liquor before or during the time of their riding on duty." Quoted in Henry, "Police Control," 33–34.

90 Henry, "Police Control," 35–37.

91 Hadden, *Slave Patrols*, 23.

92 Reichel, "Southern Slave Patrols," 83.

93 Reichel, "Southern Slave Patrols," 83–85.

The 1778 law instructed the Georgia patrols to "take up all white persons who cannot give a satisfactory account of themselves and carry them before a Justice of the Peace to be dealt with as is directed by the Vagrant Act." Quoted in Reichel, "Southern Slave Patrols," 84.

In practice, the patrols exercised control over Whites in other states as well. "Patrollers exercised their power not only against slaves in the area but also against whites who challenged the social order as it existed in each community. . . . Patrols not only cemented social bonds between whites, but also reminded

transgressors—both black and white—of what was considered acceptable behavior by the masters of Southern society." Hadden, *Slave Patrols*, 90.
94 Wintersmith, *Police and the Black Community*, 17–19.
95 Hadden, *Slave Patrols*, 25–31.
96 Hadden, *Slave Patrols*, 33–37.
97 Wintersmith, *Police and the Black Community*, 19.
98 Wintersmith, *Police and the Black Community*, 20.
99 Hadden, *Slave Patrols*, 22.
100 Hadden, *Slave Patrols*, 123.
101 Hadden, *Slave Patrols*, 110.
102 Hadden, *Slave Patrols*, 106.
103 Hadden, *Slave Patrols*, 126.
104 Quoted in Reichel, "Southern Slave Patrols," 86.
105 Hadden, *Slave Patrols*, 111–12.
106 Hadden, *Slave Patrols*, 116.
107 Quoted in Hadden, *Slave Patrols*, 113.
108 Hadden, *Slave Patrols*, 117.
109 Wintersmith, *Police and the Black Community*, 18.
110 Henry, "Police Control," 119–20.
111 Henry, "Police Control," 39–40.
112 Hadden, *Slave Patrols*, 123.
    The patrollers themselves were sworn in as agents of the state, and thus personally indemnified against lawsuits. Hadden, *Slave Patrols*, 77.
113 Quoted in Hadden, *Slave Patrols*, 89.
114 Hadden, *Slave Patrols*, 38–39.
115 Hadden, *Slave Patrols*, 54.
116 Hadden, *Slave Patrols*, 53–56.
117 Rousey, *Policing the Southern City*, 19–20.
118 Quoted in Rousey, *Policing the Southern City*, 20.
119 Quoted in Rousey, *Policing the Southern City*, 21.
120 Rousey, *Policing the Southern City*, 21–22.
121 Rousey, *Policing the Southern City*, 57.
122 Henry, "Police Control," 42.
123 Henry, "Police Control," 97.
124 Henry, "Police Control," 44.
125 Henry, "Police Control," 97.
126 Ibid.
127 Quoted in Henry, "Police Control," 102.
128 Henry, "Police Control," 99.
    For more information concerning White fears and the difficulties of subjugating an urban slave population, see: Richard C. Wade, *Slavery in the Cities: The South, 1820–1860* (London: Oxford University Press, 1964).
129 Henry, "Police Control," 43.
130 Henry, "Police Control," 51.
131 Quoted in Henry, "Police Control," 44.
132 Henry, "Police Control," 88; and Hadden, *Slave Patrols*, 114..
133 Henry, "Police Control," 51.
    For a detailed description of nineteenth-century racial segregation in Southern cities, see: Wade, *Slavery in the Cities*, 266–77.
134 Henry, "Police Control," 42.
135 Hadden, *Slave Patrols*, 54.
136 Hadden, *Slave Patrols*, 75.
137 Hadden, *Slave Patrols*, 55.
138 Quoted in Hadden, *Slave Patrols*, 63. Emphasis in original.
139 Quoted in Hadden, *Slave Patrols*, 62.
140 In North Carolina, the patrols were under court authority from their beginnings. Hadden, *Slave Patrols*, 47.
141 Bacon, "Early Development of the Modern Municipal Police, vol. 1," 359.
142 Quoted in Bacon, "Early Development of the Modern Municipal Police, vol. 1," 357.
    As recently as 1837 the Mayor of Philadelphia advised, "Every colored person found in the street after (the posting of) watch should be closely supervised by the officers of the night." Quoted in Homer Hawkins and Richard Thomas, "White Policing of Black Populations: A History of Race and Social Control in America," in *Out of Order? Policing Black People* eds. Ellis Cashmore and Eugene McLaughlin (London: Routledge, 1991), 71. Parentheses in original.

143 Hadden, *Slave Patrols*, 3–4.
　　See also: Dulaney, *Black Police*, 6.
144 Patrollers might also be compared to professional slave catchers. Slave catchers, however, were private operators, not public agents. They were hired by slaveowners for a single job, did not perform regular patrols, were not generally concerned with searching cabins or breaking up church services, and worked over a very large area, sometimes leaving the state. Hadden, *Slave Patrols*, 80–81.

　　In fact, patrollers more closely resembled overseers. Both had generalized responsibilities for keeping the slaves in line, searching for weapons, preventing gatherings, recapturing runaways, and so on. But overseers were private employees, hired by one slaveowner and responsible chiefly for one plantation. The overseer's duty was continuous, and he was paid much more than a patroller. Furthermore, in addition to his more repressive functions, the overseer also performed managerial tasks, like assigning the slaves their work and distributing food. Hadden, *Slave Patrols*, 81–82.

　　Comparisons could also be made to the constable. Like patrollers, constables regulated the movement of slaves, recaptured runaways, dispersed slave gatherings, and administered beatings. However, slave control was only one aspect of the constable's job, which also included summoning juries, transporting prisoners, process-serving, and otherwise acting as an agent of the courts. Most patrols were concerned only with the activities of slaves and rarely had reason to appear in court at all. Moreover, the patrols were interested in more than just the gathering and travels of slaves; they also searched their homes. Hadden, *Slave Patrols*, 83–84.

145 Hadden, *Slave Patrols*, 48.
146 Hadden, *Slave Patrols*, 16–17.
147 Quoted in Bacon, "Early Development of the Modern Municipal Police, vol. 2," 574. Emphasis in original.
148 Bacon, "Early Development of the Modern Municipal Police, vol. 2," 576.
149 Bacon, "Early Development of the Modern Municipal Police, vol. 2," 576–78.
150 Quoted in Bacon, "Early Development of the Modern Municipal Police, vol. 2," 581.
151 Bacon, "Early Development of the Modern Municipal Police, vol. 2," 585–86.
152 Bacon, "Early Development of the Modern Municipal Police, vol. 2," 601.
153 Quoted in Hadden, *Slave Patrols*, 58.
154 Bacon, "Early Development of the Modern Municipal Police, vol. 2," 602.
155 "[T]here can be no doubt that this city was far ahead of all others in regard to enforcement machinery at this time." Bacon, "Early Development of the Modern Municipal Police, vol. 2," 606.
156 Bacon, "Early Development of the Modern Municipal Police, vol. 2," 598–601; and Rousey, *Policing the Southern City*, 19–20.
157 Bacon, "Early Development of the Modern Municipal Police, vol. 2," 605.
158 These reforms reordered the city government, consolidating power under a mayoral figure called the intendent. They also created a daytime police force, which combined with the Charleston Watch and Guard in 1856. Bacon, "Early Development of the Modern Municipal Police, vol. 2," 616–19, 626–28, 634–35, and 643.

　　"[I]t is significant to note under what conditions it [the daytime police force] arose and with what problems it was chiefly concerned; as in the case of night policing it is the control of the slave population that dominates enforcement activity." Bacon, "Early Development of the Modern Municipal Police, vol. 2," 635.

159 Bacon, "Early Development of the Modern Municipal Police, vol. 2," 660–61.
160 In 1803, New Orleans had a population of 8,056 people. Of these, 2,273 were slaves, and another 1,335 were free Blacks. The White population at the time numbered 3,948, but this group was anything but unified. Differences of ethnicity, religion, language, and national origin all divided the White population, and sometimes produced fierce conflicts. Bacon, "Early Development of the Modern Municipal Police, vol. 2," 657.
161 Bacon, "Early Development of the Modern Municipal Police, vol. 2," 663–65; and Rousey, *Policing the Southern City*, 14–16.
162 Quoted in Bacon, "Early Development of the Modern Municipal Police, vol. 2," 669–70.
163 Rousey, *Policing the Southern City*, 16.
164 Bacon, "Early Development of the Modern Municipal Police, vol. 2," 668–69.
165 Rousey, *Policing the Southern City*, 17.
166 "Its organization was distinctly military, though a bit less so than the Gendarmerie. Unlike the gendarmes, city guardsmen did not routinely carry firearms, relying on sabers and half-pikes instead, although the use of muskets was authorized in times of emergency. Corporal punishment was abolished, and terms of enlistment ran for only six months. The city guard was dramatically closer to a military model of organization than were the northern night watches and constabulary of the same period, and slave control remained a very significant goal of the New Orleans police." Rousey, *Policing the Southern City*, 18–19.
167 Rousey, *Policing the Southern City*, 17–18.
168 Quoted in Rousey, *Policing the Southern City*, 32. Emphasis in original.
169 Quoted in Rousey, *Policing the Southern City*, 34.

170 Quoted in Rousey, *Policing the Southern City*, 33.

171 The cop was tried and acquitted, but reprimanded by the judge. Rousey, *Policing the Southern City*, 34.

172 Rousey, *Policing the Southern City*, 29.

173 Rousey, *Policing the Southern City*, 30.

174 Rousey, *Policing the Southern City*, 34–37.

175 "New Orleans initiated its military-style police in 1805 but demilitarized the police force in 1836, dropping the uniforms and weapons. At the same time a daytime police force, organizationally integrated with the night police, was formed to provide twenty-four-hour active patrolling with a unified chain of command—nine years before New York's similar reform." Rousey, *Policing the Southern City*, 6.

176 Rousey, *Policing the Southern City*, 36–37.

177 Rousey, *Policing the Southern City*, 37 and 41.

178 Rousey, *Policing the Southern City*, 45.

179 In 1847, for example, inter-governmental rivalry nearly reached conflict levels. After a series of gambling raids by the police of the First Municipality, the Third Municipality's police were ordered to arrest any cops from other jurisdictions caught trespassing on their turf. Faced with the prospect of a turf-war featuring rival police factions, the First Municipality quickly backed down. Rousey, *Policing the Southern City*, 47–48.

180 Rousey, *Policing the Southern City*, 66.

181 Rousey, *Policing the Southern City*, 69.

182 Rousey, *Policing the Southern City*, 70–72.

183 Rousey, *Policing the Southern City*, 76.

184 Rousey, *Policing the Southern City*, 78–80.

185 Robert M. Fogelson, *Big-City Police* (Cambridge, Massachusetts: Harvard University Press, 1977), 33.

186 Rousey, *Policing the Southern City*, 69–72.

187 Rousey, *Policing the Southern City*, 67 and 82–84.

188 Rousey, *Policing the Southern City*, 87–89.

189 Rousey, *Policing the Southern City*, 89.

190 Rousey, *Policing the Southern City*, 94.

191 Rousey, *Policing the Southern City*, 14.

192 Bacon, "Early Development of the Modern Municipal Police, vol. 1," 295 and 298.

193 James F. Richardson, *Urban Police in the United States* (Port Washington, NY: National University Press, 1974), 23–24; and Bacon, "Early Development of the Modern Municipal Police, vol. 1," 311–12, 316, and 322.

194 The issues of centralization and continuity are more problematic. For while the overall organization had citywide jurisdiction, the ward structure of city government insured that it would be internally fragmented, with precincts functioning for the most part as autonomous units. Likewise, though the same officers patrolled every night, the overall continuity of the organization was subject to interruption with every change in municipal politics.

195 James F. Richardson, *The New York Police: Colonial Times to 1901* (New York: Oxford University Press, 1970), 49.

196 Quoted in Richardson, *New York Police*, 233.

197 In 1816, when the Democratic political network Tammany Hall took control of the general council, it immediately replaced all city officials with federalist leanings, including a great many of the watchmen. Richardson, *New York Police*, 21.

198 Bacon, "Early Development of the Modern Municipal Police, vol. 1," 170 and 173; and Richardson, *New York Police*, 17.

  Marshals wore no uniforms and carried no weapons. They were paid by fee, and commonly neglected those duties which did not have fees attached to them. Likewise, reminiscent of the thieftakers, marshals made a priority of returning stolen goods—for a reward, of course—but not of apprehending the thief. The result was collusion between the officer and the criminal, with the former serving as a fence for the latter. Richardson, *New York Police*, 19 and 31; and Bacon, "Early Development of the Modern Municipal Police, vol. 1," 238.

199 Richardson, *New York Police*, 41.

200 Richardson, *Urban Police*, 24.

201 Richardson, *New York Police*, 83 and 86; and Richardson, *Urban Police*, 37.

202 Quoted in Richardson, *New York Police*, 87.

203 Richardson, *New York Police*, 88–89; and Richardson, *Urban Police*, 38.

204 Richardson, *New York Police*, 94–95.

205 Richardson, *New York Police*, 95–100

206 Quoted in Richardson, *New York Police*, 99.

  In the 1860s the city's fire, health, and liquor control departments were also taken under state control. "These acts were closely modeled after the Metropolitan Police Law, setting the same boundaries for the districts involved, having many of the same administrative provisions, and in some cases having the police commissioners as members of the boards ex officio." Richardson, *New York City Police*, 42–43.

207 Richardson, *New York City Police,* 101–8; and Richardson, *Urban Police,* 39.

A similar "City Hall War" occurred in Denver in 1894. There the Republican–controlled Board of Commissioners refused to resign when the governor appointed anti-gambling commissioners to their seats. Police officers, sheriff's deputies, and assorted gangsters barricaded themselves inside City Hall, facing off against the militia. Tensions were relieved when the governor ordered the militia to Cripple Creek for more important matters—breaking a strike. For a time following this incident, Denver had two police boards and three police chiefs, but the Republicans eventually surrendered to a court order. Monkkonen, *Police in Urban America,* 43.

208 Richardson, *New York City Police,* 109; and Richardson, *Urban Police,* 42–43.

Chapter 3: The Genesis of a Policed Society

1 Robert M. Fogelson, *Big-City Police* (Cambridge, Massachusetts: Harvard University Press, 1977), 17.
2 Jane's Addiction, "1%" *Jane's Addiction* (Triple X, 1987).
3 For Proudhon's famous argument, see: Pierre-Joseph Proudhon, *What Is Property?* (New York: H. Fertig, 1966).
4 They continue: "[A] specific (as opposed to general) inducement is one that can be offered to one person while being withheld from others. A *material* inducement is money or some other physical 'thing' to which value attaches. *Nonmaterial* inducements include especially the satisfaction of having power or prestige, doing good, the 'fun of the game,' the sense of enlarged participation in events and a pleasant environment. A machine, like any formal organization, offers a mixture of these various kinds of inducements in order to get people to do what it requires. But it is distinguished from other types of organization by the very heavy emphasis it places upon specific, material inducements and the consequent completeness and reliability of its control over behavior, which, of course, account for the name 'machine.'" Edward C. Banfield and James Q. Wilson, *City Politics* (Cambridge, Massachusetts: Harvard University Press and the M.I.T. Press, 1963), 115. Emphasis in original.
5 Banfield and Wilson, *City Politics,* 125.
6 Banfield and Wilson, *City Politics,* 116.
7 Fogelson, *Big-City Police,* 30.
8 Raymond B. Fosdick, *American Police Systems* (New York: The Century Company, 1920), 273–74.
9 James F. Richardson, *The New York Police: Colonial Times to 1901* (New York: Oxford University Press, 1970), 175–76.
10 James F. Richardson, *Urban Police in the United States* (Port Washington, NY: National University Press, 1974), 48.
11 Richardson, *Urban Police,* 57–58.
12 Richardson, *Urban Police,* 63.
13 Fosdick, *American Police Systems,* 101–2 and 105.
14 Richardson, *Urban Police,* 58–59; Fosdick, *American Police Systems,* 69–70.
15 Richardson, *New York Police,* 228–29.
16 Quoted in Richardson, *New York Police,* 230.
17 Richardson, *New York Police,* 229.
18 Richardson, *Urban Police,* 36.
19 Roger Lane, *Policing the City: Boston 1822–1885* (Cambridge, Massachusetts: Harvard University Press, 1967), 15–17.
20 Lane, *Policing the City,* 60.
21 Lane, *Policing the City,* 77–80.
22 Quoted in Lane, *Policing the City,* 80.
23 Fogelson, *Big-City Police,* 18–21.
24 Fogelson, *Big-City Police,* 32.
25 Richardson, *New York Police,* 182.
26 Richardson, *Urban Police,* 56.
27 Quoted in William McAdoo, *Guarding a Great City* (New York: Harper and Brothers Publishers, 1906), 86.
28 Richardson, *Urban Police,* 32–33.
29 Fogelson, *Big-City Police,* 33–34.
30 Richardson, *New York Police,* 189.
31 Charles Tilly, "War Making and State Making as Organized Crime," in *Bringing the State Back In,* Peter B. Evans et al.(Cambridge: Cambridge University Press, 1994), 170–71.
32 See: Pierre-Joseph Proudhon, *What Is Property?* (New York: H. Fertig, 1966).
33 Tilly, "War Making," 172.
34 Tilly, "War Making," 181.
35 Tilly, "War Making," 181.
36 Allen Steinberg, *The Transformation of Criminal Justice: Philadelphia, 1800–1880* (Chapel Hill, North Carolina: University of North Carolina Press, 1989), 137.
37 Steinberg, *Transformation of Criminal Justice,* 136.
38 Ibid.

39 Steinberg, *Transformation of Criminal Justice,* 145–46.

40 Steinberg, *Transformation of Criminal Justice,* 148–49.

41 Quoted in Steinberg, *Transformation of Criminal Justice,* 149.

42 Quoted in Steinberg, *Transformation of Criminal Justice,* 151.

43 Steinberg, *Transformation of Criminal Justice,* 151.

44 Richardson, *Urban Police,* 25.

45 Steinberg, *Transformation of Criminal Justice,* 166.

46 "On the whole consolidation was, in many ways, illusory. Its success depended in large part on the acquiescence of the same politicians whose activities it had been designed to control. . . . The procedures of ward politics intensified with the rise of a citywide political machine. As a result, the police became closely tied to both the existing structure of primary justice and the new structure of urban politics. " Steinberg, *Transformation of Criminal Justice,* 171.

47 Tilly, "War Making," 174–75.

48 Tilly, "War Making," 174. This was not the only path to state-formation, nor does Tilly pretend that it was. See also: Charles Tilly, *Coercion, Capital, and European States, AD 990–1990* (Cambridge, Massachusetts: Basil Blackwell, 1990).

But neither was the Tudor experience unique. Between 1620 and 1680 the French state developed along similar lines, beginning with Richelieu. Tilly, "War Making," 174.

49 The classic political machines were withering by the middle of the twentieth century, with Chicago offering one of the few examples to survive into the 1960s. But even without the machines, corruption continued to be a pervasive feature of police departments across the country. Fogelson, *Big-City Police,* 167-68 and 172.

William Chambliss describes his findings: "In my research on organized crime in Seattle, Washington, I discovered a symbiotic relationship between organized crime and the police that made it impossible to differentiate between them. Law enforcement officers, from street patrolmen to police chiefs to members of the prosecuting attorney's office, not only accepted payoffs from people who organized illegal gambling, prostitution, and drug sales, but the police and prosecutors were instrumental in organizing and managing these activities. Seattle is not the exception, it is the rule." William J. Chambliss, *Power, Politics, and Crime* (Boulder, Colorado: Westview Press, 1999), 136.

The mid and late-1990s saw a wave of corruption scandals, most notably in Los Angeles, Miami, Philadelphia, Chicago, and New Orleans—but also in smaller cities like Rochester and Cleveland. Officers were convicted of charges relating to brutality, theft, planting evidence, drug trafficking, extortion, and murder.

See, for example: Amnesty International USA, *United States of America: Rights for All* (New York: Amnesty International, 1998), 23; Human Rights Watch, *Shielded from Justice: Police Brutality and Accountability in the United States* (New York: Human Rights Watch, 1998), 36, 164-65, 259-60; and Chambliss, *Power, Politics, and Crime,* 136-37.

50 Philadelphia followed the same path as London, where "in 1829 . . . local officials helped transfer power to the centre, becoming consumers of a government service instead of providers." Elaine A. Reynolds, *Before the Bobbies: The Night Watch and Police Reform in Metropolitan London, 1720–1830* (Stanford, California: Stanford University Press, 1998), 6.

51 "Because the police organization's structure cast its net over the whole city, an unintended consequence of the adaptation of the semi-military model of communication meant that the police ended up with access to and coordinating power over the city's daily operations not achieved until the twentieth century by other parts of the city government." Eric H. Monkkonen, *Police in Urban America, 1860–1920* (Cambridge: Cambridge University Press, 1981), 159-60.

52 Reynolds, *Before the Bobbies,* 21-22.

53 Quoted in Selden Daskan Bacon, "The Early Development of the American Municipal Police: A Study of the Evolution of Formal Controls in a Changing Society, vol. 2," (PhD diss., Yale University, 1939; Ann Arbor: University Microfilms International [facsimile], 1986), 512.

54 "[T]he task was increasing the certainty of detection and the difficulty of committing a crime." Reynolds, *Before the Bobbies,* 77.

55 Both quoted in Reynolds, *Before the Bobbies,* 82.

56 Reynolds, *Before the Bobbies,* 56.

57 Quoted in Philip John Stead, *The Police in Britain* (New York: Macmillan, 1985) 40-41. Emphasis in original.

58 Clive Emsley, *The English Police: A Political and Social History* (London: Longman, 1991), 25 and 28; and Reynolds, *Before the Bobbies,* 158.

59 Richardson, *Urban Police,* 32.

60 Lane, *Policing the City,* 94.

61 Fogelson, *Big-City Police,* 16.

62 Lane, *Policing the City,* 221.

63 The slow transfer of power from the wards to the central administration, which began with an attempt to secure the influence of the machine, was later pursued by reformers as a means of limiting the machine's power. This processes will be described in detail in chapter 6.

64 Bacon, "Early Development of the Modern Municipal Police, vol. 2," 757, 761, and 767–777.

65 Bacon, "Early Development of the Modern Municipal Police, vol. 2," 779–80.

66 Cyril D. Robinson and Richard Scaglion, "The Origin and Evolution of the Police Function in Society: Notes Toward a Theory," *Law and Society Review* 21.1 (1987): 109. Parentheses in original.

67 This process is detailed in chapter 2.

68 "As long as the community was small there were sanctions more powerful than law, and when the law was invoked, the sheriffs, constables, and courts relied in practice on the initiative of the inhabitants in making complaints and swearing out warrants. . . . But as the city developed, problems arose which the community was unable to meet in traditional fashion. The creation of a professional, preventive police was both a result and a cause of the inability of citizens to deal with these matters themselves." Lane, *Policing the City*, 221.

69 Michael Stephen Hindus, *Prison and Plantation: Crime, Justice, and Authority in Massachusetts and South Carolina, 1768–1878* (Chapel Hill: University of North Carolina Press, 1980), xxv.

70 See: Wilbur R. Miller, "Police Authority in London and New York City, 1830–1870," *The Journal of Social History* (Winter 1975): 81–101. Miller does a thorough job identifying the most significant differences between the New York Municipal Police and the London Metropolitan Police.

71 Richard J. Lundman, *Police and Policing: An Introduction* (New York: Holt, Rinehart, and Winston, 1980), 29.

72 Lundman, *Police and Policing*, 29–30.

73 John C. Schneider, *Detroit and the Problem of Order, 1830–1880: A Geography of Crime, Riot, and Policing* (Lincoln: University of Nebraska Press, 1980), 55.

74 Quoted in Bacon, "Early Development of the Modern Municipal Police, vol. 2," 783.

75 Hindus, *Prison and Plantation*, 58; and Roger Lane, "Crime and Criminal Statistics in Nineteenth-Century Massachusetts," *The Journal of Social History* (Winter 1968): 162–63.

  Michael Hindus notes: "Drunkards were the refuse of society not simply because of their drinking habits, but rather due to their working habits, or lack of same." Hindus, *Prison and Plantation*, 120.

  Moreover, some employers felt they had a legitimate business interest in controlling the habits of the people who worked for them. They blamed alcohol for making workers immoral, lethargic, unhealthy, unproductive, unreliable, careless, undisciplined, and—some said—radical. One steel magnate reasoned, "Today's drinker and debaucher is tomorrow's striker for higher wages." Quoted in Sidney Harring, *Policing a Class Society: The Experience of American Cities, 1865–1915* (New Brunswick, New Jersey: Rutgers University Press, 1983), 152.

  For the classic discussion on the relationship between Protestantism and capitalism, see: Max Weber, *The Protestant Ethic and the Spirit of Capitalism* (London: Allen and Unwin, 1930).

76 "Assembly-line justice, with its tendency not simply toward efficiency, but to ruthlessness and railroading as well, was appropriate to the class-control function of many criminal prosecutions in Massachusetts. To the extent that defendants were seen as members of a deviant or dangerous class, they lost their individuality. For the offenses that characterized class-control types of prosecutions—drunkenness, riot, petty theft—error was permissible; value inculcation was the objective. Defendants seemed almost interchangeable." Hindus, *Prison and Plantation*, 124.

  Meanwhile, other forms of social control were being experimented with, especially education and the prohibition of alcohol. These too had the aim of imposing values on the poor. In a sense, they represented efforts to reform them in advance. Hindus, *Prison and Plantation*, 237.

77 Hindus, *Prison and Plantation*, 126.

78 Hindus, *Prison and Plantation*, 127.

79 "[T]he newer sources of wealth turned toward a bureaucratic police system that insulated them [elites] from popular violence, drew attack and animosity upon itself, and seemed to separate the assertion of 'constitutional' authority from that of social and economic dominance." Allan Silver, "The Demand for Order in Civil Society: A Review of Some Themes in the History of Urban Crime, Police, and Riot," in *The Police: Six Sociological Essays*, ed. David J. Bordua (New York: John Wiley and Sons, 1976), 11–12.

80 Schneider, *Detroit*, 54.

81 Monkkonen, *Police in Urban America*, 50.

82 Lundman, *Police and Policing*, 31.

83 Monkkonen, *Police in Urban America*, 50–51.

  In eighteenth century England, for example, rising crime led to harsher penalties. Reynolds, *Before the Bobbies*, 68.

84 Bacon, "Early Development of the Modern Municipal Police, vol. 2," 455.

85 Lane, "Crime and Criminal Statistics," 157. Lane bases this conclusion on an examination of lower court cases, jail sentences, grand jury proceedings, and prison records.

86 Lane, *Policing the City*, 19.

87 Richardson, *Urban Police*, 79–80.

88 Lane, "Crime and Criminal Statistics," 158–59.

89 Lane, "Crime and Criminal Statistics," 160; and Monkkonen, *Police in Urban America,* 103.

90 Harring, *Policing a Class Society,* 198.

91 Monkkonen, *Police in Urban America,* 103.
   "Private citizens may initiate the processes of justice when injured directly, but professionals are usually required to deal with those whose merely immoral or distasteful behavior hurts no one in particular. It takes real cops to make drunk arrests." Lane, "Crime and Criminal Statistics," 160.

92 Lane, *Policing the City,* 222; and Lane, "Crime and Criminal Statistics," 161.

93 Richardson, *Urban Police,* 79–80.

94 Harring, *Policing a Class Society,* 40.

95 Christine Stansell, *City of Women: Sex and Class in New York, 1789–1869* (Urbana, Illinois: University of Illinois Press, 1987), 197.

96 Stansell, *City of Women,* 172–73.

97 Stansell, *City of Women,* 173–74 and 276–77.

98 Lane, "Crime and Criminal Statistics," 160.

99 Stansell, *City of Women,* 194–95.

100 Silver, "Demand for Order," 21; and Lane, *Policing the City,* 223.

101 Stephanie Coontz, *The Social Origins of Private Life: A History of American Families, 1600–1900* (London: Verso, 1991), 222.

102 Coontz, *Social Origins,* 222.

103 Richardson, *Urban Police,* 30.

104 Lane, *Policing the City,* 173.

105 Steinberg, *Transformation of Criminal Justice,* 152.

106 Monkkonen, *Police in Urban America,* 41.

107 For example: Douglas Greenberg, *Crime and Law Enforcement in the Colony of New York, 1691–1776* (Ithaca, NY: Cornell University Press, 1976); Lane, *Policing the City;* Richardson, *New York Police;* Dennis C. Rousey, *Policing the Southern City: New Orleans, 1905–1889* (Baton Rouge: Louisiana State University Press, 1996); Schneider, *Detroit;* and Steinberg, *Transformation of Criminal Justice.*

108 Monkkonen, *Police in Urban America,* 49.

109 Monkkonen, *Police in Urban America,* 42.

110 Richardson, *Urban Police,* 3.

111 Sally E. Hadden, *Slave Patrols: Law and Violence in Virginia and the Carolinas* (Cambridge, Massachusetts: Harvard University Press, 2001), 24 and 54.

112 Lundman, *Police and Policing,* 21.

113 Richardson, *Urban Police,* 4.

114 Lane, *Policing the City,* 119.

115 Richardson, *Urban Police,* xi.

116 Quoted in Richardson, *Urban Police,* 27.

117 Bacon, "Early Development of the Modern Municipal Police, vol. 2," 487 and 538.

118 Reynolds, *Before the Bobbies,* 162.

119 Bacon, "Early Development of the Modern Municipal Police, vol. 2," 782–83.

120 Indeed, Fosdick suggests that the process of endless adaptation proved an impediment to progress. "The history of the development of American police organization. . . . presents one characteristic of outstanding prominence: the machinery of management and control has been subjected to endless experiment and modification. Change rather than stability has marked its course. With the exception of one or two cities, no carefully thought out plan of supervision has been fixed upon and maintained as a type most likely to meet legitimate demands for years to come. Instead, American cities, as if in a panic, have rushed from one device to another, allowing little or no time for the experiment last installed to prove itself." Fosdick, *American Police Systems,* 109–10.

121 Bacon, "Early Development of the Modern Municipal Police, vol. 2," 781–82.

122 Richardson, *Urban Police,* x.

123 David H. Bayley, "The Development of Modern Policing," in *Policing Perspectives: An Anthology,* eds. Larry K. Gaines and Gary W. Cordner (Los Angeles: Roxbury Publishing Company, 1999), 60.

124 Bayley, "Development of Modern Policing," 66–67.

125 This analysis should not be read to imply that all those who suffer from violence were actively resisting the authority that mobilized it. From the perspective of power, it makes little difference if the particular victims are engaged in resistance or not. The use or threat of force—especially at excess—sends a message to those who do oppose, or might come to oppose, the perpetrators. Violence demonstrates the power of the authorities and the danger of any potential opposition. In such cases, the use of violence is not only instrumental, but also communicative.

126 Roger Lane describes the idea that cities produce crime as an "anti-urban myth," arguing instead that "the growth of cities had a literally 'civilizing' effect on the population." Lane, "Crime and Criminal Statistics," 156 and 157.

127 Lane, *Policing the City,* 84.

128 "The enforcement of criminal law, in the early nineteenth century, was still the responsibility of aggrieved citizens, or of the sheriffs, courts, and constables created by the commonwealth. Much of it was in fact ignored, and an attempt to apply it could be politically disruptive as well as physically dangerous." Lane, *Policing the City*, 220–21.

129 Silver, "Demand for Order," 8.

130 Silver, "Demand for Order," 12–13.

Chapter 4: Cops and Klan, Hand in Hand

1 "The maintenance of white supremacy, and the old order generally, was a cause in which white men of all classes felt an interest. All classes had been united in a defense of slavery before the war, occasionally joining a patrol or vigilante activity for that purpose, and they had jointly fought a war to preserve the institution." Allen W. Trelease, *White Terror: The Ku Klux Klan Conspiracy and Southern Reconstruction* (New York: Harper and Row, 1971), 51.

2 The Klan was the most common type of organization, though it lacked any real coherence from place to place and could hardly be considered "one" organization. Still, the differences between the Klans and the other groups were negligible. I follow Trelease here in using the term "Klan" both to refer to the specific organizations that adopted that name, and as a generic term identifying the type of organization. Trelease, *White Terror*, xlv–xlvi.

3 Trelease, *White Terror*, 95.

4 Ibid., 17.

5 Ibid., 122.

6 Ibid., *White Terror*, 228.

7 Mary Frances Berry, *Black Resistance, White Law: A History of Constitutional Racism in America* (New York: The Penguin Press, 1994), 73–74.

8 Dennis C. Rousey, *Policing the Southern City: New Orleans, 1805–1889* (Baton Rouge: Louisiana State University Press, 1996), 116.

9 Quoted in Melinda Meek Hennessey, "To Live and Die in Dixie: Reconstruction Race Riots in the South," PhD diss., Kent State University, 1978, (Ann Arbor: University Microfilms International: 1978), 45.

10 Rousey, *Policing the Southern City*, 117–18 and 45.
  Dr. Albert Hartstuff, an Army surgeon, counted thirty-four Blacks and four whites killed, along with one-hundred-fifty-three Blacks and thirty-one whites injured. He considered this a low count, and it surely was, since it was later confirmed that five White people died, including a cop who collapsed from heat exhaustion. Hennessey, "To Live and Die in Dixie," 47.

11 Hennessey, "To Live and Die in Dixie," 46.

12 Rousey, *Policing the Southern City*, 119; and Hennessey, "To Live and Die in Dixie," 49.
  "The new police force appointed by the former Confederate mayor and commanded by the former Confederate chief was dominated by Confederate veterans." Rousey, *Policing the Southern City*, 115.

13 Hennessey, "To Live and Die in Dixie," 49–50.

14 Hennessey, "To Live and Die in Dixie," 407.

15 Hennessey, "To Live and Die in Dixie," 417–18.
  Judge Hansford Dade Duncan Twiggs of Sandersville, Georgia complained, "The *same people* who are called upon to administer & vindicate the law, are the same people who violate it." Quoted in Trelease, *White Terror*, 232. Emphasis in original.

16 Hennessey, "To Live and Die in Dixie," 133, 160, and 265, respectively.

17 Hennessey, "To Live and Die in Dixie," 123–26.

18 Quoted in Hennessey, "To Live and Die in Dixie," 129.

19 Trelease, *White Terror*, 228–30.

20 Quoted in Trelease, *White Terror*, 263.

21 Trelease, *White Terror*, 204–5.

22 Trelease, *White Terror*, 156.

23 Near Lumberton, North Carolina, this arrangement was institutionalized. Rather then forming a Klan-type group, Confederate veterans were invited to join "police guard" units. Union army officers armed and deputized them, granting them much of the responsibility for keeping order. Within limits, the military authorities ignored abuses against Black people and Union sympathizers.
  Sally E. Hadden, *Slave Patrols: Law and Violence in Virginia and the Carolinas* (Cambridge, Massachusetts: Harvard University Press, 2001), 206–7.

24 Trelease, *White Terror*, 96.

25 Quoted in Trelease, *White Terror*, 104.

26 Trelease, *White Terror*, 400.
  Even when the army made arrests, few convictions resulted. Only the worst offenders were prosecuted, and many received pardons. In 1876, the entire approach was undermined by the Supreme Court's ruling that the federal government could only protect civil rights against the actions of states, not those of individuals. Trelease, *White Terror*, 412–18.

27 Alexandria, Louisiana, provides one exception: There the sheriff armed two hundred Blacks and drove back a Klan attempt to intimidate voters. Trelease, *White Terror*, 95.

For a brief while, radical governments incorporated Blacks into the state militia and used them to enforce the provisions of martial law, intimidate Democrats on election day, engage in street battles over contested elections, and come to the aid of law enforcement officers facing violent opposition. For example, in Vicksburg, Mississippi, the Black sheriff, Peter Crosby, was illegally deposed by a committee of White citizens. The ensuing battle pitted an all-Black militia company against one hundred Whites under the leadership of a former Confederate officer. As a result, two Whites and thirty-six Blacks were killed in the battle, federal troops were sent to Vicksburg, and Crosby was returned to his position. But as White opposition persisted and the federal government softened its position on Reconstruction, the authorities became less and less willing to mobilize armed Blacks, and the militias fell into disuse. Otis A. Singletary, *Negro Militia and Reconstruction* (Austin: University of Texas Press, 1957). Details of the incident in Vicksburg appear on pages 84–85.

28 Such reservations certainly limited the use of Black militias. Mississippi Governor Adelbert Ames, among others, worried that arming Blacks could produce "a war of races." Quoted in Singletary, *Negro Militia*, 146.

29 "A racist of the lowest order, [Sheriff Bryant Peden] publicly held that the blacks were still slaves and offered ten dollars a head for the interest of any ex-slaveholder in his former chattels. He boasted of whipping his own Negroes whenever they required it, just as before the war, and still listed them as property for tax purposes." Trelease, *White Terror*, 10.

30 New Orleans writer George Washington Cable put it succinctly: "He still served, we still ruled. . . . Emancipation had destroyed private, but had not disturbed public, subjugation."
    Quoted in Trelease, *White Terror*, xvi.

31 Rousey, *Policing the Southern City*, 194; Hadden, *Slave Patrols*, 196–97 and 205; and Trelease, *White Terror*, 288 and 290.

32 This history, and especially the legacy of slavery, weighs uniquely on the position of Blacks in American society. The Black experience has been different than that of Latinos, Asians, Native Americans, Jews, gays, and other excluded groups. The experiences of these other minorities deserve more substantial treatment than they can be given in these pages. But it is specifically the subjugation of Blacks that has done so much to shape the institution of policing, at times defining its central function. The treatment of the subject here reflects that predominance.

33 Hadden, *Slave Patrols*, 219.

34 Hadden, *Slave Patrols*, 211.

35 Quoted in Hadden, *Slave Patrols*, 212–13.

For a detailed discussion of the connection between slave patrols and the KKK as they appear in Black folklore and oral histories, see: Gladys-Marie Fry, *Night Riders in Black Folk History* (Knoxville: The University of Tennessee Press, 1975).

36 "Postwar police forces would transform patrolling into a highly effective but still legal means of racial oppression, building upon the practices that many prewar police forces had used when acting as urban patrollers." Hadden, *Slave Patrols*, 202.

37 Neglect is not so incongruous with brutality and heightened scrutiny as one might assume. During the nineteenth century, "Faced with such abuse from the police, black New Orleanians became reluctant to call on the police when they were victimized by crime." Rousey, *Policing the Southern City*, 167.

38 Hadden, *Slave Patrols*, 4.

39 David A. Harris, *Profiles in Injustice: Why Racial Profiling Cannot Work* (New York: The New Press, 2002), 10–11. Emphasis in original.

40 Harris, *Profiles in Injustice*, 22.

41 Harris, *Profiles in Injustice*, 28.

42 Harris, *Profiles in Injustice*, 48.

43 Harris, *Profiles in Injustice*, 62–63.

44 Harris, *Profiles in Injustice*, 48–49.

Ron Hampton, the executive director of the National Black Police Association, complained of a similar trend in police training videos: "In a training video, every criminal portrayed is Black." Quoted in Amnesty International USA, *United States of America: Rights for All* (New York: Amnesty International, 1998), 27.

45 Quoted in Harris, *Profiles in Injustice*, 51.

46 William H. Parker, "The Police Role In Community Relations," in *Police Patrol Readings*, ed. Samuel G. Chapman (Springfield, Illinois: Charles C. Thomas, 1964), 338–39. Emphasis in original.

Parker greatly exaggerated the scientific aspects of policing. In fact, the ability of the police to track crime statistically was and is very limited. Even with the assistance of powerful computers, recent efforts to base police deployment on crime statistics have been hopelessly flawed, relying on data drawn from too narrow a sample and subject to manipulation by police managers. See: Sidney L. Harring and Gerda W. Ray, "Policing a Class Society: New York City in the 1990s," *Social Justice* (Summer 1999): 68–69 and 71.

47 Darrell Huff, *How to Lie With Statistics* (New York: W.W. Norton & Company, 1954), 92–93.

48 Faced with statistics showing that 85 percent of Volusia County's asset forfeiture cases (during the years 1989–1992) involved Black motorists, Bob Vogel offered this analysis: "What this data tells me . . . is that

the majority of money being transported for drug activities involves blacks and Hispanics." Quoted in Christian Parenti, *Lockdown America: Police and Prisons in the Age of Crisis* (London: Verso, 1999), 54.

49 Harris, *Profiles in Injustice*, 78. Emphasis in original.

50 LAPD officers unwittingly parody Parker's example in this exchange from their Mobile Digital Terminal system, made public by the Christopher Commission:

"U can c the color of the interior . . . dig."
"Ya stop cars with blk interior."
"Bees they naugahyde."
"Negrohide."
"Self tanning no doubt."

Quoted in Independent Commission on the Los Angeles Police Department [The Christopher Commission], *Report of the Independent Commission on the Los Angeles Police Department* (July 9, 1991), 76.

51 Harris, *Profiles in Injustice*, 59.

An earlier study showed that, while Blacks and Whites violated traffic laws at the same rate, and only 13.5 percent of the vehicles traveling on the New Jersey turnpike had a Black occupant, Black drivers represented 35 percent of those stopped and 73.2 precent of those arrested. Harris, *Profiles in Injustice*, 54–55.

52 Quoted in Harris, *Profiles in Injustice*, 58.

Drawing from the same well of excuses, Clayton Searle, the President of the International Narcotics Interdiction Association states: "the minorities of any major city commit most of the street drug sales and then get arrested disproportionately." Harris, *Profiles in Injustice*, 73.

53 Harris, *Profiles in Injustice*, 61–62.

54 Harris, *Profiles in Injustice*, 68.

55 Harris, *Profiles in Injustice*, 80–81.

56 Erica Leah Schmitt et al., *Characteristics of Drivers Stopped by Police, 1999* (United States Department of Justice: March 2002), 1.

57 Blacks represent 4.6 percent of the state's driving-age population, but receive 10 percent of all traffic citations; Hispanics are 5.6 percent of the driving population but 9.6 percent of those ticketed.

Bill Dedman and Francie Latour, "Traffic Citations Reveal Disparity," *Boston Globe*, January 6, 2003 [database: NewsBank Full-Text Newspapers, accessed January 26, 2003].

58 Whites were 33 percent of the drivers stopped and 29.7 percent of the population; Latinos, 38 percent of those stopped and 46.5 percent of the population.

Tina Duant and Jill Leovy, "LAPD Offers 1st Data on Traffic Stops," *Los Angeles Times*, January 7, 2003, http://www.latimes.com/news/local/la-me-lapd7jan07.story (accessed January 7, 2003).

59 Harris, *Profiles in Injustice*, 80.

60 Harris, *Profiles in Injustice*, 80.

61 Harris, *Profiles in Injustice*, 80–81.

62 Dedman and Latour, "Traffic Citations."

63 Michael Cooper, "Officers in Bronx Fire 41 Shots, And an Unarmed Man is Killed," *New York Times*, February 5, 1999; and Robert D. McFadden and Kit R. Roane, "U.S. Examining Killing of Man in Police Custody," *New York Times*, February 6, 1999.

64 Quoted in McFadden and Roane, "U.S. Examining Killing."

It seems the police can mistake practically anything for a gun when it's in the hands of a young Black man. For instance, in November 1997, a U.S. Marshal shot Andre Burgess, a seventeen-year-old Black man, as he unsuspectingly walked by an unmarked car. The Marshal explained that he mistook Burgess' candy bar for a gun. Amnesty International, *Rights for All*, 27.

65 Peter Noel, "When Clothes Make the Suspect: Portraits in Racial Profiling," *Village Voice*, March 15–21, 2000, http://www.villagevoice.com/issues/0011/noel.php (accessed April 23, 2002).

Though consisting of only 1 percent of NYPD officers, the Street Crimes Unit was responsible for 10 percent of all documented stops. Harris, *Profiles in Injustice*, 26.

A few months after Diallo's shooting, officers from the Street Crimes Unit shot another unarmed Black man, 16-year-old Dante Johnson. Johnson panicked when police stopped him for questioning. He ran, and the cops fired after him. Unlike Diallo, Johnson was fortunate enough to survive. Amnesty International, *United States of America: Rights for All; Race, Rights and Police Brutality* (London: Amnesty International, September 1999), 9.

66 Quoted in McFadden and Roane, "U.S. Examining Killing."

67 Thomas P. Bonczar and Allen J. Beck, "Lifetime Likelihood of Going to State or Federal Prison, Bureau of Justice Statistics Special Report" (United States Department of Justice: March 1997), 1.

68 Bonczar and Beck, "Lifetime Likelihood," 7.

69 Michael Stephen Hindus, *Prison and Plantation: Crime, Justice, and Authority in Massachusetts and South Carolina, 1768–1878* (Chapel Hill: University of North Carolina Press, 1980), 248.

70 Parenti, *Lockdown America*, 124–25.

71 Quoted in Parenti, *Lockdown America*, 124.

72 Parenti *Lockdown America*, 125; and Peter B. Kraska and Victor E. Kappeler, "Militarizing American Police: The Rise and Normalization of Paramilitary Units," in *Police Perspectives: An Anthology*, eds. Larry K. Gaines and Gary W. Cordner (Los Angeles: Roxbury Publishing Company, 1999), 446.

73 Randall G. Sheldon et al., *Youth Gangs in American Society* (Belmont, California: Wadsworth, 2001) 245.
    At the same time, on the other side of the continent, the Boston Police Department was conducting its "search on sight" campaign against suspected drug dealers, especially young Black men. Part of the effort included taking Black youths off of public buses and forcing their pants down in public view. Charles J. Ogletree, Jr. et al., *Beyond the Rodney King Story: An Investigation of Police Misconduct in Minority Communities* (Boston: Northeastern University Press, 1995), 137.

74 Sheldon et al., *Youth Gangs*, 244. Parentheses in original.

75 Mike Davis, *City of Quartz: Excavating the Future in Los Angeles* (London: Verso, 1991), 277–78.

76 Both quoted in Davis, *City of Quartz*, 278.

77 Christopher Commission, *Report*, 39.

78 Christopher Commission, *Report*, 74.
    Notably, the Christopher Commission both denounced and perpetuated the stereotype of Black criminality. While it disapproved of the style of policing in minority communities, it also cited the "concentration and visibility of gangs and street crime" as deserving a larger share of police attention. In other words, it takes it for granted that minority neighborhoods need higher levels of police attention, just a different kind of attention.

79 Tim Wise, "Racial Profiling and Its Apologists," *Z Magazine*, March 2002, 44.
    William Chambliss argues that it is always easier for the police to focus their attention on people who are relatively powerless. Social inequalities thus create a permanent bias in law enforcement activity. "Put quite simply, if the police treat middle and upper-class delinquents (or cocaine-snorting college students) the same way they treat lower-class delinquents (or black, ghetto crack users), they are asking for trouble from people with power. If, on the other hand, they focus their law enforcement efforts on the lower classes, they are praised and supported by 'the community', that is, by the middle and upper-class white community." William J. Chambliss, *Power, Politics, and Crime* (Boulder, Colorado: Westview Press, 1999), 115. Parentheses in original.

80 "Profiling is, by nature, overinclusive. When being black (or Latino or Asian) is used as a proxy for criminality or dangerousness in a society in which a relative few are criminals, profiles based on or including race will always sweep too widely. . . . The upshot is that even if police investigation using the profile yields some wrongdoers, it is almost certain to capture far more innocent people in its exceedingly wide net—all of whom will be stigmatized, angered, and perhaps traumatized by what happens." Harris, *Profiles in Injustice*, 106. Parentheses in original.

81 Most famously, police base this perception of deviance on race, but they also use age, economic status, and national origin.

82 David H. Bayley and Harold Mendelsohn, *Minorities and the Police: Confrontation in America* (New York: The Free Press, 1969), 93.

83 See, for example: Ishmael Reed, "Another Day at the Front: Encounters with the Fuzz on the American Battlefront," in *Police Brutality: An Anthology*, ed. Jill Nelson (New York: W.W. Norton & Company, 2000), 189–205.

84 Harris, *Profiles in Injustice*, 98–99. He also writes, "Because profiling has such a strong impact on the mobility of those subjected to it—the diminished willingness of minorities to go where they feel they will get undesirable law enforcement attention—these tactics help to reinforce existing segregation in housing and employment." Harris, *Profiles in Injustice*, 102.

85 Harris, *Profiles in Injustice*, 105–6.

86 Wise, "Racial Profiling," 44.

87 Sally Simpson describes the historical handling of elite crime: "For the most part, drug addiction (including alcohol) and violence were deemed problems for ethnics (Mexican, Chinese, Italian, Irish, and Blacks) and immigrants (predominantly Catholic working class). The 'real' crime problem was thought to rest with the constitutionally inferior and morally lax. Corporate criminals, on the other hand, were drawn from America's newly emerging capitalist Brahmins. Although perceived to be opportunistic and ruthless in their business practices, these entrepreneurs were part of the governing and newly emerging social elite. Consequently, popular definitions of and legal responses to crime and criminals were framed within divergent ideological and social–control orbits. Conventional crime was dealt with punitively but corporate misbehavior was handled through administrative agencies or relatively lenient criminal statutes." Sally S. Simpson, *Corporate Crime, Law, and Social Control* (Cambridge, UK: Cambridge University Press, 2002), 2. Parentheses in original.

88 Editorial, "Sensible Sentences" *Christian Science Monitor*, November 2, 1995, 20.
    To take just one year's figures: In 1993, three thousand people were convicted of possessing crack. 90 percent of them were Black. Neil Websdale, *Policing the Poor: From Slave Plantation to Public Housing* (Boston: Northeastern University Press, 2001), 187.
    See also: Chambliss, *Power, Politics, and Crime*, 75.

89 Simpson does note that "The social control of corporate offending increasingly is utilizing a strategy of criminalization." Simpson, *Corporate Crime*, 20.

In 2002, the Enron Scandal became a corporate Watergate—a multifaceted cluster of scandals in which questions of individual guilt overshadowed the social and institutional aspects of official malfeasance. But even now, the penalties associated with corporate offenses do not begin to approach the severity of the crimes.

"When deaths and injuries due to unsafe products, environmental hazards, and other illegal corporate acts are added to the equation, corporate crime is perhaps the most dangerous and consequential kind of crime that occurs in our society." Simpson, *Corporate Crime*, 14.

See also: Chambliss, *Power, Politics, and Crime*, 133 and 155.

90 Allen Steinberg, *The Transformation of Criminal Justice: Philadelphia, 1800–1880* (Chapel Hill: University of North Carolina Press, 1989), 128.

91 Frank Donner, *Protectors of Privilege: Red Squads and Police Repression in Urban America* (Berkeley: University of California Press, 1990), 307.

92 Michael Novick, *White Lies, White Power: The Fight Against White Supremacy and Reactionary Violence* (Monroe, Maine: Common Courage Press, 1995), 61.

93 Kenneth T. Jackson, *The Ku Klux Klan in the City, 1915–1930* (New York: Oxford University Press, 1967), 190.

See also: Seymour Martin Lipset, "Why Cops Hate Liberals—And Vice Versa," in *The Police Rebellion: A Quest for Blue Power*, ed. William J. Bopp (Springfield, Illinois: Charles T. Thomas, Publisher, 1971), 26.

94 Quoted in Jackson, *Ku Klux Klan in the City*, 208.

95 Jackson, *Ku Klux Klan in the City*, 208–9.

96 Jackson, *Ku Klux Klan in the City*, 222.

97 Jackson, *Ku Klux Klan in the City*, 287.

98 Lipset, "Why Cops Hate Liberals," 25; and Donner, *Protectors of Privilege*, 56.

99 Lipset, "Why Cops Hate Liberals," 25.

100 Herbert Jenkins, *Keeping the Peace: A Police Chief Looks at His Job* (New York: Harper & Row, 1970), 4.

101 Quoted in James F. Richardson, *The New York Police: Colonial Times to 1901* (New York: Oxford University Press, 1970), 277.

102 Thurgood Marshall, "The Gestapo in Detroit," *The Crisis* 50.8 (August 1943): 232–33.

103 Marshall, "Gestapo in Detroit," 233.

104 Marshall, "Gestapo in Detroit," 247.

105 Marshall, "Gestapo in Detroit," 232.

106 Marshall, "Gestapo in Detroit," 247.

107 Marshall, "Gestapo in Detroit," 232.

108 Quoted in National Advisory Commission on Civil Disorders [The Kerner Commission], *Report of the National Advisory Commission on Civil Disorders* (New York: E.P. Dutton & Co., Inc., 1968), 85.

109 Quoted in Seth Cagin and Philip Dray, *We Are Not Afraid: The Story of Goodman, Schwerner, and Chaney and the Civil Rights Campaign for Mississippi* (New York: MacMillan Publishing Company, 1988), 428.

110 Quoted in Donner, *Protectors of Privilege*, 306.

111 Attorney General Robert Kennedy wrote in a memo to the President John F. Kennedy: "The unique difficulty as it seems to me to be presented by the situation in Mississippi (which is duplicated in parts of Alabama and Louisiana at least) is in gathering information on fundamentally lawless activities which have the sanction of local law enforcement agencies, political officials, and a substantial segment of the white population."

Quoted in United States, Senate Select Committee to Study Governmental Operations with Respect to Intelligence Activities [The Church Committee], *Final Report of the Select Committee to Study Governmental Operations with Respect to Intelligence Activities, vol. 3* (Washington, D.C.: U.S. Government Printing Office, 1976), 240.

Ralph McGill, the publisher of the *Atlanta Constitution*, concurred: "In the small community you too often find that the sheriff is a member [of the Klan] or that the deputies are members. And the poor white man, or more particularly the poor Negro in a small community, he well knows that is has no protection at all. The law isn't going to help him because the law is, more often than not, in the Klan or sympathetic with it in the small Southern community."

Quoted in David Lowe, *Ku Klux Klan: The Invisible Empire* (New York: W.W. Norton and Company, Inc., 1967), 103.

112 Quoted in Cagin and Dray, *We Are Not Afraid*, 206.

113 Donner, *Protectors of Privilege*, 307.

114 Cagin and Dray, *We Are Not Afraid*, 111; and Donner, *Protectors of Privilege*, 306.

115 Connor told reporters: "I have said for the last twenty years that these out-of-town meddlers were going to cause bloodshed." Quoted in Cagin and Dray, *We Are Not Afraid*, 111.

116 Henry Hampton et al., *Voices of Freedom: An Oral History of the Civil Rights Movement from the 1950s through the 1980s* (New York: Bantam Books, 1990), 83.

117 Cagin and Dray, *We Are Not Afraid*, 110.

118 Church Committee, *Final Report*, vol. 3, 239.

119 Quoted Church Committee, *Final Report*, vol. 2, 13.

120 Quoted in Church Committee, *Final Report*, vol. 3, 243.

121 Donner, *Protectors of Privilege*, 308–9.

122 Church Committee, *Final Report*, vol. 3, 243.

123 Donner, *Protectors of Privilege*, 309.

124 Both quoted in Donner, *Protectors of Privilege*, 310.

125 Donner, *Protectors of Privilege*, 310.

126 Donner, *Protectors of Privilege*, 311.

127 Berry, *Black Resistance*, 164.

128 Quoted in Hampton et al., *Voices of Freedom*, 268.

129 Berry, *Black Resistance*, 164.

130 Donner, *Protectors of Privilege*, 293.

131 Berry, *Black Resistance*, 164.

132 Church Committee, *Final Report*, vol. 3, 241.

133 Both quoted in Howard Zinn, "Selma, Alabama," in *You Can't Be Neutral on a Moving Train: A Personal History of Our Time* (Boston: Beacon Press, 1994), 63.

    Unfortunately, the Justice Department's enforcement priorities have not much changed. "Not only are police misconduct cases prosecuted as the lowest rate among civil rights prosecutions, but civil rights offenses themselves are prosecuted less than any other category of offense handled by the U.S. Justice Department." Human Rights Watch, *Shielded from Justice: Police Brutality and Accountability in the United States* (New York: Human Rights Watch, 1998), 94.

134 In 1962, the Marshals were used to force the integration of the University of Mississippi.

    Rodney Stark, *Police Riots: Collective Violence and Law Enforcement* (Belmont, California: Focus Books, 1972), 135.

135 Phil Ochs, "Here's to the State of Mississippi," in *There But For Fortune* (Electra Asylum, 1990).

136 Mary Frances Berry notes: "The federal government's response to the Chaney-Goodman-Schwerner murders remained exceptional. Segregationist violence, arson, and murders of civil rights workers for trying to exercise constitutional rights continued unabated. In fact, the FBI agreed with the Southern devotion to white supremacy. FBI agents spent more time investigating the white students and black activists, who were considered a threat to national security, than worrying about the segregationist violence." Berry, *Black Resistance*, 163.

137 Quoted in Hampton et al., *Voices of Freedom*, 194.

138 Misseduc Foundation, Inc., *Mississippi Black Paper* (New York: Random House, 1965).

139 Quoted in Misseduc Foundation, Inc., "Council of Federated Organizations, et al. v L.A. Rainey, et al.," in *Mississippi Black Paper* (New York: Random House, 1965), unpaged.

    I have restricted the list here to those complaints specifically relating to the actions (or inaction) of law enforcement officials.

140 Quoted in Misseduc Foundation, Inc., *Mississippi Black Paper*, 6. The names of officers were omitted from the published version, for fear of lawsuits.

141 Quoted in Misseduc Foundation, Inc., *Mississippi Black Paper*, 25–26.

142 Quoted in Misseduc Foundation, Inc., *Mississippi Black Paper*, 25.

143 Quoted in Misseduc Foundation, Inc., *Mississippi Black Paper*, 61.

144 Cagin and Dray, *We Are Not Afraid*, en passim.

145 Cagin and Dray, *We Are Not Afraid*, 288.

146 Cagin and Dray, *We Are Not Afraid*, 436.

147 Cagin and Dray, *We Are Not Afraid*, 382.

148 Cagin and Dray, *We Are Not Afraid*, 452 and 456.

149 Cagin and Dray, *We Are Not Afraid*, 301 and 382.

150 While awaiting trial, Sheriff Rainey appeared on the platform at a Klan rally. He said: "I've been accused by the FBI . . . [of being sympathetic to] the Klan and everything and so I came down today to see the head man and investigate it and see what there was to it. And I found it so far to be mighty good. They just done a lot of lying about it. I've met some of the best fellows I think there are in Alabama and Mississippi and other places. And I've had to lay some deputies out that's been investigating it and they reported to me a while ago, they'd met some fine people and thought it was a mighty good organization. Thank you."

    Quoted in Lowe, *Invisible Empire*, 104–5.

151 Cagin and Dray, *We Are Not Afraid*, 253–54.

152 Quoted in Hampton et al., *Voices of Freedom*, 223.

153 Hampton et al., *Voices of Freedom*, 224–26.

154 Hampton et al., *Voices of Freedom*, 226–29.

155 Quoted in Darlene Clark Hine et al., *The African-American Odyssey* (Upper Saddle River, New Jersey: Prentice Hall, 2003), 535.

156 Zinn, "Selma, Alabama," 65.

157 Stark, *Police Riots*, 187.

158 "First articulated in 1966 by SNCC leader Stokely Carmichael an [sic] other young militants, Black Power stressed self-determination, the right of ethnic minorities to define their group identity, and to make the decisions that affected their lives." Bob Blauner, "Almost a Race War," in *Still the Big News: Racial Oppression in America* (Philadelphia: Temple University Press, 2001), 4.

    For an excellent overview of the aims and ideology of the Black Power movement, including a discussion of its relationship to the civil rights movement and urban rioting, see: Joe R. Feagin and Harlan Hahn, "The Continuing Struggle for Black Power," in *Ghetto Revolts: The Politics of Violence in American Cities* (New York: The Macmillan Company, 1973), 297–332.

159 The Ten Point Program:

    "1. We want freedom. We want power to determine the destiny of our black community. . . .

    2. We want full employment of our people. . . .

    3. We want an end to the robbery by the capitalists of our black community. . . .

    4. We want decent housing fit for shelter of human beings. . . .

    5. We want education for our people that exposes the true nature of this decadent American society. We want education that teaches us our true history and our role in the present-day society. . . .

    6. We want all black men exempt from military service. . . .

    7. We want an immediate end to police brutality and murder of black people. . . .

    8. We want freedom for all black men held in federal, state, county, and city prisons and jails. . . .

    9. We want all black people when brought to trial to be tried in court by a jury of their peer group or people from their black communities. . . .

    10. We want land, bread, housing, education, clothing, justice, and peace. . . ."

    Quoted in Huey P. Newton, *War Against the Panthers: A Study of Repression in America*, PhD diss., University of California, Santa Cruz, 1980 (New York: Harlem River Press, 1996), 119–121.

    Each of these general points was expanded on in a brief paragraph.

    In 1972, the Ten Point Program was revised. Gender specific-language was replaced with gender-neutral phraseology, and the new document made a clear effort to express solidarity with other oppressed groups, and other people of color in particular. Some of the demands were re-ordered. Specifically, a demand for free health care was added, "An immediate end to all wars of aggression" replaced the call for exempting Blacks from the draft, and points 8 and 9 were consolidated, with the added provision that "all wretched, inhuman penal institutions" be eliminated. Newton, *War Against the Panthers*, 123–26; quotes are from page 125.

160 Newton, *War Against the Panthers*, 34.

161 For more on the Panthers, their survival programs, and the repression they faced, see chapter 7 and the afterword.

162 Donner, *Protectors of Privilege*, 180.

163 F.K. Heussenstamm, "Bumper Stickers and the Cops," *Trans-Action* 8.4 (February 1971): 32–33.

164 Stark, *Police Riots*, 184.

165 Quoted in Stark, *Police Riots*, 214–15.

166 Novick, *White Lies*, 70–82.

    For details on White supremacist organizing among prison guards, see: Parenti, *Lockdown America*, 206–7.

167 American Friends Service Committee, Program on Government Surveillance and Citizens' Rights, *The Police Threat to Political Liberty: Discoveries and Actions of the American Friends Service Committee Program on Government Surveillance and Citizens' Rights* (Philadelphia, Pennsylvania: American Friends Service Committee, 1979), 61.

168 Novick, *White Lies*, 71.

169 Novick, *White Lies*, 73.

170 Novick, *White Lies*, 74.

171 Novick, *White Lies*, 75.

172 Novick, *White Lies*, 80.

173 Charles E. Simmons, "The Los Angeles Rebellion: Class, Race, and Misinformation," in *Why LA Happened: Implications of the '92 Los Angeles Rebellion*, ed. Haki R. Madhubuti (Chicago: Third World Press, 1993), 144.

174 Human Rights Watch, *Shielded from Justice*, 191–92.

175 Quoted in Ogletree et al., *Beyond the Rodney King Story*, 40–41. See also: Mike Davis, "LA: The Fire This Time," *CovertAction Information Bulletin* 41 (Summer 1992): 21.

176 Novick, *White Lies*, 78.

177 Novick, *White Lies*, 84–85.

178 Novick, *White Lies*, 80.

179 Christopher Commission, *Report*, 78.

    The Commission's report offers some indication of the tension within the LAPD: "The Commission was told by most of the minorities interviewed that racially derogatory remarks are made on an ongoing basis at roll call and that racist jokes and cartoons appear from time to time on the bulletin boards in the station's locker rooms. Latino officers reported they are often referred to by ethnic nicknames such as 'Chico,' 'burrito-man,' and 'Chuy.'" Christopher Commission, *Report*, 79.

The Commission's survey revealed that a substantial percentage of minority officers had heard racial slurs used by peers or supervisors: 45 percent of Black males, 40 percent of Black females, 27 percent of Latino males, 36 percent of Latina females, 31 percent of Asian males, and 24 percent of Asian females. Christopher Commission, *Report*, 81.

180 Quoted in Bill Torpy, "FBI Agent: Hate Group May Include Lawmen," *Atlanta Journal-Constitution*, March 13, 2003 [database: NewsBank Full-Text Newspapers, accessed March 14, 2003].

181 Signe Waller, "Five Alive! The Legacy of the Greensboro Massacre," *Z Magazine*, September 1999, 45.

182 Donner, *Protectors of Privilege*, 361.

183 Waller, "Five Alive!" 45–46; and Berry, *Black Resistance*, 201.

184 Waller, "Five Alive!" 45.

185 "Informer Testifies Police Knew of Klan Intent," *New York Times*, April 15, 1985.

186 Ibid.

187 Waller, "Five Alive!" 45.

188 Dawson testified that he contacted the police thirteen times in the three weeks prior to the massacre. He called them twice on the morning of November 3, reporting that they were armed and headed to the site. He claims he was shocked when the police didn't stop them. *New York Times* (April 15, 1985) B14.

189 Waller, "Five Alive!" 45.

190 Jack Fowler, Roland Wayne Wood, and Mark Sherer; David Wayne Mathews and Jerry Paul Smith; Edward Dawson; and Jerry H. Cooper and Lieutenant P.W. Spoon, repectively.

Cooper was Dawson's police handler. Spoon was in charge of the officers assigned to cover the demonstration. Fowler, Wood, Mathews, and Smith were also held liable for assaulting Paul Bermanzohn and Thomas Clark. "8 in Klan Trial Told to Pay Plaintiffs $390,000," *New York Times*, June 9, 1985, 35.

191 Some researchers have found empirical support for this view of policing. For example, based on a review of eleven cities' police expenditures during the 1960s, David Jacobs concluded: "Metropolitan areas with more blacks had stronger law enforcement agencies in 1970 but this effect was not present in the 1960 equations. Thus, economic and racial cleavages were better predictors of police strength after a decade of well publicized social upheavals which may have been threatening to elites." David Jacobs, "Inequality and Police Strength: Conflict Theory and Coercive Control in Metropolitan Areas," *American Sociological Review* 44.6 (1979): 923.

In a similar study of public spending in the 1970s, Pamela Irving Jackson found that "the evidence at hand does suggest greater collective commitment to policing in urban centers most likely to be characterized by the struggle for dominance—in regions where the minority group is, for historical reasons, likely to be viewed as threatening, and in cities in which the group is large enough to constitute a threat." Pamela Irving Jackson, *Minority Group Threat, Crime, and Policing: Social Context and Social Control* (New York: Praeger, 1989), 52.

Chapter 5: The Natural Enemy of the Working Class

1 George Orwell, *Homage to Catalonia* (San Diego: Harcourt, Brace, & Company, 1980), 124.

2 Pavlito Geshos, "Working Class Heroes," *Clamor*, March/April 2002, 50.

Greensboro was not the first time the KKK took an interest in destroying unions. To offer just one example, in the autumn of 1936, the Klan burned a cross near a rubber factory in Akron, hoping to intimidate striking workers who occupied the factory. Jeremy Brecher, *Strike!* (Boston: South End Press, 1972), 185.

3 Quoted in Dennis C. Rousey, *Policing the Southern City: New Orleans, 1805–1889* (Baton Rouge: Louisiana State University Press, 1996), 167.

The majority of the strikers were Black, but not all of them.

4 Anatole France, *The Red Lily* (New York: The Modern Library, no date), 75.

5 Quoted in Eric H. Monkkonen, *Police in Urban America, 1860–1920* (Cambridge: Cambridge University Press, 1981), 129.

6 See chapter 3 for more on this point.

7 Allen Steinberg, *The Transformation of Criminal Justice: Philadelphia, 1800–1880* (Chapel Hill, North Carolina: University of North Carolina Press, 1989), 127.

This combination of class bias and Puritanical moralism was characteristic of the period, and translated into rigid standards of conduct for women especially. Its effect was evident, for example, in New York's campaign against prostitution. "In a city so concerned with defining both women's proper place and the place of the working class, the alarm over prostitution stemmed in part from general hostilities to the milieu of laboring women from which prostitutes came." Christine Stansell, *City of Women: Sex and Class in New York, 1789–1860* (Urbana, Illinois: University of Illinois Press, 1987), 175.

8 Quoted in Steinberg, *Transformation of Criminal Justice*, 153.

9 Gang suppression is discussed in greater detail in chapter 4. The drug war, quality-of-life policies, and related efforts are addressed in chapter 9.

10 Sidney Harring, *Policing a Class Society: The Experience of American Cities, 1865–1915* (New Brunswick, New Jersey: Rutgers University Press, 1983), 201.

11 Charles J. Ogletree Jr., et al., *Beyond the Rodney King Story: An Investigation of Police Conduct in Minority Communities* (Boston: Northeastern University Press, 1995), 22–23.

12 Ann Mullen, "Harassing the Homeless," *Metro Times* (Detroit, Michigan), November 24, 1999, http://www.metrotimes.com/mtframes.asp?Page=/20/23/Features/musGimme.html (accessed September 9, 2002).

13 Harring, *Policing a Class Society*, 111.

14 Frank Donner, *Protectors of Privilege: Red Squads and Police Repression in Urban America* (Berkeley: University of California Press, 1990), 37.

15 Raymond B. Fosdick, *American Police Systems* (New York: The Century Company, 1920), 322–23. Emphasis in original.

16 See, for example: Roger Lane, *Policing the City: Boston 1822–1885* (Cambridge, Massachusetts: Harvard University Press, 1967), 206–7.

17 A Pinkerton agent, James McParland, joined the Molly Maguires, aided in the commission of crimes, and then testified against them to gain a conviction. The Pennsylvania Supreme Court upheld the practice in its 1877 *Campbell vs. Commonwealth* decision. Nineteen Molly Maguires were executed on the basis of such evidence. Donner, *Proctectors of Privilege,* 10; and Howard Zinn, *A People's History of the United States, 1492–Present* (New York: HarperPerennial, 1995), 239.

18 Donner, *Protectors of Privilege,* 24.

19 Bruce Smith, *The State Police: Organization and Administration* (New York: The Macmillan Company, 1925), 33.

20 Quoted in Donner, *Protectors of Privilege,* 25.

21 For example, the commission remarked that "the resentment expressed by many persons connected with the strike at the presence of the armed guards and militia of the State does not argue well for the peace-able character or purposes of such persons" and that "a labor or other organization whose purpose can be accomplished only by the violation of law and order of society, has no right to exist." Quoted in Katherine Mayo, *Justice To All: The Story of the Pennsylvania State Police* (New York: GP Putnam's Sons, 1917), 4.

22 Quoted in Mayo, *Justice To All,* 5.

23 Mayo, *Justice To All,* 10.

24 Diane Cecelia Weber, "Warrior Cops: The Ominous Growth of Paramilitarism in American Police Departments," *Cato Institute Briefing Papers* 30 (August 26, 1999): 6.

25 Quoted in Pennsylvanian State Federation of Labor, *The American Cossack* (New York: Arno Press & The New York Times, 1971), 17.

26 Quoted in Pennsylvanian State Federation of Labor, *American Cossack,* 28–29.

27 Quoted in Smith, *State Police,* 33–34.

28 "Capital's turn to the police to handle some aspects of the reproduction of the working class cannot be separated from a more general move by the bourgeoisie, beginning in the 1840s, with the industrial revolu-tion, to use public institutions in general for that purpose. This socialization of expenditures necessary for the reproduction and expansion of capital encompasses public expenses for education, public health, wel-fare, police and fire protection, building inspection and housing, and public works. The post–Civil War peri-od saw a rapid expansion of these early efforts, with local capitalists devoting substantial resources in order to control and direct the various components of the state apparatus to the ends of the capitalist class." Harring, *Policing a Class Society,* 27–28.

    See also: James Weinstein, *The Corporate Ideal in the Liberal State: 1900–1918* (Boston: Beacon Press, 1968), 95.

29 The Texas Rangers were an example of the military type. Created by the Republic of Texas in 1835, the Rangers, under military command, were mostly used to guard the Mexican border. Bruce Smith, *Rural Crime Control* (New York: Institute of Public Administration, 1933), 127–28.

    Massachusetts provides the model of the state-level vice squad. In 1864, the legislature created the Constables of the Commonwealth "to repress and prevent crime by the suppression of liquor shops, gam-bling places, and houses of 'ill-fame.'" Quoted in Lane, *Policing the City,* 137.

    In 1868, South Carolina's Reconstruction legislature created a state constabulary with a Chief Constable in Columbia and deputies in every county. It was intended to suppress Klan activity, but proved ineffec-tive. Allen W. Trelease, *White Terror: The Ku Klux Klan Conspiracy and Southern Reconstruction* (New York: Harper & Row, 1971), 73.

30 Bruce Smith, *Police Systems in the United States* (New York: Harper & Brothers Publishers, 1940), 187–88.

31 Quoted in Donner, *Protectors of Privilege,* 41.

32 Donner, *Protectors of Privilege,* 42–43.

33 Huey P. Newton, *War Against the Panthers: A Study of Repression in America,* PhD diss, University of California, Santa Cruz, 1980 (New York: Harlem River Press, 1996), 18.

34 See chapter 4.

35 Quoted in The Commission of Inquiry, The Interchurch World Movement, *Report on the Steel Strike of 1919* (New York: Harcourt, Brace and Howe, 1920), 238.

The brunt of repression was felt in Allegheny County and western Pennsylvania. There, the authorities responded by deputizing five thousand scabs and banning all public assemblies, including, in some places, indoor meetings. Mass arrests and physical attacks became common, with strikers facing violence from police, deputy sheriffs, scabs, company guards, vigilantes, and sometimes state troops. Many were injured, twenty were killed. Under such pressure, the strike collapsed in January, 1920. The workers returned to work, having won nothing. Samuel Yellen, *American Labor Struggles, 1877–1934* (New York: Pathfinder, 1936), 261–63 and 271; Brecher, *Strike!* 123; and Zinn, *People's History,* 371–72.

36 James F. Richardson, *Urban Police in the United States* (Port Washington, New York: National University Press and Kennikat Press, 1974), 159.

In extreme cases the police even aided strikers. During the steel strike of 1919, Cleveland Mayor Harry L. Davis had the police turn away scabs trying to enter the city. Potential strikebreakers were treated as suspicious persons, and—until a court forbade the practice—either run out of town or arrested. Richardson, *Urban Police,* 161.

Likewise in small, homogenous communities, where the police had familial and social ties with the workers, they were less likely to serve as effective strikebreaking forces. A most dramatic case of this phenomenon occurred in Mattewan, West Virginia, where the police chief himself was a former miner. Brecher, *Strike!* 136.

Such cases are noteworthy precisely because they are exceptional.

37 Smith, *State Police,* 58–59.

38 Yellen, *Labor Struggles,* 169.

39 Yellen, *Labor Struggles,* 172–73.

40 Yellen, *Labor Struggles,* 179.

On the Lawrence textile strike, see also: Zinn, *People's History,* 328–330.

41 Quoted in Peter Bollen, *Great Labor Quotations: Sourcebook and Reader* (Los Angeles: Red Eye Press, 2000), 22.

42 Yellen, *Labor Struggles,* 176.

By the end of the strike, 296 had been arrested. Yellen, *Labor Struggles,* 189.

43 Yellen, *Labor Struggles,* 178–79.

44 Yellen, *Labor Struggles,* 194.

45 Quoted in Yellen, *Labor Struggles,* 181.

A similar argument was used to convict the Haymarket defendants a quarter-century before. See chapter 7.

46 Yellen, *Labor Struggles,* 193.

47 Yellen, *Labor Struggles,* 182.

48 Quoted in Zinn, *People's History,* 328.

49 Yellen, *Labor Struggles,* 185–87.

50 Quoted in Zinn, *People's History,* 329.

51 Yellen, *Labor Struggles,* 190–91.

52 Quoted in Yellen, *Labor Struggles,* 193.

53 Yellen, *Labor Struggles,* 195–97.

54 Yellen, *Labor Struggles,* 308–13 and 316–17.

55 One oft-cited example: Oregon lumber mills shut down, because there was no way to ship the wood. Brecher, *Strike!* 151; and Yellen, *Labor Struggles,* 315.

56 David F. Selvin, *A Terrible Anger: The 1934 Waterfront and General Strikes in San Francisco* (Detroit: Wayne State University Press, 1996), 91–92.

57 Selvin, *Terrible Anger,* 93.

58 Brecher, *Strike!* 152.

59 Violence was less common in Portland and Seattle, where the persistent threat of a general strike discouraged any attempt at opening the docks. Selvin, *Terrible Anger,* 104.

The most notable incident in the northwest came as the San Francisco General Strike was winding down. Seattle Mayor Charles Smith ordered 300 police to remove 2,000 picketers from the city's pier at Smith's Cove. The cops used tear gas and nausea gas against the crowds, and the police chief resigned in protest. Selvin, *Terrible Anger,* 225; and Yellen, *Labor Struggles,* 332.

60 Selvin, *Terrible Anger,* 144–46; and Yellen, *Labor Struggles,* 318.

61 Quoted in Selvin, *Terrible Anger,* 156.

62 Yellen, *Labor Struggles,* 318.

63 Selvin, *Terrible Anger,* 149.

The police naturally reversed this chronology in their official statements, claiming that the inspectors merely defended themselves against the hail of rocks coming from the crowd. Several witnesses, including Harry Bridges, testified that nothing was thrown until after the shots were fired. Selvin, *Terrible Anger,* 14.

64 Selvin, *Terrible Anger,* 11–12 and 14.

65 Quoted in Selvin, *Terrible Anger,* 150.

66 Yellen, *Labor Struggles,* 319; and Brecher, *Strike!* 153.

67 Brecher, *Strike!* 153; and Yellen, *Labor Struggles,* 319.

68 Quoted in Selvin, *Terrible Anger*, 161–62.

69 Quoted in Yellen, *Labor Struggles*, 319.

70 Selvin, *Terrible Anger*, 166–67; and Yellen, *Labor Struggles*, 323.

71 Selvin, *Terrible Anger*, 166–67.

72 Quoted in Selvin, *Terrible Anger*, 168, 177, and 182.

73 Selvin, *Terrible Anger*, 178.

74 Yellen, *Labor Struggles*, 325.

75 Selvin, *Terrible Anger*, 185.

76 Selvin, *Terrible Anger*, 192–200; and Yellen, *Labor Struggles*, 328.

77 Selvin, *Terrible Anger*, 221 and 227.

78 Selvin, *Terrible Anger*, 224.

79 Selvin, *Terrible Anger*, 233.

80 Yellen, *Labor Struggles*, 334–35.

81 Selvin, *Terrible Anger*, 237.
   Between January 1, 1937, and August 1, 1938, 350 strikes occurred on the west coast docks, mostly brief and localized "quickies." Brecher, *Strike!* 158.

82 Quoted in Selvin, *Terrible Anger*, 240.

83 Tony Bartelme, "Indicted Longshoremen Adopted as Union Crusade," *Post and Courier* (Charleston, SC), September 3, 2001.

84 Bartelme, "Indicted Longshoremen;" and "Analysis: South Carolina Longshoremen Accuse Attorney General of Playing Politics in Riot Indictments of Union Members," *Morning Edition*, National Public Radio, July 16, 2001 (database: Newspaper source, accessed September 29, 2002).

85 Among those injured was ILA Local 1422 President Ken Riley, who was struck in the head with a baton. One ILA member was run over with a state police car. The cops later admitted they were surprised no one had been killed. Bartelme, "Indicted Longshoremen;" and Ashaki Binta, "Solidarity Grows for Dockers Victimized by 'Police Riot,'" *Labor Notes*, April 2001, 1 and 14.

86 Quoted in Morning Edition (July 16, 2001).
   Condon later sponsored an ad for Bush's presidential campaign, stating "The Charleston union riot reminds us why South Carolina is a right-to-work state." A year later, as the trial date approached, he publicly compared the ILA to the terrorists who attacked the World Trade Center. Such antics led defense attorneys to file motions accusing him of prosecutorial misconduct. Tony Bartelme, "Condon Gives Up Charleston Five Case; 1st Circuit's Walter Bailey to Prosecute Union Members on Rioting Charges," *Post and Courier* (Charleston, SC), October 11, 2001.
   The defense was not alone in the view that Condon was taking things too far. Jeff Osburn, a Charleston Police detective assigned to the case, said: "Having these guys under house arrest for this long is ridiculous. . . . These are normal, everyday, hard working citizens, the backbone of the community. They had a right to be there that night and a right to make a statement. It's just unfortunate that it got out of hand, and it's a shame that the prosecution has gone as far as it has." Quoted in Bartelme, "Indicted Longshoremen."
   Even Mayor Joseph P. Riley wrote to Condon that the case "should be resolved far short of these defendants proceeding to trial on the current charges against them." Quoted in Bartelme, "Condon Gives Up."

87 Tony Bartelme, "Remaining 'Charleston 5' Make Plea Bargain," *Post and Courier* (Charleston, SC), November 9, 2001; Tony Bartelme, "Charleston 5 Case Ends With No-Contest Pleas," *Post and Courier* (Charleston, SC), November 14, 2001; Bartelme, "Indicted Longshoremen;" Bartelme, "Condon Gives Up;" Alicia Chang, "Thousands Rally at South Carolina Statehouse to Support Dockworkers Charged in Riot" AP Worldstream (June 9, 2001) (database: Newspaper Source, accessed September 29, 2002); and Morning Edition (July 16, 2001).

88 Bartelme, "Remaining 'Charleston 5;'" and Bartelme, "Charleston 5 Case."

89 Jeremy Brecher, "Organizing the New Workforce," *Z Magazine*, July/August 1998, 71.
   A later Justice for Janitors campaign in Sacramento supplies a brief catalog of the despicable tactics still in use against union organizing. Over the course of four years, as the workers fought for a contract with Somers Building Maintenance, they faced firings, a Congressional investigation, and a citywide ban on union marches, as well as mass arrests and beatings at the hands of the police. Nevertheless, the union prevailed, and in March 1999, Somers signed a contract with SEIU. David Bacon, "Janitors Get Justice," *Labor Notes*, May 1999, 1 and 14.

90 Ann Mullen, "A Million-Dollar Question," *Metro Times* (Detroit, MI), April 19, 2000, http://www.metrotimes.com/mtframes.asp?Page=/20/23/Features/musGimme.html (accessed September 9, 2002); and Mia Butzbaugh, "Media Giants Take Aim at Newspaper Unions," *Labor Notes*, September 1995, 3.
   A Sterling Heights Police memo dated July 18, 1995, described a meeting between police and management. It said that the Detroit News Agency's representatives were "very impressed and very happy with the performance of our department and that they will do their best to assist us, so as to keep things running smoothly." Quoted in Mullen, "Million-Dollar Question."

91 David Bacon, "Labor Slaps the Smug New Face of Unionbusting," *CovertAction Quarterly* (Spring 1997): 36.

92 Butzbaugh, "Media Giants," 3; and Mia Butzbaugh, "Newspaper War in Detroit," *Labor Notes*, October 1995, 9.

93 Susan Zachem, "Sterling Heights Settles on Kicking Case," *GCUI*, March 2000, http://www.gcui.org/archives/00march/det003.shtml (accessed September 9, 2002).

94 Butzbaugh, "Newspaper War," 1 and 9.

95 Jim Dulzo, "Striking Out," *Metro Times* (Detroit, MI), January 23, 2001, http://www.metrotimes.com/editorial/story.asp?id=1210 (accessed February 13, 2003).

   Some strikers won court settlements related to excessive force and unlawful arrest. Mullen "Million-Dollar Question;" Zachem, "Kicking Case;" and "Striking Newspaper Worker Wins $2.5 Million Verdict," *Teamster Magazine*, June/July 2001, http://www.teamster.org/comm/newsletters/0601.htm#02 (accessed February 3, 2003).

96 Butzbaugh, "Newspaper War," 9.

97 Quoted in Butzbaugh, "Newspaper War," 9.

98 Quoted in Jim West, "Unions Focus on Advertiser/Circulation Boycott As Detroit Newspapers Reject Peace Offer," *Labor Notes*, November 1995, 5.

99 Paul A. Gilje, *Rioting in America* (Bloomington: Indiana University Press, 1996), 151 and 180.

100 "In March 1937, the Supreme Court upheld the constitutionality of the Wagner Act in the Jones and Laughlin case, and the machinery of the National Labor Relations Board began to work. . . . Having accepted the NLRB as a legal body with authority over employers engaged in interstate commerce, the court then set about restricting workers' rights under the Wagner Act. In 1939, it outlawed the sit-down strike in the Fansteel case, and decided that the Wagner Act could not force employers to make concessions to workers. In other decisions, the courts reinforced employers' rights and limited workers' rights by holding: (1) that the Act did not interfere with the employer's right to select employees or discharge them; (2) that, if the employers bargained to 'an impasse,' they could unilaterally impose terms, but the workers could not strike while under contract; (3) that the employees' right to strike did not include the license to 'seize the employers' plants' as in sit-down strikes; (4) that unions were institutions apart from their members and that union leaders, therefore, had to police their unions and ensure 'responsible behavior.' In sum, the courts allowed unions to engage in collective bargaining over a limited range of issues, but prohibited them from using the kind of militant, direct action that had built the CIO." James R. Green, *The World of the Worker: Labor in Twentieth-Century America* (New York: Hill and Wang, 1980), 165–66. See also: Harring, *Policing a Class Society*, 257.

101 "The institutionalization of the new unions began soon after their explosive creation in the mass strikes of the mid-thirties. The top leaders hastened this process, especially after the employers' vicious counterattack in 1937. Moreover, the whole structure of collective bargaining, as determined by the courts and the NLRB, favored a more routinized, businesslike relationship between top leaders of labor and management, with the government as referee. As a result, many of the issues, such as speedup, that precipitated the original labor revolts were shunted aside." Green, *World of the Worker*, 172.

102 One high-ranking police official attributed the General Strike to just this change of leadership: "the rank-and-file workers became convinced that their leaders were too much hand-in-glove with the industrial interests of the city." Quoted in Brecher, *Strike!* 252.

Chapter 6: Police Autonomy and Blue Power

1 "If there is any group for whom unions and job actions seemed unlikely, it was the police personnel. Their job is to preserve law and order; they have traditionally been the strike breakers; and they have been subject to the harshest restrictions against their unionization."
   Margaret Levi, *Bureaucratic Insurgency: The Case of Police Unions* (Lexington, Massachusetts: Lexington Books, 1977), 2.

2 Robert M. Fogelson, *Big-City Police* (Cambridge, Massachusetts: Harvard University Press, 1977), 196.
   FOPs were also organized geographically, rather than by department. And they sometimes formed auxiliaries including people from outside of law enforcement. William J. Bopp, "The Police Rebellion," in *The Police Rebellion*, ed. William J. Bopp (Springfield, Illinois: Charles C. Thomas, Publisher, 1971), 13.

3 Fogelson, *Big-City Police*, 196–97.

4 Fogelson, *Big-City Police*, 81; and Richard L. Lyons, "The Boston Police Strike of 1919," *The New England Quarterly* (June 1947): 164.
   In June 1919, the AFL announced that it would begin chartering police unions. By the end of August, thirty-eight such charters had been issued. Lyons, "Boston Police Strike," 151; and Francis Russell, *A City in Terror—1919—The Boston Police Strike* (New York: Viking Press, 1975), 25.

5 Russell, *City in Terror*, 50–51 and 73; and Lyons, "Boston Police Strike," 148–49.
   Of the 1,544 patrolmen, 940 voted for the union; no one voted against it. Lyons, "Boston Police Strike," 155.

6 Russell, *City in Terror*, 78.

7 Lyons, "Boston Police Strike," 148.
   Boston was not actually the country's first police strike. That honor goes to a successful walkout among

the Ithaca police in 1889. The city council voted to lower police pay, the police struck, and the council immediately rescinded their decision. Russell, *City in Terror*, 233.

8 Of 1,544 officers, 1,117 went on strike, leaving the force at about one-quarter strength. Lyons, "Boston Police Strike," 160.

9 Russell, *City in Terror*, 131, 133, and 137-38.

10 Russell, *City in Terror*, 122-25.

11 Russell, *City in Terror*, 151-52.

Additionally, 100 of the 183 state-controlled Metropolitan Park police were put at Curtis' disposal. (But fifty-eight of these refused the duty and were suspended.) Private companies armed their employees or hired guards, Harvard was patrolled by the university police and ROTC, and federal property was protected by the army. Russell, *City in Terror*, 119, 127, 150, and 166.

12 Russell, *City in Terror*, 149 and 159.

13 Russell, *City in Terror*, 162-63 and 167-70.

14 Russell, *City in Terror*, 181-82 and 217; and Lyons, "Boston Police Strike," 165.

Meanwhile, Governor Calvin Coolidge, who had initially refused Mayor Andrew Peters' request for National Guard deployment, positioned himself to take credit for breaking the strike, issuing an executive order placing himself in control of the Boston Police Department. He eventually used the strike to leverage himself into the presidency. Russell, *City in Terror*, 173-74 and 196-8; and Lyons, "Boston Police Strike," 159.

15 Lyons, "Boston Police Strike," 166.

After the strike, it took the police department a while to re-form itself. For one thing, it had lost most of its officers and, with the stigma of strikebreaking so fresh, faced considerable difficulty finding recruits. To make matters worse, tailors refused to make new uniforms. Lyons, "Boston Police Strike," 165.

16 Russell, *City in Terror*, 234 and 239; and Fogelson, *Big-City Police*, 195.

17 Russell, *City in Terror*, 48-49 and 183.

18 Fogelson, *Big-City Police*, 81-82.

19 Levi, *Bureaucratic Insurgency*, 13 and 28-29.

Carl Parsell referred to this mode of operation as "collective begging." Quoted in Fogelson, *Big-City Police*, 200.

20 Additionally, the FOP had 169 local chapters. Levi, *Bureaucratic Insurgency*, 7.

21 The mayor of Jackson, Mississippi, for example, fired thirty-six officers for organizing with an AFL affiliate. Levi, *Bureaucratic Insurgency*, 132.

22 Levi, *Bureaucratic Insurgency*, 30-31.

23 Quoted in Levi, *Bureaucratic Insurgency*, 31.

24 Levi, *Bureaucratic Insurgency*, 91-92.

25 Quoted in Levi, *Bureaucratic Insurgency*, 93.

26 Quoted in Levi, *Bureaucratic Insurgency*, 31.

27 Levi, *Bureaucratic Insurgency*, 43.

This dynamic was in effect in cities throughout the country. See: Fogelson, *Big-City Police*, 204.

28 Quoted in Levi, *Bureaucratic Insurgency*, 45.

29 Levi, *Bureaucratic Insurgency*, 49-51.

30 Levi, *Bureaucratic Insurgency*, 54-55.

31 Fogelson, *Big-City Police*, 210.

32 Rodney Stark, *Police Riots: Collective Violence and Law Enforcement* (Belmont, California: Focus Books, 1972), 202.

33 Levi, *Bureaucratic Insurgency*, 135.

34 Levi, *Bureaucratic Insurgency*, 140.

35 These strikes occurred in 1974, 1977, 1978, and 1979, respectively. Richard J. Lundman, *Police and Policing: An Introduction* (New York: Holt, Rinehart, and Winston, 1980), 41.

36 "The authorities sharply denounced these job actions; but they were so anxious to get the officers back on the street and so reluctant to tangle with the union that, instead of invoking the legal sanctions, they usually gave in to the demands and granted amnesty to the strikers." Fogelson, *Big-City Police*, 213.

37 William J. Bopp, "The Detroit Police Revolt," in *The Police Rebellion*, ed. William J. Bopp (Springfield, Illinois: Charles C. Thomas, Publisher, 1971), 165.

38 Levi, *Bureaucratic Insurgency*, 112.

39 Levi, *Bureaucratic Insurgency*, 113; and Bopp, "Detroit Police Revolt," 170.

40 Quoted in Levi, *Bureaucratic Insurgency*, 114.

41 Levi, *Bureaucratic Insurgency*, 113, 115, and 117; and Bopp, "Detroit Police Revolt," 172.

42 Bopp, "Detroit Police Revolt," 172.

43 Quoted in Levi, *Bureaucratic Insurgency*, 120.

Levi describes the City's acquiescence: "The effect of the Detroit riot on the police labor dispute was immense. . . . Officials set about appeasing patrolmen and policewomen in order to make them willing to carry out the work that had to be done. It became imperative to rebuild rank and file morale, ensure department unity and discipline in case of emergency, and develop the means of squelching community discontent without engendering protest from either the police themselves or the subject population. The first step was to reward the patrol force for their participation in putting down the black uprising. [Police Chief Ray] Girardein rescinded the earlier suspensions and pay withholdings. Two weeks after the end of the racial conflict, the Common Council rushed through its approval of the DPOA contract." Levi, *Bureaucratic Insurgency*, 119.

44 Bopp, "Detroit Police Revolt," 172.

45 Levi describes this relationship in New York: "In the next several years, the PBA leaders learned to work closely with the department hierarchy and to negotiate more effectively with the city. Issues of management prerogative remained formally outside the scope of collective bargaining. But, as one legal advisor to the association once remarked, 'What's bargainable is determined by strength, essentially.' Certainly new questions became available for discussion, and the PBA exerted greater direct influence on department policy. At the same time, the city and department learned to demand more for their money. They expected acquiescence to policy innovations in exchange for contract benefits." Levi, *Bureaucratic Insurgency*, 77. See also: Nicholas Alex, *Black in Blue: A Study of the Negro Policeman* (New York: Appleton-Century-Crofts, 1969), 61–62.

46 For example, in January 1971, a six-day wildcat strike by 85 percent of New York's patrol officers ended when each striker was fined $600. Levi, *Bureaucratic Insurgency*, 88–89.

The police faced similar reprisals when they acted in solidarity with other workers during the Baltimore AFSCME strike of 1974. The strike began among garbage collectors demanding higher pay. Soon the strikers were joined by other public employees, including jailers, park workers, zoo keepers, highway workers, and sewer engineers. After several days, on July 11, the police joined the strike, in violation of Maryland law. Looting ensued, and one rioter was killed by an on-duty officer. The next day, Governor Marvin Mandel sent in the state police, with an armored car and police dogs. The National Guard was placed on alert. By July 15, most of the city workers were back on the job, and the strike was defeated. The police union in particular was fined $25,000, and the union president was personally fined another $10,000. Russell, *City in Terror*, 242–44. See also: Pamela Irving Jackson, *Minority Group Threat, Crime, and Policing: Social Context and Social Control* (New York: Praeger, 1989), 81.

47 For more on the political machines, see chapter 3.

48 Fogelson, *Big-City Police*, 72.

49 The machines were not well equipped to defend themselves. "In short, by virtue of their extraordinary decentralization the machines could not as a rule compel the politicians, policemen, gangsters, and other members to ponder the organization's long-term interests before pursuing their own short-run opportunities." Fogelson, *Big-City Police*, 73.

50 Fogelson, *Big-City Police*, 53–54.

In areas other than policing, the business model was in the forefront. This predominance was anything but accidental. While governments were undergoing a period of rationalization, corporations were engaged in a similar process. Each set of changes sought to increase the institution's legitimacy by eliminating the appearance of partial and personalized control, replacing it with control according to "impartial" and formalized laws—legislative and administrative rules in the case of the government, the dictates of the market for corporations. "For the illusion now appears that not capital but bureaucracy, not capitalists but managers control the large corporations. . . . 'Rewards' are distributed by 'society' according to ability, or the scarcity of the skill involved and the occupation's 'functional importance.'" Maurice Zeitlin, "On Classes, Class Conflict, and the State: An Introductory Note," in *Classes, Class Conflict, and the State: Empirical Studies in Class Analysis*, ed. Maurice Zeitlin (Cambridge, Massachusetts: Winthrop Publishers, Inc., 1980), 9.

See also: Sidney Harring, *Policing a Class Society: The Experience of American Cities, 1865–1915* (New Brunswick, New Jersey: Rutgers University Press, 1983), 30.

51 Fogelson, *Big-City Police*, 56–58.

The crime-prevention focus was paired with a renewed enthusiasm for proactive tactics. "The reformers also thought that, so long as the police forces only responded to civilian complaints, they could not stamp out gambling, prostitution, and other victimless crimes or keep tabs on trade unions, radical parties, and other left-wing groups. Hence they supported departments that tempted bartenders to sell liquor after hours, enticed women to engage in prostitution, tapped public telephones, infiltrated labor organizations, employed agents provocateurs, and otherwise ignored long-standing restraints on police power." Fogelson, *Big-City Police*, 90.

52 Fogelson, *Big-City Police*, 178–80 and 184.

53 Fogelson, *Big-City Police*, 97.

54 Fogelson, *Big-City Police*, 74–77.

One place where the Chief was granted a permanent position was Los Angeles—with disastrous results. See: Independent Commission on the Los Angeles Police Department [The Christopher Commission], *Report of the Independent Commission on the Los Angeles Police Department* (July 9, 1991), 186.

55 "Most police departments . . . assumed the additional responsibility to control narcotics, censor motion pictures, curb juvenile delinquency, and infiltrate trade unions and left-wing groups." Fogelson, *Big-City Police*, 106.

56 Weber describes an ideal bureaucracy:

"Only the supreme chief of the organization occupies his position of dominance (*Herrenstellung*) by virtue of appropriation, of election, or of having been designated for the succession. But even *his* authority consists in a sphere of legal 'competence.' The whole administrative staff under the supreme authority then consists, in the purest type, of individual officials . . . who are appointed and function according to the following criteria:

(1) They are personally free and subject to authority only with respect to their impersonal official obligations.

(2) They are organized in a clearly defined hierarchy of offices.

(3) Each office has a clearly defined sphere of competence in the legal sense.

(4) The office is filled by a free contractual relationship. Thus, in principle, there is free selection.

(5) Candidates are selected on the basis of technical qualifications. In the most rational case, this is tested by examination or guaranteed by diplomas certifying technical training, or both. They are *appointed*, not elected.

(6) They are remunerated by fixed salaries in money, for the most part with a right to pensions.

(7) The office is treated as the sole, or at least the primary, occupation of the incumbent.

(8) It constitutes a career. There is a system of 'promotion' according to seniority or achievement, or both. Promotion is dependent on the judgment of superiors.

(9) The official works entirely separated from ownership of the means of administration and without appropriation of his position.

(10) He is subject to strict and systematic discipline and control in the conduct of the office."

Max Weber, *Economy and Society: An Outline of Interpretive Sociology*, ed. Guenther Roth and Claus Wittich, vol. 1 (Berkeley: University of California Press, 1978), 220–21. Emphasis in original.

57 Fogelson, *Big-City Police,* 60.

58 Fogelson, *Big-City Police,* 59.

59 Fogelson, *Big-City Police,* 169.

60 Though centralization undercut the foundation of the machine system, it can also be read as an extension of the earlier process of consolidating municipal power—the very process that established the citywide machines.

61 Fogelson, *Big-City Police,* 78–79 and 177.

62 Fogelson, *Big-City Police,* 58–59.

63 Harry Braverman, *Labor and Monopoly Capital: The Degradation of Work in the Twentieth Century* (New York: Monthly Review Press, 1974), 125.

64 In 1923, Berkeley's reform-minded police chief August Vollmer was brought to L.A. to clean up the embarrassingly corrupt department. Vollmer's plan concentrated on removing the department from political influences, but he failed to persuade the rank and file not to exploit everyday opportunities for corruption. Lundman, *Police and Policing,* 178.

65 Fogelson, *Big-City Police,* 80–81.

66 James F. Richardson, *Urban Police in the United States* (Port Washington, New York: National University Press and Kennikat Press, 1974), 85.

67 New York Police Commissioner Howard Leary invited such complaints: "If there is any criticism of the department's policies, administration, or operations, it should be directed toward the Police Commissioner, because he is the commander." Quoted in Ed Cray, "The Politics of Blue Power," in *The Police Rebellion,* ed. William J. Bopp (Springfield, Illinois: Charles C. Thomas, Publisher, 1971), 58.

James Richardson notes the political advantages of this arrangement for mayors: "A hands-off policy means that the mayors can disclaim any responsibility for police operations. . . . Thus 'no political interference' may not always be self-sacrificing. A mayor may give up police patronage or influence, but by so doing he also gives up any political responsibility for the police." Richardson, *Urban Police,* 131.

68 Egon Bittner, "The Quasi-Military Organization of the Police," in *The Police and Society: Touchstone Readings,* ed. Victor E. Kappeler (Prospect Heights, Illinois: Waveland Press, Inc., 1999), 176.

69 "Available evidence indicates that the source of support for reform in municipal government did not come from the lower or middle class, but from the upper class. The leading business groups in each city and professional men closely allied with them instituted and dominated municipal movements. "

Moreover: "These reformers, it should be stressed, comprised not an old but a new upper class. Few came from earlier industrial and mercantile families. Most of them had risen to social position from wealth created after 1870 in the iron, steel, electrical equipment, and other industries, and they lived in the newer rather than the older fashionable areas. . . . They represented not the old business community, but industries which had developed and grown primarily within the past fifty years and which had come to dominate the city's economic life." Samuel P. Hays, "The Politics of Reform in Municipal Government in the Progressive Era," *Pacific Northwest Quarterly* (July 1964): 159 and 160.

70 "From the common background and experience the reformers derived a common outlook, at the core of which were three distinct yet clearly related assumptions about American society. First, they believed that social mobility was an economic, private, and individual process, as opposed to a political, public, and collective one, and that success was a result of industry, frugality, integrity, and occasional good luck.

Second, they held that political legitimacy was a function of the public interest, the common objectives of the entire community, and not of the parochial interests of particular neighborhoods, ethnic groups, and social classes. And third, they thought that American morality was based on a commitment to abstinence and respectability, an abhorrence of self-indulgence and deviance, and a willingness to employ the criminal sanction to distinguish the one from the other." Fogelson, *Big-City Police*, 47.

Ironically, the Progressives failed to recognize the biases inherent in this perspective. Reformers identified the interests and objectives of their own class as those of the public at large. The ability to sustain such a view, of course, relies on one's own position in the dominant group; it may be that we can ascertain when a class begins to achieve dominance by the emergence of just such a perspective.

71 Both quoted in Hays, "Politics of Reform," 160.

See also: Fogelson (1977) 37; Sidney Harring, "The Development of the Police Institution in the United States," *Crime and Social Justice: A Journal of Radical Criminology* (Spring-Summer 1976): 58; and James Weinstein, *The Corporate Ideal in the Liberal State: 1900–1918* (Boston: Beacon Press, 1968), 100-4.

72 Fogelson, *Big-City Police*, 42.

73 The reformers emphasized the representative aspects of government at the expense of its participatory aspects. "According to the liberal view of the Progressive Era, the major political innovations of reform involved the equalization of political power through the primary, the direct election of public officials, and the initiative, referendum, and recall. These measures played a large role in the political ideology of the time and were frequently incorporated into new municipal charters. But they provided at best only an occasional and often incidental process of decision-making. Far more important in continuously sustained day-to-day processes of government were those innovations which centralized decision-making in the hands of fewer and fewer people." Hays, "Politics of Reform," 163.

74 Fogelson, *Big-City Police*, 47 and 62-63.

75 Edward C. Banfield and James Q. Wilson, *City Politics* (Cambridge, Massachusetts: Harvard University Press and the MIT Press, 1963), 127. Parentheses in original.

76 Fogelson, *Big-City Police*, 111-12.

77 Gramsci famously distinguished between "domination" and "intellectual and moral leadership," identifying hegemony with the latter. He argued: "A social group dominates antagonistic groups, which it tends to 'liquidate', or to subjugate perhaps even by armed force; it leads kindred or allied groups. A social group can, and indeed must, already exercise 'leadership' before winning governmental power (this indeed is one of the principal conditions for the winning of such power); it subsequently becomes dominant when it exercises power, but even if it holds it firmly in its grasp, it must continue to 'lead' as well." Antonio Gramsci, *Selections From the Prison Notebooks of Antonio Gramsci*, eds. Quintin Hoare and Geoffrey Nowell-Smith (New York: International Publishers, 1971), 57-58.

78 Femia argues along similar lines, suggesting that hegemony operates "by mystifying power relations, by justifying forms of sacrifice and deprivation, by inducing fatalism and passivity, and by narrowing mental horizons." Joseph V. Femia, *Gramsci's Political Thought: Hegemony, Consciousness, and the Revolutionary Process* (Oxford: Clarendon Press, 1981), 45.

79 Bernard Shaw, "The Doctor's Dilemma," *The Doctor's Dilemma, Getting Married, & The Shewing-Up of Blanco Posnet*, act 1 (London: Constable and Company Ltd., 1911).

80 Fogelson, *Big-City Police*, 136 and 138.

81 Fogelson, *Big-City Police*, 143; and Seymour Martin Lipset, "Why Cops Hate Liberals—And Vice Versa," in *The Police Rebellion*, ed. William J. Bopp (Springfield, Illinois: Charles C. Thomas, Publisher, 1971), 30.

82 Richardson, *Urban Police*, 137-38.

By 1940, half of the new recruits to the NYPD had bachelor degrees. This marked a significant change since the time before the Depression, when many policeman had never been to high school (6 percent in New York). Richardson, *Urban Police*, 138 and 135.

83 Robert F. Wintersmith, *Police and the Black Community* (Lexington, Massachusetts: Lexington Books, 1974), 65-66.

84 Fogelson, *Big-City Police*, 144-46.

85 Fogelson, *Big-City Police*, 150-52.

86 Fogelson, *Big-City Police*, 154-55.

Sociologists identify professions by six characteristics (1) skills based on theoretical knowledge; (2) education and training; (3) competence ensured by examinations; (4) a code of ethics; (5) provision of a service for the public good; and, (6) a professional association that organizes members. *The Peguin Dictionary of Sociology*, Nicholas Abercrombie et al. (London: Penguin Books, 2000), s.v. "Profession."

87 Fogelson, *Big-City Police*, 158; and Richardson, *Urban Police*, 131.

88 Fogelson, *Big-City Police*, 223-25.

89 Lundman, *Police and Policing*, 180.

90 Fogelson, *Big-City Police*, 225.

91 Fogelson, *Big-City Police*, 227.

92 Fogelson, *Big-City Police*, 271; and Lundman, *Police and Policing*, 181.

93 During the 1960s and 1970s, Blacks and Puerto Ricans sued police departments in Boston, Philadelphia, and Oakland, arguing that the entrance requirements were discriminatory. Fogelson, *Big-City Police*, 230.

94 Fogelson, *Big-City Police,* 227.

95 The insistence that commanders be drawn from the ranks greatly limited the pool of applicants, reduced the possibilities for innovative leadership, and institutionalized the existing police culture. The arrangement also solidified the sense of unity between beat cops and their supervisors, with predictable results for discipline.

See: Fogelson, *Big-City Police,* 229.

96 Lundman, *Police and Policing,* 181.

97 Carl B. Klockars, "The Rhetoric of Community Policing," in *The Police and Society,* ed. Victor E. Kappeler (Prospect Heights, Illinois: Waveland Press, Inc., 1999), 433.

98 Richardson, *Urban Police,* 148–49.

99 Fogelson, *Big-City Police,* 223–25.

100 Fogelson, *Big-City Police,* 226.

101 Fogelson, *Big-City Police,* 187 and 231.

102 Fogelson, *Big-City Police,* 188.

103 Fogelson, *Big-City Police,* 241–42.

104 Quoted in Fogelson, *Big-City Police,* 207. Emphasis in original.

105 In April 2001, Cincinnati Vice Mayor Minette Cooper complained: "Unfortunately, over the years, City Council has made many important concessions to the police union, creating an atmosphere of autonomy within the police division." Quoted in Kevin Osbourne, "Council Wants Police More Accountable," *Cincinnati Post,* April 10, 2001, http://www.cincypost.com/2001/apr/10/change041001.html (accessed April 25, 2002).

106 At a June 18, 2002, meeting of the Fort Worth Police Officers' Association, President John Kerr explained the union's relationship with the district attorney and its stake in his re-election: "We're going to support Tim Curry because Tim Curry will not prosecute a police officer who commits a crime." Quoted in Betty Brink, "A Pass for Bad Cops?" *Fort Worth Weekly* (Texas), October 3, 2002, http://www.fwweekly.com/issues/2002-10-03/metropolis.html (accessed February 28, 2003).

107 Margaret Levi argues that this is an aspect of all public service worker unions. She notes that public employees "organize, as do privately employed workers, when they perceive their pay to be low, their working conditions poor, and the job pressures intolerable. In addition, civil servants sometimes are motivated to form lobbies and unions when the stated aims of administrators are disagreeable." Levi, *Bureaucratic Insurgency,* 8–9.

108 Fogelson, *Big-City Police,* 212–13.

109 Jerome H. Skolnick, *The Politics of Protest: Violent Aspects of Protest and Confrontation; A Report Submitted by Jerome H. Skolnick* [The Skolnick Report; Report of the Task Force on Violent Aspects of Protest and Confrontation to the National Commission on the Causes and Prevention of Violence] (Washington, DC: Supt. of Documents, U.S. Government Printing Office, 1969), 205.

See also: Robert Reiner, *The Blue-Coated Worker: A Sociological Study of Police Unionism* (Cambridge: Cambridge University Press, 1978), 4 ; and, Stark, *Police Riots,* 210.

For a related discussion on the influence of prison guards' unions, see Clayton Szczech, "Beyond Autonomy or Dominance: The Political Sociology of Prison Expansion" (undergraduate thesis, Reed College, 2000), 78.

110 Stark goes on: "Indeed, in their new mood the police reject their historic role as the enforcers of established political and social policies. They now seek the power to determine these policies. . . . [This pursuit] causes them to challenge radically the authority of their own commanders, the courts, civil authorities, and constitutionality." Stark, *Police Riots,* 192–93.

111 In 1995, California Common Cause observed: "If legislators vote against bills supported by police interests, they know they run the risk of being labeled as 'soft on crime,' even if the legislation has nothing to do with public safety. The last thing a legislator wants in an election year is to lose the endorsement of police groups, or worse yet, end up on their hit list." Quoted in Lynne Wilson, "Cops vs. Citizen Review," *CovertAction Quarterly* (Winter 1995–96): 11.

See also: Max Gunther, "Cops in Politics: A Threat to Democracy?" in *The Police Rebellion,* ed. William J. Bopp (Springfield, Illinois: Charles C. Thomas, Publisher, 1971).

112 Frank Donner, *Protectors of Privilege: Red Squads and Police Repression in Urban America* (Berkeley: University of California Press, 1990), 206–7.

113 Fogelson, *Big-City Police,* 208.

114 Stark, *Police Riots,* 212; and Fogelson, *Big-City Police,* 208.

115 Quoted in Gunther, "Cops in Politics," 62.

116 Stark, *Police Riots,* 209; and Skolnick, *Report,* 210.

117 Donner, *Protectors of Privilege,* 252.

118 Skolnick, *Politics of Protest,* 209; and Algernon D. Black, *The People and the Police* (New York: McGraw-Hill Book Company, 1968), 211.

119 Quoted in William J. Bopp, "The New York City Referendum on Civilian Review," in *The Police Rebellion,* ed. William J. Bopp (Springfield, Illinois: Charles C. Thomas, Publisher, 1971), 129–30.

120 Quoted in Skolnick, *Politics of Protest,* 209. Emphasis in original.

121 Quoted in Black, *People and the Police,* 210-11.

122 Quoted in Stark, *Police Riots,* 194.

123 Bopp, "New York City Referendum," 133.

124 Fogelson, *Big-City Police,* 286.

125 Lynne Wilson, "Enforcing Racism," *CovertAction Quarterly* (Winter 1995-96): 9.

The efforts of Black police associations demonstrate the possibility of police support for liberal causes. But these organizations, while stark critics of department policies and a sincere voice for civil rights, always embody something of a compromise. They represent the contradictory positions occupied by Black cops. A Black officer must be constantly aware of his second-class status, even (or especially) within the department. And when he takes off his uniform he merges again, almost wholly, into the mass of people whom it is the cops' job to regard suspiciously, and sometimes to attack, and always to control. These dual roles mark the boundaries of the Black officers' political activity. If, for example, Black police associations only represent the "policing" perspective, there is neither any way to differentiate them from the other (White) police associations, nor any need to. But, if they represent only the "Black" perspective, then they exist only as social or civil rights groups—and as rather conservative ones at that. The result will always be half-measures, which seem radical only by comparison to the department as a whole, and to their White counterparts.

126 Quoted in Alex, *Black in Blue,* 167.

See also: W. Marvin Dulaney, *Black Police in America* (Bloomington: Indiana University Press, 1996), 73.

127 Quoted in Stark, *Police Riots,* 197.

A similar controversy occurred in Boston when Dick MacEachern, president of the Boston Police Patrolmen's Association, instructed members to "uphold the law and disregard any order not to do so." Quoted in William J. Bopp, "The Patrolmen in Boston," in *The Police Rebellion,* ed. William J. Bopp (Springfield, Illinois: Charles C. Thomas, Publisher, 1971), 182.

128 The maneuver was calculated to present Cassese as a tough leader and preserve his position in the PBA. Cassese was himself facing a right-wing revolt within the organization, a revolt led by the Law Enforcement Group. Skolnick, *Politics of Protest,* 207.

129 Quoted in Skolnick, *Politics of Protest,* 213.

130 Quoted in Stark, *Police Riots,* 197.

131 Quoted in Skolnick, *Politics of Protest,* 213.

132 Quoted in Fogelson, *Big-City Police,* 304.

133 Quoted in George James, "Police Dept. Report Assails Officers in New York Rally," *New York Times,* September 29, 1992.

Elsewhere the language is stronger: "The demonstrators' actions were a clear violation of the law." Ibid.

134 Ibid.

135 James, "Police Dept. Report."

The *New York Times* noted that: "In one example, an officer encouraged misconduct. More commonly, [on-duty] officers appeared to stand by and observe without taking action." "The Police Demonstration: What the Internal Investigation Found," *New York Times,* September 29, 1992.

136 Quoted in James C. McKinley, Jr., "Officers Rally and Dinkins is Their Target," *New York Times,* September 17, 1992.

137 Quoted in McKinley, Jr., "Officers Rally."

138 Quoted in James, "Police Dept. Report."

139 Giuliani's policies and police-state aspirations are discussed in chapter 9.

Ironically, the love affair between Giuliani and the PBA went sour when, as mayor, he insisted on a wage freeze for public employees. Sidney L. Harring and Gerda W. Ray, "Policing A Class Society: New York City in the 1990s," *Social Justice* (Summer 1999): 72-73.

140 In 1959, *The Nation* gleefully reported that a unionized police force could still be effectively employed against striking workers: "Members of the Bridgeport [Connecticut] police local have also proved themselves capable of enforcing the law in cases involving their brethren in other unions. Police quelled picket-line disturbances during two bitter industrial strikes in 1955, in both cases receiving expressions of thanks from the plant managers. There have been no significant picket-line battles in Bridgeport since." Edmund P. Murray, "Should the Police Unionize?" *The Nation,* June 13, 1959, 531.

141 David H. Bayley and Harold Mendelsohn, *Minorities and the Police: Confrontation in America* (New York: The Free Press, 1969), 14.

142 See, for example, Dennis C. Rousey, *Policing the Southern City: New Orleans,* 1805-1889 (Baton Rouge: Louisiana State University Press, 1996), 53.

143 In fact, in many ways the police enjoyed more favorable conditions than other workers. "These [police] jobs were quite attractive. Patrolmen earned from $600 in Kansas City to $1,200 in San Francisco, more than laborers, weavers, miners, and factory workers and about as much as painters, carpenters, teamsters, blacksmiths, and street railway conductors." Fogelson, *Big-City Police,* 19.

See also: Roger Lane, *Policing the City: Boston 1822-1885* (Cambridge, Massachusetts: Harvard University Press, 1967), 76.

144 The use of law enforcement to manage the work force is nothing new. Under the rule of Edward VI (1547–53), English law called on constables and justices of the peace to force laborers to work on farms suffering labor shortages, to wake them early in the morning, and to hurry them through mealtimes and breaks. Cyril D. Robinson and Richard Scaglion, "The Origin of the Police Function in Society: Notes Toward a Theory," *Law and Society Review* 21:1 (1987): 147.

145 Braverman offers a clear description of the middle class: "[L]ike the working class it possesses no economic or occupational independence, is employed by capital and its offshoots, possesses no access to the labor process or the means of production outside that employment, and must renew its labors for capital incessantly in order to subsist. This portion of employment embraces the engineering, technical, and scientific cadre, the lower ranks of supervision and management, the considerable numbers of specialized and 'professional' employees occupied in marketing, financial and organizational administration, and the like, as well as, outside of capitalist industry proper, in hospitals, schools, government administration and so forth." Braverman, *Labor*, 403.

146 Braverman, *Labor*, 405.

147 "This 'new middle class' takes its characteristics from *both sides*. Not only does it receive its petty share in the prerogatives and rewards of capital, but it also bears the mark of the proletarian condition." Braverman, *Labor*, 407. Emphasis in original.

148 Harring identifies several tools for dividing the police from the working class, including: stratification within the lower classes, ethnic differences, the cops' organizational culture, discipline, and the criminalization of working-class activities. Harring, *Policing a Class Society*, 144.

149 Levi, *Bureaucratic Insurgency*, 31.

150 Quoted in Fogelson, *Big-City Police*, 207.

151 These limits are significant, but they sadly do not distinguish police associations from proper labor unions. The American labor movement has often fallen far below the ideals of inter-union solidarity, rank-and-file leadership, and direct action militancy.

152 Think about it this way—if the slave patrollers had formed a union, making demands about wages, hours, discipline, and so on, would conscientious supporters of workers' rights be obliged to support them in those demands? No. And why not? Because the nature of their work was to repress and control part of the working class—the slaves. This puts the slave patrollers, and now the police, clearly on the side of the bosses, in roughly the same class position as any other manager who does not own capital, but earns his keep by acting as the proxy for the ruling class.

It should be noted that this is not intended as a legal argument about the right of the police to organize. I would not defer to the state the authority to decide who does or does not have that right. But the demands of solidarity are another matter entirely. It is these with which I am chiefly concerned.

153 For a contrary position, see: Bruce C. Johnson, "Taking Care of Labor: The Police in American Life," *Theory and Society* (Spring 1976): 89–117.

Johnson argues that police sympathize with workers (and vice versa), but he never supports his strongest claim—that the police do actually defend the interests of workers (specifically White workers) *as workers*. To the degree that White workers have an interest in racist inequalities, it is obvious that the police defend their interests in that regard—which is to say, the police defend the privileges White workers enjoy *as Whites* in a racist society. Perhaps the article would be more properly titled "Taking Care of Whitey."

154 Murray, "Should the Police Unionize?" 532.

In an ironic postscript to the infamous strike of 1919, the Boston Police Patrolmen's Association was founded in 1965, and won a contract in 1968. But when, that same year, the legislature lifted the prohibition on affiliation with other unions, the BPPA declined to attach itself to the AFL-CIO. Russell, *City in Terror*, 232.

155 Levi, *Bureaucratic Insurgency*, 89.

156 On February 27, 2003, a San Francisco grand jury stunned the city when it issued indictments against three officers involved in an off-duty beating and seven commanders who helped cover it up. Among those charged with conspiracy to obstruct justice: Police Chief Earl Sanders, Assistant Chief Alex Fagan, Sr., Deputy Chief Greg Suhr, and Deputy Chief David Robinson. Chuck Finnie, "SFPD Indictments Shock the City," *San Francisco Chronicle*, March 1, 2003 (database: NewsBank Full-Text Newspapers, accessed March 4, 2003).

157 Stark, *Police Riots*, 203–4.

158 Quoted in Levi, *Bureaucratic Insurgency*, 20–21.

159 Levi, *Bureaucratic Insurgency*, 145.

160 Colin Crouch and Ronald Dore, "Whatever Happened to Corporatism?" in *Corporatism and Accountability: Organized Interests in British Public Life*, ed. Colin Crouch and Ronald Dore (Oxford: Clarendon Press, 1990), 3. Parentheses in original.

161 Crouch and Dore, "Whatever Happened?" 3–4. Parentheses in original.

162 Michael T. Florinsky, *Fascism and National Socialism: A Study of the Economic and Social Policies of the Totalitarian State* (New York: The Macmillan Company, 1936).

For more on corporatism, see: Philippe C. Schmitter, "Still the Century of Corporatism?" *The Review of Politics* 36 (1974): 85–131.

163 If this analysis is sound, then it suggests a particular picture of the state and the role of the police union in maintaining its power. Rather than standing as a unitary sovereign with various subordinate agencies at hand to enact its will, the state would consist of a complex network comprising these agencies, and dependent on their cooperation for its power. This idea will be expanded in the pages that follow. For now, let's just note that this view complicates Crouch and Dore's definition of a "corporatist arrangement," since they identify "the state" as *one party* in the arrangement, and overlook the possibility that *the state itself* may in part consist of such corporatist relations.

164 Levi, *Bureaucratic Insurgency*, 9; and Center for Research on Criminal Justice, *Iron Fist*, 146.

Levi examines the difference between private and public employees, but not between cops and other public workers. In fact, she takes the police to be paradigmatic. But as long as the police represent the coercive apparatus of the state, they must be understood as fundamentally different than, say, sanitation workers, firefighters, and teachers.

Robert Reiner explains: "The determinants of the policeman's economic situation are to an extent diametrically opposed to those for other workers. This is because, when governments attempt to implement policies of wage restraint against union opposition, the police assume a peculiar importance due to their role in situations of industrial conflict. Then they will have to be treated as a most 'special case' in pay negotiations. Furthermore, their work situation, in particular when it involves confrontations with trade unionists at pickets, inclines them towards a conservative world-view and a sense of alienation from the labour movement. This conflicts with pressure towards forms of organization of a more or less unionate nature, deriving from their *own* concerns as employees." Reiner, *Blue-Coated Worker*, 4. Emphasis in original.

165 "[T]heir efforts to serve 'the public' often reveal how divergent conceptions of 'the public' can be. Police employee organizations demand the material and laws which enable them to protect working- and middle-class homeowners [sic]; they are far less concerned with the protection of ghetto dwellers, hippies, and political activists. The radical caucuses of social worker and teacher unions tend to make the opposite choice; they are less interested in defining and containing a problem population then in providing the impoverished and the rejected with new opportunities. The effect of battling over who is to be served—and how—is to undermine the ideology of government as a neutral servant of the citizens, able to bring together various interests under a common and equally available set of services. Instead of acting [as] the arbiter above the political struggles, the state becomes part of the fray." Levi, *Bureaucratic Insurgency*, 154.

166 Former Atlanta Police Chief Herbert Jenkins described that city's police union as "not a union at all, but in fact a thinly veiled cover for Klan membership." Herbert Jenkins, *Keeping the Peace: A Police Chief Looks at His Job* (New York: Harper & Row, 1970), 23.

167 The Miami Police Benevolent Association had a constitutional provision requiring that membership be open only to "White members of the police force." That clause was removed in January 1970, but when five Black officers applied for membership in December of that year, their applications were rejected. Dulaney, *Black Police*, 145.

Blacks were not the only group subject to discrimination like this. New York's Police Benevolent Association excluded women until 1968. Levi, *Bureaucratic Insurgency*, 27.

168 Dulaney, *Black Police*, 21.

169 Quoted in Wilson, "Enforcing Racism," 9.

170 "Shooter Cop Reinstated; What's Wrong With This Picture?" *People's Police Report* 6 (1995): 1–2.

171 Wintersmith, *Police and the Black Community*, 66–67.

172 "Before the seventeenth century, every large European state ruled its subjects through powerful intermediaries who enjoyed significant autonomy, hindered state demands that were not to their interests, and profited on their own accounts from the delegated exercise of state power. The intermediaries were often privileged members of subordinate populations, and made their way by assuring rulers of tribute and acquiescence from these populations." Charles Tilly, *Coercion, Capital, and European States, AD 990–1990* (Cambridge, Massachusetts: Basil Blackwell, 1990), 104.

173 William A. Westley, "Violence and the Police," in *Police Patrol Readings,* ed. Samuel G. Chapman (Springfield, Illinois: Charles C. Thomas, 1964), 289–90. This analysis is considered in chapter 1.

174 The degree to which this is true may be indicated by union efforts to authorize the use of force where it was prohibited by law or departmental policy. The most famous case, Cassese's rule to "enforce the law 100 percent" (Quoted in Gunther, "Cops in Politics," 65) has already been discussed, but other examples are available. In 1970, the Atlanta FOP voted to illegally carry their own guns while on duty. In Detroit, at around the same time, the DPOA was encouraging its members to use hollow-tip bullets. Levi, *Bureaucratic Insurgency*, 141.

175 Martin J. Smith, *Pressure, Power and Policy: State Autonomy and Policy Networks in Britain and the United States* (Pittsburgh: University of Pittsburgh Press, 1993), 2.

This analysis has clear implications for our understanding of other concepts, including "state autonomy," "state interests," and "reasons of state." Clayton Szczech points out that "the state cannot effectively pursue its self-interested agenda because no such unified agenda exists. . . . For example, what the Department of Defense wants and needs may not always coincide with what the Department of Commerce wants and needs, and both of them must utilize networks with social groups, elected officials and other bureaucracies to realize any goals at all." Szczech, "Beyond Autonomy or Dominance," 17.

176 Smith concurs: "It is also difficult to identify the boundaries of the state. . . . Many parts of civil society are given institutional access to the state and play a role in the development of public policy. The state also funds a number of groups within society which, although in principle autonomous, are highly dependent on the state. In addition, the boundaries of the state are continually changing through privatization, the hiving off of parts of the civil service and the creation of new regulatory bodies." Smith, *Pressure, Power and Policiy*, 2.

The absence of clearly demarcated boundaries (defining the limits of the state) seems to me a theoretical advantage. It allows us to replace a binary opposition, in which an agency is always either identified with the state or not, with a continuum in which it should be considered a part of the state to the degree that it is incorporated into the relevant power networks. Privatized services, subsidized research and development, and police unions are thus *more* a part of the state than are church-run charities, family farms, and the IWW, but *less* a part of the state than Congress, the Army, or the courts.

177 Szczech, *Beyond Autonomy or Dominance*, 19. Emphasis in original.

Again, Smith: "With policy networks, power is a relationship based on dependence and not a zero-sum. Power is something that develops within relationships between groups and state actors, and a policy network is frequently a mechanism for enhancing mutual power rather than taking power from one or the other." Smith, *Pressure, Power and Policy*, 7.

178 Again, the tendency toward corporatism is discernible.

"Monopolistic and hierarchical groups have the resources to negotiate with governments because they have the ability to implement any decisions which are agreed. Under corporatism, the role of groups is regulatory as well as representative. They are responsible for ensuring that their members accept agreed policy decisions." Smith, *Pressure, Power and Policy*, 31.

179 Szczech's thesis studies one manifestation of this process, the 1990's wave of prison expansion: "The expansion of the US prison system has clearly augmented the power of criminal justice institutions and actors considerably. This came about however, through a political process of networking that has also increased the power and resources of social actors: prison guards' and police unions, firms that contract with prisons, and rural communities that would otherwise have faced economic depression. Likewise, prison expansion has not increased the power or autonomy of the state as a whole. The fiscal costs of imprisonment have entailed severe fiscal cutbacks and reduced capacity in nearly every other governmental sector, especially social welfare." Szczech, "Beyond Autonomy or Dominance," 85.

180 "Unions, as so many authors have noted, are a source of personal mobility. Union officialdom becomes a career in itself, and union officials act to preserve their privileges. Collusive bargaining offers a number of advantages to union leaders in this position. By engaging in collusive bargaining, association leaders win concessions for their members without engaging in strikes (which are always costly and problematic in the public sector where strong prohibitions still persist). Union leaders are also likely to increase personal mobility further through access to public figures, new job opportunities, and consultantships. But those benefits are not free. In trade, the union leaders must become 'responsible' in the eyes of the city government. This means that they must be able to assure the relatively uninterrupted delivery of services and agree to some programmatic innovations." Levi, *Bureaucratic Insurgency*, 21. Parentheses in original.

181 Tilly, *Coercion*, 117.

182 George Orwell, "Looking Back on the Spanish War," in *A Collection of Essays* (Garden City, New York: Doubleday Anchor Books, 1954), 208 and 212–13.

"No group of Chileans supported the coup as strongly as did the business community, which felt its very survival to be at stake." Pamela Constable and Arturo Valenzuela, *A Nation of Enemies: Chile Under Pinochet* (New York: W.W. Norton & Co., 1991), 200.

183 See chapter 3.

Chapter 7: Secret Police, Red Squads, and the Strategy of Permanent Repression

1 Frank Donner, *Protectors of Privilege: Red Squads and Police Repression in Urban America* (Berkeley: University of California Press, 1990), 1–2.

2 Riot control strategies are discussed in the next chapter.

3 Quoted in Peter Bollen, *Great Labor Quotations: Sourcebook and Reader* (Los Angeles: Red Eye Press, 2000), 13.

4 Samuel Yellen, *American Labor Struggles, 1877–1934* (New York: Pathfinder, 1936), 59.

5 Quoted in Howard Zinn, *A People's History of the United States, 1492–Present* (New York: HarperPerennial, 1995), 264.

6 Zinn, *People's History*, 265.

See also: Paul Avrich, *The Haymarket Tragedy* (Princeton, New Jersey: Princeton University Press, 1984), 208.

7 Henry David, *The History of the Haymarket Affair: A Study in the American Social-Revolutionary and Labor Movements* (New York: Farrar and Rinehart, Inc., 1936), 528.

The Knights of Labor, for example, issued a statement that "the Knights of Labor have no affiliation, association, sympathy, or respect for the band of cowardly murderers, cut-throats, and robbers, known as anarchists." Quoted in Foster Rhea Dulles and Melvyn Dubofsky, *Labor in America: A History* (Arlington Heights, Illinois: Harlan Davidson, Inc., 1984), 188–89.

8 Jeremy Brecher, *Strike!* (Boston: South End Press, 1972), 47.

9 Quoted in Bruce C. Nelson, *Beyond the Martyrs: A Social History of Chicago's Anarchists, 1870–1900* (New Brunswick: Rutgers University Press, 1988), 190.

10 Nelson, *Beyond the Martyrs*, 190.

11 Joseph G. Rayback, *A History of American Labor* (New York: The Free Press, 1966), 168–69.

12 Among other questionable features, the jury contained members who admitted to prejudices against the defendants. Rayback, *History of American Labor*, 167–68.

13 Avrich, *Haymarket Tragedy*, 275.

14 Quoted in Nelson, *Beyond the Martyrs*, 192–93.

15 Quoted in Avrich, *Haymarket Tragedy*, 283.

16 Quoted in Yellen, *Labor Struggles*, 69.

17 Donner, *Protectors of Privilege*, 14–20.

18 Quoted in Donner, *Protectors of Privilege*, 15.

19 Donner, *Protectors of Privilege*, 20.

20 Alan Wolfe, *The Seamy Side of Democracy: Repression in America* (Reading, Massachusetts: Longman, 1978), 6.

21 Donner, *Protectors of Privilege*, 1.

22 Frank Kitson, *Low Intensity Operations: Subversion, Insurgency, Peace-Keeping* (Hamden, Connecticut: Archon Books, 1971), 49.

23 Senate Select Committee to Study Government Operations With Respect to Intelligence Activities [Church Committee], *Final Report of the Select Committee to Study Government Operations With Respect to Intelligence Activities*, 94th Congress, 2d sess., 1976, Book II, 1.

24 Donner, *Protectors of Privilege*, 10–11.

Donner's book *Protectors of Privilege: Red Squads and Repression in Urban America* is commonly recognized as the single best history of the subject, and much of the discussion here is drawn from his work.

25 Donner, *Protectors of Privilege*, 31.

26 Donner, *Protectors of Privilege*, 1–2.

27 Donner, *Protectors of Privilege*, 30.

28 Ward Churchill and Jim Vander Wall, *Agents of Repression: The FBI's Secret Wars Against the Black Panther Party and the American Indian Movement* (Boston: South End Press, 1990), 22.

29 Donner, *Protectors of Privilege*, 35–36.

30 Donner, *Protectors of Privilege*, 36–37.

31 Donner, *Protectors of Privilege*, 3.

32 Donner, *Protectors of Privilege*, 62–63.

33 Donner, *Protectors of Privilege*, 57–59.

34 Frank Donner, "Theory and Practice of American Political Intelligence," *New York Review of Books*, April 22, 1971, 29.

35 Donner, *Protectors of Privilege*, 91.

36 Donner, *Protectors of Privilege*, 66–69.

37 Donner, *Protectors of Privilege*, 260.

38 Donner, *Protectors of Privilege*, 93–95.

39 Donner, *Protectors of Privilege*, 233.

40 Donner, *Protectors of Privilege*, 318 and 330.

41 "In the early years of [the twentieth] century, police gathered information from informers planted by private agencies, employers' associations, and patriotic groups. By the thirties, big-city police had begun to recruit their own informers from the private sector and acted as the spy's 'handlers,' 'contacts,' or 'controls,' only rarely themselves resorting to impersonation, dissembling loyalties, and the fabrication of cover identities. It was one thing to have an agent as an independent contractor to do the dirty work of spying, but quite another for a public servant to do it himself. But in the sixties, police, not only in Chicago and New York but in smaller cities—San Diego, Houston, Oakland, New Orleans, and Columbus to name a few—went underground, and the 'undercover agent' became commonplace." Donner, *Protectors of Privilege*, 69–70.

42 Donner, "Theory and Practice," 33.

43 Donner, *Protectors of Privilege*, 169.

44 Donner, *Protectors of Privilege*, 260.

45 American Friends Service Committee [AFSC]. Program on Government Surveillance and Citizens' Rights, *The Police Threat to Political Liberty: Discoveries and Actions of the American Friends Service Committee Program on Government Surveillance and Citizens' Rights* (Philadelphia: AFSC, 1979), 12.

46 Ford Fessenden and Michael Moss, "Going Electronic, Denver Reveals Long-Term Surveillance," *New York Times*, December 21, 2002, http://www.nytimes.com/202/12/12/technology21PRIV.html (accessed December 21, 2002; Sarah Huntley, "Greens Criticize Cops for Spy Files," *Rocky Mountain News* (Denver, CO), September 6, 2002,
http://www.rockymountainnews.com/drmn/local/article/0,12299,DRMN15_1401560,00.html, (accessed December 11, 2002; and, Sarah Huntley, "'Spy File' Backlog Has Police Hopping," *Rocky Mountain News* (Denver, Co), September 5, 2002,
http://www.rockymountainnews.com/drmn/local/article/0,1299,DRMN_15_1374160.00 (accessed December 11, 2002).

47 AFSC, *Police Threat to Political Liberty*, 27. Parentheses in original.

48 Donner, "Theory and Practice," 32.

49 Donner, *Protectors of Privilege*, 221.

50 Donner, *Protectors of Privilege*, 207–8. Parentheses in original.

51 Donner, *Protectors of Privilege*, 209–10 and 217.

52 Quoted in Ward Churchill and Jim Vander Wall, *The COINTELPRO Papers: Documents from the FBI's Secret Wars Against Domestic Dissent* (Boston: South End Press, 1990), 92.

53 Church Committee, *Final Report*, Book II, 10.

54 Church Committee, *Final Report*, Book III, 220–223.

55 Churchill and Vander Wall, *COINTELPRO Papers*, 143.

56 Quoted in Churchill and Vander Wall, *COINTELPRO Papers*, 135–36.

57 Churchill and Vander Wall, *COINTELPRO Papers*, 139–40.

58 Churchill and Vander Wall, *COINTELPRO Papers*, 141–42.

59 Churchill and Vander Wall, *Agents of Repression*, 88.

60 Churchill and Vander Wall, *Agents of Repression*, 90.

61 Quoted in Kamal Hassan, "Justice Too Long Denied," *Z Magazine*, November 1997, 10.

62 Amnesty International, "USA: New Evidence In Murder Case Could End 25 Years of Injustice for Former Black Panther Leader," http://web.amnesty.org/ai.nsf/index/AMR510121997 (accessed December 12, 2002). Also: Hassan, "Justice," 10.

63 Quoted in Don Terry, "Los Angeles Confronts a Bitter Racial Legacy in a Black Panther Case," *New York Times*, July 20, 1997.

64 Dickey reasoned that information about Butler's connection to law enforcement might have influenced the jury's decision. His thinking seems to have been sound; Jeanne Rook Hamilton, a juror from the case said, "If we had known about Butler's background, there's no way Pratt would have been convicted." Quoted in Terry, "Los Angeles."

65 Ji Jaga sued the federal government and the city of Los Angeles and settled for $4.5 million. Todd S. Purdum, "Ex-Black Panther Wins Long Legal Battle," *New York Times*, April 27, 2000.

66 AFSC, *Police Threat to Political Liberty*, 14–15.

67 Church Committee, *Final Report*, Book II, 81.

68 Donner, *Protectors of Privilege*, 158.

69 Donner, *Protectors of Privilege*, 144.

70 Donner, *Protectors of Privilege*, 86–88, 389.

71 Church Committee, *Final Report*, Book II, 5.

72 Quoted in AFSC, *Police Threat to Political Liberty*, 66–67.

73 AFSC, *Police Threat to Political Liberty*, 50.

74 Donner, *Protectors of Privilege*, 272–73.

75 Quoted in Ben Jacklet, "The Secret Watchers," *Portland (OR) Tribune*, September 13, 2002.

76 Ben Jacklet and Anna Skinner, "The Wild, the Weird and the Plain Silly," *Portland (OR) Tribune*, September 13, 2002.

77 Ben Jacklet, "'It Should Be Noted . . .,'" *Portland (OR)Tribune*, September 17, 2002.
   See also: Ben Jacklet, "A Legacy of Suspicion" *Portland (OR) Tribune*, September 20, 2002.

78 Other biases also come into play, especially those concerning race and ethnicity. For example, in a 1972 report on the annual Rose Festival, Portland Police Sergeant Wayne Inman notes with alarm, "An abnormally high percentage of those attending carnivals are blacks and a substantial portion of blacks are normally involved in criminal activity. . . . The Carnival provides an excellent opportunity for these undisciplined blacks to gather and perform their antisocial acts within the anonymity and safety of the crowd." Quoted in Jacklet, "Legacy."

79 This tendency has been especially pronounced in police campaigns against the civil rights and labor movements. See chapters 4 and 5.

80 Donner, *Protectors of Privilege*, 286 and 359.
   "These [right-wing] organizations are prized by intelligence agencies because they share the basic intelligence assumption that the country is in the grip of a wide-spread subversive conspiracy. Intelligence agents and informers use the platform and publications of the far right to document this thesis with 'inside' information." Donner, "Theory and Practice," 29.

81 Donner, *Protectors of Privilege*, 146–50.

82 Donner, *Protectors of Privilege*, 358.

83 AFSC, *Police Threat to Political Liberty*, 105; and Donner, *Protectors of Privilege*, 297.

84 AFSC, *Police Threat to Political Liberty*, 41–42.

85 Donner, *Protectors of Privilege*, 217–20.

86 Wolfe, *Seamy Side of Democracy*, 37–38 and 51.

87 Quoted in Donner, "Theory and Practice," 36.

88 Donner, *Protectors of Privilege*, 190–91.

89 Zinn, *People's History*, 478.

90 Center for Research on Criminal Justice, *Iron Fist*, 118.

91 Donner, *Protectors of Privilege*, 196, 239–42, 350–53, 288–89, 298, 305, 319, 344, 346.

92 Quoted in Kristian Williams, "Ken Lawrence: New State Repressions [Interview]," *Portland (OR) Alliance*, April 2000.

93 Donner, *Protectors of Privilege*, 240.

94 Donner, *Protectors of Privilege*, 354–55.

95 Donner, *Protectors of Privilege*, 297.

96 AFSC, *Police Threat to Political Liberty*, 78.

97 Donner, *Protectors of Privilege*, 267.

98 Donner, *Protectors of Privilege*, 284.

99 It seems that Falk acted alone, though, oddly, the files were never reported missing. After his death in 1987, the files moldered until 2002, when they were discovered and given to reporters working for the *Portland Tribune*. Jacklet, "Secret Watchers."
   The *Tribune*'s five-part exposé is available at http://www.portlandtribune.com.

100 Jacklet, "It Should Be Noted;" and Ben Jacklet, "In Case You Were Wondering . . . " *Portland (OR) Tribune*, September 27, 2002.

101 Jacklet, "It Should Be Noted."

102 Quoted in Jacklet, "Legacy." Parentheses in original.

103 Jacklet, "Legacy;" Jacklet, "Secret Watchers;" Ibid; Jacklet, "It Should Be Noted."

104 Jacklet, "Secret Watchers."

105 Quoted in Jacklet, "Secret Watchers."

106 Ibid.

107 Quoted in Abdeen Jabara, "The Anti-Defamation League: Civil Rights and Wrongs," *CovertAction Quarterly* (Summer 1993): 28–31.

108 Subsequent lawsuits cost the ADL nearly $11 million. Barbara Ferguson, "ADL Found Guilty of Spying by California Court," *Arab News* (Jeddah, Saudi Arabia), April 25, 2002, http://www.arabnews.com/Article.asp?ID=14650 (accessed April 25, 2002).

109 Donner, *Protectors of Privilege*, 357–58.

110 Brian Glick, "The Face of COINTELPRO," forward to *The COINTELPRO Papers: Documents from the FBI's Secret Wars Against Domestic Dissent* by Ward Churchill and Jim Vander Wall (Boston: South End Press, 1990), xii. Emphasis in original.

111 See, for example: Jim Redden, "City Finds that FBI Ties are Blinding Ones," *Portland (OR) Tribune*, September 17, 2002.

112 Donner, *Protectors of Privilege*, 30–31.

113 Donner, *Protectors of Privilege*, 57.

114 Quoted in Donner, *Protectors of Privilege*, 154

115 *Alliance to End Repression, et al. v. City of Chicago*. U.S. Court of Appeals, Seventh Circuit. (January 11, 2001).

116 I can speak of this incident from my own experience. At the time of my arrest, I had been stomped by a police horse, beaten with batons, and kicked repeatedly by officer Michael Shemash. My wrist had then been cut by the cop removing my flex-cuffs. I was bleeding and blacking out; I asked repeatedly for medical attention. But before taking me to the hospital, the police interrogated me at length about political matters. At times there were as many as seven cops in the cell with me, asking questions.

117 Quoted in *Alliance to End Repression, et al. v. City of Chicago*, et al. U.S. District Court, Northern District of Illinois. (December 21, 2000) 3.

118 My own testimony was dismissed thus: "Williams appeared credible on the stand, but his actions . . . suggest a significant hostility toward the police." *Alliance to End Repression v. City of Chicago* (December 21, 2000) 20.

119 See, for example: Paul Rosenberg, "The Empire Strikes Back: Police Repression of Protest from Seattle to L.A.," *LA Independent Media Center*, August 13, 2000, http://www.r2kphilly.org/pdf/empire-strikes.pdf (accessed March 18, 2003).

120 These movements, generally overlooked by the media of the time and forgotten by textbooks since, constitute what Howard Zinn termed "The Unreported Resistance." Zinn, *People's History*, 589–618.

121 B. Hillard, "Spies, Lies, and Videotape: One Man's Campaign Against Political Surveillance," *The Progressive*, September 1991, 30–31.

122 Quoted in Mitzi Waltz, "Policing activists: Think Global, Spy Local," *CovertAction Quarterly* (Summer 1997): 27.

123 Michael Larson, *Criminal Intelligence Report* (City of Portland, Oregon: Bureau of Police, February 16, 1999), 6.

124 "Brief History of the Judi Bari Bombing Case," http://www.judibari.org/#History (accessed December 10, 2002).

125 Catherine Komp, "Justice for Judi! A Free Speech Victory," *Clamor*, November/December 2002, 61.

126 Most of the blame fell on three of the seven defendants. Former Oakland Police Lieutenant Michael Sims and retired FBI agents John Reikes and Frank Doyle were together held responsible for $4.1 million. One defendant, an FBI agent, was cleared. Mike Geniella, "Bari Juror Explains Verdicts, Marathon Deliberations," *Press Democrat*, June 14, 2002, http://www.judibari.org/jurors_talk.html (accessed December 10, 2002).

127 Quoted in Geniella, "Bari Juror."

128 Mary Nunn. Quoted in Nicholas Wilson, "Juror Talks about the Bari vs. FBI Trial," *Albion Monitor*, July 16, 2002, http://www.monitor.net/monitor/0207a/judibaritrial13.html (accessed December 10, 2002).

129 AFSC, *Police Threat to Political Liberty*, 48–49.

130 Donner, *Protectors of Privilege*, 238.

131 Ten of the eleven people killed were Black. Milton Coleman, "The Move Disaster: Life Before, The Politics After," *Washington Post*, May 26, 1985 (database: NewsBank Full-Text Newspapers, accessed December 12, 2002).

132 Quoted in Donner, *Protectors of Privilege*, 238.

133 Debbie Goldberg, "City Found Liable in Attack on MOVE," *Washington Post*, June 25, 1996 (database: NewsBank Full-Text Newspapers, accessed December 12, 2002).

134 Frank Morales, "The Militarization of the Police," *CovertAction Quarterly* (Summer 1999): 47.

135 Both quoted in Bill Peterson, "Huge Fire Destroys House of Philadelphia Radicals," *Washington Post*, May 14, 1985 (database: NewsBank Full-Text Newspapers, accessed December 12, 2002).

136 Michael Moss and Ford Fessenden, "New Tools for Domestic Spying, and Qualms," *New York Times*, December 10, 2002, http://www.nytimes.com/2002/12/10/national/10PRIV.html (accessed December 11, 2002).

137 The acceleration of JTTF expansion has been intense, especially compared to its slow start. The first JTTF was formed in New York in 1980. Chicago followed a year later. During the following fifteen years, nine JTTFs were added, bringing the total to eleven in 1996. Then, between 1996 and 2001, the number of Task Forces more than tripled; thirty-five JTTFs existed on the morning of September 11, 2001. Since then twenty-one have been added.

   Patrick J. Daly, "On Counter Terrorism: Statement of Patrick J Daly, Assistant Special Agent in Charge, Chicago Division, before the House Committee on Government Reform, Subcommittee on Government Efficiency, Financial Management, and Intergovernmental Relations," http://www.fbi.gov/congress/congress02/daly07022002.html (accessed December 11, 2002).

   Robert J. Jordan, "On Information Sharing Initiatives: Statement for the Record, before the United States Senate Committee on the Judiciary, Subcommittee on Administrative Oversight and the Courts," http://www.fbi.gov/congress/congress02/jordan041702.html (accessed December 11, 2002).

   J. T. Caruso, "On Combating Terrorism: Protecting the United States; Statement for the Record, before the House Subcommittee on National Security, Veterans Affairs, and International Relations," http://www.fbi.gov/congress/congress02/caruso032102.html (accessed December 11, 2002).

138 Jim McGee, "An Intelligence Giant In The Making: Anti-Terrorism Law Likely To Bring Domestic Apparatus of Unprecedented Scope," *Washington Post*, November 4, 2001 (database: News Collection from Dialog@CARL, accesssed November 11, 2001).

139 Quoted in Dave Mazza, "President Signs New Anti-Terrorism Bill Into Law," *Portland (OR) Alliance*, November 2001.

140 For a comparison of the Palmer Raids and ongoing immigrant detentions, see: David Cole, "The Ashcroft Raids," *Amnesty Now*, Spring 2002, http://www.amnestyusa.org/usacrisis/ashcroftraids.html (accessed December 11, 2002).

141 For an overview of the Patriot Act and its legal ramifications, see: Nancy Chang, "The USA Patriot Act: What's So Patriotic About Trampling on the Bill of Rights?" *CovertAction Quarterly* (Winter 2001): 14–18.

142 American Civil Liberties Union [ACLU], "USA Patriot Act Boosts Government Powers While Cutting Back on Traditional Checks and Balances: An ACLU Legislative Analysis," http://archive.aclu.org/congress/110101a.html (accessed December 22, 2002).

143 Mazza, "President Signs New Anti-Terrorism Bill."

144 ACLU, "USA Patriot Act."

145 ACLU, "USA Patriot Act."

146 ACLU, "USA Patriot Act."

147 Mazza, "President Signs New Anti-Terrorism Bill."

148 "These information sharing authorizations effectively put the CIA back in the business of spying on Americans: Once the CIA makes clear the kind of information it seeks, law enforcement agencies can use

tools like wiretaps and intelligence searches to provide data to the CIA. In fact, the law specifically gives the Director of Central Intelligence—who heads the CIA—the power to identify domestic intelligence requirements." ACLU, "USA Patriot Act."

149 John Ashcroft. Quoted in Eric Lichtblau, et al., "Response to Terror: Justice Dept. to Tighten Focus on Terrorism Law," *Los Angeles Times*, November 9, 2001 (database: News Collection from Dialog@CARL, accessed November 11, 2001).

150 Richard W. Stevenson, "Signing Homeland Security Bill, Bush Appoints Ridge as Secretary," *New York Times*, November 26, 2002, http://www.nytimes.com/2002/11/26/politics/26Bush.html (accessed November 28, 2002).

151 President Bush outlined these responsibilities when signing the legislation:
"First, this new department will analyze intelligence information on terror threats collected by the CIA, the FBI, the National Security Agency and others. The department will match this intelligence against the nation's vulnerabilities—and work with other agencies, and the private sector, and state and local governments to harden America's defenses against terror.
"Second, the department will gather and focus all our efforts to face the challenge of cyberterrorism, and the even worse danger of nuclear, chemical, and biological terrorism. This department will be charged with encouraging research on new technologies that can defeat these threats in time to prevent an attack.
"Third, state and local governments will be able to turn for help and information to one federal domestic security agency, instead of the more than 20 agencies that currently divide these responsibilities. This will help our local governments work in concert with the federal government for the sake of all the people of America.
"Fourth, the new department will bring together agencies responsible for border, coastline, and transportation security. There will be a coordinated effort to safeguard our transportation systems and to secure the border so that we're better able to protect our citizens and welcome our friends.
"Fifth, the department will work with state and local officials to prepare our response to any future terrorist attack that may come. . . ." "President Bush Signs Homeland Security Act: Remarks by the President at the Signing of H.R. 5005, the Homeland Security Act of 2002" Press Release (November 25, 2002), www.whitehouse.gov/news/release/2002/11/20021125-6.html (accessed December 21, 2002).

152 Human Rights Watch, "U.S. Homeland Security Bill: Civil Rights Vulnerable and Immigrant Children Not Protected," http://www.hrw.org/press/2002/11/homeland1121.html (accessed December 11, 2002).

153 Jennifer Van Bergen, "Homeland Security Act: The Rise of the American Police State (Part 3 of a Three Part Series)," *Truthout*, December 4, 2002, http://www.truthout.org/docs_02/12/03B.jub.hsa.3.html (accessed December 11, 2002).
The legal expansion of government power must be understood in the context of its simultaneous technological advance. For an overview of the surveillance technology in use, see: European Union. Parliament. Scientific and Technical Options Assessment. An Appraisal of the Technologies of Political Control: Updated Executive Summary Prepared as a Background Document for the September 1998 Part-Session. (September 1998), www.europarl.eu.int/dg4/stoa/en/publi/166499/execsum.htm, (accessed August 2, 2000).
The Homeland Security Act allegedly put the brakes on two of the administration's most controversial proposals. Operation TIPS, through which everyday citizens could report on the suspicious activities of their friends and neighbors, was explicitly barred by the law; nevertheless, it is being implemented at the state and local levels. Nat Hentoff, "Ashcroft's Shadowy Disciple: Someone to Watch Over Us," *Village Voice*, November 15, 2002, http://www.villagevoice.com/issues/0247/hentoff.php (accessed December 11, 2002).
Likewise, the work of the Total Information Awareness program, which would have been responsible for developing and employing computer technology to compile vast digital files about individual Americans, has been divided between two distinct agencies. The Pentagon is developing new dataveillance technology and The Directorate of Information Analysis and Infrastructure Protection is collecting the actual information and maintaining the files. Linda S. Heard, "Spies, Snitches and Eyes in the Sky," *CounterPunch*, December 10, 2002, http://www.counterpunch.org/heard1210.html (accessed December 11, 2002).

154 Quoted in Center for Constitutional Rights [CCR], "The State of Civil Liberties: One Year Later; Erosion of Civil Liberties in the Post 9/11 Era; A Report Issued by the Center for Constitutional Rights," http://www.ccr-ny.org/whatsnew/civil_liberties.asp (accessed December 11, 2002), 2.

155 CCR, "State of Civil Liberties," 3; and Lichtblau et al., "Response to Terror."

156 Interestingly, the police themselves have proved resistant to this idea, citing the damage it could do to their relations with immigrant communities, and, in some cases, pointing to laws to the contrary. For example, the Arizona State Police and the San Jose city police immediately announced that they would not enforce immigration laws. American Civil Liberties Union, "Ashcroft Uses Local and State Police to Enforce Complex Immigration laws; ACLU Warns Move Will Erode Immigrants' Willingness to Cooperate With Police," http://www.aclu.org/NationalSecurity/nationalSecurity.cfm?ID=10689&c=112 (accessed December 10, 2002).
Months earlier, police in San Francisco, San Jose, Detroit, Portland (OR), and elsewhere refused to assist

the Justice Department in interviews of Middle-Eastern men. Joseph Rose, "Portland Police Say No to Ashcroft," *Oregonian*, November 21, 2001; Fox Butterfield, "Police are Split on Questioning of Mideast Men," *New York Times*, November 22, 2001, http://www.newyorktimes.com (accessed November 23, 2001); and, Meg Jones, "Campus Police Refuse to Interrogate," *Milwaukee Journal Sentinel*, December 7, 2001, http://www.jsonline.com/news/state/dec01/3578.asp (acccessed December 10, 2002).

157 David Cole, "Trading Liberty for Security After September 11," *Foreign Policy in Focus Policy Report*, http://www.fpif.org/papers/post9-11_body.html (accessed December 12, 2002).

158 CCR, "State of Civil Liberties," 3. Parentheses in original.

159 In the most dramatic example, a federal appeals court overturned a year-old rule that had declared a broad range of immigration proceedings off-limits to the public. The Court wrote: "democracies die behind closed doors." Quoted in CCR, "State of Civil Liberties," 4.

160 While government surveillance of the populace has only increased, every effort has been made to make the state's activities less transparent—classifying increasing amounts of information and refusing to release many public records. Alsa Solomon, "Things We Lost in the Fire: While the Ruins of the World Trade Center Smoldered, the Bush Administration Launched an Assault on the Constitution," *Village Voice*, September 11–September 17, 2002, http://www.villagevoice.com/issues/0237/solomon.php (accessed September 27, 2002).

161 Quoted in Heard, "Spies, Snitches and Eyes."

162 CCR, "State of Civil Liberties," 4.

163 CCR, "State of Civil Liberties," 3.

164 Cole, "Trading Liberty."

For an overview of the detentions, tribunals, USA Patriot Act, Homeland Security Bill, and violations of attorney-client privilege, see: Michael Ratner, "Making Us Less Free: War on Terrorism or War on Liberty?" http://www.humanrightsnow.org (accessed December 10, 2002).

For a detailed discussion of immigrant detentions, see: Human Rights Watch, "United States: Presumption of Guilt; Human Rights Abuses of Post–September 11 Detainees," http://www.hrw.org/reports/2002/us911 (accessed December 2002).

165 Cole, "Ashcroft Raids."

166 CCR, "State of Civil Liberties," 7; and Lichtblau et al., "Response to Terror."

According to the new rules, if they cannot be deported, non-citizens suspected of terrorism can be held indefinitely. In the worst case, this suggests the possibility of life imprisonment without trial. ACLU, "USA Patriot Act."

167 Cole, "Ashcroft Raids."

168 Ibid.

169 James Sterngold, "Iranians Furious Over INS Arrests: Abuse Alleged After Men Agreed to Register in L.A.," *San Francisco Chronicle*, December 21, 2002 (database: NewsBank Full-Text Newspapers, accessed December 21, 2002).

Behrooz Arshadi reports similar conditions. Behrooz Arshadi, "Treated Like a Criminal: How the INS Stole Three Days of My Life," *The Progressive*, March 2003, 22–23.

170 Quoted in Nita Leyveld and Henry Weinstein, "INS Arrest Numbers Inflated, U.S. says: Officials Accuse Groups of Exaggerating Figures Involving Immigrants From Muslim Communities," *Los Angeles Times*, December 20, 2002 (database: NewsBank Full-Text Newspapers, accessed December 21, 2002).

171 Megan Garvey, et al., "Hundreds Are Detained After Visits to INS: Thousands Protest Arrests of Mideast Boys and Men Who Complied With Order to Register," *Los Angeles Times*, December 19, 2002 (database: NewsBank Full-Text Newspapers, accessed December 21, 2002).

172 Chisun Lee, "Spooky Goofs: Indications of Serious Flaws in a 9-11 FBI Flop," *Village Voice*, August 28, 2002–September 3, 2002, http://www.villagevoice.com/issues/0235/lee.php (accessed December 12, 2002).

173 Quoted in Lee, "Spooky Goofs."

174 Donner, *Protectors of Privilege*, 3–4.

175 Kitson, *Low Intensity Operations*, en passim; and, Ken Lawrence, *The New State Repression* (Chicago: International Network Against New State Repression, 1985), 2.

176 Kitson, *Low Intensity Operations*, 67.

177 Donner, "Practice and Theory," 35.

See also: Lawrence, *New State Repression*, 2–3.

178 Lawrence, *New State Repression*, 3.

Chapter 8: Riot Police or Police Riots?

1 Much of the discussion in this chapter is drawn from my article "The Cop and the Crowd." Kristian Williams, "The Cop and the Crowd: Police Strategies for Keeping the Rabble in Line," *Clamor*, December 2000/January 2001, 9–13.

2 This account is based primarily on my own observations, with support from the sources cited later in the chapter.

3 Seattle City Council, WTO Accountability Review Committee, *Report of the WTO Accountability Review Committee* (September 14 , 2000), 15. Emphasis in original.

4 ACLU Washington, "Out of Control: Seattle's Flawed Response to Protests Against the World Trade Organization," http://www.aclu-wa.org/ISSUES/police/WTO-Report.html (accessed August 2000).

5 Seattle City Council, *Report of the WTO,* 3.
   A more precise definition of "police riot" appears in the discussion that follows.

6 Seattle Police Department, *The Seattle Police Department After Action Report: World Trade Organization Ministerial Conference; Seattle, Washington, November 29–December 3, 1999* (April 4, 2000), 5.

7 Seattle Police Department, *Seattle Police Department After Action Report,* 41. The accuracy of this description is dubious, but it does say something about the ways the police view disorder, and exaggerate its dangers.

8 R.M. McCarthy and Associates, *An Independent Review of the Word Trade Organization Conference Disruptions in Seattle, Washington; November 29–December 3, 1999* (San Clemente, California: July 2000), 132.
   They suggest making pre-emptive arrests at earlier demonstrations and assigning National Guard troops to the area on "training/standby" status, citing—of all things—the 1968 Chicago Democratic National Convention as a precedent. R.M. McCarthy and Associates, *Independent Review,* 38.
   The 1968 Democratic Convention is examined in detail later in this chapter.

9 R.M. McCarthy and Associates, *Independent Review,* 59.

10 R.M. McCarthy and Associates, *Independent Review,* 129–30.

11 Seattle City Council, *Report of the WTO,* 13.

12 Seattle City Council, *Report of the WTO,* 3.

13 Seattle City Council, *Report of the WTO,* 10.

14 Police in DC had a secure perimeter in place considerably before the April 16, 2000 IMF/World Bank meetings. They also had about 600 protesters in jail before the meetings began; earlier in the week, they surrounded an entire march and arrested everyone present. As a result, they relied less on actual force during the conference itself, and were widely praised for their restraint. One commentator noted: "Law enforcement learned from Seattle, and changed tactics accordingly." Geov Parrish, "Lessons From D.C.," *Eat the State!* April 27, 2000, 3.
   See also: Paul Rosenberg, "The Empire Strikes Back: Police Repression of Protest from Seattle to L.A.," *LA Independent Media Center,* August 13, 2000, http://www.r2kphilly.org/pdf/empire-strikes.pdf (accessed March 18, 2003).

15 Police used nightsticks, pepper spray, and horses to forcefully attack demonstrations against the 2003 American invasion of Iraq. In New York, Washington, D.C., and Seattle, police corralled protesters and arrested them en masse. In Oakland, police fired less-lethal weapons at a crowd picketing docks where war-related cargo was being loaded onto ships; numerous protesters and several uninvolved longshore workers were injured. Silja J.A. Talui, "The Public is the Enemy," *The Nation,* May 12, 2003, 30–31.

16 Both quoted in James F. Richardson, *The New York Police: Colonial Times to 1901* (New York: Oxford University Press, 1970), 143.
   Richardson comments: "The police of the 1860's did not have either the doctrine or the materials to deal with disorder in any way other than violence. In ordinary circumstances, policemen worked alone or in small groups; their only additional training or experience came in their military drill. The only anti-riot tools they possessed were their clubs and revolvers, and their only recourse in a disorder was to bash as many people on the head as possible. There is no indication that Acton and other police officials ever thought about any other method." Richardson, *New York Police,* 143.

17 "That year there came a series of tumultuous strikes by railroad workers in a dozen cities; they shook the nation as no labor conflict in its history had done. . . . When the great railroad strikes of 1877 were over, a hundred people were dead; a thousand people had gone to jail, 100,000 workers had gone on strike, and the strikes had roused into action countless unemployed in the cities. More than half of the freight on the nation's 75,000 miles of track had stopped running at the height of the strikes." Howard Zinn, *A People's History of the United States, 1492–Present* (New York: HarperPerennial, 1995), 240 and 246.

18 Eugene L. Leach, "The Literature of Riot Duty: Managing Class Conflict in the Streets, 1877–1927," *Radical History Review,* Spring 1993, 23.

19 Quoted in Leach, "Literature of Riot Duty," 24.

20 Ibid.

21 Quoted in Jeremy Brecher, *Strike!* (Boston: South End Press, 1972), 15.

22 Leach, "Literature of Riot Duty," 23; Zinn, *People's History,* 243–44; and Brecher, *Strike!* 15.

23 "Chicago was typical: President Hayes authorized the use of Federal regulars; citizen's patrols were organized ward by ward using Civil War veterans; 5,000 special police were sworn in, freeing the regular police for action; big employers organized their reliable employees into armed companies—many of which were sworn in as special police. At first the crowd successfully out-maneuvered the police in the street fighting that ensued, but after killing at least eighteen people the police finally gained control of the crowd and thus broke the back of the movement." Brecher, *Strike!* 20.

24 Strike duty accounted for fully one-half of all deployments between 1877 and 1892. Leach, "Literature of Riot Duty," 25.

25 "The events of the [1870s] in particular led many persons to fear another insurrection, and as a result legislation was introduced to improve and provide better arms for the organized militia. In 1879, in support of this effort, the National Guard Association came into being in St. Louis, and between 1881 and 1892 every single state revised its military code to provide for an organized militia, which most states, following the lead of New York, called the National Guard. . . . Through the efforts of the National Guard Association, the Guard . . . succeeded in seeing an act in 1887 that doubled the $200,000 annual federal grant for firearms that the militia had enjoyed since 1808." Maurice Matloff, ed., *American Military History* (Washington, D.C.: United States Army, Office of the Chief of Military History, 1969), 287.

26 Leach, "Literature of Riot Duty," 25.

27 Leach, "Literature of Riot Duty," 26–28.

28 Quoted in Leach, "Literature of Riot Duty," 28.

29 Leach, "Literature of Riot Duty," 29.

30 Quoted in Leach, "Literature of Riot Duty," 30. Emphasis in original.

31 Leach, "Literature of Riot Duty," 29–30.

32 Leach, "Literature of Riot Duty," 33–34.

33 Leach, "Literature of Riot Duty," 31.

34 Quoted in Leach, "Literature of Riot Duty," 34.

35 Leach, "Literature of Riot Duty," 41.

36 Leach, "Literature of Riot Duty," 35–36.

37 In 1914, National Guard troops used a machine gun against striking workers in Ludlow, Colorado. They then set the miners' tent city on fire, burning to death two women and eleven children. All told, sixty-six people died in the clashes. Zinn, *People's History*, 243–44; and Brecher, *Strike!* 347–49.

38 Leach, "Literature of Riot Duty," 37.

39 Leach, "Literature of Riot Duty," 38–40.

40 Quoted in Leach, "Literature of Riot Duty," 41.

41 Quoted in Leach, "Literature of Riot Duty," 41–42. Emphasis in original.

42 Bellows specifically favored the riot stick because, unlike rifles, crowds understood that the troops would really use them. Leach, "Literature of Riot Duty," 41.

43 Leach, "Literature of Riot Duty," 44.

44 Clark McPhail, David Schweingruber, and John McCarthy, "Policing Protest in the United States: 1960–1995," in *Policing Protest: The Control of Mass Demonstrations in Western Democracies,* eds. Donnatella della Porta and Herbert Reiter (Minneapolis: University of Minnesota Press, 1998), 53.

45 McPhail et al., "Policing Protest," 53.

46 Donnatella della Porta and Herbert Reiter, "Introduction: The Policing of Protest in Western Democracies," in *Policing Protest: The Control of Mass Demonstrations in Western Democracies,* eds. Donnatella della Porta and Herbert Reiter (Minneapolis: University of Minnesota Press, 1998), 2.

47 "During the WTO protests, the City made decisions to clear downtown streets well away from the conference facility and streets in the Capital Hill neighborhood. The City did not do this to protect any person or thing from physical harm, but rather to pursue the ill-defined goal of gaining control of the streets." ACLU Washington, "Out of Control," 18.

48 McPhail, et al., "Policing Protest," 50–51.

49 Ward Churchill and Jim Vander Wall, *The COINTELPRO Papers: Documents from the FBI's Secret Wars Against Domestic Dissent* (Boston, Massachusetts: South End Press, 1990), 220–21.

50 Paul A. Gilje, *Rioting In America* (Bloomington: Indiana University Press, 1996), 160.

51 Rodney Stark, *Police Riots: Collective Violence and Law Enforcement* (Belmont, California: Focus Books, 1972), 5–6

52 Tariq Ali and Susan Watkins, *1968: Marching in the Streets* (New York: The Free Press, 1998), 43.

53 Stark, *Police Riots,* 6.

54 Quoted in Ronald Fraser, et al., *1968: A Student Generation in Revolt* (New York: Pantheon Books, 1988), 195.

55 Fraser, et al., *Student Generation in Revolt,* 199.

56 Gilje, *Rioting,* 164.

57 Stark, *Police Riots,* 6.

58 Ali and Watkins, *Marching in the Streets,* 72.

59 Joe R. Feagin and Harlan Hahn, *Ghetto Revolts: The Politics of Violence in American Cities* (New York: The Macmillan Company, 1973), 105.

   The Oakland police took the opportunity to have a shoot-out with the Black Panthers, who were actively (and successfully) *discouraging* rioting. The cops fired over 2,000 rounds into a house where Eldridge Cleaver and Bobby Hutton were hiding in the basement. They then filled the house with teargas, starting a fire in the process. Cleaver and Hutton surrendered. Cleaver, who stripped naked before leaving the house, was beaten by police. Hutton was shot and killed after he surrendered. He was seventeen years old. Ali and Watkins, *Marching in the Streets,* 76–77; and Henry Hampton et al., *Voices of Freedom: An Oral History of the Civil Rights Movement From the 1950s through the 1980s* (New York: Bantam Books, 1990), 514–17.

60 Stark, *Police Riots,* 4–5.

61 Stark, *Police Riots*, 6.

62 Stark, *Police Riots*, 6.
    Police vandalism was a common response to riots, especially those with a racial component. The "Soul Brother" signs that marked Black-owned businesses offered them a level of protection from the angry crowds, but made them targets for the police and National Guard. Feagin and Hahn, *Ghetto Riots*, 175 and 192–93.

63 Stark, *Police Riots*, 6.

64 Ali and Watkins, *Marching in the Streets*, 204.

65 Quoted in Ali and Watkins, *Marching in the Streets*, 201.

66 Stark, *Police Riots*, 5–6.

67 Fraser et al., *Student Generation in Revolt*, 302.

68 No exhaustive study of the year's events is available; likely, none is possible. The National Student Association counted 221 demonstrations on 101 college campuses during the first half of the year. Likewise, a review of the *New York Times* and *Washington Post* covering September 16 to October 15, 1968, shows reports of 216 separate protest events, 35 percent of which involved violence.
    Jerome H. Skolnick, *The Politics of Protest: Violent Aspects of Protest and Confrontation; A Report Submitted by Jerome H. Skolnick* [The Skolnick Report; Report of the Task Force on Violent Aspects of Protest and Confrontation to the National Commission on the Causes and Prevention of Violence] (Washington, D.C.: Supt. of Documents, U.S. Government Printing Office, 1969), 15 and 3.

69 Stark implies that television was the crucial factor in creating the DNC's infamy: "[E]vents in Chicago were unique only in the quality and quantity of media coverage." Stark, *Police Riots*, 4.

70 Gilje, *Rioting*, 166.

71 Quoted in Norman Mailer, *Miami and the Siege of Chicago: An Informal History of the Republican and Democratic Conventions of 1968* (New York: The World Publishing Company, 1968), 179.

72 Quoted in Mailer, *Miami and the Siege of Chicago*, 177.

73 Mailer, *Miami and the Siege of Chicago*, 175.

74 Daniel Walker, *Rights In Conflict: Chicago's 7 Brutal Days* (New York: Grosset and Dunlap, 1968), vii.

75 Walker, *Rights in Conflict*, xii.

76 The term "police riot" is not the hyperbole many assume it to be. During the June 19–21, 1968, disturbances in Berkeley, police not only beat, gassed, and threatened scores of peaceable citizens, they also threw rocks at crowds, broke windows, and engaged in other vandalism. "A policeman was seen knocking in a window at a bookstore. . . . Several persons reported damage to their residences after the police had forced their way inside. A number of others claimed that police beat their automobiles with riot batons, causing dents and breaking headlights." Stark, *Police Riots*, 48.

77 Stark, *Police Riots*, 18–21.

78 A Berkeley police memo dated August 21, 1968, notes, "Both civilians and officers have reported observing a sort of 'one-upmanship' phenomenon in squads without leaders of a supervisory rank. Each officer seems not to want anyone to feel he is less zealous than anyone else in the squad, and in tense encounters, a spiraling force-level was observed." Quoted in Stark, *Police Riots*, 53.

79 Walker described the attitude of the Chicago police going into the 1968 Democratic National Convention (with echoes of Henry Bellows, half a century before): "They believed that even an orderly crowd of peaceful demonstrators could easily develop into a mob led by a few determined agitators into violent action." Walker, *Rights In Conflict*, 59.

80 Stark, *Police Riots*, 138.

81 "Thus, it is not the use of violence that makes police riots unusual events, but simply the concentration of police violence in a limited time and space. . . . This is what makes it a riot—*that the police are doing collectively in a short period of time and in a small area what they would ordinarily be doing in pairs or very small groups across a very large area over a longer time.*" Stark, *Police Riots*, 12 and 84. Emphasis in original.

82 Stark, *Police Riots*, 126.

83 Stark, *Police Riots*, 128–29.

84 Quoted in Stark, *Police Riots*, 127.

85 Walker, *Rights in Conflict*, vii.

86 Stark, *Police Riots*, 186.

87 Walker, *Rights in Conflict*, xi.

88 Stark, *Police Riots*, 18.

89 Stark, *Police Riots*, 20.

90 Stark, *Police Riots*, 137.

91 President's Commission on Campus Unrest [The Scranton Commission], *The Report of the President's Commission on Campus Unrest* (Washington, D.C.: U.S. Government Printing Office, 1970), 2.

92 McPhail et al., *Policing Protest*, 52.

93 Della Porta and Reiter, "Introduction," 6–7.

94 Permit requirements have been in place since the Progressive Era, but had not previously been used to this end. Instead, permits were routinely denied, though the requirement provided a pretext for declaring gath-

erings illegal. Frank Donner, *Protectors of Privilege: Red Squads and Police Repression in Urban America* (Berkeley: University of California Press, 1990), 50.

95 John T. Brothers, "Communication Is the Key to Small Demonstration Control," *Campus Law Enforcement Journal* (September–October 1985): 13–16.

96 See, for example: National Commission on the Causes and Prevention of Violence [The Eisenhower Commission], *To Establish Justice, To Insure Domestic Tranquillity: Final Report on the Causes and Prevention of Violence* (Washington, D.C.: U.S. Government Printing Office, 1969) 88; and Scranton Commission, *Report,* 145.

97 For a critical overview of riot commission politics, see: Feagin and Hahn, *Ghetto Revolts,* 205–226.

98 Brothers, "Communication Is the Key," 15.

99 Eisenhower Commission, *To Establish Justice,* 75.

100 McPhail, et al., *Policing Protest,* 53.

101 P.A.J. Waddington, "Controlling Protest in Contemporary Historical and Comparative Perspective," in *Policing Protest: The Control of Mass Demonstrations in Western Democracies,* eds. Donnatella della Porta and Herbert Reiter (Minneapolis: University of Minnesota Press, 1998), 122. Emphasis in original.

102 As early as 1966, inspector Harry G. Fox was publicly writing of the unit's intelligence potential: "Members of a good Civil Disobedience Squad should have daily contact with the various leaders, planners and rank and file of these [protest] groups. They get to know them by name, sight and action. The CD Officer talks to them, establishing rapport. He develops intelligence about their connections, background, personal life and ambitions. He influences them to give him a phone call prior to demonstrations or meetings. . . . Prior to any group action, he secures advance copies of literature, group size, techniques to be used, routes of marches, and duration of demonstration. . . . In short, a Civil Disobedience Squad can develop files, photos, informants, plus the ability to secure advance tips on impending demonstrations. Through reports or interviews, they can alert the police administrator of the who, where, what, why, when, and how." Harry G. Fox, "The CD Man," *The Police Chief,* November 1966, 22.

103 Donner, *Protectors of Privilege,* 206.

104 Unlike their allies at the University of Kansas, Blacks in South Africa actively resisted the institutionalization of protest. "Protest, especially in the townships, was not an institutionalized expression of specific grievances but an integral part of the ANC's strategy of making the townships ungovernable." Waddington, "Controlling Protest," 137.

105 Seattle Police Department, *Seattle Police Department After Action Report,* 18.

106 Seattle Police Department, *Seattle Police Department After Action Report,* 40.

107 Seattle Police Department, *Seattle Police Department After Action Report,* 3.

108 Della Porta and Reiter, "Introduction," 30.

Robert Reiner describes the pattern as it emerged during a protest cycle in England. He writes: "Violent protest—'collective bargaining by riot'—gave way to more formalized modes of collective bargaining. Strikes became one weapon in negotiations, not all-out class war. Demonstrations and industrial conflict came to be seen as accepted processes within the confines of particular rules, not inherently subversive threats to the social order." As a result, violence decreased on both sides. However, in the 1970s, this tendency was reversed. The turning point came in 1972 when picketers closed the Saltley coke depot despite police efforts to keep it open. Following their defeat, the police returned again to open combat with strikers.

Robert Reiner, "Policing, Protest, and Disorder in Britain," in *Policing Protest: The Control of Mass Demonstrations in Western Democracies,* ed. Donnatella della Porta and Herbert Reiter (Minneapolis: University of Minnesota Press, 1998), 43 and 45.

109 In the Progressive Era, "The image of worker violence that came to dominate popular perceptions of industrial conflict was powerfully reinforced by the deployment through employers' instigation of state militias and federal troops in such conflicts. The fact that the soldiery was called out in itself served as proof that workers and their allies had once again disturbed the public order." Donner, *Protectors of Privilege,* 24.

110 In effect, the McCarthy report urges a return to Escalated Force as a primary strategy, using permits and meetings with organizers to collect intelligence and explain the rules. The report justifies this approach, in part, by constructing a revisionist history: "During the tumultuous decades of the 1960s and 1970s, there were two basic philosophies regarding law enforcement's response to large-scale demonstrations. The first doctrine held that law enforcement's response to the affected area should be limited to the normally assigned patrol force. A larger mobile force staged in preselected locations out of view would be deployed only if absolutely necessary. . . . As a result of a number of major disruptions which occurred throughout the United States, wherein police officers literally had to fight for their lives while hoping the mobile field force would arrive in time, many law enforcement administrators abandoned this approach in favor of one that had been used in the past with great success. The intent of this second doctrine was to preempt problems by deploying a sizable, highly visible mobile field force in advance of scheduled demonstrations or unrest so that the agency's response to trouble would be quickly recognized. Following this doctrine, arrests are made as soon as violations occur, whether they are the result of passive demonstrations or violent conduct." R.M. McCarthy and Associates, *Independent Review,* 129–30.

111 Seattle City Council, *Report of the WTO* 15.

112 These designated areas, or "protest pits," are one of the few real innovations in protest policing to appear during the 1990s. They generally consist of a parking lot surrounded by chain link fences and concrete barriers. While meeting the technical requirements of the First Amendment, they are designed to maximize police control and minimize the mobility of the crowd.

113 Tina Daunt and Carla Rivera, "Police forcefully break up melee after concert," *Los Angeles Times*, August 15, 2000 (database: NewsBank Full-Text Newspapers, accessed March 28, 2003).

114 Both quoted in Associated Press, "L.A. Police, Protesters Clash Outside Democratic Convention," August 15, 2000, http://www.freedomforum.org/templates/document.asp?documentID=3824 (accessed March 28, 2003).

115 Quoted in Bette Lee, "L.A. Protests: Moving Beyond Seattle Victory," *Portland (OR) Alliance*, October 2000.

116 Lee, "L.A. Protests."

117 City Council member Jackie Goldberg described the situation in L.A.: "There is an atmosphere of intimidation that is unbelievable . . . What we are doing is creating a climate of fear." Quoted in Tina Daunt, "Council Affirms Rights of Protesters," *Los Angeles Times*, August 12, 2000 (database: Full-Text Newspapers, accessed March 28, 2003).

   Christian Parenti makes a more general observation: "*[R]itualized displays of terror are built into American policing. Spectacle is a fundamental part of how the state controls poor people.*" Christian Parenti, *Lockdown America: Police and Prisons in the Age of Crisis* (London: Verso, 1999), 135. Emphasis in original.

118 McPhail et al., "Policing Protest," 54.

   Previously, the FBI had been responsible for crowd control training, since the 1964 Rochester riots. But by 1968 the responsibility for civil disorder preparation had been transferred to the military; the Defense Department spent more on riot control annually than was the Justice Department.

   See also: Frank Morales, "U.S. Military Civil Disturbance Planning: The War at Home, Part One," *CovertAction Quarterly* (Spring–Summer 2000): 82–83.

119 McPhail et al., "Policing Protest," 62–63.

120 "Perhaps the most important organizational innovation undertaken by many local police agencies was the development and utilization of special police squads. Spurred by military advocates of special antiriot task forces, the number of departments with some of these highly trained and mobile riot squads (termed 'lightning strike forces' and 'sniper control teams') increased significantly between 1966 and 1969. The overall increase was 31 percent although the greatest increase was in cities below 250,000 in population. By 1969 paramilitary police units—resembling the counterinsurgency teams developed in Department of State programs for foreign export—were now a permanent fixture in nearly half of these municipal law enforcement agencies in the United States." Feagin and Hahn, *Ghetto Revolts*, 237–38.

121 National Advisory Commission on Civil Disorders [The Kerner Commission], *Report of the National Advisory Commission on Civil Disorder* (New York: E.P. Dutton and Company, 1968), 328.

122 Waddington, "Controlling Protest," 22–23.

123 Della Porta and Reiter, "Introduction," 11–12.

124 In this respect, it is worth remembering that SWAT teams are commonly used in hostage situations—that is, they serve as a tool for negotiation.

Chapter 9: Your Friendly Neighborhood Police State

1 Peter B. Kraska, "Crime Control as Warfare: Language Matters," in *Militarizing the American Criminal Justice System: The Changing Roles of the Armed Forces and the Police,* ed. Peter B. Kraska (Boston: Northeastern University Press, 2001), 16.

2 Kraska, "Crime Control as Warfare," 16–7.

3 Militarism was more closely associated with policing before the development of the modern institution. Sally Hadden describes the connection between the slave patrols and the militia as "intimate." Sally Hadden, *Slave Patrols: Law and Violence in Virginia and the Carolinas* Cambridge: Harvard University Press, 2001), 42.

4 See chapter 6.

   Examples of the rhetoric abound, especially during the late nineteenth and early twentieth centuries. To cite one example, in 1895, New York Police Commissioner Avery D. Andrews promised to "instill . . . into our police force that spirit of military discipline and military honor which in our Army, as well as in all others, had been the true secret of success." Avery's success, by all accounts, was quite limited. Quoted in Richardson, *The New York Police: Colonial Times to 1901* (New York: Oxford University Press, 1970), 246.

5 During the sixties, the New York State Conference of mayors referred to police as "front line troops." The chief of the Cincinnati police said that each officer must become a "foot soldier." Edmund L. McNamara, the commissioner of the Boston Police Department, described the patrol force as "infantry." And President Lyndon Johnson declared a "war on crime." Quoted in Robert M. Fogelson, *Big-City Police* (Cambridge: Harvard University Press, 1977), 154.

6 Center for Research on Criminal Justice, *The Iron Fist and the Velvet Glove: An Analysis of the U.S. Police* (Bekeley, California: Center fir Research on Criminal Justice, 1975), 32.

7 Christian Parenti, "Robocop's Dream: From the Military to Your Street, Omnipresent Surveillance," *The Nation*, February 3, 1997, 22–3.

8 Quoted in Center for Research on Criminal Justice, *Iron Fist*, 36.

9 Daryl Gates with Diane K. Shah, *Chief: My Life with the LAPD* (New York: Bantam Books, 1992), 113–4.

10 Police paramilitary units (PPUs) operate under a variety of monikers, including special response teams, emergency response teams, and tactical operations teams. Christian Parenti, *Lockdown America: Police and Prisons in the Age of Crisis* (London: Verso, 1999), 112.
   Both *PPU* and *SWAT* are sometimes used as generic terms.

11 Center for Research on Criminal Justice, *Iron Fist*, 48; and Gates, *Chief*, 115.

12 Gates, *Chief*, 119-123.

13 Gates, *Chief*, 135,137; and Center for Research on Criminal Justice, *Iron Fist*, 50–1.

14 Gates, *Chief*, 137.

15 Center for Research on Criminal Justice, *Iron Fist*, 51; and Gates, *Chief*, 137.

16 Center for Research on Criminal Justice, *Iron Fist*, 49.

17 Peter B. Kraska, "The Military-Criminal Justice Blur: An Introduction" in *Militarizing the American Criminal Justice System*, ed. Peter B. Kraska (Boston: Northeastern University Press, 2001), 7.

18 Diane Cecelia Weber, "Warrior Cops: Tho Ominous Growth of Paramilitarism in American Police Departments," *Cato Institute Briefing Papers* 50 (August 26, 1999): 7.

19 A 1994 memorandum of understanding between the Department of Justice and the Department of Defense allows for the transfer of military equipment to state and local police. In the three years following the agreement, the Department of Defense gave police 1.2 million pieces of military hardware, including 112 armored personnel carriers and 73 grenade launchers. The LAPD alone received 6,000 M-16s. Weber, "Warrior Cops," 5 and 2.

20 About half (46 percent) of police paramilitary units receive training directly from the military. One SWAT officer brags, "We've had special forces folks who have come right out of the jungles of Central and South America. These guys get into the real shit. All branches of military service are involved in providing training to law enforcement. . . . We've had teams of Navy Seals and Army Rangers come here and teach us everything." Quoted in Peter B. Kraska and Victor E. Kappeler, "Militarizing American Police: The Rise and Normalization of Paramilitary Units," in *The Police and Society: Touchstone Readings*, ed. Victor E. Kappeler (Prospect Heights, Illinois: Waveland Press, Inc., 1999), 471.

21 Parenti, *Lockdown America*, 111–5

22 Quoted in Parent, *Lockdown America*, 111.
   A 10 P.M. curfew provides a useful tool for getting young people into the computer system. Enforcement is strict, but selective. Latino youth are five times more likely than Whites to be arrested for curfew violations; and Blacks are three times more likely than Whites. Parenti, *Lockdown America*, 123.

23 Parenti, *Lockdown America*, 118.

24 Kraska and Kappeler, "Militarizing American Police," 469.

25 Quoted in Kraska and Kappeler, "Militarizing American Police," 469.
   The legacy of the slave patrols is often eerily evident in these operations. One PPU commander mused: "When the soldiers ride in you should see those blacks scatter." Quoted in Kraska and Kappeler, "Militarizing American Police," 475.
   Compare with this description, dating from the 1850s: "It was a stirring scene, when the drums beat at the Guard house in the public square . . . to witness the negroes scouring the streets in all directions. . . ." Quoted in Dennis C. Rousey, *Policing the Southern City: New Orleans 1805–1899*, (Baton Rouge: Louisiana State University Press, 1996), 21.

26 Kraska and Kappeler, "Militarizing American Police."

27 Charles J. Dunlap Jr., "The Thick Green Line: The Growing Involvement of Military Forces in Domestic Law Enforcement," in Kraska, *Militarizing the American Criminal Justice System*, 39.

28 Parenti, *Lockdown America*, 131.

29 Jerome H. Skolnick and David H. Bayley, *The New Blue Line: Police Innovation in Six American Cities* (New York: The Free Press, 1986), 132.

30 Kraska and Kappeler, "Militarizing American Police," 468.

31 Quoted in Kraska and Kappeler, "Militarizing American Police," 468.

32 Gates, *Chief*, 277–80.

33 Quoted in Matt Ehling, *Urban Warrior* [video], (ETS Pictures, 2002).

34 Parenti, *Lockdown America*, 130.
   Similar cases, involving injury to suspects, bystanders, or cops are appallingly common. See: Parenti, *Lockdown America*, 127–31; and Kraska and Kappeler, "Militarizing American Police," 468.

35 The SWAT teams are deployed "not. . . [in response to] an existing high-risk situation but [in anticipation of] one generated by the police themselves." Kraska and Kappeler, "Militarizing American Police," 468.

36 Peter B. Kraska, "Epilogue: Lessons Learned" in Kraska, *Militarizing the American Criminal Justice System*, 159.

37 Quoted in Gates, *Chief*, 286–7.
   Gates later described it as his intention to "Us[e] hyperbole to draw attention to a big problem." Gates,

Chief, 297. I quote his statement here in the same spirit. The fact that Gates's quip follows from the logic of a drug "war" represents *reductio ad absurdum* at its best.

38 See chapter 3.

39 See, for instance: Human Rights Watch, *Shielded from Justice: Police Brutality in the United States* (New York: Human Rights Watch, 1998), 314.

40 Parenti, *Lockdown America*, 50–1, 53.

41 Parenti, *Lockdown America*, 54.

42 Parenti, *Lockdown America*, 52.

43 The militarization of law enforcement has two dimensions: the degree to which the police become like the military, and the degree to which the military becomes entrenched in domestic policing. Congress has authorized the military to provide equipment, research facilities, training, and advice to aid local law enforcement in anti-drug efforts, to participate directly in efforts to keep drugs from crossing the border, and, in the case of the National Guard, to join local police in drug raids and patrols. Dunlap, "Thick Green Line," 29; Weber, "Warrior Cops," 2; and Parenti, *Lockdown America*, 47–8.

Perhaps oddly, some of the strongest voices against military involvement in domestic policing come from within the armed forces. In practical terms, military commanders worry that police operations reduce combat effectiveness, are bad for morale and discipline, and damage the citizenry's trust in the military. More idealistic officers express concerns about the separation of powers, the centralization of police command, mission creep, and civil liberties. See, for example: Dunlap, "Thick Green Line."

44 It is sometimes wrongly thought that the police excursion into social work represents an entirely new phenomenon. But before the rise of the modern welfare system, the police were often the only government agency available to care for the poor. They provided overnight lodging for the homeless in an area apart from the jails, distributed free firewood, shoes, and other necessities, and sometimes ran soup kitchens and employment services. These welfare functions were eliminated during the Progressive Era, in part so that the police could focus on crime, and in part because reformers felt the poor would be better served in the workhouse.

See: Monkkonen, *Police in Urban America*, xiii, 86–127, 147; Fosdick, *American Police Systems*, 366, 370–6; Fogelson, *Big-City Police,* 60, 87, and 187; Dulaney, *Black Police in America*, 107–8; Roger Lane, *Policing the City*, 76, 114, 191–4, and 206; Rousey, *Policing the Southern City*, 132–3; Sidney L. Harring, *Policing a Class Society: The Experiment of American Cities, 1865–1915* (New Brunswick, New Jersey: Rutgers University Press, 1983) 220; and Richardson, *New York Police*, 264–5.

45 Klockars suggests that "community policing" is only a rhetorical device, used to obscure and legitimate the central place of violence in police operations. Carl B. Klockars, "The Rhetoric of Community Policing," in Kappeler, *The Police and Society*.

46 Skolnick and Bayley, *New Blue Line,* 21.

47 For case studies of early community policing programs, see: Skolnick and Bayley, *New Blue Line.*

For discussion on how specific programs fit into the community policing strategy, see: Herman Goldstein, "Toward Community-Oriented Policing: Potential, Basic Requirements, and Threshold Questions," *Crime and Delinquency* (January 1987); and Gary W. Cordner, "Elements of Community Policing," in *Policing Perspectives: An Anthology*, ed. Larry K. Gaines and Gary W. Cordner (Los Angeles: Roxbury Publishing Company, 1999).

For a discussion of early experiments with the various programs, see: Center for Research on Criminal Justice, *Iron Fist.*

48 Cordner, "Elements of Community Policing," 138–44.

49 Community Policing Consortium, "Understanding Community Policing: A Framework for Action" (Washington, D.C.: United States Department of Justice, Bureau of Justice Assistance, August 1994), 3.

50 Skolnick and Bayley, *New Blue Line,* 213.

51 In 1993, 50 percent of police administrators said they had a community policing program, and another 20 percent said they intended to establish one within a year. Neil Websdale, *Policing the Poor: From Slave Plantation to Public Housing* (Boston: Northeastern University Press, 2001) 194.

52 Gates, *Chief*, 307–9.

53 Gates, *Chief*, 308 and 267.

54 Matthew T. DeMichele and Peter B. Kraska, "Community Policing in Battle Garb: A Paradox or Coherent Strategy?" in Kraska, *Militarizing the American Criminal Justice System*, 87.

55 DeMichele and Kraska, "Community Policing in Battle Garb," 87–8.

56 "Problem-oriented policing goes a step further then what is commonly conveyed in community policing by asserting up front that the police job is not simply law enforcement, but dealing with a wide range of community problems—only some of which constitute violations of the law. It further asserts that enforcement of the law is not an end in itself, but only one of several means by which the police can deal with the problems they are expected to handle." Goldstein, "Toward Community-Oriented Policing," 16.

57 See chapter 6.

58 See chapters 2 and 3.

59 Even the Community Policing Consortium report acknowledges this fact, though of course it tries to put the best face on it: "Police became the targets of hostility, which ultimately led police leaders to concerned reflection and analysis." Community Policing Consortium, "Understanding Community Policing," 7.

60 See chapters 7 and 8.

61 A 1968 Pentagon report to President Johnson warned against increasing the number of troops in Vietnam, citing the war's unpopularity: "This growing disaffection accompanied as it certainly will be, by increased defiance of the draft and growing unrest in the cities because of the belief that we are neglecting domestic problems, runs great risk of provoking a domestic crisis of unprecedented proportions." Quoted in Howard Howard Zinn, *A People's History of the United States* (New York: HarperPerennial, 1995), 491.

62 Hubert Williams and Patrick V. Murphy, "The Evolving Strategy of Police: A Minority View," in Kappeler, *Police and Society*, 30.

63 These advantages are specifically noted by the Community Policing Consortium, though in somewhat coded language: "Cooperative problem solving . . . reinforces trust, facilitates the exchange of information, and leads to the identification of other areas that could benefit from the mutual attention of the police and the community." Community Policing Consortium, "Understanding Community Policing,"18.

64 Goldstein, "Toward Community-Oriented Policing," 10.

65 Victor E. Kappeler and Peter B. Kraska, "A Textual Critique of Community Policing: Police Adaption to High Modernity," *Policing: An International Journal of Police Strategies and Management* 21:2 (1998), 305; and Victor E. Kappeler, "Reinventing the Police and Society: The Spectacle of Social Control," in Kappeler, *Police and Society*, 488.

66 Kappeler and Kraska, "Textual Critique," 305.

67 Center for Research on Criminal Justice, *Iron Fist*, 70. Emphasis in original.
In the early 1970s, the LAPD began organizing neighborhood meetings as part of its team-policing program (called the "Basic Car Plan"). The police used these meetings to recruit informants and to circulate petitions calling for the reintroduction of the death penalty. Huey P. Newton, "A Citizen's Peace Force," *Crime and Social Justice: A Journal of Radical Criminology* 1 (Spring-Summer 1974), 39.

68 Cordner, "Elements of Community Policing," 143. See also: Center for Research on Criminal Justice, *Iron Fist*, 58.
One would think that community policing advocates would be careful about using the words "collaborate," "collaboration," and "collaborators," given their Nazi-era connotations. Oddly, the critical analyses of community policing rhetoric (e.g., Klockars, "Rhetoric of Community Policing" and Kappeler and Kraska, "Textual Critique") seem to have missed this point.

69 Goldstein, "Toward Community-Oriented Policing," 7.
Goldstein does recognize some of the inherent dangers of assigning the police such a role. "As an illustration, community organizing is almost always listed as one of the tools available to community police officers. . . . If a problem, such as residential burglaries, is identified, it is admirable when a police officer can mobilize a neighborhood in ways that deal effectively with the problem. But what if the same organizational structure is subsequently used to lobby against a half-way house for the mentally ill, or is used to prevent a minority businessman from moving into the neighborhood, or is used to endorse candidates for public office?" Goldstein, "Toward Community-Oriented Policing," 22.
Goldstein's concerns are more than hypothetical. In 1986, the police union used Los Angeles' neighborhood watch program to push for a recall election to remove liberal judges on the California Supreme Court. Mike Davis, *Ecology of Fear: Los Angeles and the Imagination of Disaster* (New York: Vintage Books, 1998), 390.

70 Michael E. Buerger and Lorraine Green Mazerolle, "Third-Party Policing: Theoretical Aspects of an Emerging Trend," Kappeler, *Police and Society*, 420.

71 In Los Angeles, prosecutors have used civil abatement laws to require landlords to remove graffiti every day and to erect fencing around their property, install lighting, tow abandoned cars, trim shrubbery, and evict tenants suspected of drug dealing. At the same time, police increase their patrols in the area.
L.A. City Attorney Gang Prosecution Section, "Civil Gang Abatement: A Community Based Tool of the Office of the Los Angeles City Attorney," *The Modern Gang Reader*, ed. Jody Miller et al. (Los Angeles: Roxbury Publishing Company, 2001), 325.

72 The dangers of allowing the state to co-opt community institutions, especially those of oppressed minorities, should be clear enough. But in case they're not, history has provided a particularly chilling example:
"Whenever the extermination process was put into effect, the Germans utilized the *existing leadership and organizations* of the Jewish community to assist them. . . . In the face of the German determination to murder all Jews, most Jews instinctively relied on their own communal organizations to defend their interests wherever possible. Unfortunately, these very organizations were transformed into subsidiaries of the German police and state bureaucracies. . . . Thus, the official agency of German Jews . . . undertook such tasks as selecting those who were to be deported, notifying the families and, finally, of sending the Jewish police to round up the victims." Richard L. Rubenstein, *The Cunning of History: The Holocaust and the American Future* (New York: Harper Torchbooks, 1978), 72 and 74. Emphasis in original.
See also: Hannah Arendt, *Eichmann in Jerusalem: A Report on the Banality of Evil* (Middlesex, England: Penguin Books, 1964) 117-25.

73 Community Policing Consortium, "Understanding Community Policing," 13.

Elsewhere, the report reads, "A concrete indication of community policing's success is the commitment of an increased level of community resources devoted to crime reduction efforts." Community Policing Consortium, "Understanding Community Policing," 47.

74 Quoted in Center for Research on Criminal Justice, *Iron Fist*, 64.

75 The Community Policing Consortium endorses this interpretation: "Community policing is democracy in action. It requires the active participation of local government, civic and business leaders, public and private agencies, residents, churches, schools, and hospitals. All who share a concern for the welfare of the neighborhood should bear responsibility for safeguarding that welfare." Community Policing Consortium, "Understanding Community Policing," 4.

76 Goldstein, for example, acknowledges that community policing opens questions about the limits of the police function, officer discretion, accountability, the means available for problem solving, and the role of the community. But, he notes: "Questions about the degree of community involvement in determining the policies of police agencies are not as open-ended as previous questions raised. Experience has taught us that, in carrying out some aspects of their functions, the police must be insulated from community influences. Some of their decision-making authority cannot be shared. . . . The standards of a neighborhood cannot be substituted for the rules of the state." Goldstein, "Toward Community-Oriented Policing," 25.

77 A discussion of corporatism appears in chapter 6.

The Iron Fist and the Velvet Glove compares "citizen participation" in policing to "worker participation" in management. Neither involve a real transfer of power. Center for Research on Criminal Justice, *Iron Fist*, 59.

78 Quoted in Skolnick and Bayley, *New Blue Line*, 30.

79 Martin J. Smith, *Pressure, Power and Policy: State Autonomy and Policy Networks in Britain and the United States* (Pittsburgh: University of Pittsburgh Press, 1993), 68.

Smith also writes: "Policy is developed through negotiations and any groups involved in the process can assist in implementation. The state agency is able to achieve its goals through the incorporation of the pressure group. Policy networks are a means of extending the infrastructural power of society by establishing mechanisms for negotiation which allow greater intervention in civil society." Smith, *Pressure, Power and Policy*, 53–4.

80 In their discussion of Detroit's community policing experiments, Skolnick and Bayley write, "Because the mini-stations organize people, they develop considerable political clout. . . . Not only do they help give voice to the security concerns of local residents, but they assist in representing communities before various public and private authorities, such as zoning boards, developers, and the sanitation and public works departments. As a result, mini-station officers develop the kind of grassroots connections politicians labor over." Skolnick and Bayley, *New Blue Line*, 71–2.

81 As we saw in chapter 6, this kind of relationship has allowed for a level of cohesion and cooperation between local governments, police departments, and police unions, even as they wage a three-way struggle for control.

82 Independent Commission on the Los Angeles Police Department [The Christopher Commission], *Report of the Independent Commission on the Los Angeles Police Department* (July 9, 1991), 102–3.

83 Christopher Commission, *Report*, 103.

Comparisons to military occupation are not wholly rhetorical. I witnessed an operation similar to Cul-de-Sac in the Logan Circle neighborhood of Washington, D.C., during the winter of 1998. National Guard troops blocked off my street with humvees. They stood in clusters at each end of the block, wearing helmets and bulletproof vests, and turning away traffic. At night they used generators to power enormous flood lights, under which the street appeared brighter than it did during the day.

A friend who lived a few blocks over reported a similar occurrence on his street some weeks earlier. He asked one of the soldiers what they were doing. The soldier replied, "Preventing crime."

And it was true. Rhode Island Avenue between Logan Circle and 13th Street was and probably is a popular spot for illicit exchanges of various kinds. During the occupation (as I thought of it), all apparent drug activity ceased. But so did practically everything else. On a typical day, even in the winter, the street would be the site of children playing, couples out for evening strolls, people walking their dogs, sitting on their front stoop, washing cars in the parking lot on the corner, and otherwise just hanging out. The National Guard put an end to all that. For a few days, the noise of cars, music, and simple human conversation was replaced with the sterile hum of an electric generator. But after a few nights, the soldiers left—moving on, surely, to someone else's neighborhood—and life returned to normal, or what passes for normal in the colony that serves as the seat of our government.

84 Goldstein writes: "Officers are frequently expected not only to respond to the full range of problems that the public expects the police to handle . . . but also to take the initiative to identify whatever community problems—beyond those within the widest definition of the police functioning—that may affect the public's sense of well-being." Goldstein, "Toward Community-Oriented Policing," 9.

A more direct statement might read: Community policing encourages the police to over-reach their authority, to look for opportunities to insert themselves into community life, and to expand the police function.

85 DeMichele and Kraska, "Commmunity Policing in Batlle Garb," 86-7. Parentheses in original.

86 Parenti, *Lockdown America*, 102.

87 Kappeler, "Reinventing the Police," 484.

88 Skolnick and Bayley, *New Blue Line*, 40.

89 Skolnick and Bayley, *New Blue Line*, 39.

90 William Wilberforce, an eighteenth-century reformer and friend to Jeremy Bentham, wrote in 1787: "[T]he most effectual way of preventing the greater crimes is punishing the smaller, and endeavoring to repress that general spirit of licentiousness which is the parent of every species of vice." Quoted in Elaine A. Reynolds, *Before the Bobbies: The Night Watch and Police Reform in Metrolpolitan London, 1720–1830* (Stanford, California: Stanford University Press, 1998), 71.

91 James Q. Wilson and George L. Kelling, "Broken Windows," *Atlantic Monthly*, March 1982, 29–38.

92 Wilson and Kelling, "Broken Windows," 31-2.

93 The Community Policing Consortium provides some specifics: "Ridding the streets of gangs, drunks, panhandlers, and prostitutes—perhaps with the help of public and private social agencies—will enhance the quality of life. Removing signs of neglect (e.g., abandoned cars, derelict buildings, and garbage and debris) will offer tangible evidence that community policing efforts are working to bring about increased order in the community." Community Policing Consortium, "Understanding Community Policing," 47. Parentheses in original.

94 And sometimes explicit: "A busy, bustling shopping center and a quiet, well-tended suburb may need almost no visible police presence. In both cases, the ratio of respectable to disreputable people is ordinarily so high as to make informal social control effective." Wilson and Kelling, "Broken Windows," 36.

95 Broken Windows theorists point to New York's statistical drop in crime during the 1990s as the empirical evidence. See, for example: William Bratton (with Peter Knobler), *Turnaround: How America's Top Cop Reversed the Crime Epidemic* (New York: Random House, 1998), 259, 289–90, and 294–5.

   There are several related problems with this argument. First, it should be remembered that crime is a complex phenomenon; its prevalence or decline is likely the result of multiple (and often, poorly-understood) factors. For a brief overview, see: James Lardner, "Can You Believe the New York Miracle?" *New York Review of Books* (August 14, 1997).

   Second, crime is notoriously difficult to measure. Third, available statistics are subject to misinterpretation and manipulation. Fourth, a managerial system that rewards "good stats" (and punishes "bad") builds in an incentive for intentionally distorting the figures. (Officials in both the NYPD and the New York Transit Police were forced to retire after they were caught skewing their numbers to fabricate drops in the crime rate.) And finally, the most reliable statistics available—those based on crime victim surveys—showed no change in the crime rate during Giuliani's reign. See: Parenti, *Lockdown America*, 83; Sidney L. Harring and Gerda W. Ray, "Policing a Class Society: New York City in the 1990s," *Social Justice* (Summer 1999) 69–71; and William J. Chambliss, *Power, Politics, and Crime* (Boulder, Colorado: Westview Press, 1999) 43.

96 There is, in fact, empirical evidence to support the idea that improved welfare services help reduce crime. See: Elliott Currie, *Crime and Punishment in America* (New York: Metropolitan Books, 1998).

97 Klockars, "Rhetoric of Community Policing," 428.

98 This gets to the core of what is wrong with Wilson and Kelling's view, ethically speaking. They don't take rights or justice seriously. For instance: "Arresting a single drunk or single vagrant who has harmed no identifiable person seems unjust, and in a sense it is. But failing to do anything about a score of drunks or a hundred vagrants may destroy an entire neighborhood." Wilson and Kelling, "Broken Windows," 35.

99 Skolnick and Bayley, *New Blue Line*, 160-3 and 167-70.

100 Skolnick and Bayley, *New Blue Line*, 175 and 178.

   Noting the NAACP's complaints, Skolnick and Bayley recommend that the police there engage in Santa Ana-style community organizing to reduce the friction.

101 Skolnick and Bayley, *New Blue Line*, 135-7.

102 Skolnick and Bayley, *New Blue Line*, 138-9.

103 Skolnick and Bayley, *New Blue Line*, 40.

104 See chapters 3 and 5.

105 Wilson and Kelling, "Broken Windows," 33.

106 Samuel Walker, "'Broken Windows' and Fractured History," *Policing Perspectives: An Anthology*, ed. Larry K. Gaines and Gary W. Cordner (Los Angeles: Roxbury Publishing Company, 1999) 110.

   Walker goes on to explain, quite rightly, that Wilson and Kelling exaggerate the depersonalization of policing in the twentieth century, over-state the cops' focus on crime control, ignore the controversy that has always surrounded the police, and idealize the nineteenth-century patrolman. Walker "'Broken Windows' and Fractured History," 117.

107 "The soldier boy for his soldier's pay obeys/the sergeant at arms, whatever he says./The sergeant will for his sergeant's pay obey/the captain till his dying day./The captain will for his captain's pay obey/the general order of battle play./The generals bow to the government, obey/the charge, You must not relent." The Clash, "Inoculated City," *Combat Rock* (New York: Epic, 1982).

108 Parenti, *Lockdown America*, 107.

109 Bratton asks rhetorically, "Why 'Glazier?' How do you fix a broken window?" Bratton, *Turnaround*, 159.

110 Bratton, *Turnaround*, 159 and 161.

111 Parenti, *Lockdown America*, 74.

112 Bratton, *Turnaround*, 173-4.

113 Quoted in Bratton, *Turnaround*, 177.

114 Bratton, *Turnaround*, 228.

115 Bratton called the squeegee workers "a living symbol of what was wrong with the city." Bratton, *Turnaround*, 212.

116 Bratton, *Turnaround*, 213-4.

117 Parenti, *Lockdown America*, 77.

Bratton's overhaul of the Transit Police had prepared him well for such one-sided class warfare. Because of his work with the transit cops, hundreds of homeless people—people who out of desperation sought refuge in the dark, wet, rat-infested subways tunnels—were driven out, onto the street, into the cold. Parenti, *Lockdown America*, 74.

118 Bratton reasoned that "if you stop kids who aren't in school, you're probably stopping kids who are no good." Quoted in Parenti, *Lockdown America*, 77.

He must have decided that the kids in school weren't much good either, since he also tripled the number of cops patrolling the public schools. Parenti, *Lockdown America*, 78.

119 Parenti, *Lockdown America*, 77-9 and 103-108.

120 Human Rights Watch, *Shielded From Justice*, 39.

121 Parenti, *Lockdown America*, 79.

122 Quoted in Human Rights Watch, *Shielded From Justice*, 373-4.

123 Parenti, *Lockdown America*, 85.

124 One witness described the situation: "[H]e was just sitting there. . . . The officers were in his face, speaking badly to him. I came back a minute later, and there were so many police cars, I thought it was a bank robbery." Quoted in Amnesty International, "United States of America; Rights for All; Race, Rights and Police Brutality" (London: Amnesty International, September 1999), 17.

125 "200 Protest Sit-Lie Rule," *Portland (Oregon) Tribune*, September 20, 2002, A6; and Chris Lydgate and Cheryl Revell, "St. Francis Showdown," *Willamette Week*, November 6, 2002, 11.

126 Megan Garvey, "Bratton is Planning a Clean Start: The Police Chief, Who Will be Sworn in Today, Sees Fighting Graffiti as Key to Reducing Crime," *Los Angeles Times*, October 25, 2002, A1.

Bratton explained police plans to round up homeless people with a comparison to his earlier anti-squeegee campaign: "The squeegee pests were symbols of fear and lack of police control and disorder. . . . The equivalent in downtown [L.A.] is begging. Some of it's benign. But it raises the degree of discomfort for the average person." Quoted in Richard Winston and Kristina Saverwein, "LAPD Tests New Police Strategy," *Los Angeles Times*, February 2, 2003, B10.

Meanwhile, Bratton also called for an "all-out assault" against gangs, describing gang activity as "homeland terrorism." Quoted in Celeste Fremon, "View From Parker Center: A One-on-One with Police Chief Bill Bratton," *LA Weekly*, January 10, 2003-January 16, 2003, www.laweekly.com/ink/03/08/news-fremon.php (accessed January 15, 2003).

127 Quoted in Kraska and Kappeler, "Militarizing American Police," 472.

128 See for example: DeMichele and Kraska, "Commmunity Policing in Batlle Garb," 89; Kraska and Kappeler, "Militarizing American Police,"469-70 and 472-3; and Parenti, *Lockdown America*, 87.

129 For example, Lt. Greg Cooper, the Area Commander of Area A in Santa Ana was responsible for overseeing the greatest successes of the community policing program there while also serving as the head of the SWAT team. Skolnick and Bayley, *New Blue Line*, 30.

Attorney Paul Richmond notes a transfer of personnel from community policing assignments to paramilitary units, usually accompanied by promotions. Paul Richmond, untitled lecture (Portland, Oregon: Liberty Hall, August 26, 2002).

130 Kraska and Kappeler, "Militarizing American Police," 470; and Parenti, *Lockdown America*, 85.

131 Quoted in Spencer S. Hsu, "D.C. Forms Network of Surveillance: Police System of Hundreds of Video Links Raises Issues of Rights, Privacy," *Washington Post*, February 17, 2002, B6.

132 The use of cameras to monitor protests worries City Councilmember Jim Graham: "These cameras have been set up to deal with demonstrations and dissent. This will have a chilling effect and discourage citizens from demonstrating openly here in the capital of the United Sates of America." Quoted in David A. Fahrenthold and David Nakamura, "Council Attacks DC Surveillance Cameras," *Washington Post*, November 8, 2002, (database: NewsBank Full-Text Newspapers, accessed May 20, 2003).

133 Kraska and Kappeler, "Militarizing American Police," 472.

134 For instance, Sergeant John Dough of the Newark Police Department described the organizational demands presented by street sweeps: "One of the underlying features of this whole activity is operating as a unit, rather than as individual action. As a unit, you have to have a game plan and report your method of operations beforehand." Quoted in Skolnick and Bayley, *New Blue Line*, 198.

135 Mark J. Osiel, *Obeying Orders: Atrocity, Military Discipline, and the Law of War* (New Brunswick: Transaction Publications, 2002), 212 and 220.

136 Osiel, *Obeying Orders*, 243–4. Parentheses in original.

137 Colonel Kenneth Estes writes in *The Marine Officer's Guide*: "The best discipline is self-discipline. To be really well-disciplined, a unit must be made up of individuals who are self-disciplined." Quoted in Osiel, *Obeying Orders*, 211.

In the community policing context, "Each officer had to be imbued with the department's values so that they could translate them into the reality of life in the unpredictable situations that would be encountered. Management's job was not to make choices for officers; it was to instruct officers about what was expected of them in all situations." Skolnick and Bayley, *New Blue Line*, 85.

138 "Circus dogs jump when the trainer cracks his whip, but the really well-trained dog is the one that turns his somersault when there is no whip." George Orwell, "As I Please" [Tribune (January 7, 1944)] *The Collected Essays, Journalism and Letters of George Orwell*, Volume III: *As I Please, 1943–1945*, eds. Sonia Orwell and Ian Angus (New York: Harcourt, Brace & World, Inc., 1968), 181.

139 Bratton, *Turnaround*, 233-4.

140 Quoted in Bratton, *Turnaround*, 238.

141 Bratton, *Turnaround*, 239.

Parenti reads one further step into the process: "[C]aptains lean on lieutenants, who lean on sergeants, who lean on beat cops, who, it could be said, lean on civilians." Parenti, *Lockdown America*, 76.

142 Skolnick and Bayley, *New Blue Line*, 217–220; and Cordner, "Elements of Community Policing," 144.

143 Skolnick and Bayley, *New Blue Line*, 218.

144 Ibid.

145 National Advisory Commission on Civil Disorders [The Kerner Commission], *Reportof the National Advisory Commission on Civil Disorders* (New York: E.P. Dutton and Company, 1968), 328.

146 The well-titled book *The Iron Fist and the Velvet Glove* was among the first to observe this relationship. "In addition to the rise of new, sophisticated technologies, another striking development in the U.S. police apparatus during the sixties was the growth of new strategies of community penetration and 'citizen participation' that sought to integrate people in the process of policing and to secure the legitimacy of the police system itself. . . . On the other side of the coin, the police have developed a variety of new 'tough' specialized units—special anti-riot and tactical patrol forces, 'special weapons' teams, and highly sophisticated intelligence units." Center for Research on Criminal Justice, *Iron Fist*, 7.

Also: Center for Research on Criminal Justice, *Iron Fist*, 30.

147 See, for example: Frank Kitson, *Low Intensity Operations: Subversion, Insurgency, Peace-Keeping* (Hamden, Connecticut: Archon Books, 1971) 67.

Kitson's work is discussed in greater detail in chapter 7.

148 Kitson, *Low Intensity Operations*, 129.

For a description of a similar structure applied to Santa Ana's block captain program, see: Skolnick and Bayley, *New Blue Line*, 28.

149 Quoted in Jennifer Anderson, "Cops Jab at Drugs, One Bust at a Time," *Portland Tribune*, December 17, 2002, A3.

The raid documented by the *Tribune* resulted in three arrests, all for misdemeanors. By the cops' own admission, such raids rarely result in jail time. Rather, the most common consequence is eviction, leading to homelessness. Anderson, "Cops Jab at Drgs," A1, A3.

150 Gates, *Chief*, 109.

151 Goldstein, "Toward Community-Oriented Policing," 12.

152 "Apparently, some police agencies are integrating a military-model approach—occupy, suppress through force, and restore the affected territory—with community policing ideology, which emphasizes taking back the neighborhood, creating a climate of order, and enacting preventive and partnership strategies. Again, New York City's style of zero-tolerance community policing is the best-known example." DeMichele and Kraska, "Commmunity Policing in Batlle Garb," 96.

See also: DeMichele and Kraska, "Commmunity Policing in Batlle Garb," 87–8.

153 This strategy can sometimes be used to divide communities that have traditionally been a source of resistance against the police. For instance, "measures that target young people are frequently cloaked in the notion that 'good citizens' must 'take back' and 'reclaim' their communities from the lawless elements that have been permitted to run amok. Increasing schisms of generation and class within communities of color demarcate the boundaries between the 'good guys' and the 'bad guys.'" Daniel HoSang, "The Economics of the New Brutality," *Colorlines* (Winter 1999-2000), 25.

154 Quoted in Martín Sánchez Jankowski, *Islands in the Street: Gangs and American Urban Society* (Berkeley: University of California Press, 1991), 256.

155 Kitson advises: "In practical terms the most promising line of approach lies in separating the mass of those engaged in the campaign from the leadership by the judicious promise of concessions, at the same time imposing a period of calm by the use of government forces. . . . Having once succeeded in providing a breathing space by these means, it is most important to do three further things quickly. The first is to implement the promised concessions so as to avoid allegations of bad faith which may enable the subversive leadership to regain control over certain sections of the people. The second is to discover and neutralize the genuine subversive element. The third is to associate as many prominent members of the popu-

lation, especially those who have been engaged in non-violent action, with the government. This last technique is known in America as co-optation." Kitson, *Low Intensity Operations*, 87.

156 "Because insurgency is bred in a climate of social malaise, U.S.-backed counterinsurgency campaigns must seek to neutralize public disaffection areas through social, political, and economic initiatives aimed at 'winning hearts and minds' for the prevailing regime."

Michael T. Klare, "The Interventionist Impulse: U.S. Military Doctrine for Low-Intensity Warfare," *Low-Intensity Warfare: Counterinsurgency, Proinsurgency, and Antiterrorism in the Eighties*, ed. Michael T. Klare and Peter Kornbluh (New York: Pantheon Books, 1988), 75.

157 Quoted in Bratton, *Turnaround*, 274.

Political rivalry between Bratton and Giuliani prevented Operation Juggernaut's implementation, though a much more modest, localized version was tried in North Brooklyn. Bratton, *Turnaround*, 278 and 296.

158 Quoted in Kraska and Kappeler, "Militarizing American Police," 473.

159 Thomas A. Marks, "Northern Ireland and Urban America on the Eve of the 21st Century," *Global Dimensions of High Intensity Crime and Low Intensity Conflict*, ed. Graham H. Turbiville, Jr. (Chicago: Office of International Criminal Justice, University of Illinois at Chicago, 1995), 76.

160 Allan Silver, "The Demand for Order in Civil Society: A Review of Some Themes in the History of Urban Crime, Police, and Riot," *The Police: Six Sociological Essays*, ed. David J. Bordua (New York: John Wiley and Sons, 1976), 8.

Afterword: Making Police Obsolete

1 Noam Chomsky, "The Manufacture of Consent," in *The Chomsky Reader*, ed. James Peck (New York: Pantheon Books, 1987), 126.

2 It is worth remembering that other sources—hip-hop albums and anarchist newspapers, for instance—do not share this assumption. To cite an example of the former, better written than most, but not unusual in its sentiment: "Five-O was outside waitin' with their vans/hopin' that shit would get out of hand/ so dat they could test their weapons/on innocent civilians,/the high tech shit costin' millions and millions/money should've spent somethin' for community/but that's O.K. 'cause we got the unity./So fuck the police! We can keep the peace!" Spearhead, "Piece 'o Peace" *Home* (Hollywood: Capitol Records, 1994).

For examples from anarchist papers, see: "Why a No Pig Zone" and "Kicking the Cops Out and Keeping Them Out," in *Profane Existence: Making Punk a Threat Again!—The Best Cuts, 1989–1993* (Minneapolis: Profane Existence, 1997), 54–55 and 73.

3 Rodney Stark, *Police Riots: Collective Violence and Law Enforcement* (Belmont, California: Focus Books, 1972), 1.

4 Carl B. Klockars, "The Rhetoric of Community Policing," in *The Police and Society: Touchstone Readings*, ed. Victor E. Kappeler (Prospect Heights, Illinois: Waveland Press, Inc., 1999), 428.

5 I am familiar with three exceptions: Center For Research on Criminal Justice, *The Iron Fist and the Velvet Glove: An Analysis of the U.S. Police* (Berkeley, California: Center for Research on Criminal Justice, 1975); Daniel Nina, "Popular Justice and the 'Appropriation' of the State Monopoly on the Definition of Justice and Order: The Case of the Anti-Crime Committees in Port Elizabeth," in *The Other Law: Non-State Ordering in South Africa*, eds. Wilfried Schärf and Daniel Nina (Lundsdowne: JUTA Law, 2001); and Dennis R. Longmire, "A Popular Justice System: A Radical Alternative to the Traditional Criminal Justice System," *Contemporary Crises* 5 (1981).

Longmire proposes pragmatic alternatives to police, courts, and prisons. His recommendations are as remarkable for their simplicity as for their radicalism.

6 For more on this point, see: George Orwell, "Thoughts on James Burnham," in *Shooting an Elephant and Other Essays* (New York: Harcourt, Brace & World, Inc., 1950), 122–48.

7 "The repressive police institution, so necessary for the maintenance of capitalism, simply could not perform any social functions at all without its legitimating crime-fighting role." Sidney L. Harring, *Policing a Class Society: The Experience of American Cities, 1865–1915* (New Brunswick, New Jersey: Rutgers University Press, 1983), 246.

Put differently—"The threat of crime, as evidenced by the myriad constructed images and narratives projected . . . serves only as the pretext for the installation of a growing and increasingly complex enterprise of social control." Victor E. Kappeler and Peter B. Kraska, "A Textual Critique of Community Policing: Police Adaption to High Modernity," *Policing: An International Journal of Police Strategies & Management* 21:2 (1998): 293.

8 My criticisms of community policing appear in chapter 9.

9 Nikolas Rose, "Government and Control," *British Journal of Criminology* 40:2 (2000): 329.

David E. Pearson argues along similar lines: "To earn the appellation 'community,' it seems to me, groups must be able to exert moral suasion and extract a measure of compliance from their members. That is, communities are necessarily—indeed, by definition—coercive as well as moral, threatening their members with the stick of sanctions if they stray, offering them the carrot of certainty and stability if they don't." David E. Pearson, "Community and Sociology," *Society* 32:5 (July–August 1995) (database: Academic Search Elite, accessed March 26, 2003).

10 Amatai Etioni, *The New Golden Rule: Community and Morality in a Democratic Society* (New York: Basic Books, 1996), 127.

11 Carl Klockars puts the point more forcefully: "Sociologically, the concept of community implies a group of people with a common history, common beliefs and understandings, a sense of themselves as 'us' and outsiders as 'them', and often, but not always, a shared territory. Relationships of community are different from relationships of society. Community relationships are based upon status not contract, manners not morals, norms not laws, understandings not regulations. Nothing, in fact, is more different from community than those relationships that characterize most of modern urban life." Klockars, "Rhetoric," 435.

12 Klockars, "Rhetoric," 435.

13 For a discussion of gang suppression activities and their impact of minority communities, see: Felix M. Padilla, *Gangs as an American Enterprise* (New Brunswick, New Jersey: Rutgers University Press, 1992), 85; and Randall G. Sheldon et al., *Youth Gangs in American Society* (Belmont, California: Wadsworth, 2001), 244.

   For an account of gangs' efforts to protect their neighborhoods from street crime, loan sharks, slum lords, price gouging, gentrification, and police brutality, see: Martín Sánchez Jankowski, *Islands in the Street: Gangs and American Urban Society* (Berkeley: University of California Press, 1991), 11–12 and 179–92.

   These under-reported aspects of gang life, and the political potential they suggest, may help to explain why the LAPD actively sought to disrupt the gang truces negotiated after the 1992 riots. See: Malcolm W. Klein, *The American Street Gang: Its Nature, Prevalence, and Control* (New York: Oxford University Press, 1995), 165; and "Bloods/Crips Proposal for LA's Face-Lift," in *Why LA Happened: Implications of the '92 Los Angeles Rebellion*, ed. Haki Madhubuti (Chicago: Third World Press, 1993), 274–82.

   Mike Davis describes the government's response to the riots and its efforts to keep the gangs at war with one another in terms of counter-insurgency: "In Los Angeles I think we are beginning to see a repressive context that is literally comparable to Belfast or the West Bank, where policing has been transformed into full-scale counterinsurgency (or 'low-intensity warfare,' as the military likes to call it) against an entire social stratum or ethnic group." Mike Davis, "L.A.: The Fire This Time," *CovertAction Information Bulletin* 41 (Summer 1992): 18.

14 Raymond J. Michalowski, "Crime Control in the 1980s: A Progressive Agenda," *Crime and Social Justice* 19 (Summer 1983): 18.

   Michalowski seems to overlook the most radical possibilities suggested by his analysis. He recommends that popular justice organizations operate parallel to, and with the assistance of, the existing police. Michalowski, "Crime Control," 19.

15 See chapter 5.

16 Pennsylvanian State Federation of Labor, *The American Cossack* (New York: Arno Press & The New York Times, 1971); Bruce Smith, *Rural Crime Control* (New York: Institute of Public Administration, 1933), 175; and Bruce Smith, *The State Police: Organization and Administration* (New York: The Macmillan Company, 1925), 62.

17 Jeremy Brecher, *Strike!* (Boston: South End Press, 1972), 107–8; and Howard Zinn, *A People's History of the United States, 1492–Present* (New York: HarperPerrenial, 1995), 368.

18 Quoted in Brecher, *Strike!* 109.

19 Brecher, *Strike!* 112–13; and Zinn, *People's History*, 369–70.

20 Quoted in Brecher, *Strike!* 111.

21 Brecher, *Strike!* 111 and 113; and Zinn, *People's History*, 369–70.

22 Brecher, *Strike!* 111; and Zinn, *People's History*, 369.

   Such good order—in the absence of police—also accompanied the Hungarian revolt of 1956 and the Havana General Strike of 1959. Colin Ward, *Anarchy in Action* (London: Freedom Press, 1988), 33–34.

23 Williams describes the first such encounter, in the summer of 1957: "[W]e shot up an armed motorcade of the Ku Klux Klan, *including two police cars*, which had come to attack the home of Dr. Albert E. Perry, vice-president of the Monroe Chapter of the National Association for the Advancement of Colored People." Robert F. Williams, *Negroes with Guns*, ed. Marc Schleifer (Chicago: Third World Press, 1973), 39. Emphasis in original.

   Faced with armed resistance, the Klan beat a hasty retreat, and the raids in Monroe ceased. Timothy Tyson, *Radio Free Dixie: Robert F. Williams & the Roots of Black Power* (Chapel Hill: The University of North Carolina Press, 1999), 88; and Williams, *Negroes with Guns*, 57.

24 Charles R. Sims (and William A. Price), "Armed Defense [Interview]," in *Black Protest: 350 Years of History, Documents, and Analyses*, ed. Joanne Grant (New York: Fawcett Columbine, 1968), 336–344.

   For a description of a similar organization, see: Harold A. Nelson, "The Defenders: A Case Study of an Informal Police Organization," *Social Problems* (Fall 1967): 127–47. In addition to protecting civil rights workers and guarding against police brutality, the Defenders also reprimanded members of the Black community who became a nuisance to their neighbors.

25 Bobby Seale, *Seize the Time: The Story of the Black Panther Party and Huey P. Newton* (New York: Random House, 1970), 93.

26 Huey P. Newton, "A Citizen's Peace Force," *Crime and Social Justice: A Journal of Radical Criminology* 1 (Spring–Summer 1974): 30–31; and Henry Hampton, et al., *Voices of Freedom: An Oral History of the Civil Rights Movement from the 1950s Thorough the 1980s* (New York: Bantam Books, 1990), 356–57.

27 Bobby Seale, "Bobby Seale Explains Panther Politics: An Interview," in *The Black Panthers Speak,* ed. Philip S. Foner (New York: De Capo Press, 1995), 86.

28 Seale, *Sieze the Time,* 412–18; and Seale, "Bobby Seale," 85.

Huey Newton identified the principle of self defense as the common theme running through all the programs. "What never became clear to the public, largely because it was always de-emphasized in the media, was that the armed self-defense program of the Party was just one form of what Party leaders viewed as self-defense against oppression. The Party had always urged self-defense against poor medical care, unemployment, slum housing, under-representation in the political process, and other social ills that poor and oppressed people suffer. The Panther means for implementing its concept of self-defense was its various survival programs. Huey P. Newton, *War Against the Panthers: A Study of Repression in America,* Phd. diss, University od California, Santa Cruz, 1980 (New York: Harlem River Press, 1996), 34.

29 Newton, *War Against the Panthers,* 35.

30 Jerome H. Skolnick, "The Berkeley Scheme: Neighborhood Police," *The Nation,* March 22, 1971, 372–73; Center For Research on Criminal Justice, *Iron Fist,* 152; Seale, *Sieze the Time,* 420–21; and, Robert M. Fogelson, *Big-City Police* (Cambridge, Massachusetts: Harvard University Press, 1977), 296.

31 Skolnick, "Berkeley Scheme," 373.

32 Center For Research on Criminal Justice, *Iron Fist,* 152; Fogelson, *Big-City Police,* 300.

33 Flores Alexander Forbes, "Point No. 7: We Want an Immediate End to Police Brutality and the Murder of Black People; Why I Joined the Black Panther Party," in *Police Brutality: An Anthology,* ed. Jill Nelson (New York: W.W. Norton & Company, 2000), 237.

The FBI put the numbers somewhat lower. In a secret report that same year, they warned President Nixon, "a recent poll indicates that approximately 25 percent of the black population has a great respect for the Black Panther Party, including 43 percent of blacks under 21 years of age." Quoted in Zinn, *People's History,* 455.

34 See: Mitchell Goodman, ed., *The Movement Toward a New America: The Beginnings of a Long Revolution* (Philadelphia: Pilgrim Press, 1970), 234–44 and 546–48.

35 Quoted in Frank Donner, *Protectors of Privilege: Red Squads and Police Repression in Urban America* (Berkeley: University of California Press, 1990), 180.

36 The repression of the BPP is detailed elsewhere in this book, especially in chapters 4 and 7.

37 Jeremy Brecher argues that the limited ambitions of the strike directly created the conditions for its defeat. Brecher, *Strike!* 112.

38 These are not, by any means, the only examples available. Ultimately all popular movements, once they develop beyond a certain point, experience conflict with the police. I have chosen here to focus on South Africa and Northern Ireland for two reasons: first, these cases are reasonably well-documented; and second, I expect that an American audience will be somewhat familiar with the politics involved.

For other examples, see: Udo Reifner, "Individualistic and Collective Legalization: The Theory and Practice of Legal Advice for Workers in Prefascist Germany," in *The Politics of Informal Justice, Volume 2: Comparative Studies,* ed. Richard L. Abel (New York: Academic Press, 1982), 81–123;

Jack Spence, "Institutionalizing Neighborhood Courts: Two Chilean Experiences," in *The Politics of Informal Justice, Volume 2: Comparative Studies,* ed. Richard L. Abel (New York: Academic Press, 1982), 215–49; Boaventura de Sousa Santos, "Law and Revolution in Portugal: The Experiences of Popular Justice After the 25th of April 1974," in *The Politics of Informal Justice, Volume 2: Comparative Studies,* ed. Richard L. Abel (New York: Academic Press, 1982), 251–80; and Barbara Isaacman and Allen Isaacman, "A Socialist Legal System in the Making: Mozambique Before and After Independence," in *The Politics of Informal Justice, Volume 2: Comparative Studies,* ed. Richard L. Abel (New York: Academic Press, 1982), 281–323.

39 Frank Kitson, *Low Intensity Operations: Subversion, Insurgency, Peace-Keeping* (Hamden, Connecticut: Archon Books, 1971), 32.

40 Wilfried Schärf, "Policy Options in Community Justice," in *The Other Law: Non-State Ordering in South Africa,* eds. Wilfried Schärf and Daniel Nina (Lundsdowne: JUTA Law, 2001), 45.

41 Quoted in Nelson Mandela, "Outlaw in My Own Land: Letter by Nelson Mandela, Released June 26, 1961, From Underground Headquarters" in *The End of Apartheid in South Africa* [by Lindsay Michie Eades] (Westport, Connecticut: Greenwood Press, 1999), 163.

42 Rebekah Lee and Jeremy Seekings, "Vigilantism and Popular Justice After Apartheid," in *Informal Criminal Justice,* ed. Dermot Feenan (Aldershot, England: Ashgate/Dartmouth, 2002), 99; Jeremy Seekings, "Social Ordering and Control in the African Townships of South Africa: An Historical Overview of Extra-State Initiatives from the 1940s to the 1990s," in *The Other Law: Non-State Ordering in South Africa,* eds. Wilfried Schärf and Daniel Nina (Lundsdowne: JUTA Law, 2001), 71; and Monique Marks and Penny McKenzie, "Alternative Policing Structures? A Look at Youth Defense Structures in Gauteng," in *The Other Law: Non-State Ordering in South Africa,* eds. Wilfried Schärf and Daniel Nina (Lundsdowne: JUTA Law, 2001), 188.

43 Andries Mphoto Mangokwana, "*Makgotla* in Rural and Urban Contexts," in *The Other Law: Non-State Ordering in South Africa,* eds. Wilfried Schärf and Daniel Nina (Lundsdowne: JUTA Law, 2001), 148–66; Seekings, "Social Ordering and Control," 81–85 and 89–90; Lee and Seekings, "Vigilantism and Popular Justice," 100 and 105–7; Schärf, "Policy Options," 47 and 52; and Daniel Nina and Wilfried Schärf, "Introduction: The Other Law?" in *The Other Law: Non-State Ordering in South Africa,* eds. Wilfried Schärf and Daniel Nina (Lundsdowne: JUTA Law, 2001), 7.

44 Lee and Seekings, "Vigilantism and Popular Justice," 103.

45 One of the harshest practices associated with Street Committees was that of "necklacing." Usually reserved for apartheid-era informers, collaborators, and political opponents, necklacing involved placing a gas-soaked tire around a suspect's neck and setting it on fire. Lindsay Michie Eades, "Second Submission of the ANC to the Truth and Reconciliation Commission, May 1997," in *The End of Apartheid in South Africa* (Westport, Connecticut: Greenwood Press, 1999), 184; and Anthony Minnaar, "The 'New' Vigilantism in Post–April 1994 South Africa," in Feenan, *Informal Criminal Justice,* 118 and 132.

46 Lee and Seekings, "Vigilantism and Popular Justice," 102; and Schärf, "Policy Options," 46.

    Here is a general definition: "Restorative Justice is an approach to dealing with the harms created by crime which views such problems as a breakdown in relationships and seeks to repair those relationships. . . . It seeks to replace the traditional focus of retributive justice on the punishment of the offender . . . with an approach which seeks to heal the injuries caused by crime to all the parties involved." Jim Auld et al., "Our Practice: The Blue Book [Designing a System of Restorative Community Justice in Northern Ireland]," http://www.restorativejusticeireland.org/ourpractice.html (accessed November 20, 2002), 1.2.

47 Lee and Seekings, "Vigilantism and Popular Justice," 100; and Minnaar, "'New' Vigilantism," 119.

48 Quoted in Lee and Seekings, "Vigilantism and Popular Justice," 103–5.

49 Schärf, "Policy Options," 49.

50 Schärf, "Policy Options," 50.

51 See: Lee and Seekings, "Vigilantism and Popular Justice," 110; and Schärf, "Policy Options," 50–51.

    An official with the South African national Civic Organization explained the change in attitude: "We used to handle cases as a movement. If we had a dispute the community would handle that, not go to the police. People were saying we had kangaroo courts. These things have changed now that we have a government of our own. Now we encourage people to go to the police, if someone is stabbed. Before it was not like that." Quoted in Lee and Seekings, "Vigilantism and Popular Justice," 109.

52 The persistent support for extra-legal violence is indicated by a 1999 survey of the Eastern Cape province. Five percent of respondents indicted that they had personally taken part in vigilante actions, and another 20 percent said that they would be willing to consider it. (Five percent of the population would equal approximately 150,000 people.) Lee and Seekings, "Vigilantism and Popular Justice," 102–3.

    Also: Lee and Seekings, "Vigilantism and Popular Justice," 104 and 109.

53 Lee and Seekings, "Vigilantism and Popular Justice," 111; and Minnaar, "'New' Vigilantism," 119–20.

54 Nina, "Popular Justice," 103.

55 Dermot Feenan, "Community Justice in Conflict: Paramilitary Punishment in Northern Ireland," in Feenan, *Informal Criminal Justice,* 42.

56 Feenan, "Community Justice", 43 and 50.

    The People's Courts collapsed for a number of reasons, including a lack of resources, procedural difficulties, security concerns, and the priority of military aims over crime control. Ronnie Munck, "Repression, Insurgency, and Popular Justice: The Irish Case," *Crime and Social Justice 21–2* (1984):88.

57 Kieran McEvoy and Harry Mika, "Republican Hegemony or Community Ownership? Community Restorative Justice in Northern Ireland," in Feenan, *Informal Criminal Justice,* 62.

58 Feenan, "Community Justice," 49–50.

    A former chief probation officer explained the problem: "The main reason punishment beatings take place is that you move a civilian police force into being the frontline fighters of terrorism, and if that terrorism is endemic in certain communities as in Northern Ireland, it is obvious that you will lose the confidence of those communities in the civilian police force." Quoted in Feenan, "Community Justice," 50.

59 Feenan, "Community Justice," 43.

    It is estimated that between 1973 and 2002, 2,300 people in Northern Ireland suffered punishment shootings—usually in the knees, thighs, elbows, or ankles. Additionally, between 1983 and 2002, 1,700 have been beaten with bats, nail-studded boards, iron bars, or other kinds of clubs. McEvoy and Mika, "Republican Hegemony or Community Ownership?" 61.

60 Munck, "Repression, Insurgency, and Popular Justice," 89.

61 Munck, "Repression, Insurgency, and Popular Justice," 87.

62 McEvoy and Mika, "Republican Hegemony or Community Ownership?" 65.

63 Quoted in McEvoy and Mika, "Republican Hegemony or Community Ownership?" 63.

64 Feenan, "Community Justice," 45.

65 Quoted in McEvoy and Mika, "Republican Hegemony or Community Ownership?" 64.

66 Auld et al., "Our Practice," 8.1.

67 Gerry Adams expresses the party's enthusiasm: "Sinn Fein is in total agreement with the use of non-violent mechanisms for making offenders more accountable for their crimes, giving victims an input and involving

communities in the ownership of the justice process." Quoted in McEvoy and Mika, "Republican Hegemony or Community Ownership?" 73.

68 McEvoy and Mika, "Republican Hegemony or Community Ownership?" 66.

69 The IRA's statement of support announced: "We want people to support the Restorative Justice approach by bringing their problems to the dedicated and highly trained workers operating in the programmes rather than to the IRA." Quoted in McEvoy and Mika, "Republican Hegemony or Community Ownership?" 74.

70 McEvoy and Mika, "Republican Hegemony or Community Ownership?" 66–67 and 69.

71 McEvoy and Mika, "Republican Hegemony or Community Ownership?" 67 and 74.

72 McEvoy and Mika, "Republican Hegemony or Community Ownership?" 66.

The Blue Book recommends the following solutions: mediated agreement, discussion, family counseling, restitution, payment of damages, referral to treatment programs, referral to statutory agency (but never to the police), community service, boycott.

"A community boycott means all relevant elements of the community, especially neighbors and traders, as well as the organizations represented on the Area Management Committee, mobilising themselves to refuse to allow the individual concerned to live normally within the community. This would mean, in effect, an organized denial of access to goods and services in the local community, such as pubs, off licenses [liquor stores], shops, etc. It is a practical closing of ranks against the person who has offended against the community in a serious way and refused to make any sort of reparation to the victim or the community as a whole." Auld et al., "Our Practice," 8.3.

73 Quoted in McEvoy and Mika, "Republican Hegemony or Community Ownership?" 74.

74 The differences between community-based systems and the modern police institution are striking. Compare, for instance, the characteristics distinguishing modern police (listed in chapter 2 of this volume) to those Richard Abel identifies with informal justice systems: "[I]nformal justice is said to be unofficial (dissociated from state power), noncoercive (dependent on rhetoric rather than force), nonbureaucratic, decentralized, relatively undifferentiated, and non-professional; its substance and procedural rules are imprecise, unwritten, demotic, flexible, ad hoc, and particularistic. No concrete informal legal institution will embody all these qualities, but each will exhibit some." Richard L. Abel, "Introduction," in *The Politics of Informal Justice, Volume 2: Comparative Studies,* ed. Richard L. Abel (New York: Academic Press, 1982), 10. Parentheses in original.

For a more detailed articulation of the ideal type, see: Heleen F. P. Ietswaart, "The Discourse of Summary Justice and the Discourse of Popular Justice: An Analysis of Legal Rhetoric in Argentina," in *The Politics of Informal Justice, Volume 2: Comparative Studies,* ed. Richard L. Abel (New York: Academic Press, 1982), 154–56.

75 McEvoy and Mika, "Republican Hegemony or Community Ownership?" 66.

Sinn Fein told the Independent Commission on Policing for Northern Ireland: "Local structures should not be seen as an alternative to formal policing. In our view restorative justice . . . is an approach which can build trust and empower individual communities affected. Effective liaison between police and community can also serve to deal more effectively with neighborhood disputes and less serious offenses in a way that also frees up police time and resources to deal with more serious crime."

But they insisted on this important caveat: "[It] needs to be clearly stated at the outset that these proposals are set in the context of a new police service that can enjoy widespread support from, and is seen as an integral part of, the community as a whole. The RUC quite clearly do not fit this criteria." Quoted in McEvoy and Mika, "Republican Hegemony or Community Ownership?" 74.

Representatives of the Community Restorative Justice program argued along similar lines: "We do want a partnership with a reformed police service in the future. . . . We intend to plan for that day. But it is not, unfortunately, here yet." Quoted in McEvoy and Mika, "Republican Hegemony or Community Ownership?" 75.

76 Auld, et al., "Our Practice," 9.2.3.

It is a little hard to know how seriously to take such a remark, since the Blue Book also notes, immediately beforehand, that "'normal policing' has not been possible in many working class nationalist communities during the violent conflict." Auld, et al., "Our Practice," 9.2.3.

It seems clear then that there was no need for the CRJ to supplant formal policing, since the military conflict had already done as much.

77 Nina, "Popular Justice," 115.

Nina also notes that in places where the civic associations refused to cooperate with the government "Peace and order existed without the state. In fact, the state was perceived as an agent of chaos and disorder." Nina, "Popular Justice," 106.

78 Of course, counter-institutions should only be one part of a broader anti-crime strategy. Common-sense measures should also be taken to add to the public safety. Some public safety tasks could simply be taken on by fire departments, health departments, and other agencies. Victimless crimes should be de-criminalized, with resources invested in drug and alcohol treatment programs and counseling services rather than law enforcement and prisons. Other elements require substantial social changes, like reducing poverty and unemployment, and combating domestic violence by improving the real opportunities available to women and thereby eliminating their dependency on men.

For other ideas, see: Center For Research on Criminal Justice, *Iron Fist and the Velvet Glove,* 162; and Elliott Currie, *Crime and Punishment in America* (New York: Metropolitan Books, 1998), especially chapters 3 and 4.

79 Lee and Seekings, "Vigilantism and Popular Justice," 113–14. Parentheses and emphasis in original.

80 Auld et al., "Our Practice," 8.2.1.

81 Auld et al., "Our Practice," 3.4.2. Parentheses in original.

82 Auld et al., "Our Practice," 3.4.

83 Auld et al., "Our Practice," 8.2.1.

84 Auld et al., "Our Practice," 9.3.2.

85 Harry Mika and Kieran McEvoy, "Restorative Justice in Conflict: Paramilitarism, Community, and the Construction of Legitimacy in Northern Ireland," *Comparative Justice Review* 4:3–4 (2001): 307–10. Parentheses and emphasis in original.

86 It has been suggested, perhaps too optimistically, that the very ideology of restorative justice puts some check on abuse, since it emphasizes a respect for diversity, human rights, and mutual understanding. McEvoy and Mika, "Republican Hegemony or Community Ownership?" 69–70.

87 Auld et al., "Our Practice," 7.2.

88 Feenan, "Community Justice," 53–54; and McEvoy and Mika, "Republican Hegemony or Community Ownership?" 68–69.

89 Quoted in Munck, "Repression, Insurgency, and Popular Justice," 87.

These concerns are real, and they should be carefully weighed. But we should also remember that the practical alternative is the justice of the state—that is, the justice of the police, the courts, overcrowded prisons, and lethal injections. As we evaluate the limitations of popular justice we should measure it, not only against our ideals, but also against the very real system of the state. In all the cases discussed here, the revolutionaries' efforts at crime control are far from perfect, but a good bit better than those of the authorities.

To offer just one point of comparison, the legal system in Northern Ireland has been characterized by arbitrary detention, torture, broad powers of search and seizure, internment without trial, courts without juries, secret evidence, constant surveillance, a reliance on paid informers, and military intervention. Munck, "Repression, Insurgency, and Popular Justice," 84–85.

SELECTED BIBLIOGRAPHY

I have tried to thoroughly document my sources in the endnotes, and I see no need to reproduce those efforts in this bibliography. Instead, I list the works I found most useful in my research, and briefly comment on them where necessary.

I begin with sources on general topics, then list those remaining, roughly following the structure of the text. There is a certain amount of unavoidable overlap between categories, but in the interest of space I have kept repetition to a minimum. The principle of organization is this: A source is assigned to the chapter for which it has the greatest significance, and then placed in the narrowest applicable topic section. For example, though I quoted from it throughout the text, Rodney Stark's book *Police Riots* is listed only once, under the heading for chapter 8 ("Riot Police or Police Riots?") in the subsection titled "Crowd Control Models." By this reasoning, it follows that a reader looking for information on the Haymarket Affair should start by looking in the "Haymarket" section among the sources for chapter 7, but she would also do well to consider the sources listed under "Red Squads" (also in chapter 7) and "Labor History" (from chapter 5).

I have focused here on print sources rather than trust internet material to remain stable from one day to the next. Moreover, I have given special priority to books, as these tend to be of more general use than the numerous magazine, newspaper, and journal articles appearing in the notes. The best articles are usually anthologized anyway; where practical, I have grouped short works together under the entries for the relevant anthologies. Unfortunately, I must warn you that many of the best books are out of print and hard to come by. That said, I managed to lay my hands on all the material I cite, so it is possible. My advice is that you ask a public librarian about inter-library loan; our public institutions are sometimes much better than we realize.

It will be observed that the majority of authors I cite are male, usually academics or police administrators. This is emphatically *not* the result of intentional selection on my part, but reflects the overall composition of the field. It is often useful to see what insiders have to say, especially about such an insular and, at times, secretive institution as the police—however, I have tried in the text to include the voices of those who are excluded from and marginalized by the institutions of social power. I have continued that effort in this bibliography.

It will also be noted that I have relied almost exclusively on secondary sources. Partly this was a practical expedient, suited to the scope of the argument. But it brings with it an additional advantage: None of my conclusions rely on the discovery of some new fact, only on a reinterpretation of what is already known. If the facts are agreed upon, those who would fault my conclusions will be forced, it is hoped, to engage my arguments.

GENERAL TOPICS

AMERICAN HISTORY

Zinn, Howard. *A People's History of the United States, 1492–Present.* New York: HarperPerennial, 1995.

Clearly written and engaging, this book presents American history "from below," emphasizing the experiences of Native Americans, African Americans, women, workers, and other oppressed peoples.

CRITICAL CRIMINOLOGY

Chambliss, William J. *Power, Politics, and Crime.* Boulder, Colorado: Westview Press, 1999.

Currie, Elliott. *Crime and Punishment in America.* New York: Metropolitan Books, 1998.

The two works listed here are each short, readable volumes demolishing the conventional wisdom about crime, its causes, the law, its enforcement, the effectiveness of prisons, and related topics.

POLICE HISTORIES

The typical police history focuses on one city and covers a century or less. If it pays attention to the early period, it traces in minute detail the gradual replacement of the night watch with the modern institution. If it discusses the latter part of the nineteenth or the first half of the twentieth century, it focuses on the interplay between official corruption and reform efforts. There are variations of scope and emphasis, but that is the standard formula.

Bacon, Selden Daskan. *The Early Development of the American Municipal Police: A Study of the Evolution of Formal Controls in a Changing Society*. 2 vols. Ph.D. diss., Yale University, 1939. Ann Arbor: University Microfilms International [facsimile], 1986.

While very dry, Bacon's dissertation presents an exhaustive account of early police systems leading up to the modern form. One is tempted to say that the account is too exhaustive, but it offers a goldmine of details for anyone willing to dig.

Bayley, David H. "The Development of Modern Policing." In *Policing Perspectives: An Anthology*, edited by Larry K. Gaines and Gary W. Cordner. Los Angeles: Roxbury Publishing Company, 1999.

Fogelson, Robert M. *Big-City Police*. Cambridge, Massachusetts: Harvard University Press, 1977.

This is the most readable of the histories listed in this section. It traces the course of reform efforts to the early 1970s.

Greenberg, Douglas. *Crime and Law Enforcement in the Colony of New York, 1691–1776*. Ithaca, New York: Cornell University Press, 1976.

Harring, Sidney. *Policing a Class Society: The Experience of American Cities, 1865–1915*. New Brunswick, New Jersey: Rutgers University Press, 1983.

Harring emphasizes the class-control aspect of the early police institution, overshadowing consideration of other features.

Lane, Roger. *Policing the City: Boston, 1822–1885*. Cambridge, Massachusetts: Harvard University Press, 1967.

Monkkonen, Eric H. *Police in Urban America, 1860–1920*. Cambridge: Cambridge University Press, 1981.

Monkkonen has a strange obsession with uniforms, but this book provides excellent coverage of the public-welfare functions of the police at the turn of the twentieth century.

Reynolds, Elaine A. *Before the Bobbies: The Night Watch and Police Reform in Metropolitan London, 1720–1830*. Stanford, California: Stanford University Press, 1998.

Richardson, James F. *The New York Police: Colonial Times to 1901*. New York: Oxford University Press, 1970.

——. *Urban Police in the United States*. Port Washington, New York: National University Press and Kennikat Press, 1974.

Robinson, Cyril D. and Richard Scaglion. "The Origin and Evolution of the Police Function in Society: Notes Toward a Theory." *Law and Society Review* 21.1 (1987).

Rousey, Dennis C. *Policing the Southern City: New Orleans, 1905–1889*. Baton Rouge: Louisiana State University Press, 1996.

Schneider, John C. *Detroit and the Problem of Order, 1830–1880: A Geography of Crime, Riot, and Policing*. Lincoln: University of Nebraska Press, 1980.

Steinberg, Allen. *The Transformation of Criminal Justice: Philadelphia, 1800–1880*. Chapel Hill: University of North Carolina Press, 1989.
Steinberg's analysis centers on the end of private prosecution, rather than the modernization of policing. Nevertheless, the book paints a fascinating picture of nineteenth-century city politics.

POLICE MEMOIRS

It is difficult to know how much credence to give these autobiographical testaments. Aside from occasional attempts to address the real difficulties police face, the genre mostly consists of self-serving polemics intended to rebuke critics, explain away problems, and justify excesses. While we should hesitate to accept such first-person accounts at face value, they are undeniably of some historical interest. It is worth noting what individual officers are willing to admit—especially after they retire. And it is interesting to see what justifications they offer, whether or not we accept their excuses.

Bratton, William. *Turnaround: How America's Top Cop Reversed the Crime Epidemic*. With Peter Knobler. New York: Random House, 1998.

Gates, Daryl F. *Chief: My Life in the LAPD*. With Diane K. Shah. New York: Bantam Books, 1992.

Jenkins, Herbert. *Keeping the Peace: A Police Chief Looks at His Job*. New York: Harper & Row, 1970.

Koon, Stacey C. *Presumed Guilty: The Tragedy of the Rodney King Affair*. With Robert Deitz. Washington, D.C.: Regnery Gateway, 1992.

McAdoo, William. *Guarding a Great City*. New York: Harper and Brothers Publishers, 1906.

CHAPTER ONE: POLICE BRUTALITY IN THEORY AND PRACTICE

RIOTS

Gilje, Paul A. *Rioting in America*. Bloomington: Indiana University Press, 1996.

National Advisory Commission on Civil Disorders [The Kerner Commission]. *Report of the National Advisory Commission on Civil Disorder*. New York Times edition. New York: E.P. Dutton and Company, 1968.

Oliver, Melvin et al. "Anatomy of a Rebellion: A Political-Economic Analysis." In *Reading Rodney King: Reading Urban Uprising*, edited by Robert Gooding-Williams. New York: Routledge, 1993.

Petersilia, Joan and Allan Abrahamse. "A Profile of Those Arrested." In *The Los Angeles Riots: Lessons for the Urban Future*, edited by Mark Baldassare. Boulder: Westview Press, 1994.

Porter, Bruce and Marvin Dunn. *The Miami Riot of 1980: Crossing the Bounds*. Lexington, Massachusetts: Lexington Books, 1984.

Sears, David O. "Urban Rioting in Los Angeles: A Comparison of 1965 with 1992." In *The Los Angeles Riots: Lessons for the Urban Future*, edited by Mark Baldassare. Boulder: Westview Press, 1994.

Simmons, Charles E. "The Los Angeles Rebellion: Class, Race, and Misinformation." In *Why L.A. Happened: Implications of the '92 Los Angeles Rebellion*, edited by Haki R. Madhubuti. Chicago: Third World Press, 1993.

THE PREVALENCE OF POLICE VIOLENCE

Reliable information on police violence is altogether rare. For reasons I discuss in chapter 1, reporting is incomplete and the presentation of data often downplays both the level of violence and its prevalence. Nevertheless, the most comprehensive studies available are supplied by the Bureau of Justice Statistics (www.ojp.usdoj.gov/bjs/) and the National Institute of Justice (www.ojp.usdoj.gov/nij/). (Unfortunately, given Attorney General John Ashcroft's recent attempts to control government information, the future value of these agencies is impossible to predict.)

Another resource for similar information is the National Criminal Justice Reference Service (www.ncjrs.org).

Bittner, Egon. "The Capacity to Use Force as the Core of the Police Role." In *The Police and Society: Touchstone Readings,* edited by Victor E. Kappeler. Prospect Heights, Illinois: Waveland Press, 1999.

Human Rights Watch. *Shielded From Justice: Police Brutality and Accountability in the United States.* New York: Human Rights Watch, 1998.

Independent Commission on the Los Angeles Police Department [The Christopher Commission]. *Report of the Independent Commission on the Los Angeles Police Department.* Los Angeles: July 9, 1991.

Justice Department. Bureau of Justice Statistics. *Contacts Between Police and the Public: Findings from the 1999 National Survey,* by Patrick A. Langan, et al. February 2001.

———. Bureau of Justice Statistics. *Policing and Homicide, 1976–98: Justifiable Homicide by Police, Police Officers Murdered by Felons,* by Jodi M. Brown and Patrick A. Langan. March 2001.

———. Bureau of Justice Statistics and National Institute of Justice. *National Data Collection on Police Use of Force,* by Tom McEwan. April 1996.

———. National Institute of Justice and Bureau of Justice Statistics. *Use of Force by Police: Overview of National and Local Data.* Washington, D.C.: October 1999.

This Justice Department document contains several reports, including: Kenneth Adams, "What We Know About Police Use of Force"; Joel Garner and Christopher Maxwell, "Measuring the Amount of Force Used By and Against the Police in Six Jurisdictions"; and Mark A. Henriquez, "IACP National Database Project on Police Use of Force."

INSTITUTIONALIZED BRUTALITY AND POLICE CULTURE

Fyfe, James T. "Police Use of Deadly Force: Research and Reform." In *Policing Perspectives: An Anthology*, edited by Larry K. Gaines and Gary W. Cordner. Los Angeles: Roxbury Publishing Company, 1999.

Justice Department and National Institute of Justice. *The Measurement of Police Integrity*, by Carl B. Klockars et al. May 2000.
———.*Police Attitudes Toward Abuse of Authority: Findings from a National Survey*, by David Weisburd et al. May 2000.

Kappeler, Victor E. et al. "Breeding Deviant Conformity: Police Ideology and Culture." In *The Police and Society: Touchstone Readings*, edited by Victor E. Kappeler. Prospect Heights, Illinois: Waveland Press, Inc., 1999.

Westley, William A. "Violence and the Police." In *Police Patrol Readings*, edited by Samuel G. Chapman. Springfield, Illinois: Charles C. Thomas, 1964.

CHAPTER TWO: THE ORIGINS OF AMERICAN POLICING

ENGLISH POLICE

Emsley, Clive. *The English Police: A Political and Social History*. London: Longman, 1991.

Miller, Wilbur R. "Police Authority in London and New York, 1830–1870." *Journal of Social History* (Winter 1975).

Reynolds, Elaine A. *Before the Bobbies: The Night Watch and Police Reform in Metropolitan London, 1720–1830*. Stanford, California: Stanford University Press, 1998.

Stead, Philip John. *The Police in Britain*. New York: Macmillan, 1985.

SLAVE PATROLS

Until quite recently, the slave patrols have occupied one of those almost-forgotten corners of our nation's story. As a result, relatively few historians have appreciated their role in the development of policing.

Dulaney, W. Marvin. *Black Police in America*. Bloomington: Indiana University Press, 1996.

Hadden, Sally E. *Slave Patrols: Law and Violence in Virginia and the Carolinas*. Cambridge, Massachusetts: Harvard University Press, 2001.

Henry, H. M. *The Police Control of the Slave in South Carolina*. Ph.D. diss., Vanderbilt University, 1913. Emory, Virginia, 1914.
Though his dissertation provides solid information on the subject, Henry's racist commentary tarnishes an otherwise excellent source.

Reichel, Philip L. "Southern Slave Patrols as a Transitional Police Type." In *Policing Perspectives: An Anthology*, edited by Larry K. Gaines and Gary W. Cordner. Los Angeles: Roxbury Publishing Company, 1999.

Rousey, Dennis C. *Policing the Southern City: New Orleans, 1905–1889*. Baton Rouge: Louisiana State University Press, 1996.

Wade, Richard C. *Slavery in the Cities: The South, 1820–1860*. London: Oxford University Press, 1964.

Wintersmith, Robert F. *Police and the Black Community*. Lexington, Massachusetts: Lexington Books, 1974.

SLAVE REVOLTS

Aptheker, Herbert. *American Negro Slave Revolts*. New York: International Publishers, 1987.

Cheek, William F. *Black Resistance Before the Civil War*. Beverly Hills, California: Glencoe Press, 1970.
Consisting of primary source material and brief introductory remarks, this volume covers the spectrum of slave resistance, from loafing and theft to escapes and organized revolt.

Wish, Harvey. "American Slave Insurrections Before 1861." In *Black Protest: 350 Years of History, Documents, and Analyses*, edited by Joanne Grant. New York: Fawcett Columbine, 1968.

CHAPTER THREE: THE GENESIS OF A POLICED SOCIETY

POLITICAL MACHINES

Banfield, Edward C. and James Q. Wilson. *City Politics*. Cambridge, Massachusetts: Harvard University Press and the M.I.T. Press, 1963.

Fogelson, Robert M. *Big-City Police*. Cambridge, Massachusetts: Harvard University Press, 1977.
See note under "General Topics: Police Histories."

Fosdick, Raymond B. *American Police Systems*. New York: Century Company, 1920.

Richardson, James F. *Urban Police in the United States*. Port Washington, New York: National University Press, 1974.

Steinberg, Allen. *The Transformation of Criminal Justice: Philadelphia 1800–1880*. Chapel Hill, North Carolina: University of North Carolina Press, 1989.
See note under General Topics: Police Histories.

Tilly, Charles. "War Making and State Making as Organized Crime." In *Bringing the State Back In*, edited by Peter B. Evans et al. Cambridge: Cambridge University Press, 1994.
Tilly doesn't directly discuss urban political machines, but he does articulate a theoretical perspective on government racketeering.

THE DEMAND FOR ORDER

The moral panic accompanying urbanization arose from multiple sources and produced complex results. Thus, many of the sources below pay little immediate attention to policing while describing nineteenth-century standards of public order in detail.

Coontz, Stephanie. *The Social Origins of Private Life: A History of American Families, 1600–1900*. London: Verso, 1991.

Harring, Sidney. *Policing a Class Society: The Experience of American Cities, 1865–1915*. New Brunswick, New Jersey: Rutgers University Press, 1983.
See note under "General Topics: Police Histories."

Hindus, Michael Stephen. *Prison and Plantation: Crime, Justice, and Authority in Massachusetts and South Carolina, 1768–1878*. Chapel Hill: University of North Carolina Press, 1980.

Lane, Roger. "Crime and Criminal Statistics in Nineteenth-Century Massachusetts." *Journal of Social History* (Winter 1968).

Schneider, John C. *Detroit and the Problem of Order, 1830–1880: A Geography of Crime, Riot, and Policing*. Lincoln: University of Nebraska Press, 1980.

Silver, Allan. "The Demand for Order in Civil Society: A Review of Some Themes in the History of Urban Crime, Police, and Riot." In *The Police: Six Sociological Essays*, edited by David J. Bordua. New York: John Wiley and Sons, 1976.

Stansell, Christine. *City of Women: Sex and Class in New York, 1789–1869*. Urbana: University of Illinois Press, 1987.

Weber, Max. *The Protestant Ethic and the Spirit of Capitalism*. London: Allen and Unwin, 1930.

CHAPTER FOUR: COPS AND KLAN, HAND IN HAND

THE KU KLUX KLAN AND RACIST TERROR

Fry, Gladys-Marie. *Night Riders in Black Folk History*. Knoxville: University of Tennessee Press: 1975.
Centering on the fear of the supernatural and its use as a means of intimidation, this study recounts the experiences of Black people as recorded in their folk tales and preserved through the oral tradition. Particular attention is given to comparisons between the slave patrols and the Ku Klux Klan.

Hadden, Sally E. *Slave Patrols: Law and Violence in Virginia and the Carolinas*. Cambridge, Massachusetts: Harvard University Press, 2001.

Hennessey, Melinda Meek. *To Live and Die in Dixie: Reconstruction Race Riots in the South*. Ph.D. diss., Kent State University, 1978. Ann Arbor: University Microfilms International, 1978.

Jackson, Kenneth T. *The Ku Klux Klan in the City, 1915–1930*. New York: Oxford University Press, 1967.

Novick, Michael. *White Lies, White Power: The Fight Against White Supremacy and Reactionary Violence*. Monroe, Maine: Common Courage Press, 1995.

Trelease, Allen W. *White Terror: The Ku Klux Klan Conspiracy and Southern Reconstruction*. New York: Harper and Row, 1971.

RACIAL PROFILING

Bayley, David H. and Harold Mendelsohn. *Minorities and the Police: Confrontation in America*. New York: The Free Press, 1969.

Harris, David A. *Profiles in Injustice: Why Racial Profiling Cannot Work*. New York: The New Press, 2002.

Justice Department. *Characteristics of Drivers Stopped by Police, 1999*, by Erica Leah Schmitt et al., March 2002.
———. Bureau of Justice Statistics. *Lifetime Likelihood of Going to State or Federal Prison*, prepared by Thomas P. Bonczar and Allen J. Beck. March 1997.

Reed, Ishmael. "Another Day at the Front: Encounters with the Fuzz on the American Battlefront." In *Police Brutality: An Anthology*, edited by Jill Nelson. New York: W.W. Norton & Company, 2000.
Reed, a Black man, recounts his own experiences with racial profiling.

Wise, Tim. "Racial Profiling and Its Apologists." *Z Magazine* (March 2002).

THE CIVIL RIGHTS AND BLACK POWER MOVEMENTS

Berry, Mary Frances. *Black Resistance, White Law: A History of Constitutional Racism in America*. New York: Penguin Press, 1994.

Cagin, Seth and Philip Dray, *We Are Not Afraid: The Story of Goodman, Schwerner, and Chaney and the Civil Rights Campaign for Mississippi*. New York: MacMillan Publishing Company, 1988.

Feagin, Joe R. and Harlan Hahn. *Ghetto Revolts: The Politics of Violence in American Cities*. New York: Macmillan Company, 1973.
A politically sophisticated sociological study, this volume provides an important antidote to the myopia of government commissions.

Hampton, Henry et al. *Voices of Freedom: An Oral History of the Civil Rights Movement from the 1950s through the 1980s*. New York: Bantam Books, 1990.
The companion volume to the documentary series Eyes on the Prize, *this book consists primarily of interviews with people who participated in or witnessed the major events of the civil rights movement.*

Misseduc Foundation, Inc. *Mississippi Black Paper*. New York: Random House, 1965.
The Black Paper *collects affidavits concerning the treatment of African Americans in Mississippi and the suppression of the civil rights movement there. It is thus a worthy historical document, but slow reading.*

Newton, Huey P. *War Against the Panthers: A Study of Repression in America*. Ph.D. diss., University of California-Santa Cruz, 1980. New York: Harlem River Press, 1996.

THE RACIAL POLITICS OF POLICE FUNDING

Jackson, Pamela Irving. *Minority Group Threat, Crime, and Policing: Social Context and Social Control*. New York: Praeger, 1989.

Jacobs, David. "Inequality and Police Strength: Conflict Theory and Coercive Control in Metropolitan Areas." *American Sociological Review* 44.6 (1979).

CHAPTER FIVE: THE NATURAL ENEMY OF THE WORKING CLASS

LABOR HISTORY

Brecher, Jeremy. *Strike!* Boston: South End Press, 1972.

Green, James R. *The World of the Worker: Labor in Twentieth-Century America*. New York: Hill and Wang, 1980.

Selvin, David F. *A Terrible Anger: The 1934 Waterfront and General Strikes in San Francisco*. Detroit: Wayne State University Press, 1996.

Yellen, Samuel. *American Labor Struggles, 1877–1934*. New York: Pathfinder, 1936.

STATE POLICE

Mayo, Katherine. *Justice to All: The Story of the Pennsylvania State Police*. New York: GP Putnam's Sons, 1917.
A reply to The American Cossack, *in defense of the state police.*

Pennsylvanian State Federation of Labor. *The American Cossack*. New York: Arno Press & The New York Times, 1971.
This volume collects evidence against the Pennsylvania State Constabulary, including affidavits, newspaper articles, and legislative debate. Unfortunately, the documents are more piled together than organized, making for a clumsy presentation.

Smith, Bruce. *Police Systems in the United States*. New York: Harper & Brothers Publishers, 1940.
———. *Rural Crime Control*. New York: Institute of Public Administration, 1933.
———. *The State Police: Organization and Administration*. New York: Macmillan Company, 1925.

CURRENT EVENTS

The newsletter *Labor Notes* (www.labornotes.org) is probably the best source for coverage of the contemporary labor movement, reported from a radical, rank-and-file perspective.

CHAPTER SIX: POLICE AUTONOMY AND BLUE POWER

POLICE REFORM

Bittner, Egon. "The Quasi-Military Organization of the Police." In *The Police and Society: Touchstone Readings,* edited by Victor E. Kappeler. Prospect Heights, Illinois: Waveland Press, Inc., 1999.

Fogelson, Robert M. *Big-City Police*. Cambridge, Massachusetts: Harvard University Press, 1977.
See note under "General Topics: Police Histories."

Lundman, Richard J. *Police and Policy: An Introduction*. New York: Holt, Rinehart, and Winston, 1980.

Richardson, James F. *Urban Police in the United States*. Port Washington, New York: National University Press and Kennikat Press, 1974.

THE PROGRESSIVE ERA AND BUREAUCRATIZATION

Banfield, Edward C. and James Q. Wilson. *City Politics*. Cambridge, Massachusetts: Harvard University Press and the MIT Press, 1963.

Hays, Samuel P. "The Politics of Reform in Municipal Government in the Progressive Era." *Pacific Northwest Quarterly* (July 1964).

Weber, Max. *Economy and Society: An Outline of Interpretive Sociology*, edited by Guenther Roth and Claus Wittich. Berkeley: University of California Press, 1978.
This unwieldy collection of notes includes a detailed analysis concerning the nature of bureaucracy.

Weinstein, James. *The Corporate Ideal in the Liberal State: 1900–1918*. Boston: Beacon Press, 1968.

HEGEMONY

Femia, Joseph V. *Gramsci's Political Thought: Hegemony, Consciousness, and the Revolutionary Process*. Oxford: Clarendon Press, 1981.

Gramsci, Antonio. *Selections From the Prison Notebooks of Antonio Gramsci*, edited by Quintin Hoare and Geoffrey Nowell-Smith. New York: International Publishers, 1971.

POLICE UNIONS AND BLUE POWER

Black, Algernon D. *The People and the Police*. New York: McGraw-Hill Book Company, 1968.
Black served as the chair of the New York Civilian Complaint Review Board.

Bopp, William J., editor. *The Police Rebellion*. Springfield, Illinois: Charles C. Thomas, 1971.
Contains William J. Bopp, "The Police Rebellion"; Seymour Martin Lipset, "Why Cops Hate Liberals—And Vice Versa"; Ed Cray, "The Politics of Blue Power"; Max Gunther, "Cops in Politics: A Threat to Democracy?"; William J. Bopp, "The New York City Referendum on Civilian Review"; William J. Bopp, "The Detroit Police Revolt"; and William J. Bopp, "The Patrolmen in Boston."

Braverman, Harry. *Labor and Monopoly Capital: The Degradation of Work in the Twentieth Century*. New York: Monthly Review Press, 1974.
Braverman barely mentions the police, but his work informs my discussion of class status.

Levi, Margaret. *Bureaucratic Insurgency: The Case of Police Unions*. Lexington, Massachusetts: Lexington Books, 1977.

Lyons, Richard L. "The Boston Police Strike of 1919." *New England Quarterly* (June 1947).

Reiner, Robert. *The Blue-Coated Worker: A Sociological Study of Police Unionism*. Cambridge: Cambridge University Press, 1978.
Reiner concentrates on the English police, but much of his analysis of their position and function in capitalist society is applicable in the U.S. context as well.

Russell, Francis. *A City in Terror—1919—The Boston Police Strike*. New York: Viking Press, 1975.

Skolnick, Jerome H. *The Politics of Protest: Violent Aspects of Protest and Confrontation; A Report Submitted by Jerome H. Skolnick* [The Skolnick Report; Report of the Task Force on Violent Aspects of Protest and Confrontation to the National Commission on the Causes and Prevention of Violence]. Washington, D.C.: GPO, 1969.

BLACK POLICE ASSOCIATIONS

Alex, Nicholas. *Black in Blue: A Study of the Negro Policeman*. New York: Appleton-Century-Crofts, 1969.

Dulaney, W. Marvin. *Black Police in America*. Bloomington: Indiana University Press, 1996.

CORPORATISM

Crouch, Colin and Ronald Dore, "Whatever Happened to Corporatism?" In *Corporatism and Accountability: Organized Interests in British Public Life*, edited by Colin Crouch and Ronald Dore. Oxford: Clarendon Press, 1990.

Schmitter, Philippe C. "Still the Century of Corporatism?" *Review of Politics* 36 (1974).
Schmitter's paper is the best introduction to corporatism I've seen, explaining its origins, its basic principles, and its various types.

THE STATE AND STATE AUTONOMY

Smith, Martin J. *Pressure, Power and Policy: State Autonomy and Policy Networks in Britain and the United States*. Pittsburgh: University of Pittsburgh Press, 1993.

Szczech, Clayton, "Beyond Autonomy or Dominance: The Political Sociology of Prison Expansion." Undergraduate thesis, Reed College, 2000.
This thesis offers a clear and empirically based explanation of prison expansion. At the same time, it goes some distance toward resolution of the "state autonomy vs. class dominance" debate.

Tilly, Charles Coercion. *Capital, and European States, AD 990–1990*. Cambridge, Massachusetts: Basil Blackwell, 1990s.

CHAPTER SEVEN: SECRET POLICE, RED SQUADS, AND THE STRATEGY OF PERMANENT REPRESSION

HAYMARKET

Avrich, Paul. *The Haymarket Tragedy*. Princeton, New Jersey: Princeton University Press, 1984.

David, Henry. *The History of the Haymarket Affair: A Study in the American Social-Revolutionary and Labor Movements*. New York: Farrar and Rinehart, Inc., 1936.

Nelson, Bruce C. *Beyond the Martyrs: A Social History of Chicago's Anarchists, 1870–1900*. New Brunswick: Rutgers University Press, 1988.

Rayback, Joseph G. *A History of American Labor*. New York: The Free Press, 1966.

REPRESSION—THEORETICAL PERSPECTIVES

Kitson, Frank. *Low Intensity Operations: Subversion, Insurgency, Peace-Keeping.* Hamden, Connecticut: Archon Books, 1971.

Kitson's book should be required reading for every radical. Not only does he offer a clear view of repression and state strategy, he also has a good grasp on how and why insurrections succeed or fail. He thus has a much better understanding of the revolutionary process than do most would-be revolutionaries.

Lawrence, Ken. *The New State Repression.* Chicago: International Network Against New State Repression, 1985.

This pamphlet serves as a kind of cheater's guide on political repression, translating the technical literature into clear and digestible prose without dumbing it down. Unfortunately, it only seems to exist in the form of third-generation photocopies.

Wolfe, Alan. *The Seamy Side of Democracy: Repression in America.* Reading, Massachusetts: Longman, 1978.

RED SQUADS

American Friends Service Committee. Program on Government Surveillance and Citizens' Rights. *The Police Threat to Political Liberty: Discoveries and Actions of the American Friends Service Committee Program on Government Surveillance and Citizens' Rights.* Philadelphia: AFSC, 1979.

Donner, Frank. *Protectors of Privilege: Red Squads and Police Repression in Urban America.* Berkeley: University of California Press, 1990.

Donner's book is without question the defining text on the history of the red squads, recounting their exploits and misadventures from the 1880s to the 1980s.

———."Theory and Practice of American Political Intelligence." *New York Review of Books* (April 22, 1971).

Rosenberg, Paul. "The Empire Strikes Back: Police Repression of Protest from Seattle to L.A." Los Angeles Independent Media Center (August 13, 2000), www.r2kphilly.org/pdf/empire-strikes.pdf (accessed March 18, 2003).

Rosenberg's essay catalogues the tactics used against antiglobalization protesters from the November 1999 WTO meeting in Seattle to the August 2000 Democratic National Convention in Los Angeles. It provides a good synopsis of recent dirty tricks—the ones we know about.

COINTELPRO

Churchill, Ward and Jim Vander Wall. *Agents of Repression: The FBI's Secret Wars Against the Black Panther Party and the American Indian Movement*. Boston: South End Press, 1990.

———. *The COINTELPRO Papers: Documents from the FBI's Secret Wars Against Domestic Dissent*. Boston: South End Press, 1990.

Churchill and Vander Wall present, analyze, and contextualize select documents stolen from the FBI's office in Media, Pennsylvania.

United States. Senate Select Committee to Study Government Operations With Respect to Intelligence Activities [Church Committee]. *Final Report of the Select Committee to Study Government Operations With Respect to Intelligence Activities*. 6 vols. 94th Congress, second session. Washington, D.C.: GPO, 1976.

Authoritative documentation of government crimes.

CURRENT EVENTS

Of the many topics discussed in this book, police intelligence activities and political repression are among those changing fastest. For coverage of developing issues, the best sources are *CovertAction Quarterly*; *CounterPunch* (www.counterpunch.org); and the *Village Voice* (www.villagevoice.com). The American Civil Liberties Union (www.aclu.org) and the Center for Constitutional Rights (www.ccr-ny.org/v2/home.asp) do their part by analyzing legislation, policies, and proposals surfacing at the federal level.

RESISTING REPRESSION

Glick, Brian. *War at Home: Covert Action Against U.S. Activists and What We Can Do About It*. Boston: South End Press, 1989.

Though I don't cite it in the text, I cannot neglect to mention Glick's War at Home. *This brief, inexpensive book touches on the history of political repression and describes some of the tactics police still use. Its real virtue, though, lies in its practical advice about fighting repression. There is no telling how many people this book has helped keep out of jail.*

CHAPTER EIGHT: RIOT POLICE OR POLICE RIOTS?

WORLD TRADE ORGANIZATION PROTESTS (SEATTLE, 1999)

ACLU Washington. *Out of Control: Seattle's Flawed Response to Protests Against the World Trade Organization.* July 2000. www.aclu-wa.org/ISSUES/police/WTO-Report.html (accessed August 2000).

R. M. McCarthy and Associates. *An Independent Review of the Word Trade Organization Conference Disruptions in Seattle, Washington; November 29–December 3, 1999.* San Clemente, California: July 2000.

Seattle City Council WTO Accountability Review Committee. *Report of the WTO Accountability Review Committee.* September 14 , 2000.

Seattle Police Department. *The Seattle Police Department After Action Report: World Trade Organization Ministerial Conference: Seattle, Washington, November 29–December 3, 1999.* April 4, 2000.

CROWD CONTROL MODELS

Leach, Eugene L. "The Literature of Riot Duty: Managing Class Conflict in the Streets, 1877–1927." *Radical History Review* (Spring 1993).

Della Porta, Donnatella and Herbert Reiter, editors. *Policing Protest: The Control of Mass Demonstrations in Western Democracies.* Minneapolis: University of Minnesota Press, 1998.
This collection features studies of crowd control in the U.S and Europe. It includes: Donnatella della Porta and Herbert Reiter, "Introduction: The Policing of Protest In Western Democracies"; Robert Reiner, "Policing, Protest, and Disorder in Britain"; Clark McPhail, David Schweingruber, and John McCarthy, "Policing Protest in the United States: 1960–1995"; and, P.A.J. Waddington, "Controlling Protest in Contemporary Historical and Comparative Perspective."

Stark, Rodney. *Police Riots: Collective Violence and Law Enforcement.* Belmont, California: Focus Books, 1972.
Stark's discussion ranges more broadly than the title would suggest, with attention to general issues of police brutality, organization, ideology, and reform. It stands among the very best books written about the police.

1968

Ali, Tariq and Susan Watkins. *1968: Marching in the Streets*. New York: The Free Press, 1998.
Using photographs, period artwork, and historical vignettes, Ali and Watkins offer a day-by-day review of the year's events.

Fraser, Ronald et al. *1968: A Student Generation in Revolt*. New York: Pantheon Books, 1988.

Gilje, Paul A. *Rioting in America*. Bloomington: Indiana University Press, 1996.

Mailer, Norman. *Miami and the Siege of Chicago: An Informal History of the Republican and Democratic Conventions of 1968*. New York: World Publishing Company, 1968.

Walker, Daniel. *Rights in Conflict: Chicago's 7 Brutal Days*. New York: Grosset and Dunlap, 1968.
The definitive account of the 1968 Democratic National Convention.

RIOT COMMISSIONS

National Advisory Commission on Civil Disorders [The Kerner Commission]. *Report of the National Advisory Commission on Civil Disorder*. New York Times edition. New York: E.P. Dutton and Company, 1968.

National Commission on the Causes and Prevention of Violence [The Eisenhower Commission]. *To Establish Justice, To Insure Domestic Tranquillity: Final Report on the Causes and Prevention of Violence*. Washington, D.C.: GPO, 1969.

President's Commission on Campus Unrest [The Scranton Commission]. *The Report of the President's Commission on Campus Unrest*. Washington, DC: GPO, 1970.

MILITARIZATION

Center for Research on Criminal Justice. *The Iron Fist and the Velvet Glove: An Analysis of the U.S. Police*. Berkeley, California: Center for Research on Criminal Justice, 1975.

This classic text of radical criminology anticipated many developments that have since reached fruition. While clearly a product of its time, much of its analysis remains relevant today.

Kraska, Peter B., editor. *Militarizing the American Criminal Justice System: The Changing Roles of the Armed Forces and the Police*. Boston: Northeastern University Press, 2001.

This brief and useful anthology includes several highly critical discussions of militarization: Peter B. Kraska, "The Military-Criminal Justice Blur: An Introduction"; Peter B. Kraska, "Crime Control as Warfare: Language Matters"; Charles J. Dunlap, Jr., "The Thick Green Line: The Growing Involvement of Military Forces in Domestic Law Enforcement" [Dunlap is an Air Force colonel, and an outspoken opponent of military involvement in domestic policing.]; Matthew T. DeMichele and Peter B. Kraska, "Community Policing in Battle Garb: A Paradox or Coherent Strategy?"; and, Peter B. Kraska, "Epilogue: Lessons Learned."

Kraska, Peter B. and Victor E. Kappeler. "Militarizing American Police: The Rise and Normalization of Paramilitary Units." In *The Police and Society: Touchstone Readings,* edited by Victor E. Kappeler. Prospect Heights, Illinois: Waveland Press, Inc., 1999.

Parenti, Christian. *Lockdown America: Police and Prisons in the Age of Crisis*. London: Verso, 1999.

Urban Warrior. Directed by Matt Ehling. ETS Pictures, 2002. Videocassette.

Weber, Diane Cecelia. "Warrior Cops: The Ominous Growth of Paramilitarism in American Police Departments." *Cato Institute Briefing Papers* 50 (August 26, 1999).

Despite the limits of its conservative libertarian ideology, the Cato Institute has produced a solid overview of police militarization.

COMMUNITY POLICING

Cordner, Gary W. "Elements of Community Policing." In *Policing Perspectives: An Anthology*, edited by Larry K. Gaines and Gary W. Cordner. Los Angeles: Roxbury Publishing Company, 1999.

Goldstein, Herman. "Toward Community-Oriented Policing: Potential, Basic Requirements, and Threshold Questions." *Crime and Delinquency* (January 1987).

Justice Department. Bureau of Justice Assistance. *Understanding Community Policing: A Framework for Action*, by Community Policing Consortium. August 1994.

Kappeler, Victor E., editor. *The Police and Society: Touchstone Readings*. Prospect Heights, Illinois: Waveland Press, Inc., 1999.
This anthology contains some of the most insightful articles written about community policing: Michael E. Buerger and Lorraine Green Mazerolle, "Third-Party Policing: Theoretical Aspects of an Emerging Trend"; Carl B. Klockars, "The Rhetoric of Community Policing"; and, Victor E. Kappeler, "Reinventing the Police and Society: The Spectacle of Social Control."

Kappeler, Victor E. and Peter B. Kraska. "A Textual Critique of Community Policing: Police Adaption to High Modernity." *Policing: An International Journal of Police Strategies and Management* 21:2 (1998).

Skolnick, Jerome H. and David H. Bayley. *The New Blue Line: Police Innovation in Six American Cities*. New York: The Free Press, 1986.

BROKEN WINDOWS

Bratton, William. *Turnaround: How America's Top Cop Reversed the Crime Epidemic*. With Peter Knobler. New York: Random House, 1998.

Walker, Samuel. "'Broken Windows' and Fractured History." In *Policing Perspectives: An Anthology*, edited by Larry K. Gaines and Gary W. Cordner. Los Angeles: Roxbury Publishing Company, 1999.

Wilson, James Q. and George L. Kelling. "Broken Windows." *Atlantic Monthly* (March 1982).

AFTERWORD: MAKING POLICE OBSOLETE

GANGS AND GANG SUPPRESSION

"Bloods/Crips Proposal for LA's Face-Lift." In *Why LA Happened: Implications of the '92 Los Angeles Rebellion*, edited by Haki Madhubuti. Chicago: Third World Press, 1993.

Davis, Mike. "L.A.: The Fire This Time." *CovertAction Information Bulletin* 41 (Summer 1992).

Jankowski, Martín Sánchez. *Islands in the Street: Gangs and American Urban Society*. Berkeley: University of California Press, 1991.

Klein, Malcolm W. *The American Street Gang: Its Nature, Prevalence, and Control*. New York: Oxford University Press, 1995.

Padilla, Felix M. *Gangs as an American Enterprise*. New Brunswick, New Jersey: Rutgers University Press, 1992.

Sheldon, Randall G. et al. *Youth Gangs in American Society*. Belmont, California: Wadsworth, 2001.

ALTERNATIVES TO POLICING

Abel, Richard L., editor. *The Politics of Informal Justice. Vol. 2, Comparative Studies*. New York: Academic Press, 1982.

The second volume of this collection is the single best source on alternative justice, providing a survey of systems around the world. It includes: Richard L. Abel, "Introduction"; Udo Reifner, "Individualistic and Collective Legalization: The Theory and Practice of Legal Advice for Workers in Prefascist Germany"; Heleen F. P. Ietswaart, "The Discourse of Summary Justice and the Discourse of Popular Justice: An Analysis of Legal Rhetoric in Argentina"; Jack Spence, "Institutionalizing Neighborhood Courts: Two Chilean Experiences"; Boaventura de Sousa Santos, "Law and Revolution in Portugal: The Experiences of Popular Justice After the 25th of April 1974"; and, Barbara Isaacman and Allen Isaacman, "A Socialist Legal System in the Making: Mozambique Before and After Independence."

Feenan, Dermot, editor. *Informal Criminal Justice*. Aldershot, England: Ashgate/
    Dartmouth, 2002.
This collection examines informal justice systems in a variety of contemporary contexts. It includes sources I cite below in the discussions of South Africa and Northern Ireland.

Longmire, Dennis R. "A Popular Justice System: A Radical Alternative to the
    Traditional Criminal Justice System." *Contemporary Crises* 5 (1981).
Longmire presents straightforward alternatives to the police, the courts, and the prisons—in short, to the entire criminal justice system as it now exists.

Michalowski, Raymond J. "Crime Control in the 1980s: A Progressive Agenda." *Crime
    and Social Justice* 19 (Summer 1983).

CIVIL RIGHTS, BLACK POWER, AND SELF DEFENSE

Goodman, Mitchell, editor. *The Movement Toward a New America: The Beginnings of
    a Long Revolution*. Philadelphia: Pilgrim Press, 1970.
A treasury of articles and artwork reprinted from the underground papers of the late 1960s, this book documents the individuals, groups, ideas, and events of the time. While well suited for browsing, it unfortunately lacks an index, thus making it very difficult to find information on any particular topic.

Hampton, Henry et al. *Voices of Freedom: An Oral History of the Civil Rights
    Movement from the 1950s through the 1980s*. New York: Bantam Books, 1990.
See note under Chapter 4: Cops and Klan, Hand in Hand; The Civil Rights and Black Power Movements.

Nelson, Harold A. "The Defenders: A Case Study of an Informal Police Organization."
    Social Problems (Fall 1967).

Newton, Huey P. *War Against the Panthers: A Study of Repression in America*. Diss.
    University of California-Santa Cruz, 1980. New York: Harlem River Press,
    1996.

Seale, Bobby. *Seize the Time: The Story of the Black Panther Party and Huey P.
    Newton*. New York: Random House, 1970.
———. "Bobby Seale Explains Panther Politics: An Interview." In *The Black Panthers
    Speak*, edited Philip S. Foner. New York: De Capo Press, 1995.

Sims Charles R. and William A. Price. "Armed Defense." In *Black Protest: 350 Years of History, Documents, and Analyses,* edited by Joanne Grant. New York: Fawcett Columbine, 1968.

Williams, Robert F. *Negroes With Guns.* Edited by Marc Schleifer. Chicago: Third World Press, 1973.

SOUTH AFRICA

Lee, Rebekah and Jeremy Seekings. "Vigilantism and Popular Justice After Apartheid." In *Informal Criminal Justice,* edited by Dermot Feenan. Aldershot, England: Ashgate/Dartmouth, 2002.

Minnaar, Anthony. "The 'New' Vigilantism in Post–April 1994 South Africa." In *Informal Criminal Justice,* edited by Dermot Feenan. Aldershot, England: Ashgate/Dartmouth, 2002.

Schärf, Wilfried and Daniel Nina, editors. *The Other Law: Non-State Ordering in South Africa.* Lundsdowne: JUTA Law, 2001.
Includes: Daniel Nina and Wilfried Schärf, "Introduction: The Other Law?"; Wilfried Schärf, "Policy Options in Community Justice"; Jeremy Seekings, "Social Ordering and Control in the African Townships of South Africa: An Historical Overview of Extra-State Initiatives from the 1940s to the 1990s"; Andries Mphoto Mangokwana, "Makgotla in Rural and Urban Contexts"; Daniel Nina, "Popular Justice and the 'Appropriation' of the State Monopoly on the Definition of Justice and Order: The Case of the Anti-Crime Committees in Port Elizabeth"; and, Monique Marks and Penny McKenzie, "Alternative Policing Structures? A Look at Youth Defense Structures in Gauteng."

NORTHERN IRELAND

Auld, Jim et al. "Our Practice: The Blue Book [Designing a System of Restorative Community Justice in Northern Ireland]." www.restorativejusticeireland.org/ourpractice.html (1997), (accessed November 20, 2002).

Feenan, Dermot. "Community Justice in Conflict: Paramilitary Punishment in Northern Ireland." In *Informal Criminal Justice,* edited by Dermot Feenan. Aldershot, England: Ashgate/Dartmouth, 2002.

McEvoy, Kieran and Harry Mika. "Republican Hegemony or Community Ownership? Community Restorative Justice in Northern Ireland." In *Informal Criminal Justice*, edited by Dermot Feenan. Aldershot, England: Ashgate/Dartmouth, 2002.

Mika, Harry and Kieran McEvoy. "Restorative Justice in Conflict: Paramilitarism, Community, and the Construction of Legitimacy in Northern Ireland." *Comparative Justice Review* 4:3–4 (2001).

Munck, Ronnie. "Repression, Insurgency, and Popular Justice: The Irish Case." *Crime and Social Justice* 21–2 (1984).

INDEX

erance, quality-of-life, and order-maintenance policing

broken windows theory, 246-247, 248-249, 249-250, 251, 330n.90, 330n.93, 330n.95; see also drug war; see also homelessness and vagrancy; see also prostitution; see also public order; see also vice laws and Prohibition; see also zero-tolerance, quality-of-life, and order-maintenance policing

Bronx, (New York, New York), 257

Brooklyn (New York, New York), 82, 215

Brooklyn Bridge, New York, 156

Brooklyn North (New York, New York), 257, 333n.157

Brooklyn South (New York, New York), 257

Brothers, John, 221, 222

Brown Berets, 267

Brown's Chapel (Selma, Alabama), 113

Brown, Willie, 281n.86

Buffalo, New York, 187, 214

Bull, William, 286n.78

Bureau of Alcohol, Tobacco, and Firearms (BATF), 117, 196

Bureau of Labor Statistics, see United States Bureau of Labor Statistics

bureaucracy and bureaucratization, 2, 70, 72-73, 80, 82, 84, 119, 145-149, 150, 151-152, 158, 162, 167-168, 170, 238-239, 252, 259, 283n.140, 291n.51, 292n.79, 307n.50, 308n.56, 308n.60, 308n.67

Burge, Jon, 278n.46

Burgess, Andre, 296n.64

Burke, Joseph, 103

Bush, George H. W., 194

Bush, George W., 198, 304n.86, 319n.151

Butkovich, Bernard, 117

Butler, Julius, 183, 316n.64

Cable, George Washington, 295n.30

Cahill, Thomas, 153

California, see individual cities

California Highway Patrol, 4, 5, 7, 93-94

California State College in Los Angeles, 114

California Supreme Court, 328n.69

Callahan, Ray, 183

Camden, South Carolina, 47

Camilla, Georgia, 89

Camp Pendleton, California, 231

Campbell v. Commonwealth (1877), 302n.17

Caniel, Peter J., 179

Cape Town, South Africa, 269

Capitol Hill (Seattle, Washington), 206, 208, 322n.47

Carey, Bernard M., 178

Carmel, Indiana, 102

Carmichael, Stokely, 300n.158

Carnell, Willie, 111

Carroll County, Arkansas, 90

Carrol, Sean, 98

Caruso, Joseph, 130

Casey, Willis, 191

Cassese, John, 142, 156, 311n.128, 313n.174

Cauce, Cesar, 117

Cawley, Bernard, 283n.132

Center for Constitutional Rights, 198

Central Intelligence Agency (CIA), 175, 184, 197, 198, 318n.148, 319n.151

Central Labor Council (San Francisco), 133

Centro, El, 180

Century City (Los Angeles, California), 135

Chambliss, William, 283n.140, 291n.49, 297n.79

Chaney, James, 109-112, 299n.136

Chapel Hill, North Carolina, 99-100

Charles II, 34

Charleston County, South Carolina, 134

Charleston Five, 134-135

Charleston, South Carolina, 39, 40-42, 45-47, 49-51, 52, 53, 74-75, 82, 89, 134-135, 283n., 288n.158, 304n.86

Charlotte-Mecklenburg, North Carolina, 279n.66

Chavez Ravine, California, 256

Cheatham, Bobby Lee, 11

Cherney, Darryl, 194-195

Chicago Bears, 178-179

Chicago Citizens' Association, 173

Chicago, Illinois, 61, 62, 64, 114, 115, 122, 140, 142, 151, 162, 171-174, 178, 179, 181, 182-183, 184, 187, 189, 190, 192, 213, 215, 216, 218-219, 278n.46, 291n.49, 315n.41, 318n.137, 321n.8, 321n.23, 323n.69, 323n.79

Chicago Times, 173-174

Chile, 170, 314n.182

Chomsky, Noam, 261

Christian Front, 104

Christie, John, 37

Christopher Commission (Independent Commission on the Los Angeles Police Department), 16, 24-25, 100-101, 116,

National Association for the Advancement of Colored People (NAACP), 105, 110, 186, 248, 266, 279n.68, 282n.126, 330n.100, 334n.23

National Black Police Association, 295n.44

"National Census of Fatal Occupational Injuries In 2000" (United States Bureau of Labor Statistics Report), 21, fig.a, 21

National Commission on the Causes and Prevention of Violence, see Eisenhower Commission

National Council of Churches, 110, 186

National Guard, 9, 132, 133, 143, 206, 209-210, 211, 213, 214, 215, 218, 226, 284n.13, 306n.14, 307n.46, 321n.8, 321n.24, 322n.25, 322n.37, 323n.62, 327n.43, 329n.83

National Institute of Justice (NIJ), 10-11, 15-16, 25, 231

National Labor Relations Act (Wagner Act), 142, 305n.100

National Labor Relations Board (NLRB), 305n.100, 305n.101

National Lawyers Guild (NLG), 191

National Organization for Women (NOW), 186

National Park Service, 226

National Security Agency (NSA), 197

National Sheriff's Association, 237

National Socialist White People's Party, 116

National Student Association, 323n.68

Nativism, 68, 150, see also Know-Nothing Party

Navy Seals, 234, 326n.20

Nazis, 116, 117, 155, 216, 328n.72

Neebe, Oscar, 172

Negotiated Management, see crowd control strategies

neighborhood watch, 237, 243, 328n.69

Nesbitt, Lenore, 8

Neshoba County, Mississippi, 110, 112

Nevada, see individual cities

New Alexandria, Pennsylvania, 125

New Hampshire, 187; see also individual cities

New Jersey, 96, 97; see also individual cities

New Orleans, Louisiana, 39, 51-56, 64, 88-89, 121, 142, 214, 288n.160, 288n.166, 289n.175, 289n.179, 291n.49, 295n.30, 295n.37, 301n.3, 315n.41

New Orleans Times (New Orleans, Louisiana), 88

New York City, New York, 5, 24, 29, 38, 56-58, 61, 63, 64, 65, 72, 75, 79, 81, 82, 98, 104-105, 115, 130, 141, 141-142, 144, 155-157, 159, 176, 178, 179, 184, 187, 189, 192, 207, 208-209, 210, 215, 231, 249-250, 251, 253-254, 257, 281n.94, 282n.123, 283n., 283n.132, 289n.175, 292n.70, 296n.65, 301n.7, 307n.45, 307n.46, 308n.67, 309n.82, 313n.167, 315n.41, 318n.137, 321n.15, 322n.25, 325n.4, 330n.95, 332n.152

New York Civilian Complaint Review Board, 24, 155-156

New York State, 191; see also individual cities

New York State Conference of Mayors, 325n.5

New York Times, 156, 209, 311n.135, 323n.68

New York Times Magazine, 282n.123

New York Transit Police, 249, 330n.95, 331n.117

Newark, New Jersey, 7, 8, 142, 155, 200, 331n.134

Newark, Ohio, 209

Newton District (South Central Los Angeles, California), 244

Newton, Huey, 114, 335n.28

Night Watch, 29, 32, 34-35, 36-39, 45, 46, 48, 49-50, 53, 55, 57, 64, 70-71, 75, 76, 82, 84, 85, 285n.47, 287n.142, 288n.166, 289n.197

Night-riding and Night Riders, see Ku Klux Klan

NIJ, see National Institute of Justice

Nina, Daniel, 270, 273, 337n.77

Nixon, Richard, 189, 335n.33

no-go areas, see Northern Ireland and popular justice

Nordana Line, 134-135

Normans, 33

Norris, John C., 89-90

North Carolina, 43, 44-45, 96-97, 99-100, 287n.140, 294n.23; see also individual cities

North Carolina Agricultural and Mechanical College, 214

North Carolina Highway Patrol, 96-97

North Carolina State Bureau of Investigation, 99-100

North Carolina State University, 96-97
North Charleston, South Carolina, 134
Northern Ireland, and Frank Kitson, 175;
    and popular justice, 270-276, 335n.38,
    336n.56, 336n.58, 336n.59, 336n.67,
    337n.69, 337n.72, 337n.75, 337n.76,
    338n.89; see also Blue Book; see also
    Community Restorative Justice (CRJ);
    see also Irish Republican Army (IRA)
Notre Dame University, 178
Novick, Michael, 115

O'Connor, Timothy J., 151
O'Neal, William, 183
Oakland, California, 114, 140-141, 182,
    183, 194-195, 248, 309n.93, 315n.41,
    318n.126, 321n.15, 322n.59
Oaks, Louis D., 103
Odom, Georgia, 187
Ohio, 191; see also individual cities
Ohio State University, 214
Oliver, Melvin, 5
Olsen, Caroline, 183
Olsen, Charles, 132
Omar, Hady Hassan, 199
100 Blacks In Law Enforcement Who Care,
    98
One Police Plaza (New York, New York), 239
Operation Cul-de-Sac, 244, 329n.83
Operation Glazier, 249
Operation Hammer, 100
Operation Juggernaut, 257, 333n.157
Operation No Case, 142
Operation Pipeline, 93-94
Operation Ready-Rock, 99-100
Operation TIPS, 319n.153
Orangeburg, South Carolina, 215
order-maintenance policing, see zero-toler-
    ance, quality-of-life, and order-main-
    tenance policing
Oregon, 303n.55; see also individual cities
Orwell, George, 121
Osburn, Jeff, 304n.86
Ostrow, Ron, 234-235

padaroes, padaroles, paddyrollers, patterol-
    ers, see slave patrols and City Guards
Pakistan-American Friendship League, 186
Palmer Raids, 176, 196, 199
Palmer, A. Mitchell, 176

panhandlers and panhandling, see home-
    lessness and vagrancy
Panthers, see Black Panther Party For Self
    Defense
Pape, Hubert, 107
paramilitary police units, see police para-
    military units
Parent-Teacher Association (PTA), 178
Parenti, Christian, 249, 325n.117,
    332n.141
Paris, France, 81, 215
Parish of St. Philip, South Carolina, 50
Parker Center (Los Angeles, California), 239
Parker, William H., 94-96, 242, 295n.46,
    296n.50
Parliament (England), 36, 81
Parsell, Carl, 141, 142-143, 306n.19
Parsons, Albert, 172, 173
Paterson, New Jersey, 215
Patriot Act, 196-198
Patriot Party, 267
Patrolman's Benevolent Associations
    (PBAs), 98, 139, 141-142, 155-157,
    159, 307n.45, 311n.128, 311n.139,
    313n.167
Paul, Jay, 190
Peace and Justice Works Iraq Affinity
    Group, 194
peace corps policing, 238, 255, 257
Peace Moratorium March (November 15,
    1969), 222
Peden, Bryant, 295n.29
Peel, Robert, 35-36, 71, 285n.41, 285n.42
Pendleton, South Carolina, 47
Pennsylvania, see individual cities
Pennsylvania State Constabulary, 125-126
Pennsylvania State Federation of Labor,
    125-126
Pennsylvania Supreme Court, 302n.17
Pennypacker, Samuel, 125
Pentagon, 20, 188, 196, 231, 239,
    319n.153, 328n.61; see also United
    States Department of Defense
People Against Racist Terror, 115
People for the Ethical Treatment of Animals
    (PETA), 197
People's Courts, see Northern Ireland and
    popular justice; see South Africa and
    popular justice
Peoria, Illinois, 182
Percy, Charles, 178
Perry, Albert E., 334n.23
Peters, Andrew, 306n.14

(PBAs); see also political machines; see also unions and labor movement

policy communities and policy networks, 166-167, 238-244, 314n.177, 329n.79; see also Smith, Martin J.

political machines, 2, 54, 55-59, 61-70, 84-85, 87, 143-145, 146-147, 148-149, 154, 167, 170, 238, 259, 289n.197, 290n.207, 290n.4, 291n.46, 291n.49, 292n.63, 307n.49, 308n.60

Pontiac, Michigan, 104

Poore, Munford J., 89

popular justice and restorative justice, 264-276, 334n.14, 335n.38, 337n.74, 337n.78, 338n.86, 338n.89; and Black Panther Party For Self Defense, 266-268; and civil rights movements, 266, 334n.23, 334n.24; and criteria for legitimacy, 275; and Havana General Strike (1959), 334n.22; and Hungary (1956), 334n.22; and Seattle General Strike (1919), 265-266, 268; restorative justice, defined, 336n.46; see also Northern Ireland and popular justice; see also South Africa and popular justice

Porter, Bruce, 8

Portland, Oregon, 104, 180, 186, 190-191, 193-194, 250, 256, 282n.127, 303n.59, 316n.78, 319n.156

Portland Police Association, 163

Portland Police Vigilantes, 104

Portland State University Hispanic Student Union, 186

Portland Telegram, 104

Portland Tribune, 256, 317n.99, 332n.149

Posse Comitatus, 115

Powell, Edmund, 116

Powell, Laurence, 4, 5

Powelton (Philadelphia, Pennsylvania), 195

PPUs, see police paramilitary units

Prague, Czech Republic, 208

Pratt, Elmer "Geronimo" (Geronimo Ji Jaga), 183-184, 316n.65

President's Commission on Campus Unrest, see Scranton Commission

Press Democrat (Santa Rosa, California), 195

preventive orientation, 2, 31, 70-72, 75, 80, 152-153, 201-203, 237, 238, 244, 246-247, 251, 258, 291n.54, 292n.83, 307n.51, 329n.83, 330n.90, 330n.95, 330n.98, 332n.152

Price, Cecil, 111-112

problem-oriented policing, 237, 238, 240, 241-242, 244, 246, 252, 254, 327n.56, 328.n63, 329n.76

profiling, see racial profiling

professionalization, 119, 150-153, 157, 158, 162, 167-168, 238-239, 259, 309n.82, 309n.86, 310n.95

progressive movement and the Progressive Era, 125, 127, 143-145, 147-149, 150-151, 211, 238, 308n.69, 308n.70, 309n.73, 323n.94, 324n.109, 327n.44

prostitution, 34, 55, 58, 64-65, 75, 79-80, 93, 144, 235, 246, 249, 250, 283n.141, 291n.49, 301n.7, 302n.29, 307n.51, 330n.93; see also broken windows theory; see also dangerous classes; see also drug war; see also homelessness and vagrancy; see also Protestant ethics; see also public order; see also vice laws and Prohibition; see also zero-tolerance, quality-of-life, and order-maintenance policing

Protestant ethics, 55, 76, 79-80, 84-85, 148-149, 292n.75, 292n.76, 301n.7, 308n.70; see also prostitution; see also public order; see also vice laws and Prohibition

Proudhon, Pierre, 62

public order, 54, 55, 75-83, 84-85, 93, 103, 122-123, 237, 240, 241, 244-246, 246-247, 248-249, 249-250, 251, 292n.68, 293n.91, 293n.126, 301n.7, 330n.93; see also broken windows theory; see also dangerous classes; see also drug war; see also homelessness and vagrancy; see also prostitution; see also Protestant ethics; see also vice laws and Prohibition; see also zero-tolerance, quality-of-life, and order-maintenance policing

quality-of-life, see zero-tolerance, quality-of-life, and order-maintenance policing

Quebec City (Canada), 208

Queens (New York, New York), 257

Quincy, Josiah, 63-64

R. M. McCarthy and Associates, 207-208, 224-225, 226, 324n.110

Shelton, Robert, 107
Shemash, Michael, 317n.116
Sherer, Mark, 301n.190
Show of Force, see crowd control strategies
Shuttleworth, Fred, 106
silent majority, 260
Silver, Allan, 85, 86, 258, 292n.79
Simi Valley, California, 5, 116
Simmons, Ricky, 134-135
Simpson, Sally, 297n.87, 298n.89
Sims, Michael, 318n.126
Sinn Fein, 272, 273, 336n.67, 337n.75
Skolnick, Jerome, 237, 245, 248, 267, 329n.80
SLA, see Symbionese Liberation Army
slave patrols and City Guards, 39-51, 52, 53, 55, 71-72, 74-75, 81-82, 84, 89, 91-92, 93, 99, 111, 112, 118-119, 121, 167, 239, 259, 285n.65, 286n.78, 286n.89, 286n.93, 287n.112, 287n.140, 288n.144, 288n.155, 288n.158, 288n.166, 294n.1, 295n.35, 295n. 36, 312n.152, 325n.3, 326n.25
Smith's Cove (Seattle, Washington), 303n.59
Smith, Bruce, 128
Smith, Charles, 303n.59
Smith, Jerry Paul, 301n.190
Smith, Martin J., 166, 243, 314n.176, 314n.177, 329n.79
Smith, Sandi, 117
SNCC, see Student Nonviolence Coordinating Committee
Socialist Women's Committee, 130
Somers Building Maintenance, 304n.89
Soulsby, Larry, 280n.79
South Africa, anti-apartheid activism in United States, 186, 190, 191, 221-222, 324n.104; apartheid, 102, 115, 191, 268-269; and popular justice, 268-270, 270, 272-273, 274-276, 335n.38, 336n.45, 336n.51, 336n.52, 337n.77
South Bethlehem, Pennsylvania, 126
South Boston Vigilance Committee, 140
South Carolina, 40-42, 44, 49, 81, 99, 286n.78, 302n.29, 304n.86; see also individual cities
South Carolina Highway Patrol, 134
South Carolina State College, 214
South Central (Los Angeles, California), 100, 244
Southern Christian Leadership Conference, 106, 186

Soviet Union, 192
Special Forces, see United States Special Forces
Special Investigations Bureau, see red squads
Special Response Team, see police paramilitary units
Special Service Unit, see police paramilitary units
Special Weapons And Tactics (SWAT), see police paramilitary units
Sperry, Howard S., 132
Spicer, Charles, 100
Spies, August, 171, 172, 173
Spoon, P. W., 301n.190
squeegee workers, 250, 331n.115, 331n.126
Squirrel, Douglas, 193-194
Stamper, Norm, 206
Stark, Rodney, 16, 22, 217, 219, 261, 262, 279n.57, 310n.110, 323n.69
State Department, see United States Department of State
State University of New York, Buffalo, 214
Staten Island (New York, York), 257
Statute of Winchester (1285), 33
Steinberg, Allen, 103
Stenvig, Charles, 154
Sterling Heights, Michigan, 135-136, 304n.90
Stewart, Potter, 11
Stockton, Richard, 211
Strategic Air Command Headquarters, 231
street committees, see South Africa and popular justice
Street Crimes Unit, 98, 296n.65
strikes, Akron Rubber Strike (1936), 301n.2; Bridgeport, Connecticut (1955), 311n.140; Chicago Social Workers Strike (1967), 162; Cripple Creek, Colorado (1894), 290n.207; Detroit Newspaper Strike (1995-2001), 135-136, 304n.90, 305n.95; eight-hour movement, 171-174, 321n.23; Great Anthracite Strike (1902), 125, 301n.21; Great Railroad Strike (1877), 208-209, 321n.17; Justice for Janitors, Los Angeles (1990), 135; Justice for Janitors, Sacramento (1999), 304n.89; Lawrence Textile Strike (1912), 129-131, 132; Ludlow Massacre (1914), 211, 322n.37; New Orleans Levee Workers' Strike (1885), 121, 301n.3;

Kristian Williams is a member of Rose City Copwatch, in Portland, Oregon.

He has written for *Dissent*, the *Progressive*, and *Labor Notes*, as well as local publications like the *Portland Alliance* and *Eat the State*.

Kristian was drawn to anarchism at a young age, thanks in large part to the Richmond, Virginia, punk scene. Despite a Reed College education and the well-meant advice of certain friends, his political views remain more or less intact.

In his spare time, he reads comic books and likes to cook.

This is his first book.

ACKNOWLEDGMENTS

This book owes its existence to many people besides me. I am especially grateful for the help of Daniel Buck, Carl Caputo, Jamie Dawson, Laura Grant, Missy Rohs, Clayton Szczech, and Shira Zucker. Their advice has guided me, and their encouragement sustained me, through many months and quite a few revisions.

I would like to thank, most of all, Emily-Jane Dawson. In addition to offering critical insights on earlier drafts, Emily-Jane helped me locate otherwise unavailable sources, aided in the production of this volume's graphics, and treated me with patience I often did not deserve. It is warmly appreciated.